PEARSON

# myHRlab

## Save Time.

## Improve Results.

More than 3 million students have used a Pearson MyLab product to get a better grade.

**MyHRLab** is an all-in-one learning and testing environment for introductory human resources. This easy-to-navigate site provides students with a variety of resources, including

- An interactive Pearson eText
- Audio and video material to view or listen to, whatever your learning style
- Personalized learning opportunities—YOU choose what, where, and when you want to study
- Self-assessment tests that create a personalized study plan to guide you on making the most efficient use of study time

To take advantage of all that MyHRLab has to offer, you will need an access code. If you do not already have an access code, you can buy one online at **www.pearsoned.ca/myhrlab.**

PEARSON

# Pearson eText

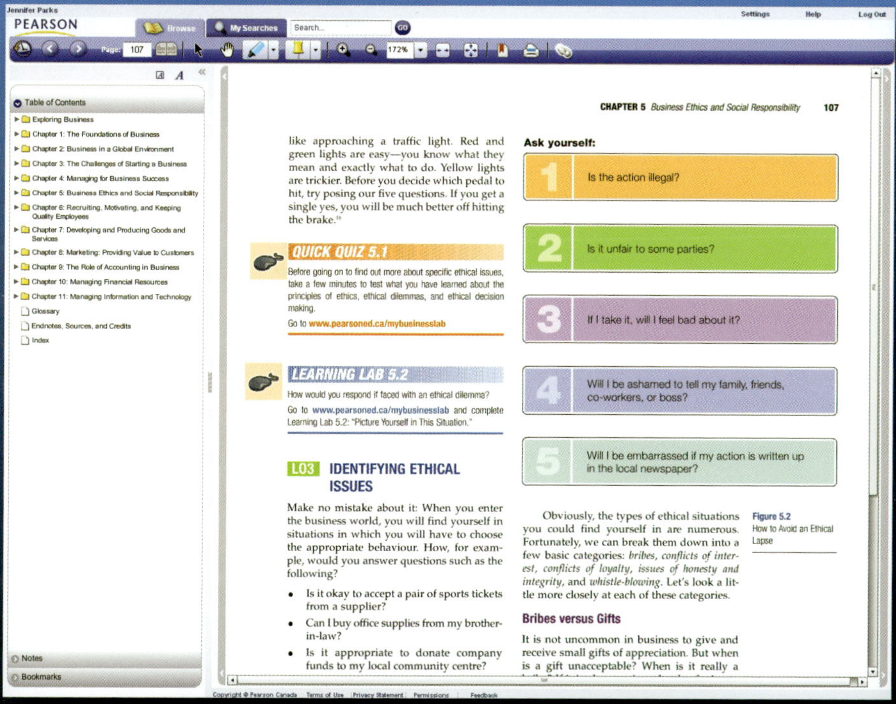


Pearson eText gives students access to the text whenever and wherever they have access to the internet. eText pages look exactly like the printed text, offering powerful new functionality for students and instructors.

Users can create notes, highlight text in different colours, create bookmarks, zoom, click hyperlinked words and phrases to view definitions, and choose single-page or two-page view.

Pearson eText allows for quick navigation using a table of contents and provides full-text search. The eText may also offer links to associated media files, enabling users to access videos, animations, or other activities as they read the text.

## Personalized Learning

In MyHRLab you are treated as an individual with specific learning needs.

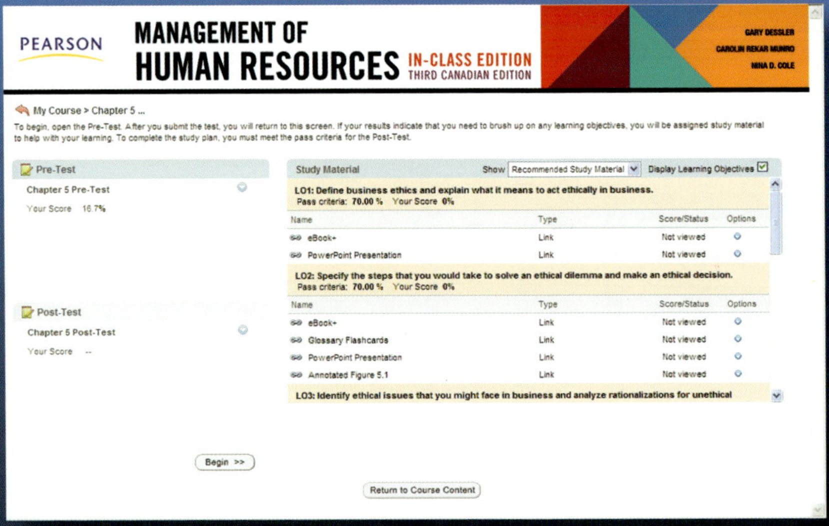


The study and assessment resources that come with your textbook allow you to review content and develop what you need to know, on your own time, and at your own pace.

### MyHRLab provides

- Auto-graded quizzes
- A personalized study plan that tells you where to study based on your quiz results
- Mini-cases let you test your analytical skills
- Annotated text figures and tables
- Glossary Flashcards
- Acadia/Pearson Video Portal featuring interviews with over 70 executives from a variety of companies, including some featured in your textbook

# Pearson eText

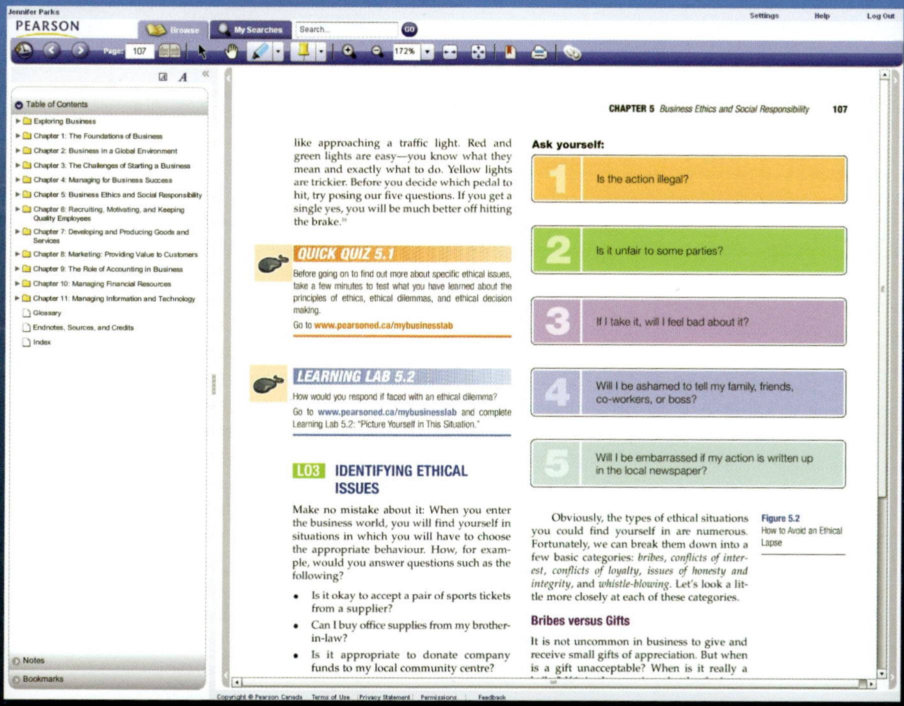


Pearson eText gives students access to the text whenever and wherever they have access to the internet. eText pages look exactly like the printed text, offering powerful new functionality for students and instructors.

Users can create notes, highlight text in different colours, create bookmarks, zoom, click hyperlinked words and phrases to view definitions, and choose single-page or two-page view.

Pearson eText allows for quick navigation using a table of contents and provides full-text search. The eText may also offer links to associated media files, enabling users to access videos, animations, or other activities as they read the text.

**Save Time. Improve Results.** www.pearsoned.ca/myhrlab

# Personalized Learning

In MyHRLab you are treated as an individual with specific learning needs.

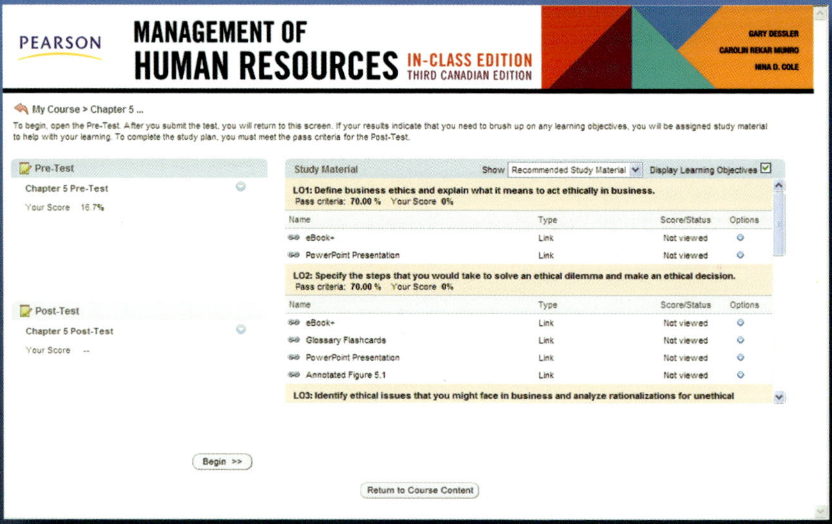


The study and assessment resources that come with your textbook allow you to review content and develop what you need to know, on your own time, and at your own pace.

## MyHRLab provides

- Auto-graded quizzes
- A personalized study plan that tells you where to study based on your quiz results
- Mini-cases let you test your analytical skills
- Annotated text figures and tables
- Glossary Flashcards
- Acadia/Pearson Video Portal featuring interviews with over 70 executives from a variety of companies, including some featured in your textbook

# MANAGEMENT OF HUMAN RESOURCES

## IN-CLASS EDITION
## THIRD CANADIAN EDITION


**GARY DESSLER**
Florida International University

**CAROLIN REKAR MUNRO**
Royal Roads University

**NINA D. COLE**
Ryerson University



**Pearson Canada**
Toronto

**Library and Archives Canada Cataloguing in Publication**

Dessler, Gary, 1942–
Management of human resources / Gary Dessler, Carolin Rekar Munro, Nina D. Cole.—3rd Canadian ed.

Previous edition had author .... [et al.] and filed under title.

Includes bibliographical references and index.
ISBN 978-0-13-814722-8

1. Personnel management—Textbooks. 2. Personnel management—Canada—Textbooks. I. Cole, Nina D. (Nina Dawn) II. Munro, Carolin Rekar, 1964– III. Title.

HF5549.M3132 2010 658.3 C2009-907105-3

---



ISBN 978-0-13-814722-8

Vice-President, Editorial Director: Gary Bennett
Editor-in-Chief: Nicole Lukach
Acquisitions Editor: Karen Elliott
Executive Marketing Manager: Cas Shields
Senior Developmental Editor: Eleanor MacKay
Production Editor: Imee Salumbides
Copy Editor: Sally Glover
Proofreader: Carol Anderson
Production Coordinator: Andrea Falkenberg
Compositor: MPS Limited, A Macmillan Company
Photo and Permissions Researcher: David Strand
Art Director: Julia Hall
Cover Designer: Miriam Blier
Interior Designer: Julia Hall
Cover Image: Getty Images/Aurora/Philip Gostelow



1 2 3 4 5 14 13 12 11 10

Printed and bound in the United States of America.

PEARSON

# Brief Contents

# Contents

# *Preface*

As part of Pearson Canada's commitment to providing students with value, choice, and the tools for educational success, *Management of Human Resources*, Third Canadian Edition, has been designed as an In-Class Study Edition. This innovative new presentation is designed to focus on student learning and self-study, and to introduce students to the evolving role of HR professionals as accountable, strategic business partners at the boardroom table.

## NEW TO THIS EDITION

While retaining the strengths of the second edition of *Management of Human Resources*, In-Class Edition, this third edition introduces several important changes.

In this edition, we highlighted the importance of collaboration amongst HR professionals and managers to identify strategic priorities, chart organizational progress and implementation, facilitate financial initiatives, and evaluate organizational effectiveness. We have also included more examples of HR theories, models, and practices.

In this age of working in a global marketplace, we have increased our coverage of how human resource management is affected on an international scale. For this edition, we have included a **new** On the International Stage feature, which exposes students to the nature and challenges of practicing human resources globally.

In individual chapters, we made the following key changes:

- expanded our discussion of attracting, engaging, and retaining employees in Chapter 1
- enhanced our coverage of how to handle diversity and discrimination in Chapter 2
- expanded our coverage on current workplace organization and on methods for analyzing jobs in Chapter 3
- incorporated coverage of new forecasting demand and supply techniques and recruitment in Chapter 4
- enhanced our coverage of employee selection, and interview and evaluation procedures in Chapter 5
- revised our coverage of training and development, including new training methods in Chapter 6
- expanded our coverage of training for appraisers, conducting interviews, and providing feedback in Chapter 7
- enhanced our discussion of managing compensation, establishing pay rates, pay equity, and incentive plans in Chapter 8
- updated our coverage of laws and policies governing employment insurance benefits, workers' compensation, and retirement benefits in Chapter 9
- updated our coverage of safe and healthy workplaces in Chapter 10
- expanded our coverage of employee engagement and privacy, and dismissal procedures in Chapter 11
- updated our coverage of the labour movement in Canada in Chapter 12

Finally, we have revised and added new end-of-chapter exercises to give students more opportunity to apply their knowledge of HR concepts and theories. **New** to this edition are our Controversial Business Topics Exercises, In the Boardroom Exercises, and On the International Stage Exercises.

# KEY FEATURES OF THE EDITION

- **Test Yourself questions** that begin each chapter focus students on the key material and stimulate their interest in the chapter material; our Chapter Review provides answers to these questions.

**Test Yourself**

1. What is human resources management and what are its objectives?
2. How do strategic HRM practices affect the bottom line?
3. What internal and external environmental factors affect HR policies and practices?
4. How has HRM evolved since its inception?
5. What are five key HR challenges in the twenty-first century?

- **In-Class Notes** throughout each chapter highlight key points and provide space for students to make their own notes.

*In-class Notes*

**Introduction to Human Resources Management**

- Serving as internal organizational consultant and strategic change agent
- Supporting employees
- Formulating policies and procedures
- Monitoring to ensure legal compliance
- Championing initiatives to attract, engage, and retain employees

- Key **Required Professional Capabilities (RPCs)** established by the Canadian Council of Human Resources' Associations (CCHRA) appear throughout each chapter. Students are tested on this material as part of the National Knowledge Exam—one of the steps required to become a Certified Human Resources Professional (CHRP).

RPC 1-7 >
Provides services to enable employee success while maintaining the well-being of the organization

- Five **Leading-Edge boxes** feature articles to stimulate discussion and critical thinking: **Strategic HR, Workforce Diversity, HR.Net, Global HRM,** and **Entrepreneurs and HR.**

**STRATEGIC HR**

**Ten Steps to the Right Fit**

For a company's recruitment expert, it's important to stay on top of innovative practices and not to fall into the trap of considering only résumés from conventional candidates. To assist in the evaluation of atypical candidates, here are some tips:

selection criteria. If "relationship management" is a key criterion, then delve into the person's qualifications in this area and follow up with references to validate the information gathered through the interview.

**GLOBAL HRM**

**Business of People behind the Great Wall**

**CANADIAN HR DELEGATION TAKES PEEK AT CHINA'S EVOLVING HR PRACTICES**
In October and November last year, a team of Canadian HR professionals visited China through the People to People Ambassadors program—a program established

Our delegation visited seven different organizations and educational institutions that offered a unique view into the complex business world of China. Make no mistake about it—China is a force to be reckoned with. The people of China embody a strong sense of commu-

**WORKFORCE DIVERSITY**

**First Female BMO Executive Opened Doors**

**MENTORING, INCLUSIVENESS AND CHARITABLE WORKS HIGHLIGHTS OF AWARD-WINNING LEADERSHIP**
Before Rose Patten joined BMO Financial Group in 1995, women held just 9 percent of the management roles at the Toronto-based bank. Considering banks

"Rose exemplifies someone who has risen to the top of her field without having to leave anyone behind. She is a very inclusive leader who has made a very deep impression on many other women coming up through her field," said Amanda Dale, director of advocacy and

**ENTREPRENEURS AND HR**

**An Innovative Occupational Health and Safety Initiative for Small Business**

Small businesses have proportionately more injuries than big businesses, but small firm owners have often felt overburdened and underserved by health and safety

on completing Part 2, which entails forming a group with other firms and furthering their health and safety program development. The rebate is calculated based

**HR.NET**

**Finding Interns Online**

Career Edge Organization is a private-sector, not-for-profit, independent Canadian organization. Career Edge Organization operates three innovative paid internship programs, including Career Edge (which promotes entry-level internships nationally for recent university

Organization and, once approved as "host" employers, post their internship positions on the Career Edge Organization website. Prospective interns visit the site, view available positions, and apply directly to the employer. The host employer staff then review the applications

- **Ethical Dilemma** questions provoke debate and discussion on the moral and ethical decisions often confronted in human resources management.

**AN ETHICAL DILEMMA**
Is it ethical for executive search firms to contact executives who are currently employed to canvass their interest in job openings in other companies?

- **Front Line Tips** indicators mark content and advice for front-line supervisors and managers.

frontLINE tips

- **Legal Compliance** indicators help practitioners avoid legal pitfalls.

- **On the International Stage** features inform students about human resource practices in other countries and prepare them for overseas assignments and international partnerships.

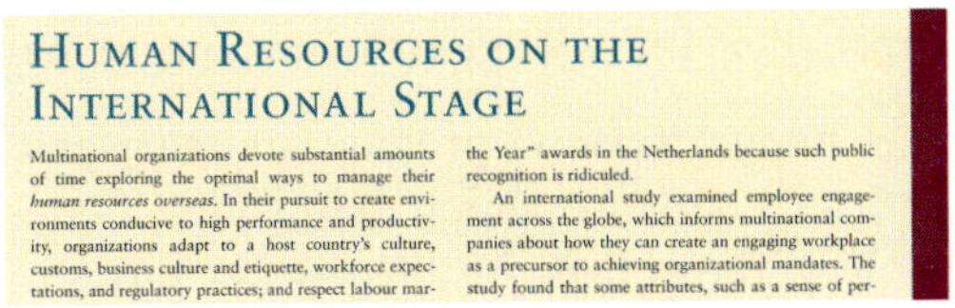


- **Key Terms and their Definitions** appear at the bottom of each right-hand page
- **Weblinks** to numerous human resources-related websites appear at the bottom of each right-hand page

- A **Study Card**, bound into the book, summarizes the key concepts taught in each chapter in a concise format. The Study Card is a great review tool for study!

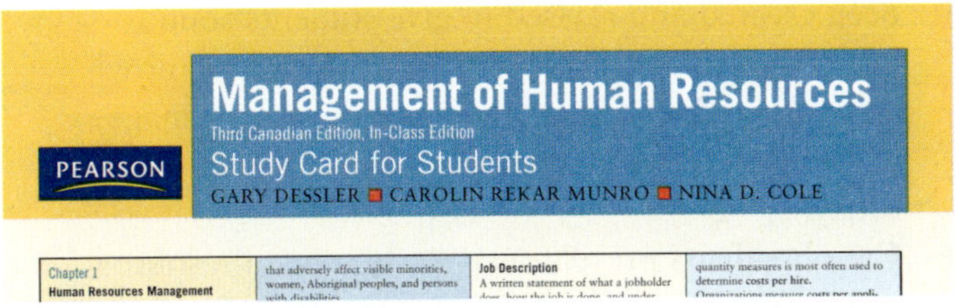


## MyHRlab

- **MyHRLab.** Supplied with every new copy of this text, MyHRLab provides students with access to a wealth of resources for a variety of learning styles, including:
  - Diagnostic tests that assess students' understanding of each learning objective and generate a customized study plan so students know exactly where they need to spend their time.
  - Chapter mini-cases with assessment, chapter quizzes and student PowerPoints
  - Audio chapter summaries and glossary flashcards
  - A media-enriched Pearson eText (see description below)

Get started with the personal access code packaged with your new copy of the text. Personal access codes for MyHRLab can also be purchased separately at **www.pearsoned.ca/myhrlab.**

- **Pearson eText.** Pearson eText gives students access to the text whenever and wherever they have access to the Internet. Pearson eText pages look exactly like those found in the printed text and offer powerful new functionality for students and instructors. Users can create notes, highlight text in different colours, create bookmarks, zoom in or out, click hyperlinked words and phrases to view definitions, and view in single-page or two-page views. Pearson eText allows for quick navigation to key parts of the text using a linkable Table of Contents and provides full-text search function. Pearson eText also offers links to associated media files enabling users to access other activities as they read the text.

# END-OF-CHAPTER MATERIAL

At the end of each chapter there are a number of features and exercises designed for students to review and apply their knowledge of managing human resources.

- **Chapter Reviews** provide summary answers to each chapter-opening Test Yourself question.
- **Key Terms** lists the chapter key terms and their page references.

> ## Chapter Review
>
> ### Answers to Test Yourself
>
> 1. What is the strategic value of the human resources planning process? Identify the techniques used to forecast human resources demand and supply.
>
>    Human resources planning is the process of analyzing and identifying the need for and availability of human resources to ensure that an organization will have the right number of employees, with the right
>
>    Forecasting the supply for human resources can be achieved through Markov analysis, skills/management inventories, replacement charts/summaries, movement analysis, and succession planning.
> 2. Identify and explain the four steps in the recruitment process.
>
>    The four steps in the recruitment process are: (1) identify job openings, (2) determine job requirements and job specifications, (3) select methods of

> ### Key Terms
>
> attrition (p. 117)
> buyout and early retirement programs (p. 117)
> computer-based simulation (p. 110)
> cost per applicant (p. 132)
> cost per hire (p. 132)
> golden parachute (p. 118)
> hiring freeze (p. 117)
> human resources planning (HRP) (p. 105)
> job posting (p. 123)
> job sharing (p. 117)

- **Required Professional Capabilities (RPCs)** lists the chapter RPCs and their page references.

> ### Required Professional Capabilities (RPCs)
>
> RPC 6-1 > (p. 180)
> RPC 6-2 > (p. 183)
> RPC 6-3 > (p. 183)
> RPC 6-11 > (p. 189)
> RPC 6-12 > (p. 192)
> RPC 6-13 > (p. 193)

- **Cases and Exercises** include a wide range of exercises at the end of each chapter. They have been created and revised to give students sound and interesting opportunities to apply their knowledge, discuss ideas, and pose solutions to management problems human resource professionals face today.
- **Case Incidents** present real-world human resource mini case problems and are accompanied by discussion questions.
- **Application Questions** ask students to apply human resources theory into practice; they are designed to give students an opportunity to experience the complexities of managing human resources and propose practical and proactive solution strategies.

> ## Cases and Exercises
>
> myHRlab
> For additional cases and exercises, go to www.pearsoned.ca/myhrlab.
>
> ### CASE INCIDENT
>
> #### Do it yourself, Enviro-Man!
>
> Ken Webster, a skilled labourer, has been working for Jansen's Manufacturing Ltd. for the past 23 years. Ken spends his days repairing machines when they break, monitoring schedules to ensure the plant has ample supplies for each shift, training new recruits on the machines, and helping out on the line when someone calls in sick. Ken has been in the same position for most of his career, and enjoys the work he does mainly because no one bothers him and he can exercise full autonomy in how he manages his day. He gets along with his colleagues and takes great pride in keeping all the machines humming on the shop floor. However, Ken is known for being outspoken, can be rebellious when things do not go his way, and often challenges management on changes made on the shop floor. He has no disciplinary record.
>
> After lunch one day, Ken was hurrying back to his work station and inadvertently put a newspaper in the wrong recycling container. Bill Hamilton, the supervisor, happened to notice this and told Ken to retrieve the newspaper and put it in the proper recycling container. Ken turned to Bill and said, "I'm not paid to sort garbage." Bill replied, "We recycle around here. Get with the program! Put the newspaper in the right recycling container! What's wrong with you?!" Ken became angry and bellowed, "I have machines to fix, and I'm not going to stop and pick up garbage. Do it yourself, Enviro-man!" Ken continued to hurl unflattering names and remarks at Bill while everyone on the shop floor stopped to watch.
>
> out pay for insubordination and use of abusive language when speaking with a supervisor. Ken was escorted by security out of the building, and Bill contacted the human resources department to inform them of the incident and the action taken.
>
> #### Questions
>
> 1. Analyze Bill's approach to disciplining Ken for not recycling according to new company protocol.
> 2. What, if anything, would you have done differently if you were in Bill's position? Explain why.
> 3. What, if anything, should Bill say to the employees who witnessed this incident?
> 4. What course of action should Bill take when Ken returns from his one-week suspension? Explain why.
> 5. If you were the HR manager in this organization, what advice would you give Bill to enhance his approach to discipline?
>
> #### Application Questions
>
> 1. For the past five years, employee turnover in your organization has been escalating.
>    a. Discuss the communications programs you will implement to get a better understanding of the root cause of the problem and the changes needed to reduce turnover.
>    b. What questions will you ask employees to get a better understanding of their concerns and needs?
> 2. There has been a rash of thefts in your factory during the third shift ("the midnight shift") over the past nine months. In an attempt to find the culprits, you decide to mount 12 cameras in the plant, yet only activate them during the third shift. Employees on the third shift are outraged by the decision and feel they are

- **Running Case: LearninMotion.com,** involving the fictional company LearninMotion.com, illustrates typical HRM challenges small business owners and front-line supervisors confront; thought-provoking critical-thinking questions accompany each case.

> ### RUNNING CASE: LEARNINMOTION.COM
>
> #### The New Training Program
>
> The case for Chapter 6, The New Training Program, describes problems that develop without a formal orientation and training program. Students must advise on how to create a suitable plan.

- **Controversial Business Topic exercises** engage students in chapter-related research and in-class debate; they are designed to expand student's skills and knowledge in current, topical areas of human resource management.

> ### CONTROVERSIAL BUSINESS TOPIC EXERCISE
>
> Your colleague, the manager of human resources at a large soft-drink manufacturer, has just alerted you to a very grave situation. The vice-president of marketing for your company—a competing soft-drink manufacturer—has

- **In the Boardroom exercises** challenge students to tackle some of the more difficult questions they might encounter in a typical boardroom setting.

> ### IN THE BOARDROOM EXERCISE
>
> You have recently been hired as the Vice President of HR for an investment banking firm in Toronto, supervising a team of 10 HR representatives who hire senior financial

- **On the International Stage exercises** serve as a follow up to the On the International Stage feature at the end of the chapter. These exercises invite students to research and explore related human resource practices in other countries.

> ### OCCUPATIONAL HEALTH AND SAFETY ON THE INTERNATIONAL STAGE EXERCISE
>
> *The exercise below relates to the Occupational Health and Safety on the International Stage feature on p. 342.*
>
> Select a company that operates its business in at least three different countries around the world. Imagine that this

- **Experiential Exercises,** individual- and group-based, promote the development of practical human resource skills.

> ### EXPERIENTIAL EXERCISE
>
> For further study of text materials and development of practical skills, select the experiential exercise module for this chapter on the companion website. This module provides two to three individual or group-based assignments per chapter.

- **Quiz Yourself: Study Guide Questions** conclude each chapter with a review of key concepts and thought-provoking questions for class discussion.

**QUIZ YOURSELF** | **STUDY GUIDE QUESTIONS**

Circle the correct answer. After completing this self-test, check your answers against the Answers to Study Guide Questions at the back of the book (p. x).

1. What is the key objective of occupational health and safety legislation?
   a. protecting the health and safety of workers by minimizing work-related stress
   b. requiring that hazardous materials in the workplace be labelled
   c. protecting the health and safety of workers by minimizing work-related accidents and illness
   d. protecting the health and safety of workers through wellness programs

5. As the supervisor of a chemical plant, Tom is responsible for disseminating information to workers and ensuring appropriate labelling is carried on hazardous material containers as provided by:
   a. WHMIS
   b. SCF
   c. *Occupational Health and Safety Act*
   d. FAE
   e. EAP

## INSTRUCTOR SUPPLEMENTS

*Management of Human Resources*, Third Canadian Edition, In-Class Edition, is accompanied by a complete supplements package:

- **MyHRlab.** Pearson Canada's online resource, MyHRLab, offers instructors and students all of their resources in one place. With MyHRLab, you will be able to enliven your lectures with a variety of material. Your students will be able to prepare and perform better on assignments and exams with customized study plans. You can assign quizzes and mini-cases that report directly into gradebook. MyHRLab is available to instructors by going to **www.pearsoned.ca/myhrlab** and by following the instructions on the opening screen. Students receive access to MyHRLab when they purchase their new text.
- **Pearson eText.** Pearson eText is accessible on the Internet and offers powerful functionality for students and instructors. Users can create notes, highlight text in different colours, create bookmarks, zoom in or out, click hyperlinked words and phrases to view definitions, and view in single-page or two page views. A linkable Table of Contents allows for quick navigation to key parts of the text and provides full-text search. The eText also offers links to associated media files enabling users to access videos or other activities.
- **MyTest.** MyTest from Pearson Canada is a powerful assessment generation program that helps instructors easily create quizzes, tests, exams, and homework or practice handouts. Instructors can author questions and tests online, which allows ultimate flexibility and efficiency in managing their marking and assessments. MyTest for *Management of Human Resources*, Third Canadian Edition, In-Class Edition, includes more than 1100 multiple-choice, true/false, and short essay questions. The questions are also available in TestGen format on the Instructor's Resource CD-ROM.

**Instructor's Resource CD-ROM (IRCD):** All the supplements that instructors need to teach and test their students are also available on one easy-to-access CD-ROM. The following are included on the IRCD:

- **Instructor's Manual:** This comprehensive guide contains a detailed lecture outline of each chapter, descriptions of the discussion boxes, answers to review and discussion questions, and suggested answers to the cases and exercises. It is available in both Word and PDF format.
- **Pearson Canada Test Generator (TestGen):** The TestGen contains more than 1100 multiple-choice, true-false, and short-essay questions. Each question is rated by level of difficulty and includes a learning-objective reference to where the material is discussed in the text. The TestGen is part of a state-of-the-art software package in the Windows platform. It enables instructors to view and edit the existing questions; create tailor-made, error-free tests; and print the tests in a variety of formats. Powerful search and sort functions make it easy to locate questions and arrange them in any desired order. The Custom Test allows instructors to create an exam, administer it traditionally or online, and evaluate and track students' results—all with the click of a mouse.
- **PowerPoint® Slides:** The PowerPoint slides feature key points and selected full-colour figures and tables from each chapter as well as the In-Class Notes.

**Pearson's Technology Specialists** work with faculty and campus course designers to ensure that Pearson technology products, assessment tools, and online course materials are tailored to meet your specific needs. This highly qualified team is dedicated to helping students take full advantage of a wide range of educational resources, by assisting in the integration of a variety of instructional materials and media formats. Your local Pearson Canada sales representative can provide you with more details about this service program.

**CourseSmart eTextbook** represents a new way for instructors and students to access textbooks online anytime from anywhere. With thousands of titles, across hundreds of courses, CourseSmart helps instructors choose the best textbook for their class and give their students a new option for buying the assigned textbook as an eText at a lower cost. For more information, visit **www.coursesmart.com.**

## INSTRUCTOR RESOURCES ON THE ONLINE CATALOGUE

The online catalogue provides instructors with additional teaching tools. The Instructor's Manual and TestGen are just some of the materials that will be available in this section. Where appropriate, this section will be password protected. To get a password, simply contact your Pearson Canada Representative or call Faculty Sales and Services at 1-800-850-5813.

## ACKNOWLEDGMENTS

The manuscript for the third Canadian edition was reviewed at various stages of its development and by a number of peers from across Canada. We wish to thank those who shared all of their valuable insights and constructive criticisms:

Ronald Alexandrowich
*York University*

George Broderick
*Kwantlen Polytechnic University*

Don Caplan
*Royal Roads University*

Thomas Foard
*Humber College/University of Guelph-Humber*

Janice Foley
*University of Regina*

Ian Gellatly
*University of Alberta*

Cheryl Pollmuller
*University of Lethbridge*

Kathryn Taft
*Capilano College*

At Pearson Canada, we are very grateful for the support and dedicated efforts of Karen Elliott, Cas Shields, Eleanor MacKay, Imee Salumbides, Sally Glover, Andrea Falkenberg, Julia Hall, and Miriam Blier.

On a personal note, I am indebted to my family—my mother, father, sister Angela and her family, Steve, Robbie, Ashleigh, and Jessica, and my brother Steven—for offering encouragement and sharing the journey with me. Thank you for being in my corner.

I am also grateful that my best friends, Wendy and Kieran Kelleher, were the wind at my back listening endlessly to my successes and challenges and offering words of wisdom.

Finally, I am blessed to work with and have the unwavering support and encouragement from my colleagues at Royal Roads University (RRU), especially Dr. Pedro Marquez, Dr. Jo Axe, Dr. Stephen Long, Dr. David Black, Dr. Rick Kool, Dr. Ingrid Kajzer-Mitchell, Dr. Connie Carter, Dr. Marilyn Taylor, Mr. Chris Duff (PhD candidate), and Mr. Don Caplan, M.Ed. You make RRU the best place to learn and work.

*Carolin Rekar Munro*

# 1 chapter THE STRATEGIC ROLE OF HUMAN RESOURCES MANAGEMENT

## Learning Objectives

1. Articulate the role and importance of human resources management (HRM).
2. Explain the importance of strategic HRM and its impact on the bottom line.
3. Identify and discuss environmental influences on HRM.
4. Describe the historical underpinnings of HRM and how history shapes today's HRM practices.
5. Discuss professional advancements in HRM.
6. Identify and discuss HRM challenges in the twenty-first century.

## Test Yourself

1. What is human resources management and what are its objectives?
2. How do strategic HRM practices affect the bottom line?
3. What internal and external environmental factors affect HR policies and practices?
4. How has HRM evolved since its inception?
5. What are five key HR challenges in the twenty-first century?

## 1.1 INTRODUCTION TO HUMAN RESOURCES MANAGEMENT

**Human resources management (HRM)** refers to the management of people in organizations. The goal of HRM is to:

1. attract the best qualified applicants to an organization;
2. engage employees to fully commit skills, abilities, and energy to the organization and to their jobs;
3. maximize employees' contributions in order to achieve optimal productivity and effectiveness while attaining individual objectives (such as having a challenging job and obtaining recognition) and societal objectives (such as legal compliance and social responsibility); and
4. retain employees so they are not tempted to leave the organization in pursuit of more lucrative employment opportunities.

A growing number of companies are beginning to view human resources as a value-adding competitive advantage.[1] As one HR practitioner says, "We can make a difference in terms of how organizations operate, how productive they are, and the success of the organizations, by putting the right people in the right place at the right time."[2] The realization that employees can be central to achieving competitive advantage has led to the development of **strategic human resources management**, defined as "the linking of HRM with strategic goals and objectives in order to improve business performance and develop (an) organizational culture that fosters innovation and flexibility . . . "[3] The term *strategic HR* recognizes an HR department's partnership role in the strategic planning process, while the term *HR strategies* refers to specific HR actions a company might use to achieve its strategic objectives.[4]

Managers are concerned with HRM, since their goals are met through the efforts of others, which requires the effective management of people. This is particularly true in small and medium-sized firms, where the HR department is small or may not exist at all. Every supervisor and line manager has responsibilities related to a wide range of HRM activities, including analyzing jobs, planning labour needs; selecting, orienting, and training employees; managing compensation; communicating (which includes counselling and disciplining); and maintaining employee commitment. HRM might also include ensuring fair treatment; appraising performance; ensuring employee health and safety; building and maintaining good employee/labour relations; handling complaints and grievances; and ensuring compliance with human rights, occupational health and safety regulations, labour relations, and other legislation affecting the workplace.

**RPC 1-1 >**

**Contributes to an environment that fosters effective working relationships**

According to one expert, "The direct handling of people is, and always has been, an integral part of every . . . manager's responsibility, from president down to the lowest-level supervisor."[5] In small organizations, line managers may carry out all of their HRM duties without the assistance of an HR department and must continually focus on HR matters as they manage their employees day by day. As an organization grows, however, they often need assistance, specialized knowledge, and advice from a separate HR staff.[6]

Organization size and complexity are generally major factors in a senior management team's decision to establish an HR department. As an organization grows, managing human resources effectively and ensuring legal compliance become more of a challenge. When department managers and first-line supervisors find that HRM activities interfere with their other responsibilities, the benefits of delegating some of their HRM tasks to a separate HR department are generally seen to exceed the costs of establishing such an entity.

### Human Resources Management Responsibilities

Once an HR department has been created, it is the unit that has overall responsibility for HRM programs and activities. The primary role of the HR department is to create a working environment that is conducive to engagement, collaboration, strong employer–employee relations, and maximum productivity, and that empowers employees to exercise their full potential. The HR department strives to ensure that the organization's human resources are utilized effectively and managed in compliance with company policies and procedures, government legislation, and, in unionized settings, collective agreements. HR department staff members are involved in five distinct types of activities: serving as an internal organizational consultant and strategic change agent; supporting employees; formulating policies and procedures; championing initiatives to attract, engage, and retain employees; and monitoring to ensure compliance.

Many studies have shown that employees are more committed to their jobs when their participation is valued and encouraged. Here, assembly line workers in a Tokyo Nissan factory participate in a worker productivity session attended by managers and supervisors.

**SERVING AS INTERNAL ORGANIZATIONAL CONSULTANT AND STRATEGIC CHANGE AGENT** In most firms, HR professionals serve as internal organizational consultants offering advice to senior management and managers of other departments. HR professionals are often referred to as "right-hand advisors" to senior management and give a human resources perspective on strategic directives and organizational change while informing senior management of employees' concerns, needs, and expectations. Senior managers often seek HR expertise on a wide range of issues: human resources planning, to make sure the right people with the right skills are hired to meet strategic targets; compliance with legislation; labour market trends; strategies for enhancing engagement and decreasing turnover; sustaining a safe and healthy work environment; approaches to maintaining cooperative management–employee relations; and the administration of collective agreements. In seeking HR expertise, senior management not only stay informed but gain advice about initiatives that should be implemented in order to increase organizational efficiency and effectiveness and to create an environment in which employees want to work. HR professionals also provide insight to departmental managers in solving HR issues such as recruitment, job evaluation, training, and approaches for managing employees who are not performing to standard.

**RPC 1-2 >**

**Develops requests for proposals (RFPs) and reviews submissions by third parties**

**RPC 1-3 >**

**Monitors expenditures and timeliness**

**RPC 1-4 >**

**Develops budgeting, monitors expenditures, and evaluates activities of contractors**

In addition to serving as consultants, HR specialists are expected to be "change agents" who exercise leadership in planning, implementing, and evaluating initiatives that help an organization enhance efficiency and effectiveness in reaching its strategic goals. For example, an HR professional may be asked by senior management to investigate the root cause of high turnover in an organization and then implement solution strategies. If the source is lagging salaries and substandard benefits, then the HR professional is expected to develop and implement an equitable compensation system and test its effectiveness. A cost-benefit analysis is often part of the evaluation process in determining whether an initiative adds value to an organization and to what degree.

**RPC 1-5 >**

**Operates within organizational guidelines for procurement of equipment and services**

**SUPPORTING EMPLOYEES** Employees at all levels frequently consult HR department staff for expert advice and counsel. Members of the HR team are expected to be completely familiar with employment legislation, HR policies and procedures, collective agreements, past practices, and the outcome of recent arbitration hearings and court decisions so that they

**human resources management (HRM)** The activities, policies, and practices involved in obtaining, utilizing, and retaining the appropriate number of skilled employees to accomplish an organization's objectives.

**strategic human resources management** The linking of HRM with strategic goals and objectives in order to improve business performance.

can provide sound guidance and suggest solutions. Employees in non-management positions often seek advice from HR professionals when they are experiencing problems with their immediate supervisor and need guidance on how to manage the situation. HR is also a key source of information for employees trying to understand how company policies and procedures directly apply to the work they do.

**RPC 1-6 >**

**Advises clients on status of dependent and independent contractor and elements of employee status**

**FORMULATING POLICIES AND PROCEDURES** The HR department takes the lead in formulating policies and procedures that are compatible with current economic conditions, collective bargaining trends, and applicable employment legislation. A *policy* is a predetermined guide established to provide direction in decision making. Policies define an organization's position on given issues, communicate management's expectations of employees, articulate acceptable/unacceptable behaviour, ensure consistency in the treatment of employees and continuity and predictability in the course of action, and serve as standards against which performance can be measured. HR *procedures* specify a prescribed sequence of steps to be followed when implementing HR policies. To maximize effectiveness, HR policies and procedures should be put into writing in a policy manual or made available online so that they are readily accessible. HR policies and procedures are common in such areas as recruitment, selection, training and development, performance management, compensation, and discipline.

**CHAMPIONING INITIATIVES TO ATTRACT, ENGAGE, AND RETAIN EMPLOYEES** The HR department generally provides services in the following areas on an ongoing basis: recruitment, selection, orientation, training and development, performance management, compensation and benefits administration, labour relations, and occupational health and safety. HR professionals develop initiatives that meet employees' needs and expectations to encourage potential applicants to join the organization and so that existing staff are so engaged in their work and the company that they are not motivated to leave. An increasing number of HR departments are exploring **electronic human resources (e-HR)**, which is the use of technology to deliver HR services and to promote self-service of HR transactions.

Examples of technology in action include the use of social networking tools for recruitment, online orientation and training courses, videoconferencing for staff meetings, and online benefits systems such as pension calculators that help employees determine how long they need to work to achieve the pension earnings they desire. IBM uses Second Life, a virtual community where employees are represented by avatars, for training, recruiting, and team collaborations on "islands." Employees also post their work in Second Life to allow colleagues access to it.[7] Automated HR transactions give employees access to services such as updating personal data, enrolling in and making changes to benefits plans, and accessing personal payroll information. An example of how Best Buy implemented an online pay system is provided in the HR.Net box on page 5.

**RPC 1-7 >**

**Provides services to enable employee success while maintaining the well-being of the organization**

**RPC 1-8 >**

**Develops and maintains a departmental or project budget**

**MONITORING TO ENSURE LEGAL COMPLIANCE** An HR team is generally responsible for monitoring for compliance with employment legislation (this is explained in detail in Chapter 2) and with HR policies and procedures. The department collects and analyzes recruitment, selection, and promotion data to ensure compliance with human rights and employment equity legislation. HR staff also assess salary and benefits data for compliance with employment standards and pay equity requirements and examine accident investigation and grievance reports to ensure that they meet with health and safety and labour relations legislation. They may also analyze data pertaining to absenteeism and turnover or accident rates, for example, to identify problems with policy implementation or failures to comply with specified procedures.

As the HR department's mandate and accountabilities continue to burgeon, organizations are outsourcing some HR functions. **Outsourcing**, the practice of contracting with outside vendors to handle specified functions on a permanent basis, has emerged as a worldwide business trend. The rapid emergence of the use of the Internet to manage everyday business processes electronically, from supply chain to delivery,

HR.NET

## Online Pay System Best Practice for Best Buy

**CANADA POST'S ONLINE DELIVERY SYSTEM SAVES TIME, LABOUR, AND PAPER FOR BEST BUY CANADA'S PAYROLL STAFF**

Getting pay stubs to employees can be a time-consuming, labour-intensive process. Just ask Best Buy Canada Ltd.

Every two weeks, the Burnaby, B.C.-based retailer would print a paper pay statement and stuff it in an envelope, a process it repeated thousands of times for its more than 18 000 permanent employees. Then it would box up the statements and ship them to its 197 stores across the country.

The system was working fine, according to Janice Antaya-Finlayson, Best Buy Canada's vice-president of HR. But the process was time consuming for payroll staff, and the company made a decision that it needed to become more efficient in how it was paying employees.

It decided to look into online delivery of pay statements, something that was not only more efficient but was also in line with the company's commitment to reducing its carbon footprint.

With that in mind, Best Buy Canada approached ePost—Canada Post's electronic delivery service—to have it provide electronic delivery of pay statements to employees.

**How it works**

Employees who opt in to receive electronic pay statements are set up with a password-protected ePost account.

The payroll staff at Best Buy Canada then prepares the payroll with its regular payroll system, Peoplesoft v.8.8, and sends encrypted files of the pay statements to ePost. Those statements are then delivered to employees via e-mail, and they can look at them online at any time. Antaya-Finlayson says ePost accommodated Best Buy Canada's payroll system and none of the other components of payroll processing changed as a result of introducing electronic pay documents. The only change was the creation of new processes in Peoplesoft to record employees' selection of the delivery method and to allow the creation of a pay documents file that provides details of the method of delivery to ePost.

**Tech-savvy employees**

Given the nature of what Best Buy Canada sells—largely electronics—most of its staff are technologically savvy and are online a lot already, said Antaya-Finlayson. As a result, the shift to online payroll didn't encounter much resistance.

When the change was rolled out in late summer, about 45 percent of employees signed up immediately. A detailed communication plan was developed and a strategy was created to challenge employees to "Help Best Buy Canada Ltd. reduce its use of paper."

Best Buy Canada informed employees of the new system through written communications, pay inserts, Intranet postings, newsletters and reminders from HR managers across the country. Stores and regions across Canada were challenged to see who could recruit the highest number of participants, with the winners choosing an environmental charity to send a company donation.

Best Buy Canada staff are happy with the change, said Antaya-Finlayson. With the number of paper statements going out across the country, there were sometimes issues with them arriving late or getting lost on the way to the stores. And it's made things easier for the 8000 or so seasonal employees the retailer hires each December. A lot of the pay statements and T4s the company mailed to those workers would be returned because they had moved after they left the company.

And since a good chunk of employees are paid an hourly rate, with some on commission, speedier electronic delivery means they get their statements a few days before they are paid. This gives them certainty on the amount of their pay and allows them to plan ahead or let payroll know if there are any discrepancies on the statement that need to be fixed.

**More time for payroll staff**

Since they no longer have to stuff so many envelopes and box up as many statements, payroll staff are able to focus more on helping employees and other administrative duties to make payroll run smoother, said Antaya-Finlayson. As a result, payroll staff are enjoying the new system.

**electronic human resources (e-HR)** The use of technology to deliver HR services and to promote self-service of HR transactions.

HRM Guide Canada
**www.hrmguide.net/hrm/Links/can.htm**
CFT Recruitment and Human Resources Consulting
**www.cfthr.com**

**outsourcing** The practice of contracting with outside vendors to handle specified functions on a permanent basis.

"Payroll is such a time-sensitive area with short windows to produce pay and if something goes wrong, you don't have a lot of time to spare," she said. "Freeing up payroll employees from the manual labour of sorting envelopes and courier boxes allows them to do their jobs better."

Before the ePost delivery system was implemented, it took four days of work before payday to ensure employees were paid on time and they received their statements by payday. With the nearly half of employees using the ePost system, preparation time has been cut to about two days, said Antaya-Finlayson.

**Environmental benefits**

Best Buy Canada used to use more than one million pieces of paper to produce pay statements and envelopes, a number that will be reduced by more than 200 000 over a year by sending electronic statements to the nearly 8000 employees that had signed up as of December.

**Employees have a choice**

Best Buy Canada wants as many employees as possible to use the ePost system, but so far employees still have a choice if they're more comfortable with getting paper statements. Employees who have opted into the electronic method can opt out and return to paper by unsubscribing to their ePost account, which will automatically inform payroll of their choice, said Antaya-Finlayson. New employees also can choose which method they prefer.

Source: J. Smith, "Online pay system best practice for Best Buy: Canada Post's online delivery system saves time, labour, and paper for Best Buy Canada's payroll staff," *Canadian Payroll Reporter*, February 19, 2009. Reprinted with permission.

## *In-class Notes*

**Introduction to Human Resources Management**

- Serving as internal organizational consultant and strategic change agent
- Supporting employees
- Formulating policies and procedures
- Monitoring to ensure legal compliance
- Championing initiatives to attract, engage, and retain employees

______________________________

______________________________

______________________________

______________________________

______________________________

______________________________

______________________________

is having a dramatic impact on the outsourcing environment—even in the HR field.[8] Counselling services, payroll administration, and benefits administration are common HR responsibilities that have been outsourced to external experts. Outsourcing administrative tasks enables HR professionals to focus their limited resources on serving as internal organizational consultants and strategic change agents; advising employees; formulating HR policies and procedures; championing initiatives to attract, engage, and retain employees; and monitoring for legal compliance—the core responsibilities in the HR portfolio.

## 1.2 STRATEGIC HR: THE IMPACT OF EFFECTIVE HRM PRACTICES ON THE BOTTOM LINE

HRM is in the midst of a fundamental shift from being a cost item on the income statement to being able to justify its existence as an asset through return on investment. Historically, the HR department performed administrative functions such as payroll, pensions, and benefits administration. This role changed with the advent of technology and then outsourcing, leaving HR professionals free to devote their time to developing a new role, one that could help the company reach its strategic objectives.[9]

Canada's HR professionals are reinventing themselves—changing what they do for the companies that employ them and how they relate to those on the operations side of the business. Their goal is a seat at the senior management table alongside decision makers such as the chief operating, information, and financial officers. This goal will be achieved by quantifying and harnessing the **human capital** resources of the organization, including the knowledge, education, training, skills, and expertise of the company's workers. HR departments are also expected—like other units within the organization—to justify their existence through metrics that illustrate in concrete and measurable terms the value-added contribution that HR programs bring to the organization's bottom line. It no longer suffices for HR to ask for funding of its initiatives without offering return-on-investment data to justify its expenditures.[10]

Research findings indicate that strategic HRM practices have a positive effect on the bottom line if properly implemented and accompanied by a supportive company culture and climate. Studies have established that 15 percent of the relative profit performance of an organization derives from HR strategy. Furthermore, HR systems can affect a firm's market value by $15 000 to $45 000 per employee, and HR systems can affect the probability of new-venture survival by as much as 22 percent.[11]

There is growing research evidence, however, that, in addition to high-involvement HR practices, a complementary workplace culture and climate is required. Studies involving more than 1200 Canadian firms and almost 800 local union leaders found that the highest performance levels are associated with high-involvement HR practices combined with a supportive work environment characterized by participative decision making and open communication.[12]

In addition, HR managers now have numbers to take to the boardroom to prove just how much the department can contribute to the bottom line in the form of the Human Capital Index (HCI), developed by Watson Wyatt. Based on a year-long study analyzing HR practices at more than 400 companies, which were matched with objective financial measures, the HCI outlines 30 key HR practices and indicates, in best-case scenarios, their contributions to shareholder value. These 30 practices were then summarized in five categories: (1) recruiting excellence; (2) clear rewards and accountability; (3) collegial and flexible workplaces; (4) communications integrity; and (5) the imprudent use of resources—the negative impact of poorly implemented HR policies and practices.[13]

A study by Watson Wyatt went beyond previous correlational findings to investigate whether strong HRM drove financial performance or whether successful companies simply had more resources to put into HRM. Results showed that strong HRM was driving company performance. Looking at 51 large companies in North America and Europe, the study found that those with the best HR practices provided a 64-percent total return to shareholders over a five-year period, more than three times the 21-percent return for companies with weaker HR practices. Bruce Pfau, head of organizational effectiveness consulting at Watson Wyatt and author of the study, says, "Evidence from this new research clearly favours superior human capital management as a leading—rather than lagging—indicator of improved financial outcomes."[14] The bottom line is that effective human capital practices drive business outcomes more than business outcomes lead to good HR practices.[15]

A recent Pulse Survey conducted by the *Canadian HR Reporter* and the Human Resources Professionals Association (HRPA) found that 63.5 percent of HR professionals think their organizational leaders perceive them as business partners in the quest to achieve the organization's strategic mandate. The majority of HR professionals (52.4 percent) also reported that they were involved in consultations with senior management before important decisions were made. This is a significant milestone for the HR profession, which has struggled to carve a signature identity as a key player in the boardroom for a number of years. Yet the struggles continue, as only 11 percent of HR professionals declared it was relatively easy for them to establish their business partnership with organizational leaders. Overwhelmingly, 77 percent of HR professionals believe it is more difficult to establish credibility in their field than in any other professional discipline because of the lingering stigma of HR as an administrative function instead of a

**human capital** The knowledge, education, training, skills, and expertise of a firm's workers.

IBM—Cognos 8 Workforce Performance
**www-01.ibm.com/software/data/cognos**

Watson Wyatt Worldwide Human Capital Index
**www.watsonwyatt.com/services/servicerender.asp?ID=21007**

strategic contributor. Approximately one-third (32.9 percent) of HR professionals said they needed to continuously prove themselves as legitimate business partners.

Survey respondents urged the HRPA to raise awareness of HR professionals as business partners by raising the profile of the Certified Human Resources Professional designation (CHRP), allowing the business community to recognize it as a standard of excellence in the profession. Half (50.2 percent) of respondents acknowledged that the profession can do a better job informing the public of HR's positive contribution to society, and 90.3 percent believe the profession should manage its image in a more proactive way. Figure 1.1 showcases key findings from the *Pulse Survey.*[16]

Encouragingly, 81.3 percent of respondents in another survey of HR professionals think HRM and the CHRP designation will be more widely recognized within the next decade, and 76.9 percent believe the profession will play a more strategic role. In part, changing demographics will place a greater accountability on the HR function to recruit, engage, and retain a workforce that brings different values, preferences, attitudes, and behaviours to the workplace.[17]

## 1.3 ENVIRONMENTAL INFLUENCES ON HRM

Internal and external environmental influences play a major role in HRM. Internal organizational climate, culture, and management practices help shape HR policies and practices, which in turn have an impact on the quality of candidates that a firm can attract as well as its ability to retain desired workers. There are also a number of external challenges that dramatically influence the environment of HRM, requiring it to play an ever more crucial role in organizations.

### Internal Environmental Influences

How a firm deals with the following three internal environmental influences has a major impact on its ability to meet its objectives.

First, **organizational culture** consists of the core values, beliefs, and assumptions that are widely shared by members of an organization. It serves a variety of purposes:

- communicating what the organization "believes in" and "stands for"
- providing employees with a sense of direction and expected behaviour (norms)
- shaping employees' attitudes about themselves, the organization, and their roles
- creating a sense of identity, orderliness, and consistency
- fostering employee loyalty and commitment

Culture is often conveyed through an organization's mission statement as well as through stories, myths, symbols, and ceremonies.

All managers with HR responsibilities play an important role in creating and maintaining the type of organizational culture desired. For example, they may organize recognition ceremonies for high-performing employees and be involved in decisions regarding

*In-class Notes*

**Strategic HR**

- HR shifting from administrative to strategic orientation
- Focus on harnessing human capital to achieve strategic goals
- Justifying value-added contribution of HR initiatives by providing return on investment data
- Strong HRM drives company performance
- Slow to evolve in many Canadian organizations

## *figure* 1.1 Pulse Survey: HR Increasingly a Business Partner

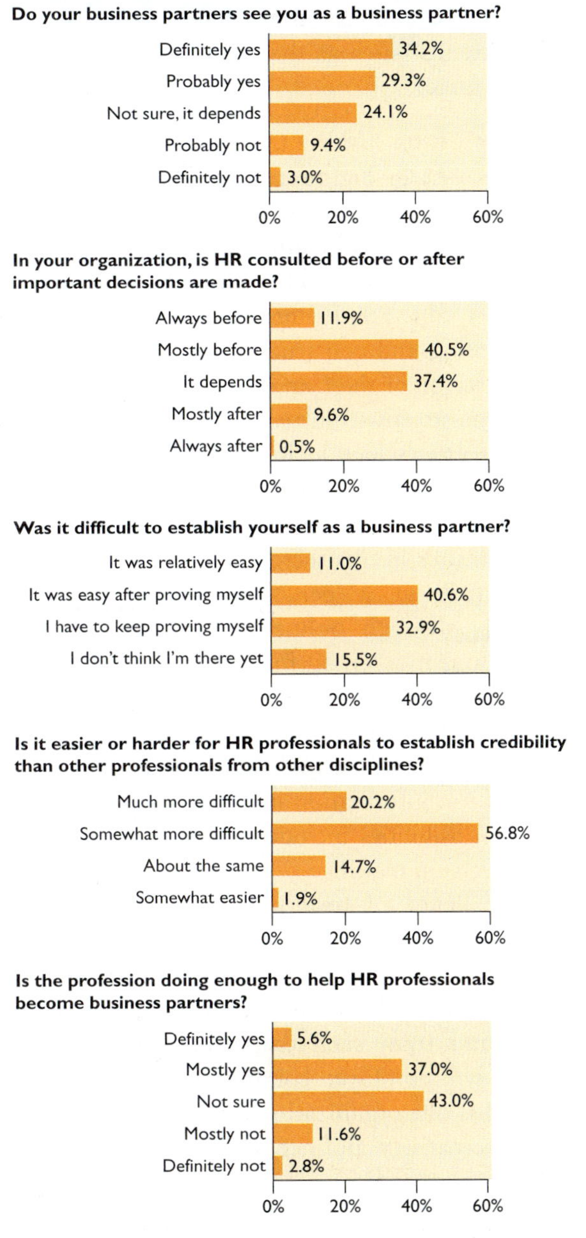


Source: S. Klie, "HR increasingly a business partner: Survey." Pulse Survey. *Canadian HR Reporter,* January 26, 2009, p. 11. Reprinted with permission.

symbols, such as a logo or the design of new company premises. A positive culture has a positive impact on both retention and recruitment. Lloyd Craig, president and CEO of Surrey Metro Savings Credit Union in British Columbia, says, "The most important thing for the head of HR is an appreciation of the culture of the organization. Everything you try to do in HR will fit or not, depending on culture."[18]

Second, **organizational climate** refers to the prevailing atmosphere or "internal weather" that exists in an organization and its impact on employees.[19] Organizations have personalities, just like people. They can be friendly or unfriendly, open or secretive, rigid or flexible, innovative or stagnant. The major factors influencing the climate are management's leadership style, HR policies and practices, and the amount and style of organizational communication. The type of climate that exists is generally reflected in the level of employee motivation, job satisfaction, performance, and productivity and thus has a direct impact on organizational profits and/or ongoing viability. HR department staff members play a key role in helping managers throughout the company to establish and maintain a positive organizational climate.

Third, many new management practices are emerging, with many HRM implications. For example, flatter organizational forms are replacing the traditional *bureaucratic structure* that is characterized by a pyramid shape and hierarchies with many levels of management. These generally emphasize cross-functional teams and improved communication flow, with corresponding de-emphasis on "sticking to the chain of command" to get decisions made.[20] Since managers have more people reporting to them in flat structures, they cannot supervise their employees as closely. Employee **empowerment** is thus becoming more common, and work is increasingly organized around teams and processes rather than specialized functions. *Boundaryless organization structures* are also emerging. In this type of structure, relationships (typically joint ventures) are formed with customers, suppliers, and/or competitors to pool resources for mutual benefit or encourage co-operation in an uncertain environment. Finally, managers today must build employee engagement and commitment in order to ensure the success of client-focused and customer-responsive organizations.

## External Environmental Influences

To be effective, all managers, including those with responsibility for HR, must monitor the environment on an ongoing basis; assess the impact of any changes;

**organizational culture** The core values, beliefs, and assumptions that are widely shared by members of an organization.

**organizational climate** The prevailing atmosphere that exists in an organization and its impact on employees.

**empowerment** Providing workers with the skills and authority to make decisions that would traditionally be made by managers.

and be proactive in implementing policies and programs to deal with such challenges.

**LABOUR MARKET ISSUES** Three labour market issues are particularly relevant to HR professionals: economic conditions, the service sector and the concept of "human capital," and labour unions.

**Economic Conditions** Economic conditions affect supply and demand for products and services, which in turn have a dramatic impact on the **labour force** by affecting the number and types of employees required as well as an employer's ability to pay wages and provide benefits. The **labour market** is the geographic area from which an organization recruits employees and where individuals seek employment.

When the economy is healthy, companies often hire more workers as demand for products and services increases. Consequently, unemployment rates fall, there is more competition for qualified employees, and training and retention strategies increase in importance.[21] Conversely, during a downturn, some firms reduce pay and benefits in order to retain workers. Other employers are forced to downsize, by offering attractive early retirement and early leave programs or by laying off and terminating employees. Unemployment rates rise and employers are often overwhelmed with applicants when vacancies are advertised.

As illustrated in Figure 1.2, **productivity** refers to the ratio of an organization's outputs (goods and services) to its inputs (people, capital, energy, and materials).[22] For example, a shoe manufacturer could measure worker productivity as the number of shoes produced each year per employee. To improve productivity, managers must find ways to produce more outputs with current input levels or to use fewer resources to produce current output levels. In most organizations today, productivity improvement is essential for long-term success. Canada's relatively low productivity growth rate and high labour costs are of grave concern, since competition with foreign companies has become increasingly important.

Organizations must constantly monitor and track trends affecting supply and demand of human resources. By doing so, they can gather information about the prevailing pay rates for employees with particular talents or skills and estimate how difficult it is likely to be to attract and recruit staff. Labour market conditions should also be monitored to determine present and emerging trends (such as the changing composition of the labour force).

**The Service Sector and the Concept of "Human Capital"** As can be seen in Figure 1.3, employment trends in Canada have been experiencing dramatic changes. The *primary sector*, which includes agriculture, fishing and trapping, forestry, and mining, now represents less than 5 percent of jobs. Employment in the *secondary sector* (manufacturing and construction) has also been dropping. The sector of the Canadian economy accounting for the greatest growth in recent decades is the *tertiary or service sector*, which includes public administration, personal and business services, finance, trade, public utilities, and transportation/communications.

Since all jobs in this sector involve the provision of service, often in a person-to-person format but increasingly through online technologies, effectively managing and motivating human resources is critical. Although there are some lesser-skilled jobs (in housekeeping and food services, for example), many service-sector jobs demand **knowledge workers**—employees who transform information into a product or service—whose responsibilities include planning, problem solving, and decision making.

The challenge of fostering intellectual or human capital lies in the fact that knowledge workers must be managed differently from workers of previous generations. New HRM systems and skills are required to select and train such employees, encourage self-discipline, win employee commitment, and spark creativity. 3M is one organization that has learned how to encourage creativity and access the skills and ideas of all of its employees:[23]

> At 3M, there is a corporate policy that 30 percent of its annual revenues must come from products that are less than 4 years old. Thus, over the years, 3M has

*figure* 1.2 **Productivity Ratio**

$$\text{Productivity} = \frac{\text{Outputs (Goods and Services)}}{\text{Inputs (People, Capital, Energy, Materials)}}$$

## *figure* 1.3 Employment by Industry

**Employment by Industry**

| | 2004 | 2005 | 2006 | 2007 | 2008 |
|---|---|---|---|---|---|
| | | | thousands | | |
| **All industries** | **15 947.0** | **16 169.7** | **16 484.3** | **16 866.4** | **17 125.8** |
| Goods-producing sector | 3989.8 | 4002.4 | 3985.9 | 3993.0 | 4021.3 |
| Agriculture | 326.0 | 343.7 | 346.4 | 337.2 | 327.0 |
| Forestry, fishing, mining, oil, and gas | 286.6 | 306.4 | 330.1 | 339.3 | 340.1 |
| Utilities | 133.3 | 125.3 | 122.0 | 138.0 | 151.8 |
| Construction | 951.7 | 1019.5 | 1069.7 | 1133.5 | 1232.2 |
| Manufacturing | 2292.1 | 2207.4 | 2117.7 | 2044.9 | 1970.3 |
| Services-producing sector | 11 957.2 | 12 167.3 | 12 498.4 | 12 873.5 | 13 104.5 |
| Trade | 2507.1 | 2574.6 | 2633.5 | 2682.4 | 2678.8 |
| Transportation and warehousing | 799.4 | 793.6 | 802.2 | 822.8 | 857.7 |
| Finance, insurance, real estate, and leasing | 960.6 | 987.8 | 1040.5 | 1060.4 | 1075.4 |
| Professional, scientific, and technical services | 1018.3 | 1050.0 | 1089.9 | 1136.9 | 1200.0 |
| Business, building, and other support services[1] | 630.2 | 654.4 | 690.0 | 702.1 | 686.5 |
| Educational services | 1035.7 | 1106.1 | 1158.4 | 1183.2 | 1192.8 |
| Health care and social assistance | 1733.4 | 1734.6 | 1785.5 | 1846.1 | 1903.4 |
| Information, culture, and recreation | 738.0 | 735.1 | 745.0 | 782.0 | 759.6 |
| Accommodation and food services | 1012.4 | 1004.5 | 1015.0 | 1069.4 | 1073.5 |
| Other services | 696.6 | 693.4 | 701.0 | 723.5 | 751.1 |
| Public administration | 825.5 | 833.1 | 837.4 | 864.6 | 925.7 |

1. Formerly Management of companies, administrative and other support services.

Source: Statistics Canada, "Employment by industry." www40.statcan.gc.ca/l01/cst01/econ40-eng.htm, Nov. 5, 2009.

mastered the art of motivating employees to come up with new and useful ideas. Scientists and engineers are actively encouraged to form small groups to come up with new ideas and launch new products. If they are unable to obtain funding from the managers of their own business units, they can seek money from other business groups. If that fails, they can appeal to a panel of scientists from across the firm to obtain a "Genesis Grant," which provides up to $50 000 in funding. For example, 3M executives tried to end the Thinsulate project at least five times. Innovators within 3M persisted, however, and the light, waterproof, synthetic fibre is now used in sporting goods, shoes, and car doors.

**Labour Unions** A labour union is an officially recognized association of employees who have joined together to present a united front and collective voice in dealing with management. Once a union has been certified or recognized to represent a specific group of employees, the company is required by law to recognize the union and bargain with it in good faith.

Labour unions affect organizations in several ways. Management has less discretion in implementing and administering HR policies, procedures, and practices when dealing with unionized employees. Labour unions also influence HR policies and practices in

**labour force** Individuals who are employed and those actively seeking work.

**labour market** The geographic area from which an organization recruits employees and where individuals seek employment.

**productivity** The ratio of an organization's outputs (goods and services) to its inputs (people, capital, energy, and materials).

**knowledge worker** An employee who transforms information into a product or service, whose responsibilities include planning, problem solving, and decision making.

non-unionized organizations wishing to remain union-free. Such organizations monitor bargaining activities in their community and industry and ensure that their employees are provided with terms and conditions of employment equal to or better than those being negotiated by unions.

**AN ETHICAL DILEMMA**

The maintenance department supervisor has just come to you, the HR manager, voicing concern about the safety of two of her reporting employees whom she recently discovered are functionally illiterate. What are your responsibilities to these employees, if any?

Many firms are using more **contingent employees**—defined as workers who do not have regular full-time or part-time employment status—to handle vacation and leave coverage, peak-period demands, extra workload, and specialized tasks or assignments. Included are contract workers, seasonal workers, casual and non-regular part-time employees, temporary employees, independent contractors (freelancers), consultants, and leased employees. Contingent workers represent 25 percent of all jobs in Canada, according to 2010 projections.[24]

There are more regular part-time employees in Canada than ever before, as shown in Figure 1.4. The fact that part-time workers are often paid as much as 50 percent less than their full-time counterparts—and may not have benefits coverage—has raised some major equity concerns. Loblaw, Canada's largest grocery chain, employing over 140 000 employees in 1000 stores, faces a turnover crisis with its part-time staff. In retail, including grocery, approximately 77 percent of staff are employed part-time, and the industry has a part-time employee turnover rate of 50 percent every three months, compared to the turnover rate for full-time employees, which is 90 percent lower. Loblaw is converting about 10 percent of its workforce to full-time as part of a plan to enhance productivity and retention.[25]

**DEMOGRAPHIC TRENDS AND INCREASING WORKFORCE DIVERSITY** **Demographics** refers to the characteristics of the workforce, including age, sex, marital status, and education level.[26] The fact that Canada's labour force is becoming increasingly diverse is one of the major challenges confronting HR managers today. **Diversity** refers to "any attribute that humans are likely to use to tell themselves, 'that person is different from me,'" and thus includes such factors as race, gender, age, values, and cultural norms.[27]

**Population Growth** Since Canada's population growth has slowed to less than 1 percent per year, the average age of the workforce is increasing. Canada admits more immigrants per capita than any other country, which

*figure* 1.4 **Labour Force Characteristics**

**Labour Force Characteristics**

| | 2004 | 2005 | 2006 | 2007 | 2008 |
|---|---|---|---|---|---|
| | | | thousands | | |
| **Population 15 years and over** | **25 443.4** | **25 805.5** | **26 185.1** | **26 553.4** | **26 924.7** |
| Labour force | 17 182.3 | 17 342.6 | 17 592.8 | 17 945.8 | 18 245.1 |
| Employed | 15 947.0 | 16 169.7 | 16 484.3 | 16 866.4 | 17 125.8 |
| Full time | 12 998.1 | 13 206.2 | 13 509.7 | 13 803.1 | 13 976.6 |
| Part time | 2948.9 | 2963.5 | 2974.7 | 3063.3 | 3149.2 |
| Unemployed | 1235.3 | 1172.8 | 1108.4 | 1079.4 | 1119.3 |
| Not in the labour force | 8261.1 | 8462.9 | 8592.3 | 8607.6 | 8679.6 |
| **Actual hours worked** | **530 362.0** | **541 729.9** | **548 306.8** | **562 182.6** | **566 022.9** |
| | | | % | | |
| Employment to population ratio | 62.7 | 62.7 | 63.0 | 63.5 | 63.6 |
| Participation rate | 67.5 | 67.2 | 67.2 | 67.6 | 67.8 |
| Unemployment rate | 7.2 | 6.8 | 6.3 | 6.0 | 6.1 |

Source: Statistics Canada, "Labour force characteristics." www40.statcan.gc.ca/l01/cst01/econ10-eng.htm, Nov. 5, 2009.

has created a very diverse labour force. Currently, the fastest-growing groups in the Canadian workforce are women, visible minorities, Aboriginal people, and persons with disabilities.

**Age** The **baby boomers**, born between 1946 and 1964, are characterized as driven to succeed, questioning authority, and valuing power, personal growth, and achievement. Baby boomers are also considered loyal, logical, and bottom-line focused. They began crowding into the labour market in the late 1960s and today represent the largest of the generational cohorts (9.6 million Canadians). The oldest of the baby boomers are now reaching the age of 60, and there are grave concerns as to whether there will be sufficient employees in the labour pool to replace them. Statistics Canada reported that the labour force is precariously balanced, with one employee leaving for every one employee entering, yet in 10 years a sharp negative replacement ratio is expected, with more retirees than workforce entrants.[28] The Conference Board of Canada forecasts an accelerated rate of retirement beginning in 2012, when 30 percent of older, "front-end" baby boomers, who represent 6.6 million workers, will turn 65.[29] By 2030, a quarter of Canada's population will be 65 or older and ready to retire (assuming an age-65 departure). By 2016, a shortage of a million workers is predicted,[30] and even more disturbing is the forecast of 10 million more jobs than people capable of filling them by 2010.[31] Instinctively, Canada looks to the United States as a source of labour, but that country faces the same dilemma. Approximately 60 million U.S. baby boomers are expected to retire in the next 15 years,[32] with 19 percent in management positions forecast to retire in five years.[33] To further exacerbate the situation in Canada, under its current immigration policy, entrance quotas will be deficient in closing the gap.[34] International recruitment offers little resolution, as census data show that 61 countries are experiencing below-average birth rates needed to meet workforce replacement needs.[35]

**Generation X** (individuals born between 1965 and 1980) employees are the smallest generational cohort, consisting of 18 percent (6 million) of the population; these workers will replace the aging boomers. Their workplace needs and preferences consist of flexible work arrangements, continuous skill development, and a balance between work and personal life. Generation X workers are not averse to hard work but place a premium on personal time, value a life-friendly work culture, want to be valued immediately for the skills they bring to the workplace, and like to be active participants in decision making. They view command- and authority-based cultures with disdain and believe that security comes from transferability of skills rather than corporate loyalty.[36] The message to employers is that having workers of diverse ages may create a need to bridge the generation gap.

**Generation Y** (also known as echo boomers or the Net generation), born since 1980, are the children of the baby boomers, who represent 23 percent (8.1 million) of the population. A major challenge facing organizations employing this group is how to attract, engage, and retain Generation Y individuals, who, because of their experiences and attitudes toward work, are markedly different in their workplace needs and expectations. Generation Y is characterized as entrepreneurial and independent; digitally savvy; rejecting micromanagement; and valuing empowerment, challenge, and excitement.[37] They have low levels of trust and loyalty to corporate cultures, which can be attributed to intense media scrutiny of corporations tainted with scandal[38] and having witnessed several instances of organizational downsizing.[39] Consequently, they have become skeptical, mistrustful, and apathetic toward traditional hierarchies and authority.[40] With Generation Y declared "the most entrepreneurial generation in history," organizations are confronted with the added weight of convincing young workers that working for a corporation has greater appeal than self-employment.[41]

**contingent employees** Workers who do not have regular full-time or part-time employment status.

**demographics** The characteristics of the workforce, which include age, sex, marital status, and education level.

**diversity** Any attribute that humans are likely to use to tell themselves, "that person is different from me," and thus includes such factors as race, gender, age, values, and cultural norms.

**baby boomers** Individuals born between 1946 and 1964.

3M Canada Innovation Centre **http://cms.3m.com/cms/CA/en/1-30/crcFzFW/view.jhtml**

Canadian Union of Public Employees (CUPE) **www.cupe.ca**

**Generation X** Individuals born between 1965 and 1980.

**Generation Y** Individuals born since 1980.

Many middle-aged employees are caught in the **Sandwich Generation**, with responsibilities for raising young dependants as well as assisting elderly relatives who are no longer capable of functioning independently. Although some employers, such as the Royal Bank, have been proactive in assisting their "sandwiched" employees, only about 10 percent of Canadian businesses have programs specifically designed to assist workers providing eldercare.[42] Leave for palliative care responsibilities is now provided in most jurisdictions, and Employment Insurance (EI) benefits are payable for six weeks.[43]

**Education** The level of education of the Canadian labour force is increasing at a significant rate. Today, the number of Canadians involved in adult education and training activities rivals the number of students enrolled in the entire elementary, secondary, and post-secondary education systems, a trend that many organizations encourage through tuition-assistance programs.[44] Given the higher expectations of the better-educated labour force, managers are expected to try to ensure that the talents and capabilities of employees are fully utilized and that opportunities are provided for career growth.

Very few Canadians are illiterate in the sense of not being able to read, but a startlingly high proportion (43 percent) have only marginal literacy skills, defined as the ability to understand and use printed and written documents in daily activities to achieve goals and to develop knowledge and potential.[45] A frightening reality is that inadequate reading and writing skills have replaced lack of experience as the major reason for rejecting entry-level candidates.[46] About one in six working-age Canadians is **functionally illiterate**, unable to read, write, calculate, or solve problems at a level required for independent functioning or the performance of routine technical tasks.[47] Since these individuals are in the labour force, their functional illiteracy will affect the ability of their employers to compete in the global economy.

**Visible and Ethnic Minorities** The proportion of visible and ethnic minorities entering the Canadian labour market is growing, in jobs ranging from general labour to technical, professional, and skilled trades. This increase is largely the result of immigration. More than three-quarters of those who came to Canada during the 1990s were members of a visible minority group.[48] Ethnic diversity is also increasing. HR specialists must ensure that policies and programs are developed in their organizations to accommodate and celebrate the diverse cultural characteristics of visible and ethnic minority employees. At Assiniboine Credit Union in Winnipeg, one of Mediacorp Canada's *Best Diversity Employers 2009*, new Canadians are offered three-month paid work placements to help them integrate into the Canadian workplace. The credit union collaborates with the Manitoba government and two other credit unions to facilitate a five-week training program, offer mentorship, and provide regular feedback on performance. At the end of the term, new recruits are considered for permanent jobs at one of the credit unions. So far, 80 percent of the new hires have been offered permanent jobs.[49]

**Women** The growing presence of women has been one of the dominant trends in Canada's labour force since the 1950s.[50] Factors contributing to the dramatic increase in the female participation rate include smaller family sizes, increased divorce rates, the need and desire for dual family incomes, increased educational levels, and the availability of more-flexible working hours and part-time jobs.

Figure 1.5 illustrates the employment participation rates by industry for men and women. Since 1946, the employment rate for adult women has tripled, while that for men has fallen by 30 percent.[51]

During the 1990s, the unemployment rate for women fell below that of men and has remained there.

Of particular significance to employers is the increasing number of women with dependent children in the workforce. A recent study found that 33 percent of highly skilled women take a leave of absence from their careers, and while 93 percent want to return to work, only 74 percent succeed in doing so, with 40 percent returning to full-time status.[52] Many organizations are making a determined effort to accommodate working women and shared parenting responsibilities and offer family-friendly benefits such as on-site daycare and flexible work programs. The University of Western Ontario's Ivey Business School in London has launched a leadership renewal program called ReConnect for professional women returning to work. It is designed for women who have been out of the workforce for at least two years and need to update their skills and knowledge in such areas as governance, finance, and global issues.[53]

**Aboriginal Peoples** Between 1996 and 2006, the number of First Nations (North American Indians, Inuit, and Métis) in the prime working and family-rearing age group (35 to 54) increased by 41 percent, which has exacerbated their current situation and will continue to do so unless drastic measures are taken.[54] First Nations peoples face considerable difficulty in

## *figure* 1.5 Employment by Industry and Sex

| Employment by Industry and Sex | | | |
|---|---|---|---|
| | | 2008 | |
| | | Number employed | |
| | Both sexes | Men | Women |
| | | thousands | |
| **All industries** | **17 125.8** | **9021.3** | **8104.5** |
| Goods-producing sector | 4021.3 | 3123.2 | 898.1 |
| Agriculture | 327.0 | 230.5 | 96.5 |
| Forestry, fishing, mining, oil, and gas | 340.1 | 279.4 | 60.7 |
| Utilities | 151.8 | 115.6 | 36.1 |
| Construction | 1232.2 | 1087.3 | 144.8 |
| Manufacturing | 1970.3 | 1410.4 | 559.9 |
| Services-producing sector | 13 104.5 | 5898.1 | 7206.4 |
| Trade | 2678.8 | 1353.3 | 1325.4 |
| Transportation and warehousing | 857.7 | 647.5 | 210.2 |
| Finance, insurance, real estate, and leasing | 1075.4 | 465.0 | 610.4 |
| Professional, scientific, and technical services | 1200.0 | 693.7 | 506.3 |
| Business, building, and other support services[1] | 686.5 | 366.7 | 319.8 |
| Educational services | 1192.8 | 405.9 | 787.0 |
| Health care and social assistance | 1903.4 | 342.4 | 1561.0 |
| Information, culture, and recreation | 759.6 | 400.3 | 359.4 |
| Accommodation and food services | 1073.5 | 433.0 | 640.4 |
| Other services | 751.1 | 336.3 | 414.8 |
| Public administration | 925.7 | 454.0 | 471.7 |

1. Formerly Management of companies, administrative and other support services.

Source: Statistics Canada, "Employment by industry and sex." www40.statcan.gc.ca/l01/cst01/labor10a-eng.htm, Nov. 5, 2009.

obtaining jobs and advancing in the workplace. The Aboriginal Human Resources Council (AHRC) introduced a training program on recruiting, retaining, and advancing Aboriginal workers to enhance awareness of the gifts and talents they bring to the workplace, to capitalize on Aboriginal perspectives, and to explore how Canadian organizations can build partnerships with First Nations communities.[55]

**Persons with Disabilities** Despite the fact that human rights legislation in every Canadian jurisdiction prohibits discrimination against individuals with disabilities, Canadians with disabilities continue to confront physical barriers to equality every day. Inaccessibility is the rule, not the exception. Even though studies show that there are no performance differences in terms of productivity, attendance, and average tenure between employees who classify themselves as having a disability and those who do not, persons with disabilities continue, on average, to experience high rates of unemployment and underemployment, and lower pay levels.

According to a recent Royal Bank of Canada study, people with disabilities have employment rates

**Sandwich Generation** Individuals with responsibility for raising young dependents as well as for assisting elderly relatives who are no longer capable of functioning independently.

**functionally illiterate** Unable to read, write, calculate, or solve problems at a level required for independent functioning or the performance of routine technical tasks.

HR Technology **www.advantech.com**

## WORKFORCE DIVERSITY

# LGBT Employees Still Face Barriers

**LACK OF AWARENESS, OVERT DISCRIMINATION AND LACK OF ROLE MODELS BLOCK CAREER PATHS**

Esther Dryburgh, a partner in the financial services sector at IBM Canada, struggled for years in deciding whether or not she should come out at work. As a woman, she was already trying to prove she was as capable as men and she worried being out as a lesbian would mean she would have even more to prove.

As she got closer and closer to an executive position in a company with a strong track record of supporting diversity, it became a question of being true to herself and those she worked with.

"What really struck me was authenticity," she said. "I didn't realize the benefits of being truly yourself—you actually realize your potential that way. I realized I was only showing a couple of dimensions of myself."

Two years after coming out, Dryburgh was promoted to an executive position and became the first out lesbian executive at IBM Canada.

Unfortunately, despite laws protecting the rights of lesbian, gay, bisexual and transgender (LGBT) individuals in Canada, a report has found LGBT employees still face barriers in the workplace.

"Legislative protection is not enough. LGBT employees face workplace barriers that create a less inclusive workplace and limit career advancement opportunities," said Deborah Gillis, vice-president for North America at Catalyst, a New York-based advocacy group for the advancement of women.

**Traditional leader straight, white male**

The findings of the Catalyst report Building LGBT-Inclusive Workplaces: Engaging Organizations and Individuals in Change are consistent with other Catalyst research looking at women, visible minorities and women of colour, she added.

"Essentially, the more different you are from the traditional definition of a successful leader—typically a straight, white male—the more challenging you find the workplace," said Gillis.

Catalyst's third report on LGBT-inclusive workplaces is based on the results of two surveys, one of 232 self-identified LGBT employees and one of 17 908 workers, 466 of whom identified as LGBT.

Both LGBT women and men reported exclusion from the "old boys' club," but LGBT women reported facing a less friendly workplace and even greater hurdles than their male counterparts.

About three-quarters (76 percent) of LGBT women reported their manager is comfortable interacting with them, compared to 85 percent of LGBT men. Also, 70 percent of LGBT women reported their manager evaluated performance fairly compared to 80 percent of LGBT men.

LGBT men are also out to more of their colleagues—72 percent of colleagues, compared to 50 percent for LGBT women.

**Stereotypes at root of problem**

The report found a lack of awareness, which may cause other employees to rely on stereotypes, was at the root of the barriers LGBT employees faced. Just 8 percent of respondents reported colleagues are very informed about LGBT issues and just 13 percent said managers are very informed.

However, more LGBT employees felt colleagues and managers are very comfortable with LGBT people (41 percent and 43 percent respectively).

Discriminatory behaviours against LGBT employees—such as homophobia and inappropriate humour, exclusion from important connections inside and outside the organization, and a lack of role models—also affected career advancement.

Respondents gave two main reasons for not coming out at work: a preference to keep personal and professional identities separate and a fear of potential repercussions. Those who decided to come out at work cited several reasons, including a desire to be more authentic, form stronger relationships, become role models and combat homophobia.

Before coming out at work, some respondents first ensured they were seen as good performers or they determined to whom it would be safe to disclose their true identity. For most LGBT employees, coming out at work is a never-ending process because there are always new employees, new work teams and new clients, said Gillis.

Location can make a big difference to an employee's choice to come out. When Dryburgh was working for IBM Canada in Edmonton and Winnipeg, she wasn't comfortable coming out in those areas because, as communities, they aren't as accepting of LGBT people as Toronto, she said.

"It's definitely tougher in those more rural locations," said Dryburgh.

Role models can also make coming out easier. While Michael Bach, national director of diversity, equity and inclusion for KPMG Canada in Toronto, came out in his personal life at age 15, he didn't feel comfortable coming out to his employers. It wasn't until the late 1990s, when he began working for George Smitherman, the first openly gay MPP in Ontario, that Bach felt comfortable enough to come out in the workplace.

While he knew he might face overt discrimination, Bach said coming out meant he could live an authentic life and no longer worry about changing pronouns when talking about his boyfriend.

"I would sleep well at night," he said.

**Inclusiveness builds loyalty**

An LGBT-inclusive environment increases employee engagement by allowing employees to be authentic and spend less time self-editing, which creates employee loyalty and reduces turnover, stated the report. An inclusive environment can also increase revenue by encouraging LGBT employees to help an organization tap new markets.

At IBM, it's an important business strategy for the workforce to represent customers because it builds customer loyalty, said Dryburgh. When she came out to one of her customers, an openly gay man, she was able to tell him about how the company supports LGBT employees.

"He felt good about doing business with a company that supported his diversity group," she said.

If LGBT employees don't feel their organization is inclusive, they'll choose not to disclose their sexual orientation, which makes them "invisible" to the organization. As a result, the organization won't be able to fully understand the benefits, needs, and challenges of these employees, decreasing the likelihood of the workplace becoming more inclusive, said Gillis.

Efforts aimed at creating LGBT-inclusive workplaces, such as diversity training, employee networks and mentoring programs, result in LGBT employees having better workplace relationships, improved perceptions about workplace fairness, and increased organizational commitment and career satisfaction, which are linked to increased productivity, found the report.

"Having an inclusive workforce is part of our strategy to ensure we retain and attract the best talent possible," said Cory Garlough, Toronto-based vice-president of global employment strategies at Scotiabank.

One year ago, Scotiabank created Scotia Pride, an employee group for LGBT employees and their allies, and the bank was recently named one of Canada's Best Diversity Employers by Mediacorp Canada. But Sylvia Chrominska, global head of global human resources and communications with Scotiabank in Toronto, knows there's still more work to be done.

"We also understand we must keep working to make our environment more inclusive in the years to come," she said. "In the business community we know there's still a lot that needs to be done to achieve ultimate inclusion."

**Pride at work**

*Making workplaces LGBT-inclusive*

Lesbian, gay, bisexual and transgender (LGBT) employees working in organizations with effective and inclusive diversity practices report better workplace relationships and greater organizational commitment and career satisfaction, according to "Building LGBT-Inclusive Workplaces: Engaging Organizations and Individuals in Change," a report from Catalyst.

To help organizations become more inclusive, Catalyst has the following recommendations:

- Increase awareness by identifying and tackling organizational issues related to LGBT employees company-wide.
- Create and enforce anti-discriminatory policies and practices and communicate these externally as well as internally to all employees.
- Implement diversity training to help dispel LGBT myths and stereotypes.
- Help LGBT employees find mentors and form employee groups.
- Make consistent and inclusive communications a core goal. For example, organizations should make it clear that partners of employees, regardless of sex, are invited to corporate events and that discrimination, in any form, will not be tolerated.
- Include LGBT identity in diversity metrics to help ensure these employees, and candidates, aren't overlooked in recruiting and promotion.
- Leverage general talent management practices to support all employees. Broad talent management practices without a specific focus on diversity and inclusion will help develop all employees and improve workplace experiences.

Source: S. Klie, "LGBT employees still face barriers. Lack of awareness, overt discrimination, and lack of role models block career paths." *Canadian HR Reporter,* July 13, 2009. Reprinted with permission.

that are about 30 full percentage points below those without a disability. Men with a severe disability who secure full-time employment earn almost 24 percent less than their non-disabled counterparts.[56]

Overall, organizations such as IBM have led the way in seeking the benefits of workforce diversity, as described in the Workforce Diversity box on page 16.

**AN ETHICAL DILEMMA**

How much responsibility does a firm have toward employees whose skills will soon become obsolete due to changing technology?

**TECHNOLOGY** Manufacturing advances, such as robotics and computer-aided design/computer-aided manufacturing (CAD/CAM), have eliminated many blue-collar jobs, replacing them with fewer but more highly skilled positions. When robots were introduced to the automobile industry, for instance, there was a major decrease in the demand for welders and painters but a new demand for technicians who could program, install, and service automated equipment.[57] Unfortunately, the training of the Canadian labour force has not kept pace with the rate of technological change and innovation. Consequently, there is a scarcity of skills in certain fields.

While much of the impact of information technology has been positive, it has also led to some organizational problems. For many employees, it has created anxiety, tension, resentment, and alienation. Unions have consistently expressed concerns about job displacement and health hazards, such as those related to video display terminals. Questions concerning data control accuracy, the right to privacy, and ethics are at the core of a growing controversy brought about by information technologies.

As discussed earlier, technology is increasingly used as a delivery mechanism for HR services. Originally, many firms introduced a *Human Resources Information System (HRIS)* to store detailed information on employees, HR policies and procedures, government laws and regulations, and collective agreements; to track statistics on absenteeism, grievances, and health and safety; to collect data for government statistical reporting and employment equity purposes; to advertise jobs and recruit candidates; and to communicate with employees.

Robotics is revolutionizing work in many fields. Such technology requires highly trained and committed employees.

More recently, some companies have implemented *enterprise resource software* systems (SAP being the most common) that include an HRM module. Today, Canadian employers are using HR Intranet portals and e-HR to provide personalized service to employees.[58] The majority of Canadian organizations use HR technology in office and HR administration, document and file handling, HR transactions, employee research, payroll, benefit self-service, education, skills inventory, and career planning.[59]

**GOVERNMENT** Various laws enacted by governments have had and will continue to have a dramatic impact on the employer–employee relationship in Canada. In one recent survey, 70 percent of the HR specialists responding cited changing regulatory requirements as a major factor altering their work environment.[60]

Some employment-related legislation is aimed at prohibiting discrimination in various aspects and terms and conditions of employment, such as human rights, employment equity, and pay equity. Other laws require employers to meet certain obligations, such as occupational health and safety regulations and employment standards regarding holidays, hours of work, and labour relations. Still others provide social benefits, such as Workers' Compensation, Employment Insurance, and the Canada/Quebec Pension Plans, which require financial contributions from employers and/or employees.

One of the factors that make the laws affecting employment in Canada so challenging is *multiple jurisdictions*. Each province and territory (13 in all) has its own human rights, employment standards, labour relations, health and safety, and workers' compensation legislation. While there is some commonality across jurisdictions, there is also considerable variation. This means that companies with employees in more than one jurisdiction have different rules applying to different employees.

LEGALcompliance

To complicate matters even further, employees in certain organizations that operate across Canada are not covered by provincial/territorial legislation but

## In-class Notes

**Environmental Influences on HRM**

Internal
- organizational culture
- organizational climate
- new management practices

External
- labour market issues
- demographic trends and increases in workforce diversity
- technology
- government
- globalization

by federal employment law. These employees represent about 10 percent of the Canadian workforce, including employees of the federal government and Crown corporations, chartered banks, airlines, national railways, and the Canadian armed forces. There are also certain laws that apply to all employers and employees across Canada. These federal laws include Employment Insurance and the Canada/Quebec Pension Plan.

The laws mentioned above and their accompanying regulations have important implications for all managers. HR professionals inform managers of changes to the laws; develop and administer legally compliant policies and practices to avoid losing government contracts, fines, or other penalties for noncompliance; and guard against adverse publicity.

**GLOBALIZATION** **Globalization** refers to the growing tendency of firms to extend their sales, service, or manufacturing to new markets abroad. As one international business expert put it, "The bottom line is that the growing integration of the world economy into a single, huge marketplace is increasing the intensity of competition in a wide range of manufacturing and service industries."[61] Canadian-based Four Seasons Hotels and Resorts is an example of an organization that has aggressively targeted the global marketplace. The company operates 75 hotels in 31 countries including Europe, the Middle East, and Africa.

There are increasing numbers of multinational corporations—firms that conduct a large part of business outside the country in which they are headquartered and that locate a significant percentage of their physical facilities and human resources in other countries. Many organizations are locating new plants in areas where wages and other operating costs are lower. For example, Hewlett Packard's computers are assembled in Mexico, and 3M has located one of its newest plants in India.[62] Many multinational firms also set up manufacturing plants abroad to utilize that country's professionals and engineers. From boosting the productivity of a global labour force to formulating selection, training, and compensation policies for expatriate employees, managing globalization and its effects on competitiveness will thus continue to be a major HR challenge in the years to come.

As organizations become more intrigued with doing business on the international stage, their attention

**globalization** The tendency of firms to extend their sales, service, or manufacturing to new markets abroad.

Human Resources and Skills Development Canada - **www.hrsdc.gc.ca/eng/home.shtml**

## GLOBAL HRM

# Business of People behind the Great Wall

**CANADIAN HR DELEGATION TAKES PEEK AT CHINA'S EVOLVING HR PRACTICES**

In October and November last year, a team of Canadian HR professionals visited China through the People to People Ambassadors program—a program established in 1956 under the leadership of former United States president Dwight Eisenhower.

It marked the first time Canadian HR professionals had participated in the program and the delegation included senior HR practitioners from across the country. The group travelled to Hong Kong, Beijing, Guilin and Shanghai where we had the opportunity to examine population demographics, organizational development, recruitment and retention, the impact of supply and demand demographics on business, total compensation structures, cost of living and standard of living, learning and development infrastructures, the impact of geographic location and the supply of a skilled workforce in China—and the overall relevance to Canada.

**North America—advanced people management**

In North America, the business of people management has existed for many decades. It has evolved from an industrial relations model to an administrative management model to a strategic model leveraging organizational effectiveness.

We have many practices that work very well and, by the same token, many practices that have evolved into a complex web of taxing bureaucracies rooted in serious inefficiencies. We sport layers upon layers of complex legislation, regulations and rules that often have competing objectives. As a result, it is becoming increasingly difficult for businesses to operate efficiently under this system.

**China—emerging market in people management**

In what was described by our team as the "land of opposites," we had a rare opportunity to get a glimpse into the vast land, immense diversity, ancient traditions and ultra-modern society that is China.

It's common to see high-end cars zip along crowded streets, passing old rusted bicycles carrying various wares to market. The contrast between the two is striking, an interesting mix of commerce under communism.

Companies in China are now beginning to instill a corporate spirit and sense of community among workers. This clearly demonstrates the universal appreciation that a happy workforce is a productive workforce and, in turn, is good for the bottom line.

Our delegation visited seven different organizations and educational institutions that offered a unique view into the complex business world of China. Make no mistake about it—China is a force to be reckoned with. The people of China embody a strong sense of community, have strong family values, take great pride in their country and have a daring, entrepreneurial spirit. HR practices in many Chinese organizations are highly sophisticated and are evolving at such a rapid pace China may certainly achieve strategic HR across its companies and organizations before its Canadian counterparts.

The following is a brief overview of some of the organizations and educational institutions we visited:

**Professional HR associations:** The HR Association for Chinese and Foreign Enterprises has many Fortune 500 companies as members and is strategic in its ability to leverage communication between business and government, even providing input on new labour laws. It has developed a certification model for HR professionals and is facing many of the same opportunities and challenges Canadian HR associations are experiencing—growing memberships and difficulty engaging senior practitioners, to name a few.

**Consulting firms:** The Value Added Consulting Firm as well as the China International Intellectech (Shanghai) are examples of consulting firms that are evolving and prospering. They offer a wide range of sophisticated, innovative, progressive and forward-thinking methodologies that provide clients with highly developed professional services and technical savvy to maintain a competitive advantage in China, and beyond.

**Private companies:** Firms such as Taikang Life Insurance and Yanjing Li Spring Beer know retaining a talented workforce is the key to success. They use sophisticated compensation and bonus programs, as well as pension, benefit and leave programs, in rewarding top talent. Both companies have an impressive track record under rapid expansion and development and have experienced mergers, acquisitions and cultural transformation.

**Academic institutions:** Schools such as the Guangxi Normal University and the Shanghai Normal University struggle to keep up with the demand for HR development, experienced instructors, and curriculum development to meet rapidly changing business needs and requirements. Remarkably, many programs have only been in existence for less than five years, which again is a testament to the Chinese capacity for vigorous development and implementation.

**The impact of China's "one-child policy"**
China's "one-child policy" has had a dramatic effect, resulting in a serious imbalance in demographics. This issue will have a long-lasting ripple effect on the population that will be felt around the world, affecting family units, organizations, educational institutions, companies, and countries.

Traditionally, the male child cares for the aging family, so male children have been preferred by many Chinese families. Vast numbers of female children have been adopted by families outside of China. This lopsided demographic will present significant challenges to China in the years to come.

The one-child policy has also resulted in the development of Western-style expectations among the younger generation. As parents devote all their love, attention, and financial resources to their one offspring, this has led to a generation of "little emperors." So companies in China, the U.S., and Canada will have the same challenges in motivating and retaining young talent who have high expectations and demands.

**The role of China's government**
Much has been said, speculated, and written about China's communist regime. While undoubtedly no government is perfect, we experienced a genuine desire by the government to improve the quality of life for its people.

Enhancements such as national wellness strategies, improved labour laws, and increased education will enable China to maintain its increased presence as a dominate world leader. By the same token, the government also has the capacity to enact large-scale change, such as cleaning up the highly polluted Li River by closing all the factories along the river.

All of these factors—supply and demand, demographics, government regulations, and organizational development—are entwined in economic development, company profitability, and HR management practices. They form a web of complex factors that have remarkably similar features clear across the globe.

Source: D. Wiesenthal, "Business of people behind Great Wall (Guest Commentary), Canadian HR delegation takes peek at China's evolving HR practices," *Canadian HR Reporter,* May 4, 2009. Reprinted with permission of the author.

focuses to better understanding other countries and how they operate. The Global HRM box on page 20 features a summary of the experiences of a delegation of Canadian HR professionals during a recent visit to China, where they explored the culture, legislation, and business practices.

In order to be fully skilled in a global workplace, an increasing number of Canadians are enrolling in language training. Employees cite a host of advantages associated with learning a second or third language: greater career options (72 percent), more job options (66 percent), stronger relationships with colleagues (77 percent), flexible job locations (62 percent), accelerated promotions (48 percent), and higher salaries (44 percent). Unilingual Canadians have agreed that not having a second language restricted their career options (38 percent). Languages earmarked as the most beneficial for navigating in a global economy include Spanish, Mandarin, and Cantonese.[63]

## 1.4 A BRIEF HISTORY OF HRM

HRM has changed dramatically over time and has assumed an increasingly important role. The demands on HR department staff members and expectations regarding the types of assistance they should provide have increased correspondingly. HR practices have been shaped by society's prevailing beliefs and attitudes about workers and their rights. Table 1.1 outlines the three distinct stages in the general evolution of management thinking about workers, each of which had a different focus: scientific management, human relations, and human resources.[64]

### Scientific Management: Concern for Production

Frederick Taylor was the driving force behind **scientific management**, the process of "scientifically" analyzing

**scientific management** The process of "scientifically" analyzing manufacturing processes, reducing production costs, and compensating employees based on their performance levels.

Frederick Taylor (1856–1915), the father of scientific management.

manufacturing processes, reducing production costs, and compensating employees based on their performance.[65] The scientific management movement had a significant impact on management practices in the late 1800s and early 1900s. Taylor emphasized task simplification and performance-based pay.

Based on his underlying assumptions about workers and the appropriate role of managers (explained in Table 1.1), Taylor advocated achieving operational efficiency through work simplification and paying workers a piece rate, with extra pay for pieces produced in excess of the daily standard. It was his belief that such incentives would lead to higher wages for workers, increased profits for the organization, and workplace harmony.

All management theorists did not accept Taylor's views. For example, Mary Parker Follett, a writer who was ahead of her time, advocated the use of self-management, cross-functional cooperation, empowerment, and managers as leaders rather than dictators.[66]

## The Human Relations Movement: Concern for People

The primary aim of the **human relations movement**, which emerged in the 1920s and 1930s but was not fully embraced until the 1940s, was to consider jobs from an employee's perspective. Managers who treated workers as machines were criticized. This management philosophy was based on the results of the Hawthorne Studies, a series of experiments that examined factors influencing worker morale and productivity. The conclusions had a significant and far-reaching impact on management practices.

The researchers discovered that the effect of the social environment is equal to or greater than that of the physical environment. They learned that workers' feelings and morale are greatly influenced by such factors as working conditions, the supervisor's leadership style, and management's philosophy regarding employees. Treating workers with dignity and respect was found to lead to higher job satisfaction and productivity levels; economic incentives were of secondary importance.

In the many firms embracing the human relations approach, working conditions improved substantially. Based on the beliefs about workers and managers highlighted in Table 1.1, managerial approaches to motivation had a strong social emphasis. To overcome low morale, feelings of alienation, and prevailing poor performance, managers focused on establishing better channels of communication, allowing employees to exercise more self-direction, and treating them with consideration.

This movement came under severe criticism for its overcompensation of the dehumanizing effects of scientific management by failing to recognize the importance of structure and work rules, for oversimplifying the concept of employee motivation, and for its lack of recognition of individual differences in beliefs, needs, and abilities.

## The Human Resources Movement: Concern for People and Productivity

HRM is currently based on the theoretical assumptions of the **human resources movement**, listed in Table 1.1. Arriving at this joint focus on people and productivity involved four evolutionary phases in the HR function.[67]

**PHASE ONE** In the early 1900s, "personnel administration," as it was then called, played a secondary or even non-existent role. During this era, personnel administrators assumed responsibility for hiring and firing (a duty formerly looked after by first-line supervisors), ran the payroll department, and administered benefits. Their job consisted largely of ensuring that procedures were followed.

**PHASE TWO** As the scientific management movement gained momentum, operational efficiency increased. However, wages generally fell behind productivity growth, causing workers to distrust management.

*table* 1.1 **Theories of Management**

| Scientific Management Model | Human Relations Model | Human Resources Model |
|---|---|---|
| **Assumptions** | **Assumptions** | **Assumptions** |
| 1. Work is inherently distasteful to most people. | 1. People want to feel useful and important. | 1. Work is not inherently distasteful. People want to contribute to meaningful goals that they have helped establish. |
| 2. What workers do is less important than what they earn for doing it. | 2. People desire to belong and to be recognized as individuals. | 2. Most people can exercise far more creative, responsible self-direction and self-control than their present job demands. |
| 3. Few want or can handle work that requires creativity, self-direction, or self-control. | 3. These needs are more important than money in motivating people to work. | |
| **Policies** | **Policies** | **Policies** |
| 1. A manager's basic task is to closely supervise and control employees. | 1. A manager's basic task is to make each worker feel useful and important. | 1. A manager's basic task is to make use of "untapped" human resources. |
| 2. A manager must break tasks down into simple, repetitive, easily learned operations. | 2. A manager should keep employees informed and listen to their objections to his/her plans. | 2. A manager must create an environment in which all members may contribute to the limits of their ability. |
| 3. A manager must establish detailed work routines and procedures and enforce these firmly but fairly. | 3. A manager should allow employees to exercise some self-control on routine matters. | 3. A manager must encourage full participation on important matters, continually broadening employees' self-direction and control. |
| **Expectations** | **Expectations** | **Expectations** |
| 1. People can tolerate work if the pay is decent and the boss is fair. | 1. Sharing information with employees and involving them in routine decisions will satisfy their basic needs to belong and to feel important. | 1. Expanding employee influence, self-direction, and self-control will lead to direct improvements in operating efficiency. |
| 2. If tasks are simple enough and people are closely controlled, they will produce up to standard. | 2. Satisfying these needs will improve morale and reduce resistance to formal authority—employees will "willingly co-operate." | 2. Work satisfaction may improve as a "byproduct" of employees making full use of their resources. |

Source: Abridged and adapted from Raymond E. Miles, *Theories of Management*, (McGraw-Hill: New York, 1975). Reprinted with permission of Raymond E. Miles, Professor Emeritus and former Dean, Haas School of Business, University of California, Berkeley.

Many turned to unions for support. The increase in unionizing activities dramatically changed the role of personnel departments. Personnel managers were expected to develop policies and practices that would enable the firm to retain non-union status, if possible, and, if not, to serve as the primary contact for union representatives. Following the depression of the 1930s, workers sought government intervention to provide some form of financial protection in the case of job loss and to recognize their right to form and join unions. Various laws were enacted, including a minimum wage act, an unemployment insurance program, and protection of workers' right to belong to unions. Legal compliance was subsequently added to the responsibilities of personnel managers.

During the 1940s and 1950s, personnel managers were also involved in dealing with the impact of the human relations movement. Orientation, performance appraisal, and employee relations responsibilities were added to their portfolio.

**PHASE THREE** The third major phase in personnel management was a direct result of government laws passed during the 1960s, 1970s, and 1980s that affected employees' human rights, wages and benefits, working conditions, and health and safety, and established penalties for failure to meet them. The role and accountability of personnel departments expanded dramatically. They continued to provide expertise in such areas as recruitment, screening, and training, but in an expanded capacity. During the latter part of this era, the term "human resources management" emerged. This change represented a shift in emphasis—from maintenance and administration to corporate contribution, proactive management, and initiation of change.[68]

**PHASE FOUR** The fourth phase of HRM is ongoing. Most managers today believe that employees are motivated primarily by the nature and scope of the job, social influences, the nature of the compensation and incentive systems, organizational culture and climate, management's leadership style, and individual needs and values. It is widely recognized that employees do not all seek the same rewards and that most of them sincerely want to make a contribution. To harness this drive and determination, organizations must develop strategies to maximize employee performance and potential such that the goals and aims of both management and employees are achieved. In today's flattened, downsized, and responsive organizations, highly trained and committed employees—not machines—are an organization's best competitive advantage. The role of the HR department has thus shifted from protector and screener to planner and change agent.

## 1.5 GROWING PROFESSIONALISM IN HRM

Today, HR practitioners must be professionals in terms of both performance and qualifications, concerning themselves with all aspects of HRM and their impact on organizational performance and society as a whole. Every profession has four major characteristics—a common body of knowledge, certification of members, self-regulation, and a code of ethics.

### *In-class Notes*

**A Brief History of HRM**

- Scientific management—concern for production
- Human relations movement—concern for people
- Human resources movement—concern for people and productivity
- Today, focus on people as a competitive advantage

The Canadian Council of Human Resources Associations (CCHRA) is the national body through which nine provincial HR associations are affiliated. International Personnel Management Association (IPMA) Canada is the national association for public-sector and quasi-public-sector HR professionals.[69] Other important associations for HR specialists include the Canadian Society for Training and Development, the Canadian Association of Management Consultants, the Canadian Industrial Relations Association, WorldatWork (formerly the Canadian Compensation Association), the Industrial Accident Prevention Association, the Construction Safety Association, and Safe Communities Canada.

**AN ETHICAL DILEMMA**

Suppose that you, an HR professional, have discovered that an HR colleague, who is a good friend, has been "leaking" confidential information about employees to other employees. How would you handle this situation?

**RPC 1-9 >**

**Stays current in terms of professional development**

## Certification of HR Professionals

The HR profession in Canada requires member **certification**, which is recognition for having met certain professional standards. The CCHRA offers a national Certified Human Resources Professional (CHRP) designation involving a National Knowledge Exam (NKE), an experience requirement (effective May 2010), and a recertification process every three years.[70] Academic requirements to be fulfilled before taking the National Knowledge Exam vary by province. The academic requirements for Ontario are shown in Figure 1.6. Effective January 1, 2011, CHRP applicants will require a degree—in any discipline—to be granted the CHRP designation.

As of May 2010, a new requirement was added in order to attain the CHRP designation—individuals must have had at least three years of demonstrated experience in HR at a professional level. Candidates must demonstrate the following:[71]

- Activities are at the professional level, and
- At least 51 percent of his or her daily activities are with the HR function, OR
- An individual has direct supervision of those who deliver HR services.

In 2009, four provinces launched the Senior Human Resources Professional designation (SHRP) to recognize senior human resources professionals who have made a significant strategic contribution to their organization and to the HR profession. Ontario, Saskatchewan, Nova Scotia, and PEI led the way in promoting this designation as a way to celebrate and showcase senior HR leaders and what they can do for an organization, as well as to provide a goal for HR professionals who are working toward or have already earned their CHRP designation. The interprovincial task force responsible for the designation modelled it after senior HR designations offered by the Society for Human Resources Management in the United States and the Chartered Institute of Personnel and Development in the United Kingdom. Candidates interested in the designation complete a detailed questionnaire that is evaluated by an assessment committee consisting of SHRP volunteers.[72]

## Code of Ethics

The professionalization of HRM has created the need for a uniform code of ethics that deals with what is good or bad and right or wrong and with moral duty and obligation. Professional associations create codes of ethics to promote and maintain the highest possible standards of personal and professional conduct among members and to assist them in handling ethical dilemmas. Agreement to abide by the code of ethics is one of the requirements of maintaining professional status. The Code of Ethics of the CCHRA is shown in Figure 1.7.

**human relations movement** A management philosophy based on the belief that the attitudes and feelings of workers are important and deserve more attention.

**human resources movement** A management philosophy focusing on concern for people and productivity.

International Personnel Management Association
**www.ipma-aigp.ca**

Canadian Council of Human Resources Associations (CCHRA) **www.cchra-ccarh.ca**

Human Resource Professionals Association
**www.hrpa.ca/Pages/home.aspx**

Ethics Resource Center
**www.ethics.org**

**certification** Recognition for having met certain professional standards.

**RPC 1-10 >**

**Understands and adheres to the Canadian Council of Human Resources Association's Code of Ethics**

**AN ETHICAL DILEMMA**

Can or should an employee reveal information about a troubled co-worker that was disclosed in confidence, and if so, under what circumstances?

The most prevalent ethical issues confronting Canadian firms today pertain to security of information, employee and client privacy, environmental issues, governance, and conflicts of interest.[73] The major reasons for the failure of ethics programs to achieve their desired results are lack of effective leadership and inadequate training.

**RPC 1-11 >**

**Contributes and promotes the development of the profession**

Positive outcomes associated with effectively implemented ethics programs include:

- increased confidence among stakeholders, such as clients, partners, and employees
- greater client/customer and employee loyalty
- decreased vulnerability to crimes committed against the public and legal liability issues
- reduced absenteeism
- increased employee productivity
- reduced losses due to internal theft
- increased profits and public trust.[75]

## 1.6 HUMAN RESOURCES MANAGEMENT CHALLENGES IN THE TWENTY-FIRST CENTURY

### Formulating and Implementing Corporate Strategy

Perhaps the most striking change in the role of HR professionals is their growing importance in formulating and implementing strategy. Traditionally, **strategy**—a company's plan for how it will balance its internal strengths and weaknesses with external opportunities and threats in order to maintain a competitive advantage—was formulated without HR input. Today, things are very different. Strategies increasingly depend on strengthening organizational responsiveness and building committed work teams, and these put HRM in a central role.

Thus, it is increasingly common to involve HR professionals in the earliest stages of formulating and implementing a company's strategic plan. More and more organizations have come to realize that HR professionals are of greatest benefit to a company when they become strategic partners, responsible for leading organizational change initiatives, formulating business

***figure* 1.6 Ontario CHRP Academic Requirements**

In order to meet the varying needs of HR professionals, HRPAO supports a variety of paths to completing the academic requirements for the CHRP designation:

| Option 1<br>Complete a Nine Course Academic Program | Option 2<br>Take Challenge Exams | Option 3<br>Participate in an Executive Certificate Program |
|---|---|---|
| Human Resources Management<br>Organizational Behaviour<br>Finance and Accounting<br>Training and Development<br>Occupational Health and Safety<br>Employee and Labour Relations<br>Human Resources Planning<br>Compensation<br>Staffing (Recruitment) | If a candidate has significant work experience in a specific HR field, did not achieve the minimum grade requirement in a course, or took courses more than 10 years prior, he or she can choose to write challenge exams to qualify for writing the National Knowledge Exam (NKE). | HRPAO has partnered with several post-secondary institutions to offer programs for senior-level HR professionals interested in achieving the Certified Human Resources Professional (CHRP) designation (e.g., Rotman Advanced Program in Human Resources Management; Sprott School of Business Executive Certificate in Strategic Human Resources Leadership).[74] |

Source: Excerpted from Human Resources Professionals Association of Ontario, *Become a Certified Human Resources Professional (CHRP): Your Road to Excellence and Professionalism.* Copyright © 2005. Used with permission of the HRPAO, www.hrpao.org.

## *figure* 1.7 CCHRA National Code of Ethics

### 1. Preamble

As HR Practitioners in the following categories—

- Certified Human Resources Professionals,
- CHRP Candidates, or
- CHRP Exam Registrants

we commit to abide by all requirements of the Code of Ethics of the Canadian Council of Human Resources Associations (CCHRA), as listed in this document. (Where provincial codes are legislated, those will prevail.)

### 2. Competence

- Maintain competence in carrying out professional responsibilities and provide services in an honest and diligent manner.
- Ensure that activities engaged in are within the limits of one's knowledge, experience and skill.
- When providing services outside one's level of competence, or the profession, the necessary assistance must be sought so as not to compromise professional responsibility.

### 3. Legal Requirements

- Adhere to any statutory acts, regulation or by-laws which relate to the field of Human Resources Management, as well as all civil and criminal laws, regulations and statutes that apply in one's jurisdiction.
- Not knowingly or otherwise engage in or condone any activity or attempt to circumvent the clear intention of the law.

### 4. Dignity in the Workplace

- Support, promote, and apply the principles of human rights, equity, dignity and respect in the workplace, within the profession and in society as a whole.

### 5. Balancing Interests

- Strive to balance organizational and employee needs and interests in the practice of the profession.

### 6. Confidentiality

- Hold in strict confidence all confidential information acquired in the course of the performance of one's duties, and not divulge confidential information unless required by law and/or where serious harm is imminent.

### 7. Conflict of Interest

- Either avoid or disclose a potential conflict of interest that might influence or might be perceived to influence personal actions or judgments.

### 8. Professional Growth and Support of Other Professionals

- Maintain personal and professional growth in Human Resources Management by engaging in activities that enhance the credibility and value of the profession.

### 9. Enforcement

- The Canadian Council of Human Resources Associations works collaboratively with its Member Associations to develop and enforce high standards of ethical practice among all its members.

Source: The CCHRA National Code of Ethics © 2005. Reprinted with the permission of the Canadian Council of Human Resources Associations.

Professional associations create codes of ethics to promote and maintain high standards of professional conduct.

strategies in cooperation with operational managers, and building effective HR strategies.

In today's intensely competitive and globalized marketplace, maintaining a competitive advantage by becoming a cost leader and/or differentiator puts a heavy premium on having a highly committed and competent workforce. Many experts emphasize the strategic role that committed employees play in helping organizations achieve competitive advantage.

**ROLE IN FORMULATING STRATEGY** HR professionals, often together with line managers, can play a role in what strategic planners call **environmental scanning**, which involves identifying and analyzing external opportunities and threats that may be crucial to an organization's success. These managers can also supply *competitive intelligence* that may be useful as the company formulates its strategic plans. Examples include details regarding a successful incentive plan being used by a competitor, consumer surveys, and information about pending legislative changes.

HR professionals also participate in the strategy formulation process by supplying information regarding a company's internal strengths and weaknesses. Once weaknesses have been identified, corrective action can be planned and taken. Some companies even build their strategies around an HR-based competitive advantage. For example, in the process of automating its factories, farm-equipment manufacturer John Deere developed a workforce that was exceptionally talented and expert in factory automation. This in turn prompted the company to establish a new technology division to offer automation services to other companies.[76]

**RPC 1-12 >**

**Gathers, analyzes, and reports relevant business and industry information, including global trends**

In the Canadian public sector, a serious labour shortage is looming, with 30 percent of employees forecast to retire in the next seven years.[77] Specifically, the public sector is expecting a leadership crisis that must be addressed immediately. Strong leadership is critical given

## In-class Notes

**Growing Professionalism in HRM**

- Canadian Council of Human Resources Associations (CCHRA)
- Certified Human Resources Professional (CHRP) designation
- National Knowledge Exam (NKE)
- an experience requirement
- recertification every three years
- Code of Ethics

the magnitude of accountabilities for domestic and international affairs, including education, health care, disaster preparedness, foreign relations, and new trade prospects.[78] In order to meet future human resources needs, the public sector must formulate an aggressive strategy to recruit applicants and to train and mentor them for management positions.

**RPC 1-13 >**

**Encourages interaction between the organization and external stakeholders (e.g., public, government, educational institutions, community groups) that supports the development and implementation of the HR plan**

**ROLE IN EXECUTING STRATEGY** According to leading HR researcher Brian Becker, "It isn't the content of the strategy that differentiates the winners and losers, it is the ability to execute."[79] Strategy execution has traditionally been the "bread and butter" of HRM's strategy role. For example, the competitive strategy may involve differentiating the organization from its competitors by offering superior customer service through a highly committed, competent, and customer-oriented workforce.[80]

HR professionals support strategy implementation in numerous other ways. For example, they are heavily involved in the execution of most firms' downsizing and restructuring strategies through establishing training and retraining programs, arranging for outplacement services, instituting pay-for-performance plans, and helping to redesign jobs. In addition, HR professionals and line managers jointly play a critical role in strategies to increase organizational effectiveness through better performance management.[81]

## Improving Product and Service Quality

Organizations known for product and service quality strongly believe that employees are the key to their reputation and that proper attention to employees improves both quality and productivity. A review of management practices in such companies as GE, FedEx Canada, and 3M Canada indicates that top-level commitment, employee involvement, and a conscious strategy to encourage innovation are critical for productivity improvement.[82] All of these require the presence of strategic HRM policies and procedures.

HR professionals and line managers play a pivotal role in lowering labour costs—the single largest operating expense in many organizations, particularly in the service sector. Doing so might involve introducing strategies to reduce turnover, absenteeism, and/or the rate of incidence of occupational illnesses and injuries. It could also mean adopting more effective recruitment, selection, and/or training programs. At one international tire-manufacturing firm, for example, adopting a behavioural interview strategy as the basis for selection of entry-level engineers resulted in savings of $500 000 in three years. These savings were due to lower turnover, lower training costs, and improved capabilities of the engineering staff because of a better fit.[83]

Employee behaviour is particularly important in organizations providing personal services. All other efforts to attract a customer will have been wasted if the customer is confronted by someone who is discourteous or unprepared to discuss the pros and cons of different products or services. Many such organizations have little other than superior service to differentiate them from their competitors, and that makes them uniquely dependent on their employees' attitudes and motivation—and thus on effective HRM. As noted by Kevin Scott, senior manager of HRM at the Bank of Montreal, "In the financial-services sector, just about everything that's new can be copied by competitors pretty quickly. What distinguish a company are the "people" business aspects. People are the critical differentiating component. . . ."[84]

## Increasing Responsiveness to Change

Making an enterprise more responsive to product/service innovations and technological change involves flattening the pyramid, empowering employees, and organizing around teams. This in turn facilitates communication and makes it easier for decisions to be made so that the organization can respond quickly to its customers' needs and competitors' challenges. HR professionals, together with all other managers and employees, play a crucial role in accomplishing these objectives.

**strategy** A company's plan for how it will balance its internal strengths and weaknesses with external opportunities and threats in order to maintain a competitive advantage.

**environmental scanning** Identifying and analyzing external opportunities and threats that may be crucial to an organization's success.

A recent study isolated the top five workforce challenges that HR executives will need to address over the next decade. HR executives are expected to champion change initiatives in the following areas:[85]

- Retaining top talent
- Honing management's leadership skills
- Recruiting top talent
- Maximizing employee engagement
- Developing future leaders

The Strategic HR box below provides a glimpse into the working world in 2020. HR professionals must contemplate how they will lead their organizations through the changes.

**STRATEGIC HR**

## What Will the Working World Look Like in 2020?

**HR MUST PROVE ITS WORTH OR RISK BEING SIDELINED**

The business world is going to change drastically in the next decade and HR professionals need to figure out how to make themselves relevant in the future or risk being pushed aside, according to a report from PricewaterhouseCoopers (PwC) in the United Kingdom.

In examining what the world of work might look like in 2020, PwC found there is significant opportunity for the HR function to become one of the most powerful parts of the business. But if HR doesn't step up, the function could be almost completely outsourced or absorbed by other departments, according to the report Managing Tomorrow's People: The Future of Work to 2020.

Previous PwC surveys of chief executive officers found they are increasingly focused on the people agenda. But CEOs also worry HR is not equipped to do what the CEOs want, said Michael Rendell, partner and leader of human resource services for PwC in London.

There are several steps HR professionals can take to ensure they deliver and help organizations thrive. The first is to understand the business in which they're operating, said Rendell.

"Without that kind of knowledge, that kind of relevance to the business, they are hopelessly at sea when it comes to talking about what's the people impact of the particular things the organization is trying to do," he said.

HR also needs to use metrics that show the link between talent and profits to prove the department's value to the executive team.

"The HR function needs to become more relevant again and the only way to do that is to link into the planning process and really understand what it needs to evolve to and then start measuring its effectiveness," said Ellen Corkery-Dooher, partner in PwC Canada's advisory services practice.

**Three possible worlds**

Knowing where the business is going is crucial for HR because the people they recruit today and the programs they put in place will shape the business of the future, said Rendell. To help them better predict the evolution of their business, Managing Tomorrow's People gives HR professionals a glimpse into three possible worlds of work in 2020.

Blue World: Large corporations turn into mini-states and take on a prominent role in society.

Orange World: The focus is on specialization and the rise of collaborative networks of workers.

Green World: The environmental agenda drives the business strategy.

Most likely all three worlds will co-exist in some form, with aspects of one becoming more prominent in certain regions or sectors, said Rendell.

"I think we'll see a world that has a blend of the different characteristics of the different worlds," he said.

**The Blue World**

In the Blue World model, corporations will lock in the best talent by providing employees with benefits such as housing, health care and tuition. But despite these perks, top talent will still be hard to find and senior executives will use personal agents to seek out the best deals. Young people will be profiled at age 16 and most of the top talent will be linked to an organization, which will pay for their education, by the age of 18.

This kind of link between corporations and education can be seen today, said Rendell. For example, one automotive manufacturer in the U.K. couldn't find enough qualified graduates so it started its own university.

"Increasingly we're seeing, especially in the U.K., academies and schools that are sponsored by and set up by particular employers," he said.

In the Blue World, the people and performance model is the closest to what many companies aspire to today, linking HR interventions to business performance and using human capital metrics to evaluate corporate activity.

In this world, individuals will have long careers with a single employer and corporations will have a lot of control over employees, at work and at home.

"The question is, how much freedom are people prepared to trade for a certainty about a future?" asked Rendell.

There is already a clear desire among the younger generation for stability and regularity, according to a PwC survey of 2739 graduates from China, the United States and the U.K. More than three-quarters (78.4 percent) expect they'll have just two to five employers throughout their career.

And while 74 percent of respondents believe they'll work from a mix of locations (home and office), 75 percent expect to work regular office hours. Despite that result, employers shouldn't abandon their move toward more flexible workplaces, said Rendell.

"Flexibility in the working environment is a critical element of attracting and retaining the best people," he said, adding new graduates probably need to work for a few years before they truly value flexibility.

**The Orange World**

The Orange World is the diametric opposite of the Blue World. In this world, networks will prosper while large companies fall. Trade barriers will be non-existent and the global village will become a global network of small, linked communities.

In this world, individuals will develop specialized portfolio careers, usually working on a short-term, contract basis. They will join craft guilds that manage career opportunities and provide development opportunities, medical insurance and pensions.

Within organizations, the people strategy will be replaced with a sourcing strategy to maintain an optimum supply of people and HR will work with expertise networks and guilds to attract the talent the organization needs.

**The Green World**

In the Green World, consumers will demand ethics and environmental credentials, forcing companies to develop a social conscience. Audits and quarterly reports will include a measurement of greenness and companies that fail to meet government regulations will be penalized.

In this world, HR will play a critical role in developing the corporate social responsibility program to recruit new graduates who are looking for socially responsible employers.

This is something graduates are already looking for today, according to PwC's graduate survey. Nearly nine in 10 respondents (86.9 percent) said they would deliberately seek out an employer with corporate responsibility behaviour that reflects their own values. Unfortunately, businesses have been slow to catch on, said Rendell.

"I'm not sure that message has got through yet to the boardrooms," he said.

Employers in the Green World will also take a holistic approach to learning, with secondments and paid sabbaticals to work on worthy causes becoming common. This is something young workers are already looking for, according to the PwC survey. Nearly all of the survey respondents (93.9 percent) expect to work across more geographic borders than their parents did.

"There's a real expectation for mobility," said Corkery-Dooher in Canada. Usually this is reserved for more experienced employees, but relocation is becoming more important to people early in their careers.

"That's viewed as a real incentive to work somewhere," she said.

While it's hard to predict what the working world will look like in 2020, the most important thing for employers today is to be adaptable, said Rendell.

"The key for me is flexibility in the way employers recruit, retain and develop their people," he said.

Source: S. Klie, "What will working world look like in 2020? HR must prove its worth or risk being sidelined." *Canadian HR Reporter*, September 22, 2008. Reprinted with permission.

## Building Employee Engagement

Intense global competition and the need for more responsiveness put a premium on *employee engagement*—the commitment of employees to the organization and to their jobs. There is also the added challenge of bridging the differences between four generational cohorts in the workplace: traditionalists, baby boomers, Generation X, and Generation Y. Each brings a unique profile of work expectations, preferences, work behaviours, and personality characteristics that can sometimes contribute to workplace conflict. The challenge for HR professionals is to help employees see their differences as opportunities in order to build collaborative and high-performance work teams. Building employee engagement is often championed by HR professionals but requires active involvement and commitment from everyone in an organization. Companies focused on employee engagement also tend to engage in *actualizing practices*, which aim to ensure that employees fully use their skills and gifts at work and become all that they can be. Building employee engagement will be discussed later in the textbook.

## Licensing of the HR Profession

Boardroom tables are buzzing with discussion about whether HR professionals should be licensed. The Pulse

Survey found that 48 percent of HR professionals are in favour of some form of licensing, with 43.7 percent opposed. Those who reject licensing say there are no guarantees that a licensed HR professional will offer better or more accurate advice, and it would be difficult to license people who provide HR advice because many line managers also perform HR duties. Most respondents in favour of licensing believe it would guarantee a certain level of competence among HR professionals, which would protect employers and the public. Licensing would raise the credibility of the profession and give employers more reassurance, especially when HR professionals are offering advice around legislation.[86] Figure 1.8 illustrates highlights of the survey.

*figure* 1.8 **Pulse Survey: Growing Professionalism**

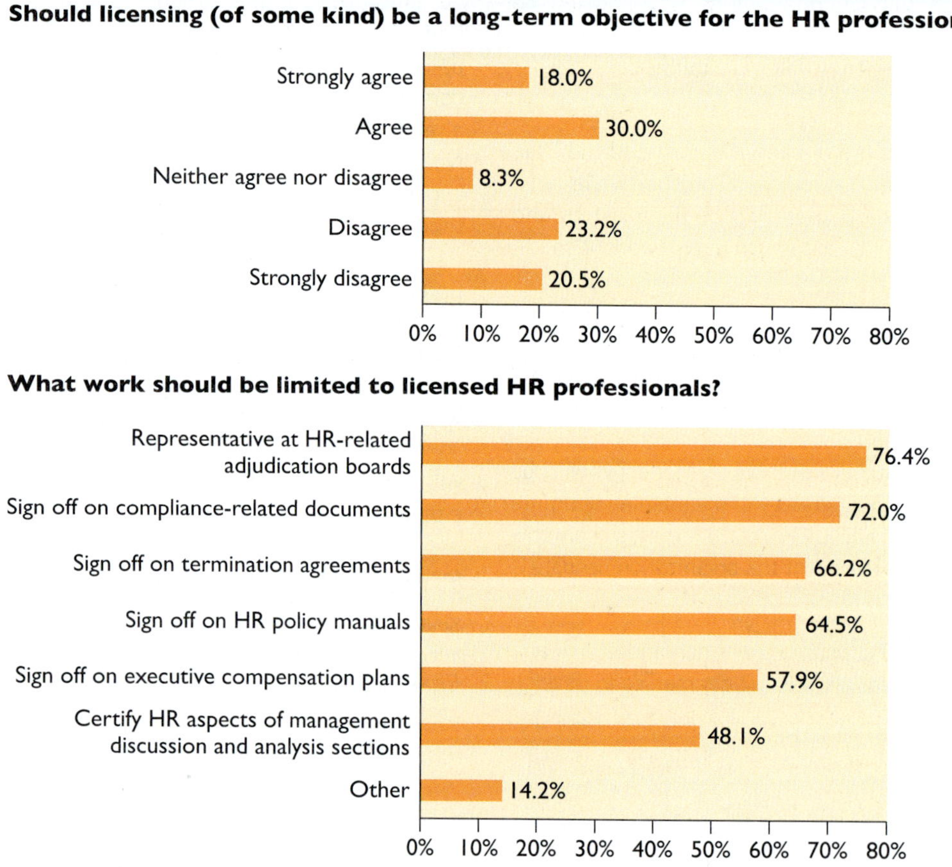


Source: S. Klie, "HR divided on need for licensing: Survey." *Canadian HR Reporter,* January 12, 2009, p. 8. Reprinted with permission.

## *In-class Notes*

**Human Resources Management Challenges in the Twenty-First Century**

- Formulating and implementing corporate strategy
- Improving product and service quality
- Increasing responsiveness to change
- Building employee engagement
- Licensing of the HR profession

# Human Resources on the International Stage

Multinational organizations devote substantial amounts of time exploring the optimal ways to manage their *human resources overseas.* In their pursuit to create environments conducive to high performance and productivity, organizations adapt to a host country's culture, customs, business culture and etiquette, workforce expectations, and regulatory practices; and respect labour market conditions and stages of economic development. For example, multinational organizations initiate aggressive succession-planning initiatives in India, given that the most important motivator to the Indian workforce is promotional opportunities. Employers in China augment their training budgets because Chinese workers report higher levels of engagement with companies that offer professional development. In Russia, local and international companies poach talent at such a staggering and expensive rate that companies establish cash reserves so that in the event employees are approached by the competition, current employers can match or exceed the salary offer. Employers refrain from introducing "Employee of the Year" awards in the Netherlands because such public recognition is ridiculed.

An international study examined employee engagement across the globe, which informs multinational companies about how they can create an engaging workplace as a precursor to achieving organizational mandates. The study found that some attributes, such as a sense of personal accomplishment, are universal, but there are notable differences. In China, engagement occurs when employees are given fair pay for their contributions, awarded comparable benefits to industry, provided with opportunities for training, and have confidence in senior management. Engagement in the United Kingdom stems from regular feedback on performance, workplace cooperation, and strong connections with customers and clients.[87]

As organizations expand into the global marketplace, it is incumbent on them to adapt to international protocol, legislation, and business practices so that their collaborations with host countries will result in the achievement of organizational mandates.

# CHAPTER REVIEW

## Answers to Test Yourself

1. What is human resources management and what are its objectives?

   Human resources management (HRM) refers to the management of people in organizations. The goal of HRM is four-fold: (a) to attract qualified candidates; (b) to engage them in the organization and their jobs; (c) to maximize employees' contributions in order to achieve optimal productivity and effectiveness while simultaneously attaining individual objectives (such as having a challenging job and obtaining recognition) and societal objectives (such as legal compliance and demonstrating social responsibility); and (d) to retain employees so they are not tempted to leave for more lucrative employment opportunities.

2. How do strategic HR practices affect the bottom line?

   Historically, HRM has performed administrative functions such as payroll, benefits, and pensions. With changes in technology and the availability of outsourcing, the HR function has changed and developed into a role that helps a company reach its strategic objectives. Recent research shows that strategic HR practices have a positive effect on the bottom line. Fifteen percent of relative profit performance has been found to derive from HR strategy.

3. What internal and external environmental factors affect HR policies and practices?

   Internal environmental factors influencing HRM include organizational culture, organizational climate, and management practices, such as the shift from traditional bureaucratic structures to flatter organizations where employees are empowered to make more decisions. External factors include labour market issues, demographic trends and increasing workforce diversity, technology, government, and globalization.

4. How has HRM evolved since its inception?

   When the Industrial Revolution occurred in the late 1800s, the scientific management philosophy viewed people as machines and led to a focus on achieving operational efficiency through work simplification and performance-based pay. During the early part of the twentieth century, the Hawthorne Studies, which showed the effect of the social environment to be equal to or greater than that of the physical environment, led to the emergence of the human relations movement, and concern for people became the focus. Based on a concern for both people and productivity, the human resources movement evolved as the century progressed. In the early 1900s, personnel administration largely consisted of ensuring that procedures were followed. In the 1930s, an increase in unionizing activities changed the role of personnel managers to serving as the primary contact for union representatives. During the second half of the twentieth century, the term "human resources management" emerged when the role of personnel departments expanded dramatically as a result of government legislation. The latest phase of HRM is ongoing and recognizes that highly trained and committed employees—not machines—are often a firm's best competitive advantage.

5. What are five key HR challenges in the twenty-first century?

   Five key HR challenges in the twenty-first century are: developing and implementing corporate strategy; improving product and service quality; increasing responsiveness to change; building employee engagement; and licensing of the HR profession.

## Key Terms

baby boomers (p. 13)
certification (p. 25)
contingent employees (p. 12)
demographics (p. 12)
diversity (p. 12)
electronic human resources (e-HR) (p. 4)
empowerment (p. 9)
environmental scanning (p. 28)
functionally illiterate (p. 14)
Generation X (p. 13)
Generation Y (p. 13)
globalization (p. 19)
human capital (p. 7)
human relations movement (p. 22)
human resources management (HRM) (p. 2)
human resources movement (p. 22)

knowledge workers (p. 10)
labour force (p. 10)
labour market (p. 10)
organizational climate (p. 9)
organizational culture (p. 8)
outsourcing (p. 4)
productivity (p. 10)
Sandwich Generation (p. 14)
scientific management (p. 21)
strategic human resources management (p. 2)
strategy (p. 28)

## Required Professional Capabilities (RPCs)

RPC 1-1 > (p. 2)
RPC 1-2 > (p. 3)
RPC 1-3 > (p. 3)
RPC 1-4 > (p. 3)
RPC 1-5 > (p. 3)
RPC 1-6 > (p. 4)
RPC 1-7 > (p. 4)
RPC 1-8 > (p. 4)
RPC 1-9 > (p. 25)
RPC 1-10 > (p. 26)
RPC 1-11 > (p. 28)
RPC 1-12 > (p. 28)
RPC 1-13 > (p. 29)

# Cases and Exercises

**myHRlab**

For additional cases and exercises, go to **www.pearsoned.ca/myhrlab.**

## CASE INCIDENT

### Launching HR at Briar Construction Ltd.

Briar Construction Ltd. is a medium-sized construction company serving Durham Region in Ontario. It employs 415 construction workers: 45 administrative staff, 7 managers, and a contingency workforce of approximately 65 people who work for the company during the busy season. Over the past three years, Briar has successfully landed a number of lucrative residential and commercial contracts in the growing Durham community. For its outstanding craftsmanship and service, Briar Construction was recognized by the Chamber of Commerce as the "community's choice"—a prestigious award sought after by many companies in the region.

The management team at Briar Construction, headed by CEO Don Cavlan, met to discuss the strategic direction of the company over the next 10 years. They are targeting 300 percent growth in business by expanding into metropolitan Toronto. In order to achieve this goal, Don realizes that a considerable investment in human resources is required, as the existing staff cannot manage the overwhelming workload that is expected from this expansion. Briar Construction does not have an HR department as part of its organizational structure. The management team takes responsibility for human resources issues in their units. Yet, given the expansion plans, it is not realistic or feasible for management to manage human resources issues, as it takes away from their daily responsibilities as line managers overseeing construction projects. Don proposes they hire an HR manager to provide leadership in establishing an HR department and looking after all human resources-related activities. The management team vehemently opposes the idea, arguing that the hiring of another senior person is a waste of money, that HR does little more than hire and monitor employee benefits, and that there is no return on investment and impact on the bottom line from an HR department. Don ignores management's criticism and proceeds to hire an HR manager.

Congratulations! You have been hired as the HR Manager for Briar Construction Ltd.!

#### Questions

1. What is your first task as the new HR Manager for Briar Construction Ltd.?
2. When you establish an HR department that adds value to an organization, what does it look like?
3. How will you deal with management's concerns about the legitimacy of an HR department in the company?

4. Discuss how you will position yourself as a business partner at the boardroom table.
5. After a year on the job, how will you determine if you are adding value to the company's bottom line?

### Application Questions

1. The human resources department is considered one of the most important contributors to organizational success and viability. Present key business arguments to defend this position.
2. Identify challenges that HR professionals face as they fulfill their mandate in the organization and discuss how they should manage these challenges.
3. The measure of effective human resources functionality within an organization is based on the degree to which the HR department demonstrates its strategic relevance. What should HR professionals do to assume greater accountability for strategic management in an organization?
4. What practices and programs should HR professionals implement to accommodate the changing demographic profile of the workforce?
5. Discuss approaches that HR practitioners should take to create an organizational culture that embraces diversity.

## RUNNING CASE: LEARNINMOTION.COM

### Introduction

The case for Chapter 1, "Introduction," familiarizes students with a new company—LearninMotion.com, its owner–managers, and the first two years of its history.

To read this case, go to www.pearsoned.ca/myhrlab and click on *Management of Human Resources,* Third Canadian Edition, In-Class Edition, cover. Click on the case module in Chapter 1. The Running Case illustrates a variety of challenges often confronted by HRM professionals, small-business owners, and front-line supervisors. It places students in the role of HR management consultants to help the fledgling LearninMotion.com develop HR policies, strategies, and long-term goals. Each case is accompanied by assignments in the form of critical-thinking questions posed to the student.

## CONTROVERSIAL BUSINESS TOPIC EXERCISE

For the past seven years, you have facilitated an orientation program for new recruits with the aim of acclimatizing them to the workplace. You decided to collect data this year to determine what value the orientation has for new employees. Regrettably, the feedback indicates that the orientation does not add value and actually makes their transition to the workplace more difficult. You decide to shred the data and not report your findings at the next HR meeting. Was this the right thing to do? Why or why not?

## IN THE BOARDROOM EXERCISE

As manager of human resources for a large software development company, you deliver an annual report to the board of directors on HR achievements, progress on current initiatives, and strategic goals for the next year. This year, you announce that you are enrolled part-time to take courses toward the CHRP designation. The board is flabbergasted and not sure why you are doing this. They argue that it is a waste of time since you have been practising in the HR field for the past nine years and could probably teach the courses. The board does not see the value of the designation and refuses to provide financial support or release time for you to pursue your designation. How will you respond to this situation?

## HUMAN RESOURCES ON THE INTERNATIONAL STAGE EXERCISE

*The exercise below relates to the Human Resources on the International Stage feature on p. 33.*

Select a multinational organization that you would be interested in working for when you graduate. Assume you are the human resources manager, accountable for managing human resources overseas, and that the organization is expanding its business into a global community that it has not yet explored. Identify the new country in which this organization should do business, and outline the approach you will take to create a work environment that is conducive to engagement and productivity for locals.

## EXPERIENTIAL EXERCISE

For further study of text materials and development of practical skills, select the Experiential Exercise module for this chapter on www.pearsoned.ca/myhrlab. This module provides two to three individual or group-based assignments per chapter.

# Quiz Yourself

**STUDY GUIDE QUESTIONS**

Circle the correct answer. After completing this self-test, check your answers against the Answers to Study Guide Questions section at the back of the book (p. 433).

1. The activities, policies, and practices involved in obtaining, developing, utilizing, evaluating, maintaining, and retaining the appropriate number and skill mix of employees to accomplish the organization's objectives is called:
   a. human resources management
   b. people management
   c. personnel management
   d. strategic HR management
   e. all of the above
2. The HR department has overall responsibility for HRM programs and activities. Its primary role is to ensure that the organization's human resources are utilized effectively and managed in compliance with policies and procedures and government legislation. The role that HR is expected to perform is:
   a. consultant
   b. change agent
   c. compliance monitor
   d. advisor
   e. all of the above
3. Research findings indicate that strategic HRM practices have a positive effect on the bottom line if properly implemented and accompanied by a supportive company and culture. The Human Capital Index developed by Watson Wyatt outlines key HR practices and their contributions to shareholder value. The practices include:
   a. recruiting excellence and high pay
   b. clear rewards and performance appraisal
   c. collegial and flexible workplaces
   d. communications integrity and high pay
   e. all of the above
4. Organizational culture consists of core values, beliefs, and assumptions that are widely shared by members of an organization. All managers with HR responsibilities play an important role in creating and maintaining the type of organizational culture desired. Organizational culture can be conveyed through:
   a. mission statement
   b. HR strategy
   c. organizational strategy
   d. policies
   e. procedures
5. The Black Company is in the IT industry and has been in business for only three years. The organization has a hierarchical structure and many levels of management. What kind of an organizational structure does this company have?
   a. empowerment
   b. bureaucratic
   c. flat
   d. boundary-less
   e. none of the above
6. Management expert Peter Drucker has said, "The foundation of an organization is not money or capital or technology—it's knowledge and education." The knowledge, education, training, and expertise of a firm's workers is known as
   a. human resources
   b. competencies
   c. human capital
   d. knowledge workers
   e. human assets
7. Summer is the busiest season in the hotel industry in eastern Canada. Tom is the HR specialist for a chain of hotels. In anticipation of the peak periods, Tom wants to recruit extra staff only for the summer season. What can Tom do to get additional people?
   a. hire people on contract
   b. hire contingent employees
   c. hire permanent staff
   d. hire other staff to do the jobs
   e. all of the above
8. Modern Company is a large manufacturing firm with more than 250 staff members. The company has been in operation for more than 50 years, and most of its staff are baby boomers with long service at the company. These workers are part of the Sandwich Generation. As the HR manager of Modern Company, what benefit could you provide that would be of particular help to your Sandwich Generation employees?
   a. workers compensation
   b. vision care
   c. eldercare
   d. employment insurance
   e. legal insurance
9. The growing presence of women in the Canadian labour force has been a dominant trend for more than five decades. Smaller family size, increased divorce rate, and increased educational levels are some of the contributing

factors. Keeping this in mind, what can an organization do to accommodate women in the workplace?
   a. provide childcare assistance
   b. provide on-site daycare
   c. provide flexible work programs
   d. provide family-friendly benefits
   e. all of the above

10. Multiple legal jurisdictions are one of the factors that make Canadian employment law so challenging. There are certain organizations that operate across Canada that are not covered by provincial/territorial legislation but by federal employment law. What are some of those organizations?
    a. manufacturing
    b. airlines
    c. national retailers
    d. supermarkets
    e. police force

11. HRM has changed dramatically over time and has assumed an increasingly important role. What are the three distinct stages in the general evolution of management thinking (in order)?
    a. human relations, human resources, scientific management
    b. human resources, scientific management, human relations
    c. scientific management, human relations, human resources
    d. scientific management, human resources, human relations
    e. human relations, scientific management, human resources

12. Which of the following models places emphasis on a management philosophy focused on concern for both people and productivity?
    a. scientific management
    b. human resources movement
    c. human relations movement
    d. human resources productivity
    e. personnel management

13. The most prevalent ethical issues confronting Canadian firms today pertain to security of information, employee and client privacy, environmental issues, governance, and conflict of interest. The key outcomes associated with properly implemented ethics programs are:
    a. reduced absenteeism and increased productivity
    b. increased profits and increased public trust
    c. greater client and employee loyalty
    d. increased confidence among stakeholders
    e. all of the above

14. An organization's plan for how it will balance its internal strengths and weaknesses with external opportunities and threats in order to maintain a competitive advantage is defined as:
    a. HR strategy
    b. strategy
    c. SWOT
    d. PEST
    e. mission

15. HR professionals together with line managers can supply competitive intelligence that may be useful for an organization as it forms its strategic plans. Which of the following is an example of competitive intelligence?
    a. headcount plans
    b. productivity ratios
    c. performance management
    d. consumer surveys
    e. employee opinion surveys

# 2 chapter

# The Legal Environment

## Learning Objectives

1. Explain the legal framework for employment law in Canada.
2. Explain employment standards legislation.
3. Describe the fundamental freedoms under the Charter of Rights and Freedoms.
4. Explain human rights legislation in Canada.
5. Discuss employer accountabilities under employment equity and pay equity legislation.
6. Discuss the impact of employment legislation on HRM.
7. Summarize best pathways for managing diversity.

## Test Yourself

1. What is the legal framework for employment law in Canada?
2. What are the types of behaviour that could constitute harassment, and what are employers' responsibilities pertaining thereto?
3. What is employment standards legislation, and what does the requirement for "equal pay for equal work" mean?
4. What is the purpose and intent of employment equity and pay equity legislation?
5. What are the characteristics of successful diversity management initiatives?

## 2.1 INTRODUCTION TO THE LEGAL ENVIRONMENT

As discussed in Chapter 1, government legislation presents some major challenges to managers and small-business owners. In this chapter, we will look at the legal framework in Canada as well as some of the major pieces of legislation affecting HRM.

Many laws have been written to protect employers and employees. Although an HR department normally acts in an advisory capacity regarding legislation, all managers must be aware of the legal environment of HRM and the implications of their actions regarding employees and prospective employees. Ignorance of the law is not an excuse, and all managers in all organizations are accountable for intentional, and even unintentional, violations.

Today, many organizations have moved beyond legal compliance and begun to initiate and promote workplace diversity initiatives, recognizing that a diverse workforce makes good business sense. In fact, it is no longer an option: it is a requirement.

### The Legal Framework for Employment Law in Canada

The *Constitution Act* of 1867 (formerly the *British North America Act*) gave each of the provinces and territories the power to legislate in relation to employment law for all those who are not employed by the federal government or not employed in federally regulated industries such as banks or airlines. Provincial legislation covers such industries as manufacturing, retail, schools, hospitals, and a myriad of other businesses operating in a particular province or territory. This results in approximately 90 percent of Canadian employees being covered by their respective provincial legislation and the remaining 10 percent being covered by federal legislation. Each of Canada's 14 jurisdictions (federal, 10 provincial, and three territorial) is distinct and is responsible for laws pertaining to human rights, employment standards, labour relations, health and safety, employment equity, and other employment-related legislation.

There is a great deal of commonality between federal and provincial legislation, but there are also some differences. For example, vacations, statutory holidays, and minimum wage are all covered by various employment (labour) standards legislation, but entitlement may vary from jurisdiction to jurisdiction.

In addition, the legal framework for employment includes constitutional law, particularly the Charter of Rights and Freedoms; acts of parliament; **common law**, which is the accumulation of judicial precedents that do not derive from specific pieces of legislation; and **contract law**, which governs collective agreements and individual employment contracts. Such laws impose specific requirements and constraints on management policies, procedures, and practices. One example of common law as it relates to the workplace is a court's decision regarding an employee's allegations of wrongful dismissal by an employer.

To avoid flooding the courts with complaints and the prosecutions of relatively minor infractions, the government in each jurisdiction creates special regulatory bodies to enforce compliance with the law and aid in its interpretation. Such bodies, which include human rights commissions and ministries of labour, develop legally binding rules, called **regulations**, and evaluate complaints.

## 2.2 EMPLOYMENT STANDARDS LEGISLATION

All employers and employees in Canada are covered by **employment (labour) standards legislation.** Those under federal jurisdiction are covered by the Canada Labour Code; the ten provinces and three territories each have an employment (or labour) standards act. These laws establish minimum employee entitlements pertaining to such issues as wages; paid holidays and vacations; leave for some mix of maternity, parenting, and adoption; bereavement leave; termination notice; and overtime pay. They also set a limit on the maximum number of hours of work permitted per day or week.

The Northwest Territories went through a major transition as the *Labour Standards Act, Wage Recovery Act*, and Employment Agencies Act were replaced with the *Employment Standards Act*. Overall, the new *Employment Standards Act* addresses many areas of the employment relationship that were neglected by the territory's old legislation, which had left employers to negotiate their own standards. A number of new provisions are realized under the new legislation, including:[1]

- Time off in lieu of overtime pay (the old legislation did not have provisions for lieu time)
- 1.5 hours of paid time off for every hour of overtime worked
- Overtime permitted up to an overall daily total of 10 hours
- Two consecutive days of rest over two work weeks or three consecutive days over three work weeks

## In-class Notes

**Introduction to the Legal Environment**

- Provincial/territorial responsibility for employment law (90 percent of employees)
- Federal employment law for employees of federally regulated industries, such as civil service, banks, and airlines (10 percent of employees)
- Multiple laws apply to businesses with employees in more than one province/territory
- Common law (judicial decisions) and contract law (union contracts) also affect employment

- Lowering of the age at which employment restrictions are enforced, from 17 to 16
- Employment of an employment standards officer to investigate complaints and make recommendations
- A minimum of five sick-leave days each year and up to eight weeks of compassionate care leave

Every jurisdiction in Canada has legislation incorporating the principle of equal pay for equal work. In most jurisdictions, this entitlement is found in the employment (labour) standards legislation; otherwise, it is covered by human rights legislation. **Equal pay for equal work** specifies that an employer cannot pay male and female employees differently if they are performing substantially the same work, requiring the same degree of skill, effort, and responsibility under similar working conditions. This principle makes it illegal, for example, for a school board to classify male employees as janitors and female employees doing virtually the same work as housekeepers, and provide different wage rates based on these classifications.

Pay differences based on a merit system or employee productivity are permitted; it is only sex-based discrimination that is prohibited. Enforcement is complaint-based and violators can be fined.

## 2.3 THE CHARTER OF RIGHTS AND FREEDOMS

The legal cornerstone for issues of equality is the **Charter of Rights and Freedoms**, which is part of Canada's Constitution. The Charter regulates all other laws and is thus far-reaching in scope. It provides

**common law** The accumulation of judicial precedents that do not derive from specific pieces of legislation.

**contract law** Legislation that governs collective agreements and individual employment contracts.

**regulations** Legally binding rules established by the special regulatory bodies created to enforce compliance with the law and aid in its interpretation.

**employment (labour) standards legislation** Laws present in every Canadian jurisdiction that establish minimum employee entitlements and set a limit on the maximum number of hours of work permitted per day or week.

**equal pay for equal work** The stipulation, specified in the employment (labour) standards or human rights legislation of every Canadian jurisdiction, that an employer cannot pay male and female employees differently if they are performing substantially the same work, requiring the same degree of skill, effort, and responsibility under similar working conditions.

**Charter of Rights and Freedoms** Federal law enacted in 1982 that guarantees fundamental freedoms to all Canadians.

Government of Canada **www.canada.gc.ca**

## In-class Notes

**Employment Standards Legislation**

- Minimum entitlements regarding wages, holidays, maternity leave, and more
- Maximum limits on hours worked
- Requires equal pay for equal work by men and women

four fundamental freedoms to every Canadian:

1. Freedom of conscience and religion
2. Freedom of thought, belief, opinion, and expression, including freedom of the press and other media of communication
3. Freedom of peaceful assembly
4. Freedom of association

In addition to these four freedoms, the Charter also provides the right to democracy, the right to live and seek employment anywhere in Canada, the right to due process in criminal proceedings, equality rights, minority language education rights, Canadian multicultural heritage rights, and First Peoples' rights. Section 15 of the Charter prohibits discrimination in Canadian society and is the foundation for human rights legislation.[2]

A violation of the Charter of Rights and Freedoms was played out in 2008 when three former justices of the peace fought and won their constitutional challenge of the profession's mandatory retirement-age rule. They argued that it was unlawful to force them to retire at age 70, especially when provincial court justices can hear cases until age 75. The Ontario Superior Court ruled it unlawful to force justices of the peace to retire at age 70 because it violates the equality rights section of the Charter of Rights and Freedoms. New language was added that allows for justices of the peace to serve until age 75 if they so choose.[3]

## In-class Notes

**The Charter of Rights and Freedoms**

- Part of Canada's constitution that regulates other laws
- Four fundamental freedoms:
  1. conscience and religion
  2. thought, belief, opinion, and expression
  3. peaceful assembly
  4. association
- Prohibits discrimination in Canadian society

## 2.4 HUMAN RIGHTS LEGISLATION

Every employer in Canada is affected by **human rights legislation**, which prohibits intentional and unintentional discrimination in its dealings with the public and in its policies pertaining to all aspects and terms and conditions of employment.

Human rights legislation affects virtually all aspects of HRM. The manner in which employees should be treated on the job every day and the climate in which they work are also addressed by this legislation. For this reason, it is critical that all supervisors and managers are thoroughly familiar with the human rights legislation and their legal obligations and responsibilities specified therein.

As indicated in Figure 2.1, the protected grounds are similar across jurisdictions, and the provincial and territorial laws are similar to the federal law. All jurisdictions prohibit discrimination on the grounds of race, colour, religion or creed, physical and mental disability,

*figure* 2.1 **Prohibited Grounds of Discrimination in Employment by Jurisdiction**

| Prohibited Grounds of Discrimination | Federal | Alta. | B.C. | Man. | N.B. | Nfld. | N.S. | Ont. | P.E.I. | Que. | Sask. | N.W.T. | Yukon | Nunavut |
|---|---|---|---|---|---|---|---|---|---|---|---|---|---|---|
| Race | ◆ | ◆ | ◆ | ◆ | ◆ | ◆ | ◆ | ◆ | ◆ | ◆ | ◆ | ◆ | ◆ | ◆ |
| Colour | ◆ | ◆ | ◆ | ◆ | ◆ | ◆ | ◆ | ◆ | ◆ | ◆ | ◆ | ◆ | ◆ | ◆ |
| Ethnic or national origin | ◆ | | | ◆ | ◆ | ◆ | ◆ | ◆ | ◆ | ◆ | ◆ | ◆ | ◆ | ◆ |
| Ancestry or place of origin | | ◆ | ◆ | ◆ | ◆ | | | ◆ | | | ◆ | ◆ | ◆ | ◆ |
| Creed or religion | ◆ | ◆ | ◆ | ◆ | ◆ | ◆ | ◆ | ◆ | ◆ | ◆ | ◆ | ◆ | ◆ | ◆ |
| Sex | ◆ | ◆ | ◆ | ◆ | ◆ | ◆ | ◆ | ◆ | ◆ | ◆ | ◆ | ◆ | ◆ | ◆ |
| Marital status | ◆ | ◆ | ◆ | ◆ | ◆ | ◆ | ◆ | ◆ | ◆ | ◆ | ◆ | ◆ | ◆ | ◆ |
| Family status | ◆ | ◆ | ◆ | ◆ | | | ◆ | ◆ | ◆ | ◆ | ◆ | ◆ | ◆ | ◆ |
| Age | ◆ | ◆ 18+ | ◆ 19–65 | ◆ | ◆ | ◆ 19–65 | ◆ | ◆ 18+ | ◆ | ◆ | ◆ 18–64 | ◆ | ◆ | ◆ |
| Mental & physical disability | ◆ | ◆ | ◆ | ◆ | ◆ | ◆ | ◆ | ◆ | ◆ | ◆ | ◆ | ◆ | ◆ | ◆ |
| Pardoned offence | ◆ | | ◆ | | | | | ◆ | | ◆ | | ◆ | | ◆ |
| Record of criminal conviction | | | ◆ | | | | | | ◆ | ◆ | | | ◆ | |
| Sexual orientation | ◆ | ◆ | ◆ | ◆ | ◆ | ◆ | ◆ | ◆ | ◆ | ◆ | ◆ | ◆ | ◆ | ◆ |
| Dependence on alcohol/drugs | ◆ | ◆ | ◆ | ◆ | ◆ | ◆ | ◆ | ◆ | ◆ | ◆ | ◆ | | | ◆ |

Note: The legislation providing human rights protection and equal pay for equal work in Nunavut is titled the *Fair Practices Act.*

Source: *Canadian Master Labour Guide:* 16th Edition 2002. Toronto, ON: CCH Canadian Ltd., p. 402; "Recent Changes in Canadian Labour Law—Northwest Territories: Human Rights Act; Bill 1, Assented to October 30, 2002," *Workplace Gazette* (Spring 2003), pp. 95–96; Legislative Assembly of Nunavut, Bill 12 Human Rights Act, www.nunavutcourtofjustice.ca/library/statutes/2003/Snu_2003_12.pdf (June 14, 2005).

**human rights legislation** A family of federal and provincial/territorial laws that have a common objective: providing equal opportunity for members of protected groups in a number of areas, including accommodation, contracts, provision of goods and services, and employment.

## In-class Notes

**Human Rights Legislation**

- Prohibits both intentional and unintentional discrimination on specified grounds including age, sex, religion, and so on
- Exemption for *bona fide* occupational requirements
- Requires reasonable accommodation of differences, to the point of undue hardship

sex (including pregnancy and childbirth), and marital status. All prohibit age-based discrimination (although the protected age groups differ), and all jurisdictions other than British Columbia and Alberta prohibit discrimination on the basis of national or ethnic origin. Discrimination on other grounds, such as sexual orientation and criminal history, are prohibited in some jurisdictions, but not all.

Human rights laws do not restrict employers' ability to reward outstanding performers or to penalize employees who do not meet productivity standards or follow company rules and regulations as long as such rewards or punishments are based on work-related criteria rather than age, sex, or other prohibited grounds.

Federally, human rights legislation is covered by the ***Canadian Human Rights Act***, which covers all businesses under federal jurisdiction. Each province/territory has its own human rights legislation. As indicated earlier, all jurisdictions prohibit discrimination based on specific grounds. Appendix 2.1 provides an example related to screening and selecting employees.

## Discrimination Defined

The word **discrimination** has taken on a negative connotation. When someone is accused of discrimination, it generally means that he or she is perceived to be acting in an unfair or prejudicial manner. However, definitions of the term in the *Webster's Encyclopedic Dictionary* include "choosing with care" and "good taste, discernment"; in other words, making choices based on perceived differences, which is something people do every day. Deciding which college or university to attend, for example, involves discriminating on the basis of such criteria as cost, reputation, and convenience.

What the law prohibits is *unfair discrimination*—making choices on the basis of perceived but inaccurate differences, to the detriment of specific individuals and/or groups. Standards pertaining to unfair discrimination have changed over time.

## Types of Discrimination Prohibited

**INTENTIONAL DISCRIMINATION** Except in specific circumstances that will be described later, **intentional discrimination** is prohibited. An employer cannot discriminate *directly* by deliberately refusing to hire, train, or promote an individual, for example, on any of the prohibited grounds. It is important to realize that deliberate discrimination is not necessarily overt. In fact, overt (blatant) discrimination is quite rare today. Subtle, direct discrimination can be difficult to prove. For example, if a 60-year-old applicant is not selected for a job and is told that there was a better-qualified candidate, it is often difficult for the rejected job-seeker to determine if someone else truly did match the company's specifications more closely or if the employer discriminated on the basis of age.

An employer is also prohibited from intentional discrimination in the form of *differential or unequal treatment*. No individuals or groups may be treated differently in any aspects or terms and conditions of employment based on any of the prohibited grounds. For example, it is illegal for an employer to request that only female applicants for a factory job demonstrate their lifting skills or to insist that any candidates with a

It is illegal in every jurisdiction in Canada to discriminate on the basis of age.

physical disability undergo a pre-employment medical, unless all applicants are being asked to do so.

It is also illegal for an employer to engage in intentional discrimination *indirectly*, through another party. This means that an employer may not ask someone else to discriminate on his or her behalf. For example, an employer cannot request that an employment agency refer only male candidates for consideration as management trainees or instruct supervisors that women of childbearing age are to be excluded from consideration for promotions.

*Discrimination because of association* is another possible type of intentional discrimination listed specifically as a prohibited ground in six Canadian jurisdictions. It involves the denial of rights because of friendship or other relationship with a protected group member. An example would be the refusal of a company to promote a highly qualified white male into senior management on the basis of the assumption that his wife, who was recently diagnosed with multiple sclerosis, will require too much of his time and attention and that her needs may restrict his willingness to travel on company business.

**UNINTENTIONAL DISCRIMINATION** Unintentional discrimination, also called **constructive** or **systemic discrimination,** is the most difficult to detect and combat. Typically, it is embedded in policies and practices that, although appearing to be neutral on the surface and implemented impartially, have an adverse impact on specific groups of people for reasons that are not job related or required for the safe and efficient operation of the business. Examples are given in Figure 2.2.

### *figure* 2.2 Examples of Systemic Discrimination

- Minimum height and weight requirements, such as formerly existed for the Canadian Forces and many police forces, which screened out disproportionate numbers of women and Canadians of Asian origin, who tend to be shorter in stature
- Internal hiring policies or word-of-mouth hiring in workplaces that have not embraced diversity
- Limited accessibility of buildings and facilities, which poses a barrier to persons with mobility limitations
- Culturally biased or non–job-related employment tests, which discriminate against specific groups
- Job evaluation systems that undervalue jobs traditionally held by women
- Promotions based exclusively on seniority and experience in firms that have historically been dominated by white males
- Lack of explicit anti-harassment guidelines, or an organizational climate in which certain groups feel unwelcome and uncomfortable.

Source: Based on material provided by the Ontario Women's Directorate and the Canadian Human Rights Commission.

***Canadian Human Rights Act*** Federal legislation prohibiting discrimination on a number of grounds; applies to federal government agencies, Crown corporations, and businesses and industries under federal jurisdiction.

**discrimination** As used in the context of human rights in employment, a distinction, exclusion, or preference, based on one of the prohibited grounds, that has the effect of nullifying or impairing the right of a person to full and equal recognition and exercise of his or her human rights and freedoms.

**intentional discrimination** Deliberately using criteria such as race, religion, sex, or other prohibited grounds when making employment decisions.

**constructive/systemic discrimination** Discrimination that is embedded in policies and practices that appear neutral on the surface and are implemented impartially but have an adverse impact on specific groups of people for reasons that are not job related or required for the safe and efficient operation of the business.

*Canadian Human Rights Act* **http://laws.justice.gc.ca/en/H-6/index.html**

A recent study found that many visible minority managers, professionals, and executives believe they need to "Canadianize" themselves in order to progress in their careers. In their determination to climb the corporate ladder, visible minorities believe they need to downplay their heritage, sometimes going as far as trying to eradicate their accent. Visible minorities report the following insights about their career progression:[4]

- 66 percent of visible minorities say they are satisfied with their career progress, compared with 78 percent of Caucasians.
- 69 percent of visible minorities say "who you know" is more important than "what you know," compared with 57 percent of Caucasians.
- 54 percent of visible minorities believe there are few role models for them in their organizations, compared with 39 percent of Caucasians.
- 73 percent of Caucasians received one or more developmental opportunities in the three years leading up to the study, compared with 64 percent of visible minorities.

The results of the study indicate that even though we have a diverse workforce, visible minorities do not perceive it to be as inclusive as it could be. There are a number of unintentional barriers impeding their career progression.

## Specific Human Rights Legislation Issues

**_BONA FIDE_ OCCUPATIONAL REQUIREMENTS** Employers are permitted to discriminate if employment preferences are based on a ***bona fide*** **occupational requirement (BFOR)**, which is defined as a justifiable reason for discrimination based on business necessity (i.e., required for the safe and efficient operation of the organization) or a requirement that can be clearly defended as intrinsically required by the tasks that an employee is expected to perform. There are some settings in which a BFOR exception to human rights protection is fairly obvious. For example, if a boutique handling ladies' apparel requires its salespersons to model the merchandise, sex is clearly a BFOR. When casting in the theatre, there may be specific roles that justify using age, sex, or national origin as a recruitment and selection criterion.

An example of a situation in which company standards were not deemed to represent a BFOR can be found in *Great Blue Heron Charity Casino v. Ontario* (Human Rights Commission). The tribunal ruled that there was a case of discrimination on the basis of sex because a female employee was denied a full-time housekeeping position vacated by a male co-worker because she was a woman. Even though the company had a policy around workers cleaning the bathrooms of the same sex because they had to be cleaned while still open to patrons, the casino did not prove that having a male housekeeper for the men's washroom was a BFOR. The casino had not explored alternatives to replacing a man with a woman that could have been implemented without undue hardship. Employers are reminded that even though they have a gender preference that might be beneficial for the company and its patrons, such a preference is still discrimination and will not automatically be considered a BFOR simply because of the benefits it provides.[5]

**REASONABLE ACCOMMODATION** Employers who believe there is a BFOR for denying employment or assignment to a specific job may encounter the legal principle of **reasonable accommodation.** This principle requires the adjustment of employment policies and practices so that no individual is denied benefits, disadvantaged in employment, or prevented from carrying out the essential components of a job on the basis of prohibited grounds of discrimination. This may involve making adjustments to meet needs based on the group to which an individual belongs, such as scheduling adjustments to accommodate religious beliefs, or on an individual employee basis, such as workstation redesign to enable an individual with a physical disability to perform a particular task.

Employers are expected to accommodate to the point of **undue hardship**, a term for which there is no definitive definition. Therefore, the definition of what constitutes undue hardship might vary from employer to employer, depending on the particular circumstances in question. Generally, however, to claim undue hardship, employers must present evidence that the financial cost of the accommodation (even with outside sources of funding) or health and safety risks to the individual concerned or other employees would make accommodation impossible. Factors that cannot be taken into consideration include business inconvenience, customer preference, or disruption to a collective agreement.[6] Failure to make every reasonable effort to accommodate employees is a violation of the *Canadian Human Rights Act*:[7]

> In some situations, duty to accommodate may be related to testing standards. Employers requiring a high standard of fitness, for example, may face problems developing fair tests. If standards are set too

Persons with disabilities are now employed in a wide range of fields and occupations.

> low, people's lives may be endangered; too high a standard may mean losing otherwise highly qualified people—particularly women—to an arbitrary standard. For example, the Supreme Court ruled that the physical fitness testing being used to screen British Columbia forest firefighters was illegal, since it failed to accommodate the physiological differences between men and women.[8]

The following examples illustrate two different outcomes of arguing undue hardship as a reason for not making workplace accommodations. In the first case, the Supreme Court of Canada found that Hydro-Québec met the standard of proving undue hardship after numerous modifications were made to accommodate an employee's medical condition, including reduced duties and gradual returns to work. After doctors determined that the employee was unable to resume work in the foreseeable future, Hydro-Québec was justified in terminating her. In another case, the Ontario Divisional Court upheld an $80 000 award against ADGA Group Consulting Inc. when it failed to prove that it was impossible to accommodate an employee with a bipolar disorder. ADGA said the new recruit misrepresented his ability to perform the job and it could not accommodate him without undue hardship. The Divisional Court ruled that the company did not engage in consultation with experts to explore alternatives for how to manage bipolar disorder.[9]

**HARASSMENT** Federal legislation and laws in Ontario, Quebec, and the Yukon prohibit harassment on all proscribed grounds. In a number of other jurisdictions, only sexual harassment is expressly banned. **Harassment** includes a wide range of behaviour that a reasonable person ought to know is unwelcome; however, it also encompasses actions and activities that were once tolerated, ignored, and considered horseplay or innocent flirtation, provided that the individual who feels that he or she is being harassed makes it clear that such behaviour is unwelcome and inappropriate and asks that it be discontinued. Examples of the types of behaviour that may constitute harassment are included in Figure 2.3. In the case of blatantly inappropriate actions such as physical assault, one incident may constitute harassment, but generally, harassment involves a series of incidents. Protection against harassment extends to incidents occurring at or away from the workplace, during or outside normal working hours, provided such incidents are employment related.[10] An employer is also responsible for dealing with employee harassment by clients or customers once it has been reported. Air Canada Jazz provides "respect in the workplace" training for unionized and management employees. In collaboration with the Canadian Auto Workers Union, the airline carrier's training programs are aimed at enhancing awareness of harassment, discrimination, and diversity in the workplace.[11]

**Psychological Harassment** The escalating number of psychological harassment complaints in Canada can be attributed to workplace bullying. **Psychological harassment**—unlike other forms of harassment covered under human rights legislation—is based on grounds other than race, religion, and gender. It

***bona fide* occupational requirement (BFOR)** A justifiable reason for discrimination based on a business necessity (that is required for the safe and efficient operation of the organization) or a requirement that can be clearly defended as intrinsically required by the tasks an employee is expected to perform.

**reasonable accommodation** The adjustment of employment policies and practices that an employer may be expected to make so that no individual is denied benefits, disadvantaged in employment, or prevented from carrying out the essential components of a job because of grounds prohibited in human rights legislation.

**undue hardship** The point to which employers are expected to accommodate under human rights legislative requirements.

**harassment** A wide range of behaviours that a reasonable person ought to know are unwelcome. This includes actions and activities that were once tolerated, ignored, and considered horseplay or innocent flirtation, provided that the individual who feels that he or she is being harassed makes it clear that such behaviour is unwelcome and inappropriate and asks that it be discontinued.

**psychological harassment** Harassment based on physical or verbal intimidation, such as name-calling, unfounded yelling, insults, and spiteful comments.

## *figure* 2.3 Examples of Behaviours That May Constitute Harassment

- Physical assault
- Unnecessary physical contact, such as patting, pinching, touching, or punching
- Verbal abuse or threats
- Unwelcome invitations or requests, whether subtle or explicit, and intimidation
- Unwelcome remarks, jokes, innuendos, or taunting about a person's body, attire, age, marital status, ethnic or national origin, religion, etc.
- Leering or other gestures
- Displaying pornographic, racist, or other offensive or derogatory pictures
- Practical jokes that cause awkwardness or embarrassment
- Condescension or paternalism that undermines self-respect

Source: Based on material provided by the Ontario Women's Directorate and the Canadian Human Rights Commission.

includes physical or verbal intimidation, name-calling, unfounded yelling, insults, spiteful comments, assaults on character, attempts to defame an individual, workplace isolation, and assigning demeaning work that makes minimal use of an employee's competencies. In 2004, Quebec was the first province to amend the *Labour Standards Act* to include psychological harassment and hold employers accountable for creating a harassment-free zone.

The best-known case of psychological harassment in Canada is that of *Shah v. Xerox Canada Ltd.* The court ruled in favour of Shah after he described an intolerable work climate, including poor performance ratings based on unsubstantiated concerns and unjustified probation from a manager characterized as being "authoritarian, impatient, and intolerant." The court agreed that the manager's behaviour constituted bullying and ruled that the employer's failure to protect Shah from a toxic workplace was constructive dismissal.[12]

**Sexual Harassment** The type of harassment that has attracted the most attention in the workplace is **sexual harassment**. According to one noted scholar, sexual harassment can be divided into two categories: sexual coercion and sexual annoyance.[13]

**Sexual coercion** involves harassment of a sexual nature that results in some direct consequence to the worker's employment status or some gain in or loss of tangible job benefits. Typically, this involves a supervisor using control over employment, pay, performance appraisal results, or promotion to attempt to coerce an employee to grant sexual favours. If the worker agrees to the request, tangible job benefits follow; if the worker refuses, job benefits are denied.

**Sexual annoyance** is sexually related conduct that is hostile, intimidating, or offensive to the employee but has no direct link to tangible job benefits or loss thereof. Rather, a "poisoned" work environment is created for the employee, the tolerance of which effectively becomes a term or condition of employment.

**Harassment Policies** It is mandatory for all organizations operating under federal jurisdiction to develop and implement sexual harassment policies. Many organizations under provincial/territorial or municipal jurisdiction or receiving government funding have a similar legal obligation. Increasingly, however, organizations are developing policies to deal with harassment, whether or not they are required by law to do so.

A poisoned work environment may exist even if no direct threats or promises are made.

Complying with the legal obligation to provide a "poison-free" workplace and exercise due diligence after a complaint is lodged does not necessarily require severe discipline in every case. In fact, imposing unduly harsh discipline (in view of the specific circumstances) can lead to a wrongful or constructive dismissal lawsuit.[14] Figure 2.4 provides guidelines for establishing a policy for a harassment-free work environment.

Retaliation against someone exercising his or her rights under human rights legislation is prohibited. Whether filing charges, testifying, or participating in a human rights action in another way, individuals are protected. Thus, it is against the law for a supervisor to attempt to "get even" with an employee who has testified in a case by disciplining or demoting him or her.

The **Canadian Human Rights Commission (CHRC)** is the body responsible for enforcing the *Canadian Human Rights Act*. Its members are appointed by the Governor-in-Council. All of the provinces and territories have their own human rights commissions (HRCs) or equivalent bodies, with similar powers of enforcement.

## *figure* 2.4 Anti-Discrimination/Harassment Policy

The following is a guide to some best practices that an employer should consider when developing this policy.

*Content of the Policy:*

- A statement setting out the employer's commitment to a fair and equitable workplace free of discrimination and harassment and that discrimination/harassment will not be tolerated by the employer/organization.
- A statement of rights and obligations, including:
  - employee rights
  - employer/supervisor obligations
  - union obligations
  - an explanation of corporate liability for the behaviour of officers, managers, employees, etc.
  - a statement indicating that no reprisals are permitted or will be taken against an individual making a complaint
- A list of the prohibited grounds of discrimination listed in the *Code.*
- The *Code* definitions of "harassment" and of "sexual harassment/solicitation."
- An explanation of the concept of a "poisoned environment" as a violation of the *Code.*
- Description/examples of unacceptable behaviour, such as:
  - refusal to hire/promote based on a ground listed in the Code
  - examples of harassment based on a ground listed in the Code
  - examples of what would constitute sexual harassment, etc.
- How internal complaints will be handled, including:
  - to whom is the complaint made
  - confidentiality
  - length of time for complaint to be investigated, etc.
- Disciplinary measures that will be applied if a claim of harassment or discrimination is proven.
- Remedies that will be available if the claim of harassment or discrimination is proven, such as:
  - an oral or written apology from the harasser/person who discriminated and company
  - recovery of lost wages, benefits, job or promotion that was denied, and/or a compensation for injury to dignity
- A statement reinforcing the right of employees to go to the Commission at any time during the internal process, as well as an explanation of the six-month time requirement in the *Code.*

Source: *Human Rights at Work,* 3rd ed., 2008, prepared by the Ontario Human Rights Tribunal, published by Carswell Thomson. © Queen's Printer for Ontario, 2004. Reproduced with permission.

**sexual harassment** Harassment on the basis of gender or physical attractiveness or unattractiveness.

**sexual coercion** Harassment of a sexual nature that results in some direct consequence to the worker's employment status or some gain in or loss of tangible job benefits.

**sexual annoyance** Sexually related conduct that is hostile, intimidating, and offensive to the employee, but that has no direct link to tangible job benefits or loss thereof.

**Canadian Human Rights Commission (CHRC)** The body responsible for the implementation and enforcement of the Canadian Human Rights Act.

Canadian Human Rights Commission **www.chrc-ccdp.ca**

## 2.5 EMPLOYMENT EQUITY AND PAY EQUITY LEGISLATION

The Charter of Rights and Freedoms and human rights legislation focus on prohibiting various kinds of discrimination, thereby attempting to create a level playing field in the employment relationship. However, over time, it became obvious that there were certain groups for whom this complaint-based, reactive approach was insufficient. Investigation revealed that four identifiable groups—women, Aboriginal peoples, persons with disabilities, and visible minorities—had been subjected to pervasive patterns of differential treatment by employers, as evidenced by lower pay on average, occupational segregation, higher rates of unemployment, underemployment, and concentration in low-status jobs with little potential for career growth.

For example, historically, 60 percent of all women worked in 20 of 500 possible occupational classifications. This is known as **occupational segregation.** Advancement of women and other designated group members into senior management positions has been hindered by the existence of a **glass ceiling**, an "invisible" barrier caused by attitudinal or organizational bias, which limits the advancement opportunities of qualified designated group members.

The results of recent studies conducted by Catalyst (a nonprofit group that works for the advancement of women in business) are highlighted in Figures 2.5 and 2.6. There is concrete evidence of **underutilization** of female employees. While women make up almost half of the Canadian workforce, they are still underrepresented on executive teams, comprising 39 percent of management positions, 16.9 percent of corporate officers, and 13 percent of boards of directors. It is projected that over the next decade, female representation in the Canadian workforce and around the world will increase, yet the percentage of females on executive teams will remain relatively the same. Companies such as BMO Financial Group (as explained in the Workforce Diversity box on page 53) are taking proactive initiatives to advance women into leadership roles.[15]

In most companies, there has tended to be a **concentration** of women in certain professions, which have been undervalued and underpaid. The 2008 *Employment Equity Act* Annual Report noted that women represent 75.5 percent of administrative and senior clerical personnel, 66 percent of clerical personnel, and 26.4 percent of intermediate and skilled sales

*figure* 2.5 **Canadian Women in Business**

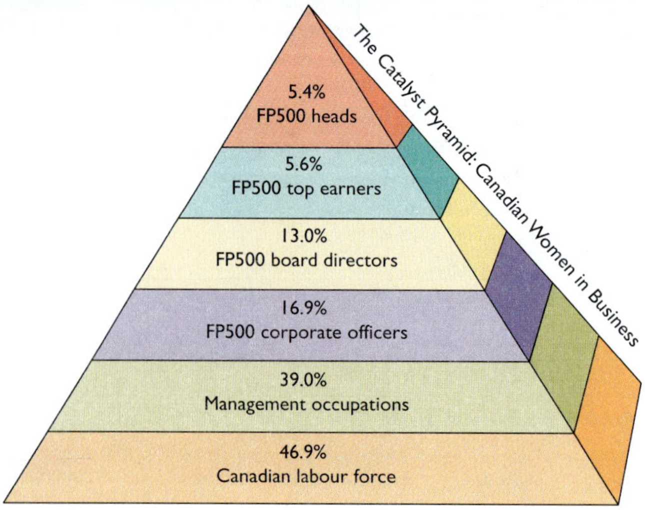


Note: Although there are 26 companies headed by women, there are only 23 women who head those companies.

Sources: © Catalyst, December 2008 for Census and © Catalyst, June 2009 for Global Women Quick Takes.

*figure* 2.6 **Women and Men in the Labour Force, 2009 and Projected 2020, Ages 15+**

| | Number of Women in the Labour Force, 2009 | Number of Men in the Labour Force, 2009 | Number of Women in the Labour Force, Projected 2020 | Number of Men in the Labour Force, Projected 2020 |
|---|---|---|---|---|
| **Latin America & Caribbean** | 115 694 000 | 161 899 000 | 140 593 000 | 185 871 000 |
| Central America | 23 094 000 | 40 332 000 | 29 862 000 | 46 355 000 |
| Caribbean | 7 316 000 | 10 634 000 | 8 134 000 | 11 753 000 |
| South America | 85 284 000 | 110 933 000 | 102 596 000 | 127 763 000 |
| **Europe** | 165 917 000 | 190 635 000 | 164 309 000 | 182 141 000 |
| Northern Europe | 23 677 000 | 27 118 000 | 24 592 000 | 27 672 000 |
| Western Europe | 42 301 000 | 49 757 000 | 43 058 000 | 48 302 000 |
| Eastern Europe | 71 880 000 | 76 032 000 | 66 966 000 | 69 782 000 |
| Southern Europe | 28 058 000 | 37 729 000 | 29 693 000 | 36 384 000 |
| **Africa** | 164 442 000 | 233 087 000 | 226 887 000 | 305 386 000 |
| Northern Africa | 19 952 000 | 50 898 000 | 26 594 000 | 61 215 000 |
| Western Africa | 41 819 000 | 64 061 000 | 60 692 000 | 84 839 000 |
| Eastern Africa | 72 538 000 | 78 030 000 | 100 487 000 | 107 281 000 |
| Middle Africa | 20 643 000 | 28 875 000 | 28 696 000 | 39 811 000 |
| Southern Africa | 9 490 000 | 11 224 000 | 10 418 000 | 12 240 000 |
| **Northern America** | 83 567 000 | 97 272 000 | 90 429 000 | 104 130 000 |
| Canada | 8 989 000 | 10 008 000 | 9 881 000 | 20 487 000 |
| United States | 74 578 000 | 87 264 000 | 80 548 000 | 93 523 000 |
| **Oceania** | 7 946 000 | 9 440 000 | 9 301 000 | 10 613 000 |
| Australia | 5 046 000 | 6 054 000 | 5 724 000 | 6 507 000 |
| New Zealand | 1 061 000 | 1 226 000 | 1 173 000 | 1 334 000 |
| **Asia** | 772 057 000 | 1 227 475 000 | 875 770 000 | 1 385 000 000 |
| Western Asia | 19 994 000 | 58 120 000 | 24 649 000 | 70 551 000 |
| South-Central Asia | 214 507 000 | 497 857 000 | 279 077 000 | 599 864 000 |
| South-Eastern Asia | 122 784 000 | 173 273 000 | 145 039 000 | 202 245 000 |
| Eastern Asia | 414 772 000 | 498 225 000 | 427 004 000 | 513 191 000 |

Source: © Catalyst, December 2008 for Census and © Catalyst, June 2009 for Global Women Quick Takes.

and service personnel. Women continue to be underrepresented in engineering, natural sciences, mathematics, and skilled crafts and trades—a trend unlikely to change in the near future, since women are also underrepresented in university programs in these fields.[16]

Women are not the only group that is underrepresented. Although the number of young Aboriginal workers has increased dramatically in recent years (in western Canada, this group accounts for a large portion of labour market growth), many are concentrated in low-paying, unstable employment, especially in urban centres.

Based on 2006 Census information, there is a large gap between Aboriginal representation and their labour market availability. In 2006, 60.5 percent of First Nations people between 25 and 54 years of age were employed. Although this figure is lower than the employment rate

**occupational segregation** The existence of certain occupations that have traditionally been male dominated and others that have been female dominated.

**glass ceiling** An invisible barrier caused by attitudinal or organizational bias, which limits the advancement opportunities of qualified designated group members.

**underutilization** Having a smaller proportion of designated group members in particular jobs, occupations, departments, or levels of the organization than is found in the labour market.

**concentration** Having a higher proportion of designated group members in specific jobs, occupations, departments, or levels of an organization than is found in the labour market.

## *In-class Notes*

**Employment Equity and Pay Equity Legislation**

- Four disadvantaged groups in employment with pervasive patterns of lower pay, occupational segregation, high unemployment, and low job status:
  1. women
  2. Aboriginals
  3. people with disabilities
  4. visible minorities
- Employment equity legislation (federal only) requires goals and timetables to achieve better representation for designated groups at all levels of the organization
- Pay equity legislation requires equal pay for work of equal value in male-dominated and female-dominated jobs

for non-Aboriginal Canadians in the same age group (81.6 percent), it represents an increase of close to 4 percentage points over 2001. First Nations people living on reserves had an employment rate of 51.9 percent in 2006, as compared with 66.3 percent for those living off reserves. The unemployment rate among First Nations people living on reserves in 2006 was 23.1 percent. First Nations people earned approximately $11 000 less, on average, than non-Aboriginals—$14 517, compared with $25 955. Overall, First Nations people living on reserves had a lower median income ($11 224) than those living off reserves ($17 464).[17]

A number of organizations are committed to supporting Aboriginal communities. IBM Canada offers a range of programs aimed at First Nations, Métis, and Inuit students to encourage them to remain in school, earn diplomas and degrees, and pursue careers in science, engineering, business, and technology.[18]

The 2008 *Employment Equity Act* Annual Report indicated that only 3.2 percent of persons with disabilities are represented in the workforce. This number is well below the labour availability benchmark for persons with disabilities in the Canadian labour market workforce, which is 5.4 percent.[19] Persons with disabilities face attitudinal barriers, physical demands unrelated to actual job requirements, and inadequate access to the technical and human support systems that would make it possible for them to obtain productive employment. Encouragingly, the number of persons with disabilities in the banking sector has increased as a result of a number of workplace initiatives designed to increase representation of this designated group. For example, the BMO Financial Group collaborated with Jewish Vocational Services (JVS) and the Job Opportunity Information Network (JOIN) to co-create and conduct a pre-employment training program for persons with disabilities. The team provides coaching and training to close the gap often experienced by candidates with little or no work experience.[20]

Representation of members of visible minorities in the federally regulated workforce increased to 13.1 percent in 2008, which surpassed their labour market availability rate of 12 percent.[21] This increase marks a significant improvement from 20 years ago, when visible minorities represented 5 percent of the workforce. Among the occupational groups that have experienced dramatic increases in minority representation are sales and service personnel, clerical personnel, administrative

WORKFORCE DIVERSITY

## First Female BMO Executive Opened Doors

**MENTORING, INCLUSIVENESS AND CHARITABLE WORKS HIGHLIGHTS OF AWARD-WINNING LEADERSHIP**

Before Rose Patten joined BMO Financial Group in 1995, women held just 9 percent of the management roles at the Toronto-based bank. Considering banks attract a high proportion of women at the entry level, the pool from which to choose women for management positions was quite deep. With such low representation in the management ranks, Patten knew something had to be blocking their move up the ladder.

"We recognized that one of the factors inhibiting peoples' progress, and particularly with the advancement of women, was the work-life balance dimension," she said.

In response, Patten advocated for the implementation of policies that are common now, but at the time were on the cutting edge, such as job sharing, flexible hours and elder-care support.

Today, women hold 35 percent of management roles at BMO. While there are many factors, such as education, that have helped the proportion grow over the past decade, family-friendly policies are a key component of that growth, said Patten, who is the bank's senior executive vice-president of HR.

"We were certainly pioneers and quite passionate about work-life balance and all the policies you need to help that process," she said.

She's pleased with the bank's progress but there is still more work to be done to get more women into senior roles, said Patten.

While women make up more than 30 percent of management at BMO and other large organizations, there are still many organizations that don't have anywhere near that high a proportion, she said. And the percentage drops significantly at the executive level and on boards of governance.

"We've come a very long way and we've broken down some of the systemic barriers, attitudinally," said Patten, who is the first woman to sit on the executive committee of BMO. "There are still new levels to be attained, because while we've managed well in the general management ranks, when it gets to being presidents and CEOs we've got a ways to go."

Patten's work for the advancement of women through family-friendly policies at BMO is just one of the reasons she was awarded the 2008 YWCA Toronto Woman of Distinction award for corporate leadership.

"Rose exemplifies someone who has risen to the top of her field without having to leave anyone behind. She is a very inclusive leader who has made a very deep impression on many other women coming up through her field," said Amanda Dale, director of advocacy and communications at the YWCA Toronto.

The YWCA award exemplifies leadership that is inclusive, shares power instead of hoarding it, invites others to the table and ultimately contributes to the development of everyone, said Dale. This kind of leadership is the exact opposite of what is seen in popular culture, on television and in the news, she added.

"We see a vision of leadership that valorizes a kind of top-down authoritarian leadership," she said. "We offer, through these awards, an opportunity to imagine a leadership where nobody loses just because somebody is on the leading side."

One way Patten exemplifies this kind of leadership is by including people from all levels and all backgrounds in various projects.

"When you have a large body of people, why wouldn't you tap into as many as possible?" said Patten. "It's really a matter of having better outcomes, having better solutions and getting better decisions because you have the richness."

Her senior rank gives her the ability to role model this inclusive and collaborative form of leadership and make it part of the bank's culture, she said.

"I have the position of influence to be able to set that tone," she said.

Mentoring is another important component of Patten's leadership style for which the YWCA recognized her.

"I try to, by nature and in a deliberate way, make every encounter I have a bit of a mentoring encounter," she said.

This can include helping someone break through a barrier or offering a bit of advice to help an employee be successful at work or in life. At any given time, Patten also has about 20 formal mentees.

The YWCA also recognized Patten for her charitable contributions to help society's less fortunate, especially disadvantaged and abused women. At BMO, she has been a strong advocate for charities that help battered women and encouraged the bank to become the corporate sponsor for Shelter from the Storm, the Canadian Women's Foundation's campaign to fund shelters across the country.

She has funded several bursaries and scholarships at the University of Toronto and Memorial University in St. John's, Nfld., to help single parents, women and new Canadians who don't have the financial resources to attend university.

Giving people access to education gives them access to the opportunity to improve themselves, said Patten.

"Education is quite an equalizer in today's world," she said.

Throughout her career, which spans more than three decades, Patten has never worried about overstepping her bounds or taking on a project that wasn't necessarily in her job description.

"Whenever the opportunity existed, I tried to do new things that would give me new skills," she said.

It is that kind of openness and willingness to work hard that Patten would like to pass on to the next generation of women climbing the corporate ladder. By being open to new experiences, women will be prepared when job opportunities present themselves, she said.

Source: Shannon Klie, "First female BMO executive opened doors," *Canadian HR Reporter*, June 16, 2008. Reprinted with permission.

and senior clerical personnel, and professionals. Many visible minority workers are relatively new immigrants, and they often obtain employment in jobs that do not take full advantage of their skills and qualifications; this is known as **underemployment**. Systemic barriers that have a negative impact on employment opportunities for visible minorities range from culturally biased aptitude tests to language-skills demands in excess of job requirements to lack of recognition of credentials gained elsewhere.[22] Recognizing how difficult it is for employers to assess educational equivalencies, various governments, professional bodies, and educational institutions have established assessment centres.

Many employers have developed internship programs to help women, Aboriginal peoples, persons with disabilities, and visible minorities develop skills and acquire work experience. For example, Global Ontario, a division of Canwest Media Inc., created an awards/internship program specifically aimed at members of these groups. The "Broadcaster of the Future" awards are a series of scholarship, internship, and mentorship programs designed to encourage and help young Canadians establish or further careers in the Canadian broadcast industry. Through these programs, Global Ontario provides industry experience to interns and mentors them through the career decision-making process.[23]

After realizing that simply levelling the playing field would not correct underemployment, underutilization, and occupational segregation, a number of jurisdictions passed two categories of legislation:

1. *Employment equity*, aimed at identifying and eliminating systemic barriers to employment opportunities that adversely affect these four groups.
2. *Pay equity*, which focuses on mechanisms to redress the imbalance in pay between male-dominated and female-dominated job classes resulting from the undervaluing of work traditionally performed by women.

## Employment Equity

A royal commission in the 1980s made recommendations to institute legislation regarding how the four traditionally disadvantaged groups identified above could be brought into the mainstream of Canada's labour force. They recommended the use of the term "employment equity" to distinguish Canada's approach from the "affirmative action" found in the United States. Affirmative action had by then come to be associated with quotas, which had become a divisive political issue.[24]

The federal ***Employment Equity Act*** is intended is to remove employment barriers and promote equality for members of the four designated groups. The Act requires employers under federal jurisdiction having more than 100 employees to develop annual plans that set out specific goals to achieve better representation of the designated group members at all levels and timetables for goal implementation.

A large number of employers under provincial/territorial jurisdiction are subject to federal employment equity requirements. Under the **Federal Contractors Program**, a provision of the *Employment Equity Act*, firms with 100 or more employees wishing to bid on federal contracts of $200 000 or more are required to certify their commitment to employment equity in writing and implement an employment equity program as a condition of the bid.

Mandatory equity programs are virtually nonexistent in provincial and territorial jurisdictions. Voluntary employment equity programs are legalized under human rights legislation in most Canadian jurisdictions. Provincial/territorial human rights commissions often provide assistance to employers wishing to implement such initiatives.

**EMPLOYMENT EQUITY IMPLEMENTATION** An **employment equity program** is designed to identify and correct existing discrimination, redress past discrimination, and achieve a balanced representation of designated group members in an organization. As such, it is much more than a formal document prepared by an HR specialist; it is a major change-management exercise. Successful implementation requires that employment equity be incorporated in the organization's strategic planning process,[25] Different groups within an organization should be involved in the implementation process, including senior management, HR specialists, all other managers and supervisors, and union/non-union employee representatives. The process includes six main steps, which are tailored to suit the unique needs of the firm:

1. Obtaining senior management commitment and support
2. Conducting data collection and analysis
3. Reviewing the employment systems
4. Developing the plan, including goals and timetables
5. Implementing the plan
6. Monitoring, evaluating, and revising the plan

**BENEFITS OF EMPLOYMENT EQUITY** Employment equity makes good business sense, since it contributes to the bottom line. National Grocers is one organization that recognized this fact years ago. As Robert Rocon, director of employment equity at the firm, stated:[26]

> Regardless of any legislative requirement, [employment equity] is a good business decision for us. When you consider the changing face of Canada, it just makes good business sense to reflect the customers that you serve.

**RPC 2-1 >**

**Evaluates programs on deliverables**

One of the benefits derived from implementing employment equity is being able to attract and keep the best-qualified employees, which results in greater access to a broader base of skills. Other benefits include higher employee morale due to special measures employed, such as flexible work schedules or job sharing; and improved corporate image in the community.[27]

According to the Canadian Human Rights Commission, employment equity programs can make a difference. In a recent report, representation of women and visible minority group members has seen improvement, although Aboriginal peoples and persons with disabilities are not faring as well.[28]

## Pay Equity

The overall wage gap between men and women remains substantial: Women employed full-time, year-round make only 73 percent of what men take home. This chronic gap is in part due to the fact that men still are not assuming an equal share of responsibility at home. As a result, women are more likely to be absent from work, to work part-time or in other nonstandard arrangements, and to work shorter weeks than men.[29]

While the lack of shared responsibility at home may account for some of the difference in wages, according to a Statistics Canada study, the remaining portion of this wage differential cannot be attributed to differences in work experience, education, major field of study, occupation, or industry of employment. Researchers concluded that "much of the wage gap still remains a puzzle, leaving at least half of the discrepancy unaccounted for."[30] Pay equity legislation is aimed at reducing the "unaccounted-for" portion of the wage differential.

**underemployment** Being employed in a job that does not fully utilize one's knowledge, skills, and abilities (KSAs).

***Employment Equity Act*** Federal legislation intended to remove employment barriers and promote equality for members of four designated groups: women, visible minorities, Aboriginal peoples, and persons with disabilities.

**Federal Contractors Program** A provision of the Employment Equity Act that requires firms with 100 or more employees wishing to bid on federal contracts of $200 000 or more to certify their commitment to employment equity in writing and to implement an employment equity program.

**employment equity program** A detailed plan designed to identify and correct existing discrimination, redress past discrimination, and achieve a balanced representation of designated group members in the organization.

Aboriginal Canada Portal **www.aboriginalcanada.gc.ca**

Canadian Information Centre for International Credentials **www.cicic.ca**

Public Service Alliance of Canada **www.psac.com/what/index-e.shtml**

**Pay equity**, also known as "equal pay for work of equal value," is designed to augment the "equal pay for equal work" legislation mentioned at the beginning of the chapter. In some jurisdictions, such as Ontario, pay equity is covered under separate legislation. For employers under federal jurisdiction, however, pay equity is incorporated into the human rights legislation. The federal jurisdiction, Quebec, and Ontario have the most comprehensive pay equity legislation, covering virtually all public- and private-sector employers. A number of other jurisdictions have laws that are restricted to the public sector.

**AN ETHICAL DILEMMA**

"Employment equity sometimes leads to reverse discrimination, which is legal, as long as it fulfills the spirit of the law." Is this ethical?

Pay equity requires an employer to provide equal pay to male-dominated job classes and female-dominated job classes of equal value on the basis of skill, effort, responsibility, and working conditions, which may require comparing jobs that are quite different, such as nurses and firefighters. This principle is known as "**equal pay for work of equal value**." The focus is on eliminating the historical income gap between male- and female-dominated jobs attributable to the undervaluing of work traditionally performed by women.

The federal pay equity legislation applies to all organizations under federal jurisdiction, regardless of size. It involves a complaint-based system, which means that action is taken once a complaint has been filed by an individual, a group of employees, or a bargaining agent.[31]

## 2.6 IMPACT OF EMPLOYMENT LEGISLATION ON HRM

### HR Functions

Equal opportunity and equity legislation has an impact on virtually every manager and every HR function. Human rights legislation applies to all aspects and terms and conditions of employment. Pay equity affects job evaluation and compensation administration, and employment equity systems reviews involve an examination of all policies, procedures, and practices in the workplace. Implementing required changes necessitates much more than revising documents. Understanding, acceptance, and commitment are essential, which means that education and communication must be given high priority.

### Reverse Discrimination

Organizations sometimes decide to adopt a "quota" approach to employment equity, as the Ontario College of Art did in 1990 (at which time a decision was made to hire only women for a 10-year period in order to correct a grave imbalance in the male-to-female ratio of faculty members).[32] Or, sometimes, a specific numerical goal is imposed to overcome past discrimination, as in the case of Canadian National Railways (CN).[33] In either of these situations, the employer may be accused of **reverse discrimination**. This involves giving preference to designated group members to the extent that non-members believe they are being discriminated against.

Charges of reverse discrimination put HR managers in a difficult position. On the one hand, they are responsible for eliminating concentration and underutilization resulting from past discriminatory practices. On the other hand, they must also deal with those who feel disadvantaged because of special measures for designated group members. Preferential treatment will always raise questions of fairness; however, the *Canadian Human Rights Act* and provincial/territorial human rights legislation declare employment equity programs to be nondiscriminatory if they fulfill the spirit of the law.

It is possible to avoid the issue of reverse discrimination if the approach taken to employment equity is not one of quotas, the adoption of which gave affirmative action a mixed reaction in the United States. Unlike the United States, Canadian legislation does not require quotas; rather, it specifies that organizations are to establish reasonable goals and timetables based on external labour force availability data.

### Managerial Decision Making

In firms that have not done a good job of educating front-line supervisors and other managers and/or have failed to build responsibility for conforming to all aspects of employment legislation in their performance appraisals, HR department specialists may have a final say in hiring, transfer, and promotion decisions in order to ensure that the organization conducts itself legally. Losing the authority to make such decisions is demoralizing to the individuals concerned and has a detrimental impact on the quality of the work environment, and should therefore be avoided.

A characteristic of successful adherence to all legislative requirements is commitment on the part of all managers across an organization. Achieving this commitment requires extensive education and training.

## The Role of the HR Department and Line Manager

The HR department is generally assigned overall responsibility for legal compliance with human rights legislation and employment equity program results—whether voluntary or legally required—as well as pay equity plan implementation. HR department staff members are expected to keep up to date with changing regulations, court decisions, and emerging legal developments, and to generally take a leadership role in acquiring information, establishing communication and training strategies, developing programs to ensure company compliance, and filing government reports. However, supervisors and managers throughout a firm should be assigned responsibility and held accountable for compliance with human rights legislation, collecting accurate information about jobs for pay-equity purposes, hiring/promoting/training in a non-discriminatory manner, and otherwise conducting themselves in a legal and ethical manner.

**AN ETHICAL DILEMMA**

As the hiring manager, how would you inform a white male that he was not selected because preference was given to an equally qualified visible minority candidate in accordance with the firm's employment equity policy?

## 2.7 MANAGING DIVERSITY

Although many people perceive "management of diversity" to be another term for employment equity, the two are very distinct. Managing diversity goes far beyond legal compliance or even implementing an employment equity plan voluntarily. **Diversity management** is broader and more inclusive in scope. It involves a set of activities designed to integrate all members of an organization's multicultural workforce and use their diversity to enhance the firm's effectiveness. Although organizations have made progress in managing diversity, work still needs to be done. Diversity was cited as a priority in 85 percent of organizations in Canada in 2007, yet 42 percent do not have a strategic plan to accompany it.[34]

While 58 percent of senior managers reported having a stated commitment to diversity in a study conducted by Catalyst in 2007, only 48 percent of visible minorities believe this is to be true, as compared to 60 percent of Caucasians.[35] Another study, conducted in 2007 by the Human Resources Professional Association, found that only 25 percent of companies have a diversity recruitment plan and only 15 percent have an approach for enhancing retention of diverse groups.[36]

As discussed in Chapter 1, the ethno-cultural profile of Canada has been changing since the 1960s and will continue to change dramatically over the next 20 years. Canada has seen continued immigration from many lands during the past four decades. Managers at organizations ranging from McDonald's and Holiday Inn to Bell Canada and Levi Strauss are learning to manage in diverse work environments. While there are ethical and social responsibility issues involved in embracing diversity, there are also more pragmatic reasons for doing so:

1. It makes economic sense. The annual spending power of Canada's visible minorities is over $300 billion.[37]
2. Employees with different ethnic backgrounds often possess foreign-language skills, knowledge of different cultures and business practices, and may even have established trade links in other nations, which can lead to competitive advantage.
3. Having a workforce representative of a company's clientele is of value both morally and economically. As expressed by Dominic D'Alessandro, president and CEO at Manulife Financial:

> Given that we operate in a global marketplace, it is to be expected that our workforce would mirror our customer base. Not only does this allow us to better understand our customer needs, but it also helps us to be a more creative, responsive organization. Through a diverse workforce, we generate creative ideas—ideas about products and services for our diverse markets, ideas for solutions to business problems, and ideas about future directions. Our diversity will help us achieve improved performance.[38]

**pay equity** Providing equal pay to male-dominated job classes and female-dominated job classes of equal value to the employer.

**equal pay for work of equal value** Paying dissimilar jobs equally on the basis of skill, effort, responsibility, and working conditions.

**reverse discrimination** Giving preference to designated group members to the extent that non-members believe they are being discriminated against.

**diversity management** Activities designed to integrate all members of an organization's multicultural workforce and use their diversity to enhance the firm's effectiveness.

## In-class Notes

**Impact of Employment Legislation on HRM**

- HR function
- Reverse discrimination
- Managerial decision making
- Role of HR department and line manager

A dramatic example of how a more diverse workforce can help a company to identify differences in customer needs or preferences that might otherwise be overlooked is provided by Levi Strauss, at which the Dockers line of casual pants, now worth more than U.S.$1 billion a year, has been credited to ideas obtained from Argentinean employees.[39]

4. Visible minorities can help increase an organization's competitiveness and international savvy in the global business arena. Specifically, cultural diversity can help fine-tune product design, marketing, and, ultimately, customer satisfaction.[40]

Although embracing employee diversity offers opportunities to enhance organizational effectiveness, transforming an organizational culture presents a set of challenges that must be handled properly. Diversity initiatives should be undertaken slowly, since they involve a complex change process. Resistance to change may have to be overcome, along with stereotypical beliefs or prejudices and employee resentment. The aim is to ensure group cohesiveness, effective communication, retention of outstanding performers, and maximum opportunity for all employees.

## Organizational Characteristics for Successful Diversity Management

Organizations that have been most successful in managing diversity tend to share the following eight characteristics:

**TOP MANAGEMENT COMMITMENT** As with any major change initiative, unless there is commitment from the top, it is unlikely that other management staff will become champions of diversity. It is no coincidence that organizations that have established themselves as leaders in diversity management, such as the Bank of Montreal, Royal Bank of Canada, and Warner-Lambert Canada, Inc., have had senior-level commitment over an extended period of time.[41] Leaders in diversity management commit to understanding what motivates employees and what gifts and talents they bring to the workplace. Managers give visible minorities high-profile assignments, when appropriate, to showcase their skills and abilities, and expose them to a wider organizational network.[42]

**DIVERSITY RECRUITMENT INITIATIVES** Organizations committed to diversity management broaden their recruitment initiatives to better reflect the community. They cast a wide net in their recruitment campaigns so that advertised positions are visible to diverse employee groups. For example, the recruitment drive for the Edmonton Police Service (EPS) includes postcards, posters, bus wraps, and online ads that feature images of a diverse police force, coupled with getting out into the community and building relationships with various ethnic groups. The EPS partners with ethnic community leaders to help promote a positive image of the force. It also has a mentorship program for job candidates who marginally fail the written and fitness tests that are part of the job application process.[43] At the Canadian Imperial Bank of Commerce (CIBC), training is delivered on topics such as Aboriginal awareness, Aboriginal recruitment, skills for interviewing persons with disabilities, interacting with persons with disabilities, and recruiting diverse talent.[44]

**DIVERSITY TRAINING PROGRAMS** Diversity training programs are designed to provide awareness of diversity issues and to educate employees about specific gender and cultural differences and appropriate ways to respond. Supervisors must be taught strategies to effectively manage and motivate a diverse group of employees. Often, it is appropriate to bring in an outside consulting firm with the requisite expertise to provide the training, at least initially. To be successful, diversity training must be ongoing, not a one-day workshop. Elements of diversity must be incorporated into all core-training programs, based on the needs of specific business units or employee groups.[45] At KPMG Canada, for example, web-based diversity training is mandatory for all employees, and training is provided to managers on how to manage diverse work styles, including culturally different work styles. KPMG's workforce is composed of 54 percent women, 23 percent visible minorities, 1.5 percent disabled persons, and 0.6 percent Aboriginal persons (the remainder are Caucasian males).[46]

**INCLUSIVE AND REPRESENTATIVE COMMUNICATIONS** Organizations wishing to incorporate the value of diversity into their corporate culture must ensure that all of their internal communications and external publications convey this message. Inclusive language, such as gender-neutral terms and broad representation of age, gender, race, and so on in company publications are strategies used. A diversity advisory board is an important addition to an organization, as it can help shape the diversity management strategy, champion diversity initiatives, and address questions from employees.[47]

**ACTIVITIES TO CELEBRATE DIVERSITY** Diversity must also be celebrated in organizational activities. During orientation for new learners and convocation ceremonies at Royal Roads University in Victoria, for example, a traditional First Nations blessing and tribute play a prominent role.

**SUPPORT GROUPS, MENTORING PROGRAMS, AND NETWORKING OPPORTUNITIES** An aim of diversity programs is to ensure that employees encounter a positive and welcoming organizational climate, not one that is insensitive to their culture or background. To ensure that no one experiences feelings of alienation, isolation, or tokenism, support groups have been established in some firms to provide a caring climate and a means for employees who share the same background to find one another. For example, at Royal Bank of Canada there are four employee resource groups: Reach (for people with disabilities); Royal Eagles (for Aboriginals); Pride (for lesbian, gay, bisexual, and transgendered people [LGBT]); and Mosaic (for visible minorities and new Canadians).[48]

Organizations have also established mentoring programs. Ernest & Young has a reverse mentoring program that matches non-visible minority employees with visible minority employees to share their workplace experiences and to offer each other support. The company also has a "Just Ask" mentoring program that matches LGBT Generation Y employees with senior staff who have expressed interest in learning more about LGBT workplace issues and concerns.[49] Many organizations with mentoring programs have established links with school boards, colleges, and community organizations. At Rogers, for example, employees participate in a Goodwill program, through which call-centre training is provided to youths and people with disabilities who, because of long-term unemployment, are not eligible for Employment Insurance. After two-and-a-half years of participation, Rogers had fully employed 20 graduates of the Goodwill program.[50]

**DIVERSITY AUDITS** To assess the effectiveness of an organization's diversity initiatives, **diversity audits** should be conducted. Criteria that can be used to assess diversity management initiatives include:[51]

- *representation*, which involves an assessment of the type of employees and their representation and focuses on demographic and socioeconomic features. Surveys are helpful in identifying these types of data.
- *competency*, which requires determining the diversity KSAs (knowledge, skills, and abilities) of employees. Self-assessments may be involved, as well as feedback from managers, peers, reporting employees, and customers.
- *progress*, which is an assessment of organizational movement from an initial state of little or no diversity commitment and infrastructure to an ideal state in which diversity is integrated into the fabric

**diversity audits** Audits to assess the effectiveness of an organization's diversity initiatives.

Diversity Central **www.diversitycentral.com**

of the organization. This may involve a subjective approach (questions about how employees perceive such key corporate functions as recruitment and such processes as policy development) and objective measures (such as budgets and staff time).

- *results*, which require measuring the extent to which diversity management strategies are perceived to have succeeded in promoting diversity or corporate objectives (and other subjective criteria) and increasing such objective criteria as increased morale, productivity, and/or market share and decreasing turnover and absenteeism.

Organizations that have robust diversity management strategies tend to track diversity metrics, and visible minorities report greater satisfaction in organizations that have these tracking systems. Royal Bank of Canada (RBC) sets the standard for exemplary tracking of diversity metrics. At RBC, where 23 percent of the workforce and 10 percent of executives represent visible minorities, managing diversity is a long-term investment.[52] Regrettably, studies have found that tracking is one of the least reported practices in Canadian companies.

### MANAGEMENT RESPONSIBILITY AND ACCOUNTABILITY

As with employment equity, diversity management initiatives will not receive high priority unless supervisors and managers are held accountable and results are part of their formal assessment. Having managers throughout a firm committed to diversity is a major factor in program success. At Scotiabank, for example, the co-operation of line managers in making a strong business case for diversity is cited as the key reason for the success of the firm's diversity initiatives.

## In-class Notes

**Managing Diversity**

- Set of activities designed to integrate all members of a multicultural workforce and use their diversity to enhance the firm's effectiveness
- Effective diversity management requires:
  - top management commitment
  - diversity recruitment initiatives
  - diversity training programs
  - inclusive and representative communications
  - activities to celebrate diversity
  - support groups or mentoring programs
  - diversity audits
  - management responsibility and accountability
- Some multinational firms extend diversity management to their global workforce

# MANAGING DIVERSITY ON THE INTERNATIONAL STAGE

An increasing number of organizations have decided to ensure that the rights of all their employees around the world are respected and that operations outside of Canada meet acceptable labour and human rights standards. Taking a stand on international human rights and labour standards requires more than a code of conduct, however. It also requires ensuring that the practices of the company's international clients or customers are both legal and ethical and that the firm is not inadvertently supporting less-than-desirable practices in any country around the world. The World Bank and its diversity management practices are featured in the Global HRM box.

## GLOBAL HRM

### A Global Workforce

A true global community, the World Bank staff is made up of people representing 161 countries. The work of IBRD and IDA is performed by about 8600 staff working in Washington, DC, and in almost 120 country offices worldwide. Today, 36 percent of Bank staff works in country offices, where an increased presence in the field helps the Bank better understand, work more closely with, and provide faster service to its partners in client countries.

Staff diversity is critical to the World Bank's organizational effectiveness, enriching its talent base, reflecting its global membership, and bringing a wide range of perspectives to bear on its poverty reduction work. In 2007, the Bank Group adopted a five-year Diversity & Inclusion Strategy for Bank Group staff, emphasizing four key themes—the role of leadership; more inclusive staffing processes; new learning to promote behavior change; and fresh metrics that focus on developing-country nationals, gender, and Sub-Saharan African and Caribbean nationals. Future metrics and research will focus on language, education, and previous experience, together with more sustainable diversity in the workplace.

The Bank Group continues to deploy a comprehensive diversity and inclusion agenda supportive of staff with disabilities and any sexual orientation, in country offices as well as Washington. Nationals of developing countries account for 62 percent of all staff and 45 percent of management and senior technical positions. Women account for 52 percent of all staff and 38 percent of management and senior technical positions. Sub-Saharan African and Caribbean nationals represent 17 percent of all staff and 12 percent of management and senior technical positions. The Bank's 24 senior managers include 10 developing-country nationals, seven women, and four Sub-Saharan African nationals.

The intention of the Bank's decentralization initiative was to increase the Bank's responsiveness to clients and to better integrate global and country knowledge. The experience in recent years suggest that, since this process was started a decade ago, the Bank has become a more responsive and effective institution. Although the pace of decentralization has slowed in recent years, there continues to be a call for the Bank, most recently as part of the IDA 15 replenishment, to decentralize further, particularly in Africa and in fragile and conflict-affected countries. As a result, the move to deploy more resources from headquarters into the field has continued during fiscal 2008. The cost of maintaining a field presence continues to place significant pressure on the annual budget. The major drivers for this increase in many countries have been higher-than-expected salary growth and office expenses and, in some countries, security costs. These costs have been exacerbated by the depreciation of the U.S. dollar against a number of currencies worldwide. The Bank is developing a strategy to guide future decentralization efforts as well as to adapt its human resource policies and support services to facilitate the decentralization process.

**Staff knowledge and learning**

Knowledge and learning are key to the Bank Group's ability to achieve its mission. A menu of learning activities and knowledge products is available to staff so that they can continuously sharpen their skills and expertise to fight poverty. Options include activities to foster technical expertise, expand cultural awareness, and strengthen interpersonal and client engagement skills. Learning with and from partners is an increasingly critical stepping stone for teams in producing results. The Bank is expanding its use of technology and innovative methods to reach country offices and help these teams harness global expertise in the search for local solutions.

Source: "Doing Business 2007—A Global Workforce." International Bank for Reconstruction and Development/The World Bank.

# Chapter Review

## Answers to Test Yourself

1. What is the legal framework for employment law in Canada?

   The *Constitution Act* of 1867 gives each of the provinces and territories the power to legislate in relation to employment law for all those who are not employed by the federal government or not employed in federally regulated industries, such as banks or airlines. Provincial/territorial legislation covers such businesses as manufacturing, retail, schools, hospitals, and a myriad of other businesses.

2. What are the types of behaviour that could constitute harassment, and what are employers' responsibilities pertaining thereto?

   Harassment includes a wide range of behaviour that a reasonable person ought to know is unwelcome. It also encompasses actions and activities that were once tolerated, ignored, and considered horseplay or innocent flirtation, provided that the individual who feels that he or she is being harassed makes it clear that such behaviour is unwelcome and inappropriate and asks that it be discontinued. An employer is also responsible for dealing with employee harassment by clients or customers once it has been reported.

3. What is employment standards legislation, and what does the requirement for "equal pay for equal work" mean?

   Employment standards legislation is present in every Canadian jurisdiction. It establishes minimum employee entitlements and sets a limit on the maximum number of hours of work permitted per day or week. Equal pay for equal work specifies that an employer cannot pay male and female employees differently if they are performing substantially the same work, requiring the same degree of skill, effort, and responsibility, under similar working conditions.

4. What is the purpose and intent of employment equity and pay equity legislation?

   Employment equity is aimed at identifying and eliminating systemic barriers to employment opportunities that adversely affect visible minorities, women, Aboriginal peoples, and persons with disabilities. Pay equity focuses on mechanisms to redress the imbalance in pay between male- and female-dominated job classes resulting from the undervaluing of work traditionally performed by women.

5. What are the characteristics of successful diversity management initiatives?

   Diversity management, which is much broader and more inclusive than employment equity, involves a set of activities designed to integrate all members of a firm's multicultural workforce and use their diversity to enhance organizational effectiveness. Characteristics of a successful program include top management commitment, recruitment, training, communication, activities to celebrate diversity, mentoring programs, audits, and management responsibility/accountability.

## Key Terms

*bona fide* occupational requirement (BFOR) (p. 46)
*Canadian Human Rights Act* (p. 44)
Canadian Human Rights Commission (CHRC) (p. 49)
Charter of Rights and Freedoms (p. 41)
common law (p. 40)
concentration (p. 50)
constructive/systemic discrimination (p. 45)
contract law (p. 40)
discrimination (p. 44)
diversity audits (p. 59)
diversity management (p. 57)
employment (labour) standards legislation (p. 40)
*Employment Equity Act* (p. 54)
employment equity program (p. 55)
equal pay for equal work (p. 41)
equal pay for work of equal value (p. 56)
Federal Contractors Program (p. 54)
glass ceiling (p. 50)
harassment (p. 47)
human rights legislation (p. 43)
intentional discrimination (p. 44)
occupational segregation (p. 50)
pay equity (p. 56)
psychological harassment (p. 47)
reasonable accommodation (p. 46)
regulations (p. 40)
reverse discrimination (p. 56)
sexual annoyance (p. 48)
sexual coercion (p. 48)
sexual harassment (p. 48)
underemployment (p. 54)
underutilization (p. 50)
undue hardship (p. 46)

## Required Professional Capabilities (RPCs)

RPC 2-1 > (p. 55)

# Cases and Exercises

myHRlab
For additional cases and exercises, go to www.pearsoned.ca/myhrlab.

## CASE INCIDENT

### Harassment

Maria was hired two months ago to supervise the compensation area of the HR department, which you manage. She seems to have been accepted by her peers and reporting employees, but you have noticed for the past three weeks that she has been the last to arrive at staff meetings and always sits as far away as possible from Bob, another supervisor.

Yesterday afternoon, you had a very upsetting conversation with her. She claimed that for more than a month Bob had been repeatedly asking her to go out with him and that her constant refusals seemed to be making the situation worse. Bob had accused her of being unfriendly and suggested that she thought she was too good for him. She said that he had never touched her but that he discussed how "sexy" she looked with the other men in the department, who seemed embarrassed by the whole situation. Maria also said that Bob's advances were escalating the more she refused him and his behaviour was interfering with her job performance to such an extent that she was thinking of resigning.

With Maria's consent, you have just spoken to Bob, who denied her allegations vehemently and believably.

### Questions

1. How would you proceed in dealing with this situation?
2. What are your responsibilities to Maria and Bob?
3. If Maria is telling the truth, are you or Bob legally liable in any way? If so, under what conditions?
4. How would you resolve this matter?

Source: Based on a case in *Equity Works Best: A Manual for Practitioners,* developed by the Ontario Ministry of Labour and published by the Ontario Women's Directorate, 1991. © Queen's Printer for Ontario, 1991. Reproduced with permission.

## Application Questions

1. Conduct an audit of either your workplace or your school, searching for evidence of systemic discrimination.
   a. What did you discover?
   b. If there is evidence of systemic discrimination, what impact does it have on the workplace/school and what are the consequences of not taking action to correct the situation?
   c. What recommendations would you make to management once your audit has been completed?
2. Review the *Employment Standards Act* for your province. Based on your knowledge of and/or experiences in the workplace,
   a. What are the strengths and weaknesses of the Act? Defend your critique.
   b. What changes would you make to the Act and what impact would these changes have on the employer–employee working relationship?
3. Review Figure 2.1 on page 43 on the prohibited grounds of discrimination in employment by jurisdiction.
   a. What does Figure 2.1 reveal about employment in Canada?
   b. Based on your review of Figure 2.1, what changes would you like to see in Canada's employment landscape? Why would these changes be beneficial?
4. Your company decides to abolish all employment equity initiatives because there has been no return on investment after two years of committing human and financial resources.
   a. What are the potential consequences of this decision?
   b. How would you convince management to reconsider this decision?
5. Assume you are in the role of manager of human resources in charge of enhancing your company's commitment to employment equity. Discuss the approaches you would take to minimize occupational segregation, underutilization, underemployment, and the glass ceiling.

## RUNNING CASE: LEARNINMOTION.COM

### A Question of Discrimination

The case for Chapter 2, A Question of Discrimination, discusses legal issues that arise as a company begins to institute and implement some HR policies.

To read this case, go to www.pearsoned.ca/myhrlab and click on the *Management of Human Resources,* Third Canadian Edition, In-Class Edition, cover. Click on the case module in Chapter 2. The running case illustrates a variety of challenges confronted by HR professionals, small-business owners, and front-line supervisors. It places students in the role of HR management consultants to help the fledgling LearninMotion.com develop HR policies, strategies, and long-term goals. Each case is accompanied by assignments for the management consultants in the form of critical-thinking questions posed to the student.

## CONTROVERSIAL BUSINESS TOPIC EXERCISE

You are the owner of a financial services agency in a downtown Toronto building complex that was declared a heritage building because it is over 100 years old. The location is ideal, as it is in the heart of the financial district and affords your clients easy access to your business, with ample free parking. Clients often comment that the exquisite architecture and prestigious decor set a highly professional atmosphere for your business. Alongside the excellent service you provide, the location might be a key reason you attract high-end clients.

However, business has been steadily declining over the past year, and, in an attempt to regain your competitive advantage, you want to hire a "star" financial expert who can pull your company out of this slump. A number of candidates vie for the position, but only a few are even remotely qualified. They either have education and no experience, or experience but no current financial training. One of the candidates is a "star"—top of her class in financial management with an exemplary track record of achievements in the financial sector, a robust list of high-end clients who are prepared to seek out her services when she relocates, references from well-known financial experts across the country, and a history of helping organizations prosper. She is someone who would fit well with the existing team. She is the perfect candidate—but you cannot offer her the job. The candidate uses a wheelchair and the heritage building in which you are stationed does not have wheelchair accessibility. In fact, the building is so old that if attempts are made to build ramps and elevators, it would jeopardize its structural integrity. What course of action should you take in this situation?

## IN THE BOARDROOM EXERCISE

At yesterday's management meeting, your supervisor did not support your recommendation that the management team be schooled in the legal framework for employment in Canada, including the Charter of Rights and Freedoms, employment standards legislation, and human rights legislation. "I am a business owner of a food distribution company," said your supervisor, "and I don't need to be aware of the legal framework for employment! My primary concern is making money, maintaining business contacts with suppliers and clients, balancing the books, and making sure we stay ahead of the competition. Let the lawyers look after the legal issues." How would you respond to your supervisor?

## MANAGING DIVERSITY ON THE INTERNATIONAL STAGE EXERCISE

*The exercise below relates to the Managing Diversity on the International Stage feature on p. 61.*

In the Global HRM box at the end of Chapter 2, you read about the World Bank and its operations in 120 countries around the world. Assume the organization wants to establish itself as a benchmark leader with regards to diversity management. Map out the approach you would take to develop and sustain a strong diversity management presence in the company so that the World Bank is known as a leader in this area.

## EXPERIENTIAL EXERCISE

For further study of text materials and development of practical skills, select the Experiential Exercise module for this chapter on www.pearsoned.ca/myhrlab. This module provides two to three individual or group-based assignments per chapter.

# QUIZ YOURSELF

## STUDY GUIDE QUESTIONS

Circle the correct answer. After completing this self-test, check your answers against the Answers to Study Guide Questions at the back of the book (p. 433).

1. The legal cornerstone for issues of equality is the Charter of Rights and Freedoms, which is part of Canada's constitution. The Charter regulates all other laws and is thus far-reaching in scope. The Charter provides the following fundamental rights to every Canadian:
   a. freedom of conscience, religion, peaceful assembly, association, thought, belief, opinion, and expression
   b. freedom of conscience, thought, belief, opinion, expression, race, and occupation
   c. freedom of association, thought, belief, opinion, expression, education, and race
   d. freedom of conscience, religion, assembly, association, thought, belief, opinion, and expression
   e. freedom of association, unionization, assembly, race, religion, opinion, and expression
2. As the hiring manager, you will be interviewing people from varying backgrounds. If you discriminate on the grounds of race, colour, religion or creed, physical and mental disability, sex (including pregnancy and childbirth), or marital status in the selection process, what legislation will you be violating?
   a. *Employment Standards Act*
   b. *Employment Equity Act*
   c. human rights legislation
   d. intentional discrimination
   e. systemic discrimination
3. When someone is accused of discrimination, it generally means that he or she is perceived to be acting in an unfair or prejudicial manner. The Acme Company is a manufacturing firm in the pharmaceutical industry. Recently, the hiring manager interviewed a woman and made her an offer of employment. However, the woman stated that she was three months pregnant, and the company withdrew the offer immediately. This constitutes:
   a. intentional discrimination
   b. unintentional discrimination
   c. harassment
   d. systemic discrimination
   e. all of the above
4. The recruitment manager of an apparel firm insists on hiring females for its sales positions. Under human rights legislation in Canada, this is illegal. However, human rights legislation allows employers to discriminate if employment preferences are based on:
   a. unintentional discrimination
   b. *bona fide* occupational requirements
   c. reasonable accommodation
   d. differential treatment
   e. unequal treatment
5. An employee of a manufacturing firm injured his lower back. His physician required him to use an ergonomic

chair in order to ensure that he did not suffer further damage or fail to heal as quickly as possible. The firm provided the worker with the required equipment. The company's action is known as:
a. employee assistance program
b. return to work program
c. reasonable accommodation
d. *bona fide* requirements
e. none of the above

6. Harassment includes a wide range of behaviour that a reasonable person ought to know is unwelcome, such as:
a. leering
b. physical assault
c. practical jokes that cause embarrassment
d. unwelcome invitations or requests
e. all of the above

7. A female employee in an apparel company filed a complaint with HR regarding a male supervisor who had threatened that she would not be given a wage increase if she did not grant him sexual favours. This is known as:
a. sexual harassment
b. sexual coercion
c. sexual insult
d. sexual annoyance
e. psychological harassment

8. All employees and employers in Canada are covered by employment (labour) standards legislation. These laws establish minimum employee entitlement pertaining to such issues as:
a. paid holidays
b. wages
c. leave
d. termination notice
e. all of the above

9. A manufacturing plant employs 50 female and 30 male machine operators. The work performed by all employees requires a similar amount of skill, effort, and responsibility under similar working conditions. They are all paid similar wages. This is known as:
a. internal pay equity
b. equal pay for equal work
c. employment equity
d. external pay equity
e. none of the above

10. New immigrant workers have a difficult time finding employment in Canada in keeping with their qualifications and past work experiences. This is known as:
a. concentration
b. systemic discrimination
c. the glass ceiling
d. underutilization
e. underemployment

11. In order to correct patterns of discrimination faced by the four designated groups—women, Aboriginal peoples, visible minorities, and people with disabilities—a number of jurisdictions have passed the following two categories of legislation:
a. pay equity, employment equity
b. pay equity, employment standards
c. human rights laws, employment standards
d. employment standards, employment equity
e. equal pay for equal work, pay equity

12. An employment equity program is designed to identify and correct existing discrimination, redress past discrimination, and achieve a balanced representation of designated group members. These programs have a six-step process. What is the first step?
a. conducting data collection/analysis
b. implementing the plan
c. reviewing the employment systems
d. revising and evaluating the plan
e. obtaining management support

13. Pay equity is designed to redress the undervaluation of "women's work." Most pay equity legislation covers only public-sector workers. Which jurisdictions have pay-equity legislation affecting both the public and private sectors?
a. Alberta and Ontario
b. Yukon, Nunavut, Nova Scotia
c. federal, Quebec, Ontario
d. British Columbia, Alberta, Saskatchewan
e. none of the above

14. Diversity management is broader than employment equity and more inclusive in scope. It involves a set of activities designed to integrate all members of an organization's multicultural workforce and use their diversity to enhance the firm's effectiveness. Why is it important to embrace diversity?
a. it is required by legislation
b. it makes economic sense
c. to support new Canadians
d. to save money
e. all of the above

15. Diversity initiatives should be undertaken slowly, since they involve a complex change process. Organizations that have been most successful in managing diversity tend to have:
a. top management commitment
b. diversity training programs
c. mentoring programs
d. diversity audits
e. all of the above

# APPENDIX 2.1

## A GUIDE TO SCREENING AND SELECTION IN EMPLOYMENT

| Subject | Avoid asking | Preferred | Comment |
|---|---|---|---|
| **Name** | about name change<br><br>whether it was changed by court order, marriage, or other reason<br><br>maiden name | | ask after selection if needed to check on previously held jobs or educational credentials |
| **Address** | for addresses outside Canada | ask place and duration of current or recent address | |
| **Age** | for birth certificates, baptismal records, or about age in general | ask applicants if they are eligible to work under Canadian laws regarding age restrictions | if precise age required for benefit plans or other legitimate purposes, it can be determined after selection |
| **Sex** | males or females to fill in different applications<br><br>about pregnancy, child-bearing plans, or child care arrangements | ask applicant if the attendance requirements can be met | during the interview or after selection, the applicant, for purposes of courtesy, may be asked which of Dr., Mr., Mrs., Miss, or Ms. is preferred |
| **Marital status** | whether applicant is single, married, divorced, engaged, separated, widowed, or living common-law<br><br>whether an applicant's spouse may be transferred<br><br>about the spouse's employment | if transfer or travel is part of the job, the applicant can be asked whether he or she can meet these requirements<br><br>ask whether there are any circumstances that might prevent completion of a minimum service commitment | information on dependents can be determined after selection, if necessary |
| **Family status** | number of children or dependents<br><br>about child care arrangements | ask if the applicant would be able to work the required hours and, where applicable, overtime | contacts for emergencies and/or details on dependents can be determined after selection |
| **National or ethnic origin** | about birthplace, nationality of ancestors, spouse, or other relatives<br><br>whether born in Canada<br><br>for proof of citizenship | since those who are entitled to work in Canada must be citizens, permanent residents, or holders of valid work permits, applicants can be asked whether they are legally entitled to work in Canada | documentation of eligibility to work (papers, visas, etc.) can be requested after selection |
| **Military service** | about military service in other countries | inquire about Canadian military service where employment preference is given to veterans by law | |
| **Language** | mother tongue<br><br>where language skills obtained | ask if applicant understands, reads, writes, or speaks languages required for the job | testing or scoring applicants for language proficiency is not permitted unless job-related |
| **Race or colour** | any inquiry into race or colour, including colour of eyes, skin, or hair | | |
| **Photographs** | for photo to be attached to applications or sent to interviewer before interview | photos for security passes or company files can be taken after selection | |

continued

## A GUIDE TO SCREENING AND SELECTION IN EMPLOYMENT—continued

| Subject | Avoid asking | Preferred | Comment |
|---|---|---|---|
| **Religion** | whether applicant will work on a specific religious holiday<br><br>about religious affiliation, church membership, frequency of church attendance<br><br>for references from clergy or religious leader | explain the required work shift, asking whether such a schedule poses problems for the applicant | reasonable accommodation of an employee's religious beliefs is the employer's duty |
| **Height and weight** | no inquiry unless there is evidence they are genuine occupational requirements | | |
| **Disability** | for a list of all disabilities, limitations, or health problems<br><br>whether applicant drinks or uses drugs<br><br>whether applicant has ever received psychiatric care or been hospitalized for emotional problems<br><br>whether applicant has received worker's compensation | | The employer should:<br>• disclose any information on medically related requirements or standards early in the application process.<br>• ask whether the applicant has any condition that could affect his or her ability to do the job, preferably during a pre-employment medical examination.<br><br>A disability is only relevant to job ability if it:<br>• threatens the safety or property of others<br>• prevents the applicant from safe and adequate job performance even when reasonable efforts are made to accommodate the disability |
| **Medical information** | whether the applicant is currently under a physician's care<br><br>name of family doctor<br><br>whether receiving counselling or therapy | | medical exams should be conducted after selection and only if an employee's condition is related to job duties<br>offers of employment can be made conditional on successful completion of a medical exam |
| **Pardoned conviction** | whether an applicant has ever been convicted<br><br>whether the applicant has ever been arrested<br><br>whether the applicant has a criminal record | if bonding is a job requirement, ask whether the applicant is eligible | inquiries about criminal record or convictions are discouraged unless related to job duties |
| **Sexual orientation** | about the applicant's sexual orientation | | contacts for emergencies and/or details on dependants can be determined after selection |
| **References** | the same restrictions that apply to questions asked of applicants apply when asking for employment references | | |

Source: Canadian Human Rights Association, *A Guide to Screening and Selection in Employment*, www.chrc-ccdp.ca/publications/screening_employment-en.asp, June 15, 2005. Reproduced with the permission of the Minister of Public Works and Government Services Canada, 2009.

# 3 chapter

# Designing and Analyzing Jobs

## Learning Objectives

1. Distinguish between different types of organizational structures.
2. Explain the key components of job design.
3. Articulate the purpose of job analysis.
4. Explain the process of conducting a job analysis.
5. Discuss the methods of collecting job analysis information.
6. Outline the steps in writing job descriptions and job specifications.
7. Explain the future of job descriptions.

## Test Yourself

1. What are the industrial, behavioural, human engineering, and flexible work arrangement considerations involved in job design?
2. What is job analysis and what seven steps are involved?
3. What is a job description and what are its key components?
4. What are the basic methods of collecting job analysis information and what quantitative techniques are available?
5. What are the current trends in the nature of jobs and job descriptions?

## 3.1 ORGANIZING WORK

The new landscape in which companies do business is characterized by the global marketplace, international competition, shifts in demographic needs and expectations, and unprecedented technological advancements. Many organizations are reconfiguring their organizational structures and redesigning jobs in response to the demands placed on their operations as a result of shifts in how the work world functions.

An organization consists of one or more employees who perform various tasks. The relationships between people and tasks must be structured in such a way that the organization can achieve its goals in an efficient and effective manner.

**Organizational structure** refers to the formal relationships among jobs in an organization. An **organization chart** is often used to depict the structure. As illustrated in Figure 3.1, such a chart indicates the types of departments established and the title of each manager's job and, by means of connecting lines, clarifies the chain of command and shows who is accountable to whom. An organization chart presents a "snapshot" of the firm at a particular point in time but does not provide details about actual communication patterns, degree of supervision, amount of power and authority, or specific duties and responsibilities.

There is no best recipe for designing an organizational structure. Designs that work for one organization are not necessarily effective in another company. Designing an organization involves choosing a structure that is appropriate given the company's strategic goals. Each organization must research, design, and implement a structure that supports its strategy, and must be prepared to change its structure when the strategy undergoes changes. For example, Proctor & Gamble, which is known for innovation and responsiveness to customer needs in the global marketplace, continually reconfigures its organizational structure to allow for flexibility in growth opportunities both inside and outside the organization.[1]

There are three basic types of organizational structure, depicted in Figure 3.2: bureaucratic, flat, and

*figure* 3.1 **A Sample Organization Chart**

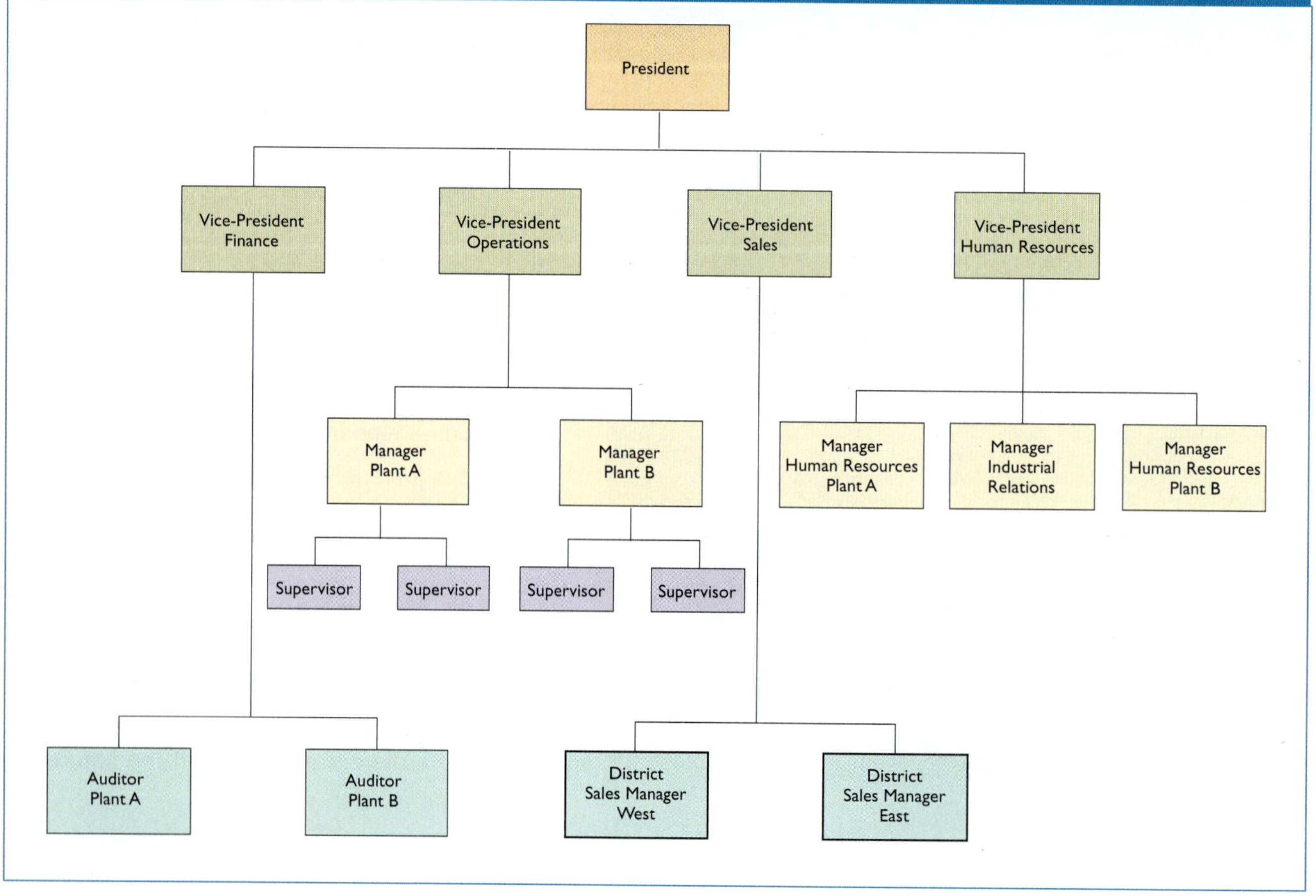

## *figure* 3.2 Bureaucratic, Flat, and Boundaryless Organizational Structures

**Structure**

**Characteristics**

BUREAUCRATIC

A typical educational institution

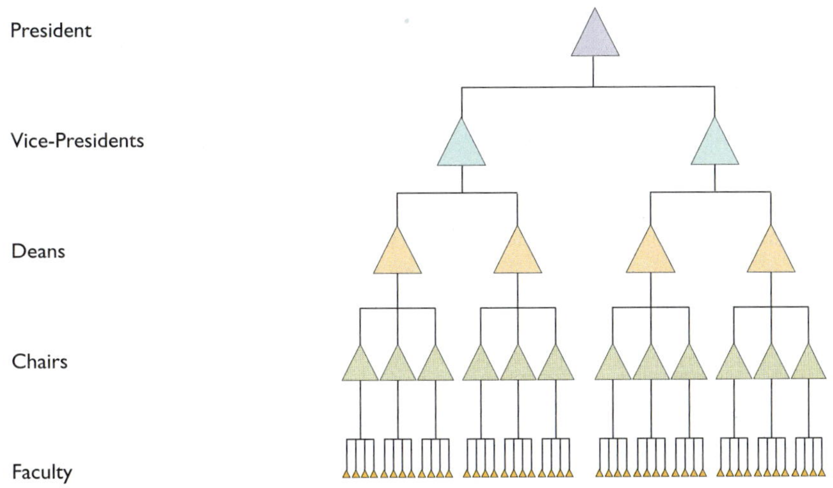


- Top-down management approach
- Many levels, and hierarchical communication channels and career paths
- Highly specialized jobs with narrowly defined job descriptions
- Focus on independent performance

FLAT

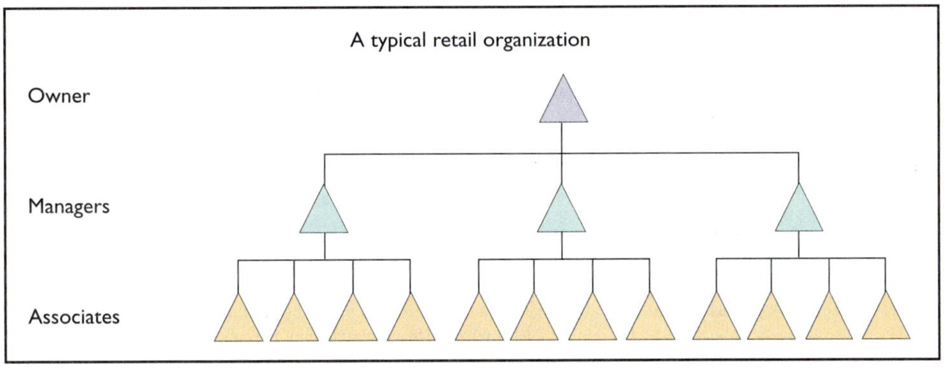


- Decentralized management approach
- Few levels and multi-directional communication
- Broadly defined jobs, with general job descriptions
- Emphasis on teams and on customer service

BOUNDARYLESS

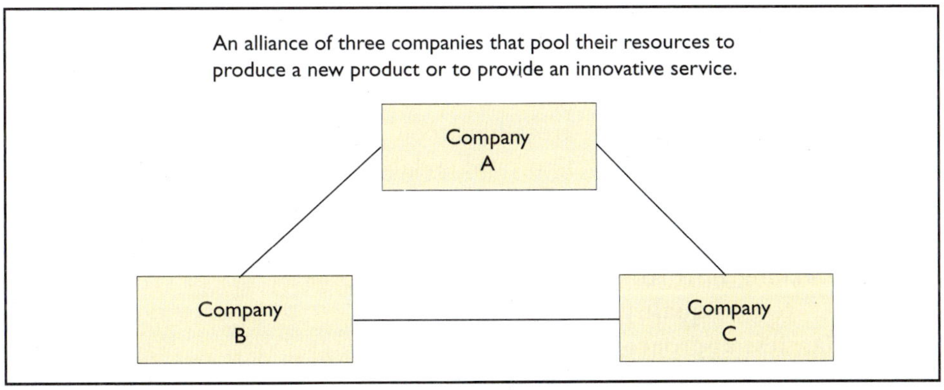


- Joint ventures with customers, suppliers, and/or competitors
- Emphasis on teams whose members may cross organizational boundaries

**organizational structure** The formal relationships among jobs in an organization.

**organization chart** A "snapshot" of a firm at a particular point in time, depicting the organization's structure in chart form.

boundaryless. *Bureaucratic* designs are becoming less common; *flat* structures are increasingly the norm; and *boundaryless* organizations, characterized by alliances and joint ventures, have started to evolve. Another emerging form of organization is the virtual organization. These organizations do not have a formal structure or any one physical location and coordinate their operations using the Internet.

**FLAT ORGANIZATIONS** Instead of pyramid-shaped organizations with seven or more management layers, **flat organizations** with just three or four levels are becoming more prevalent. Many firms have already cut their management layers from a dozen to six or fewer. As the remaining managers are left with more people reporting to them, they can supervise them less, so every employee's job ends up involving greater breadth and depth of responsibilities. For example, the federal public service is undergoing a major initiative to design flatter organizational structures so that it can become more efficient and more responsive to public needs.[2]

**BOUNDARYLESS ORGANIZATIONS** The phrase "boundaryless organization" was coined by Jack Welch, CEO of General Electric, in the late 1980s. The term is reserved for organizations that remove obstacles that stifle productivity, efficiency, and communication, and dismantle labels such as "management," "salaried," and "hourly," which often hinder collaboration.[3] **Boundaryless organization** structures emerge when relationships (typically joint ventures) are formed with customers, suppliers, and/or competitors to pool resources for mutual benefit or encourage cooperation in an uncertain environment. As in team-based organizations, barriers are broken down—in this case, between the organization and its suppliers, customers, or competitors—and teams are emphasized. In such structures, jobs are defined in very general terms, since the emphasis is on the overall best interests of the organization. Companies are likely to design boundaryless organization structures when they are breaking into foreign markets or implementing total quality management initiatives. The boundaryless approach is best suited in these cases because it enables companies to quickly make changes as needed. Examples of boundaryless organizations include Allied Signal, PPG, and Unilever.

## Work Teams

Over the past decade, work has become increasingly organized around teams and processes rather than around specialized functions. In teams, employees' jobs change daily; the effort to avoid having employees view their job as a limited and specific set of responsibilities is thus intentional.

The use of teams has been steadily escalating as a result of international competition that is pressuring organizations to employ more efficient ways of doing business in order to compete in the global marketplace. Studies have found that over 70 percent of organizations have integrated teams into their organizational structures, with most employees holding membership in more than one team.[4] Companies that structure work around teams report better quality products and services, decreased employee turnover and absenteeism, and greater employee commitment and sense of accomplishment.[5] Teams also have a proven track record for resilience in times of change, especially given their ability to collectively pool resources to manage transitions.[6] In many organizations, the widespread use of teams means that the boundaries that typically separate organizational functions (like sales and production) and hierarchical levels are reduced and made more permeable. Responsiveness is fostered by encouraging employees to rid themselves of the "it's not my job" attitude that typically creates walls between one employee area and another. Instead, the focus is on defining the job at hand in terms of the overall best interests of the organization, as is the case at WestJet Airlines, described in the Strategic HR box on page 73.

Hewlett-Packard and Motorola switched to a focus on building multifunctional teams as a result of business necessity. Twenty years ago, both organizations were unable to meet market demands for their products because of problems with their structures and coordination of labour. They developed decentralized, cross-functional, and cross-organizational teams that improved collaboration across departments and generated innovative products that were delivered to customers in a timely manner.[7]

## Virtual Teams

The technology boom allows inexhaustible ways to arrange work, including virtual teams. **Virtual teams** are groups of employees who are physically separated but interact electronically to complete assigned work.

There is widespread integration of these teams in the workplace as more organizations partner with companies around the world on global initiatives. Virtual teams support a continuous cycle of workflow, as employees can work anywhere at any time; allow employers to recruit employees for their skills and not their physical location; and enable employees to collaborate and take products and services to market without the added expense and inconvenience of travel to meet face-to-face. Team members come together for meetings and exchange information using a number of tools: email, teleconferencing, videoconferencing, intranets, cellphones, and shareware, such as Wikis and blogs.[8]

However, virtual teams face a number of challenges. Team members report a sense of isolation and a lack of team cohesion, and feel that work performance is hindered across different time zones, especially when critical decisions need to be made.[9] To enhance the effectiveness of virtual collaborations, teams are given training in leadership, decision making, e-communication, and conflict management. They are also encouraged to discuss how they envision effectively working together, and to establish a code of conduct to be periodically reviewed.[10]

Ottawa-based computer manufacturer Dy4 Systems Inc., which services the U.S. military and NASA with navigational systems for tanks, submarines, and space shuttles, advocates the use of virtual teams. Through the use of technology, employees stationed around the world in such places as Turkey, Australia, and Japan join in quarterly town hall meetings. These

## STRATEGIC HR

### WestJet Airlines

While most North American airlines are cutting staff and slashing costs in a desperate fight for survival, Calgary-based WestJet Airlines Ltd. continues to defy the odds and add more jobs. Employees are key to the cost-cutting culture at the no-frill, low-fare airline. When hiring new employees, the company often looks for individuals who are fun-loving, energetic, gregarious and optimistic rather than those with previous airline experience. In fact, those with little or no airline experience are preferred as " . . . they don't bring any preconceived notions of how things are done, because at WestJet we don't do things like traditional airlines do," said company spokesperson Siobhan Vinish.

While the company does set some standards and expectations, training is focused on motivation of employees. The company stresses teamwork and is managed from the bottom—reducing a costly level of supervisory management. Since there are no job descriptions, employees are given a high degree of latitude to perform their jobs and are expected to pitch in and perform all tasks necessary to keep the flights on schedule. It is not uncommon to have WestJet pilots unload luggage, and after a plane lands, every employee on the flight, including employees flying on their own time, are expected to join in cleaning the aircraft for its next take-off. Even the CEO helps out during flights and can often be found greeting customers at the ticket counter. This team-based "jobless" culture means an annual savings of $2.5 million and enables a quick turnaround, making WestJet one of the most profitable and successful airlines in North America.

Source: P. Fitzpatrick, "Wacky WestJet's Winning Ways: Passengers Respond to Stunts That Include Races to Determine Who Leaves the Airplane First." *National Post* (October 16, 2000), pp. C1, C2; J. Bryan, "WestJet Puts Friendly Back in the Skies: The Upstart Western Airline is Praised for Its Low Fares, On-time Flights, Trouble-free Flying, and Helpful, Cheerful Employees." *National Post* (September 6, 1999), p. C6; "WestJet Flies Against Trends by Adding Employees and Aircraft." Canadian Press Newswire (September 12, 2002); P. Verburg, "Prepare for Takeoff (Entrepreneur of the Year)." *Canadian Business* (December 25, 2000), pp. 94–96.

**flat organization** An organizational structure with three or four levels.

**boundaryless organization** Organizations in which barriers between the company and its suppliers, customers, or competitors are broken down so that products and services can be efficiently and effectively delivered.

**virtual teams** Groups of employees who are physically separated but interact electronically to complete assigned work.

Human Resource Consultants **www.hrcjobs.com**

two-and-a-half-hour meetings, which include a presidential address, updates from each department, and a Q&A session, are broadcast live on the Internet using video and audio streams. Employees from around the world log on to a predetermined URL, enter the site using a password, and follow the presentation onscreen. Webcasts allow them to view speeches live, watch PowerPoint presentations, and participate in Q&A sessions using email.[11]

## Re-Engineering

**Re-engineering** is defined as "the fundamental rethinking and radical redesign of business processes to achieve dramatic improvements in critical, contemporary measures of performance, such as cost, quality, service, and speed."[12] Experts argue that traditional principles like highly specialized divisions of work should be retired. Instead, organizations should emphasize combining tasks into integrated, unspecialized processes that are then carried out by committed employees.

Re-engineering is achieved in several ways. Specialized jobs are combined into one so that formerly distinct jobs are integrated and compressed into enlarged, enriched positions.[13] Workers become collectively responsible for overall results rather than being individually held to account for just their own tasks. As a result, their jobs change dramatically. To that extent, re-engineering also contributes to de-jobbing an enterprise.

Companies are most likely to commit to re-engineering during an economic downturn, at which time all operations are examined for possible cost reductions and development of competitive advantages. Toyota, for example, coined the term "Lean Thinking," which focuses on streamlining operations and removing wasteful and unnecessary processes so that activities add the most value to customers. "Lean Thinking" is not meant to be a one-time event practised during economic hardship, but a commitment to continuous improvement.[14]

# 3.2 JOB DESIGN

In any organization, work has to be divided into manageable units and ultimately into jobs that can be performed by employees. **Job design** is the process of systematically organizing work into tasks that are required to perform a specific job. A **job** consists of a group of related activities and duties. Ideally, the duties of a job should be clear and distinct from those of other jobs and involve natural units of work that are similar and related. This helps minimize conflict and enhance employee performance. A job may be held by a single employee or may have a number of incumbents. The collection of tasks and responsibilities performed by one person is known as a **position.** To clarify, in a department with 1 supervisor, 1 clerk, 40 assemblers, and 3 tow-motor operators, there are 45 positions and 4 jobs.

**SPECIALIZATION AND INDUSTRIAL ENGINEERING CONSIDERATIONS** The term "job" as it is known today is largely an outgrowth of the efficiency demands of the industrial revolution.[15] Work simplification is based on the premise that work can be broken down into clearly defined, highly specialized, repetitive tasks to maximize efficiency. This approach to job design involves assigning most of the administrative aspects of work (such as planning and organizing) to supervisors and managers, while giving lower-level employees narrowly defined tasks to perform according to methods established and specified by management.

**Industrial engineering** is concerned with analyzing work methods and establishing time standards to improve efficiency. Industrial engineers systematically identify, analyze, and time the elements of each job's work cycle and determine which, if any, elements can be modified, combined, rearranged, or eliminated to reduce the time needed to complete the cycle. Differences in industrial engineering practices are evident when contrasting the U.S. automobile industry with Toyota. The former increases the numbers of cars and models it produces by dramatically increasing the number of employees hired. Toyota's employee base grows slowly, while yielding dramatic growth in the numbers of cars and models produced. Much of this difference is due to Toyota's lean manufacturing and just-in-time organization design and work systems, which use people and their skills effectively.[16]

While work simplification can increase operating efficiency in a stable environment, it is not effective in a changing environment in which customers/clients demand custom-designed products and/or high-quality services, or one in which employees want challenging work. Moreover, among educated employees, simplified jobs often lead to lower satisfaction, higher rates of absenteeism, and turnover, and demands for premium pay to compensate for the repetitive nature of the work.

Since jobs are created primarily to enable an organization to achieve its objectives, industrial engineering cannot be ignored as a disciplined and objective approach to job design. However, too much emphasis on the concerns of industrial engineering—improving efficiency and simplifying work methods—may result in human considerations being neglected or downplayed.

**BEHAVIOURAL CONSIDERATIONS** By the mid-1900s, reacting to what they viewed as the "dehumanizing" aspects of pigeonholing workers into highly repetitive and specialized jobs, management theorists proposed ways of broadening the numbers of activities in which employees engaged. **Job enlargement (horizontal loading)** involves assigning workers additional tasks at the same level of responsibility to increase the number of tasks they have to perform. Also known as *horizontal loading*, job enlargement reduces monotony and fatigue by expanding the job cycle and drawing on a wider range of employee skills. Another technique to relieve monotony and employee boredom is **job rotation**. This involves systematically moving employees from one job to another. Although the jobs themselves do not change, workers experience more task variety, motivation, and productivity. The company gains by having more versatile, multi-skilled employees who can cover for one another efficiently.

More recently, psychologist Frederick Herzberg argued that the best way to motivate workers is to build opportunities for challenge and achievement into jobs through **job enrichment (vertical loading)**.[17] This is defined as any effort that makes an employee's job more rewarding or satisfying by adding more meaningful tasks and duties. Also known as *vertical loading*, job enrichment involves increasing autonomy and responsibility by allowing employees to assume a greater role in the decision-making process.

*frontLINE tips* Enriching jobs can be accomplished through such activities as:

- increasing the level of difficulty and responsibility of the job
- assigning workers more authority and control over outcomes
- providing feedback about individual or unit job performance directly to employees
- adding new tasks requiring training, thereby providing an opportunity for growth
- assigning individuals specific tasks or responsibility for performing a whole job rather than only parts of it

Richard Hackman and Greg Oldham's job design studies identified various job dimensions that would simultaneously improve the efficiency of organizations and the satisfaction of employees.[18] Their *job characteristics model* proposes that employee motivation and satisfaction are directly linked to five core characteristics:[19]

1. *Skill variety.* The degree to which the job requires a person to do different tasks and involves the use of a number of different talents, skills, and abilities.
2. *Task identity.* The degree to which the job requires completion of a whole and identifiable piece of work; that is, doing a job from beginning to end, with a visible outcome.
3. *Task significance.* The degree to which the job has a substantial impact on the lives and work of others—both inside and outside the organization.
4. *Autonomy.* The amount of freedom, independence, and discretion the employee has in terms of scheduling work and determining procedures.
5. *Feedback.* The degree to which the job provides the employee with clear and direct information about job outcomes and the effectiveness of his or her performance.

As illustrated in Figure 3.3, these core job characteristics create the conditions that enable workers to experience three critical psychological states that are related to a number of beneficial work outcomes:[20]

1. *Experienced meaningfulness.* The extent to which the employee experiences the work as important, valuable, and worthwhile.

**re-engineering** The fundamental rethinking and radical redesign of business processes to achieve dramatic improvement in contemporary measures of performance.

**job design** The process of systematically organizing work into tasks that are required to perform a specific job.

**job** A group of related activities and duties held by a single employee or a number of incumbents.

**position** The collection of tasks and responsibilities performed by one person.

**industrial engineering** A field of study concerned with analyzing work methods; making work cycles more efficient by modifying, combining, rearranging, or eliminating tasks; and establishing time standards.

**job enlargement (horizontal loading)** A technique to relieve monotony and boredom that involves assigning workers additional tasks at the same level of responsibility to increase the number of tasks they have to perform.

**job rotation** Another technique to relieve monotony and employee boredom, which involves systematically moving employees from one job to another.

**job enrichment (vertical loading)** Any effort that makes an employee's job more rewarding or satisfying by adding more meaningful tasks and duties.

*figure* 3.3 **The Job Characteristics Model**

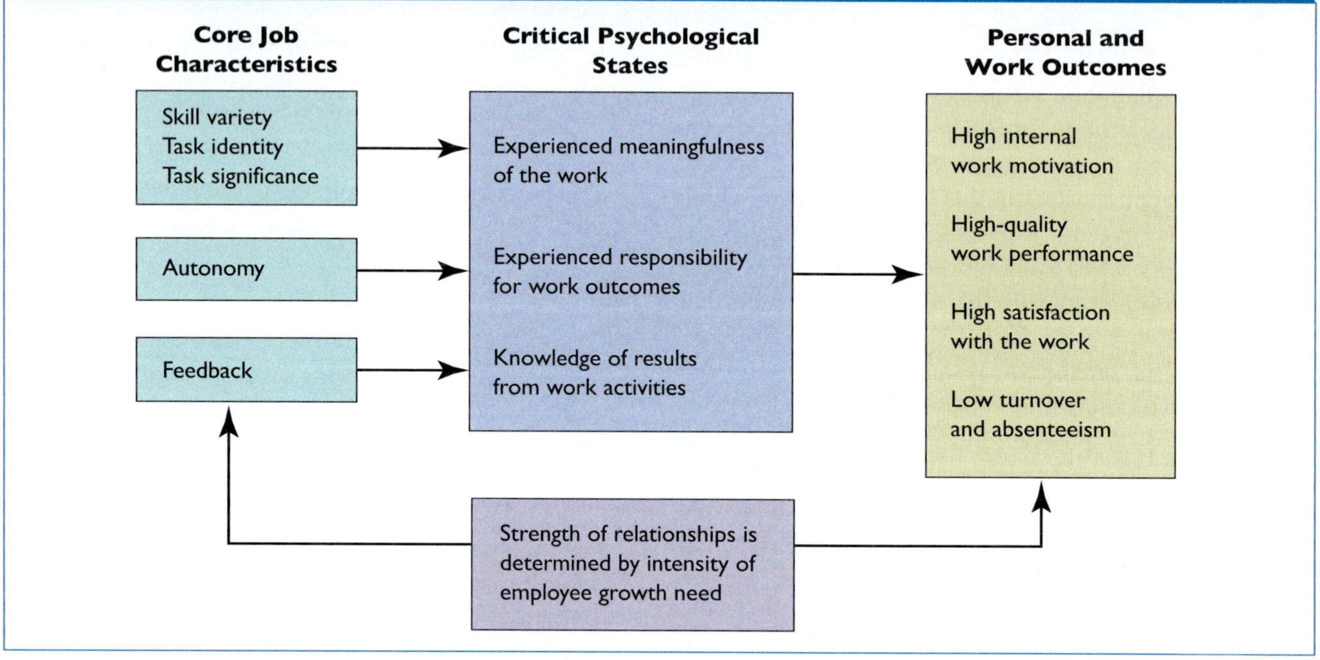


2. *Experienced responsibility.* The degree to which the employee feels personally responsible or accountable for the outcome of the work.
3. *Knowledge of results.* The degree to which the employee understands, on a regular basis, how effectively he or she is performing.

A job with characteristics that allows an employee to experience all three critical states provides internal rewards that sustain motivation. The benefits to the employer include high-quality performance, higher employee satisfaction, and lower absenteeism and turnover.

Job enrichment and the inclusion of the five core dimensions in jobs is not, however, a panacea. Job enrichment programs are more successful in some jobs and settings than in others. Moreover, not all employees want additional responsibility and challenge. Hackman and Oldham stress that the strength of the linkage among job characteristics, psychological states, and work outcomes is determined by the intensity of an individual employee's need for growth.[21] Some people prefer routine jobs and may resist job redesign efforts. In addition, job redesign efforts almost always fail when employees lack the physical or mental skills, abilities, or education needed to perform the job. Furthermore, neither approach will correct job dissatisfaction problems related to inequitable compensation, inadequate benefits, or lack of job security. Unions have sometimes resisted job enrichment, fearing that management will expect workers to take on more responsibility and challenge without additional compensation. Managers, fearing a loss of authority and control or worried about possible elimination of supervisory jobs, have also been sources of resistance.

**HUMAN ENGINEERING CONSIDERATIONS** Over time, it became apparent that, in addition to considering psychological needs, effective job design must also take physiological needs and health and safety issues into account. The typical office worker spends eight hours seated at a desk using a computer and telephone, and the wrong workstation set-up can lead to physical stresses and ailments that lower productivity and increase absenteeism. Studies have found that one of every ten Canadian workers suffers from repetitive motion injury that limits daily activity.[22]

**Human engineering** (ergonomics) aims to adapt the entire job system—the work, environment, machines, equipment, and processes—to match human characteristics. Doing so results in eliminating or minimizing product defects, damage to equipment, and worker injuries or illnesses caused by poor work design. Over a 10-year period, the injury rates and lost workdays

In this auto factory, team members with complementary skills work toward common goals for which they hold joint responsibility and accountability.

associated with work-related musculoskeletal disorders (WMSDs) decreased by 80 percent and compensation costs decreased by 70 percent in companies that made ergonomic modifications in the workplace.[23]

**AN ETHICAL DILEMMA**

If a supervisor decides to make changes to jobs in her department based on the job characteristics model, is she obligated to consult with employees before making the changes?

In addition to designing jobs and equipment with the aim of minimizing negative physiological effects for all workers, human engineering can aid in meeting the unique requirements of individuals with special needs. For example, over the past few years, as the aging of the workforce has become apparent, human engineering has been used to adapt jobs for older workers. The key for employers dealing with the effects of their aging workforce is to ensure that jobs requiring physical activity are designed with ergonomic principles in mind. Physical demands, such as manual materials-handling (lifting, pushing, pulling, and carrying) and upper-limb movements (reaching, grasping, pinching, and fingering), should be performed using good working postures and as little force and repetition as possible. Items such as mechanical assists for lifting (scissor-lift tables, tilters, vacuum lifts) and assembly (screw guns and adjustable tables) are therefore becoming more essential.[24]

### FLEXIBLE WORK ARRANGEMENTS

**Flexible work arrangements** give employees autonomy over when to start and finish their work day. Employees are still mandated to work 40 hours per week at the workplace, but are given a range of hours within which to do so. Most companies expect employees to be at their workstations during a core time, usually between 11:00 and 3:00, for meetings and other team-based activities.[25] Flexible work arrangements are not suitable for some organizations, such as manufacturing, that require workers to be available during the entire run of the production line.

Many organizations also offer **telecommuting**, which provides flexibility around when and where employees complete their work. Technological advances have created opportunities for employees to work from home or other off-site facilities while staying connected to the workplace. The number of Canadian companies offering telecommuting increased from 30 to 42 percent between 2007 and 2009, which equates to approximately 800 000 Canadians who telecommute daily and about 2.5 million who telecommute at least one day a week.[26]

**human engineering (ergonomics)** An interdisciplinary approach that seeks to integrate and accommodate the physical needs of workers into the design of jobs. It aims to adapt the entire job system—the work, environment, machines, equipment, and processes—to match human characteristics.

**flexible work arrangements** A work arrangement that gives employees autonomy over when to start and finish their work day.

**telecommuting** A work arrangement that gives employees autonomy to work from home or other off-site facilities.

## *In-class Notes*

**Organizing Work**

- Organization chart depicts organizational structure of relationships among jobs
- Job-design process organizes work into groups of tasks called jobs
- Industrial engineering approach creates specialized, repetitive jobs
- Behavioural approach (based on job characteristics theory) broadens job tasks to increase motivation
- Human engineering approach (ergonomics) adapts job tasks to physical characteristics of employee
- Flexible work arrangements give employees autonomy over when they start and finish their work day.

Studies have found that telecommuting results in improved productivity, organizational loyalty and commitment, job satisfaction, and employee retention and attraction.[27] One reason for the increase in productivity is the distraction-free environment often provided by telework, which is not as likely in traditional offices where proximity can result in regular interruptions.

Studies have also found that telecommuters exhibit better work–life balance and lower levels of absenteeism than their office-based colleagues.[28] With employees exercising the telecommuting option, companies report annual real estate savings of $5000 for each employee.[29] Some organizations have implemented "hot desking," which involves having a limited number of workstations available for workers to share when they are in the office.[30]

The enhanced flexibility offered by telecommuting is used to attract new employees and retain existing staff under conditions of labour shortage. One study found that over 30 percent of teleworkers would have quit their jobs if telecommuting was not available.[31] Some studies indicate that employees are even willing to accept employment in another company and forfeit a promotion in order to obtain flexible work arrangements.[32]

In late 2006, the Telus Vancouver office experimented with telecommuting by offering 170 employees the option of working from home full-time for six months. The participating employees saved 14 000 hours of time in traffic and 114 tonnes of greenhouse gas emissions by not commuting, and exhibited morale and productivity improvements. Today, 18 000 Telus employees work at home at least once a week. In the call centres alone, there are approximately 500 staff working at home full-time, a number that is expected to increase by another 400 before 2011. Other companies offering telecommuting programs include IBM Canada, Boeing, Bell Canada, Bank of America, and Sun Microsystems.[33]

The following questions help determine if an employee is a candidate for telecommuting:

- Can this employee manage time well without supervision?
- Is the employee a self-starter who can meet deadlines without supervision?
- Is the employee able to work alone for long periods of time?

## Employee Engagement in Job Redesign

Successful organizations realize that job redesign requires the collective wisdom and expertise of all staff. The complexities of job redesign demand that everyone in an organization be part of the process so that a variety of ideas are generated around what changes need to be made. Delegating the decision making around job design to lower organizational levels enhances employee involvement, empowerment, and commitment to change.[34] Employees who fulfill their job requirements on a daily basis are in the best position to identify where changes are required. If supervisors exclusively hold accountability for job redesign, they run the risk of making changes to jobs that may not necessarily reflect the needs and expectations of employees in the actual positions. With employee input, job redesign can be executed in a way that has employee support and commitment and allows the organization to efficiently and effectively achieve its strategic goals.

Employee engagement in job redesign also increases the probability that employees will remain with an organization, because employees know they have played a role in shaping the intrinsic job quality and increasing the meaningfulness of the job.[35] Studies have found that companies with highly engaged employees experience 26 percent higher productivity, lower turnover, a greater ability to attract skilled labour, and 13 percent higher returns to shareholders over a five-year period. As well, highly engaged employees have a 20 percent lower absenteeism rate, exceed expectations in performance reviews, and are more supportive of organizational change. Companies with engaged employees boosted operating income by 19 percent compared with companies that had the lowest percentage of engaged employees.[36]

## 3.3 THE NATURE OF JOB ANALYSIS

Once jobs have been designed or redesigned, an employer's performance-related expectations need to be defined and communicated based on job analysis, a process by which information about jobs is systematically gathered and organized. **Job analysis** is the procedure that firms use to determine the tasks, duties, and responsibilities of each job and the human attributes (in terms of knowledge, skills, and abilities) required to perform it. In contrast to job design, which reflects subjective opinions about the ideal requirements of a job, job analysis is concerned with objective and verifiable information about the actual requirements. Once this information has been gathered, it is used for developing **job descriptions** (what the job entails) and **job specifications** (what the human requirements are).[37]

Accuracy of job analysis information is very important, as it provides the basis for many HR-related decisions. However, job analysis is usually based on human judgment, a process that is known to be fallible and subject to considerable inaccuracy. Inaccuracies can be created by the effects of social influence, enhancement of self-presentation, and limited or biased information processing.[38] Thus, one point of view is that caution should be taken to ensure that potential inaccuracies do not occur—such as by having more than one job analyst at work and reviewing any discrepancies between the results.[39] Others believe that accuracy is possible if job analysis is properly conducted and focused on concrete, specific behaviours.[40]

A growing number of organizations prefer **competency analysis** instead of traditional job analysis.[41] Competency analysis identifies the behaviours, skills, and knowledge that all employees are expected

**job analysis** The procedure for determining the tasks, duties, and responsibilities of each job and the human attributes (in terms of knowledge, skills, and abilities [KSAs]) required to perform it.

**job descriptions** A list of the duties, responsibilities, reporting relationships, and working conditions of a job—one product of job analysis.

**job specifications** A list of the "human requirements"; that is, the requisite knowledge, skills, and abilities (KSAs) needed to perform the job—another product of job analysis.

**competency analysis** Reviewing an organizations' values, mission statement, and strategic direction to identify behaviours, skills, and knowledge that all employees in a company must demonstrate.

Job Analysis Internet Guide **www.job-analysis.net**

Job Analysis **http://harvey.psyc.vt.edu**

to demonstrate regardless of their position within an organization. This list of universal capabilities is generated through a study of the organization's values, mission statement, and strategic direction. For example, the snack food company Frito Lay has used a competency-based approach to inform its compensation decisions for over 10 years. The four competencies at the managerial level include: 1) leading for results; 2) building workforce effectiveness; 3) leveraging technical and business systems; and 4) modelling, teaching, and coaching company values.[42] A competency-based approach reinforces the capabilities that are valued by the organization and rewards employees when they demonstrate or exceed organizational expectations. Raising competency levels ultimately enhances competitive advantage. Many leading companies, including the Canadian public service, 3M, American Express, IBM, Metlife, Shell, and Marriott Hotels, use competency analysis.

## Uses of Job Analysis Information

Job analysis is sometimes called the cornerstone of HRM. As illustrated in Figure 3.4, information gathered, evaluated, and summarized through job analysis is the basis for a number of interrelated HR activities. Having accurate information about jobs and their human requirements—which should be gathered in a gender-neutral, bias-free manner—is essential for legal compliance in each of these areas:

**HUMAN RESOURCES PLANNING** Knowing the actual requirements of jobs is essential for planning future staffing needs and assessing how a firm's employment equity goals can most effectively be met.

**RECRUITMENT AND SELECTION** Job description and job specification information should be used to decide what sort of person to recruit and hire. Identifying *bona fide* occupational requirements and ensuring that all activities related to recruitment and selection (such as advertising, screening, and testing) are based on these requirements is necessary for legal compliance in all Canadian jurisdictions.

**COMPENSATION** Job analysis information is also essential for determining the relative value of each job and its appropriate compensation. The relative value of jobs is one of the key factors used to determine appropriate compensation and justify pay differences if challenged under human rights or pay equity legislation.

**PERFORMANCE APPRAISAL** To be legally defensible, the criteria used to assess employee performance must be directly related to the duties and responsibilities identified through job analysis. Performance standards should be based on actual job requirements.

*figure* 3.4 **Uses of Job Analysis Information**

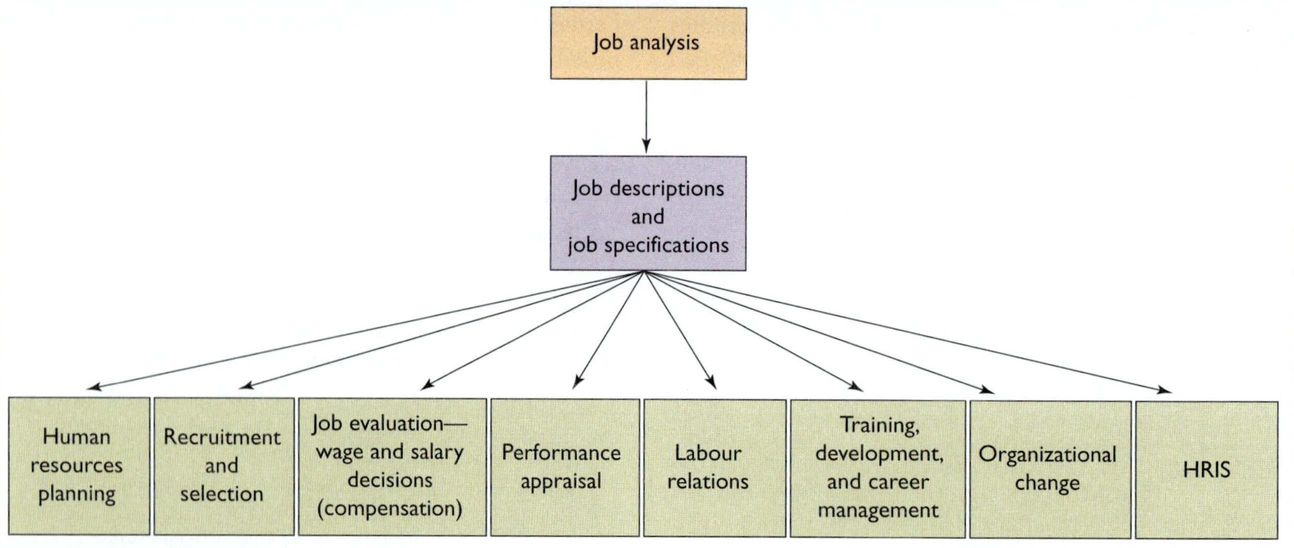

**LABOUR RELATIONS** In unionized environments, job descriptions developed from analysis information are generally subject to union approval prior to finalization. Union-approved descriptions then become the basis for classifying jobs and bargaining over wages, performance criteria, and working conditions. Once approved, significant changes to job descriptions may have to be negotiated.

**TRAINING, DEVELOPMENT, AND CAREER MANAGEMENT** By comparing the knowledge, skills, and abilities (KSAs) that employees bring to a job with those that are identified by job analysis, managers can determine the gaps. Training programs can then be designed to bridge these gaps.

**DESIGNING HRIS** Job descriptions and job specifications inform the design of human resources information systems (HRIS). Information collected from both sources, such as main duties, qualifications, supervisory responsibilities, education, experience, skills, abilities, and work environment, are used as major categories or links for HRIS. This enables fast retrieval of information as needed for HR audits.

**ORGANIZATIONAL CHANGE INITIATIVES** When organizations search for ways to enhance efficiency and effectiveness in their operations, job descriptions reveal what needs to be modified, eliminated, or added.

## 3.4 STEPS IN JOB ANALYSIS

The seven steps involved in analyzing jobs are as follows:

**Step 1.** *Identify how the information will be used.* This will determine the types of data that should be collected and the techniques used. Some data-collection techniques—such as interviewing the employee and asking what the job entails and what his or her responsibilities are—are good for writing job descriptions and selecting employees. Other job analysis techniques (such as the position analysis questionnaire, described later) do not provide qualitative information for job descriptions but rather numerical ratings for each job; these can be used to compare jobs with one another for compensation purposes.

**Step 2.** *Review relevant background information such as organization charts, process charts, and job descriptions.*[43] As explained earlier, organization charts show how a job relates to other jobs and where it fits in the overall organization. A **process chart** provides a more detailed understanding of the workflow than is obtainable from the organization chart alone. In its simplest form, a process chart (like the one in Figure 3.5) shows the flow of inputs to and outputs from the job under study. (In Figure 3.5, the inventory control clerk is expected to receive inventory from suppliers, take requests for inventory from the two plant managers, provide requested inventory to these managers, and give information to these managers on the status of in-stock inventories.) Finally, the existing job description, if there is one, can provide a starting point for building the revised one.

**Step 3.** *Select representative positions and jobs to be analyzed.* This is necessary when there are many incumbents for a single job and when a number of similar jobs are to be analyzed, since it would be too time-consuming to analyze every position and job. Clearly communicate to supervisors, employees, and,

***figure* 3.5 Process Chart for Analyzing a Job's Workflow**

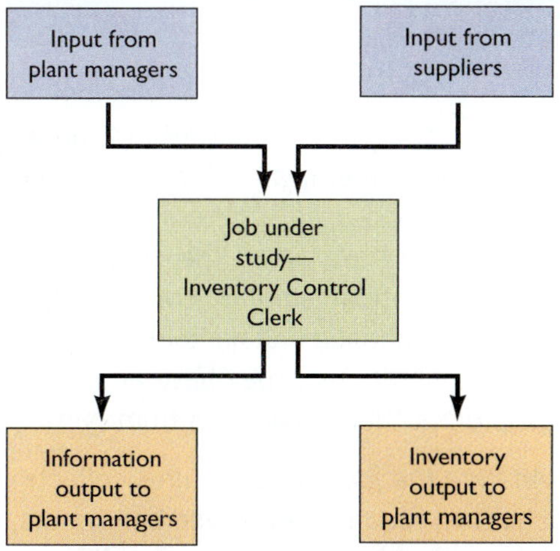


Source: R. I. Henderson, *Compensation Management in a Knowledge-based World*, 9th ed. © 2003 Adapted by permission of Pearson Education, Inc., Upper Saddle River, NJ.

**process chart** A diagram showing the flow of inputs to and outputs from the job under study.

## In-class Notes

**The Nature of Job Analysis**

- Job analysis determines tasks, duties, and responsibilities of a job and the human attributes required to perform it.
- Job analysis is used to create job descriptions and job specifications that form the cornerstone of many HR activities.
- Seven steps in job analysis are:

1. identify how the information will be used
2. review background information
3. select representative jobs to be analyzed
4. analyze the jobs
5. review information with job incumbents
6. develop job descriptions and job specifications
7. review and update job descriptions and job specifications

possibly, union stewards, the purpose of job analysis, what is required of them, and how data will be collected, validated, and used. Address any questions or concerns they may have about the process or use of data. This is a critical step in conducting the job analysis, as it enhances stakeholder support and reduces the likelihood that they have any reservations that might prompt them to abstain from participating.

**Step 4.** *Analyze the jobs.* This requires collecting data on job activities, required employee behaviours, working conditions, and human traits and abilities needed to perform the job, using one or more of the job analysis techniques explained later in the chapter.

**Step 5.** *Review the information with job incumbents.* Job analysis information should be verified with the worker(s) performing the job and with the immediate supervisor. This will help confirm that the information is factually correct and complete. By providing an opportunity for review and modification, if necessary, this step can also help gain employees' acceptance of the job analysis data as well as the documents derived from these data and subsequent decisions reached.

**Step 6.** *Develop a job description and job specification.* A job description and job specification are the two concrete products of the job analysis. As explained earlier, the *job description* is a written statement that describes the activities and responsibilities of the job as well as important features of the job (such as working conditions and safety hazards). The *job specification* summarizes the personal qualities, traits, skills, and background required. While there may be a separate document describing the human qualifications, job descriptions and specifications are often combined in a single document, generally titled "Job Description."

**Step 7.** *Review and update the job description and job specification.* Annually canvass feedback from supervisors and employees on the degree to which the job description and job specification continue to reflect the actual job duties and requirements. For example, both documents can be reviewed during an employee's performance appraisal interview or during the recruitment drive when a job vacancy occurs.

## 3.5 METHODS OF COLLECTING JOB ANALYSIS INFORMATION

Various techniques are used for collecting information about the duties, responsibilities, and requirements of a job; the most important ones will be discussed in this section. In practice, when the information is being used for multiple purposes, several techniques may be used in combination. Since each data collection method has a unique set of strengths and limitations, using a combination of methods can often counterbalance each method's weaknesses. For example, surveys are prone to generating vague responses, which can be offset by interviews that encourage probing for details.

Collecting job analysis data usually involves a joint effort by an HR specialist, the incumbent, and the jobholder's supervisor. In smaller firms, it may be a line manager who collects this information. The HR specialist or line manager analyzes the work being done and then develops a job description and specification. The supervisor and incumbent typically review and verify the job analyst's conclusions regarding the job's duties, responsibilities, and requirements.

### The Interview

The interview is probably the most widely used method for determining the duties and responsibilities of a job. Three types of interviews are used to collect job analysis data: *individual* interviews with each employee; *group* interviews with employees having the same job; and *supervisory* interviews with one or more supervisors who are thoroughly knowledgeable about the job being analyzed. The group interview is used when a large number of employees are performing similar or identical work, and it can be a quick and inexpensive way of learning about the job.

Whichever interview method is used, the interviewee should fully understand the reason for the interview, since there's a tendency for such interviews to be misconstrued as "efficiency evaluations." When they are, interviewees may not be willing to accurately describe their jobs or those of their reporting employees.

Some typical interview questions include:

1. What is the major purpose of the job?
2. What are the major duties? What percentage of time is spent on each?
3. What are the major responsibilities?
4. What types of equipment, machinery, and/or tools are used?
5. What are the education, experience, skill, and (where applicable) certification and licensing requirements?
6. What are the basic accountabilities or performance standards that typify the work?
7. What are the job's physical demands? What are its emotional and mental demands?
8. In what physical location(s) is the work performed? What working conditions are involved?
9. What are the health and safety conditions? To what hazard(s) is there exposure, if any?

Interviews should follow a structured or checklist format. A job analysis questionnaire with detailed questions like the one presented in Figure 3.6 may be used to interview job incumbents or may be filled out by them. A job analyst who collects information by personally observing the work being done can also use this questionnaire. These two methods will be explained shortly.[44]

**INTERVIEW GUIDELINES** When conducting a job analysis interview, supervisors and job analysts should keep several things in mind:

1. The job analyst and supervisor should work together to identify the employees who know the job best, as well as those who might be expected to be the most objective in describing their duties and responsibilities.
2. Rapport should be established quickly with the interviewee by using the individual's name, speaking in easily understood language, briefly reviewing the purpose of the interview (job analysis, not performance appraisal), and explaining how the person came to be chosen.

*frontLINE tips*

3. A structured guide or checklist that lists questions and provides spaces for answers should be used. This ensures that crucial questions are identified ahead of time so that complete and accurate information is gathered and that all interviewers (if there is more than one) glean the same types of data, thereby helping ensure comparability of results. However, leeway should also be permitted through including some open-ended questions, such as, "Was there anything we didn't cover with our questions?"
4. When duties are not performed in a regular manner—for instance, when the incumbent does not perform the same tasks or jobs over and over again many times a day—the incumbent should be asked to list

## *figure* 3.6 Job Analysis Questionnaire

Job title: ____________________ Job grade: ____________________
Department: ____________________ Location: ____________________
Prepared by: ____________________ Date: ____________________

**1. Purpose of job**

- What is the purpose of the job? Why does the job exist?

______________________________________________________
______________________________________________________
______________________________________________________

**2. Major responsibilities and essential functions (list in order of importance)**

- What are the responsibilities?
- How are they done?
- Percentage of time?
- Why is the activity performed?
- What is the measure of success?
- What direction of others is involved?

______________________________________________________
______________________________________________________
______________________________________________________
______________________________________________________

**3. Knowledge**

- What techniques and/or practices are necessary? Why?

______________________________________________________
______________________________________________________

- List specific education requirement(s).

______________________________________________________
______________________________________________________

- List experience requirement(s) and number of years required in each.

______________________________________________________
______________________________________________________

- List required licences or certificates.

______________________________________________________
______________________________________________________

**4. Problem solving and decision making**

- List how the jobholder solves problems (i.e., planning, scheduling, creativity techniques, complexity of procedures, degree of independent thinking, and resourcefulness or ingenuity required). List examples of required development of new methods. What are the consequences if problems are not solved?

______________________________________________________
______________________________________________________
______________________________________________________
______________________________________________________
______________________________________________________

**5. Resource responsibility**

- List annual pay of personnel who report to jobholder: ____________________
- List annual operating budget (include pay): ____________________
- List any other financial resources (i.e., annual project value/cost, shop order value, total sales, total unit payroll, gross sales booked,

purchasing/contracts volume, transportation costs, facilities budget, assets, investment income, program development costs, and gross sales billed):

______________________________________________

______________________________________________

- What is the jobholder's role in planning, organizing, acquiring, or monitoring these resources?

______________________________________________

______________________________________________

- What is the jobholder's impact in planning, organizing, acquiring, or monitoring these resources?

______________________________________________

______________________________________________

**6. Skills of persuasion**

- Describe the communication skills required in the job (e.g., explaining, convincing, and selling).
- Are contacts inside or outside?
- What are the levels of contacts?
- What types of oral or written communications are involved?
- Who is communicated with and why?

______________________________________________

______________________________________________

______________________________________________

______________________________________________

______________________________________________

______________________________________________

**7. Working conditions**

Read the list of working conditions below and put a check mark if they impact on your job.

| **Condition** | **Amount of Exposure** | | |
|---|---|---|---|
| | *Occasional* | *Regular* | *Frequent* |
| Dust, dirt, fumes | ______ | ______ | ______ |
| Heat, cold | ______ | ______ | ______ |
| Noise | ______ | ______ | ______ |
| Vibration | ______ | ______ | ______ |
| Inclement weather | ______ | ______ | ______ |
| Lighting | ______ | ______ | ______ |

Describe any health or safety hazards related to the job.

______________________________________________

______________________________________________

______________________________________________

Source: *Carswell's Compensation Guide*, ed. D. E. Tyson, CHRP, Tab 3 Job Analysis and Evaluation, Chapter 9, "Job Analysis and Job Descriptions," by T. J. Hackett and E. G. Vogeley, adapted by S. Weeks, P. Drouillard, and D. E. Tyson, pp. 9–21 and 9–23, "Job Analysis Questionnaire—Management and Professional." Reprinted by permission of Carswell, a division of Thomson Reuters Canada Limited.

his or her duties in order of importance and frequency of occurrence. This will ensure that crucial activities that occur infrequently—like a nurse's occasional emergency room duties—are not overlooked.

5. The data should be reviewed and verified by both the interviewee and his or her immediate supervisor.

## Questionnaires

Having employees fill out questionnaires to describe their job-related duties and responsibilities is another good method of obtaining job analysis information. The major decision involved is determining how structured the questionnaire should be and what questions to include. Some questionnaires involve structured checklists listing an inventory of perhaps hundreds of specific duties or tasks (such as "change and splice wire"), and the employee is asked to indicate whether or not he or she performs each and, if so, how much time is normally spent on it. At the other extreme, the questionnaire can be open-ended and simply ask the employee to describe the major duties of his or her job. In practice, a typical job analysis questionnaire often falls between the two extremes. As illustrated in Figure 3.6, there are often several open-ended questions (such as "state your main job duties") as well as a number of structured questions (concerning, for instance, job requirements).

## Observation

Direct observation is especially useful when jobs consist mainly of observable physical activities. Jobs like those of a janitor, assembly-line worker, and accounting clerk are examples. On the other hand, observation is usually not appropriate when the job entails a lot of mental activity that cannot be measured (lawyer, design engineer). Nor is it useful if the employee engages in important activities that might occur only occasionally, such as year-end reports.

Direct observation and interviewing are often used together. One approach is to observe the worker on the job and note all observed job activities. Then, after as much information as possible is accumulated, the incumbent is interviewed, asked to clarify points not understood, and explain what additional activities he or she performs that were not observed. Another approach is to observe and interview simultaneously while the jobholder performs his or her tasks.

## Participant Diary/Log

Another technique involves asking employees to keep a diary/log or a list of what they do during the day. Each employee records every activity in which he or she is involved (along with the time) in a log. This can produce a very complete picture of the job, especially when supplemented with subsequent interviews with the employee and his or her supervisor. However, it is too time-consuming to be practical in most of today's organizations and generates highly repetitive entries if an employee is in a highly routine job completing the same daily tasks.

## The World Café

Although not typically associated with job analysis, the **World Café** is an innovative and simple approach that can be modified for data collection purposes. As the name implies, the World Café is meant to replicate the café experience, where conversations are continually evolving. It is an approach for hosting a number of simultaneous, free-flowing, and relaxed conversations about issues that matter to a group. Facilitation of the session is grounded in the following principles: establishing a hospitable space, exploring questions that matter, encouraging everyone's contribution, connecting diverse views, listening for patterns, and sharing collective discoveries.[45]

Tables are set up around a room with a question or issue assigned to each station. Participants travel to each table sharing their insights, opinions, experiences, and stories. Each time participants move to a new table, they bring with them the experiences from the last round of discussions. As the rounds progress the conversations move to deeper levels.

The World Café fosters dialogue in which the goal is thinking together, and makes evident the collective wisdom of the group. As a data collection method, the World Café can be used to capture the depth and breadth of essential job duties and requirements as well as risks, challenges, time pressures, and constraints.

## Advantages and Disadvantages of the Conventional Data Collection Methods

Interviews, questionnaires, observation, and participant diaries are known as the conventional data collection methods, and they are all qualitative in nature. They are the most popular methods for gathering job analysis data and provide realistic information about what job incumbents actually do and the qualifications and skills required. Associated with each are certain advantages and disadvantages, summarized in Table 3.1.

***table* 3.1 A Summary of Conventional Data Collection Methods for Job Analysis and the Advantages/ Disadvantages of Each**

| Method | Variations | Brief Descriptions | Advantages | Disadvantages |
|---|---|---|---|---|
| **Observation** | Structured | • Watch people go about their work; record frequency of behaviours or nature of performance on forms prepared in advance | • Third-party observer has more credibility than job incumbents, who may have reasons for distorting information<br>• Focuses more on reality than on perceptions | • Observation can influence behaviour of job incumbents<br>• Meaningless for jobs requiring mental effort (in that case, use information processing method)<br>• Not useful for jobs with a long job cycle |
| | Unstructured | • Watch people go about their work; describe behaviours/ tasks performed | | |
| | Combination | • Part of the form is prepared in advance and is structured; part is unstructured | | |
| **Questionnaire** | Structured | • Ask job incumbents/supervisors about work performed using fixed responses | • Relatively inexpensive<br>• Structured questionnaires lend themselves easily to computer analyses<br>• Good method when employees are widely scattered or when data must be collected from a large number of employees | • Developing and testing a questionnaire can be time-consuming and costly<br>• Depends on communication skills of respondents<br>• Does not allow for probing<br>• Tends to focus on perceptions of the job |
| | Unstructured | • Ask job incumbents/supervisors to write essays to describe work performed | | |
| | Combination | • Part of the questionnaire is structured; part is unstructured | | |
| **Diary/Log** | Structured | • Ask people to record their activities over several days or weeks in a booklet with time increments provided | • Highly detailed informaton can be collected over the entire job cycle<br>• Quite appropriate for jobs with a long job cycle | • Requires the job incumbent's participation and co-operation<br>• Tends to focus on perceptions of the job |
| | Unstructured | • Ask people to indicate in a booklet over how long a period they work on a task or activity | | |
| | Combination | • Part of the diary is structured; part is unstructured | | |
| **Individual Interview** | Structured | • Read questions and/or fixed response choices to job incumbent and supervisor; must be face to face | • Provides an opportunity to explain the need for and functions of job analysis<br>• Relatively quick and simple way to collect data<br>• More flexible than surveys<br>• Allows for probing to extract information and provides the interviewee with an opportunity to express views and/or vent frustrations that might otherwise go unnoticed<br>• Activities and behaviours may be reported that would be missed during observation | • Depends heavily on rapport between interviewer and respondent<br>• May suffer from validity/ reliability problems<br>• Information may be distorted due to outright falsification or honest misunderstanding |
| | Unstructured | • Ask questions and/or provide general response choices to job incumbent and supervisor; must be face to face | | |
| | Combination | • Part of the interview is structured; part is unstructured | | |

continued

***table* 3.1 A Summary of Conventional Data Collection Methods for Job Analysis and the Advantages/ Disadvantages of Each—continued**

| Method | Variations | Brief Descriptions | Advantages | Disadvantages |
|---|---|---|---|---|
| **Group Interview** | Structured | • Same as structured individual interviews except that more than one job incumbent/supervisor is interviewed | • Groups tend to do better than individuals with open-ended problem solving<br>• Reliability and validity are likely to be higher than with individuals because group members cross-check each other | • Cost more because more people are taken away from their jobs to participate<br>• Like individual interviews, tends to focus on perceptions of the job |
| | Unstructured | • Same as unstructured individual interviews except that more than one job incumbent/supervisor is interviewed | | |
| | Combination | • Same as combination individual interview except more than one job incumbent/supervisor is interviewed | | |

Source: Adapted from W. J. Rothwell and H. C. Kazanas, *Planning and Managing Human Resources: Planning for Personnel Management*, 2nd ed. (Amherst, MA: Human Resources Development Press, 2003), pp. 66–68. Reprinted by permission of the publisher.

## Quantitative Job Analysis Techniques

Although most employers use interviews, questionnaires, observations, and/or diaries/logs for collecting job analysis data, there are many times when these narrative approaches are not appropriate. For example, when the aim is to assign a quantitative value to each job in order that jobs can be compared for pay purposes, a more quantitative job analysis approach may be best. The position analysis questionnaire and functional job analysis are two popular quantitative methods.

**POSITION ANALYSIS QUESTIONNAIRE** The **position analysis questionnaire (PAQ)** is a very structured job analysis questionnaire.[46] The PAQ itself is filled in by a job analyst, who should already be acquainted with the particular job to be analyzed. The PAQ contains 194 items, each of which represents a basic element that may or may not play an important role in the job. The job analyst decides whether each item plays a role, and, if so, to what extent. In Figure 3.7, for example, "written materials" received a rating of four, indicating that materials such as books, reports, and office notes play a considerable role in this job.

The advantage of the PAQ is that it provides a quantitative score or profile of a job in terms of how that job rates on five basic dimensions: (1) decision-making/communication/social responsibilities, (2) skills, (3) physical activity, (4) vehicles/equipment operation, and (5) information processing. Since it allows the assignment of a quantitative score to each job based on these five dimensions, the PAQ's real strength is in classifying jobs. Results can be used to compare jobs with one another; this information can then be used to determine appropriate pay levels.[47]

**FUNCTIONAL JOB ANALYSIS** **Functional job analysis (FJA)** rates a job on responsibilities pertaining to data, people, and things. It also includes the following dimensions: the extent to which specific instructions, reasoning, and judgment are required to perform the task; the mathematical ability required; and the verbal and language facilities involved. This quantitative technique also identifies performance standards and training requirements. Thus, FJA allows the analyst to answer the question, "To do this task and meet these standards, what training does the worker require?"[48]

**NATIONAL OCCUPATIONAL CLASSIFICATION** The *National Occupational Classification (NOC)*, which was revised and updated in 2001, is an excellent source of standardized information. It contains comprehensive descriptions of approximately 25 000 occupations and the requirements for each. To illustrate the types of information included, the *NOC* listing for Specialists in Human Resources is shown in Figure 3.8.

## *figure* 3.7 Portions of a Completed Page from the Position Analysis Questionnaire

**INFORMATION INPUT**

1 INFORMATION INPUT

1.1 Sources of Job Information

Rate each of the following items in terms of the extent to which it is used by the worker as a source of information in performing the job.

| | *Extent of Use (U)* |
|---|---|
| NA | Does not apply |
| 1 | Nominal/very infrequent |
| 2 | Occasional |
| 3 | Moderate |
| 4 | Considerable |
| 5 | Very substantial |

1.1.1 Visual Sources of Job Information

1 | 4 Written materials (books, reports, office notes, articles, job instructions, signs, etc.)

2 | 2 Quantitative materials (materials that deal with quantities or amounts, such as graphs, accounts, specifications, tables of numbers, etc.)

3 | 1 Pictorial materials (pictures or picturelike materials used as *sources* of information, for example, drawings, blueprints, diagrams, maps, tracings, photographic films, x-ray films, TV pictures, etc.)

4 | 1 Patterns/related devices (templates, stencils, patterns, etc., used as *sources* of information when *observed* during use; do *not* include here materials described in item 3 above)

5 | 2 Visual displays (dials, gauges, signal lights, radarscopes, speedometers, clocks, etc.)

6 | 5 Measuring devices (rulers, calipers, tire pressure gauges, scales, thickness gauges, pipettes, thermometers, protractors, etc., used to obtain visual information about physical measurements; do *not* include here devices described in item 5 above)

7 | 4 Mechanical devices (tools, equipment, machinery, and other mechanical devices that are *sources* of information when *observed* during use or operation)

8 | 3 Materials in process (parts, materials, objects, etc., that are *sources* of information when being modified, worked on, or otherwise processed, such as bread dough being mixed, workpiece being turned in a lathe, fabric being cut, shoe being resoled, etc.)

9 | 4 Materials *not* in process (parts, materials, objects, etc., not in the process of being changed or modified, that are *sources* of information when being inspected, handled, packaged, distributed, or selected, etc., such as items or materials in inventory, storage, or distribution channels, items being inspected, etc.)

10 | 3 Features of nature (landscapes, fields, geological samples, vegetation, cloud formations, and other features of nature that are observed or inspected to provide information)

11 | 2 Man-made features of environment (structures, buildings, dams, highways, bridges, docks, railroads, and other "man-made" or altered aspects of the indoor or outdoor environment that are *observed* or *inspected* to provide job information; do not consider equipment, machines, etc., that an individual uses in the work, as covered by item 7)

Note: The 194 PAQ elements are grouped into six dimensions. This exhibits 11 of the "information input" questions or elements. Other PAQ pages contain questions regarding mental processes, work output, relationships with others, job context, and other job characteristics.

Source: E. J. McCormick, P. R. Jeanneret, and R. D. Mecham, *Position Analysis Questionnaire*, 1989. Purdue Research Foundation, West Lafayette, IN. Reprinted with permission.

**World Café** An approach for hosting a number of simultaneous, free-flowing, and relaxed conversations about issues that matter to a group.

**position analysis questionnaire (PAQ)** A questionnaire used to collect quantifiable data concerning the duties and responsibilities of various jobs.

**functional job analysis (FJA)** A quantitative method for classifying jobs based on types and amounts of responsibility for data, people, and things, as well as the extent to which instructions, reasoning, judgment, and verbal facility are necessary for performing assigned tasks. Performance standards and training requirements are also identified.

***National Occupational Classification (NOC)*** A reference tool for writing job descriptions and job specifications. Compiled by the federal government, it contains comprehensive, standardized descriptions of about 25 000 occupations and the requirements for each.

## *figure* 3.8 NOC (2001) Job Description for Specialists in Human Resources

Specialists in Human Resources develop, implement, and evaluate human resources and labour relations policies, programs, and procedures and advise managers and employees on personnel matters. Specialists in Human Resources are employed throughout the private and public sectors, or may be self-employed.

**Examples of titles classified in this unit group**

Business Agent, Labour Union
Classification Officer
Classification Specialist
Compensation Research Analyst
Conciliator
Consultant, Human Resources
Employee Relations Officer
Employment Equity Officer
Human Resources Research Officer
Job Analyst
Labour Relations Officer
Mediator
Union Representative
Wage Analyst

**Main duties**

Specialists in Human Resources perform some or all of the following duties:

- Develop, implement, and evaluate personnel and labour relations policies, programs, and procedures
- Advise managers and employees on the interpretation of personnel policies, benefit programs, and collective agreements
- Negotiate collective agreements on behalf of employers or workers, and mediate labour disputes and grievances
- Research and prepare occupational classifications, job descriptions, and salary scales
- Administer benefit, employment equity and affirmative action programs, and maintain related record systems
- Coordinate employee performance and appraisal programs
- Research employee benefit and health and safety practices and recommend changes or modifications to existing policies.

**Employment requirements**

- A university degree or college diploma in a field related to personnel management, such as business administration, industrial relations, commerce, or psychology

or

- Completion of a professional development program in personnel administration is required.
- Some experience in a clerical or administrative position related to personnel administration may be required.

**Additional information**

- Progression to management positions is possible with experience.

**Classified elsewhere**

- Human Resources Managers (0112)
- Personnel and Recruitment Officers (1223)
- Personnel Clerks (1442)
- Professional Occupations in Business Services to Management (1122)
- Training officers and instructors (in 4131 College and Other Vocational Instructors)

Source: *National Occupation Classification* (NOC 2001)—1121—Specialists in Human Resources. Catalogue MP53-25/2001-E. Human Resources and Skills Development Canada, 2001. Reproduced with the permission of the Minister of Public Works and Government Services Canada, 2009.

## In-class Notes

**Methods of Collecting Job Analysis Information**

- Interviews: individual, group, supervisory
- Questionnaires: varying degrees of structure
- Observation: by job analyst
- Participant diary/log: employees record activities during the day
- World Café
- Quantitative techniques:
  - position analysis questionnaire (PAQ)
  - functional job analysis (FJA)
  - *National Occupational Classification* (NOC)

The *NOC* and its counselling component, the *Career Handbook*, both focus on occupations rather than jobs. An **occupation** is defined as a collection of jobs that share some or all of a set of main duties.

The jobs within each group are characterized by similar skills.[49]

To provide a complete representation of work in the Canadian economy, the *NOC* classifies occupations into major groups based on two key dimensions—skill level and skill type. The major groups, which are identified by two-digit numbers, are then broken down further into minor groups, with a third digit added, and unit groups, at which a fourth digit is added. Within these three levels of classification, a unit group provides the actual profile of an occupation.[50] For example:

- Major Group 31—Professional Occupations in Health
- Minor Group 314—Professional Occupations in Therapy and Assessment
- Unit Group 3142—Physiotherapists

One of the benefits of the *NOC* is that it has helped promote a greater degree of uniformity in job titles and descriptions used by employers across Canada. This has facilitated the exchange of information about salaries and benefits for compensation administration purposes and about labour supply and demand for human resources planning.

## 3.6 WRITING JOB DESCRIPTIONS AND JOB SPECIFICATIONS

### Job Descriptions

A job description is a written statement of what the jobholder actually does, how he or she does it, and under what conditions the job is performed. No standard format is used in writing job descriptions, but most include the following types of information: job identification, job summary, relationships, duties

**occupation** A collection of jobs that share some or all of a set of main duties.

The World Café **www.theworldcafe.com**

and responsibilities, authority of incumbent, performance standards, and working conditions. The description in Figure 3.9—in this case for a marketing manager—provides an example. As can be seen, the description is quite comprehensive and includes such essential elements as identification, summary, and duties and responsibilities, as well as the human qualifications for the job. As explained in the HR.Net box below, online assistance is also available.

**JOB IDENTIFICATION** The job identification section generally contains several types of information. The *job title* specifies the title of the job, such as marketing manager, recruiter, or inventory control clerk. The *department* or location is also indicated, along with the title of the immediate supervisor—in this case, under the heading *reports to*. The *date* refers to the date the job description was actually written, and *prepared by* identifies the person who wrote it. There is also an indication of *who approved the description* and the *approval date*. Many job descriptions also include a *job code*, which permits easy referencing. While some firms devise their own coding systems based on wage classification, for example, many use *NOC* codes to facilitate external comparison and employment equity reporting.

**JOB SUMMARY** The *job summary* should describe the general nature of the job, listing only its major functions or activities. Thus, the marketing manager "plans, directs, and co-ordinates the marketing of the organization's products and/or services." For the job of materials manager, the summary might state that she or he "purchases economically, regulates deliveries of, stores, and distributes all material necessary on the production line," while that for a mailroom supervisor might indicate that he or she "receives, sorts, and delivers all incoming mail properly, and he or she handles all outgoing mail, including the accurate and timely posting of such mail."[51]

**RELATIONSHIPS** There is sometimes a relationships section, which indicates the jobholder's relationships with others inside and outside the organization. The relationships section in the job description of an HR manager, for example, might look like this:[52]

- *reports to*: vice-president of human resources
- *supervises*: HR specialist, test administrator, labour relations specialist, and one administrative assistant
- *works with*: all department managers and senior management team members
- *contacts outside the company*: employment agencies, executive recruiting firms, union representatives, benefit consultants, and various suppliers.

**DUTIES AND RESPONSIBILITIES** This section presents a detailed list of the job's major duties and responsibilities. Each of the job's major duties should be listed separately and described in a few sentences. The duties of the marketing manager include establishing marketing goals to ensure share of market and profitability and developing and recommending pricing strategy.

**HR.NET**

## Writing Job Descriptions Online

Thanks to the Internet, assistance in writing job descriptions may be just a few keystrokes away. A comprehensive, individual, professional job description can be created in minutes—it is fast, easy, and done completely online. At www.jobdescription.com, there are more than 3700 built-in job descriptions in the existing job library, and specific competencies can be added to further define and individualize the job description to meet the needs of a specific organization.

After completing the job description, jobdescription.com helps create and publish professional job advertisements and generate a job-specific interview form that contains suggested behavioural interview questions.

Source: Compiled from the Knowledge Point website, www.jobdescription.com (March 26, 2005). Used with permission of Knowledge Point, LLC, Petaluma, CA. 

*figure* 3.9 **Sample Job Description—Automotive Service Manager**

**OLEC CORP.**
**Job Description**

| | | | |
|---|---|---|---|
| **Job Title:** | Automotive Service Manager | **Prepared By:** | Larry Weber |
| **Department:** | Automotive Repair | **Prepared Date:** | October 12, 2005 |
| **Reports To:** | General Manager | **Approved By:** | Anne Massard |
| **FLSA Status:** | Non-Exempt | **Approved Date:** | October 18, 2005 |

**SUMMARY**
Directs and coordinates activities concerned with acquisition of automotive equipment and operation and maintenance of automotive fleet repair and storage facilities by performing the following duties personally or through subordinate supervisors.

**ESSENTIAL DUTIES AND RESPONSIBILITIES** include the following. Other duties may be assigned.

Coordinates activities of personnel conducting research and testing program on automotive equipment considered for acquisition based on such factors as operational performance, costs of operation and maintenance, operational safety, and compliance with environmental laws and regulations.

Reviews and submits staff proposals for modifications to vendor or manufacturer.

Directs procurement of all types of company owned and operated automotive equipment and materials, supplies, and parts required to maintain automotive equipment, garages, and storage facilities.

Coordinates automotive repair and maintenance services to obtain maximum utilization of automotive equipment and prevent operational delays in other departments.

**SUPERVISORY RESPONSIBILITIES**
Manages total of 7 employees in the Automotive Department. Carries out supervisory responsibilities in accordance with the organization's policies and applicable laws. Responsibilities include interviewing, hiring, and training employees; planning, assigning, and directing work; appraising performance; rewarding and disciplining employees; addressing complaints and resolving problems.

**QUALIFICATIONS**
To perform this job successfully, an individual must be able to perform each essential duty satisfactorily. The requirements listed below are representative of the knowledge, skill, and/or ability required. Reasonable accommodations may be made to enable individuals with disabilities to perform the essential functions.

**EDUCATION and/or EXPERIENCE**
Fifth year college or university program certificate; or two to four years related experience and/or training; or equivalent combination of education and experience.

**LANGUAGE SKILLS**
Ability to read and interpret documents such as safety rules, operating and maintenance instructions, and procedure manuals. Ability to write routine reports and correspondence. Ability to speak effectively before groups of customers or employees of organization.

**MATHEMATICAL SKILLS**
Ability to calculate figures and amounts such as discounts, interest, commissions, proportions, percentages, area, circumference, and volume. Ability to apply concepts of basic algebra and geometry.

**REASONING ABILITY**
Ability to solve practical problems and deal with a variety of concrete variables in situations where only limited standardization exists. Ability to interpret a variety of instructions furnished in written, oral, diagram, or schedule form.

**COMPUTER SKILLS**
Inventory Smog Tester Certificate

**PHYSICAL DEMANDS**
While performing the duties of this job the employee is regularly required to stand; walk; use hands to finger, handle, or feel; reach with hands and arms; and talk or hear. The employee is occasionally required to sit; climb or balance and stoop, kneel, crouch, or crawl. The employee is regularly required to lift up to 10 pounds and up to 25 pounds. The employee is frequently required to lift up to 50 pounds. The employee is occasionally required to lift up to 100 pounds. The vision requirements include: close vision.

**WORK ENVIRONMENT**
While performing the duties of this job the employee is regularly exposed to moving mechanical parts and fumes or airborne particles. The employee is frequently exposed to outside weather conditions. The employee is occasionally exposed to high, precarious places; toxic or caustic chemicals and risk of electrical shock.

The noise level in the environment is high.

Source: Compiled from the Knowledge Point website, www.jobdescription.com (March 26, 2005). Used with permission of Knowledge Point, LLC, Petaluma, CA. 

The *NOC* may be a helpful reference tool when itemizing a job's duties and responsibilities. As shown in Figure 3.8, a specialist in human resources might be expected to: "develop, implement, and evaluate personnel and labour relations policies, programs, and procedures"; "advise managers and employees on the interpretation of personnel policies, benefit programs, and collective agreements"; and "research and prepare occupational classifications, job descriptions, and salary scales."

Most experts state unequivocally that one item frequently found but that should never be included in a job description is a "cop-out clause," such as "other duties, as assigned,"[53] since this leaves open the nature of the job and the people needed to staff it and can be subject to abuse. Instead, a statement such as "The duties and responsibilities outlined above are representative but not all-inclusive" may meet a firm's need for flexibility without sacrificing the quality and usefulness of the job description.

**AUTHORITY** This section of a job description should define the limits of the jobholder's authority, including his or her decision-making authority, direct supervision of other employees, and budgetary limitations. For example, the jobholder might have authority to approve purchase requests up to $5000, grant time off or leaves of absence, discipline department employees, recommend salary increases, and interview and hire new employees.[54]

**PERFORMANCE STANDARDS** Some job descriptions also contain a performance standards section, which indicates the standards the employee is expected to achieve in each of the job description's main duties and responsibilities.

Setting standards is never an easy matter. Simply telling employees to "do their best" does not provide enough guidance to ensure top performance. One straightforward way of setting standards is to finish the statement: "Work will be considered completely satisfactory when. . . ." This sentence, if completed for each duty listed in the job description, should result in a usable set of performance standards, as follows:[55]

Duty: Accurately Posting Accounts Payable

- all invoices received are posted within the same working day;
- all invoices are routed to the proper department managers for approval no later than the day following receipt;
- no more than three posting errors per month occur on average; and
- by the end of the third working day of each month, the posting ledger is balanced.

Duty: Meeting Daily Production Schedule

- work group produces no less than 426 units per working day;
- no more than 2 percent of units are rejected at the next workstation on average; and
- work is completed with no more than 5 percent overtime per week on average.

**WORKING CONDITIONS** The job description should also list the general working conditions involved in the job. This section generally includes information about noise level, temperature, lighting, degree of privacy, frequency of interruptions, hours of work, amount of travel, and hazards to which the incumbent may be exposed.

**JOB DESCRIPTION GUIDELINES** Some helpful guidelines to assist those writing job descriptions include:[56]

1. *Be clear.* Portray the job so well that the duties are clear without reference to other job descriptions.
2. *Indicate scope of authority.* Indicate the scope and nature of the work by using such phrases as "for the department" or "as requested by the manager." Include all important relationships.
3. *Be specific.* Select the most specific words to show (1) the kind of work, (2) the degree of complexity, (3) the degree of skill required, (4) the extent to which problems are standardized, (5) the extent of the worker's responsibility for each phase of the work, and (6) the degree and type of accountability. Use action words such as *analyze*, *gather*, *assemble*, *plan*, *devise*, *infer*, *deliver*, *transmit*, *maintain*, *supervise*, and *recommend*. Positions at the lower levels of the organization generally have the most detailed explanations of duties and tasks, while higher-level positions tend to have broader responsibility statements.
4. *Be brief.* Use short, accurate statements, since they usually best accomplish the purpose.

The job specifications for previously trained candidates, such as the call centre operators shown here, should clearly indicate which skills, like computer literacy, are job requirements.

5. *Recheck.* Finally, to check whether the description fulfills the basic requirements, ask, "Will a new employee understand the job if he or she reads the job description?"

**JOB DESCRIPTIONS AND HUMAN RIGHTS LEGISLATION** Job descriptions are not legally required but are highly advisable. Human rights legislation requires employers to ensure that there is no discrimination on any of the prohibited grounds in any aspect or terms and conditions of employment. Essential job duties should be clearly identified in the job description. Indicating the percentage of time spent on each duty and/or listing duties in order of importance are strategies used to differentiate between essential and non-essential tasks and responsibilities. It must be remembered that even when an employee cannot perform one or more of the essential duties due to reasons related to a prohibited ground, such as a physical disability or religion, reasonable accommodation to the point of undue hardship is required.

## Job Specifications

Writing the job specification involves examining the job's duties and responsibilities and answering the question, "What human traits and experience are required to do this job?" Both skill and effort factors should be considered, as well as the human implications of the working conditions. The job specification clarifies what kind of person to recruit and for which qualities that person should be tested. Often—as in Figure 3.9—it is presented as part of the job description.[57]

The usual procedure for obtaining the required information is to ask questions on the job analysis questionnaire, such as, "What does it take in terms of education, knowledge, training, and experience to do this job?" When developing job specifications, the *NOC* and *Career Handbook* can provide helpful reference information, including requirements for vision, colour discrimination, hearing, body position, limb coordination, and strength.[58]

Once again, complying with human rights legislation means keeping a few things in mind. All listed qualifications must be justifiable, based on the current job duties and responsibilities. For example, unjustifiably high educational and/or lengthy experience requirements can lead to systemic discrimination. For that reason, many employers are no longer indicating that a degree or diploma is mandatory; rather, they specify that the position calls for a university degree in a specific area, a college diploma in that area, or an equivalent combination of education and work experience.

## Legal Compliance

The qualifications of the current incumbent should not be confused with the minimum requirements, since he or she might be under- or overqualified. To avoid overstating or understating qualifications, it is helpful to ask the question, "What minimum qualifications would be required if this job were being filled in the immediate future?"

For entry-level jobs where no experience is required, identifying the actual physical and mental demands is critical. For example, if the job requires detailed manipulation on a circuit-board assembly line, finger dexterity is extremely important and is something for which candidates should be tested. A **physical demands analysis**—which identifies the senses used and type, frequency, and amount of physical effort involved in the job—is often used to supplement the job specification. Having such detailed information is particularly beneficial when determining accommodation requirements.

To illustrate the types of information and amount of detail that should be provided in a well-written job specification, a sample has been included as Figure 3.10.

**physical demands analysis** Identification of the senses used and type, frequency, and amount of physical effort involved in the job.

Monster Board Canada **www.monster.ca**

Canadian Human Rights Commission
**www.chrc-ccdp.ca/default-en.asp**

## *figure* 3.10 Job Specification

### Job Title: Lifeguard

| | |
|---|---|
| Location: | Lethbridge Community Pool |
| Job Code: | LG1 |
| Supervisor: | Head Lifeguard |
| Department: | Recreation |
| Division: | Parks and Recreation |
| Date: | May 1, 2006 |

**Job Summary**

The incumbent is required to safeguard the health of pool users by patrolling the pool, rescuing swimmers in difficulty, treating injuries, advising pool users of safety rules, and enforcing safety rules.

**Skill**

Formal Qualifications: Royal Life Saving Society Bronze Medallion or equivalent

Experience: No prior experience required but would be an asset.

Communication Skills: Good oral communication skills are required. Proficiency in one or more foreign languages would be an asset. The incumbent must be able to communicate courteously and effectively. Strong interpersonal skills are required. All interaction with the public must be handled with tact and diplomacy.

**Effort**

Physical Effort: The incumbent is required to stand during the majority of working hours. In the event of an emergency where a swimmer is in distress, the incumbent must initiate rescue procedures immediately, which may involve strenuous physical exertion.

Mental Effort: Continuous mental attention to pool users. Must remain vigilant despite many simultaneous demands on his or her attention.

Emotional Effort: Enforcement of safety rules and water rescue can be stressful. Must maintain a professional demeanour when dealing with serious injuries or death.

**Working Conditions**

Job is performed in humid temperature-controlled indoor environment. No privacy. Shift work to cover pool hours of 7 a.m. to 11 p.m. seven days a week. Some overtime and split shifts may be required.

**Approval Signatures**

Incumbent: ____________

Supervisor: ____________

Date: ________________

## *In-class Notes*

**Writing Job Descriptions and Job Specifications**

- Job descriptions include:
  - job identification
  - job summary
  - relationships
  - duties and responsibilities
  - authority
  - performance standards
  - working conditions
- Job descriptions should be clear, specific, and brief
- Job specifications include knowledge, skills, and abilities (KSAs) required of an employee to do the job
- Qualifications in a job specification must be justifiable, particularly education and experience

## 3.7 THE FUTURE OF JOB DESCRIPTIONS

Most organizations today utilize job descriptions and rely on jobs as traditionally defined. However, it is clear that more and more companies are moving toward new organizational configurations, ones built around jobs that are broad and that may change every day. In some cases, job descriptions have been abandoned because they are too rigid and lack the flexibility needed in today's workplace. They fail to communicate the need for an extensive competency profile, including the capacity to manage multiple assignments and exercise leadership on special projects as needed. Hence, job descriptions have been replaced by goal statements. These statements articulate the objectives that employees are expected to reach, encouraging employees to chart their own pathways for goal attainment. In doing so, employees exercise the highest degree of autonomy, innovation, leadership, and critical thinking. In the workplace of the future, flexibility in job roles will be the most important competency requirement and measure of job success.[59]

**AN ETHICAL DILEMMA**

Because job descriptions are not required by law and some organizations have found them no longer relevant, would abolishing job descriptions raise any moral or legal concerns?

# Flexible Work Arrangements on the International Stage

Flexible work arrangements vary significantly in the international workplace. In China, the major advance in flexible work has been the implementation of the five-day work week, with nearly 80 percent of companies implementing this policy. Only 13 percent of companies in China have policies in place for flexible working hours, and only 8 percent allow employees to telecommute.[60] In the UK, more than two-thirds of managers "never" or only "occasionally" permit employees to work from home. The main reason for denying permission is that managers are afraid they do not have sufficient control over employees when they are away from the office. Although 60 percent of companies in the UK claim to offer telecommuting options, the majority of these only occasionally accept employees' requests.[61] Flexible work arrangements are gaining popularity in Spain, with an increasing trend to let employees work from home at least once a week. Employers realize their employees want to manage their own time and acknowledge the benefits of helping staff achieve work–life balance. The increase in flexible working opportunities has partly been fuelled by technological advances that make it possible for more employees to work remotely and reduce the need for them to visit the workplace to conduct face-to-face meetings.[62]

# Chapter Review

## Answers to Test Yourself

1. What are the industrial engineering, behavioural engineering, human engineering, and flexible work arrangement considerations involved in job design?

   Industrial engineers systematically identify, analyze, and time the elements of job cycles and use the information to modify, eliminate, or rearrange work to reduce time to improve efficiency. Behavioural engineering proposes job enlargement, job rotation, and job enrichment to overcome dehumanization and other problems associated with industrial engineering. The job characteristics model proposes that employee motivation and satisfaction are directly linked to five core job characteristics: skill variety, task identity, task significance, autonomy, and feedback. Human engineering takes into consideration ergonomics and tries to adapt the entire job system to match human characteristics. Flexible work arrangements give employees autonomy over when to start and finish their work days. Telecommuting, a popular type of work arrangement, gives employees autonomy over not only when they work but also where they work.

2. What is job analysis and what seven steps are involved?

   Job analysis is concerned with objective and verifiable information about the actual requirements of a job. Once this information has been gathered, it is used for developing job descriptions (what the job entails) and job specifications (what the human requirements are). Job analysis involves six steps: (1) determine the use to which the information will be put, (2) collect background information, (3) select the representative positions and jobs to be analyzed, (4) collect data, (5) review the information collected with the incumbents and their supervisors, (6) develop the job descriptions and job specifications, and (7) review and update job descriptions and job specifications.

3. What is a job description and what are its key components?

   A job description is a written statement of what the jobholder actually does, how the job is done, and under what conditions the job is performed. Typical information included is the job identification, a job summary, relationships, duties and responsibilities, authority of incumbent, performance standards, and working conditions.

4. What are the basic methods of collecting job analysis information and what quantitative techniques are available?

   The basic methods of collecting job analysis information are interviews, questionnaires, direct observation, participant diary/log, and World Café. Quantitative job analysis techniques include the position analysis questionnaire (PAQ) and functional job analysis (FJA).

5. What are the current trends in the nature of jobs and job descriptions?

   The concept of a "job" is in the midst of change, as organizations are becoming flatter and boundaryless and focus on work teams. Although organizational techniques used to foster responsiveness to change have helped to blur the meaning of job as a set of well-defined and clearly delineated responsibilities, most firms today continue to utilize job descriptions and to rely on jobs as traditionally defined. In some cases, competency/skill analysis and brief role descriptions are being used instead.

## Key Terms

boundaryless organization (p. 72)
competency analysis (p. 79)
flat organization (p. 72)
flexible work arrangements (p. 77)
functional job analysis (FJA) (p. 88)
human engineering (ergonomics) (p. 76)
industrial engineering (p. 74)
job (p. 74)
job analysis (p. 79)
job descriptions (p. 79)
job design (p. 74)
job enlargement (horizontal loading) (p. 75)
job enrichment (vertical loading) (p. 75)
job rotation (p. 75)
job specifications (p. 79)
*National Occupational Classification (NOC)* (p. 88)
occupation (p. 91)
organization chart (p. 70)
organizational structure (p. 70)
physical demands analysis (p. 95)
position (p. 74)
position analysis questionnaire (PAQ) (p. 88)
process chart (p. 81)
re-engineering (p. 74)
telecommuting (p. 77)
virtual teams (p. 72)
World Café (p. 86)

# Cases and Exercises

**myHRlab**

For additional cases and exercises, go to **www.mypearsoned.ca/myhrlab**.

## CASE INCIDENT

### Linking Job Analysis and Pay

Until the CEO's secretary, Fay Jacobs, retired, no one in the Winnipeg Engineering Company's HR department realized how much variation there was in the compensation of the company's secretaries.

To Tina Jessup, compensation specialist, it was quite apparent why there were inconsistent standards for secretarial pay. With the advance of office-automation technology, managers' differing styles of delegation, and secretaries' varying degrees of willingness to take on increasing managerial responsibilities, the job had assumed a variety of profiles. As the jobs now existed, it was quite likely that two individuals with the same title might be performing very different jobs.

Knowing that updated job analysis information was essential, and prepared for resistance from those who might want to protect their status and pay, Tina decided to use an objective method to gather information about each of the secretaries' jobs. She developed a questionnaire that she planned to distribute to each member of the firm's secretarial staff and his or her manager following a brief explanatory interview. The interviews would, she hoped, give her a chance to dispel fears on the part of any of the secretaries or managers that the purpose of the analysis was to eliminate jobs, reduce salaries, or lower the grade level of positions.

Before finalizing the questionnaire, Tina shared it with a small group of secretaries in her own department. Based on their input, she made some modifications, such as adding questions about the use of office technology and its impact on the job.

The questionnaire now covered nearly every aspect of the secretarial role, from processing mail and making travel arrangements to editing and preparing company correspondence, budgets, and reports. The questions also captured information about how much time was spent on each activity and how much supervision each task required. Tina hoped that in addition to establishing standards on which Winnipeg Engineering could base a more equitable pay structure, the survey would allow the HR staff members to assess training needs, examine the distribution of work, determine accurate specifications for recruitment and selection, and develop employment tests to be used in the future.

Just as Tina was about to begin the interviews and the distribution of questionnaires, she got a telephone call from Janet Fried, vice-president of sales. She had heard about the upcoming analysis and was very upset. Janet claimed to be worried about how much time Avril, the secretary assisting her, would have to take away from her work in order to meet with Tina and fill out the questionnaire. She also expressed concern that Avril might feel that her job was threatened and start looking for a position elsewhere. Tina agreed to meet with Janet to discuss her reservations, for which Janet thanked her profusely. Just before hanging up, Janet added, "You know, Tina, I sure wouldn't want to see Avril's job rated at a lower grade level than the secretary assisting the vice-president of operations!"

## Questions

1. What do you think is the real "problem," from Janet's point of view?
2. How should Tina address each of Janet's concerns?
3. What can Tina do to prepare herself for any resistance to her job analyses on the part of the secretaries themselves?
4. Given the current advances in office technology, such as sophisticated spreadsheet programs, voicemail systems, and email, as well as the elimination of many middle-management positions through corporate downsizings, secretaries in many firms are taking on quasi-managerial responsibilities. How can Tina account in her job analyses for the degrees to which individual secretaries at Winnipeg Engineering are doing so?

## Application questions

1. You are assigned to write job descriptions for a shirt factory in Nova Scotia employing workers who have English as a second language. Identify the most effective methods you would use to collect job analysis data and explain why these methods are most effective.
2. Discuss how you can enrich the job referred to in question 1 using Hackman & Oldham's Job Classification Model. How will you determine if you proposed the right set of changes to the job?
3. With reference to your current or former part-time job, what job design changes would you make to enhance job satisfaction and productivity? Your proposal should refer to industrial engineering, behavioural engineering, human engineering, and flexible work arrangement considerations.
4. Congratulations! You have just received funding to finance the start-up of your own business.
   a. Describe the type of business you will launch and state your company's goals.
   b. Create an organizational chart that illustrates the organizational structure and types of jobs in your organization. Explain the rationale for the type of structure and jobs you propose.

## RUNNING CASE: LEARNINMOTION.COM

### Who Do We Have to Hire?

The case for Chapter 3, Who Do We Have to Hire?, asks the student to develop job descriptions and specifications and to assess other job requirements based on the needs of LearninMotion.com.

To read this case, go to www.pearsoned.ca/myhrlab and click on the *Management of Human Resources*, Third Canadian Edition, In-Class Edition, cover. Click on the case module in Chapter 3. The running case illustrates a variety of challenges confronted by HR professionals, small-business owners, and front-line supervisors. It places students in the role of HR management consultants to help the fledgling LearninMotion.com develop HR policies, strategies, and long-term goals. Each case is accompanied by assignments for the management consultants in the form of critical-thinking questions posed to the student.

## CONTROVERSIAL BUSINESS TOPIC EXERCISE

You have completed three weeks of one-on-one interviews as part of a job analysis for a mechanical engineering position at a large manufacturing plant in Ontario. As you analyze the data, you realize there is a discrepancy in the findings. The supervisors and mechanical engineers who were interviewed disagree on the essential duties and requirements for the job. The supervisors stated that mechanical engineers work as a team to design and develop machines and that the minimum academic requirement for entry into the profession is a Master's degree in engineering. The employees stated that mechanical engineers supervise the design of machinery and require a college diploma in engineering or business to enter the profession. Discuss your action plan for resolving the inconsistencies.

## IN THE BOARDROOM EXERCISE

"I don't understand why this is taking so long," bellows the CEO as you explain the comprehensive schedule for conducting a job analysis of all information technology staff in your company. "Just use the job descriptions that are on file from 1998 to make your HR decisions. Actually, I can't understand why we are spending all this money on job analysis to update job descriptions that get filed away somewhere—never to be used. It's just another make-work administrative task." Discuss how you will respond to the CEO's position on job analysis and job descriptions, and how you will convince him/her to see the value of the work you will be doing in this area.

## FLEXIBLE WORK ARRANGEMENTS ON THE INTERNATIONAL STAGE EXERCISE

*The exercise below relates to the Flexible Work Arrangements on the International Stage feature on p. 98.*

You are a successful entrepreneur launching your Canadian enterprise overseas. Select two countries in which you would like to do business and research the employment practices in each of these countries. Based on your findings, will you present flexible work arrangements to your employees in each of these countries? Why or why not? In the case where you do plan to offer flexible work arrangements, what specific policies and practices will you put in place?

## EXPERIENTIAL EXERCISE

For further study of text materials and development of practical skills, select the experiential exercise module for this chapter on www.pearsoned.ca/myhrlab. This module provides two or three individual or group-based assignments per chapter.

# Quiz Yourself

## STUDY GUIDE QUESTIONS

Circle the correct answer. After completing this self-test, check your answers against the Answers to Study Guide Questions at the back of the book (p. 433).

1. Which of the following outlines the structure of relationships between people and tasks, giving a "snap shot" view of the organization?
   a. organization structure
   b. organization chart
   c. organizational analysis
   d. organization design
   e. none of the above
2. Smith Company used a job design method that helped it redesign its jobs to increase organization efficiency. The method systematically identified, analyzed, and timed the key elements of job cycles. The information was then used to make modifications and rearrangements that increase efficiency. What work simplification method was used?
   a. organization redesign
   b. job redesign
   c. industrial re-engineering
   d. job enrichment
   e. all of the above
3. Amila and Chan work for a leading financial institution. During the past three years, Amila worked in the HR department, first as a receptionist, then an office

administrator, and then as an HR assistant. Chan worked as an accountant for two years and was recently given additional job responsibilities and a payroll clerk reporting to him. What job broadening techniques were used in the cases of Amila and Chan?
a. job rotation; job enrichment
b. job rotation; job enlargement
c. job redesign
d. job analysis; job redesign
e. job enrichment; job enlargement

4. Richard Hackman and Greg Oldham's job design studies identified five core characteristics that could enhance organizational effectiveness and increase employee satisfaction. Which answer below correctly lists these characteristics?
a. skill variety, task identity, task significance, redesign, task management
b. task identification, skill identification, skill variety, feedback, autonomy
c. skill variety, task identity, task significance, feedback, autonomy
d. skill variety, task variety, tasks, suggestions, autonomy
e. skill identification, skill variety, task identity, feedback, autonomy

5. The procedure used to determine the tasks, duties, and responsibilities of a job and the human attributes required to perform the job is known as:
a. job description
b. job analysis
c. job design
d. job re-engineering
e. none of the above

6. Job analysis is the cornerstone of HR activities. The information gathered is used for key HR activities such as:
a. recruitment and selection
b. human resources planning
c. compensation
d. performance and career management
e. all of the above

7. Jessica, who is the HR assistant at a manufacturing firm, was given the task of analyzing the firm's jobs. She was told to collect data on job activities, employee behaviours, and working conditions and to identify skills required to perform the jobs. This was part of a project to complete a job analysis project. Which step in the job analysis process corresponds to what Jessica is supposed to do?
a. analyze the jobs
b. review relevant background information
c. select representative positions and jobs to be analyzed
d. review job analysis with job incumbents
e. develop job description and job specification

8. Harry is the HR manager of Harris Inc. One of his key objectives is to reassess the company's compensation structures and salary grades. The most suitable job analysis technique Harry can use for this purpose is:
a. interview
b. salary survey
c. functional job analysis
d. position analysis questionnaire
e. none of the above

9. There are a number of techniques used to conduct job analysis. The following lists the common conventional job analysis techniques:
a. diary/log, observation, interview, questionnaire
b. interview, PAQ, job description, diary/log
c. interview, observation, functional analysis
d. PAQ, functional analysis, questionnaire
e. all of the above

10. A reference tool compiled by the federal government that contains comprehensive job descriptions is called the:
a. Federal Occupational Classification
b. National Occupational Analysis
c. job description bank
d. standard national occupations
e. National Occupational Classification

11. A list of duties, responsibilities, reporting relationships, and working conditions of a job, which is a product of a job analysis exercise, is called:
a. job specification
b. job description
c. job class
d. job design
e. process chart

12. A job description written for a VP of sales and marketing included the following areas: job identification, relationships, duties and responsibilities, performance standards, and working conditions. What other key areas need to be included to complete the description?
a. job specification, job title
b. department, prepared date
c. authority, job summary
d. job summary, job title
e. authority, job specification

13. The Brown-Dobson Company hired a consultant to launch a project to develop job descriptions for key positions in the organization. The consultant decided to prepare a document with guidelines to assist the line managers who will play a key role in writing the job descriptions. What are some of the guidelines included in the document?
a. be clear, be specific, use action words
b. conduct interviews, ask specific questions

c. write the job descriptions and share with employees
d. use action words, get employee commitment
e. all of the above

14. Over the past few years, the concept of a "job" has been changing quite rapidly due to changes in technology, globalization, deregulation, and many other reasons. This has forced organizations to be more responsive, flexible, and competitive in a global marketplace. What are some of the key techniques that have contributed to the "blurring" of the concept of a "job"?
a. reduced organizational hierarchy
b. emphasis on team and team process
c. re-engineering
d. creation of boundaryless organizations
e. all of the above

15. Due to rising competition, Hi-Tech Inc. had to take a number of measures to ensure its competitiveness. One of the measures it used reduced a number of management layers in the organization, which has contributed to faster decision making so that the firm is more responsive and nimble. What technique did the organization use to achieve its responsiveness?
a. introduced staff layoffs
b. workforce reduction
c. flattened the organization
d. downsized
e. job redesign

chapter 4

# Human Resources Planning and Recruitment

## Learning Objectives

1. Articulate the strategic role of human resources planning.
2. Describe the approaches used to forecast future human resources demand.
3. Describe the approaches used to forecast supply of human resources to meet labour demands.
4. Select the most appropriate approaches for responding to imbalances in supply and demand of human resources.
5. Trace the recruitment process and explain why each step is important.
6. Describe the process for recruiting within an organization.
7. Determine which recruitment methods should be used based on the human resources plan (HRP).
8. Plan your strategy for recruiting a diverse workforce.

## Test Yourself

1. What is the strategic value of the human resources planning process? Identify the techniques used to forecast human resources demand and supply.
2. Identify and describe the four steps in the recruitment process.
3. What are the advantages of using internal and external recruitment methods?
4. What should organizations do to make their websites effective in order to attract potential candidates for job vacancies?
5. Identify and discuss the four approaches for evaluating the effectiveness and efficiency of the recruitment process.

## 4.1 THE STRATEGIC ROLE OF HUMAN RESOURCES PLANNING

Through strategic planning, organizations set major objectives and develop comprehensive plans for achieving them. Determining whether people will be available to carry out these plans is a critical element of the strategic planning process. **Human resources planning (HRP)** is the process of analyzing and identifying the need for and availability of human resources to ensure that an organization will have the right number of employees, with the right skills, at the right times, and in the right jobs to meet its strategic objectives.[1] Imagine the complexity of the human resources planning process for Vancouver's 2010 Winter Olympics. The human resources staff hired 1200 paid employees and 25 000 volunteers representing 115 countries and 60 languages in order to achieve the vision and mandate of the event. To meet the HRP mandate, the HR staff hired approximately 100 employees per month.[2]

Key steps in the HRP process include forecasting demand for labour, analyzing labour supply, and planning and implementing HR programs to balance supply and demand, as illustrated in Figure 4.1. Alternative solutions to imbalances in supply and demand are shown in Figure 4.2. Effective HRP helps an organization achieve economies in hiring new workers; anticipate and avoid shortages and surpluses of human resources; control and/or reduce labour costs; establish employment equity goals and timetables that are realistic and attainable; and meet its short- and long-range strategic goals.

Corning, Inc. is a leader in the integration of HRP and strategic planning, where managing human capital has as much value to the company as managing financial or tangible assets. Human capital planning (HCP) is used to determine the effect of corporate strategy on HR services and to improve HR services to support the execution of the business strategy. In each annual planning cycle, HR and line managers identify the number and type of employees needed, identify and prioritize the talent gaps and determine the best approach for closing the gaps, and chart actions to ensure that the organization gets the highest and best use of the available talent. A comprehensive formula is used to ensure HR remains within the boundaries of appropriate total cost to deliver required services, such as HR expenditure as a percentage of the company's revenues. With HCP, HR retains its role as a key strategic decision-maker at the boardroom table.[3]

### *In-class Notes*

**The Strategic Role of Human Resources Planning**

- Review of future HR requirements to ensure the right number of employees with the right skills, at the right times, and in the right jobs are available to meet strategic objectives
- Key steps in HR planning are:
  1. forecasting demand for labour
  2. analyzing labour supply
  3. planning and implementing HR programs to balance supply and demand

______________________________

______________________________

______________________________

______________________________

______________________________

______________________________

______________________________

**human resources planning (HRP)** The process of analyzing and identifying the need for and availability of human resources to ensure that an organization will have the right number of employees, with the right skills, at the right times, and in the right jobs to meet its strategic objectives.

## *figure* 4.1 Human Resources Planning Model

### Step 1: Forecast Demand for Labour

**Considerations**
- Organizational strategic plans
- Organizational tactical plans
- Economic conditions
- Market and competitive trends
- Political and legislative factors
- Social and cultural factors
- Technological changes
- Demographic trends
- Globalization

**Techniques Utilized**
- Trend analysis
- Ratio analysis
- Scatter plot
- Regression analysis
- Computerized-based simulation forecasting
- Nominal group technique
- Delphi technique
- Managerial judgment
- Impact analysis
- Scenario analysis
- New-venture analysis

### Step 2: Analyze Supply of Labour

**Internal Analysis**
- Markov analysis
- Skills inventories
- Management inventories
- Replacement charts and development tracking
- Replacement summaries
- Succession planning
- Linear programming
- Movement analysis

**External Analysis**
- General economic conditions
- Labour market conditions (national and local)
- Occupational market conditions

### Step 3: Respond to Imbalances in Supply and Demand

**Labour Shortage**
- Overtime
- Hire temporary employees
- Subcontract work
- Recruitment
- Transfer
- Promotion
- Employee leasing

**Labour Surplus**
- Hiring freeze
- Attrition
- Buyouts
- Early and phased retirement offers
- Job sharing
- Part-time work
- Work sharing
- Reduced work week
- Internal transfers
- Loaning or flexforce
- Layoffs (reverse seniority or juniority)
- Supplemental unemployment benefits (SUBs)
- Termination
- Severance pay
- Outplacement assistance

### *figure* 4.2 Solutions to Imbalances in Supply and Demand

**Conditions and Possible Solutions**

**A. When labour demand exceeds labour supply**

- Scheduling overtime hours
- Hiring temporary workers
- Subcontracting
- External recruitment
- Internal promotions and transfers
- **Employee leasing** involves outsourcing job functions to companies specializing in a specific field, such as training or payroll.
- Performance management, training and retraining, and career development play a critical role.

**B. When labour supply exceeds labour demand**

- Hiring freeze: reassigning current workers to job openings
- Attrition: standard employee resignation, retirement, or death
- Incentives to leave the organization: buyouts or early retirement programs
- Job sharing
- Reducing positions to part-time
- Work sharing and reduced work week
- Finding employees alternative jobs within the organization
- Employee layoffs
- Termination of employment
- Loaning or flexforce is an alternative to layoffs where employees are loaned to other organizations in need of staff for special projects.
- Evaluating the effectiveness of layoffs and downsizing is critical, as is managing "survivor sickness."

**C. When labour demand equals labour supply**

- Vacancies are filled internally through transfers or promotions, or externally by hiring new employees.
- Performance management, training, and career development are critical in achieving balance.

Lack of or inadequate HRP within an organization can result in significant costs—both tangible and intangible. For example, vacant positions can lead to costly inefficiencies, including lengthy training for new hires and overtime for current employees, which can lead to lower productivity, fatigue, stress-related illnesses, and accidents, as well as the overtime cost itself. There are also costs associated with overstaffing, such as severance pay. Ineffective HRP can result in situations in which one department is laying off employees while another is hiring individuals with similar skills. This can have a devastating impact on morale and productivity; turnover, especially among high performers who are denied opportunities for lateral moves or promotions; difficulties in meeting employment equity goals; and the inability to accomplish short-term operational plans and/or long-range strategic plans.

## Environmental Scanning

Environmental scanning is the monitoring of major external factors to identify trends that might affect an organization. It is a critical component of HRP and strategic planning processes, since the most successful organizations are prepared for changes before they occur. Effective HRP involves following key environmental indicators, forecasting their impact, and devising strategies to deal with them. The environmental factors most frequently monitored include economic conditions, market and competitive trends, political and legislative issues, social issues (health care, childcare, and educational priorities), technological changes, and demographic trends.

One of the most significant environmental factors in HRP in Canada relates to dramatic changes in labour-force composition.[4] A labour shortage is expected to create serious challenges for Canadian employers.[5] The Conference Board of Canada forecasts an accelerated rate of retirement beginning in 2012, when 30 percent of baby boomers, who represent 6.6 million Canadian workers, will reach the age of 65.[6] Studies have found that by 2012, one employee will replace every four employees retiring from the workplace.[7] In the Canadian public sector, 30 percent of employees are forecast to retire by 2015, which will result in a major loss of leadership talent.[8] This trend has major implications for the HR activities of recruitment, selection, training, retention, succession planning, compensation, and benefits.

Once the HR implications of an organization's strategic plans have been analyzed, there are three subsequent processes involved in HRP, which will be discussed next. The processes are as follows:

1. Forecasting future human resources needs (demand)
2. Forecasting availability of internal and external candidates (supply)
3. Planning and implementing solutions to imbalances in supply and demand

In their HR planning, employers include close monitoring of such trends as the availability of entry-level labour.

## 4.2 FORECASTING FUTURE HUMAN RESOURCES DEMAND (STEP 1)

A key component of HRP is forecasting the number and type of people needed to meet organizational objectives. Managers should consider several factors when forecasting such requirements.[9] Beginning with a sales projection for the organization's product or service is paramount.[10] The staff required to maintain this volume of product or service is then estimated, along with several other factors, including:

1. *Quality and nature of employees* in relation to what management sees as the strategic needs of the organization.
2. *Decisions to upgrade* the quality of products or services *or enter into new markets,* which might change the required employee skill mix.
3. *Planned technological and administrative changes aimed at increasing productivity and reducing employee headcount*, such as the installation of new equipment or the introduction of a financial incentive plan.
4. The *financial resources* available to each department; for example, a budget increase may enable managers to pay higher wages and/or hire more people. Conversely, a budget crunch might result in wage freezes and/or layoffs.
5. *Organizational restructuring and job redesign* to accommodate new product lines or service delivery, which may either increase or decrease the demand for labour.

HR forecasting should project labour needs in three phases: (1) *short range* within six months to one year, (2) *intermediate range* within one to five years, and (3) *long range* beyond five years. A three-phase approach enables organizations to allocate resources to HRP in a more efficient manner based on whether the demand for labour is immediate or a long-term projection.

In large organizations, needs forecasting is primarily quantitative in nature and is the responsibility of highly trained specialists. *Quantitative techniques* for determining human resources requirements are mathematical and include trend analysis, ratio analysis, scatter plot analysis, regression analysis, and computer-based simulations. *Qualitative approaches* to forecasting are more subjective estimates and range from sophisticated analytical models to informal expert opinions about future needs.[11]

## Quantitative Approaches

**TREND ANALYSIS** **Trend analysis** involves studying the relationship between an organizational indicator such as sales and the number of employees required over the previous five years or so to identify employment trends that might continue into the future. Although sales level is most often used in the calculations, other indicators include the number of units produced, the number of clients served, and production hours. Even though trend analysis generates a simple forecast, it is one of the most commonly used HRP approaches for calculating labour needs across an entire organization, division, or a specific operational team. An example of a trend analysis is shown in Figure 4.3.

**RATIO ANALYSIS** Another approach, **ratio analysis,** involves making forecasts based on the ratio between (1) some causal factor (such as sales volume) and (2) the number of employees required (for instance, number of salespeople). For example, suppose a salesperson traditionally generates $500 000 in sales and that plans call for increasing the firm's sales by $3 million in the next year. In this case, if the ratio of sales revenue to salespeople remains the same, six new salespeople would be required (each of whom produces an extra $500 000 in sales).

Like trend analysis, ratio analysis assumes that productivity will remain about the same—for instance, that each salesperson cannot be motivated to produce much more than $500 000 in sales. If sales productivity were to increase or decrease, then the ratio of sales to salespeople would change. A forecast based on historical ratios would then no longer be accurate.

**SCATTER PLOT** A **scatter plot** is a graphic method used to determine whether two factors—a measure of business activity and staffing levels—are related. If they are and if the measure of business activity is forecast, HR requirements can also be estimated. An example based

*figure* 4.3 **Example of Trend Analysis of Demand for Staff**

| Year | Business Factor (Sales in Thousands) divided by . . . . | Labour Productivity (Sales/Employee) = | Human Resources Demand (number of employees required) |
|---|---|---|---|
| 2006 | $5433 | 15.22 | 357 |
| 2007 | $5666 | 15.33 | 370 |
| 2008 | $4800 | 14.30 | 335 |
| 2009 | $4630 | 14.22 | 326 |
| 2010 | $4010 | 14.10 | 284 |
| 2011* | $4200 | 14.18 | 296 |
| 2012* | $4500 | 14.18 | 317 |
| 2013* | $4610 | 14.18 | 325 |
| 2014* | $4810 | 14.18 | 340 |

*projected figures

**trend analysis** Study of a firm's past employment levels over a period of years to predict future needs.

**ratio analysis** A forecasting technique for determining future staff needs by using ratios between some causal factor (such as sales volume) and the number of employees needed.

**scatter plot** A graphical method used to help identify the relationship between two variables.

*figure* 4.4 **Determining the Relationship between Hospital Size and Number of Nurses**

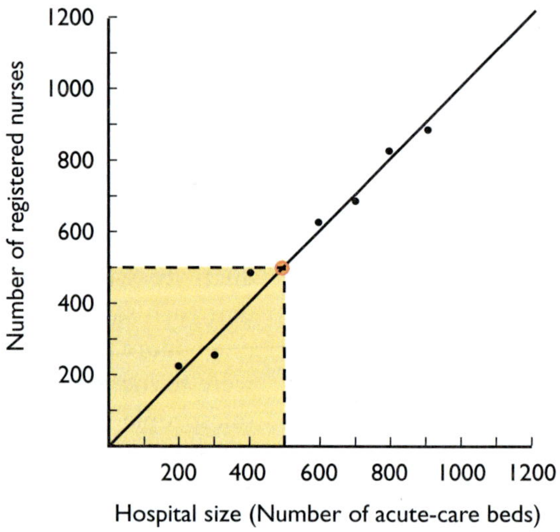


Note: After fitting the line, the number of employees needed, given projected volume, can be extrapolated (projected).

on the relationship between the number of registered nurses (RNs) and hospital size (based on number of acute-care beds) is depicted in the scatter plot shown in Figure 4.4. If the two factors are related, then the points representing data from a number of actual hospitals sampled will tend to fall along a straight line, as they do in this case. Carefully drawing a line that minimizes the distances between the line and each of the plotted points permits an estimate of the number of nurses required for hospitals of various sizes. For a new hospital with 500 acute-care beds, the estimated number of RNs needed is 500.

**REGRESSION ANALYSIS** **Regression analysis** is a more sophisticated statistical technique to determine the "best-fit" line. It involves the use of a mathematical formula to project future demands based on an established relationship between an organization's employment level and some measurable factor of output, such as revenue, sales, or production level.

**COMPUTER-BASED SIMULATION** **Computer-based simulation** is a sophisticated and complex series of mathematical formulas that use a number of key internal and external indicators to calculate future human resources needs. The computer program simulates and forecasts changes in demand for labour caused by workforce factors, competition, technological changes, social challenges, political changes, and economic factors. Large organizations that seek a high degree of precision in the HRP process commonly use computer-based simulations.

## Qualitative Approaches

In contrast to quantitative approaches, which utilize statistical formulas, qualitative techniques rely solely on expert judgments. Approaches used to gather such opinions in order to forecast demand for human resources include the nominal group technique, the Delphi technique, and scenario planning.

**NOMINAL GROUP TECHNIQUE** The **nominal group technique** involves a group of experts (such as first-line supervisors and managers) meeting face to face.[12] Each member of the group independently writes down his or her ideas on a problem or issue (in this case, the causes of demand). Going around the table, each member then presents one idea. This process continues until all ideas have been presented and recorded, typically on a flipchart or chalkboard. No discussion is permitted during this step. Clarification is then sought, as necessary, followed by group discussion and evaluation. Finally, each member is asked to rank the ideas. This is done independently and in silence.

Advantages of this technique include the involvement of key decision makers, a future focus, and the fact that the group discussion can facilitate the exchange of ideas and greater acceptance of results. Drawbacks include subjectivity and the potential for group pressure to lead to less accurate assessments than could be obtained through other means.

**THE DELPHI TECHNIQUE** While managers generally handle short-term forecasting, the **Delphi technique** is useful for long-range forecasting and other strategic planning issues. It typically involves outside experts as well as company employees, in order to increase objectivity.[13] A problem is identified (in this case, the causes of demand) and each group member is requested to submit a potential solution by completing a carefully designed questionnaire. Direct face-to-face contact is not permitted. After each member independently and anonymously has completed the initial questionnaire, the results are compiled at a centralized location. Each group member is then given a copy of the results. If there are differences in opinion, each individual uses the feedback from other experts to fine-tune his or her independent assessment. Review of the results and feedback are repeated and continue as often as necessary until a consensus is reached.

As with the nominal group technique, advantages include involvement of key decision makers and a future focus. The Delphi technique also permits the group to critically evaluate a wider range of views. Drawbacks include the fact that judgments may not efficiently use objective data, the time and costs involved, and the potential difficulty in integrating diverse opinions.

**SCENARIO PLANNING** This method invites managers to envision the trends that will affect their organizations in the future and to predict the products, services, and workforce composition that need to be in place. Scenarios are used for long-range planning by understanding trends that are at least 20 years in the future. Organizations start on the demand side by thinking about implications for future products and services, including what products will be successful and how to foster innovation. Organizations then assess the implications for the supply network needed to support and enhance these products and services. Lego, the Danish toymaker, experimented with scenario planning as part of its 2009 budget. It also developed contingency plans for each scenario to allow it to respond quickly to environmental changes. Senior managers meet monthly to pool knowledge of what is happening in the market and to make predictions about what is likely to happen in the next 12 months. One benefit of **scenario planning** is that it discourages companies from becoming too fixated on the present at the expense of the future.[14]

**regression analysis** A statistical technique involving the use of a mathematical formula to project future demands based on an established relationship between an organization's employment level (dependent variable) and some measurable factor of output (independent variable).

**computer-based simulation** A complex series of mathematical formulas that use a number of key internal and external indicators to calculate future human resources needs.

**nominal group technique** A decision-making technique that involves a group of experts meeting face to face. Steps include independent idea generation, clarification and open discussion, and private assessment.

**Delphi technique** A judgmental forecasting method used to arrive at a group decision, typically involving outside experts as well as organizational employees. Ideas are exchanged without face-to-face interaction, and feedback is provided and used to fine-tune independent judgments until a consensus is reached.

**scenario planning** A method that invites managers to envision the trends that will impact their organizations in the future and to predict the products, services, and workforce composition that need to be in place.

Industry Canada **http://strategis.ic.gc.ca**

## 4.3 FORECASTING FUTURE HUMAN RESOURCES SUPPLY (STEP 2)

Short-term and long-range HR demand forecasts provide only half of the staffing equation by answering the question, "How many employees will we need?" The next major concern is how the projected openings will be filled. There are two sources of supply:

1. *Internal*—present employees who can be transferred or promoted to meet anticipated needs
2. *External*—people in the labour market not currently working for the organization. Included are those who are employed elsewhere as well as those who are unemployed.

### Forecasting the Supply of Internal Candidates

Before estimating how many external candidates will need to be recruited and hired, management must determine how many candidates for projected openings will likely come from within a firm. Approaches for determining the supply of internal candidates include Markov analysis, skills/management inventories, replacement charts/summaries, movement analysis, and succession planning.

**MARKOV ANALYSIS** **Markov analysis** is a statistical technique that predicts the internal supply of candidates by determining the pattern of movement to and from jobs throughout an organization. The analysis uses transition matrices to show the number of people who remain in their jobs from year to year, and the number of people who are promoted, transferred, or leave an organization. Many organizations use the previous year's transition data for predicting the following year's movements. Markov analysis is a popular forecasting approach because it is easy to use and enables the organization to trace the specific number of replacements needed at any organizational level. With this information, organizations can plan more accurately for promoting and training internal employees, and calculate external recruitment needs if internal candidates are not available.

*In-class Notes*

**Forecasting Future Human Resources Demand**

- Quantitative approaches include:
  - trend analysis based on past employment levels
  - ratio analysis based on ratio of employees to a business activity indicator
  - scatter plot and regression analysis using graphs of employees and a business activity indicator
  - computer-based simulation using mathematical formulas to calculate future human resources needs
- Qualitative approaches include:
  - nominal group technique where experts meet and make predictions
  - Delphi technique where experts in separate locations make predictions and share them
  - managerial judgment
  - scenario planning

**SKILLS/MANAGEMENT INVENTORIES** **Skills inventories** contain comprehensive information about the capabilities of current employees. An example of a skills inventory and development record is shown in Figure 4.5. Prepared manually or using a computerized system, data gathered for each employee include educational background, previous work history, skills, abilities, interests, and career aspirations. Information about current performance and readiness for promotion is also generally included. Data pertaining to managerial

### *figure* 4.5 Skills Inventory Form Appropriate for Manual Storage and Retrieval

HUMAN RESOURCES SKILLS
INVENTORY AND DEVELOPMENT RECORD

Date: month, year

| Department | Area or sub-department | Branch or section | Location |
|---|---|---|---|
| | | | |

| Company service date (month, day, year) | Birthdate (month, day, year) | Job title |
|---|---|---|
| | | |

Education — Diploma or degree and major field of study

Grade school: 6 7 8 | High school: 9 10 11 12
College and/or University: 1 2 3 4 5

Courses (company sponsored)

| Type of course | Subject or course | Year | Type of course | Subject or course | Year |
|---|---|---|---|---|---|
| | | | | | |
| | | | | | |
| | | | | | |
| | | | | | |

Career and development interests

| Are you interested in an alternative type of work? Yes ☐ No ☐ | Would you accept transfer to another division? Yes ☐ No ☐ | Would you accept lateral moves for further development? Yes ☐ No ☐ |
|---|---|---|

If yes, specifically what type? | Comment on any qualifying circumstances

What type of training do you believe you require to:
A) Improve your skills and performance in your present position?
B) Improve your experience and abilities for advancement?

Last name

First name

Middle name

What other assignments do you believe you are qualified to perform now?

| Languages | Written | | Spoken | |
|---|---|---|---|---|
| | ☐ | ☐ | ☐ | ☐ |
| | ☐ | ☐ | ☐ | ☐ |

Societies and organizations — Memberships in community organizations, etc., within last five years. Indicate name of association and office held, if any.

Skills

| Type of skill | Certification, if any | Type of skill | Certification, if any |
|---|---|---|---|
| | | | |
| | | | |
| | | | |
| | | | |

Other significant work experience (omit repetitive experiences)

| | Location | From yr. | To yr. |
|---|---|---|---|
| | | | |
| | | | |
| | | | |

Comments: Other significant experience, recreational activities, hobbies, interests, or personal data

**Markov analysis** A statistical technique that predicts the internal supply of candidates by determining the pattern of movement to and from jobs throughout an organization.

**skills inventories** Manual or computerized records summarizing employees' education, experience, interests, skills, and so on, which are used to identify internal candidates eligible for transfer and/or promotion.

*figure* 4.6 **Management Replacement Chart**

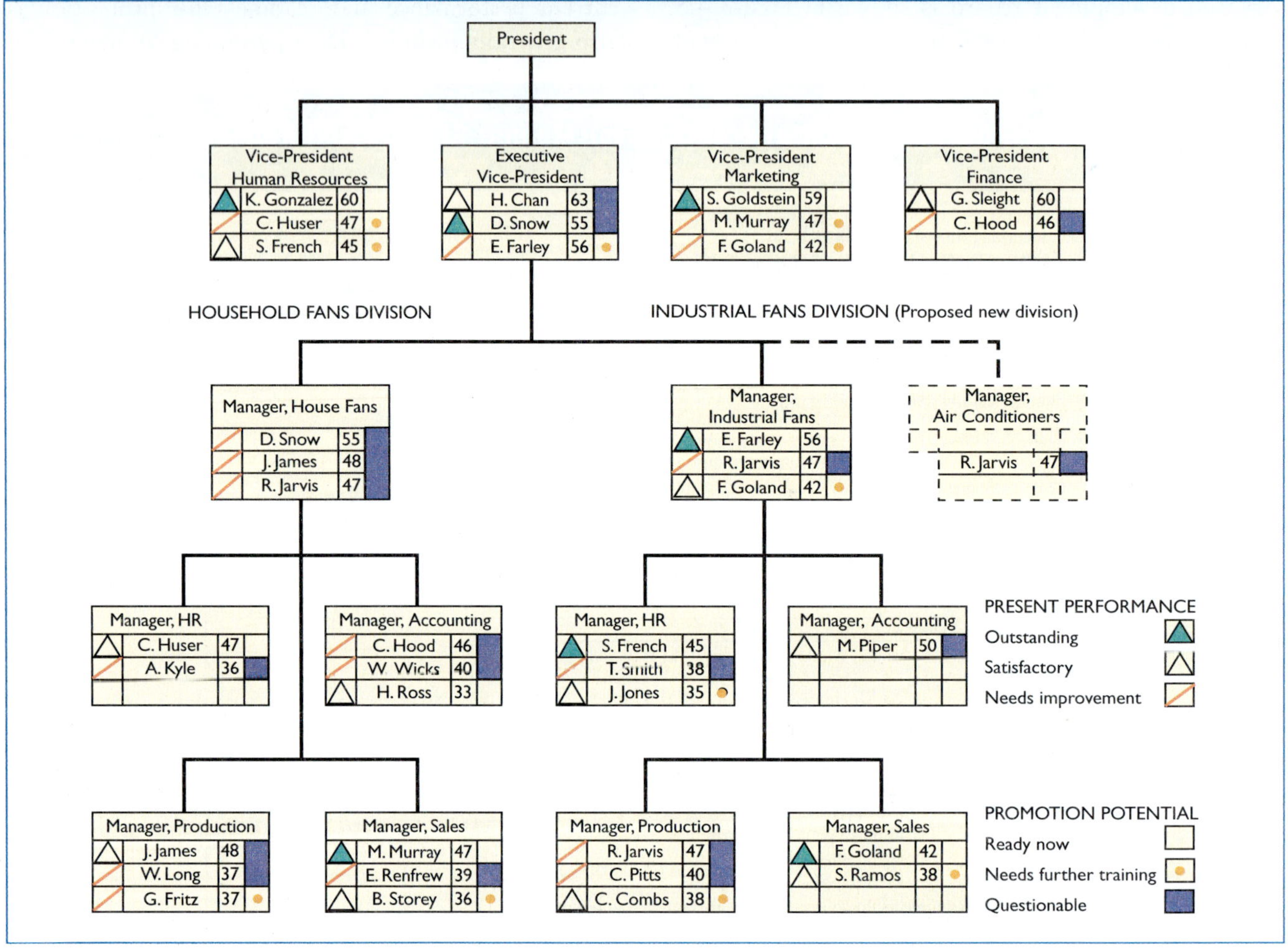


staff are compiled in **management inventories.** In addition to the information listed above, such inventories also include the number and types of employees supervised, duties of such employees, total budget managed, previous managerial duties and responsibilities, and managerial training received. Organizations search skills and management inventories when looking for staff with the skills required for a specific job. Inventories can also help an organization depict workforce strengths and weaknesses, plan training, and identify which job vacancies need to be filled from external sources because current employees lack the skills required. For this reason, skills and management inventories must be updated regularly.

### REPLACEMENT CHARTS/REPLACEMENT SUMMARIES

**Replacement charts** are a visual representation of who will replace whom in the event of a job opening and are typically used to keep track of potential internal candidates for a firm's most important positions. As can be seen in Figure 4.6, such charts, which are structured much like organizational charts, typically indicate age and replacement status of potential internal candidates. While age cannot be used as a criterion in making selection or promotion decisions, such information is necessary to project retirement dates, plan lateral moves, and so on. Replacement status consists of present performance (from performance appraisals) and future promotability, based on information provided by the employee about future career aspirations and assessments by the employee's immediate supervisors of likelihood of future success.

**Replacement summaries** are the preferred method of many firms, as replacement charts provide an excellent quick reference tool but contain very little information. Replacement summaries list likely replacements for each position and their relative strengths and weaknesses, as well as information about current position, performance, promotability, age, and experience. These additional data can be extremely helpful to decision makers, although caution must be taken to ensure that there is no discrimination on the basis of age, gender, and so on.

**MOVEMENT ANALYSIS** **Movement analysis** is a technique used to trace and analyze the ripple effect that promotions and job losses have on the movement of other employees in an organization. When one employee vacates a job, organizations calculate the total number of positions that become open. Movement analysis is conducted for a specific profession, department, or the entire organization depending on needs. Organizations that rely heavily on internal hiring are most likely to see a huge ripple effect as the number of movements is always equal to or greater than the number of vacant positions. When the ripple effect is challenging to manage, firms may choose to establish a hiring policy that includes a mix of promotion-from-within and external recruitment practices.

**SUCCESSION PLANNING** **Succession planning** is the process of identifying and coaching key individuals to assume executive positions. Succession planning requires balancing an organization's requirements for top managers with the potential and career aspirations of available internal candidates. Two types of succession planning initiatives exist: (1) long-term succession, which provides leadership development to prepare employees for future roles, and (2) short-term succession, which prepares key employees for emergency replacement if individuals unexpectedly quit, are terminated, or go on short- or long-term disability. The succession planning process often involves a series of fairly complicated and integrated steps. For example, potential successors for top positions might be routed through the top jobs in several key divisions, as well as overseas, and sent through a university-graduate level, advanced management program. Succession planning is a critical organizational mandate in today's economic climate. All sectors of the Canadian economy share a concern about an escalating leadership deficit resulting primarily from baby boomers leaving the workforce. Studies have found that 78 percent of organizations are having difficulty securing skilled leaders, with 50 percent predicting that the degree of difficulty will escalate.[15] Succession planning is a critical component of HRP as it enables organizations to maintain work continuity when employees unexpectedly leave, and provides motivation and an incentive for staff to stay.

## Forecasting the Supply of External Candidates

It is not possible to fill all future openings with current employees. External sources of supply must be considered when entry-level jobs need to be filled or when there are no qualified internal replacements. To project the supply of outside candidates, employers assess general economic conditions, national labour market conditions, local labour market conditions, and occupational market conditions.

**RPC 4-1 >**

**Maintains an inventory of HR talent for the use of the organization**

The first step is to forecast general economic conditions and the expected prevailing *rate of unemployment*. In the short run, the national unemployment rate serves as an approximate measure of how difficult it will be to acquire new employees. In general terms, the lower the rate of unemployment, the smaller the labour supply will be, and the more difficult it will be to recruit employees. It is important to note, though, that

**management inventories** Manual or computerized records summarizing the background, qualifications, interests, skills, etc., of management employees, as well as information about managerial responsibilities, duties in current and previous position(s), and management training, used to identify internal candidates eligible for transfer and/or promotion opportunities.

**replacement charts** Visual representations of who will replace whom in the event of a job opening. Likely internal candidates are listed, along with their age, present performance rating, and promotability status.

**replacement summaries** Lists of likely replacements for each position and their relative strengths and weaknesses, as well as information about current position, performance, promotability, age, and experience.

**movement analysis** A technique used to trace and analyze the ripple effect that promotions and job losses have on the movement of other employees in an organization.

**succession planning** The process of ensuring a suitable supply of successors for current and future senior or key jobs so that careers of individuals can be effectively planned and managed.

SkillSoft **www.skillsoft.com**

Statistics Canada **www.statcan.gc.ca**

Human Resources and Skills Development Canada **www.hrsdc.gc.ca/en/home.shtml**

(1) even when unemployment rates are high, some positions will still be difficult to fill, and (2) unemployment rates vary for different groups, as well as from province to province and from one city to another.

**RPC 4-2 >**

**Identifies potential sources of qualified candidates**

Second, demographic trends that have a significant impact on *national labour market* conditions must be considered. Fortunately for organizations, these trends are well measured and projected and there is a wealth of information available from government and private sources.[16] For example, Statistics Canada publishes annual, monthly, quarterly, and occasional reports on labour force conditions, including total labour force projections based on demographic, geographic, and occupation data.

Third, *local labour markets* are affected by many conditions, including community growth rates and attitudes (if growth is frowned upon or businesses receives little support, present employers and young workers may move elsewhere). Chambers of commerce and provincial/local development and planning agencies can be excellent sources of local labour market information.

**RPC 4-3 >**

**Identifies potential sources and the markets in which the organization competes for qualified candidates**

Finally, in addition to looking at the overall labour market, organizations generally want to forecast the availability of potential candidates in *specific occupations* for which they will be recruiting. In recent years, for example, there has been an undersupply of information technology (IT) specialists, physiotherapists, and physicians in many parts of the country. Forecasts for various occupations are available from a number of sources, including Human Resources and Skills Development Canada (HRSDC), which publishes short- and long-term labour force projections by occupation.[17]

## 4.4 RESPONDING TO IMBALANCE IN SUPPLY AND DEMAND (STEP 3)

Forecasting the supply and demand for human resources is not an exact science, as there are many internal and external factors that can skew forecasting calculations. Organizations might experience two possible scenarios:

1. Expected labour supply exceeds expected labour demand (*surplus*).

### *In-class Notes*

**Forecasting Future Human Resources Supply**

- Forecasting internal supply using:
  - Markov analysis
  - skills/management inventories
  - replacement charts/replacement summaries
  - movement analysis
  - succession planning
- Forecasting external supply by projecting:
  - future unemployment levels
  - national labour market trends
  - local labour market trends
  - supply in specific occupations

2. Expected labour demand exceeds expected labour supply (*shortage*).

## Labour Surplus

A labour surplus exists when the internal supply of employees exceeds an organization's demand. Most employers respond initially by instituting a **hiring freeze**, which means that openings are filled by reassigning current employees. The surplus is slowly reduced through **attrition**, which is the normal separation of employees due to resignation, retirement, or death. A major drawback of this approach is that the firm has no control over who stays and who leaves. Thus, valuable high performers may leave, while less-needed or lower-performing employees stay. Also, remaining employees may be overburdened with work, resulting in decreased or inferior performance, increased accident and incident rates, and stagnation due to the lack of new skills and ideas.

Some organizations attempt to accelerate attrition by offering incentives for employees to leave, such as **buyout and early retirement programs.** Staffing levels are reduced by offering attractive buyout "packages" or the opportunity to retire on full pension, with an attractive benefits package, at a relatively early age (often as young as 50 or 55). A drawback of this approach is that a great deal of money is required upfront, but the option appeals to employers because they can reduce payroll costs over time. For example, Chrysler Canada offered salaried employees in its assembly plant in Windsor a buyout package worth up to $75 000 cash and a voucher of up to $25 000 toward a new Chrysler vehicle. A quarter of its salaried employees—237 people—took the package. Layoffs would have followed if not enough of the 950 salaried employees in Canada took the buyout.[18] In an attempt to slash $300 million of operating expenses in 2003, Telus offered early retirement and voluntary departure packages to 11 000 of its 17 000 unionized employees. The packages were offered to Telus and Telus Mobility employees in British Columbia and Alberta to reduce its workforce by approximately 10 percent.[19] Care must be taken to ensure that early retirement is voluntary, since forced early retirement is a contravention of human rights legislation, the consequences of which can be extremely costly.

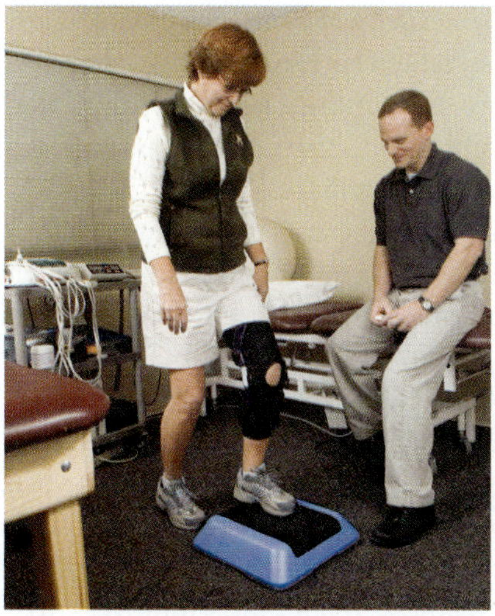

Physiotherapy is a skills-shortage occupation: The demand for physiotherapists exceeds the supply.

Another strategy used to deal with an employee surplus involves reducing the total number of work hours. Although the employees involved work fewer hours and thus have less pay, they are still employed and may enjoy having more free time at their disposal. The organization benefits by retaining good employees. **Job sharing** involves dividing the duties of a single position between two or more employees.[20] Reducing full-time positions to part-time work is sometimes more effective, especially if there are peak demand periods. A major challenge for HR is deciding whether employees who share a job should get full benefits or benefits that are scaled down to reflect the employees' hours.[21] A **reduced work week** is an arrangement whereby employees simply work fewer hours and receive less pay. The organization retains a skilled workforce, lessens the financial and emotional impact of a full layoff, and yet manages to reduce production costs. The only potential drawback is that it is sometimes difficult to predict in advance, with any degree of accuracy, how many hours of work should be scheduled each week.

**hiring freeze** A common initial response to an employee surplus. Openings are filled by reassigning current employees, and no outsiders are hired.

**attrition** The normal separation of employees from an organization due to resignation, retirement, or death.

**buyout and early retirement programs** Strategies used to accelerate attrition, which involve offering attractive buyout (early leave) packages or the opportunity to retire on full pension, with an attractive benefits package.

**job sharing** A strategy that involves dividing the duties of a single position between two or more employees.

**reduced work week** A layoff-avoidance strategy involving employees working fewer hours and receiving less pay.

Some highly resourceful organizations use **loaning or flexforce**, whereby staff are loaned to other organizations that are experiencing a labour shortage. Loaning is popular in seasonal companies, where there is a temporary slowdown in the need for services but management wants to retain the option of recalling employees when the busy season returns.

**Layoffs**, the temporary withdrawal of employment for economic or business reasons, are also used to correct employee surpluses. Layoffs may be short in duration, as when plants close for brief periods to adjust inventory levels or retool for a new product line, or they can last months or even years if caused by a major change in the business cycle. Transcontinental Inc., a Montreal-based publisher and printer, slashed 10 percent of its North American workforce as a result of clients clamping down on advertisements during the recession of 2008–09. Over 1500 layoffs and other cost-cutting measures were implemented to save the company $75 million annually. Half the cuts occurred in the organization's U.S. operations, 10 percent at printing plants in Mexico, and the remaining 40 percent were in Canada, with half of those in Quebec.[22] To ease the financial burden of layoffs, some organizations offer **supplemental unemployment benefits (SUBs)**, which increase income levels closer to what an employee would receive if on the job. SUB programs are generally negotiated through collective bargaining. Benefits are payable until the pool of funds set aside has been exhausted.

*frontLINE tips*

When employees are no longer required, the employment relationship may be severed. **Termination** is a broad term that encompasses permanent separation from an organization when positions that are no longer critical to its strategic direction are identified. Termination differs from firing, whereby an employee is discharged for substandard performance, violating policies or procedures, insubordination, or high absenteeism. **Severance pay** is a lump-sum payment that is given to employees who are being permanently terminated. In addition to pay, severance packages often include benefits continuation for a specified period of time. **Outplacement assistance** may be provided to lessen the impact of termination. Generally offered by an outside agency, such programs are designed to assist affected employees in finding employment elsewhere. Typical aids provided include job-search resources, skills training, and the use of office space and office services. Executives may be protected by a **golden parachute** clause in their contract of employment—a guarantee by the employer to pay specified compensation and benefits in the case of their termination due to downsizing or restructuring. The *Employment Standards Act* and the Canada Labour Code require employers to give notice to employees who are being terminated. The amount of notice and severance given to employees varies across federal and provincial jurisdictions.

**AN ETHICAL DILEMMA**

What are the employee and organizational consequences of scheduling long stretches of overtime hours as the initial response to a labour shortage?

While restructuring initiatives ranging from layoffs to mergers and acquisitions have been prevalent in Canadian firms in recent years, in many instances, the consequences have not been as positive as anticipated. Almost one in three mergers and acquisitions fails to achieve its business goals because of mishandled people issues and the inability to garner employee buy-in.[23]

In a study involving a sample of almost 500 Canadian organizations, employers who had resorted to workforce reductions reported significant expenditure cuts. They also reported a decline in the firm's reputation and financial performance, pressure on managers to focus on short-term profit or budget goals, present employee concern about job security, difficulty in retaining top performers, and increased stress among managers. Permanent workforce reductions were also found to be associated with significantly lower overall employee satisfaction rates; higher rates of grievances and absenteeism; more conflict within the organization; and somewhat lower productivity, product/service quality, and market share.[24]

A high cost associated with downsizing is **survivor sickness**, a range of emotions that can include feelings of betrayal or violation, guilt, and detachment. The remaining employees, anxious about the next round of terminations, often suffer stress symptoms, including depression, proneness to errors, and reduced performance. To avoid survivor sickness in downsizing situations, supervisors should provide abundant, honest communication; treat victims and survivors with dignity and respect; allow remaining employees to grieve and deal with repressed feelings and emotions; and use ceremonies, such as special meetings or small-group sessions, to provide people with a chance to acknowledge the changes and their reactions to these changes.[25]

## Labour Shortage

A labour shortage exists if the internal supply of human resources cannot

## *In-class Notes*

**Balancing Supply and Demand**

- Labour surplus managed by:
  - hiring freeze and attrition
  - early retirement programs
  - job sharing, reduced work week, and loaning/flexforce
  - layoffs and terminations
- Labour shortage managed by:
  - overtime
  - temporary employees and subcontracting
  - transfers
  - external hiring of permanent employees

fulfil an organization's needs. Scheduling overtime hours is often the initial response. Another short-term solution is to hire temporary employees. Employers may also subcontract work (if not prohibited by a collective agreement) on a temporary or permanent basis. As vacancies are created within a firm, opportunities are generally provided for employee transfers and promotions. Although this internal movement does not eliminate a shortage, resultant vacancies will be for entry-level jobs, which can be filled more easily externally.

A *transfer* involves lateral movement from one job to another that is relatively equal in pay, responsibility, and/or organizational level. Such a move can lead to the more effective use of human resources. It can broaden an employee's knowledge, skills, and perspectives in preparation for future promotional opportunities, result in additional technical or interpersonal challenges that lead to improved motivation and/or satisfaction, or offer some variety, which may also increase employee motivation and satisfaction. A *promotion* involves the movement of an employee from one job to another that is higher in pay, responsibility, and/or organizational level. Promotions should be based on an objective measure of performance.

The human resources planning (HRP) process enables firms to project a labour shortage and take steps to manage it, as discussed in the Strategic HR box on page 120. When the HR planning process identifies a labour shortage, the next step is internal and/or

**loaning or flexforce** A strategy that involves loaning staff to other organizations that are experiencing a labour shortage.

**layoff** The temporary withdrawal of employment for workers for economic or business reasons; another strategy used to correct an employee surplus.

**supplemental unemployment benefits (SUBs)** A top-up to employment insurance generally negotiated through collective bargaining, to bring income levels closer to what an employee would receive if they were on the job.

**termination** A broad term that encompasses permanent separation from an organization for any reason.

**severance pay** A lump-sum payment that is given to employees who are being permanently terminated.

**outplacement assistance** A program designed to assist terminated employees in finding employment elsewhere.

**golden parachute** A guarantee in an executive's employment contract to pay specified compensation and benefits in case of the executive's termination due to downsizing or restructuring.

**survivor sickness** A range of negative emotions experienced by employees remaining after a major restructuring initiative, which can include feelings of betrayal or violation, guilt, and detachment that result in stress symptoms such as depression, proneness to errors, and reduced productivity.

STRATEGIC HR

## Pumping Up People Supply to Build Heart Valves

**WORKFORCE PLANNING AT SORIN GROUP CANADA FOCUSES ON FINDING HIGHLY SPECIALIZED TALENT**

Building an aortic pericardial heart valve is no easy task. The intricate medical device—measuring mere millimetres—requires highly specialized skills in it productions and engineering. So for a Burnaby, B.C.-based company that manufactures this product, workforce planning is particularly challenging, thanks to a small talent pool.

Sorin Group Canada is the only Canadian company to make a tissue heart valve, through its Mitroflow division. Last year the company received approval from the Food and Drug Association (FDA) in the United States, which meant it had to fill 60 new positions in anticipation of increased production in 2009.

"The nature of our product requires us to kind of ramp up our hiring at certain points," says Judith Thompson, senior manager at Sorin Group. "We needed to know ahead of time, so to speak, what our sales forecasts are going to be. So it does take some planning and some crunching at times."

The 300-employee company has three main employee areas of focus: engineers, for custom-engineered machinery and equipment; quality assurance, to ensure regulations are followed; and production technicians.

"But these aren't folks punching out pieces from equipment, they are production technicians that hand-suture a heart valve, which is quite small, so there's a certain skill set we need to test for," says Thompson. "We have 85 who do hand-sewing and 25 who do hand-suturing."

At one time, Sorin could see 250 responses to job ads but with low unemployment in B.C., fewer candidates fit the bill.

"Canada isn't well-known for its biomedical engineers so even when we hire now, to ask for medical device experience, we wouldn't get it," says Thompson. "So we hire an engineer or scientist and train on the rest of it."

The company has also come to realize the benefits, and necessity, of new immigrants as a major source of talent.

"Our culture here is very diverse. About 90 percent of staff speak English as a second language, from production people to vice-presidents, so we don't look for Canadian-born, Canadian-educated, Canadian experience because in these economic times that would set us back," she says. "I would never have filled 60 positions last year with that criteria."

Training is extensive as it takes three to four months before workers, wearing gowns and gloves in a super-clean environment, can make a product that is usable. And even then they can only make a certain number of valves or components per week—it takes another six months to ramp up to regular production, says Thompson.

Sorin supports its employees with in-house English-language training, through a partnership with Immigration Services. And it provides subsides to foreign-trained engineers who want to pursue an engineering degree in B.C.

"We just can't speak enough about the program and the return on investment we've gotten," says Thompson. "We're getting better feedback on problems on the floor because the employees are more comfortable speaking to the researchers and scientists and surgeons who come in on tours. The confidence level of the group has gone up and they are very devoted to the company and the product they make."

Workforce planning is done largely on a year-by-year basis, she says, depending on the production levels at the manufacturing plant (which has about 250 employees, while the Toronto sales office has about 50). The 25-year-old company has a young workforce—the average age is 40—and has not yet had an employee retire. Twenty years ago there were only nine staff and when Thompson came on 10 years ago, only 45.

"Being a young company and privately owned at that time, young engineers and scientists came on board, and new graduates," she says.

For planning purposes, HR meets with the vice-president, director of operations and director for quality assurance on a weekly basis. They bring information on their different groups and projects, and assess what skill sets are needed in developing or bringing someone onboard. Sometimes that can mean bringing someone under another person's direction, or splitting people up, "to be as efficient as we can," she says.

More recently, Sorin has focused on the areas of succession planning and talent management. Last year it slotted high potentials for their next roles, assessing what would be required, and this year the development programs will kick off.

"We would prefer not to go outside the company for those skill sets, we prefer to keep them in-house and build that here. So we've put a lot into certain individuals who have shown an interest in certain areas, to support them in that."

The planning should only increase in importance as demand grows for the Mitroflow product, with aging baby boomers and surgeons leaning away from mechanical valves to tissue valves, she says.

Source: S. Dobson, "Pumping up people supply to build heart valves: Workforce Planning at Sorin Group Canada focuses on finding highly specialized talent," *Canadian HR Reporter*, February 23, 2009, p. 16. Reprinted with permission.

*figure* 4.7 **An Overview of the Recruitment Process**

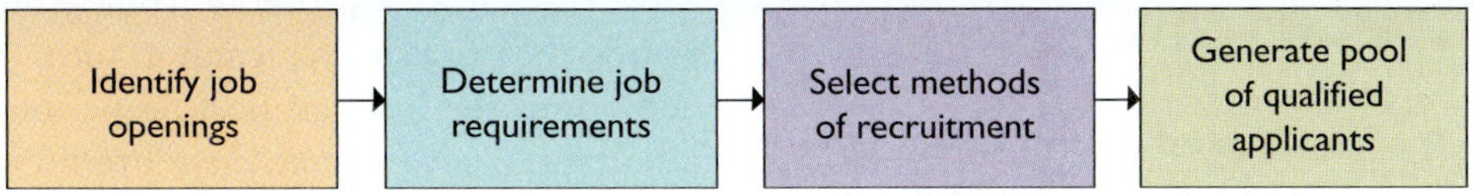


external recruitment. In particular, the HRP process is often considered a necessary first step before large-scale recruiting efforts can begin, particularly with respect to planned company expansion or growth.

## 4.5 THE RECRUITMENT PROCESS

**Recruitment** is the process of searching for and attracting an adequate number of qualified candidates, from among whom the organization may select the most appropriate to meet its staff requirements. In large organizations, in which recruiting is done on an almost continuous basis, the HR team typically includes specialists, known as recruiters, whose job it is to find and attract qualified applicants. The process begins when the need to fill a position is identified and ends with the receipt of résumés and/or completed application forms.

Recruitment is a critical HR function. Its purposes are to ensure that the required number of applicants with the required skills is generated at minimum possible cost; to eliminate poorly qualified candidates, thus improving the success rate of the selection process; to find and attract individuals who are also suited to the organization's unique culture and climate; and to help the firm meet its employment equity goals by attracting a diverse applicant pool.[26]

As illustrated in Figure 4.7, there are a number of steps in the recruitment process:

1. ***Identify job openings.*** HR plans provide valuable information to recruiters by indicating how many candidates will be required for various positions, when they will be needed, and whether positions should be filled internally or externally.
2. ***Determine job requirements and job specifications.*** This involves reviewing the job description and job specification to determine the knowledge, skills, abilities, and general characteristics necessary to perform the job according to standard. Manager

### *In-class Notes*

**The Recruitment Process**

- Recruitment process has four steps:
  1. identify job openings
  2. determine specific job requirements and job specifications
  3. select methods of recruitment
  4. generate pool of qualified recruits

**recruitment** The process of searching for and attracting an adequate number of qualified candidates, from among whom the organization may select the most appropriate to meet its staff requirements.

comments may also prove helpful in identifying requirements, particularly pertaining to personality and fit. A hiring criteria list is generated that includes the essential and desirable requirements that recruiters will search for on applicants' résumés.

3. ***Select methods of recruitment.*** Filling vacant job openings can be achieved by recruiting within or outside an organization. There is no single best recruiting technique, and the most appropriate for any given position depends on a number of factors, which will be discussed next.
4. ***Generate a pool of qualified applicants.*** External environmental conditions, such as changes in the labour market, unemployment rate, economy and legislation, and the recruiting activities of labour-market competitors, affect a recruiter's ability to generate a pool of qualified applicants. To ensure that the assumptions on which the HR plan was based are valid at the time of recruitment, recruiters check leading economic indicators such as Statistics Canada. If these indices signal a sudden downturn or upturn in the economy, recruiting plans may have to be modified. Yet studies have found that only 18 percent of recruiters have strategies in place to handle the imminent labour shortage in Canada that will compel organizations to compete for talent.[27]

**RPC 4-4 >**

**Implements deployment procedures ensuring that necessary compensation and benefit changes and education plans are addressed**

## 4.6 RECRUITING WITHIN AN ORGANIZATION

Most firms have a promote-from-within policy, which means that a recruiter cannot start recruiting externally until the internal posting period is over, even if he or she is aware that there are no suitable internal candidates.

Filling open positions with inside candidates has major advantages:

1. The firm is likely to have a more accurate assessment of a person's skills and performance level than with an outside candidate.
2. Employees see that competence is rewarded, thus enhancing commitment, morale, performance, and the likelihood that employees will stay with the organization.
3. Internal recruitment lowers overall recruitment costs.
4. Inside candidates require less orientation than do outsiders.
5. Managers are provided with a longer-term perspective when making business decisions.
6. Since internal candidates are familiar with the organization and its culture, they are more likely to achieve job mandates faster than external candidates.

Promotion from within also has major drawbacks:

1. Employees who apply for jobs and do not get them may become discontented and are more likely to leave the organization.

### *In-class Notes*

**Recruiting within an Organization**

- Review human resources records/files for qualified employees
- Post available positions on traditional or online bulletin boards
- Skills inventories, replacement charts, and succession plans often used to supplement job posting

## *figure* 4.8 Advantages and Disadvantages of Job Posting

**Advantages**

- Provides every qualified employee with a chance for a transfer or promotion
- Reduces the likelihood of special deals and favouritism
- Demonstrates an organization's commitment to career growth and development
- Communicates to employees the organization's policies and guidelines regarding promotions and transfers
- Provides equal opportunity to all qualified employees

**Disadvantages**

- Unsuccessful job candidates may become demotivated, demoralized, discontented, and unhappy if feedback is not communicated in a timely and sensitive manner
- Tensions may rise if it appears that a qualified internal candidate was passed over for an equally qualified or less qualified external candidate
- The decision about which candidate to select may be more difficult if there are two or more equally qualified candidates

2. Time may be wasted if managers are required to post all job openings and interview all inside candidates even when they already know who they wish to hire.
3. Employees may be less satisfied and accepting of a boss appointed from within their own ranks than they would a newcomer.
4. It is sometimes difficult for a newly chosen leader to adjust to no longer being "one of the gang."[28]
5. There is a possibility of "inbreeding," meaning a tendency to make decisions "by the book" and to maintain the status quo when a new and innovative direction may be needed.
6. Competition among internal candidates can strain cooperation and team dynamics.

Promotion from within requires using job posting, human resources records, and skills inventories. **Job posting** is a process of notifying current employees about vacant positions. This may involve placing a form outlining the title, duties (as listed in the job description), qualifications (taken from the job specification), hours of work, pay range, posting date, and closing date on designated bulletin boards throughout the firm, in employee publications, special-announcement handouts, or posting jobs on the company's intranet. For example, DuPont Canada has computerized job-posting systems, such that information about vacancies can be found on the company's intranet or is accessible 24 hours a day by calling a specific telephone number. As illustrated in Figure 4.8, there are advantages and disadvantages to using job postings to facilitate the transfer and promotion of qualified internal candidates.

Human resources records are often consulted so that qualified individuals can be notified, in person, of vacant positions. An examination of employee files may uncover employees who are working in jobs below their education or skill levels, people who already have the requisite KSAs for another job, or persons with the potential to move into the vacant position if given some additional training.

Skills inventories, replacement charts and summaries, and succession plans are even better reference tools. While such tools may be used instead of job postings, they are more often used as a supplement. Referring to these documents and plans helps ensure that qualified internal candidates are identified and considered for transfer or promotion when opportunities arise.

**AN ETHICAL DILEMMA**

Is it ethical to write job postings with specific internal candidates in mind to increase the probability that they will apply for the position?

**job posting** The process of notifying current employees about vacant positions.

Information and Communications Technology Council (ICTC) **www.ictc-ctic.ca**

Canada Labour Market Information **www.labourmarketinformation.ca**

## 4.7 RECRUITING OUTSIDE AN ORGANIZATION

Not all recruiting can be done internally. First of all, external candidates fill most entry-level positions. Hiring someone from outside may be preferable in order to acquire the latest knowledge and expertise or gain new ideas and revitalize a department or organization.[29] In addition, external recruiting is required when middle- and upper-level jobs are vacated unexpectedly, with no internal replacements yet qualified or ready for transfer or promotion; or when the jobs require such specialized training and experience that there are no potential internal replacements.

Application forms are commonly used in external recruiting. It is important to remember that these forms cannot ask questions that would *directly* or *indirectly* classify candidates on the basis of any of the prohibited grounds under human rights legislation (e.g., race, religion, disability, and so on). Employers with operations in a number of provinces have to ensure that their application forms comply with the human rights code provisions in each one. Specific guidelines regarding questions that can and cannot be asked on application forms are available through the human rights commissions in each jurisdiction. Appendix 4.1, a sample application form developed by the Ontario Human Rights Commission, illustrates the types of information that can legally be requested. As indicated therein, employers have the right to elicit detailed information about educational qualifications, employment history, and job-related skills—all of the data required to compare the qualifications of each candidate with the job specifications.

The advantages of external recruitment include the generation of a larger pool of qualified candidates; the availability of a more diverse applicant pool to assist in meeting employment equity goals and timetables; the acquisition of skills or knowledge not currently available within an organization and/or new ideas and creative problem-solving techniques; the elimination of rivalry and competition caused by employees jockeying for transfers and promotions; and the potential cost savings resulting from hiring individuals who already have required skills, rather than providing extensive training.

When choosing external recruitment method(s), there are two other factors that should be taken into consideration. First, the type of job to be filled has a major impact on the recruitment method selected. Recruiters normally rely on professional search firms for recruiting executive-level employees. In contrast, local newspaper advertising can be used to hire general

### *In-class Notes*

**Recruiting Outside an Organization**

- Online recruiting has experienced explosive growth
- Traditional print advertising must spark attention, interest, desire, action
- Private employment agencies find candidates for client firms.
- Executive search firms specialize in executive positions
- Educational institutions provide candidates for entry-level jobs
- Non-permanent staff are sourced through temporary help agencies, contract workers, employee leasing, and outsourcing/subcontracting

labour. Online recruitment is effective for jobs ranging from IT and engineering professionals to writers, teachers, nurses, managers, and sales people.[30]

Second, the budget for recruitment is a driving force in determining what external recruitment methods will be used to canvass job applicants. The costs of telephone calls, travel, advertising, and so on must be taken into consideration. Some positions can be filled at a low cost; others will require extensive advertising and considerable time and travel, especially if international recruitment is conducted. Careful HRP and forethought by recruiters can minimize expenses. For example, recruiting for several job openings simultaneously can reduce the cost per recruit. However, reliance on inexpensive techniques, such as word-of-mouth hiring, can result in systemic discrimination.

## Online Recruiting

The majority of companies now recruit online. Online recruiting can involve accessing one or more Internet job boards; using an application service provider's recruitment software; using the firm's intranet for internal job postings and generating employee referrals; and using a corporate website for external recruiting. Most recently, social networks and blogging tools are used to actively seek and connect with prospective employees. Several of these sites have gained prominence, including Yahoo! Groups, Friendster, YouTube, MySpace, Facebook, Second Life, LinkedIn, and Select Minds. Organizations use social networking tools for **relationship marketing**, which is the process of attracting and sustaining relationships with a wide range of people who the organization is interested in pursuing as possible employees. Online job descriptions are interactive and reflect the employment brand of an organization.[31] Electronic Arts, an international company based in Vancouver that develops and publishes interactive software for computer-based games such as PlayStation, replaced print-based job ads with social networks and blogs to foster relationships with potential candidates.[32] Vancouver-based lululemon athletica, which sells activewear, followed suit, using blogs to communicate hiring needs and information about the organization, such as its culture and benefits, and to provide updates on organizational changes. Social networks and blogs are also advantageous for job seekers, who can post their profiles and include career goals for recruiters to review. The use of social networking as a recruitment tool is featured in Figure 4.9.

**RPC 4-5 >**

**Evaluates recruiting effectiveness**

Building on the popularity of social networks, some organizations post guided virtual tours of their workplace along with online job advertisements. Virtual tours showcase the company's culture and career opportunities and help job seekers determine if the employer is a good fit with their career ambitions. Given the surge in international recruitment, video can clarify what it is like to work in an organization before travel costs are incurred to bring candidates for face-to-face interviews. The B.C. retail chain Dollar Giant uses virtual tours to convey its culture and the magnetic personality of its president, Joe Calvano. The online feature is more effective than print ads in communicating the enthusiasm Calvano brings to his industry and workers.[33]

Using a company's website for recruiting has other advantages. Studies have found that 62 percent of recruiters favour social networking tools over traditional methods such as print advertisements.[34] It tends to reduce cycle times, particularly if prescreening is done online, and is much less costly than print-based advertising. It has been estimated online recruitment can reduce time-to-hire by weeks and save companies at least 30 percent on cost-per-hire. By targeting star candidates and acting immediately, firms can gain competitive advantage.[35] Recruitment via company websites reduces the use of recruitment agencies by up to

**relationship marketing** Attracting and sustaining relationships with a wide range of people who an organization is interested in pursuing as possible employees.

Job Fair **www.lauriercc.ca/career/employers/cf-jf.htm**

Canadian Association of Career Educators & Employers **www.cacee.com**

Yahoo HotJobs **http://hotjobs.yahoo.com**

Service Canada Job Bank **www.jobbank.gc.ca**

Careers in the Federal Public Service **http://jobs-emplois.gc.ca/index-eng.htm**

Canadajobs.com **www.canadajobs.com**

Workopolis.com **www.workopolis.com**

Service Canada Job Bank **www.jobsetc.ca**

Recruiting news site with analysis, polls, and stats **www.ere.net**

Recruiting.com **www.recruiting.com**

Service Canada's Human Resources Management for Employers **www.hrmanagement.ca**

Canjobs.com **www.canjobs.com**

Monster Canada **www.monster.ca**

## *figure* 4.9 Recruiting in the Age of Social Networking

Sites like Facebook, Second Life can be high-impact, low-cost way to find talent

In a bright, spacious room, the benches are neatly lined up in rows. A giant screen at the front is ready to play a PowerPoint presentation. Young people—some with spiky hairdos or unconventional outfits—take a seat. In walks a police officer who begins his pitch to join the Vancouver Police Department (VPD).

The only thing real here is the message. The police officer and potential recruits are avatars, computer-generated digital characters interacting in a virtual community known as Second Life.

More than seven million avatars—real-life players logging on from around the globe—inhabit this world, opening up a new, and very large, audience to recruiters.

"When I first heard about this, I thought it was kind of whacked," says Const. Howard Chow of the VPD recruiting unit. "But it's given us major exposure."

Many organizations are turning to social networking sites, such as Second Life, Facebook, MySpace and LinkedIn, to find young, tech-savvy, leading-edge hires.

Some, such as VPD, set up virtual recruitment booths or seminars. Others create company sites where they can post jobs and sell their organization's assets to millions of people with a click of the mouse.

Ernst & Young started a "sponsored wall" a few years ago on Facebook. There are now 13 000 members—some are employees, others graduates interested in a job. The wall provides both information and interaction. It boasts of Ernst & Young's success and achievements, what the organization has to offer and how to apply.

The site also lets surfers interact with employees, either by posting questions and comments on the wall or in discussion boards.

Daniela Carcasole, Ernst & Young's national director of campus recruiting in Toronto, says Facebook has given the firm a brand and credibility in a sea of opportunities for young graduates. The company is not only hearing from recruiters, it's also hearing from employees.

"Testimonials are big for Generation Y. To hear someone else, close to their age group, say 'I've gone through this experience' is really credible," she says.

Carcasole says a major reason for using a social networking site is to tap into a demographic that favours technology over conventional practices.

"We could have just said, 'Forget it, we want them to conform to us' or we could say 'This is a new generation, they are taking over the marketplace and we need to start speaking their language,'" she says.

Unlike users of traditional job sites such as Workopolis or Monster, the people surfing social networking sites aren't necessarily looking for jobs. Sometimes this works in the employer's favour, says Brandy Douglas, an HR administrator at Labtronics, a technology firm in Guelph, Ont.

"Actively looking candidates are not always the ones you want to attract," she says. "The best candidates are those who don't know they are looking. Having our ad up and our name there on the site—where they don't expect to see it—can draw those candidates in."

Social networking sites expose companies to people beyond the typical borders, says Douglas. Facebook, for example, claims to have 69 million users worldwide.

"There are many options for fresh-thinking, skilled employees. It's our job to come up with a way to brand ourselves and differentiate ourselves from other employers," she says.

Sometimes, however, there are unintended consequences of this platform, for both parties, says Douglas. Potential recruits have requested to be her "friend" which potentially allows them to view her personal information or, at times, have given her "more information than I need as a recruiter."

The casual nature of social networking sites is a reason for caution, says Lynne Perry-Reid, a graduate recruitment specialist with Corporate Connections in Calgary. She says the "barrier of professionalism" is often dropped online.

"When you meet face-to-face, you're dressed nicely and you have your manners. That doesn't happen in a casual place like Facebook," she says. "You don't get people who check their spelling when they send you a message."

The other pitfall of these sites is also a great asset: Access to millions of potential employees, says Perry-Reid. What if thousands of them flood your inbox? And what if, after weeding through the résumés, only a few are even worth calling for an interview?

"It could be more work for the recruiter," she says. "You automatically question the candidates' credibility when they have spelling mistakes in their messages, when they want to add you as a friend or all these kinds of things that seem a little bit weird—that would not happen if you met face-to-face."

There's also the possibility an applicant who was turned down might take revenge online. At Ernst & Young, Carcasole says though people occasionally post disparaging remarks on her site, she doesn't censor them.

"We want to be credible," she says. "We respond openly and honestly."

Considering many of these sites are free or cost less than $20 a month, many of these organizations say it's not worth it not to be out there.

It's about getting your company's name out there first, to a generation of people who are less likely to be seeing your name in the newspaper, on television or walking down the street, says Perry-Reid.

"Generation Y is attached at the hip to technology—all the time," she says. "You can't change that force. This is interactive and it creates a presence."

Const. Chow says he has no way of knowing how many police recruits have arrived through the virtual world. None of the other firms has found a way to keep track either.

But it doesn't matter how VPD attracts potential hires, he says. Ultimately, they "still have to come in and face the same questions and go through the same procedures as the 21-year-old guy who's wanted to be a police officer his whole life."

Hopefully, there will just be more of them to choose from, he says.

Source: D. Harder, "Recruiting in the age of social networking: Sites like Facebook, Second Life can be high-impact, low-cost way to find talent," *Canadian HR Reporter,* April 28, 2008, p. 13. Reprinted with permission.

80 percent and is popular with many organizations, regardless of size.[36]

Another advantage of using a website for recruitment purposes is that company recruiters at one location can mine the candidate database and share résumés and candidate profiles with hiring managers and/or recruiters at other sites. Most software enables recruiters to track individual candidates through the recruitment and selection processes and permits candidates to keep their profiles up to date. Using prescreening strategies is essential, however. As the HR department staff members at Bombardier have discovered, the volume of résumés definitely does not diminish when the firm accepts them online. At Hewlett Packard, more than a million online applications are received each year.[37] One way of coping with volume is to generate automatic replies acknowledging receipt of applications. These replies are an excellent public relations tool and can help avoid numerous follow-up emails and/or telephone calls.[38]

In order for company websites to be effective, they must be user-friendly.[39] According to iLogos, a research company that monitors trends in online recruiting, best practices to attract a large applicant pool include: a link to career sections from the homepage, a recruiting section for recent college and university graduates, information about company benefits and culture, complete and updated job descriptions, job search by job category, choice of cut-and-paste form or résumé builder, application automatically attached to a job, reuse of candidate information for multiple jobs, and online user feedback.[40]

A website can become even more powerful if used in combination with commercial job boards.[41] There are more than 150 job boards in Canada: Some are general in nature, others are student-oriented, and still others specialize in particular types of postings ranging from acting to health care and physical therapy. The top five job boards based on the number of unique visits from Canadian surfers are Monster, Workopolis, HotJobs, JobBoom, and CareerClick.[42]

The Internet provides recruiters with a large audience for job postings and a vast talent pool.[43] A presence on the web is necessary if firms want the best talent working for them. Online recruitment does not replace the need for interviews, testing, and thorough reference checking, however.

**RPC 4-6 >**

**Implements and monitors processes for attracting qualified candidates**

## Traditional Recruitment Methods

**PRINT ADVERTISING** With the advent of online recruitment, print advertising is less common as a recruiting method. For advertising to bring the desired results, two issues must be addressed: the medium to be used and the construction of the ad.[44] The selection of the best medium—whether it is the local newspaper, a national newspaper, or a technical journal—depends on the types of positions for which the organization is recruiting. Reaching individuals who are already employed and not actively seeking alternative employment requires a different medium from the one appropriate to attract those who are unemployed.

To achieve optimum results from an advertisement, the following four-point guide, called *AIDA*, should be kept in mind as the ad is being constructed. These guidelines are also beneficial for constructing online advertisements.

1. *The ad should attract attention.* The ads that stand out have borders, a company logo or picture, and effective use of empty white space. To attract attention, key positions should be advertised in display ads, not lost in the columns of classified ads.
2. *The ad should develop interest in the job.* Interest can be created by the nature of the job itself, by pointing out the range of duties and/or the amount of challenge or responsibility involved. Sometimes, other aspects of the job, such as its location or working conditions, are useful in attracting interest. To ensure that the individuals attracted are qualified, the job specifications should always be included.
3. *The ad should create a desire for the job.* This may be done by capitalizing on the interesting aspects of the job itself and by pointing out any unique benefits or opportunities associated with it, such as the opportunity for career development or travel. The target audience should be kept in mind as the ad is being created.
4. *The ad should instigate action.* To prompt action, ads often include a closing date and a statement, such as "Email your résumé today," "Check out our website for more information," or "Go to the site of our next job fair."

If properly constructed, advertisements can be an effective instrument for recruiting and for communicating an organization's corporate image to the general public. A newspaper ad incorporating the AIDA guidelines is shown in Figure 4.10.

**PRIVATE EMPLOYMENT AGENCIES** Private employment agencies are often called upon to provide assistance to employers seeking intermediate- to senior-level clerical staff and professional, technical, or managerial employees. The staffing services business in Canada has grown into a $4-billion industry that places hundreds of thousands of job seekers in full-time, temporary, and contract-work assignments.[45] Such agencies take an employer's request for recruits and then solicit job seekers, relying primarily on advertising and walk-ins/write-ins. They serve two basic functions: expanding the applicant pool and performing preliminary interviewing and reference checking. It should be noted, though, that the amount of service provided varies widely, as do the level of professionalism and the calibre of staff. Generally, it is the employer who pays the agency fee, often equal to 15 to 30 percent of the first year's salary of the individual hired through agency referral.

An agency is likely to be used when the organization does not have an HR department, the firm has experienced difficulty in generating a pool of qualified candidates in the past, an opening must be filled quickly, or there is a desire to recruit a greater number of designated group members than the firm has been able to attract on its own.

There are many advantages to using a professionally operated private employment agency. The agency can save the organization a great deal of time by finding, interviewing, and selecting qualified candidates for referral to the hiring manager; cut down on the number of people for the employer to interview; and help ensure that only candidates matching the job specifications are interviewed. To ensure that the agency–employer relationship is positive and to avoid any legal compliance problems, references provided by the agency should be contacted to confirm suitability and professionalism. In addition, it is recommended that organizations give agencies an accurate and complete job description, specify the tools for screening applicants on a firm's behalf, periodically review data on accepted and rejected candidates, and develop a long-term relationship with one or two agencies.

**EXECUTIVE SEARCH FIRMS** Employers retain executive search firms to seek out middle- to senior-level professional, technical, and managerial employees. While the percentage of an organization's positions filled by such firms is generally small, they typically include the most critical jobs. For executive positions, using a search firm may be an organization's only recruitment method.

Executive search firms can be very useful. They often specialize in a particular type of talent, such as executives or technical employees. They typically know and understand

**AN ETHICAL DILEMMA**

Is it ethical for executive search firms to contact executives who are currently employed to canvass their interest in job openings in other companies?

## *figure* 4.10 Recruitment Advertisement Illustrating AIDA Principles

Source: Reprinted with permission of Horizon Utilities.

the marketplace, have many contacts, and are especially adept at contacting qualified candidates who are employed and not actively looking to change jobs (which is why they have been given the nickname "headhunters").

Executive search firms can keep their client organization's name confidential until late in the search process and save considerable top-management time by looking after advertising, prescreening what could turn out to be hundreds of applicants, and doing careful reference checking. Search firms' fees range from 25 to 50 percent of the annual salary for the position, with one-third of the fee generally payable as a retainer at the outset.

**EDUCATIONAL INSTITUTIONS** Recruiting at educational institutions is extremely effective when candidates require relatively little full-time work experience and will be trained by the organization. Universities and colleges supply qualified applicants for positions ranging from police officer to management trainee. Most Canadian universities and community colleges have placement centres. Organizations provide such centres with information about their job openings, which are then posted. In addition, many companies throughout Canada visit selected educational institutions each year to conduct on-campus recruitment activities.[46]

Most colleges and universities have counselling centres that provide job-search assistance to students through such activities as skills assessment testing and workshops on résumé preparation and interview strategies. Sometimes, they arrange on-site job fairs, at which employers set up displays outlining the types of job opportunities available. The largest such job fair in Canada is held at Wilfrid Laurier University each February, attracting 175 to 200 companies and 2500 to 3000 students.[47]

Cooperative education (co-op) and field placement programs have become increasingly popular in Canada. These programs require students to spend a specified period of time working in organizations as an integral part of their academic program, thereby gaining some hands-on skills in an actual work setting. Summer internship programs are part of the recruitment strategy at such organizations as Celestica, Shell Canada, Royal Bank of Canada, and Infosys Technologies Inc., which offers a competitive global internship program called InStep.[48] Internship, co-op, and field placement programs can produce a win–win result. The employer is provided with an excellent opportunity to assess the skills and abilities of a potential employee without incurring any significant costs, while benefiting from the current knowledge and enthusiasm of bright, talented individuals. It is now possible for firms to recruit graduate interns online through Career Edge, described in the HR.Net box.

**HR.NET**

## Finding Interns Online

Career Edge Organization is a private-sector, not-for-profit, independent Canadian organization. Career Edge Organization operates three innovative paid internship programs, including Career Edge (which promotes entry-level internships nationally for recent university and college graduates), Ability Edge (a national internship program for recent graduates with disabilities), and Career Bridge (the newest program to be launched under the Career Edge Organization banner, providing internships for internationally qualified immigrants to Canada).

The original goal of the Career Edge organization was to provide a service to address youth unemployment and underemployment in Canada. Recognizing the existence of these problems, charter member companies including the TD Bank, Boston Consulting Group of Canada Limited, Noranda Inc., PanCanadian Petroleum Limited, Nortel, and Bell Canada launched Career Edge Organization in 1996. Ability Edge was subsequently introduced in 1999 to assist with the employment of recent graduates with disabilities, and the Career Bridge program was added in 2003 to assist recent professional, internationally trained immigrants to launch their Canadian careers.

This innovative business enabler is used by employers to select from an online talent pool of more than 10 000 recent graduates who have registered for the Career and Ability Edge programs from a nationwide variety of university and college programs, as well as to select from more than 1500 recent immigrant professionals from the pre-screened Career Bridge registrant pool. Interested employers register with Career Edge Organization and, once approved as "host" employers, post their internship positions on the Career Edge Organization website. Prospective interns visit the site, view available positions, and apply directly to the employer. The host employer staff then review the applications and select the intern(s).

Intern payroll is administered by Career Edge Organization. Interns are paid a modest stipend that is paid for by the host employer. The cost for a 12-month internship, including intern stipend, applicable taxes, and a non-refundable program delivery fee paid to Career Edge Organization, is less than $27 000 for Career Edge and less than $30 000 for both the Ability Edge and Career Bridge programs. No government funding or other subsidies are involved in providing these internships.

Host employers provide a professional workplace; meaningful intern positions building on the skills, experience, and education of the intern; and a designated mentor to coach for six-, nine-, and twelve-month internship periods. A four-month internship under the Career Bridge program is also available. By completing an internship, participating graduates gain the skills and experience they need to become more marketable, and professional immigrants acquire experience in the Canadian workplace that help them launch careers in Canada. Host employers benefit by gaining fresh ideas from creative, committed candidates from the online database. More than 7000 interns have been placed in over 1000 participating host organizations.

Source: Career Edge for Recent Graduates, www.careeredge.org.

**EMPLOYEE REFERRALS** Current employees may encourage people they know to apply for job vacancies. Studies have found that referrals are an inexpensive recruitment method and that employees hired through referrals stay with an organization longer, demonstrate greater loyalty, and experience higher job satisfaction than employees recruited by other means.[49] New recruits are often familiar with an organization as a result of the employees who referred them and are more attracted to the organization than employees hired through other recruitment methods.[50] Some companies, such as food maker Mars Canada Inc, Bank of Canada, and Vancouver software developer Upside Software Inc., offer bonuses to employees who refer candidates who are eventually hired.[51] Employees are more likely to refer people who are similar to themselves in work ethics and practices. A disadvantage of this recruitment method is that current employees tend to refer candidates who are demographically similar to themselves, which can create potential employment equity and human rights problems. Organizations are advised to use employee referrals along with other recruitment methods when filling job vacancies.

**OTHER** There are many other less-often-used methods of external recruiting, including walk-ins, write-ins, the HRSDC online job bank, professional and trade associations, alumni associations, labour organizations, military establishments, open houses, information sessions, and job fairs.

## Recruiting Non-permanent Staff

In many firms, contingent workers are key to attaining labour flexibility and acquiring special expertise on an as-needed basis. In these organizations, recruiters spend more time seeking temporary (term, seasonal, casual) and contract workers and less time recruiting permanent staff.

**TEMPORARY HELP AGENCIES** Temporary help agencies, such as Kelly Services and Office Overload, exist in all major cities in Canada. They provide **temporary** employees (temps) to fill in for vacationing, sick, or on-leave employees as well as extra staff for seasonal work, peak workloads, and special projects.[52] Temps provide employers with three major benefits. First, they cost much less than permanent employees. Second, if a temp performs unsatisfactorily, a substitute can be requested immediately. Generally, a suitable replacement is sent to the firm within one business day. Third, individuals working as temps who are seeking full-time employment are often highly motivated, knowing that many firms choose full-time employees from the ranks of their top-performing temps.

**CONTRACT WORKERS** Contract workers are employees who develop work relationships directly with the employer for a specific type of work or period of time.[53] Some contract workers wish to remain self-employed; others hope to obtain a full-time position eventually. Sometimes they are contracted to provide specialized services one or two days a week on a permanent basis. PPL Marketing Services—a mid-sized firm in Mississauga with a core staff of 80 people—uses contract workers on a regular basis, both project-based and permanent. As projects come and go, so do the writers or production people contracted to complete the jobs. PPL also has a senior HR professional on contract, working two days a week to handle critical issues such as hiring, exit interviews, and developing salary structures.[54]

Because contract workers are not part of the company head count, managers can rely on their services while honouring staffing restrictions aimed at reducing payroll costs. Contract workers may be more productive and efficient than permanent employees because they can focus on the task at hand and do not get involved in countless meetings or organizational politics. The major drawback of using contract workers is that their commitment to the employer may be somewhat lower than that of permanent staff, and the demands and deadlines of their multiple clients may conflict at times.

**OUTSOURCING/SUBCONTRACTING** Outsourcing or subcontracting is the process by which employers transfer work to another organization specializing in that type of work, which therefore has the ability to perform it more efficiently. Outsourcing agreements may result in a long-term relationship between the employer and subcontractor, although both parties retain the ability to renew or sever the relationship at their convenience. While data processing, security, cafeteria services, and housekeeping have been outsourced for many years, companies have recently begun to hire subcontractors to provide services that are important to the business but not within its core capabilities, including research and development, marketing research, product design, specific HR functions, and payroll.

## 4.8 EVALUATING RECRUITMENT EFFECTIVENESS AND EFFICIENCY

Like other organizational initiatives, recruitment processes and practices should be evaluated to gauge their effectiveness and efficiency in attracting first-rate job applicants. Common approaches include:

1. *Cost measures* to ascertain costs incurred during a recruitment drive, such as advertising, travel, search firm fees, referral bonuses, and salary costs of staff involved in the recruitment process
2. *Time measures* to trace the time between when the need to hire staff is identified and the time new employees are in their positions. Time measures for recruitment vary depending on economic conditions and rates of unemployment, but organizations can study them to detect which steps in the process helped and hindered the length of time taken to fill job vacancies.
3. *Quantity measures* concentrate on the number of applicants generated through each recruitment method. Yield ratios are commonly used to indicate which recruitment methods are the most effective at producing qualified job candidates. A **yield ratio** is the percentage of applicants that proceed to the next stage of the selection process. A recruiting yield pyramid, such as that shown in Figure 4.11, can be devised for each recruiting method by calculating the yield ratio for each step in the selection process. Using this particular recruitment method, 1200 leads must be generated in order to hire 50 new accountants. By calculating and comparing yield pyramids for each recruiting method, it is possible to determine which method results in the most new hires for each type of job.
4. *Quality measures* focus on the extent to which recruiting activities locate and attract people who have the right skill set for the job. Typical measures include assessments of how many applicants are qualified for the job as well as measures of turnover and performance of the people hired.

**figure 4.11** A Recruiting Yield Pyramid

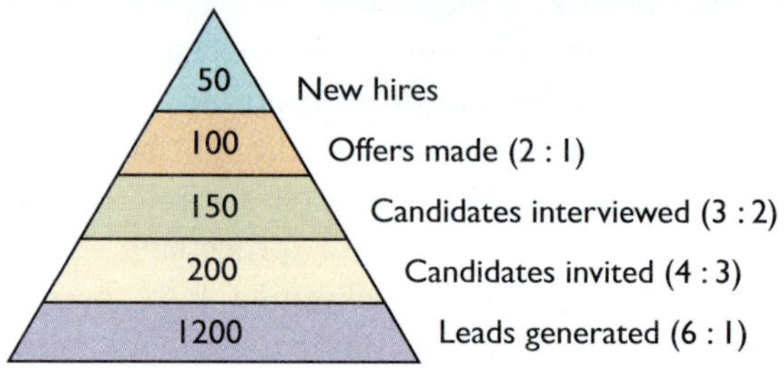


The most common assessment approach is a combination of cost and quantity measures to determine the **cost per hire**. Cost per hire is calculated by dividing the total costs of a recruitment drive by the number of qualified applicants it generated. Organizations use these calculations to pinpoint where they can reduce recruitment costs. Another measure is **cost per applicant**, which is calculated by dividing the cost of a recruiting method, such as newspaper advertising, by the number of qualified applicants who respond. This measure allows organizations to assess the relative value of different recruitment methods and decide which methods they will continue using.

Determining recruitment effectiveness and efficiency puts organizations at a strategic advantage because they are recognizing their strengths in attracting high-calibre applicants and examining areas for improvement. Organizations that annually review their recruitment processes and practices can detect trends over time, and compare and contrast the impact of new practices on the hiring process.

## 4.9 RECRUITING A MORE DIVERSE WORKFORCE

Recruiting a diverse workforce is not just socially responsible—it is a necessity.[55] As noted earlier, the composition of Canada's workforce is changing dramatically. Trends of particular significance include a decrease in the availability of young workers, a dramatic increase in the average age of employees, and an increase in the number of women, visible minorities, Aboriginal peoples, and persons with disabilities in the workforce. The number of employees trying to balance work with child- and elder-care responsibilities is also increasing.

## Attracting Older Workers

Employers are beginning to encourage retirement-age employees to stay with the company and are actively recruiting employees who are at or beyond retirement age. Studies have found that organizations acknowledge the value of hiring workers over the age of 50, but they do not have HR policies and programs in place for them. The few organizations that have tailored HR policies and programs for older workers have been successful at attracting them (see the Workforce Diversity box). Only 11 percent of firms indicate they are actively focused on attracting and recruiting mature workers and 7 percent formally consider mature workers as a distinct employee group.[56] There are significant benefits to hiring and retaining older employees, including high job satisfaction; a strong sense of loyalty and organizational commitment; a strong work ethic; good people skills, such as patience, empathy, and helpfulness; willingness to work in a variety of roles, including part-time; high potential for successful retraining; and a greater likelihood of staying with the firm.[57] Studies have also shown that since

### WORKFORCE DIVERSITY

### Age-Free Culture Goal of Top Employers

**5 ORGANIZATIONS AWARDED FOR EFFORTS TO ENTICE, RETAIN 50-PLUS WORKER**

In Edmonton, there is a 91-year-old man who greets customers entering Wal-Mart. He's the oldest employee at the chain, which has no maximum age for its workers.

"We've had retired dentists come back to work as greeters because it's a very social position and allows them to be engaged with the community. Certainly the greeter is one of the most popular positions for the 50-plus," said Karin Campbell, manager of corporate affairs for Wal-Mart Canada, based in Mississauga, Ont.

That inclusive culture is one of the reasons the 77000-employee retailer, along with four other organizations, received the 2009 Best Employer Award for 50-Plus Canadians—the fifth annual award from the Workplace Institute which recognizes great workplaces for Canadians aged 50 and above. Judges evaluate entries based on innovative approaches to retirement, management practices and attraction and retention of mature workers.

Wal-Mart and the other winners for 2009—Bethany Care Society, the Catholic Children's Aid Society of Toronto, HSBC Bank Canada and Seven Oaks General Hospital—are constantly innovating and continuing to work on different aspects to strengthen the value proposition for older workers, said Barbara Jaworski, founder of the awards and author of *Kaa-Boom! How to Engage the 50-Plus Worker* and *Beat the Workforce Crisis.* "They may find, for whatever reason, it's strategically important to their business to retain those folks or attract them."

Wal-Mart has ambitious goals for expansion and for hiring, and it sees the 50-plus category as a really important one, said Campbell.

"Certainly our objective is to let them know we have these opportunities available and we do offer flexible and rewarding work for them, in a variety of different positions, not just at the store level but home office."

In 2008, Wal-Mart Canada introduced "progressive retirement services," a program to help the company effectively retain and recruit more experienced workers through work-life flexibility options. Workers are encouraged to return as consultants, special project managers or mentors.

"We were doing it on an ad hoc basis and really wanted to formalize it so everyone had access," said Campbell. "We really saw an opportunity to use the knowledge and expertise of these 50-plus individuals, in markets particularly where we couldn't find younger associates, and we have seen the value of their experience firsthand.

**yield ratio** The percentage of applicants that proceed to the next stage of the selection process.

**cost per hire** Calculated by dividing the total costs of a recruitment drive by the number of qualified applicants it generated.

**cost per applicant** Calculated by dividing the cost of a recruiting method, such as newspaper advertising, by the number of qualified applicants who respond.

There is also a diversity council at Wal-Mart that was established to create a culture of inclusion by encouraging the special qualities of each associate and celebrating how individual differences bring value to customers and the workplace. And for each store, the retailer looks at the surrounding area to assess the different demographics, customer ages and multicultural clusters, both for the selection of merchandise and for hiring.

"We look at what we need to do at the store level to recruit," said Campbell. "For a store where there are a lot of boomers working in the community, you see a lot of boomers in the store."

The 50-plus awards recognize several specific areas, such as career development, recruitment practices, workplace culture, health supports, benefits, pensions or recognition. For career development, that can mean continued, targeted training for workers, even if they are approaching retirement age, and the chance to move to different positions if so desired, to keep work interesting. Or it can mean a tailored career development plan for each employee, regardless of age.

"Continuing to offer training can be an important message to older workers that they're not being put on the back shelf," said Jaworski.

All of these strategies are very tied in to business needs, as companies see a gap and then ask employees, through focus groups, for example, about alternatives, she said.

"Flexibility is number one. Organizations that don't offer that flexibility are asking for trouble, asking their older workers to leave to go to competitors where they may get greater flexibility or work on a part-time basis," said Jaworksi.

Organizations are also focusing more on marketing to older workers. While many companies are afraid to take such an approach for fear of "offending" Gen Ys, whom they also hope to attract, "smart organizations are trying to attract the total labour pool—all age groups, different skill levels," she said.

And while younger workers may be concerned more senior employees will lock jobs, preventing them from moving forward, "what's interesting about older workers, especially when rehired after 50, is they generally are not that interested in moving up in the organization," said Jaworski.

"They are interested in what they do well and helping younger workers attain some of those supervisory positions they may be looking for," she said. "They're not always interested in taking on more responsibility. They want to contribute and to do a good job."

Source: S. Dobson, "Age-free culture goal of top employers," *Canadian HR Reporter*, January 12, 2009, p. 11. Reprinted with permission.

older employees are less likely to get work injuries and have lower rates of turnover and absenteeism, their employers benefit from significantly reduced costs.[58]

Recruiting and attracting older workers generally requires a comprehensive effort before recruiting begins, to make a company attractive to them. Specifically, organizations should:[59]

- deal with stereotypical attitudes toward older workers through education and proactive efforts to eliminate discriminatory practices
- check HR policies, procedures, and practices to ensure that they do not discourage recruitment of seniors or encourage valuable older people to leave (for example, promoting early retirement)
- develop flexible work options, such as part-time positions and phased retirement
- redesign or create jobs; for example, to accommodate older adults experiencing a decrease in dexterity and strength (e.g., manufacturing jobs may need to be redesigned).

## Attracting Younger Employees

Many firms recognize the benefits of a multigenerational workforce. They not only try to attract older workers but also take steps to address the pending shortage of younger employees. Younger workers are characterized as entrepreneurial and independent; digitally savvy; and valuing empowerment, challenge, and excitement.[60] They seek career opportunities that offer fast-track promotions, raises, perks, independence, flexible work arrangements, and an opportunity to have fun.[61] With the younger workforce declared "the most entrepreneurial generation in history," organizations are confronted with the added weight of convincing them that working for a corporation has greater appeal than self-employment.[62]

BMO Bank of Montreal has taken numerous steps to achieve a more representative workforce, including establishing a "Possibilities Foundation."

## Recruiting Designated Group Members

Employers need to formulate comprehensive plans for attracting members of the employment equity–designated groups—women, visible minorities, Aboriginal peoples, and persons with disabilities, including overcoming stereotypes and biases, re-evaluating HR policies and practices, developing flexible work options, redesigning jobs, and investing in training and career development.[63] The employer's commitment to equity and diversity must be made clear to all involved in the recruitment process—whether it is employees asked for referrals or private employment agencies. This can also be stressed in all recruitment advertising. Alternative publications targeting the designated groups should be considered for advertising, and linkages can be formed with organizations and agencies interested in or specializing in assisting designated group members. For example, the Canadian Council for Aboriginal Business is making available a national database of résumés of qualified Aboriginal peoples, as well as careers and jobs of interest to Aboriginal peoples, in partnership with the employment portal Monster.ca.[64]

BMO Bank of Montreal, which is committed to both education and employment equity, established an $8-million Possibilities Foundation aimed at visible minority, Aboriginal, and disabled high-school students moving on to post-secondary education. Selected students are eligible for summer employment and a $1000 scholarship.[65] This program enables BMO to benefit from the many advantages to hiring individuals with disabilities, including access to a broader pool of job candidates, enhanced corporate image, lower staff turnover, a workforce better prepared to deal with customers or clients with disabilities, improved staff morale, and better customer service.[66]

### *In-class Notes*

**Recruiting a More Diverse Workforce**

- Older workers require flexible work arrangements and redesigned jobs for physical changes due to aging
- Younger workers want flexibility and the opportunity to grow
- Recruiting designated group members involves overcoming stereotypes and biases, providing flexible work arrangements, redesigning jobs, and investing in training and career development

# Recruiting on the International Stage

A talent shortage is looming as baby boomers are due to start retiring in 2010. To prepare for the deficit, organizations are expanding their search for qualified candidates by tapping into the international market. Given Canada's strong ties to the European Union, Europe offers a rich supply of candidates with labour and management expertise. An important contribution of European executives to the Canadian market is their ability to interact and negotiate within a multicultural context. This aptitude strengthens Canadian companies' ability to expand overseas and to function in Canada's increasingly multicultural environment. For Europeans, Canada offers an opportunity for advancement that might not be available at home. Studies have found that 76 percent of European executives identify lack of career advancement opportunities as the premier motivator to leave a company. In Italy, for example, it is almost impossible to advance into management positions unless you have devoted at least 20 years to the company. The response that differed most significantly in the studies was the perceived importance of travel and international relocation when considering a job opportunity. European and North American executives rated this much lower than Asia Pacific executives: While 38 percent of Asia Pacific executives rated it as extremely important, 31 percent of Europeans and 54 percent of North Americans stated it was not important at all. Americans are used to relocating nationally when considering job opportunities but are not keen, like Europeans, to relocate internationally. Deloitte & Touche in the United States would like its executives to have international experience, but the organization finds it difficult to convince employees to travel overseas for many reasons, including family, schooling, spousal careers, and a concern about working in another culture.[67]

# Chapter Review

## Answers to Test Yourself

1. What is the strategic value of the human resources planning process? Identify the techniques used to forecast human resources demand and supply.

   Human resources planning is the process of analyzing and identifying the need for and availability of human resources to ensure that an organization will have the right number of employees, with the right skills, at the right times, and in the right jobs to meet its strategic objectives. Organizations would be hard pressed to reach their strategic targets if employees did not have the required skills and abilities.

   Forecasting the demand for human resources can be achieved through quantitative and qualitative approaches. Quantitative approaches include trend analysis, ratio analysis, scatter plots, regression analysis, and computer-based simulations. Qualitative approaches include nominal group technique, Delphi technique, and scenario planning.

   Forecasting the supply for human resources can be achieved through Markov analysis, skills/management inventories, replacement charts/summaries, movement analysis, and succession planning.

2. Identify and explain the four steps in the recruitment process.

   The four steps in the recruitment process are: (1) identify job openings, (2) determine job requirements and job specifications, (3) select methods of recruitment, and (4) generate a pool of qualified applicants.

   *Identify job openings.* HR plans provide valuable information to recruiters by indicating how many candidates will be required for various positions, when they will be needed, and whether positions should be filled internally or externally.

   *Determine job requirements and job specifications.* This involves reviewing the job description and job specification to determine the knowledge, skills, abilities, and general characteristics necessary to perform the job according to standard.

*Select methods of recruitment.* Filling vacant job openings can be achieved by recruiting within or outside an organization.

*Generate a pool of qualified applicants.* External environmental conditions, such as changes in the labour market, the unemployment rate, economy and legislation, and the recruiting activities of labour-market competitors, affect a recruiter's ability to generate a pool of qualified applicants. To ensure that the assumptions on which the HR plan was based are valid at the time of recruitment, recruiters check leading economic indicators such as Statistics Canada.

3. What are the advantages of using internal and external recruitment methods?

   The advantages of internal recruitment include a more accurate assessment of the person's skills and performance level than with an outside candidate; employees see that competence is rewarded, thus enhancing commitment, morale, performance, and the likelihood that employees will stay with the organization; lower overall recruitment costs; inside candidates require less orientation than do outsiders; managers are provided with a longer-term perspective when making business decisions; and, since internal candidates are familiar with the organization and its culture, they are more likely to achieve job mandates faster than external candidates.

   The advantages of external recruitment include the generation of a larger pool of qualified candidates; the availability of a more diverse applicant pool to assist in meeting employment equity goals and timetables; the acquisition of skills or knowledge not currently available within the organization and/or new ideas and creative problem-solving techniques; the elimination of rivalry and competition caused by employees jockeying for transfers and promotions; and the potential cost savings resulting from hiring individuals who already have required skills, rather than providing extensive training.

4. What should organizations do to make their websites effective in order to attract potential candidates for job vacancies?

   In order for company websites to be effective, they must be user-friendly. According to iLogos, a research company that monitors trends in online recruiting, best practices to attract a large applicant pool include: a link to career sections from the homepage, a recruiting section for recent college and university graduates, information about company benefits and culture, complete and updated job descriptions, job search by job category, choice of cut-and-paste form or résumé builder, application automatically attached to a job, reuse of candidate information for multiple jobs, and online user feedback.

5. Identify and discuss the four approaches for evaluating the effectiveness and efficiency of the recruitment process.

   The four approaches for evaluating the effectiveness and efficiency of the recruitment process include: cost measures, time measures, quantity measures, and quality measures. Cost measures ascertain costs incurred during the recruitment drive, such as advertising, travel, search firm fees, referral bonuses, and salary costs of staff involved in the recruitment process. Time measures trace the time between when the need to hire staff is identified and the time new employees are in their positions. Quantity measures concentrate on the number of applicants generated through each recruitment method. Yield ratios are commonly used to indicate which recruitment methods are the most effective at producing qualified job candidates. A yield ratio is the percentage of applicants that proceed to the next stage of the selection process. Quality measures focus on the extent to which recruiting activities locate and attract people who have the right skill set for the job. Typical measures include assessments of how many applicants are qualified for the job, as well as measures of turnover and performance of the people hired.

## Key Terms

attrition (p. 117)
buyout and early retirement programs (p. 117)
computer-based simulation (p. 110)
cost per applicant (p. 132)
cost per hire (p. 132)
Delphi technique (p. 111)
employee leasing (p. 107)
golden parachute (p. 118)
hiring freeze (p. 117)
human resources planning (HRP) (p. 105)
job posting (p. 123)
job sharing (p. 117)
layoff (p. 118)
loaning or flexforce (p. 118)

management inventories (p. 114)
Markov analysis (p. 112)
movement analysis (p. 115)
nominal group technique (p. 110)
outplacement assistance (p. 118)
ratio analysis (p. 109)
recruitment (p. 121)
reduced work week (p. 117)
regression analysis (p. 110)
relationship marketing (p. 125)
replacement charts (p. 114)
replacement summaries (p. 114)
scatter plot (p. 109)
scenario planning (p. 111)
severance pay (p. 118)
skills inventories (p. 113)
succession planning (p. 115)
supplemental unemployment benefits (SUBs) (p. 118)
survivor sickness (p. 118)
termination (p. 118)
trend analysis (p. 138)
yield ratio (p. 132)

## Required Professional Capabilities (RPCs)

RPC 4-1 > (p. 115)
RPC 4-2 > (p. 116)
RPC 4-3 > (p. 116)
RPC 4-4 > (p. 122)
RPC 4-5 > (p. 125)
RPC 4-6 > (p. 127)

# CASES AND EXERCISES

myHRlab
For additional cases and exercises, go to www.mypearsoned.ca/myhrlab.

## CASE INCIDENT

### Management Trainees at Nova

It's that time of year again at Nova! Each year, Carl Adams, recruitment officer at the head office of the retail chain, visits colleges and universities across Canada to recruit graduates for sales, marketing, human resources, and purchasing management-trainee positions for its 26 locations.

In order to predict the number of management trainees required, HRP is done each year based on the budget and sales forecast. The previous year's plan is also reviewed. There has been virtually no change in the HR plan over the past 10 years.

Natalie Gordon, vice-president of human resources, is feeling rather concerned about what happened last year and is wondering how to prevent it from happening again. Based on the HR plan, 50 new management trainees were hired. Unfortunately, six months after they started, the company experienced a drastic drop in sales due to a downturn in the economy, combined with increased foreign competition. Half of the recently hired management trainees had to be laid off.

Carl started at Nova as a management trainee when he had completed the Business Administration–Human Resources Management program at Central Community College. He has just returned from an on-campus recruitment campaign, which happened to be at his alma mater, and reported that his experience was not as pleasant as usual. One of the candidates that he interviewed knew someone who had been hired and laid off last year. She indicated she was rather worried about considering a position with the firm in light of that fact, despite Nova's excellent reputation for promotion from within and overall stability. (Nova, which currently employs more than 8000 people in its head office and retail stores, has been in business for more than 70 years.)

Carl has just finished telling Natalie how embarrassed he was by this candidate's probing questions about job security and how uncomfortable he felt. He ended up simply reassuring the candidate that such a situation could never happen again. Natalie is now wondering how to make Carl's reassurance a reality.

## Questions

1. What are the consequences of poor HRP at Nova?
2. What problems do you see with Nova's present HRP process?
3. What should Natalie do to more accurately forecast the demand for management trainees for the coming year before Carl does any more on-campus recruiting?

## Application Questions

1. Imagine you are on the human resources planning team for the human resources program at your college or university.
   a. Demand: How will you determine the number of students that should be permitted into the HR program next year? Will you cap class size? Why or why not?
   b. Supply: From where will you recruit qualified applicants for the program? What entrance requirements will be set?
   c. Oversupply: How will you deal with oversupply (i.e., too many students applying to the program)?
2. Discuss the approach that should be taken by a human resources planning team to measure the success of its forecasting initiatives. What criteria should be put in place for evaluation?
3. Select a Canadian organization that interests you and conduct an environmental scan to determine the factors that will have an impact on how this organization will recruit qualified candidates over the next five years.
4. You are a member of the recruitment team responsible for attracting qualified applicants to job vacancies in your organization. Select one of the following six options and discuss the sources from which you will recruit qualified applicants. Design the ad you will post to attract applicants to the position.
   a. Pilots to fly for Virgin Atlantic Airlines
   b. Firefighters for your local fire department
   c. Senior computer programmers for NASA's next shuttle launch to MARS
   d. Special agents for the Central Intelligence Agency (CIA) working on homeland security
   e. Head coach of the Toronto Maple Leafs
   f. Entertainers to play the roles of Mickey Mouse, Donald Duck, Tinkerbell, and Goofy at Walt Disney's Magic Kingdom
5. After completing question 4, identify the measures your team will use to determine the effectiveness and efficiency of your recruitment practices. How will the evaluation inform your team's practices in the future?

## RUNNING CASE: LEARNINMOTION.COM

### Getting Better Applicants

The case for Chapter 4, Getting Better Applicants, follows the owners as they begin to hire staff and are faced with a series of disappointments. The students must assess the selection process and give recommendations to improve it. To read this case, go to the companion website at www.pearsoned.ca/myhrlab and click on the *Management of Human Resources*, Third Canadian Edition, In-Class Edition, cover. Click on the case module in Chapter 4.

## CONTROVERSIAL BUSINESS TOPIC EXERCISE

You are the manager of recruitment for a large retail chain with branches across Canada. Your recruitment team launched a national search for qualified applicants to fill the position of vice president of marketing. The team analyzed the job description and job specifications, designed and posted job advertisements, contracted search firms across the country to assist with the search, and has been receiving résumés from employee referrals. The CEO of the company approached you in private today to request that you put his brother-in-law at the top of the qualified applicant list to ensure that he gets an interview. The CEO also expects you to "sell" his brother-in-law as the top contender for the job and do whatever it takes to make sure he gets it. You are reminded that this is a confidential discussion and if you leak the information to anyone, the CEO will fire you. Discuss the course of action you will take and present a rationale for your proposed direction.

## IN THE BOARDROOM EXERCISE

As a member of the executive team for a large software development company in Montreal, you are sitting at a boardroom table listening to the CEO's report on the economic hardships that have hit your organization. For the past year, the company has had an oversupply of human resources by 10 percent, and in order to face its fiscal reality must lay off 380 staff within the next three months. You begin to argue against layoffs, stating that there are other options that can be exercised, but before you can go any further the CEO bellows, "I don't care about other options! This is a crisis and we need to do something fast! Just lay them off and be done with it so we can salvage our operation and get back to business. Every other organization in Canada is laying off staff so it must be the right thing to do!" Discuss the approach you would use to argue that layoffs may not be the best and only option available to the organization. Present your recommendations in class to a team of three or four students. Invite someone to play the role of devil's advocate and challenge the options that are presented.

## RECRUITING ON THE INTERNATIONAL STAGE EXERCISE

*The exercise below relates to the Recruiting on the International Stage feature on p. 136.*

Select three organizations that conduct international searches to find qualified applicants for job vacancies. Research their recruitment practices by examining their websites. Compare and contrast the recruitment approaches they employ. In your opinion, which organization has the most effective international recruitment strategy and why?

## EXPERIENTIAL EXERCISE

For further study of text materials and development of practical skills, select the experiential exercise module for this chapter on www.pearsoned.ca/myhrlab. This module provides two to three individual or group-based assignments per chapter.

# QUIZ YOURSELF

## STUDY GUIDE QUESTIONS

Circle the correct answer. After completing this self-test, check your answers against the Answers to Study Guide Questions at the back of the book (p. 433).

1. Acme Inc. comprises four departments. One of the departments went through a downsizing exercise due to declining sales over the past two years. The head of that department recently found out that her colleague, who is the head of one of the other departments, has been recruiting staff over the same time period. Productivity of the organization and staff morale has suffered severely. What could have reduced the productivity and morale problems at Acme Inc.?
   a. better downsizing strategies
   b. better HR planning
   c. better recruitment methods
   d. drop in sales
   e. better strategic planning
2. One of the key components of HRP is forecasting the number and type of people an organization requires in order to meet its objectives. Several qualitative and quantitative techniques can be used for forecasting purposes. Which of the following indicates a qualitative and a quantitative technique, respectively?
   a. nominal group technique; Delphi technique
   b. Delphi technique; job analysis
   c. regression analysis; nominal group technique
   d. nominal group technique; trend analysis
   e. all of the above
3. Seretonic Ltd. is a leading pharmaceutical company that is sales driven and does not manufacture locally. For 2011, they have a sales target of $9 billion. Each salesperson is estimated to bring in $1.8 million during the year. The HR department is planning to conduct a forecasting session to arrive at the number of people the organization will require for 2011. What is the most appropriate technique to use for this forecasting, considering the information the HR department has?
   a. trend analysis
   b. regression analysis
   c. Delphi technique
   d. ratio analysis
   e. scatter plot analysis
4. Nigel, who is an HR consultant, facilitated a forecasting session for one of his client organizations. He used a panel of outside experts, but none of the members of the panel met face to face during the session—they presented their solutions via an email questionnaire. What is the technique used by Nigel?
   a. questionnaire technique
   b. nominal group technique
   c. Delphi technique
   d. managerial judgment
   e. trend analysis
5. Succession planning is an important component of HR planning. Succession planning:
   a. forecasts availability of internal candidates for key executive positions
   b. involves a series of integrated and complicated steps
   c. needs to balance organization requirements with potential/career aspirations of internal candidates

d. can be highly confidential
e. all of the above

6. A golden parachute clause in an employment contract guarantees executives compensation and benefits in case of:
   a. illness
   b. leave of absence
   c. termination due to downsizing or restructuring
   d. global reassignment
   e. exceeding company financial objectives

7. To avoid survivor sickness in downsizing situations, supervisors should:
   a. provide limited information to survivors
   b. ignore the situation
   c. provide more work to survivors
   d. allow survivors to grieve and deal with emotions
   e. provide job rotation

8. IT Recruiters Inc. recently won a project that requires the company to recruit 15 software professionals from outside sources. They need experienced hands to get the project off the ground smoothly, but software professionals are in short supply worldwide. What conditions does the company need to be mindful of during the recruitment process?
   a. local labour market conditions
   b. national labour market conditions
   c. occupational market conditions
   d. economic conditions
   e. all of the above

9. A labour shortage requires a company to recruit more people. However, a labour surplus requires companies to take a number of measures to reduce staff to meet requirements. The following activities can be used to address a labour surplus:
   a. hiring freeze, early retirement programs
   b. succession planning, attrition
   c. job sharing, job enrichment
   d. job sharing, job rotation
   e. none of the above

10. Jeffrey is a recruiter at MegaCity. He needs to recruit an IT manager and an HR manager. Jeffrey is finding it hard to get good, qualified candidates for the IT manager position due to a global shortage of qualified candidates. He has found a suitable candidate for the HR manager position, but the individual has stated a salary requirement that is beyond the company's pay ranges. Jeffrey is confronted with the following constraints:
    a. environmental conditions
    b. internal pay structures and environmental conditions
    c. inducements of competitors
    d. job specifications
    e. organizational policies and plans

11. Selecting candidates internally can have advantages to both the employer and the employee. However, it can also have a number of disadvantages. Which of the following is a disadvantage of recruiting candidates from within?
    a. dissatisfaction with newly appointed superiors from within the ranks
    b. increased employee motivation and commitment
    c. better "fit" in terms of organizational culture
    d. accuracy of skill assessment by the employer
    e. need for succession planning

12. The ABC Company uses a number of methods to attract workers from outside the organization. The new recruiter wanted to identify which recruitment method brought the best results in terms of producing the best-qualified candidates. The technique used calculated the percentage of applicants who moved to the next stage of the process. The technique used was:
    a. ratio analysis
    b. regression analysis
    c. yield ratio
    d. Delphi technique
    e. none of the above

13. The HR assistant of a firm is planning to place an advertisement in a local paper for an account manager position. As a recruitment consultant, what tips can you give her so that she can achieve optimum results from the ad?
    a. exclude the company's address
    b. exclude the company's name
    c. develop the ad to create desire for the job and to instigate action
    d. ask a recruitment agency for help
    e. none of the above

14. A newly formed IT company has only 20 employees. The CEO finds that the company has an urgent need for an HR professional to provide HR services. However, its budget does not have enough money to hire such an individual. The CEO can overcome this problem by:
    a. outsourcing/subcontracting HR services
    b. asking the controller to take care of HR
    c. doing it himself/herself
    d. succession planning
    e. job rotation

15. Which of the following combinations accurately outlines the four designated groups in employment equity programs?
    a. women, visible minorities, Aboriginal peoples, low-income people
    b. visible minorities, older workers, Aboriginal peoples, people with disabilities
    c. women, people with disabilities, Aboriginal peoples, visible minorities
    d. people with disabilities, low-income people, older workers
    e. visible minorities, Aboriginal peoples, people with disabilities

# APPENDIX 4.1

**SAMPLE APPLICATION FORM**

**Position being applied for:** | **Date available to begin work:**

**PERSONAL DATA**

Last name | Given name(s)

**Address**

Street | Apt. No.

City | Province | Postal Code

Home Telephone Number:

Business Telephone Number:

Are you eligible to work in Canada? Yes ☐ No ☐

Are you 18 years or more and less than 65 years of age? Yes ☐ No ☐

Are you willing to relocate in Ontario? Preferred Location

☐ Yes ☐ No

To determine your qualification for employment, please provide below and on the reverse side, information related to your academic and other achievements including volunteer work, as well as employment history. Additional information may be attached on a separate sheet.

**EDUCATION**

**Secondary School** ☐ | **Business or Trade School** ☐

Highest grade or level completed | Name of program | Length of program

Licence, certificate, or diploma awarded? | Type:

☐ Yes ☐ No

**Community College** ☐ | **University** ☐

Name of Program | Length of Program | Diploma/Degree awarded

Major subject | ☐ Yes ☐ No ☐ Honours

Other courses, workshops, seminars, Licences, Certificates, Degree

**WORK-RELATED SKILLS**

Describe any of your work-related skills, experience, or training that relate to the position being applied for.

**SAMPLE APPLICATION FORM—continued**

## EMPLOYMENT

| | |
|---|---|
| Name of present/last employer | Job title |
| Type of Business | Period of employment (includes leaves of absence related to maternity/parental leave, Works' Compensation claims, handicap/disability, or human rights complaint)<br>From To<br>Reason for leaving (do not include leaves of absence related to maternity/paternal leave, Workers' Compensation claims, handicap/disability, or human rights complaints) |
| Functions/Responsibilities | |
| Name of previous employer | Job title |
| Type of Business | Period of employment (including leaves of absence related to maternity/parental leave, Workers' Compensation claims, handicap/disability, or human rights complaints)<br>From To<br>Reason for leaving (do not include leaves of absence related to maternity/paternal leave, Workers' Compensation claims, handicap/disability, or human rights complaints) |
| Functions/Responsibilities | |

For employment references we may approach:

Your present/last employer? ☐ Yes ☐ No

Your former employer(s) ☐ Yes ☐ No

List references if different from above on a separate sheet.

## PERSONAL INTERESTS AND ACTIVITIES (civic, athletic, etc.)

I hereby declare that the foregoing information is true and complete to my knowledge. I understand that a false statement may disqualify me from employment or cause my dismissal.

Have you attached an additional sheet? ☐ Yes ☐ No

Signature ______________________________ Date ______________________________

Source: *Human Rights at Work*, 3rd ed., 2008, prepared by the Ontario Human Rights Tribunal, published by Carswell Thomson. © Queen's Printer for Ontario, 2004. Reproduced with permission.

# 5 chapter SELECTION

## Learning Objectives

1. Articulate the strategic role of selection in the hiring process.
2. Explain the process of prescreening applicants.
3. Describe how to conduct a selection interview.
4. Discuss the value of employment tests in the selection process.
5. Explain the approaches used to conduct background investigations and reference checks.
6. Describe how to make a hiring decision.
7. Explain the value of reliability and validity in the selection process.

## Test Yourself

1. What is selection and what is its purpose and importance for an organization?
2. What are the major steps in the selection process?
3. What are the major types of selection interviews and the problems that can undermine their effectiveness?
4. What are the four types of testing used in selection, and what are the legal and ethical concerns related to medical examinations and drug testing?
5. What is the importance of reference checking? What strategies can make reference checking effective? What are the legal issues involved?

## 5.1 THE STRATEGIC IMPORTANCE OF SELECTION

**Selection** is the process of choosing individuals with the relevant qualifications to fill existing or projected job openings. Whether considering current employees for a transfer or promotion or outside candidates for a first-time position with an organization, information about the applicants must be collected and evaluated. Each step in the selection process, from preliminary reception and initial screening to the hiring decision, is performed under legal, organizational, and environmental constraints that protect the interests of both the applicant and the organization.[1]

### Purpose and Importance of Selection

The purpose of selection is to find the "best" candidate for the job—an individual who possesses the required knowledge, skills, abilities (KSAs), and personality, and who will perform well, embrace the corporate mission and values, fit the organizational culture, and help the organization achieve its strategic goals. More and more organizations are recognizing the importance of fit. In fact, in a recent survey of 200 Canadian companies, fit with organizational culture was identified as the second most important hiring criterion for business graduates, surpassed only by relevant areas of study.[2] Human capital is the largest investment a company makes, with the average cost of a company's workforce calculated to be 36 percent of its revenue. Human resources have become more important than tangible assets such as technology as the primary source of competitive advantage because tangible assets can be copied by competitors. With human capital as the leading source of competitive advantage, it is essential for companies to implement effective hiring systems to attract star candidates.[3] Proper selection is important for four key reasons: (1) its impact on company performance, (2) the costs involved, (3) its legal and ethical implications, and (4) its impact on company budget.

**COMPANY PERFORMANCE** While proper selection was important during the years when the Canadian economy was predominantly production oriented, it is even more vital now that the major part of the nation's gross national product is based on the provision of services. Managers have come to realize that the quality of a company's human resources is often the single most important factor in determining whether the organization is going to survive, be successful in reaching the objectives specified in its strategic plan, and realize a satisfactory return on its investment. In fact, after increasing profits, the top priority of 300 CEOs participating in a recent survey was attracting and retaining key employees.[4]

It is not always possible to attract a large pool of qualified recruits. In fields in which there is a *supply shortage*, such as nursing, management, and university faculty, there is often a very small selection ratio.[5] A **selection ratio** is the ratio of the number of applicants hired to the total number of applicants. A small selection ratio means that there is a limited number of applicants, many of whom might be under-qualified. If this is the case, it is generally better to start the recruitment process again, even if it means a hiring delay, rather than taking the risk of hiring an employee who will be a marginal performer at best. Some companies offer jobs to candidates who do not have all the essential job skills but demonstrate potential because the company is willing to invest in training to enhance job competency.

**COST** The cost of recruitment and selection has risen substantially, especially the costs of making a poor hiring decision. Hiring a new employee costs approximately $1580, but can reach two or three times an individual's salary if relocation expenses and signing bonuses are included. Terminating or replacing one employee after six months of employment costs a firm, on average, $68 112.[6] A study by the Society for HR Management estimated the cost of a poor hire for an intermediate position at $20 000, the cost of a poor hire for a senior management position at $100 000, and the cost of hiring a poorly selected sales representative at $300 000.[7] There are a number of direct and indirect costs that result from a poor hire. Direct costs, which are easier to measure, include interview preparation; conducting the interview, including travel, hotel, and meal costs; conducting background checks; administering and evaluating

**selection** The process of choosing individuals with the relevant qualifications to fill existing or projected job openings.

**selection ratio** The ratio of the number of applicants hired to the total number of applicants.

Market Yourself: Canadian Careers.com
**www.canadiancareers.com/resandcl.html**

employment tests; relocation costs for the new hire; orientation and training; termination costs, including litigation costs if the employee sues for wrongful dismissal; and outplacement costs. Indirect costs are more challenging to measure and include customer dissatisfaction, lost customers, lost sales, decreased morale, low productivity, and increased overtime payouts for employees juggling the responsibilities of multiple positions.[8]

> **AN ETHICAL DILEMMA**
>
> What would you do as the HR manager if one of the external job candidates is someone you have previously worked with and with whom you have a personality conflict, yet the candidate is qualified for the job vacancy?

Much emphasis has been placed on effective training and development and various motivational techniques as ways of ensuring that employees make worthwhile contributions. However, if the wrong employee is selected initially, no training program or motivational strategy—no matter how well conceived and designed—is likely to compensate adequately or offset the cost of the original hiring error.

LEGAL**compliance**

**LEGAL ISSUES** Organizations must ensure that all of their selection criteria and procedures are free of both intentional and systemic discrimination. Failure to do so may result in *human rights* complaints. Those organizations required by law to implement an *employment equity* plan must ensure that the selection process is bias-free and does not have an adverse impact on members of the four designated groups—women, visible minorities, Aboriginal peoples, and persons with disabilities.

Another legal implication is employer liability for *negligent or wrongful hiring*. Courts are increasingly finding employers liable when employees with unsuitable backgrounds are hired and subsequently engage in criminal activities falling within the scope of their employment. For example, the British Columbia Supreme Court held the United Church and the Canadian government liable for sexual assaults perpetrated by a dormitory supervisor on children living in a residential school.[9]

Finally, there is the legal issue of *wrongful dismissal*. According to wrongful dismissal case law, employees who are unable to perform a job may be dismissed without any notice or severance. While it is often difficult to prove gross incompetence, companies that satisfy the court's standards (such as warning the employee and giving him or her an opportunity to improve) have been successful. On the other hand, courts typically reject gross incompetence arguments when the employee's poor performance is the result of a flawed selection decision.[10]

**BUDGET REALITIES** A realistic *budget* for the selection process should be established and adhered to. To make the best use of an organization's funds, selection strategies, including testing and reference

## *In-class Notes*

**The Strategic Importance of Selection**

- Selecting the best candidate for a job from a group of applicants
- Critical to achieving the strategic goals of an organization
- Poor selection decisions are very costly
- Legal issues regarding human rights, employment equity, negligent hiring, and wrongful dismissal

*figure* 5.1 **Typical Steps in the Selection Process**

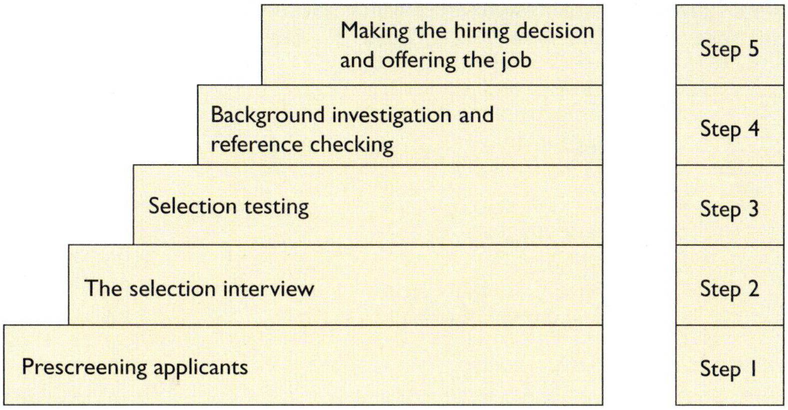


checking, must be cost-effective. *Compensation policies* can pose a constraint on recruiting, but not being able to meet the starting salary expectations of a chosen candidate can, and often has, led to a refusal on the candidate's part to accept the position.

## The Selection Process

While an HR department generally assumes overall responsibility for the selection process, HR managers collaborate with supervisors and managers throughout the organization. HR managers provide leadership in structuring the selection process; handle initial screening, testing, and reference checking; and advise supervisors and managers on selection criteria, interview questions, and the most effective and legally defensible approaches for evaluating applicants. The final hiring decision ultimately rests with the immediate supervisor.

In order to gain an accurate picture of each applicant's potential for success on the job, organizations typically rely on a number of sources of information. The types of selection instruments and screening devices used are not standardized. Even within a firm, the number and sequence of steps often varies with type and level of job. Figure 5.1 illustrates the steps commonly involved.

After applicants have been prescreened, there are a number of selection methods that employers use to determine which candidate is best suited for the job. Figure 5.2 shows the results of a study that asked HR practitioners to assess the effectiveness of various selection methods.

The type and level of job also make a difference. For example, while 58 percent of those responding to a recent survey of 202 Canadian organizations indicated that they use letters of reference for at least some jobs, as illustrated in Figure 5.3, such letters are requested least frequently for blue-collar jobs and most frequently for white-collar professional positions.[11]

Each of the steps commonly involved in the selection process, as identified in Figure 5.1, will now be described.

## 5.2 STEP 1: PRESCREENING APPLICANTS

An effective recruitment process will provide a pool of applicants who have provided résumés and/or submitted application forms either through the mail, over the Internet, or in person. Companies also receive unsolicited résumés or applications that they might keep for a specified period of time in the event of a suitable opening.

### *figure* 5.2 The Effectiveness of Selection Methods

In a survey of 201 HR executives, participants were asked which selection methods produce the best employees. The mean rating for nine methods on a 5-point scale (1 = not good, 3 = average, 5 = extremely good):

| | |
|---|---|
| Work samples | 3.68 |
| References/recommendations | 3.49 |
| Unstructured interviews | 3.49 |
| Structured interviews | 3.42 |
| Assessment centres | 3.42 |
| Specific aptitude tests | 3.08 |
| Personality tests | 2.93 |
| General congnitive ability tests | 2.89 |
| Biographical information blanks | 2.84 |

Source: This article was originally published in IOMA's monthly newsletter *HRFocus* and is republished here with the express written permission of IOMA. Copyright © 2009. For more information, go to www.ioma.com.

**RPC 5-1 >**

**Establishes screening and assessment procedures**

Members of the HR department generally perform prescreening by reviewing application forms and résumés. Those candidates not meeting the "must-have" selection criteria are eliminated first. Then, the remaining applications are examined, and those candidates who most closely match the remaining job specifications are identified and given further consideration. Seventy-eight percent of HR managers say that half of the résumés they receive are from unqualified candidates, according to research. Approximately 25 percent of these managers receive more than 75 résumés for each job posting and 38 percent spend no more than two minutes reviewing each one.[12]

Some applicants include webcam-recorded presentations along with their résumés to address questions posted by employers. Video responses showcase applicants' skills and abilities that are not evident in a résumé, such as verbal communication skills,

## *In-class Notes*

**Prescreening Applicants**

- Review résumés and application forms
- Eliminate applicants without "must have" criteria
- Rank remaining applicants who most closely match job specifications
- Conduct telephone screening

*figure* 5.3 **Letters of Reference as a Selection Strategy**

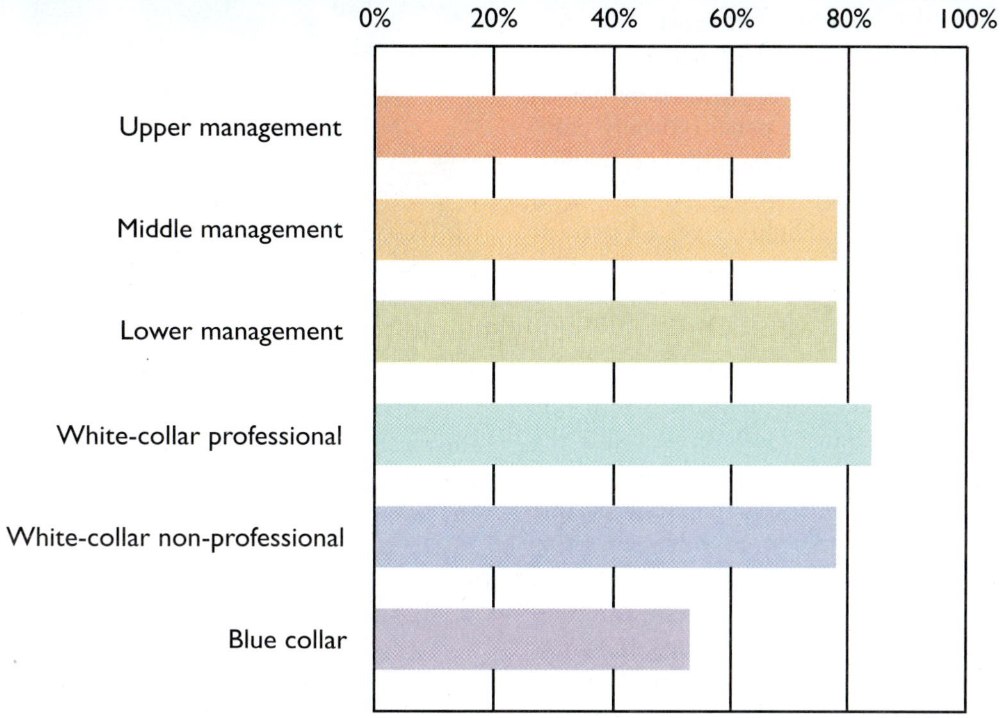


Source: S. A. Way and J. W. Thacker, "Selection Practices: Where Are Canadian Organizations?" *HR Professional* 16(5) (October/November 1999), p. 33. Reprinted by permission of Professor James W. Thacker.

enthusiasm for the position, and specific details about how the applicant's education and past experiences link to the job vacancy. This additional information about suitability for a job reduces the risks and costs of inviting non-local applicants for interviews.[13]

At this stage, a preliminary contact may be made via phone. This initial contact by the HR department is often used to verify information on the résumé, to confirm interest in the applicant to proceed through the next steps, to ensure that salary requests are compatible with the salary being offered, or for any reason that might eliminate the candidate early in the process. Holt Renfrew, a leading Canadian retailer, uses a web-based screening system that asks applicants role-specific questions in order to sort them into one of three buckets: (1) "what were they thinking," for unqualified applicants; (2) "interesting, but will pass," for those who are borderline acceptable for the job; or (3) "dream employee," for qualified applicants.[14]

Preliminary screening can save both the organization and the applicant the time and money that a face-to-face interview would cost. Applicants are usually grateful not to have their valuable job-hunting time wasted by coming in for an initial interview that will not proceed on to the next steps of the process. The company may disqualify an applicant at this stage or some applicants may self-select out of the process. If the organization and the applicant agree to proceed, the next step is to ask the person to come in for an interview.

## 5.3 STEP 2: THE SELECTION INTERVIEW

The **selection interview** involves a process of two-way communication between an interviewee and the interviewer(s) and can be defined as "a procedure designed to predict future job performance on the basis of applicants' oral responses to oral inquiries."[15] In smaller organizations where there is no HR department, the immediate supervisor is most likely to conduct the interview. In most organizations, interviews are conducted by a panel. A **panel interview** involves the candidate being interviewed simultaneously by a group. The panel typically comprises a representative of the HR department, the hiring manager, and potential coworkers, superiors, and/or reporting employees. Slightly over 64 percent of HR managers conduct interviews as a member or lead of an interview panel.[16] There are many advantages to this format, including having several people hearing and recording the same information, saving time and money by condensing the process into one interview, and reducing interviewer errors and the possibility of human rights violations. Panel interviews are perceived as more fair than one-on-one interviews, thus reducing the probability of complaints or litigation.[17]

The interview is one of the most common and popular devices used for selecting job applicants. In fact, it was the only selection method being used by 100 percent of the respondents in a recent survey of 202 Canadian organizations.[18] The ironic thing about interviews is that while virtually all employers use them, much of the earlier research gave selection interviews low marks in terms of validity. Today, however, studies affirm that the interview is "generally a much better predictor of performance than previously thought and is comparable with many other selection techniques," as long as the proper administration technique is selected.[19]

## Classification of Interviews

Selection interviews can be classified in three ways: according to structure, the type of questions, and the type of interviews.

**THE STRUCTURE OF THE INTERVIEW** First, interviews can be classified according to the degree to which they are structured. In an **unstructured interview**, questions are asked as they come to mind. While questions may be specified in advance, they usually are not, and there is seldom a formalized guide for scoring the quality of each answer. Interviewees for the same job thus may or may not be asked the same or similar questions, and the interview's unstructured nature allows the interviewer to ask questions based on the candidate's last statements and to pursue points of interest as they develop. While extremely friendly, unstructured interviews lack reliability and are used for selection purposes by only 17 percent of Canadian organizations.[20]

A panel interview is an efficient and cost-effective way of permitting a number of qualified persons to assess a candidate's KSAs.

The interview can also be structured. In the classic **structured interview**, the questions and acceptable responses are specified in advance and the responses are rated for appropriateness of content.[21] In practice, however, most structured interviews do not involve specifying and rating responses in advance. Instead, each candidate is asked a series of predetermined, job-related questions based on the job description and specification. However, a totally structured interview does not provide the flexibility to pursue points of interest as they develop, which may result in an interview that seems quite mechanical to all concerned.

Between these two extremes is the **semi-structured interview**, which involves a combination of preset, structured questions based on the job description and specification and a series of preset, candidate-specific, job-related questions based on information provided on the application form and/or résumé. Gaps in a candidate's employment history are explored to determine why and what the candidate did during times of unemployment. The questions asked of all candidates facilitate candidate comparison, while the job-related, candidate-specific questions make the interview more conversational. A realistic approach that yields comparable answers and in-depth insights, the mixed interview format is extremely popular.

**THE TYPES OF QUESTIONS** Interviews can also be classified according to the way the questions are designed. A **situational interview (SI)** is one in which the questions focus on the individual's ability to project what his or her behaviour would be in a given situation.[22] The underlying premise is that stated intentions predict behaviour. For example, a candidate for a supervisory position might be asked how he or she would respond to an employee coming to work late three days in a row. The interview can be both *structured/semi-structured* and *situational,* with predetermined questions requiring the candidate to project what his or her behaviour would be. In this situation, the applicant could be evaluated, say, on whether he or she would try to determine if the employee was experiencing some difficulty in getting to work on time or would simply issue a verbal or written warning.

The **behavioural interview**, also known **as a behaviour descriptive interview (BDI)**, involves describing various situations and asking interviewees how they behaved *in the past* in such situations.[23] Thus, while situational interviews ask interviewees to describe how they *would* react to a situation, the BDI asks interviewees to describe how they *did* react to situations in the past, giving specific examples and explaining the consequences of their actions.[24] The underlying assumption is that the best predictor of future performance is past performance in similar circumstances.

Studies have found that BDI questions are included in interviews with the following regularity: "always" (48.2 percent) or "most of the time" (37.5 percent). Situational interview questions are asked as well, but with greater variability—"always" (17.6 percent), "most of the time" (26.6 percent), or "sometimes" (34.6 percent). Only 16 percent of HR managers report always including both BDI and SI questions.[25]

**TYPES OF INTERVIEWS** While most interviews are conducted by a panel of interviewers, there are other approaches used: one on one, sequentially, computerized, or via videoconferencing.

Interviews can be administered *one on one*. As the name implies, this process involves one interviewer and one interviewee. One-on-one interviews are generally easier to arrange and conduct, yet there is greater probability of error in determining candidate suitability for a position. Since the hiring decision is made exclusively by one person, the advantage of multiple interviewers discussing their perceptions of the candidate and challenging each other's assumptions does not exist. Because these checks are not in place, there is a greater likelihood that bias can seep into the hiring decision.

In a **sequential interview**, several people interview the applicant in sequence before a selection decision is made. In an unstructured sequential interview, each interviewer may look at the applicant from his or her own point of view, ask different questions, and form an independent opinion of the candidate. On the other hand, in a structured sequential or serialized interview, each interviewer rates the candidate on a standard evaluation form, and the ratings are compared before the hiring decision is made.[26]

Increasingly, interviews are not administered by people at all but are computerized. A **computerized selection interview** is one in which a candidate's oral and/or computerized responses are obtained in response to computerized oral or written questions and/or situations. The basic idea is to present to each

**selection interview** A procedure designed to predict future job performance on the basis of applicants' responses to oral inquiries.

**panel interview** An interview in which a group of interviewers questions the applicant.

**unstructured interview** An unstructured, conversational-style interview in which the interviewer pursues points of interest as they come up in response to questions.

**structured interview** An interview following a set sequence of questions.

**semi-structured interview** An interview format that combines the structured and unstructured techniques.

**situational interview** A series of job-related questions that focus on how the candidate would behave in a given situation.

**behavioural or behaviour descriptive interview (BDI)** A series of job-related questions that focus on relevant past job-related behaviours.

**sequential interview** An interview in which the applicant is interviewed sequentially by several persons, who each rate the applicant on a standard form.

**computerized selection interview** An interview technique involving a computer rather than a person. A candidate's oral and/or computerized responses to computer-generated oral or written questions and/or situations are obtained and assessed.

Microsoft Online Résumé Building and Pre-screening **www.microsoft.com/jobs**

Cisco Career Site **www.cisco.com/jobs**

applicant a series of questions (often multiple choice) regarding his or her KSAs for the job for which he or she has applied. Once the questions have been answered, they are automatically scored, and the candidates are ranked according to a predetermined weighting scale based on the relative importance of each of the selection criteria.

**Videoconferencing** is a recent technology that uses webcams to bring the interviewer(s) and the interviewee together for an interview when they are separated by distance. The advantages of videoconferencing include speeding up the search process; eliminating costs associated with travel and hotel accommodations, especially for candidates in remote locations; and reducing time demands on candidates. While videoconferencing can help employers save time and money, applicants often have difficulty making a positive first impression when speaking into a camera rather than being in a room with a panel. At the U.S. division of UBS, a Switzerland-based international investment banking firm, videoconferencing has been used to interview candidates for the past five years. It is mainly used to interview candidates who would work in the United States but would have work responsibilities in the company's international offices. For example, if the job is in New York and involves working in the London branch, a videoconference interview can be set up to allow the candidate to be interviewed by panels in New York and London. According to the company's HR manager, their interview panels get about 90 percent of the same information from the videoconference as they get from face-to-face meetings.[27] Some companies prefer to record video interviews to share with managers who did not participate in the original interview. In order to do this, written permission from candidates is required beforehand.

## Interviewing and the Law

As a selection procedure, interviews must comply with human rights legislation. Doing so requires keeping the following guidelines in mind:

1. Interviewers cannot ask questions that would violate human rights legislation, either directly or indirectly. Questions cannot be asked about candidates' marital status, childcare arrangements, ethnic background, political affiliation, religion, or workers' compensation history, for example.
2. All interviewees must be treated in the same manner. An interviewer cannot ask only female applicants for a factory position to demonstrate their lifting abilities, for example, or question female applicants for sales positions about their willingness to travel, but not male candidates.

LEGALcompliance

3. Cutting short an interview based on preconceived notions about the gender or race of the "ideal" candidate should also be avoided, since this is another example of illegal differential treatment.
4. A helpful phrase to keep in mind when designing interview questions is: "This job requires . . . " Interviewers who focus on the job description and job specification can gather all of the information required to assess applicants without infringing on the candidates' legal rights.

## Common Interviewing Mistakes

There are several common interviewing errors that undermine the usefulness of interviews. These include:

**POOR PLANNING** All those involved in the process should plan the interview well in advance. What type of interview will it be? Who will do it? When? How will it be structured and administered? And, most importantly, what job-related questions will be asked?

**SNAP JUDGMENTS** One of the most consistent research findings is that interviewers tend to jump to conclusions—make snap judgments—during the first few minutes of the interview or even before the interview begins, based on the candidates' test scores or résumé data. Not only might it be unlawful to do this, it is probably unwise—you might jump to the wrong conclusions and overlook an excellent candidate.

**NEGATIVE BIAS** Some interviewers seem to have a consistent negative bias. They are generally more influenced by unfavourable than favourable information about the candidate. Also, their impressions are much more likely to change from favourable to unfavourable than vice versa. It is thus common for interviewers to turn interviews into a search for negative information, which means that most interviews are probably loaded against the applicant.[28]

**HALO EFFECT** It is also possible, though, for a positive initial impression to distort an interviewer's rating of a candidate, such that subsequent information is judged with a positive bias. This is known as the halo effect. An applicant who has a pleasant smile and firm handshake, for example, may be judged positively before the interview even begins. Having gained that positive initial impression, the interviewer may not seek contradictory information when listening to the candidate's answers to the questions posed.

**POOR KNOWLEDGE OF THE JOB** Interviewers who do not know precisely what the job entails and what sort of candidate is best suited for it usually make their decisions based on incorrect stereotypes about what a good applicant is. They then erroneously match interviewees with their incorrect stereotypes. On the other hand, interviewers who have a clear understanding of what the job entails conduct more effective interviews.

**PRESSURE TO HIRE** Pressure to hire also undermines an interview's usefulness, since interviewers often lower their standards in such situations. In one study, a group of managers was told to assume that they were behind in their recruiting schedule. A second group was told that they were ahead of schedule. Those "behind" evaluated the same recruits much more highly than did those "ahead."

**INFLUENCE OF NON-VERBAL BEHAVIOUR** Interviewers are influenced by the applicant's non-verbal behaviour. For example, several studies have shown that applicants who demonstrate greater eye contact, head movement, smiling, and other such non-verbal behaviours are rated more highly. In fact, these non-verbal behaviours often account for more than 80 percent of the applicant's rating.[29] An applicant's attractiveness and gender also play a role.[30] In general, studies find that more favourable traits and successful life outcomes are ascribed to physically attractive people.[31]

**TELEGRAPHING** Some interviewers are so anxious to fill a job that they help the applicants respond correctly to their questions by telegraphing the expected answer.[32] An obvious example might be a question like, "This job calls for handling a lot of stress. You can do that, can't you?" The telegraphing is not always so obvious. For example, favourable first impressions of candidates tend to be linked to use of a more positive interview style. This can translate into sending subtle cues regarding the preferred response, such as a smile or nod.[33]

**TOO MUCH/TOO LITTLE TALKING** Providing too much or too little guidance is another common interviewer error. If the applicant is permitted to dominate the interview, the interviewer may not have a chance to ask his or her prepared questions and often learns very little about the candidate's job-related skills. At the other extreme, some interviewers talk so much that the interviewee is not given enough time to answer questions.[34] As a general rule, candidates should talk at least 75 percent of the time so that the panel can gather sufficient data to make an informed hiring decision.[35]

## Designing an Effective Interview

Problems such as those just described can be avoided by training panel members how to design and conduct effective interviews. Training helps the panel develop approaches for minimizing common interview mistakes; develop legally defensible questions that target specific knowledge, skills, and abilities; articulate the responses they are looking for; collect and evaluate interview data; and make good hiring decisions. To allow for probing and to prevent an interview from becoming too mechanical in nature, a semi-structured format is recommended. Given their higher validity in predicting job performance, the focus should be on situational and behavioural questions.

Featured in the following Strategic HR box on page 154 are examples of companies in Alberta that are using innovative approaches to hiring in response to a 30-year low in the unemployment rate.

Designing an effective interview involves composing a series of job-related questions—primarily situational and behavioural—to be asked of all applicants for a particular job, as well as a few job-related,

**videoconferencing** A recent technology that uses webcams to bring the interviewer(s) and the interviewee together for an interview when they are separated by distance.

STRATEGIC HR

## Extreme Hiring in Alberta

With an unemployment rate hitting a 30-year low at 3.0 percent and an anticipated shortfall of 86 000 workers by the year 2015, according to the province's numbers, employers in Alberta have had to approach hiring differently from others in the rest of the country. Signing bonuses are common, with employers offering $5000 or so to new hires at the one-year mark, said Judy Harcourt of Edmonton-based Harcourt Recruiting Specialists. More companies are willing to pay for employees' moving costs if they're from out of town, she added.

Most often, though, companies are offering not just financial incentives but lifestyle sweeteners: flex time, four weeks' vacation to start, telecommuting options, gym memberships, child-care support or on-site daycare services and parking—an increasingly lucrative item in Calgary these days, said Murray Bandura, recruiting manager at the Calgary office of staffing firm Robert Half.

But apart from sweetening the pot with perks, employers have had to change the way they recruit. Trish Ham, team leader at the Calgary office of recruiting agency About Staffing, recalled one oil and gas company seeking a senior accounting person to fill a controller position. "We got our paperwork in place within the day. The following day they interviewed a candidate and by the end of the second day they had hired that candidate," said Ham. "They were intelligent about it. They knew they had found a good person and they didn't waste any time. They made the offer."

At Sutton Place Hotel in Edmonton, HR director Sherry Scott echoed this need for speed. If a résumé comes to her via a fax or an email, she can no longer afford to get to it later, as HR managers in a less frenzied market might be wont to do. "I can't just put (it) in an envelope and hope the department manager will look at it today because they won't. They're so busy," said Scott. "I have to get right up in their face and say, 'Okay. I've found a really great person. Let's get them in the door and meet them and hire them.'" The same goes for job fairs. Scott has to call back the candidates the next day because she knows that's exactly what the 120 other employers at the job fair will be doing.

Scott also found a way to keep recruiting around the clock. She distributed a special set of business cards among managers and even personal contacts whose judgment she trusts. The business cards read, "You impress me." Managers hand them out to whomever they encounter in their daily lives—a cashier at the grocery store, a waitress at a restaurant—they think would make a good employee at Sutton Place. The back of the business card invites the recipient to give Scott a call if they're looking for a second job.

At the Calgary office of Apache Corporation, an oil and gas firm, decisiveness is paramount. In recent months, managers have been expected to clear their plates and make themselves available whenever a hiring opportunity comes up. That's according to a directive from the very top.

"The president has said during these challenging last few months that hiring and recruitment is an absolute priority for the managers, that they need to make themselves available. Even if they have operational issues and production issues and technical issues, they need to do whatever it takes. So stay late, come early, meet through lunch, whatever," said HR manager Barbara Atkinson.

Like Scott of Sutton Place, Atkinson can no longer afford to mull over a good résumé for a few days. Nor can she expect to find four best candidates for every position and select the one from among them. It's certainly a different modus operandi for Atkinson, who launched her HR career in the late 1970s at a staffing and recruiting firm. "In a different environment you wouldn't say to your manager, 'I've only got one. Here he is, now hire him,'" said Atkinson. "But now you do. 'Here's a guy. He's excellent, he's available, he fits our culture and the job description. If you want him, hire him.'"

At Apache, the demand for professionals is such that, even if a candidate is not suited for an immediate opening, but is otherwise a strong fit, the company might still be inclined to hire that person. "There are so many opportunities in so many different areas that it's just a matter of saying, 'Well, maybe we don't take him for this position but we want him to grow in that position because that's where he's strong. We weren't going to hire that next but let's do so anyway,'" she said.

Some companies even go further and do away with job descriptions, said Byrne Luft, regional vice-president of staffing firm Manpower.

"They don't hire people for the box in the organizational chart. Instead, they try to find positions that work around a person's competency," said Luft. That would involve managers understanding employees enough to know what their strengths are, what they want to stay focused on and what aspects of the job they'd rather hand off to someone else. Manpower is among those adopting this concept, said Luft. "We're bringing people in and looking at their talent and seeing how we can maximize their talent when we integrate them in the company," he said. The advantage of such a practice is that it completely engages the employees—"they're doing exactly what they love to do"—and retention improves, he said. What's more, it puts employees in positions where they're performing at their best, thereby raising performance across the organization.

This is an example of the kind of innovation employers in a tight labour market have had to adopt, said Byrne. It's where the future lies, he thinks, and what organizations will have to move toward in several years' time. But in a market such as Alberta, it's already here.

Source: Extracted from U. Vu, "Under Extreme Pressure," *Canadian HR Reporter.* Toronto: November 20, 2006, 19(20), p. 9. Reprinted with permission.

candidate-specific questions. Doing so involves the following five steps; the first two should occur prior to recruitment.[36]

**Step 1.** *Deciding Who Will Be Involved in the Selection Process and Developing Selection Criteria.* Members of the interview panel should be selected as soon as the job opening is identified, since they will be involved in developing the selection criteria and interview questions. Panels are most effective when they comprise three to four key stakeholders, including the candidate's prospective manager, an HR representative, and a prospective colleague. Panels with more than six members are discouraged as they often create a high degree of anxiety for candidates.[37] Once selected, the panel members develop selection criteria by thoroughly examining the job description and job specification.

**Step 2.** *Specifying Musts and Wants.* Based on a review of the job description and job specification, the panel should reach consensus on the competencies—knowledge, skills, abilities, and attributes—required to fulfill the vacancy and the desired degree of proficiency required in each domain. The list of competencies should include technical skills and performance skills. **Technical skills** are the specific knowledge and skills required to perform the job that are usually learned from one's formal education, such as accounting skills or knowledge of Excel. **Performance skills** are attributes that are learned through life experience, such as organizational skills, leadership, and coping skills. Once agreed upon, the competencies should be divided into two categories: musts and wants. This step should also occur prior to recruitment. **Must criteria** are those that are absolutely essential for the job and include a measurable standard of acceptability or are absolute and can be screened initially on paper or online.

The **want criteria** include skills and abilities that cannot be screened on paper (such as verbal communication skills) or are not readily measurable (such as leadership ability, teamwork skills, and enthusiasm), as well as qualifications that are desirable but not critical (such as knowledge of the specific word processing software package used at a firm). Want criteria should be weighted by level of importance.

**Step 3.** *Determining Assessment Strategies and Developing an Evaluation Form.* Once the must and want criteria have been identified, appropriate strategies for learning about each should be specified. For example, word processing skills are best assessed through hands-on testing rather than interview questions. Want criteria become the basis for candidate comparison and evaluation, as illustrated in Figure 5.4. During each step of the selection process, including verification of references, information about each of the want criteria should be gathered and recorded. At the end,

**technical skills** Specific knowledge and skills required to perform a job that are usually learned from one's formal education, such as accounting skills or knowledge of Excel.

**performance skills** Attributes that are learned through life experiences, such as organizational skills, leadership, and coping skills.

**must criteria** Requirements that are absolutely essential for a job and include a measurable standard of acceptability or are absolute and can be screened initially on paper.

**want criteria** Those criteria that have been culled from the must list. They represent qualifications that cannot be screened on paper or are not readily measurable as well as those that are highly desirable but not critical.

## *figure* 5.4 Worksheet—Comparison of Candidates for a Secretarial Position

| Criteria | Alternatives | | | | | |
|---|---|---|---|---|---|---|
| | **A** Smith | | **B** Brown | | **C** Yuill | |
| **Must** | **Info** | **Go/No** | **Info** | **Go/No** | **Info** | **Go/No** |
| Education — Office Admin. diploma or equivalent experience (3 years' clerical/secretarial experience) | Office admin. diploma | Go | Office admin. diploma | Go | No diploma | No Go |
| Experience — At least 2 years' secretarial/clerical experience | 3 years' experience | Go | 2 years' experience | Go | 1 year related experience | |

| **Wants** | **Wt.** | **Info** | **Sc.** | **Wt. Sc.** | **Info** | **Sc.** | **Wt. Sc.** | **Info** | **Sc.** | **Wt. Sc.** |
|---|---|---|---|---|---|---|---|---|---|---|
| Keyboarding/word processing | 10 | Word processing test | 9 | 90 | Word processing test | 10 | 100 | | | |
| Good oral communication | 9 | Interview assessment | 9 | 81 | Interview assessment | 9 | 81 | | | |
| Good spelling/grammar | 9 | Test results | 8 | 72 | Test results | 9 | 81 | | | |
| Organizational ability | 9 | Interview questions/simulation/ reference checking | 8 | 72 | Interview questions/simulation/ reference checking | 9 | 81 | | | |
| Initiative | 8 | Interview questions/simulation/ reference checking | 7 | 56 | Interview questions/simulation/ reference checking | 8 | 64 | | | |
| High ethical standards | 7 | Interview questions/simulation/ reference checking | 7 | 49 | Interview questions/simulation/ reference checking | 7 | 49 | | | |
| Shorthand skills (or speed writing) | 4 | Interview question and test results | 4 | 16 | Interview question and test results | 0 | 0 | | | |
| Designated group member, other than white female | 2 | Application form | 2 | 4 | Application form | 0 | 0 | | | |
| | | | | 440 | | | 456 | | | |

TOP CANDIDATE

each candidate can be assessed and given an overall score by adding his or her score on each of the wants. (Note: Using this scoring process, designated group member status will only become a deciding factor if two candidates are equally qualified. That is what employment equity is supposed to mean!)

**RPC 5-2 >**

**Analyzes position requirements to establish selection criteria**

**Step 4.** *Developing Interview Questions to Be Asked of All Candidates.* Questions should be prepared to specifically target the competencies identified in step 2 and be consistent with business necessity so that panelists can gather data that determine which candidate is best suited for the job. Questions relating to the technical aspects of the job are known as *job-knowledge questions,* which assess whether candidates have the basic knowledge needed to perform the job. *Worker-requirements* or *willingness questions* gauge the applicants' motivation and willingness to perform under prevailing working conditions. Examples include questions about shift work, travel, or relocation associated with the job.

**Step 5.** *Developing Candidate-Specific Questions.* Next, a few open-ended, job-related questions that are candidate specific should be planned, based on each candidate's résumé and application form. Examples might include: "What specific duties did you perform at SaskPower that would be transferable to the job for which you are applying here?" or "You indicated on your résumé that you were president of the students' council when you were in high school. What knowledge or skills did you acquire through this position that would be beneficial to performing the job here?"

## Conducting an Effective Interview

While the following discussion focuses on a semi-structured panel interview, the steps described should be involved in every in-person selection interview.[38]

**PLANNING THE INTERVIEW** One panelist, usually the HR representative, is appointed the facilitator. The facilitator's responsibilities include introducing panel members to candidates, explaining the interview process, facilitating communication during the interview, keeping the interview on track, and ensuring that all competencies are covered in the interview and that no one panel member dominates the discussion.[39]

Prior to conducting interviews, agreement should be reached on the procedure that will be followed. Sometimes, all members of the team ask a question in turn; in other situations, only one member of the team asks questions and the others serve as observers. A comfortable, quiet, non-stressful setting should be selected. Sitting around a large table in a conference room is much more appropriate and far less stressful than having all panel members seated across from the candidate behind a table or desk, which forms both physical and psychological barriers. Special planning is required when assessing candidates with disabilities. An example is provided in the Workforce Diversity box on page 158.

**ESTABLISHING RAPPORT** The main reason for an interview is to find out as much as possible about the candidate's fit with the job specifications, something that is difficult to do if the individual is tense and nervous. The candidate should be greeted in a friendly manner and put at ease. Generally, easy, non-controversial questions are asked at the beginning of an interview in order to reduce the applicant's tension.

Tips for conducting effective interviews are discussed in the Strategic HR Box on page 159.

**ASKING QUESTIONS AND TAKING NOTES** The questions written in advance should then be asked in order. Interviewers should listen carefully and encourage the candidate to express his or her thoughts and ideas fully. During the interview, all panel members should record each of the applicant's responses on the interview questionnaire. Taking notes increases the utility of the interview process, since doing so:[40]

1. reduces the likelihood of forgetting job-relevant information and subsequently reconstructing forgotten information in accordance with biases and stereotypes
2. reduces the likelihood of making a snap judgment and helps prevent the halo effect, negative emphasis, and candidate-order errors
3. helps ensure that all candidates are assessed on the same criteria

**frontLINE tips**

Studies have found that interviewers take either summary (52.8 percent) or verbatim (31.9 percent) notes during an interview. Notes about candidates not selected are

**WORKFORCE DIVERSITY**

## Looking for a Few Good Workers?

Given the impending labour shortage, hiring persons with disabilities is not only legally required and good public relations, it is a necessity. Employees who are visually impaired are an asset to any organization as they have excellent attendance records and a greater retention rate in organizations for which they are employed. Many companies that employ visually impaired individuals find that they are very loyal and productive employees. However, when a company encounters a visually impaired candidate, it needs to consider altering its selection processes to help accommodate the applicant. Tips to assist visually impaired applicants include:

- have the application available in electronic form. Visually impaired applicants then can use computers with Braille, speech output or screen magnification to read and complete the application.
- provide the application in advance of the interview so the applicant can complete it at home.
- ask if the applicant wants assistance in an unfamiliar environment. Some people with visual impairments prefer to take someone's arm above the elbow, others prefer to follow verbal directions.
- when entering the interview room, describe the setting to the applicant. For example, you might say, "We are going to sit at a round table. Your chair is on the left."
- if pre-employment tests are routinely administered, discuss accommodations with the applicant to make the test accessible. For example, the test could be given electronically using appropriate assistive technology. Or another employee could read the questions and record the applicant's answers.
- focus on an applicant's qualifications, not his or her visual impairment.
- never pet a guide dog. Although it may be friendly, a guide dog is a working animal.
- don't be afraid to use terms like "Do you see what I mean?" Visually impaired people use them, too.

Source: Excerpted from K. Tyler, "Looking for a Few Good Workers?" *HR Magazine*, December 2000, pp. 129–134. Reprinted with permission of *HR Magazine*, published by the Society for Human Resource Management, Alexandra, VA.

The rapport established with a job applicant not only puts the person at ease but also reflects the company's attitude toward its public.

often retained for more than two years (23.2 percent) or one to two years (31.2 percent); however, 43 percent of interviewers retain their notes for less than one year. Based on time limits for human rights complaints, organizations should keep interview notes for at least one year.[41]

**GIVING INFORMATION** As candidates also need to make a decision as to whether a position and organization meet their professional and career goals, it is important to ensure that all relevant information is given regarding the position, the organization, and career prospects. Candidates should be given an opportunity at the end of the interview to ask questions about the job and the organization that were not addressed.

It is recommended that candidates be given a **realistic job preview (RJP)**. Doing so is an excellent strategy for creating appropriate expectations about the job.[42] As the name indicates, an RJP presents realistic information about the job demands, the organization's expectations, and the work environment. Candidates thereby learn about both the positive and negative aspects of the job and firm. RJPs should be tailored to the needs of the organization.

**CLOSING THE INTERVIEW** All interviews should be ended on a positive note. The interviewee should be thanked and informed about subsequent steps in the selection process and their timing. As well, candidates should be told when and how they will be notified.

**REVIEWING NOTES AND EVALUATING THE CANDIDATE** Immediately following each interview, the applicant's interview performance should be rated by each panel

STRATEGIC HR

## Ten Steps to the Right Fit

For a company's recruitment expert, it's important to stay on top of innovative practices and not to fall into the trap of considering only résumés from conventional candidates. To assist in the evaluation of atypical candidates, here are some tips:

- If you're not familiar with the industry or type of work outlined in a résumé, conduct some research to broaden your understanding of the skills presented and to better determine their transferability. Don't make the excuse you're too busy—taking the time to learn now will provide you with a competitive edge as the recruitment market tightens.
- Begin interviews by asking individuals to tell their work history in a chronological order, including how it transpired. Investigate any inconsistencies or areas of concern to ensure you are satisfied with the narrative. For example, if there are gaps in experience, explore why and how they have been managed, and find out whether there are valid reasons behind them or if they are indicative of someone with a serious attitude problem.
- Determine the individual's core competencies, how they align with the job and the organizational profile.
- Drill down to uncover specifics that enable the evaluation of someone's candidacy against stated selection criteria. If "relationship management" is a key criterion, then delve into the person's qualifications in this area and follow up with references to validate the information gathered through the interview.
- Probe to get a clear sense about their vision for successfully navigating or delivering in the position.
- Make every effort to ascertain their true motivation for assuming this new path and find out if the candidate is running away from or toward an opportunity.
- Ask questions that enable you to assess whether someone can make the shift both successfully and happily into a "T-4 person."
- Consider using a reliable assessment tool that will measure the individual's behaviour against the organizational and job profile.
- Employ the services of a qualified professional career coach to conduct an in-depth analysis of the individual's competencies, attributes and values.
- Take the time to confirm references. Perform background checks—for credit, criminal history, and education—and carry out a full 360-degree reference check to validate key data.

Source: "Ten steps to the right fit," *Canadian HR Reporter*. Toronto: Feb 13, 2006. Vol. 19, Issue 3; p. 17. Reprinted with permission.

member independently, based on a review of his or her notes. Since interviews are only one step in the process and a final decision cannot be reached until all assessments (including reference checking) have been completed, these evaluations should not be shared at this point in time.

## 5.4 STEP 3: SELECTION TESTING

Selection testing, also known as psychometric assessment, is a common screening device used by organizations for hiring and promotion purposes. There are more than 5000 selection tests available to assess specific job-related skills in addition to general intelligence, personality characteristics, mental abilities, interests, and preferences.[43] Testing techniques provide efficient, standardized procedures for screening candidates.

The use of valid tests can significantly assist in the selection of the most qualified candidate and increase output substantially. Studies have found that selection testing is a more accurate predictor of job performance than interviews, background investigation, or reference checks. Selection testing enables panelists to move away from subjective criteria toward more objective means of ascertaining whether a candidate is the right fit for the job.[44] Even though selection tests are good

**realistic job preview (RJP)** A strategy used to provide applicants with realistic information—both positive and negative—about the job demands, the organization's expectations, and the work environment.

## *In-class Notes*

**The Selection Interview**

- Selection interviews vary by:
  - structure (unstructured, structured, semi-structured)
  - type of questions (situational, behavioural)
  - type of interviews (one-on-one, sequential, computerized, or via videoconferencing)
- Common interviewing mistakes include poor planning, snap judgments, negative bias, halo effect, poor knowledge of the job, pressure to hire, influence of non-verbal behaviour, telegraphing, and too much/too little talking
- Designing an effective interview involves deciding who will be involved, specifying "must" and "want" criteria, determining assessment strategies and developing an evaluation form, developing interview questions, and developing candidate-specific questions.
- Conducting an effective interview requires planning, establishing rapport, asking questions, giving information, closing the interview, and reviewing notes.

predictors of job performance, they are not 100 percent accurate in assessing candidates. For this reason, assessments should not represent more than 30 percent of the hiring decision.[45]

The use of tests to assist with hiring and/or promotion decisions is becoming more common. In a recent study involving 202 Canadian firms, two-thirds of the respondents indicated that they use at least one type of testing method in their selection process to supplement interview results.[46] Off-the-shelf tests are preferred by 89 percent of employers, with 8 percent preferring to use tests that have been specifically designed for their own use, such as testing at senior management levels. Tests to determine specific skills are most popular (48 percent), followed by general ability tests (41 percent), literacy and numeracy tests (40 percent), and aptitude tests (35 percent).[47] In general, testing is more prevalent in larger organizations. This reflects their greater need for efficient, standardized procedures to screen large numbers of candidates and their ability to finance testing programs.

The Internet has had a significant impact on selection testing, with 65 percent of employers administering some of their tests online. Web-based testing makes for a better experience, as the candidate can complete the instrument when and where it is convenient, answers can be matched against a profile of the position, and results can be delivered to the interview panel without delay.[48] However, while 91 percent of employers believe online testing is easier and faster to administer, 78 percent still consider paper-based testing the most popular medium.

## Fundamental Guidelines to Effective Testing

The Canadian Psychological Association has developed and published comprehensive testing standards

To assess the traits on which job success depends, many firms, such as those that rely on computer literacy, administer a skills assessment test before hiring.

covering such areas as test instrumentation, test use and administration, scoring, and reporting.[49] Selection testing involves many different varieties of tests that purport to measure such diverse attributes of candidates as job performance and honesty. It is important, therefore, that firms do a great deal of planning, analysis, and experimentation to ensure that the tests they use best satisfy their needs. They also need to ensure that tests produce accurate results, that they are administered appropriately, and that they do not contravene legislation.

## Types of Tests

A number of the tests commonly used in selection can conveniently be classified according to whether they measure cognitive (thinking) abilities, motor and physical abilities, personality and interests, or achievement.[50] Other potential testing strategies include work sampling, management assessment centres, situational testing, honesty testing, medical examination, and drug testing.

**TESTS OF COGNITIVE ABILITIES** Included in this category are tests of general reasoning ability (intelligence), tests of emotional intelligence, and tests of specific thinking skills such as memory and inductive reasoning.

**Intelligence quotient (IQ) tests** are tests of general intellectual abilities. They do not measure a single "intelligence" trait but rather a number of abilities, including memory, vocabulary, verbal fluency, and numerical ability. Intelligence is often measured with individually administered tests, such as the Stanford-Binet Test or the Wechsler Test.

**Emotional intelligence (EI) tests** measure the ability to monitor one's own emotions and the emotions of others and use that knowledge to guide thoughts and actions. Someone with a high emotional quotient (EQ) is self-aware, can control his or her impulses, motivates himself or herself, and demonstrates empathy and social awareness.

Tests that measure specific thinking skills, such as inductive and deductive reasoning, verbal comprehension, memory, and numerical ability, are often called **aptitude tests**, since they purport to measure an applicant's aptitudes for the job in question—that is, the applicant's potential to perform the job once given proper training. An example is the test of mechanical comprehension, which tests the applicant's understanding of basic mechanical principles. It may therefore reflect a person's aptitude for jobs—like that of machinist or engineer—that require mechanical comprehension.

Some firms administer and score aptitude tests online. At Microsoft, for example, after completing an online aptitude test, potential candidates are provided with a list of recommended jobs.

**TESTS OF MOTOR AND PHYSICAL ABILITIES** There are many *motor abilities* that a firm might want to measure. These include finger dexterity, manual dexterity, speed of arm movement, and reaction time. The Crawford Small Parts Dexterity Test, as illustrated in Figure 5.5, is an example. It measures the speed and accuracy of simple judgment, as well as the speed of finger, hand, and arm movements. Tests of physical abilities—such as static strength (lifting weights),

**intelligence quotient (IQ) tests** Tests that measure general intellectual abilities, such as verbal comprehension, inductive reasoning, memory, numerical ability, speed of perception, spatial visualization, and word fluency.

**emotional intelligence (EI) tests** Tests that measure ability to monitor one's own emotions and the emotions of others and use that knowledge to guide thoughts and actions.

**aptitude tests** Tests that measure an individual's aptitude or potential to perform a job, provided he or she is given proper training.

*figure 5.5* **Crawford Small Parts Dexterity Test**

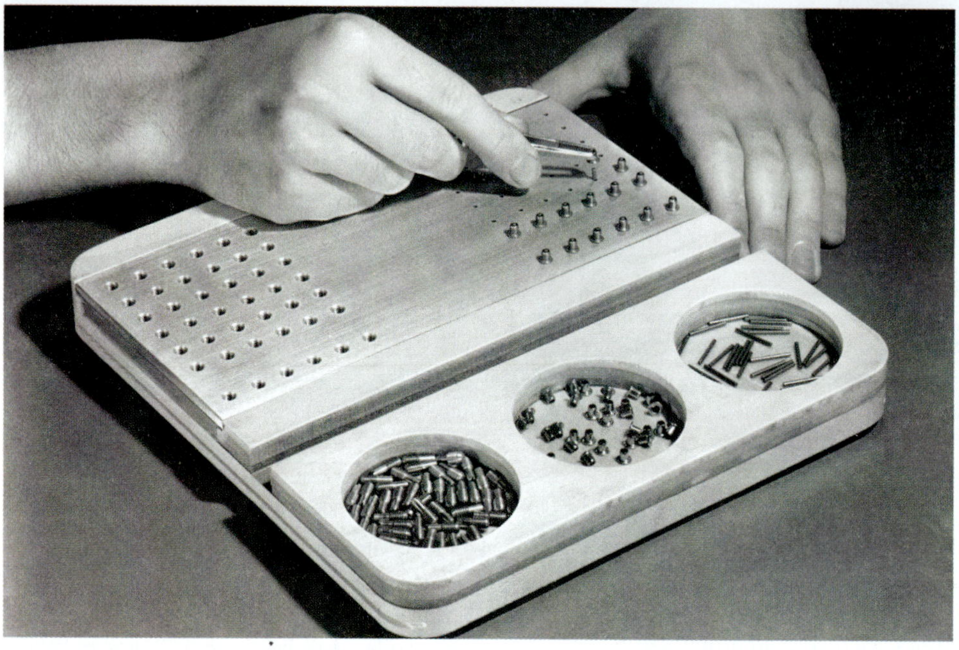

Source: The Psychological Corporation.

dynamic strength (like pull-ups), body coordination (as in jumping rope), and stamina[51]—may also be required.[52] For example, some firms use *Functional Abilities Evaluations (FAE)* to assist with placement decisions. An FAE, which measures a series of physical abilities ranging from lifting to pulling and pushing, sitting, squatting, climbing, and carrying— is particularly useful for positions with a multitude of physical demands, such as firefighter and police officer.[53] It is important to ensure that physical abilities tests do not violate human rights legislation.

**TESTS OF PERSONALITY AND INTERESTS** A person's mental and physical abilities are seldom sufficient to explain his or her job performance. Other factors, such as the person's motivation and interpersonal skills, are also important. Personality and interests inventories are sometimes used as predictors of such intangibles.

**Personality tests** can measure basic aspects of an applicant's personality, such as introversion, stability, and motivation. Many of these tests are *projective*. An ambiguous stimulus (like an inkblot or clouded picture) is presented to the test taker, and he or she is asked to interpret or react to it. Since the pictures are ambiguous, the person's interpretation must come from within—he or she supposedly *projects* into the picture his or her own emotional attitudes about life. The Thematic Apperception Test is one such test. Thus, a security-oriented person might describe the woman in Figure 5.6 as "my mother worrying about what I will do if I lose my job."

**AN ETHICAL DILEMMA**

As the employment manager, how would you inform an applicant that he or she is being eliminated from a competition based on personality test results?

Personality tests—particularly the projective type—are the most difficult tests to evaluate and use. An expert must analyze the test taker's interpretations and reactions and infer from them his or her personality. The usefulness of such tests for selection then assumes that it is possible to find a relationship between a measurable personality trait (such as introversion) and success on the job.[54]

A third study confirms the potential usefulness of personality tests for selection while underscoring the importance of job analysis. Researchers concluded that the predictive power of a personality test can be quite high.[55] However, they also found that the full potential of

***figure*** **5.6 Sample Picture from Thematic Apperception Test**

How do you interpret this picture?

Source: Reprinted by permission of the publishers from Henry A. Murray, "Thematic Apperception Test," Plate 12F, Cambridge, Mass.: Harvard University Press, 1943.

personality testing in selection will be realized only when careful job analysis becomes the "standard practice for determining which traits are relevant to predicting performance on a given job."[56] In summary, personality tests can help employers predict which candidates will succeed on the job and which will not. However, the job analysis and validation study must be carefully executed.

**ACHIEVEMENT TESTS** An *achievement test* is basically a measure of what a person has learned. Most of the tests taken in school are achievement tests. They measure knowledge and/or proficiency in such areas as economics, marketing, or HRM.

Achievement tests are also widely used in selection. For example, the Purdue Test for Machinists and Machine Operators tests the job knowledge of experienced machinists with such questions as, "What is meant by 'tolerance'?" Other tests are available for electricians, welders, carpenters, and so forth. In addition to job knowledge, achievement tests measure an applicant's abilities; a keyboarding test is one example.

**WORK SAMPLING TESTS** *Work samples* differ from most of the tests that we have discussed because they focus on measuring job performance directly.[57] Personality and interest inventories aim to predict job performance by measuring such traits as extroversion or interests. Work sampling measures how a candidate actually performs some of the job's basic tasks: The clear link between the work sample and actual job requirements makes such testing more legally defensible. Work sampling can be used to identify top performing candidates for jobs ranging from entry level to executive management. As each applicant performs the crucial tasks, the test administrator monitors his or her work and completes a checklist to record the approach taken. This ensures that an organization can identify who can do the work, instead of identifying who can only tell you they know how to do the work. Studies have found work sampling to be the most powerful and cost-effective approach currently available, with advantages including decreases in the areas of turnover (20 percent), selection costs (40 percent), and number of interviews required (75 percent), as well as significant improvements in the quality and productivity of new recruits.[58]

It is important to determine the relationship between applicants' scores on work samples and their actual performance on the job, in order to validate the work sampling test. Then, once it has been shown that the work sample is a valid predictor of job success, the employer can begin using it for selection.

Zappos, a company that sells shoes online, is renowned for its culture of customer service and its unique approach to work sampling. Hiring the right team members for its call centre is one of its most pressing concerns. All new recruits go through a four-week customer loyalty training program that pays them full salary. After one week in intensive training, during which new recruits are exposed to call centre operations and expected to demonstrate their ability to function in a high-volume customer-service environment, Zappos offers each recruit $1000 to quit. If they take the money, it demonstrates that they are lacking the commitment to customer service that is required to work at Zappos. Approximately 10 percent of new recruits take the cash.[59]

**personality tests** Instruments used to measure basic aspects of personality, such as introversion, stability, motivation, neurotic tendency, self-confidence, self-sufficiency, and sociability.

AllInterview.com **www.allinterview.com**

Queendom Online Testing **www.queendom.com/tests**

American Psychological Association Testing and Assessment **www.apa.org/science/testing.html**

A management game or simulation is a typical component in a management assessment centre.

Interactive employment tests administered via computer are becoming popular as screening devices at many firms.

**MANAGEMENT ASSESSMENT CENTRES** In a two- to three-day **management assessment centre**, the management potential of top candidates is assessed by expert appraisers who observe them performing realistic management tasks. The centre may be a plain conference room, but it is often a special room with a one-way mirror to facilitate unobtrusive observation. The possible benefits of this high-cost testing must be carefully weighed if an organization considers using it.

**SITUATIONAL TESTS** In *situational tests*, candidates are presented with hypothetical situations representative of the job for which they are applying and are evaluated on their responses.[60] Video-based situational testing is growing in popularity. In a typical test, a number of realistic video scenarios are presented, and each is followed by a multiple-choice question with several possible courses of action, from which candidates are asked to select the "best" response, in their opinion.[61] While the evidence is somewhat mixed, the results of several recent studies suggest that video-based situational tests can be useful in employee selection.[62]

**HONESTY TESTS** Honesty tests, such as polygraphs/"lie detector" tests, are generally considered to be inaccurate and invasive and are illegal in many Canadian jurisdictions; therefore, they are not widely used. However, paper-and-pencil honesty tests are used to predict job applicants' proneness to dishonesty and other forms of counterproductivity.[63] Most measure attitudes such as tolerance of others who steal, acceptance of rationalizations for theft, and admission of theft-related activities.

While several psychologists initially raised concerns about the validity of many of the paper-and-pencil honesty tests on the market, several recent studies support the validity of honesty testing as a selection technique.[64] Even where legally permissible, until more widespread evaluations are done, such tests should never be used as the sole selection strategy but rather as a supplement to other techniques, such as interviewing and reference checking.

**PHYSICAL EXAMINATION** Although physical examinations may be considered a form of "testing," they must only be conducted after a written offer of employment has been extended (except in cases where a *bona fide* occupational requirement exists, such as for food handlers). There are three main reasons why firms may include a medical examination as a step in the selection process:

1. To determine that the applicant *qualifies for the physical requirements* of the position and, if not, to document any *accommodation requirements*.
2. To establish a *record and baseline* of the applicant's health for the purpose of future insurance or compensation claims.
3. To *reduce absenteeism and accidents* by enabling the applicant and physician to identify any health- or safety-related issues or concerns that need to be addressed.

LEGALcompliance A number of legal issues regarding physical testing must be kept in mind. First, human rights laws require that if medical exams are used, they must be required of all applicants for the job in question. Second, a person with a disability cannot be rejected for a job if he or she is otherwise qualified and could perform the job duties with reasonable accommodation. Third, companies have no right to request information regarding the nature of a candidate's disability, either from the applicant or the physician performing the medical examination. The physician should only be asked to indicate, in writing, whether or not the applicant is capable of performing the essential job duties and, if not, what type of accommodation might be required.

**SUBSTANCE ABUSE TESTING** The purpose of pre-employment substance abuse testing is to avoid hiring employees who would pose unnecessary risks to themselves or others and/or perform below expectations. However, in Canada, employers are not permitted to screen candidates for substance abuse.[65] Alcohol and drug addiction is considered to be a handicap under human rights codes, and an employee cannot be discriminated against during the selection process based on a handicap.[66] What complicates the legal situation even further are employers' obligations under health and safety legislation.[67] Certainly, employers can legally discipline employees for being obviously impaired on the job, with sanctions up to and including discharge, but the right to conduct random testing is very limited. Employers are encouraged to offer workplace accommodation through such services as employee assistance programs.

Random *alcohol tests*, such as breathalyzers, can detect current impairment at the time of the test and therefore is permissible in Canada under certain circumstances. A recent Ontario court case, *Entrop v. Imperial Oil Ltd.*, determined that an employer's right to conduct random alcohol testing of employees in safety-sensitive positions depends on whether the tests are considered to be a *bona fide* occupational requirement (BFOR). In order to determine if such tests are legally permissible as a BFOR, a company must meet a three-step requirement as set out by the Supreme Court of Canada:

1. The alcohol test must be adopted for a purpose rationally connected to the performance of the job.
2. The testing provisions must be adopted in an honest and good-faith belief that they are necessary to accomplish the company's purpose.
3. The testing provisions must be reasonably necessary to accomplish a company's purpose.

## *In-class Notes*

**Selection Testing**

- Tests assess personal characteristics and specific job-related KSAs
- Tests of personal characteristics include cognitive/thinking abilities, motor/physical abilities, achievement/learning, personality/interests, and honesty tests
- Tests of job-related KSAs include work sampling tests, management assessment centres, situational tests, and medical tests such as physical examinations and substance abuse testing

**management assessment centre** A strategy used to assess candidates' management potential using a combination of realistic exercises, management games, objective testing, presentations, and interviews.

*Drug testing* remains a grey area for employers. Pre-employment testing is not permitted, even for safety-sensitive positions, as current drug testing technology does not measure actual impairment at the time of the test—it can only detect past usage. Random testing is generally not permitted, with the possible exception of safety-sensitive positions (such as truck drivers) or upon reinstatement following a workplace incident in which impairment affected performance, but only if it is one facet of a larger process of assessment of drug abuse. Only about 2 percent of Canadian companies conduct drug testing, compared with 80 percent in the United States.[68]

## 5.5 STEP 4: BACKGROUND INVESTIGATION AND REFERENCE CHECKING

An interview panel determines the kind of references it needs in order to provide a 360-degree view of the candidate. Background investigation and reference checking serve two key purposes:

1. Verifying the accuracy of the information pertaining to job-related educational qualifications and experience provided by candidates on their application forms and résumés.
2. Validating the information obtained during the other steps in the selection process.

In a recent study, for example, 99 percent of employers surveyed reported that they find reference checking to be either useful or very useful. Three-quarters conduct telephone discussions with individuals suggested by executive candidates, and 88 percent conduct reference checks for managerial, supervisory, professional, technical, and other salaried candidates. In addition, 97 percent of respondents rated verification of education licences or designations as useful or very useful.[69] Online social and business networking sites such as LinkedIn are popular vehicles for reference checking, because they provide information about the candidates that may not be evident from their résumés or interviews, and can be used to verify details.[70]

It is estimated that one in four applicants overstates his or her qualifications or achievements, attempts to hide negative information, or is deliberately evasive or untruthful.[71] More than 93 percent of the respondents in a recent survey said that they had found exaggerations on résumés, and 86 percent had found outright misrepresentations.

Whether requesting reference information in writing or asking for such information over the phone, questions should be written down in advance.

Figure 5.7 is an example of a form used for written reference checking.

### Obtaining Written Permission

As legal protection for all concerned, applicants should be asked to indicate, in writing, their willingness for the firm to check with current and/or former employers and other references. There is generally a section on the application form for this purpose. Many employers will not give out any reference information until they have received a copy of such written authorization. Educational institutions generally require written permission and the payment of a small fee prior to issuing a transcript.

With the fear of civil litigation increasing, more Canadian companies are adopting a "no-reference" policy regarding previous employees or are only willing to confirm the position held and dates of employment—especially in the case of discharged employees.[72] If complete details cannot be obtained due to a company's reference-checking policy or the unwillingness of the contacted individual to provide more than minimal information, the applicant should be asked to identify other information sources, such as individuals working within the organization who might be willing to provide reference data or people who are no longer with the firm. As with all other references, their relevance and impartiality should be taken into account.[73]

Failure to check references can lead to *negligent or wrongful hiring* suits that may involve significant damages. For example, in one case, a man became involved in an altercation at a bar, was escorted from the tavern, and was assaulted by two bouncers in the parking lot. The man was left with severe and permanent brain damage that rendered him permanently unemployable and incapable of managing his day-to-day affairs. While liability was imposed directly against the bouncers, the court went further and held the employer vicariously liable for failing to properly check the references or

**AN ETHICAL DILEMMA**

How would you respond if a former employee with a poor performance record who made few significant contributions to the company asked you to write a reference letter for him/her?

## *figure* 5.7 Form Requesting Written Reference Information

We are in the process of considering James Ridley Parrish (SIN Number: 123-456-789) for a sales position in our firm. In considering him/her, it would be helpful if we could review your appraisal of his/her previous work with you. For your information, we have enclosed a statement signed by him/her authorizing us to contact you for information on his/her previous work experience with you. We would certainly appreciate it if you would provide us with your candid opinions of his/her employment. If you have any questions or comments you would care to make, please feel free to contact us at the number listed in the attached cover letter. At any rate, thank you for your consideration of our requests for the information requested below. As you answer the questions, please keep in mind that they should be answered in terms of your knowledge of his/her previous work with you.

1. When was he/she employed with your firm? From _______ to _______
2. Was he/she under your direct supervision? ☐ Yes ☐ No
3. If not, what was your working relationship with him/her? ______________________________
4. How long have you had an opportunity to observe his/her job performance? ________________
5. What was his/her last job title with your firm? ________________________________________
6. Did he/she supervise any employees? ☐ Yes ☐ No If so, how many?
7. Why did he/she leave your company? _______________________________________________

Below is a series of questions that deal with how he/she might perform at the job for which we are considering him/her. Read the question and then use the rating scale to indicate how you think he/she would perform based on your previous knowledge of his/her work.

8. For him/her to perform best, how closely should he/she be supervised?
   - ☐ Needs no supervision
   - ☐ Needs infrequent supervision
   - ☐ Needs close, frequent supervision
9. How well does he/she react to working with details?
   - ☐ Gets easily frustrated
   - ☐ Can handle work that involves some details but works better without them
   - ☐ Details in a job pose no problems at all
10. How well do you think he/she can handle complaints from customers?
    - ☐ Would generally refuse to help resolve a customer complaint
    - ☐ Would help resolve a complaint only if a customer insisted
    - ☐ Would feel the customer is right and do everything possible to resolve a complaint
11. In what type of sales job do you think he/she would be best?
    - ☐ Handling sales of walk-in customers
    - ☐ Travelling to customer locations out-of-town to make sales
12. With respect to his/her work habits, check all of the characteristics below that describe his/her work situation:
    - ☐ Works best on a regular schedule
    - ☐ Works best under pressure
    - ☐ Works best only when in the mood
    - ☐ Works best when there is a regular series of steps to follow for solving a problem
13. Do you know of anything that would indicate if he/she would be unfit or dangerous (for example, in working with customers or co-workers or in driving an automobile) in a position with our organization? ☐ Yes ☐ No

    If "yes" please explain. ____________________________________________
14. If you have any additional comments, please write them on the back of this form.

Your Name: ____________________________________________

Your Title: ____________________________________________

Address: ____________________________________________

City State ZIP

Company: ____________________________________________

Telephone: ____________________________________________

Thank you for your time and help. The information you provided will be very useful as we review all application materials.

## *In-class Notes*

**Background Investigation and Reference Checking**

- Two key purposes are verifying the accuracy of the information provided on qualifications and experience and validating information obtained at other steps in the selection process
- Many applicants provide information that is not accurate
- Applicants should be asked to provide written permission for reference checking
- Some employers have a "no reference" policy for fear of litigation by former employees who may believe the reference provided for them is inaccurate (concept of qualified privilege protects those who provide honest references)
- Failure to check references can result in negligent/wrongful hiring litigation

criminal backgrounds of the bouncers involved. The application form for one of the bouncers was missing, and the form for the other contained false information. He had also previously been convicted of assault. The judge awarded damages of more than CDN$2 million against the bar's bouncers, the company that operated the bar, and two shareholders, both of whom were officers of the company.

LEGALcompliance

In providing reference information, the concept of *qualified privilege* is important. Generally speaking, if comments are made in confidence for a public purpose, without malice, and are honestly believed, the defence of "qualified privilege" exists. Thus, if honest, fair, and candid references are given by an individual who is asked to provide confidential information about the performance of a job applicant, then the doctrine of qualified privilege generally protects the reference giver, even if negative information about the candidate is imparted.

However, if a statement that is known to be untrue is made in an attempt to sabotage the employee's chances of finding another job or is contained in an employment evaluation or performance review, it is likely that malice will destroy the qualified privilege, and the court will not come to the rescue of the reference giver.[74]

## 5.6 STEP 5: THE HIRING DECISION AND JOB OFFER

After all the interviews have been completed, information from the multiple predictors—interviews, selection testing, background investigation, and reference checking—must be combined to make a hiring decision. The panel should evaluate candidates across each competency to determine the degree to which they meet the standards required for the job. The panel should conduct the evaluation first independently, then as a group. This ensures that each panelist's assessment of the candidates is taken into consideration. The evaluation discussion usually consists of two parts: a rating and a ranking of each candidate.

Panelists should address the following questions when evaluating candidates:

1. Can the candidate perform the job as described in the job description?
2. Can the candidate reach the performance standards set for the job?
3. Does the candidate fit into the department?
4. Does the candidate fit into the organization?
5. Does the candidate demonstrate potential for growth and development in the organization?

Organizations generally use a **clinical strategy** for evaluation, which involves making a subjective assessment of all of the information gleaned about each candidate and arriving at an overall judgment. The validity and reliability of judgments made using the clinical strategy can be improved by using tests that are objectively scored and devising a candidate rating sheet based on the weighted want criteria.

There is also a **statistical strategy**, which involves combining all of the pieces of information according to a formula and giving the job to the candidate with the highest score. Although research studies have indicated that the statistical strategy is generally more reliable and valid, most organizations use the clinical strategy.[75]

Even though the panel provides valuable insight during the evaluation of candidates, the supervisor is ultimately responsible for making the final selection decision, for a number of reasons:

1. The supervisor tends to know the technical aspects of the job best and is the most qualified to assess the applicants' job knowledge and skills.
2. The supervisor is typically best equipped to answer any job-specific questions.
3. The immediate supervisor generally has to work closely with the selected individual and must feel comfortable with that person.
4. If the supervisor is not committed to the selected individual, he or she can easily set the new hire up for failure.
5. The selected individual must fit with the current members of the department or team, something the supervisor is often best able to assess.

Once the selection decision has been made, a job offer is extended to the successful candidate. HR department staff members generally handle offers of employment, both the initial offer by phone and the follow-up in writing.

If there are two candidates who are both excellent, and the second choice would be quite acceptable to all concerned, the runner-up is often not notified until after the first-choice candidate has accepted the position. Should the first-choice candidate decline the offer, the runner-up can then be offered the job.

When the supervisor recommends hiring an individual, he or she has made a psychological commitment to assist the new employee. If the candidate turns out to be unsatisfactory, the supervisor is much more likely to accept some of the responsibility for his or her failure.

**AN ETHICAL DILEMMA**

As the HR manager, how much feedback should you provide to those individuals not selected for a position?

**RPC 5-3 >**

**Establishes appointment procedures**

## Evaluating the Selection Process

Evaluating the selection process involves considering whether the selection procedures used are effective in identifying qualified, capable, productive employees; whether the techniques used are efficient and worth the costs and trouble; and whether there are ways the process could be streamlined or improved.

**clinical strategy** A decision-making technique used to select the candidate to whom the job should be offered, which involves making a subjective evaluation of all of the information gleaned about each candidate and arriving at an overall judgment.

**statistical strategy** An objective technique used to determine to whom a job should be offered, which involves identifying the most valid predictors and weighting them through statistical methods, such as multiple regression.

Kroll Consulting—Substance Abuse Testing - **www.krollworldwide.com/services/screening/substance_abuse_testing**

CHRC Policy on Drug and Alcohol Testing **www.chrc-ccdp.ca/pdf/poldrgalceng.pdf**

## *In-class Notes*

**The Hiring Decision and Job Offer**

- Hiring decision made using either a clinical strategy (subjective evaluation of interview and test results) or a statistical strategy (scoring results of interviews and tests and giving the job to the highest-scoring candidate)
- Job offer extended to selected candidate
- Evaluation of selection process involves comparing the value of the contribution of the individual selected to the costs of selection

To answer these questions, feedback is required. Retention data and performance appraisal results can help identify successes. Feedback on failures is typically ample and includes complaints from supervisors, poor performance ratings, turnover and/or absenteeism, low employee satisfaction, union grievances or unionization attempts, and even legal challenges.

Constructive feedback can also be obtained from employees and supervisors. A questionnaire can be administered to newly hired and newly transferred or promoted employees asking for their impressions of the steps involved in the selection process. Supervisors can be asked for information about how easily and how well their recent hires seem to be adapting to the job, team, and organizational culture. In addition, an informal assessment of the performance of each newly hired and newly transferred or promoted employee can be made long before a formal appraisal is due.

In the long run, the utility of the selection procedure must be determined by looking at the quality and productivity of the chosen individuals, as well as the costs incurred in the process.

## 5.7 RELIABILITY AND VALIDITY

Because the selection process is so critical to an organization, every effort must be made to ensure that all aspects of the process are reliable and valid.

### Reliability

The degree to which interviews, tests, and other selection procedures yield comparable data over a period of time is known as **reliability**. Reliability is thus concerned with the degree of dependability, consistency, or stability of the measures used.[76] For example, if a group of interviewers selects three candidates as their top choices today but not those they chose yesterday, their judgments are obviously not reliable. Similarly, a test that results in widely variable scores when it (or an equivalent version of the test) is administered on different occasions to the same individual is unreliable.

Reliability also refers to the extent to which two or more methods (such as tests and reference checking) yield the same results or are consistent, as well as the extent to which there is agreement between two or more raters (interrater reliability). Another measure of reliability that is taken into account for tests is internal consistency. For example, suppose that there were 10 items on a vocational interest test, all of which were supposed to measure, in one way or another, the person's interest in working outdoors. To assess internal reliability, the degree to which responses to those 10 items vary together would be statistically analyzed. (This is one reason why tests often include questions that appear rather repetitive.)

There are at least four sources of unreliability:

1. The selection instrument might do a poor job of sampling. For example, one version of a college

## *In-class Notes*

**The Selection Process**

- Common steps include:
  1. prescreening applicants
  2. selection interview
  3. selection testing
  4. background investigation and reference checking
  5. hiring decision and making the job offer
- Some steps may be conducted by external parties, such as employment agencies

course test might focus on specific chapters more than the supposedly equivalent version does. Similarly, interview questions may be worded in such a way that they do not do a good job of measuring what they were supposed to, such as knowledge about a particular subject.

2. Errors may result from chance-response tendencies. For example, a test may be so hard or so boring that the candidate gives up and starts answering questions at random.
3. The conditions under which the instrument is administered might create variability. An interview room with construction noise outside may unnerve a candidate, for example, resulting in a far worse performance than if the interview had been conducted in a quiet setting.
4. There could be changes within the applicant. Interview performance after a sleepless night is typically far different from that when a candidate is well rested, for example.

## Validity

**Validity** refers to the accuracy with which a predictor measures what it is supposed to measure. In the context of selection, validity is an indicator of the extent to which data from a selection technique, such as a test or interview, are related to or predictive of subsequent performance on the job.[77] Selection procedures must, above all, be valid. Without proof of validity, there is no logical or legally permissible reason to continue using the technique to screen job applicants. To ensure that the selection techniques being used are valid, validation studies should be conducted.

**reliability** The degree to which interviews, tests, and other selection procedures yield comparable data over a period of time; in other words, the degree of dependability, consistency, or stability of the measures used.

**validity** The accuracy with which a predictor measures what it is supposed to measure.

Personnel Selection: Tips and FAQs **www.hr-guide.com/data/G362.htm**

## *In-class Notes*

**Reliability and Validity**

- Reliable interviews and tests yield consistent results over time
- Threats to reliability include poor sampling of material being assessed, chance responses, environmental distractions, and candidate factors
- Validity of interviews and tests refers to accuracy of measurement of how well the candidate will perform on the job
- Only use interviews and tests on which validation studies have been conducted

# Selection on the International Stage

When a Canadian company decides to expand its business into other countries, attracting local talent is far more complicated than translating the job posting from English into another language. What Canadians consider professional hiring practices may not be appropriate in other parts of the world. As a result, HR managers are advised to conduct extensive research on the country in which they want to do business, including culture, business practices such as hiring and compensation, customs, employee needs, expectations and motivations, legislation, political structure, and current affairs—including the relationship between Canada and the host country. With this information in hand, Canadian companies are less likely to offend candidates or violate foreign customs or legislation; hence, they can carry out their selection initiatives with greater ease.

An example of hiring differences exists in the type of interview questions asked. During job interviews in Canada, it is illegal to ask questions that are not job-related or do not have business necessity, such as questions about age, marital status, and number of children. In Latin America and Latin Europe, candidates disclose their age, marital status, and number of children on their résumés and in interviews. Pictures of the candidate and his or her family are often attached to the résumé. Canadian interviewers who do not initiate conversations around these topics are often perceived by Latin American and Latin European candidates as disinterested in getting to know them as people and only interested in the contribution they will make to the company's bottom line. As a result, Canadian employers are less likely to make a favourable impression and risk losing good candidates.

When creating selection policies and procedures for foreign operations, Canadian companies must look for a way to marry their corporate objectives with the host country's practices, customs, and culture. Attracting the best local talent overseas requires familiarity with the country and a willingness to adapt their interview process. Adapting to local practices benefits the company in two ways: (1) It enhances the probability that candidates will be interested in working for the company, and (2) it ensures that candidates are evaluated in the context of the qualifications required for the local market.[78]

# Chapter Review

## Answers to Test Yourself

1. What is selection and what is its purpose and importance for an organization?

   Selection is the process of choosing individuals with the relevant qualifications to fill existing or projected job openings. The purpose is to find the "best" candidate who possesses the required KSAs and personality, and who will perform well, embrace the corporate mission and values, and fit the organizational culture. Proper selection is important because (1) the quality of the company's human resources are frequently the single most important factor in a company's performance and success, (2) there are high costs associated with inappropriate or poor hiring, and (3) there are legal implications related to human rights and employment equity legislation.

2. What are the major steps in the selection process?

   There are five major steps involved in the selection process: (1) prescreening applicants, (2) selection interview, (3) selection testing, (4) background investigation and reference checking, and (5) making the hiring decision and offering the job.

3. What are the major types of selection interviews and the problems that can undermine their effectiveness?

   Interviews used for selection purposes can be classified by structure: unstructured, structured, or mixed; by type of question: situational or behavioural; and by how they are conducted: sequential, computerized, or via videoconferencing. Problems that can undermine the effectiveness of an interview include poor planning, making snap judgments, having a negative or positive bias, not knowing the job requirements, lowering standards under pressure to hire, not allowing for the contrast effect, being unduly influenced by non-verbal behaviour, telegraphing desired responses to the interviewee, talking too much or too little, or being influenced by the attractiveness or gender of the applicant.

4. What are the four types of testing used in selection, and what are the legal and ethical concerns related to medical examinations and drug testing?

   The different types of tests used for selection include intelligence tests, emotional intelligence tests, aptitude tests, tests of motor and physical abilities, personality tests, achievement tests, work sampling, management assessment centres, honesty testing, and medical testing. Alcohol and drug testing are controversial in many situations and are subject to numerous constraints under human rights legislation.

5. What is the importance of reference checking? What strategies can make reference checking effective? What are the legal issues involved?

   Background investigation and reference checking are extremely important, for two key reasons: (1) for verifying information provided by the candidate, and (2) for validating information obtained during the other steps in the selection process. Reference checking can be made more effective by using a structured form to ensure that important questions are not overlooked, using the references offered by the applicant as a source for other references, and being persistent. Failure to check references can lead to negligent or wrongful hiring suits that may involve significant damages.

## Key Terms

aptitude tests (p. 161)
behavioural or behaviour descriptive interview (BDI) (p. 151)
clinical strategy (p. 169)
computerized selection interview (p. 151)
emotional intelligence (EI) tests (p. 161)
intelligence quotient (IQ) tests (p. 161)
management assessment centre (p. 164)
must criteria (p. 155)
panel interview (p. 150)
performance skills (p. 155)
personality tests (p. 162)
realistic job preview (RJP) (p. 158)
reliability (p. 170)
selection (p. 145)
selection interview (p. 149)
selection ratio (p. 145)
semi-structured interview (p. 150)

sequential interview (p. 151)
situational interview (p. 151)
statistical strategy (p. 169)
structured interview (p. 150)
technical skills (p. 155)
unstructured interview (p. 150)
validity (p. 171)
videoconferencing (p. 152)
want criteria (p. 155)

## Required Professional Capabilities (RPCs)

RPC 5-1 > (p. 148)
RPC 5-2 > (p. 157)
RPC 5-3 > (p. 169)

# Cases and Exercises



## CASE INCIDENT

### Why are they leaving so quickly?

Elford Printing Inc. is a medium-sized company that prints and distributes popular magazines and newspapers throughout Ontario. It has been in business for the past 20 years and employs approximately 560 factory staff and 65 office staff. This past year has been flagged as one of the best in the company's history, with an astounding 200 percent increase in revenue. Steve, the company's CEO, is extremely pleased with the growth and takes advantage of every networking opportunity in the community to boast about the company's success. This is a great achievement, considering other companies in the region have been hit hard by the economic downturn and have had to aggressively contain costs and lay off staff.

On Monday morning, Angela, the new HR director, met with Steve to present her first report on HR operations. Regrettably, Angela brought some distressing news. Over the past 12 months, turnover has been steadily increasing and currently hovers at a staggering 14 percent. This means that, on average, employees are only staying four to five months with the organization before resigning. Steve admits that he has been so focused on the revenue increase and making sure that customer demands are met that he has been oblivious to the fact that they are losing people at a faster rate than usual.

Steve is unable to figure out what is happening and asks Angela to outline the hiring process for him. Angela explains that the overwhelming leap in revenue has created new challenges for her team of three HR representatives. They have been feverishly rushing to fill vacancies in a number of key areas: production, maintenance, distribution, marketing, research, and sales. Angela explains that her team has a specific hiring system in place. When a line manager has a vacancy in his or her department, he or she calls HR with a few details about the job, an ad is placed in the local newspaper, and incoming résumés are quickly scanned to see who has the technical skills for the job. Candidates are invited for an interview, which usually lasts about 20 minutes. Since the HR team has so many interviews to conduct each day, they rarely have more than 20 minutes to offer each candidate, and often have to make up questions as they are conducting the interview. Since there are only three people on the HR team, they all spread out and conduct one-on-one interviews. Given the immediate need for staff, candidates are told at the end of the interview if they have the job. For those who are offered a job, they are asked to show up the next day to start work.

Steve stares in amazement—he cannot believe what the HR director has told him about hiring practices in his company.

#### Questions

1. What errors are being made in the current approach to hiring and what are the consequences of each?
2. What are the potential violations of human rights legislation at play in the company's hiring practices?

3. Besides turnover, what other problems might surface as a result of poor hiring decisions and what are the consequences of each?
4. What advice would you offer to help the company enhance the validity and reliability of its hiring process?

## Application Questions

1. In a team comprising four people, imagine you are on the selection committee at Labatt's Brewery, interviewing recent college and university graduates for an entry-level position as a regional salesperson.
   a. Identify four skills required to be an effective regional salesperson and for each skill design a behaviour-based interview question to determine candidate suitability for this position.
   b. Pair with another team of four people and practise answering the behaviour-based interview questions designed by each team.
   c. Critique the behaviour-based interview questions designed by each team.
   d. Discuss your experiences as a job candidate answering these behaviour-based interview questions.
2. Over the next six months, a mining company in northern Ontario will be interviewing candidates for eight senior management positions. The HR team wants to enhance the validity and reliability of the hiring decision by administering selection tests. What three selection tests would you recommend to the HR team? Explain the benefits of each test.
3. Work sampling is identified as one of the most reliable and valid selection tests that can be used to determine a candidate's competency in a specific area. With reference to your current job or a job you have held in the past, map out the work sampling test that you could administer to candidates seeking employment in this area to determine who is best qualified for the job. What are the technical and performance skills that must be demonstrated?
4. Some applicants include webcam-recorded presentations along with their résumés when applying for jobs. With reference to the job you would like to secure when you graduate, produce a two-minute webcam presentation that showcases your skills and abilities to a potential employer. In groups of two or three, present your videos and offer feedback to each other on the content and marketing appeal of the presentations.
5. Assume there is a prescreening process for all students who have applied for entrance into your college or university. In teams of three, design the questions that should be asked in the prescreening phone interview. Conduct a role play that showcases how the interview should progress. One person is the HR representative, one person is the student, and the other person is the observer who gives feedback on the interview.

## RUNNING CASE: LEARNINMOTION.COM

### The Better Interview

The case for Chapter 5, The Better Interview, asks the student to assess the group's interviewing skills and to develop a plan to better quantify the merits of each candidate.

To read this case, go to www.pearsoned.ca/myhrlab and click on the *Management of Human Resources*, Third Canadian Edition, In-Class Edition, cover. Click on the case module in Chapter 5. The running case illustrates a variety of challenges confronted by HRM professionals, small-business owners, and front-line supervisors. It places students in the role of HR management consultants to help the fledgling LearninMotion.com develop HR policies, strategies, and long-term goals. Each case is accompanied by assignments for the management consultants in the form of critical-thinking questions posed to the student.

## CONTROVERSIAL BUSINESS TOPIC EXERCISE

Ashleigh, the assistant to the Vice President of a small academic institution, was thrilled to be invited to an interview for the position of Executive Assistant to the President of a larger academic institution in a nearby city. She has been waiting for a vacancy in the company for over five years and this is exactly the position she wants. It is her dream job. Unfortunately, she just discovered that her current boss, the Vice President, will be serving as an external member on the interview panel. When Ashleigh expressed concern about the situation to the HR Manager on the interview panel, she was informed that there was no reason for her boss to resign from the panel. Ashleigh is very uncomfortable about the situation and is not sure what to do. What advice would you give to Ashleigh on how to handle the situation?

## IN THE BOARDROOM EXERCISE

You have recently been hired as the Vice President of HR for an investment banking firm in Toronto, supervising a team of 10 HR representatives who hire senior financial staff in 25 locations across the city. In your conversations with your team, it is evident that they have never received formal training in how to conduct interviews. At your first boardroom meeting you request funds to send your HR representatives on a one-week intensive training program to enhance their interviewing skills. The CEO does not support your request. She says, "That's a waste of good money! Who needs training to determine if a candidate is right for the job? You can tell if you are going to hire someone the minute they walk through the door." Discuss the approach you would use to argue the value of training for your HR staff.

## SELECTION ON THE INTERNATIONAL STAGE EXERCISE

*The exercise that follows relates to the Selection on the International Stage feature on p. 172.*

You are the HR Manager for a five-star hotel that is interested in expanding its operations overseas. Select an international destination and research its culture, business practices such as hiring and compensation, customs, legislation, political structure, and current affairs, including the relationship between Canada and the host country. Present your findings to the class, showcasing the similarities and differences. Given what you discover about doing business in the host country, discuss your approach for hiring local candidates.

## EXPERIENTIAL EXERCISE

For further study of text materials and development of practical skills, select the experiential exercise module for this chapter on www.pearsoned.ca/myhrlab. This module provides two to three individual or group-based assignments per chapter.

# QUIZ YOURSELF

## STUDY GUIDE QUESTIONS

Circle the correct answer. After completing this self-test, check your answers against the Answers to Study Guide Questions at the back of the book (p. 433).

1. Selection is the process of identifying qualified candidates to fill open or projected positions within an organization. Proper selection is important for the following three key reasons:
   a. impact on organizational performance, associated costs, legal and ethical implications
   b. organizational performance, culture fit, KSAs of the new hire
   c. culture fit, organizational performance, involved costs
   d. company performance, costs involved, management time involved
   e. costs involved in training new hires, hiring costs, impact on company performance

2. The Acme Company uses a personality test as a selection tool. The test aims to identify candidates' suitability for a sales representative position. The test was first administered by an HR specialist and then at a later stage was administered on the same candidate by a supervisor. At the decision-making stage, the panel discovered that the test results did not match. The test failed to show:
   a. reliability
   b. validity
   c. validity and reliability
   d. accuracy
   e. none of the above

3. IT.com is in the process of selecting individuals for the position of software developer for its technical team. The selection process is in the stage where the manager of the technical team is interviewing potential candidates. What step in the selection process is the company in?
   a. the initial selection interview stage
   b. the selection testing stage
   c. the behavioural interview stage
   d. the supervisory interview stage
   e. the prescreening stage

4. The Smith Company uses interviews as a key component of its selection process. The HR division has designed the interviews based on competencies identified for each position in the organization. Interviewers are required to rate answers on a rating scale. The company has a:
   a. semi-structured interview process
   b. structured interview process
   c. unstructured interview process
   d. panel interview process
   e. situational interview process

5. Mary recently attended an interview for the position of HR Generalist. At the interview, Mary was given specific situations and was asked to describe how she reacted to each of the situations in the past by giving specific examples. What type of interview did Mary face?
   a. structured interview
   b. situational interview
   c. behavioural interview
   d. panel interview
   e. unstructured interview

6. The new HR manager of a pharmaceutical company decided to change the interview process by replacing the existing method with the following method. The interview was designed for the interviewers to describe specific situations and then to ask each applicant how he/she would behave in the same situation. The interview also involved three interviewers interviewing the candidate at the same time. The interview process combined:
   a. behavioural and panel interviews
   b. situational and panel interviews
   c. situational and sequential interviews
   d. behavioural and sequential interviews
   e. situational and behavioural interviews

7. If interviews are used as part of the selection process, the company must ensure that they comply with human rights legislation. Which of the following questions, if asked, would be considered a violation of human rights?
   a. questions about marital status
   b. questions about the age of a candidate
   c. questions about ethnic background
   d. questions about the number of children
   e. all of the above

8. Although interviews are used by all organizations as a key component of the selection process, there are interviewing errors that can undermine their effective use. Which of the following are common interviewing errors?
   a. halo effect, poor planning, playing psychologist
   b. negative bias, poor planning, pressure to hire
   c. poor knowledge of the job, halo effect, negative bias
   d. influence of non-verbal behaviour, halo effect, telegraphing
   e. all of the above

9. Amal is the new recruitment specialist for Murray's Paint Company. One of his first tasks is to design an effective interview. At present, he is in the process of specifying "must" and "want" criteria. Once he has specified "musts" and "wants," what should he do?
   a. determine assessment strategies and develop a form
   b. identify those who are involved in the selection process
   c. weight the "want" criteria that have been specified
   d. develop interview questions to be asked of candidates
   e. do nothing, since he has completed the process

10. The purpose of using a management assessment centre for selection testing is to:
    a. test intelligence
    b. observe personality
    c. test achievement
    d. test emotional intelligence
    e. observe the results of performing realistic management tasks

11. Substance abuse testing brings with it a number of restrictions under the human rights legal framework, despite employers' obligations under health and safety laws. For which of the following is it permissible to test during the selection process?
    a. alcohol only
    b. smoking only
    c. alcohol and drugs
    d. no pre-employment testing is permitted
    e. drugs only

12. Reference and background checking is an important component of the selection process. How can reference checking be made more productive?
    a. by outsourcing
    b. by using a structured form
    c. by obtaining permission
    d. by getting personal references
    e. by calling past employers

13. Providing candidates with realistic information about job demands, organization expectations, and the work environment creates appropriate expectations of the job. This helps the candidates learn about both positive and

negative aspects of the job and the firm. This is known as realistic job:

a. representation
b. expectations
c. preview
d. performance
e. experience

14. A company uses a strategy whereby a hiring decision is arrived at after examining all the information collected throughout the selection process. All individuals involved in the process get together, share the information collected, and make a subjective evaluation on who should be extended an offer. This method of making a hiring decision is known as the:
    a. statistical strategy
    b. clinical strategy
    c. hiring strategy
    d. selection strategy
    e. selection ratio

15. Lee is a recruiter working for a manufacturing company. At the start of the financial year, the company planned to recruit 60 production staff equally divided over the four quarters of the year. However, due to a downward trend in the market, sales took a sudden and sharp hit. As a result, the company decided to impose a hiring freeze until the market situation improved. What kind of a constraint is Lee facing in terms of selecting new production staff?
    a. legislative constraint
    b. job requirements
    c. supply changes
    d. organizational policies and plans
    e. compensation policies

6 chapter

# Orienting and Training Employees for High Performance

## Learning Objectives

1. Explain the individual and organizational relevance of orienting employees.
2. Describe best practices for orienting new staff and assessing the effectiveness of orientation programs.
3. Communicate the strategic relevance of training and development.
4. Describe how to conduct organizational, task, and person analyses (needs analysis).
5. Discuss how to choose the most appropriate training method to match training objectives (instructional design).
6. Explain the process for moving training plans into action and testing their validity (implementation and delivery of training).
7. Identify best practices for moving classroom training into workplace practice (transfer of learning).
8. Discuss the quantitative and qualitative approaches to assessing the effectiveness of a training program (evaluation and follow-up).
9. Identify and describe special-purpose training programs.

## Test Yourself

1. What is the purpose of orientation from an employer's perspective?
2. What are the three approaches to evaluating orientation programs?
3. What is the strategic relevance of training and development?
4. What are the five steps in the training process?
5. Why has the need to deliver training through e-learning escalated in the past few years?
6. What is the organizational value of leadership development?

## 6.1 ORIENTING EMPLOYEES

Once employees have been recruited and selected, the next step is orienting them to their new company and its industry, and their new job. **Employee orientation** provides new employees with information about the employer, the industry, and the job for which they were hired, in order to perform their jobs to their full potential. Orientation is actually one component of the employer's new-employee socialization process. **Socialization** is the ongoing process of instilling in all employees the prevailing attitudes, standards, values, and patterns of behaviour that are expected by the organization and its departments.[1]

The purpose of orientation is to familiarize employees with a company's culture, rules, policies, and practices so that they understand the environment within which they will be working and can start performing according to organizational expectations. Orientation is valuable in communicating to new employees how their jobs contribute to the organization's goals and strategic mandate. Understanding the strategic value of their jobs helps employees establish a task identity, which we discussed in Chapter 3. Orientation can reduce the anxiety new employees often experience and minimize the **reality shock** that surfaces when they realize there are differences between their personal expectations of the job and the realities of it. From an employer's perspective, a comprehensive orientation contributes to lower turnover, increased productivity, improved employee morale, and lower training costs.[2] Developing strong orientation programs to lower turnover is especially critical at a time when Generation Y's definition of long-term commitment to an organization is one year[3] and only one in five anticipates staying with the same company for six years or longer.[4] Job jumping every few years in search of better compensation or more meaningful work is the new norm.[5]

## 6.2 CONTENT OF ORIENTATION PROGRAMS

Orientation programs range from brief, informal introductions to lengthy, formal programs. In the latter, the new employee is usually given a handbook or printed materials that cover such matters as working hours, performance reviews, getting on the payroll, benefits information, training courses, vacations, safety procedures, and probationary periods. A tour of the company facilities and introductions to the employee's supervisor and coworkers are also included. BASF Canada used a high-tech approach and produced a CD-ROM to provide consistent orientation information to new employees across the country. The information was so useful that existing employees asked for copies and took them home to show their families. The CD-ROM was also adapted as one of BASF's recruitment tools.[6]

Online orientations in the form of synchronous and asynchronous presentations are also being used to acclimatize new employees to their workplaces. The advantages of online orientations include cost-effectiveness, the convenience of delivering consistent messages to new recruits located in widespread geographical regions, and their ability to help acclimatize new employees to their organizations prior to their official employment start date.[7] For example, the orientation program at Verizon Wireless consists of three online virtual tours that include the company's code of conduct and benefits, a meeting with staff, and highlights of the company's history, mission, and values.

At Ernst & Young, after a review of both internal and external best practices, the orientation program was redesigned to include:[8]

- a presentation providing an overview of the firm
- an administrative checklist of tasks to be conducted prior to a new employee's start date and during the first three months of employment
- a binder explaining the firm's vision, values, strategies, and structures
- a form for employee feedback, and
- an intranet site with information about the firm.

**RPC 6-1 >**

**Develops orientation policies and procedures for new employees**

**LEGALcompliance**

Note that some courts have found that content in an employee-handbook represents a contract with the employee. Therefore, disclaimers should be included that make it clear that statements of company policies, benefits, and regulations do not constitute the terms and conditions of an employment contract, either expressed or implied. Organizations should think twice before including in the handbook such statements as, "No employee will be fired without just cause," or statements that imply or state that employees have tenure; these could be viewed as legal and binding commitments.

## Responsibility for Orientation

The first part of the orientation is usually performed by an HR specialist, who provides an overview of the company's mission, values, and strategic direction; explains such matters as payroll dates, company benefits, building security, working hours, and vacation; and addresses any questions the new employee might have. The employee is then introduced to his or her new supervisor, who continues the next phase of orientation by explaining the exact nature of the job, such as shift hours, lunch break times, and customer service expectations; introduces the person to his or her new colleagues; and familiarizes the new employee with the workplace. Supervisors also explain how the job contributes to the organization, which helps the new employee understand the value of his or her efforts. Sometimes, another employee at a peer level will be assigned as a "buddy" or mentor for the newly hired employee during the first few weeks or months of employment. It is a good idea for the HR department to follow up with each new employee about three months after the initial orientation to address any remaining questions and to check in on the new employee's progress on the job.

## Problems with Orientation Programs

A number of potential problems can arise with orientation programs. Often, too much information is provided in a short time (usually one day) and the new employee is overwhelmed. New employees commonly find themselves inundated with forms to fill out for payroll, benefits, pensions, and so on. Another problem may be that little or no orientation is provided, which means that new employees must seek answers to each question that arises and start working without a solid understanding of what is expected of them. Finally, the orientation information provided by the HR department can be too broad to be meaningful to a new employee, especially on the first day, whereas the orientation information provided by the immediate supervisor may be too detailed to realistically expect the new employee to remember it all.

In an orientation, the supervisor explains the exact nature of the job, introduces new colleagues, and familiarizes new employees with the workplace.

## Evaluation of Orientation Programs

Organizations are encouraged to evaluate their orientation programs on an annual basis to assess whether they are providing timely and useful information to new employees and the degree to which they are cost-effective. Doing so enables the company to determine what it does well and where it should make changes.

Three approaches to evaluating orientation programs are:

1. *Employee Reaction:* Interview (either individually or in focus groups) or survey new employees for their opinions on the usefulness of the orientation program in helping them transition into the company and their new jobs.
2. *Cost/Benefit Analysis:* Calculate the return on investment from orientation programs by comparing orientation costs (e.g., printing handbooks, spending time orienting new employees by HR staff and immediate supervisors) and the benefits of orientation (e.g., reduction in errors, rate of productivity, efficiency levels, accident rates, and reduction in turnover).
3. *Employee Evaluation:* Assess the degree to which orientation contributed to new employees' on-the-job performance as part of their first performance evaluation. We will discuss the link between orientation and performance evaluations in Chapter 7.

**employee orientation** A procedure for providing new employees with information about the company and its industry, and the job.

**socialization** The ongoing process of instilling in all employees the prevailing attitudes, standards, values, and patterns of behaviour that are expected by the organization.

**reality shock** A new employee's realization that there are differences between his or her personal expectations about the job and the realities of it.

## *In-class Notes*

**Orienting Employees**

- Providing new employees with information about the company and its industry, and the new job
- Socialization of new employees to adopt the organization's values, behaviours, and attitudes
- Orientation may be formal or informal depending on what organizations perceive as the best way to introduce employees to the company
- Orientation conducted by HR and immediate supervisor
- A presentation providing an overview of the firm
- An administrative checklist of tasks to be conducted prior to a new employee's start date and during the first three months of employment

## 6.3 WHAT IS TRAINING AND WHAT CAN IT DO FOR YOUR ORGANIZATION?

**Training** is the process by which organizations equip employees with the knowledge, skills, and abilities needed to perform their jobs according to organizational standards. It has a short-term focus on developing an employee's ability to perform tasks as described in the job description and, for example, might involve sending an employee to a one-day training workshop to learn how to use a new software package. This differs from **development**, which provides employees with the competencies required for future success, such as leadership skills for junior staff to prepare them for roles as front-line managers. Development involves long-term, extensive programs, such as mentoring, leadership development, and job rotation, and is often associated with grooming employees for managerial careers.

Boston Pizza, Nike, Labatt's, and WestJet have made a strong commitment to training and developing their employees as a hallmark of competitiveness and profitability. Companies such as these face many competing demands, including globalization, breakneck revolutions in information technology, shifting demographic and social trends, escalating stakeholder demands, the need to improve product and service quality, and the pressure to be environmentally responsible. To be industry leaders in this complex and changing global economy requires employees that have the knowledge, skills, and tools to respond quickly to challenges and to chart new and innovative directions for products and services. Training employees to be fully functional in their jobs and to make contributions to the strategic direction of the company helps organizations meet their goals and objectives. According to industry experts, within the next five to ten years up to 85 percent of jobs in North America and Europe will demand extensive industry knowledge that spans international borders.[9] To achieve these outcomes, organizations must invest in training and developing their workforces. Training and development initiatives are fundamental to an organization's long-range strategy and strategic advantage.

For example, Space Systems/Loral, a U.S.-based company that designs and produces satellites and satellite systems, aligns all of its training initiatives with the company's strategic mandate. The executive management team meets regularly with the training and development staff to map out new training initiatives that support the company's strategic goals. Whenever changes are made in a strategic direction, the training team is the first one consulted about what kind of training is required to support the work that needs to be done. Management at Space Systems/Loral understand that the success of the organization is based on the strength of the knowledge capital that employees are able to offer on a day-to-day basis.

Training and development are gaining even greater importance in our steadily dwindling Canadian labour market. According to Statistics Canada, the generation of workers now in the workforce and available to replace the boomers is 20 percent smaller in number. Millennium busters—those still in school preparing for workforce entry—are an additional 15 percent fewer in number, so finding talent in a declining workforce will continue to be a daunting task in the next decade and beyond.[10] Our labour force is delicately balanced, with one employee leaving for every one employee entering the labour market; in ten years, however, a sharp negative replacement ratio is expected, with more retirees than workforce entrants. By 2016, a shortage of a million workers is predicted. Even more disturbing is the forecast of over 10 million more jobs than people capable of filling them as of 2010.[11] International recruitment offers little, if any, resolution, as census data indicate that 61 countries are experiencing below-average birth rates and will be unable to meet workforce-replacement needs.[12] The aging workforce and the scarce skills associated with new workforce entrants necessitate that we create more innovative ways to leverage the knowledge of older workers to bring new employees up to speed quickly. Clearly, Canadian organizations need to increase their investment in human capital in order to compete effectively.

**RPC 6-2 >**

**Ensures the application of appropriate development methods and techniques based upon generally accepted principles of adult learning**

**RPC 6-3 >**

**Using a variety of methods, facilitates the delivery of development programs to groups and individual learners**

## Legal Aspects of Training

LEGALcompliance

Under human rights and employment equity legislation, several aspects of employee training programs must be assessed with an eye toward the programs' impact on designated group members.[13] For example, if relatively few women or visible minorities are selected for a training program, there may be a requirement to show that the admissions procedures are valid—that they predict performance on the job for which the person is being trained. In some cases, there may be government sources of funding available for training of designated group members or for occupations with skills shortages.

**RPC 6-4 >**

**Identifies and accesses external sources of training funding available to employees**

Negligent training is another potential problem. *Negligent training* occurs when an employer fails to train adequately and an employee subsequently harms a third party.[14] Employees who are dismissed for poor performance or disciplined for safety infractions may claim that the employer was negligent because the training was inadequate. Precautions include:[15]

- confirming claims of skill and experience for all applicants
- reducing the risks of harm by extensively training employees who work with dangerous equipment, materials, or processes
- ensuring that the training includes procedures to protect third parties' health and safety (including that of other employees)
- evaluating the training activity to determine its effectiveness in reducing negligence risks

**training** The process by which organizations equip employees with the knowledge, skills, and abilities to perform their current jobs according to organizational standards.

**development** A long-term initiative, such as mentoring, leadership development, or job rotation, designed to prepare employees for future jobs within the organization.

**RPC 6-5 >**

**Ensures legislated training obligations are met within the organization**

## The Five-Step Training Process

Developing an effective training program requires a structured process, as summarized in Figure 6.1. The steps include:

- needs analysis
- instructional design
- implementation and delivery of training
- transfer of learning
- evaluation and follow-up

### *figure* 6.1 The Five Steps in the Training and Development Process

**1. NEEDS ANALYSIS**

- Conduct organizational analysis, task analysis, and person analysis.
- Identify specific job performance skills needed to improve performance and productivity.
- Analyze the audience to ensure that the program will be suited to their specific levels of education, experience, and skills, as well as their attitudes and personal motivations.

**2. INSTRUCTIONAL DESIGN**

- Gather instructional objectives, methods, media, description and sequence of content, examples, exercises, and activities. Organize them into a curriculum in accordance with adult learning theory.
- Make sure all materials (such as video scripts, leaders' guides, and participants' workbooks) complement each other, are written clearly, and blend into unified training geared directly to the stated learning objectives.
- Carefully and professionally prepare all program elements—paper-based or electronic—to guarantee quality and effectiveness.

**3. IMPLEMENTATION AND DELIVERY OF TRAINING**

- Design training agenda.
- Run a pilot study to assess effectiveness of a program in achieving its objectives.
- Implement a program with revisions from pilot study.

**4. TRANSFER OF LEARNING**

- Enhance the probability that learning from the training classroom is applied in workplace practice.
- Minimize the barriers that impede the transfer of learning from classroom to workplace.

**5. EVALUATION AND FOLLOW-UP**

- Assess program success according to:
  REACTION—Document the learners' immediate reactions to the training.
  LEARNING—Use feedback devices or pre- and post-tests to measure what learners have actually learned.
  BEHAVIOUR—Note supervisors' reactions to learners' performance following completion of the training. This is one way to measure the degree to which learners apply new skills and knowledge to their jobs.
  RESULTS—Determine the level of improvement in job performance and assess needed maintenance.

Source: This article was originally published in IOMA's monthly newsletter *HRFocus* and is republished here with the express written permission of IOMA.  For more information, go to www.ioma.com.

## 6.4 STEP 1: NEEDS ANALYSIS

Needs analysis is the most important and complex step in developing a training program. It is a form of research that is used to discover what training and development needs are required by an organization. Needs analysis consists of organizational analysis, task analysis, and person analysis. An **organizational analysis** is an assessment of an entire organization that investigates the strategies, resources, and support systems the organization has in place for training. Specifically, it involves identifying how the company's strategic direction supports training, how management will support training initiatives, and what training resources and support systems will be required. An organizational analysis helps trainers understand the context within which they will design and deliver training programs in order to enhance the probability that they will design training programs that are aligned with the organization's strategy.

A **task analysis** is a comprehensive study of a job, including the skills, knowledge, abilities (KSAs), and behaviours required to perform it; the challenges an employee faces in performing the job; the conditions under which the employee works; and the performance standards the employee is expected to achieve. Identifying the broad competencies and specific skills required to perform job-related tasks is used for determining the training needs of employees who are new to their jobs. The job description and job specification are helpful because they list the specific duties and skills required on the job and become the basic reference point when determining what training is required. The competencies and specific skills or knowledge required for each of the tasks and subtasks should be listed, specifying exactly the knowledge or skills that must be taught.

A **person analysis** identifies those employees who require training and what specific training they need in order to reach organizational expectations. A person analysis involves a review of company data such

### In-class Notes

**The Training Process**

- Training needs analysis including organizational, task, and personal analyses
- Instructional design of content of training program
- Implementation and delivery of training
- Transfer of learning from the training classroom into workplace practice
- Evaluation of reactions, learning, behaviour, results

**organizational analysis** An assessment of an entire organization that investigates the strategies, resources, and support systems it has in place for training.

**task analysis** A detailed study of a job to identify the skills and competencies it requires so that an appropriate training program may be designed.

**person analysis** Identifies which employees require training and what specific training they require to reach organizational expectations.

Canadian Management Centre www.cmctraining.org

Saba People Management www.saba.com

Excel Group Management Development Training www.growingcoaches.com

Canadian Society for Training and Development www.cstd.ca

as customer feedback, performance evaluation results, and accident records, and speaking with supervisors to determine which employees would benefit from training.

Person analysis means verifying whether there is a deficiency of knowledge or a deficiency of execution on the part of the employee. If there is a gap between employees' actual performance and the company's expectations, an important question must be asked—is training the solution to closing this gap? If employees are not performing to standard because they have not been trained or do not know how to do the job, then this is a training opportunity. A lack of skills, knowledge, and abilities to do a job according to standard is referred to as a **deficiency of knowledge** and is solved through training. On the other hand, when employees lack the interest or motivation to perform their jobs to expected standards, they are displaying a **deficiency of execution**. In such cases, training is not the solution. Organizations need to discover the root cause of why employees are not committed to completing the work as expected, and then implement a non-training solution. For example, employees may be disengaged because they are not receiving recognition for their work, and therefore reward systems should be considered. They may also be frustrated by breakdowns in their equipment, which hinder ability to complete tasks according to standard. In this case, technology upgrades might be required so that fewer obstacles prevent completion of work.

*frontLINE tips*

**RPC 6-6 >**

Conducts training need assessments by identifying individual and corporate learning requirements

**RPC 6-7 >**

Establishes priority of responses to needs assessment results

**RPC 6-8 >**

Develops training budgets, monitors expenditures, and documents activities associated with training

**RPC 6-9 >**

Ensures arrangements are made for training schedules, facilities, trainers, participants, and equipment and course materials

## 6.5 STEP 2: INSTRUCTIONAL DESIGN

Concrete, measurable training and development objectives should be set after the trainer has identified employees' specific training and development needs. Objectives specify what the trainee should be able to accomplish after successfully completing the training or development program. For example, if a needs analysis found that response times to service calls were

### *In-class Notes*

**Needs Analysis**

- Needs analysis is a form of research used to discover what training and development needs are required by an organization
- Needs analysis consists of organizational analysis, task analysis, and person analysis
- Ascertain whether there is a deficiency of knowledge or deficiency of execution before designing a training program

______________________

______________________

______________________

______________________

______________________

______________________

slow, trainers would set as an objective that trainees should be able to respond to all service calls from customers within one minute. Objectives provide a focus for the efforts of trainees and serve as a roadmap for trainers in determining the content they should cover and the types of activities they should include to achieve their objectives. Objectives also serve as a benchmark for evaluating the success of the training or development initiative.

After training objectives have been set, the training or development program can be designed and delivered. Determining which training and development techniques to use depends on many factors: objectives to be achieved, budget, timelines for completion of training, trainer's expertise in the use of training methods, trainees' learning style preferences and capabilities, and organizational culture.

Descriptions of the most popular traditional training and development techniques follow in this section. Traditional training techniques are being replaced with more flexible, personalized, and cost-effective techniques, known as e-learning, which will be discussed in the next section.[16]

**RPC 6-10 >**

**Recommends the most appropriate way to meet identified learning needs (e.g., courses, secondments, and on-the-job activities)**

## Traditional Training Techniques

**ON-THE-JOB TRAINING** **On-the-job training** (OJT) involves having a person learn a job by actually performing it. It usually entails assigning new employees to experienced workers or supervisors who then do the actual training.[17]

There are several types of on-the-job training. The most familiar is the *coaching* or *understudy* method. Here, the employee is trained on the job by an experienced worker or by the trainee's supervisor. *Job rotation*, in which an employee (usually a management trainee) moves from job to job at planned intervals, is another OJT technique. *Special assignments* are another on-the-job training technique designed to give lower-level executives first-hand experience in working on actual problems. OJT is beneficial when trainees are learning complex tasks that require more immediate feedback, and it enables them to experience the organizational climate while training.

On-the-job training is structured and concrete. Here, a supervisor teaches an employee to use a drum-forming machine.

**APPRENTICESHIP TRAINING** Apprenticeship training is a structured process by which individuals become skilled workers through a combination of classroom instruction and on-the-job training. It is widely used to train individuals for many occupations, including those of electrician and plumber. Apprenticeship training basically involves having the learner/apprentice study under the tutelage of a master craftsperson.[18]

**JOB INSTRUCTION TRAINING** Many jobs consist of a logical sequence of steps and are best taught step by step. This step-by-step process is called **job instruction training** (JIT). To begin, all necessary steps in the job are listed, each in its proper sequence. Alongside each step, a corresponding "key point" (if any) should be noted. The steps show *what* is to be done, while the key points show *how* it is to be done and *why*. Here is an example of a job instruction training sheet for teaching a right-handed trainee how to operate a large, motorized paper cutter.

**deficiency of knowledge** Lack of skills, knowledge, and abilities to do a job according to company standards, which can be solved by training.

**deficiency of execution** Lack of interest or motivation to work to standard, which can be solved by non-training interventions such as reward systems and job redesign.

**on-the-job training (OJT)** Learning a job while performing it.

**job instruction training (JIT)** Listing of each job's basic tasks, along with key points, in order to provide step-by-step training for employees.

| *Steps* | *Key Points* |
|---|---|
| 1. Start motor. | None. |
| 2. Set cutting distance. | Carefully read scale—to prevent wrong-sized cut. |
| 3. Place paper on cutting table. | Make sure paper is even—to prevent uneven cut. |
| 4. Push paper up to cutter. | Make sure paper is tight—to prevent uneven cut. |
| 5. Grasp safety release with left hand. | Do not release left hand—to prevent hand from being caught in cutter. |
| 6. Grasp cutter release with right hand. | Do not release right hand—to prevent hand from being caught in cutter. |
| 7. Simultaneously pull cutter and safety releases. | Keep both hands on corresponding releases—to avoid hands being on cutting table. |
| 8. Wait for cutter to retract. | Keep both hands on releases—to avoid having hands on cutting table. |
| 9. Retract paper. | Make sure cutter is retracted; keep both hands away from releases. |
| 10. Shut off motor. | None. |

**LECTURES** Classroom training continues to be the primary method of providing corporate training in Canada, and lectures are a widely used method of classroom training delivery.[19] Lecturing has several advantages. It is a quick, simple, and cost-effective way of providing knowledge to large groups of trainees, such as when a sales force must be taught the special features of a new product. Building in time for interactive classroom discussion can be a good way to ensure that training is successful.

**VIDEOCONFERENCING** Videoconferencing, where an instructor is televised live to multiple locations, is a common method for training employees. Videoconferencing allows people in one location to communicate live with people in another city or country or with groups in several other cities, which is a cost-effective method of delivering training.[20] For example, Owen-Illinois, a manufacturer of glass products that employs 34 000 employees in 140 locations worldwide, saves U.S.$500 000 annually on travel costs by delivering government-mandated training by videoconferencing.

**PROGRAMMED LEARNING** Whether the programmed instruction device is a textbook or a computer, **programmed learning** consists of three functions:

1. Presenting questions, facts, or problems to the learner
2. Allowing the person to respond
3. Providing feedback on the accuracy of his or her answers

The main advantage of programmed learning is that it reduces training time by about one-third.[21] Programmed instruction facilitates learning because it lets trainees learn at their own pace and provides immediate feedback. On the other hand, trainees do not learn much more from programmed learning than they would from a traditional textbook. Therefore, the cost of developing the manuals and/or software for programmed instruction has to be weighed against the accelerated, but not improved, learning that should occur.

**VESTIBULE OR SIMULATED TRAINING** **Vestibule or simulated training** is a technique by which trainees learn on the actual or simulated equipment that they will use on the job but are trained off the job. It is virtually a necessity when it is too costly or dangerous to train employees on the job. For example, putting new assembly-line workers right to work could slow production. When safety is a concern—as with pilots—simulated training may be the only practical alternative. In pilot training, for instance, the main advantages of flight simulators are:[22]

1. *Safety.* Crews can practise hazardous flight manoeuvres in a safe, controlled environment.
2. *Learning efficiency.* The absence of the conflicting air traffic and radio chatter that exists in real flight situations allows for total concentration on the business of learning how to fly the craft.
3. *Cost savings.* The cost of flying a flight simulator is only a fraction of the cost of flying an aircraft. This includes savings on maintenance costs, pilot cost, fuel cost, and the cost of not having the aircraft in regular service.

Simulated training simulates underwater conditions of a space walk at Johnson Space Center.

## E-Learning

Over the past few years, electronic training techniques have been developed that allow training professionals to provide learning in a flexible, personalized, and cost-effective manner.[23] **E-learning** is the delivery and administration of learning opportunities and support via computer, networked, and web-based technology to enhance employee performance and development.[24] The use of e-learning represents a state-of-the-art approach to how knowledge is acquired and human capital is developed. Canadian employers are using e-learning to become more productive and innovative and to create self-directed, lifelong learners of their employees.[25] Studies have found that 72 percent of training challenges are time sensitive, and organizations cannot wait until trainers design and develop learning curricula for classroom delivery. In 2004, the Canadian corporate market for e-learning reached about $900 million ($15 billion in the United States) and increased to $18 billion in 2005.[26] E-learning boasts a 75-percent retention rate of material—favourable compared to the 5-percent retention rate for lectures.[27]

According to a Conference Board of Canada survey, three-quarters of all employers in Canada use e-learning technology, and nearly half of them have used the Internet to deliver training to employees.[28] The survey also found that three major obstacles are slowing further investment in e-learning—high costs, lack of time, and content shortage.[29] With the arrival of an escalated number of Generation Y employees, who bring an impressive portfolio of requisite skills in technology to the workplace and who expect that organizations will capitalize on computer access and knowledge, Canada will need to look carefully at the rate at which it adapts new e-learning technology.[30]

**RPC 6-11 >**

**Participates in course design and selection/delivery of learning materials via various media**

There are three major types of e-learning—computer-based training, online training, and electronic performance support systems (EPSS).

**COMPUTER-BASED TRAINING** In computer-based training (CBT), the trainee uses a computer-based system to interactively increase his or her knowledge or skills. Computer-based training almost always involves presenting trainees with integrated computerized simulations and the use of multimedia (including video, audio, text, and graphics) to help them to learn how to do the job.[31]

A new generation of simulations has been developed to simulate role-play situations that are designed to teach behavioural skills and emotional intelligence. Body language, facial expressions, and subtle nuances are programmed into the simulation. These new simulations offer authentic and relevant scenarios involving pressure-filled situations that tap users' emotions and force them to act.[32]

*Multimedia training* is most often implemented with CD-ROM technology, but it is also available through the Internet and other sources.[33] Due to its interactive nature, interactive multimedia has been found to be more effective than text-based instruction for training people.[34]

A higher percentage of Canadian firms use CBT compared with American firms, primarily because of Canada's geography. CBT is often more cost-effective than traditional training methods that require instructors

**programmed learning** A systematic method for teaching job skills that involves presenting questions or facts, allowing the person to respond, and giving the learner immediate feedback on the accuracy of his or her answers.

**vestibule or simulated training** Training employees on special off-the-job equipment, as in airplane pilot training, so that training costs and hazards can be reduced.

**e-learning** The delivery and administration of learning opportunities and support via computer, networked, and web-based technology to help individual performance and development.

*figure* 6.2 **For What Do You Currently Use E-Learning?**

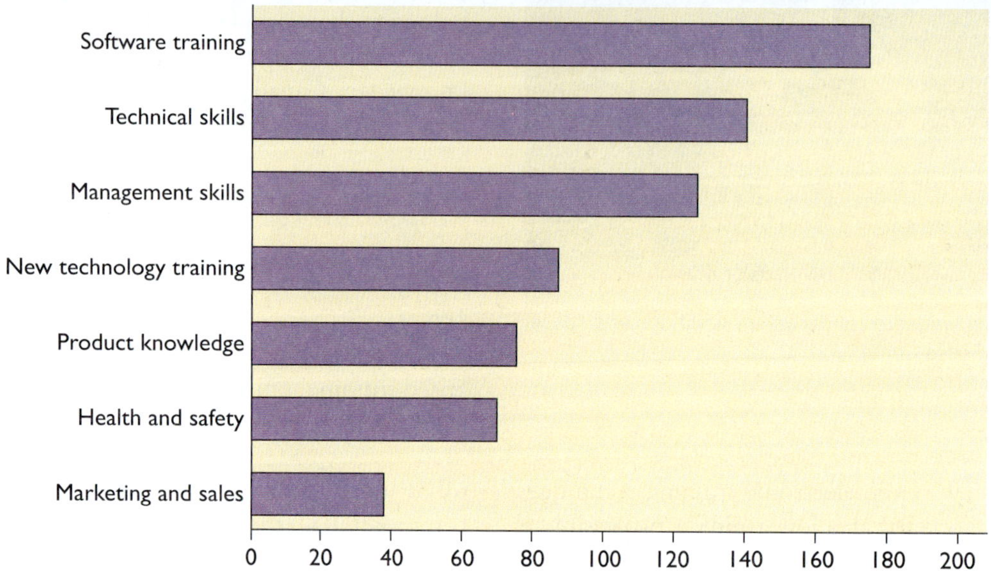


Source: M. Bloom, "E-Learning in Canada, Findings from 2003 E-Survey," p. 4, The Conference Board of Canada, www.conferenceboard.ca/Libraries/EDUC_PUBLIC/TopLine_report.sflb. Reprinted with permission.

and/or trainees to travel long distances to training sites.[35] Alberta Pacific Forest Industries (AL-Pac) has had such good results from using CBT as a staple of its training program that it is about to launch a new component that will enable employees to pick up the skills of another trade. Employees benefit from having training that is accessible 24 hours a day in order to address shift work and different learning styles. This training program also helps keep non-union staff members satisfied, as the multiskilling resulting from CBT enables many employees to rotate jobs.[36] Trainers at Mount Sinai Hospital, an internationally renowned health care facility in Toronto, developed CBT as a key approach to delivering training when they realized that clinical staff were too busy to attend training programs. Using a series of real-world health care simulations, staff develop skills in electronic clinical documentation, electronic medication administration, and computerized physician order entry.[37]

CBT programs can be very beneficial. Studies indicate that interactive technologies reduce learning time by an average of 50 percent.[38] The new forms of training can also be very cost-effective; while traditional training costs less to develop, new media-based training has a lower cost of delivery over its lifespan.[39] Other advantages include instructional consistency (computers, unlike human trainers, do not have good days and bad days), mastery of learning (if the trainee does not learn it, he or she generally cannot move on to the next step in the CBT), increased retention, flexibility for the trainee, and increased trainee motivation (resulting from the responsive feedback of the CBT program).

**ONLINE TRAINING** Current uses of e-learning in Canada are shown in Figure 6.2.[40] Use of this technology as a tool for workplace learning is here to stay, in part because it is generally estimated that web-based training costs about 50 percent less than traditional classroom-based training. Web-based learning is ideal for adults who learn what they want, when they want, and where they want.[41] Online training is often the best solution for highly specialized business professionals with little time available for ongoing education.[42] Students (the workers of tomorrow) thrive in online learning environments. They do not find it to be an isolated or lonely experience, and they find that they have more time to reflect on the learning material, which leads to livelier interaction.[43]

However, critics point out that content management, sound educational strategy, learner support, and system administration should receive more attention because they are often the critical determining factors in successful training outcomes.[44] In the past few years, "learner content management systems" have been developed to deliver personalized content in small "chunks" or "nuggets" of learning. These systems complement "learning management systems" that are focused on the logistics of managing learning. Together, they form a powerful combination for an e-learning platform.[45] This development is considered to be part of the "second wave" of e-learning, involving greater standardization and the emergence of norms.[46] Another problem is that the freedom of online learning means that unless learners are highly motivated, they may not complete the training. It is estimated that learners fail to complete 50 to 90 percent of web-based courses.[47] In general, it is important to seek "blended learning" that includes both personal interaction and online training tools.[48]

Studies are beginning to focus on teaching effectiveness in technology-based distance learning programs to see what teachers can do to be more effective in these kinds of environments. The results of one such study suggest the following:[49]

1. Use cameras and technology layouts that allow instructors to maintain eye contact with both local and remote audiences.
2. Use the variety of media available (CD-ROMs, graphs, videos, and so forth).
3. Do not focus on the technology at the expense of the students.
4. Try to emphasize technology that is reliable and of high quality (little delay in audio and video signals is particularly important).
5. Learn how to use the technology effectively, and understand the importance of a participative style of teaching.
6. Have adequate technical support staff.

Research comparing the effectiveness of educational television or interactive video to face-to-face instruction has found little or no difference in student achievement.[50] The preliminary evidence, at least, seems to suggest that technology-supported (and particularly video-based) training can be effective.[51] However, this assumes that the technology is effective and that the instructors are (as previously explained) specially trained to utilize it for maximum impact.

**VIRTUAL REALITY** **Virtual reality** is one of the most sophisticated forms of computer technology. It can be used to create realistic three-dimensional images of work environments. A virtual reality training environment allows employees to step into a 3D image that is equipped with a typical workplace. In this environment, the trainee learns to handle objects and respond to coworkers as though it were in real life. Virtual reality training has proven successful in training employees for high-risk jobs such as firefighting, flying an aircraft, and paramedic emergency services.[52]

**ELECTRONIC PERFORMANCE SUPPORT SYSTEMS (EPSS)** **Electronic performance support systems (EPSS)** are computer-based job aids or sets of computerized tools and displays that automate training, documentation, and phone support. EPSS provides support that is faster, cheaper, and more effective than traditional paper-based job aids, such as manuals. When a customer calls a Dell Computer service representative about a problem with a new computer, he or she is probably asking questions prompted by an EPSS that takes the service representative and the customer through an analytical sequence, step by step. Without the EPSS, Dell would have to train its service representatives to memorize an unrealistically large number of solutions. Learners say that EPSS provides significant value in maximizing the impact of training. If a skill is trained at one point in time but the trainees do not need to use it until several weeks or months later, the learning material is always available through the EPSS.[53]

## On-the-Job Management-Development Techniques

On-the-job training is one of the most popular development methods. Important techniques include developmental job rotation, the coaching/understudy approach, mentoring, and action learning.

**DEVELOPMENTAL JOB ROTATION** **Developmental job rotation** involves moving management trainees from

**virtual reality** Involves the use of advanced computer technology to create a realistic three-dimensional image of a work environment that allows trainees to act and react as though it were in real life.

**electronic performance support systems (EPSS)** Computer-based job aids or sets of computerized tools and displays that automate training, documentation, and phone support.

**developmental job rotation** A management-training technique that involves moving a trainee from department to department to broaden his or her experiences; identifies the candidate's strong and weak points.

department to department in order to broaden their understanding of all parts of a business.[54] In addition to providing a well-rounded training experience for each person, job rotation helps prevent stagnation through the constant introduction of new points of view in each department. It also tests the trainee and helps identify his or her strong and weak points.[55] Job rotation does have disadvantages. It encourages generalization and tends to be more appropriate for developing general line managers than functional staff experts. Firms also have to be careful not to inadvertently forget a trainee at some deserted outpost.

The Royal Bank offers a program called Graduate Leadership (GLP), which gives newly hired business school graduates the chance to "shop around" for two years by working in several areas of the RBC Financial Group. The program was specially designed to attract some of the most talented graduates in the country.[56]

**RPC 6-12 >**

**Facilitates the implementation of cross-functional development work experiences for employees**

**COACHING/UNDERSTUDY APPROACH** In the *coaching/understudy approach*, a trainee works directly with the person that he or she is to replace. Normally, the understudy relieves the executive of certain responsibilities, thereby giving him or her a chance to learn the job.[57] This helps to ensure that the employer will have trained managers to assume key positions when such positions are vacated due to retirement, promotion, transfer, or termination. To be effective, the executive has to be a good coach and mentor.

**MENTORING** Mentoring is a leading employee-development tool, especially for leadership training.[58] Mentoring differs from coaching in that it focuses on senior staff providing junior staff with career-development guidance and support. Specifically, senior staff support junior staff in adapting to an organizational culture, preparing them for job promotion, developing their professional networks, managing office politics, and dealing with workplace conflicts. Studies have found that between 70 and 90 percent of workplace learning occurs through mentoring, and at least one-third of organizations with a minimum of 500 employees launch formal mentoring programs.[59] Mentoring accelerates career progression, acclimatizes new employees to organizational culture and values, reduces job ambiguity, and decreases absenteeism and turnover.[60] Those who have had mentoring experiences are shown to have higher incomes, greater career commitment, stronger leadership skills, and greater career and job satisfaction.[61]

**ACTION LEARNING** **Action learning** releases managers from their regular duties in order to allow them to work full-time on projects to analyze and solve problems in departments other than their own.[62] The trainees meet periodically with a project group of four or five people with whom their findings and progress are discussed and debated. This gives trainees real experience with actual problems, thereby developing such skills as problem analysis and planning. The main drawback of action learning is that, in releasing trainees to work on outside projects, the employer loses the full-time services of a competent manager.

## Off-the-Job Management-Development Techniques

There are many techniques that are used to develop managers off the job, perhaps in a conference room at headquarters or off the premises entirely at a university or special seminar.

**THE CASE STUDY METHOD** The **case study method** presents a trainee with a written description of an organizational problem. The person then analyzes the case in private, diagnoses the problem, and presents his or her findings and solutions in a discussion with other trainees.[63] The case method approach is aimed at giving trainees realistic experience in identifying and analyzing complex problems in an environment in which their progress can be subtly guided by a trained discussion leader.

Trainees participating in a case-study discussion.

**MANAGEMENT GAMES** In a computerized **management game**, trainees are divided into five- or six-person companies, each of which has to compete with the others in a simulated marketplace. Each company sets a goal and is told that it can make several decisions relating to advertising, production, inventory, and so on. Like the real world, each company usually cannot see what decisions the other firms have made, although these decisions do affect its own sales. For example, if a competitor decides to increase its advertising expenditures, it may end up increasing its sales at the expense of the other firms.[64]

Management games help trainees develop their problem-solving skills and leadership skills while fostering cooperation and teamwork. For example, *Making Sense of Business: A Simulation* is a board game that provides hands-on experience in executive decision making by having a group of two to five people run a business. This simulation, developed by Development Dimensions International, allows participants to learn how money travels through a business, how to create strategic plans, how their own job relates to other jobs, and how to make the tough decisions and trade-offs that business leaders deal with every day.[65]

**OUTSIDE SEMINARS** Many organizations offer special seminars and conferences aimed at providing skill-building training for managers. For example, the Canadian Management Centre offers a wide variety of seminars on management topics, ranging from "Secrets of Power Marketing" to "High-Performance Business Writing" and "Behavioural Interviewing." The seminars range in length from two to five days. Outdoor experiential expeditions, such as those available through the Canadian Outward Bound Wilderness School, are sometimes used to enhance leadership skills, team skills, and risk-taking behaviour.[66]

**RPC 6-13 >**

**Assesses and reports on the costs and benefits of engaging internal and external suppliers of development programs given the organizational constraints and objectives**

**COLLEGE/UNIVERSITY-RELATED PROGRAMS** Colleges and universities provide three types of management-development activities. First, many schools provide *executive-development programs* in leadership, marketing, HRM, operations management, and the like. Second, many colleges and universities also offer *individualized courses* in areas like business, management, and health-care administration. Finally, many schools also offer *degree programs*, such as the Master of Business Administration (MBA) or Executive MBA. The employer usually plays a role in university-related programs.[67] Many organizations offer *tuition refunds* as an incentive for employees to develop job-related skills. Employers are also increasingly granting technical and professional employees extended *sabbaticals*—periods of time off—for attending a college or university to pursue a higher degree or to upgrade skills.

**RPC 6-14 >**

**Develops requests for proposals (RFP) and reviews submissions by third parties**

Adventure-learning participants enhancing their leadership skills, team skills, and risk-taking behaviour.

**action learning** A training technique by which management trainees are allowed to work full-time analyzing and solving problems in other departments.

**case study method** A development method in which a trainee is presented with a written description of an organizational problem to diagnose and solve.

**management game** A computerized development technique in which teams of managers compete with one another by making decisions regarding realistic but simulated companies.

Simulation Training **www.learningcircuits.org**

Online Schools and Distance Learning **www.schoolfinder.com/schools/online.asp**

Pensare Inc. (e-learning) **www.trinity.edu/rjensen/000aaa/prest/penzare/pensare02.htm**

Blackboard (software products and services for e-learning) **www.blackboard.com**

Computer Based Training Planet **www.cbtplanet.com**

Career Key Networking **www.careerkey.com**

World Institute for Action Learning **www.wial.org**

**RPC 6-15 >**

**Recommends the selection of external training consultants and contractors such as public education institutions**

**ROLE-PLAYING** The aim of **role-playing** is to create a realistic situation and then have the trainees assume the parts (or roles) of specific persons in that situation.[68] Role-playing can trigger a spirited discussion, particularly when all participants throw themselves into the roles. The idea of the exercise is to solve the problem at hand and thereby develop trainees' skills in areas like leadership and delegation. For example, a supervisor could experiment with both a considerate and an autocratic leadership style, whereas in the real world, the person might not have this harmless avenue for experimentation. According to psychologist Norman Maier, role-playing also trains a person to be aware of and sensitive to the feelings of others.[69]

In order to maximize the effectiveness of role-playing, the instructor must prepare a wrap-up explanation of what the participants were to learn. Knowing the audience is important because some trainees may feel that role-playing is childish and others may be uncomfortable with acting.

**BEHAVIOUR MODELLING** **Behaviour modelling** involves: (1) showing trainees the right (or "model") way of doing something; (2) letting each person practise the right way to do it; and then (3) providing feedback regarding each trainee's performance.[70] It has been used for training in common supervisor–employee interactions and interpersonal situations, such as taking and giving criticism and establishing mutual trust and respect.

The basic behaviour-modelling procedure can be outlined as follows:

1. *Modelling.* First, trainees watch films or videos that show model persons behaving effectively in a problem situation. The film or video might thus show a supervisor effectively disciplining an employee if teaching how to discipline is the aim of the training program.
2. *Role-playing.* Next, the trainees are given roles to play in a simulated situation; here they practise and rehearse the effective behaviours demonstrated by the models.
3. *Social reinforcement.* The trainer provides reinforcement in the form of praise and constructive feedback based on how the trainee performs in the role-playing situation.
4. *Transfer of training.* Finally, trainees are encouraged to apply their new skills when they are back on their jobs.

**IN-HOUSE DEVELOPMENT CENTRES** Some employers have **in-house development centres**, also called "corporate universities." These centres usually combine classroom learning (lectures and seminars, for instance) with other techniques, such as assessment centres, in-basket exercises, and role-playing, to help develop employees and other managers. Two of the best-known centres in Canada are Bank of Montreal's Institute for Learning and CIBC's Leadership Centre.

## Leadership Development

**Leadership development** is the process by which employees with leadership potential are equipped with the knowledge, skills, and abilities needed to serve as organizational leaders. In a complex and competitive global arena, where success is measured by one's ability to respond to change quickly and effectively, exemplary leadership is the hallmark of competitive advantage.[71] Studies affirm that an organization's leadership- development initiatives have a direct impact on key financial metrics, including shareholder returns, growth in market share, and return in sales. These studies also report that 34 percent of organizations that achieve superior financial results are supported by comprehensive, first-rate leadership-development programs.[72] Yet in the midst of developing leadership talent, organizations face a leadership crisis. All sectors of the Canadian economy share a concern about an escalating leadership deficit resulting primarily from baby boomers leaving the workforce. Organizations are troubled by the low quantity of potential employees available to take on leadership roles to meet their future needs. In the *Leadership Forecast Study* of 2005–2006, 78 percent of organizations reported having difficulty securing skilled leaders, and 50 percent predicted that this degree of difficulty would increase.[73] The need to respond to the leadership crisis is intensely present in the Canadian public sector, where 30 percent of employees are forecast to retire in the next seven years.[74] The quest for leadership expertise has been dubbed the "war for talent."[75]

An example of how organizations develop leadership capacity can be found at Shoppers Drug Mart. The leadership-development program at Shoppers Drug Mart is imperative to the strategic viability of the pharmacy chain because it provides a rich supply of managers to fill the constantly growing need for leaders as new stores are built across Canada. Training involves presenting weekly seminars to stores across the country by satellite, engaging leadership trainees in self-directed study, and coaching at each store. Managers regularly conduct learning assessments to determine if their training design and delivery methods meet employees' needs and if the training still contributes to the company's strategic direction.

The Strategic HR box below provides an in-depth look at Labatt's management training program.

STRATEGIC HR

## Brewing Up Management Trainee Programs

**GRADS LAND PLUM ROLES IN RECORD TIME AT LABATT**

For the past two months, Luca Lorenzoni has gone to work every day in a lab coat and goggles—not exactly where the University of Waterloo business major expected to find himself after graduating a couple of years ago.

"If you'd told me that I'd be in the quality control lab, analyzing chemicals in beer, I would have laughed at you," he says. "But that's the opportunity we're given here."

Lorenzoni is in the midst of Labatt Breweries of Canada's global management trainee program, a cross-sectional program aimed at building leaders who understand the beer business from start to finish.

Having learned about brewing, Lorenzoni is now going on the road with sales reps to learn how to sell beer. In the new year, he'll move to head office, where he'll train in the HR, information technology, legal and corporate affairs side of the business. Then he'll be assigned to a five-month project before moving into his first management role with the company.

In all, Lorenzoni will spend 10 months in the program, where he'll learn every aspect of the business and travel across the country—all while receiving a full salary.

"If you went to a restaurant and there are five good things on the menu and you want to eat everything, what if they cooked you all five things and said you could try it out?" he says. "That's kind of what we're experiencing."

Labatt introduced the management trainee program in 2004, when its parent company, Interbrew, merged with Brazil's AmBev, to form InBev. The program has helped Labatt entice the best and brightest as future leaders, says Amy Secord, manager of people development. Last year, 3000 students and recent graduates (within two years of graduating) applied for the program. Only 15, including Lorenzoni, were chosen.

The selection process involves five rigorous rounds of interviews, including a business simulation that resembles the game of Risk, says Secord. Applicants are divided into teams and assigned a continent where they manage a beer company.

"We go through different rounds to represent different years. We throw in factors such as another entry into the market, perhaps they had a bad year with weather," she says. "It's not so much to see what their results are but how they interact as a team and who steps up as a natural leader."

Lorenzoni jokes that he still has nightmares about the intense selection process but says that's what attracted him to the program in the first place. It also gives him the time and experience to decide whether Labatt is the right fit for him and vice versa.

"Any time you spend that much time and dedicate that many resources to actually finding candidates, you know the company has a lot behind the program," he says. "You get to see round through round who's staying on and see if you really fit with them."

Before applying for the program, Lorenzoni did consulting work in Toronto with little vision for the future. The management trainee program has opened up more opportunities than he could have imagined, he says.

**role-playing** A training technique in which trainees act out the parts of people in a realistic management situation.

**behaviour modelling** A training technique in which trainees are first shown good management techniques, then asked to play roles in a simulated situation, and finally given feedback regarding their performance.

**in-house development centres** A company-based method for exposing prospective managers to realistic exercises in order to develop improved management skills.

**leadership development** The process by which employees with leadership potential are equipped with the knowledge, skills, and abilities needed to serve as leaders within an organization.

"You see a path. It's something that at every step you have to earn but, at the same time, there is a lot of opportunity here," he says.

The program is already paying off for Labatt, says Secord. Several trainees from the first intake have shot straight up the corporate ranks, landing roles just below the director level—roles that have traditionally taken 10 to 15 years to achieve.

"These are people two to three years out of school," she says. "(The program) is imperative. We have to make sure we have the right people in the right places."

Some components of the program have been modified along the way and, more significantly, Labatt has condensed the interview process to have candidates in the door by November, instead of December.

"We've had to speed up our recruitment process quite a bit," says Secord. "Even in this tough market, more and more companies are trying to get the best talent. Last year, in Luca's year, we actually lost a lot of candidates because we were only offering to them at the beginning of December."

Labatt is also trying to reach a broader audience, through a Facebook group and trainees' blogs. Secord declines to say how much the program costs per trainee but will say it's one of the company's more expensive—and valued—programs.

"If we don't take the time to make sure that we have the right people, who are trained the right way, we're in a lot of trouble further down the line. We need them now."

Source: D. Harder, "Brewing up management trainee programs: Grads land plum roles in record time at Labatt," *Canadian HR Reporter*, December 15, 2008, p. 8. Reprinted with permission.

**AN ETHICAL DILEMMA**

Is it ethical to require employees to participate in role-playing exercises when they are uncomfortable in this situation?

Leadership-development needs must first be assessed at the overall corporate level based on an organization's strategy. For example, if global expansion is planned, then managers with cross-cultural management competencies would be required. Each individual department would need to review its role in the strategic plan and assess its development needs. If employees have recently received new hardware or software, department managers with knowledge of these new resources will be required.

When a leadership-development program is aimed at filling a specific senior management position, such as CEO, the process is called **succession planning.** Succession planning is particularly challenging in today's downsized organizations because the pool from which to choose future leaders has grown smaller and is filled with employees who need a compelling reason to remain with the organization. A formal succession plan can aid in employee retention by encouraging promising employees to pursue their careers within the firm by offering a reasonable return for loyalty and effort.

A succession program typically takes place in stages. First, an *organizational projection* is made. Here, each department's management needs are anticipated based on such factors as planned expansion or contraction. Next, the HR department reviews its *management-skills inventories* to identify the management talent now employed. *Management-replacement charts* are then drawn. These summarize potential candidates for each of the management slots as well as each person's development needs, such as *job rotation*, *executive-development* activities, and assignment to an *in-house management-development centre*.[76]

Succession planning has its challenges. A persistent difficulty is the age-old problem of executives wanting to hire someone in their own image. Another challenge is today's highly mobile workforce. One way to offset these issues is to publicize the succession planning process, letting high performers know they are being considered for a senior position. This is an approach used by Enbridge Gas, JetForm, and the pharmaceutical firm Schering Canada Inc.[77]

Effective executive development is particularly challenging because leaders need the opportunity to learn it, try it out, and be supported in the process. The Banff Centre for Management in Alberta uses a five-step process that involves competency modelling and learning contracts in order to maximize the effectiveness of its executive development programs:[78]

**Step 1:** *Evaluation of leadership competencies.* Competency profiles have been researched for the leader's specific position and can provide a mechanism for peers, colleagues, and supervisors to provide feedback. Table 6.1 illustrates key competencies for leading strategically.

**RPC 6-16 >**

**Facilitates coaching and post-training support activities to ensure transfer of learning to the workplace**

### *table* 6.1 Leading Strategically: Competency Map

| Core Competency | Category A Behaviour | Category B Behaviour | Category C Behaviour | Category D Behaviour |
|---|---|---|---|---|
| 1. Fashions clear vision and passion for quality, innovation and business strategy across organization/ division. | Shows a personal sense of quality, passion and innovation for the organization and its products/services. | Engages the team in developing general quality direction/standards for the organization. Key points of contact for decision making around new ideas and processes are clear. | Input from all departments in the organization and customers is utilized to drive goals and "future state." Customers and stakeholders are regularly tapped to suggest improvements and new processes. | Stakeholder input, competitive benchmarks, and organization/ customer knowledge are utilized to create continuously improving standards, values, and goals for the orgaization, department, and individuals. High level of passion and commitment to this end is maintained. |
| 2. Is capable of leading strategic planning processes. | Correlates plans and orchestrates activities for short-term results and fire fighting. | Involves key stakeholders in longer-term, strategic discussions on selected issues. Leads own team effectively in business planning process. | Leads a complete strategic planning process (to action plans) with senior management, including input from internal stakeholders. Departmental "outcome measures" are defined, business risk assessed, and realignment of organization considered. | Establishes interactive and integrated strategic planning process with all stakeholders based on an accurate scanning of the environment, audience tastes and client needs. Goals and outcomes are clearly defined for the organization within evolving organization. |
| 3. Vision development and enunciation within sector and in keeping with global trends. | Shows a personal sense of the general direction of the organization. | Engages team in developing a common understanding of future direction. | Establishes the process and gathers input from key stakeholders for the purpose of describing a desired future state shared by the management team. | Develops a clear and shared picture of the future state based on an accurate reading of sector, global trends and forces within the environment. Consistently communicates to multi-stakeholders so it is understood. |
| 4. Is able to recognize "big picture" patterns and relationships and understands how to make balanced decisions suitable for the organization. | Has good problem-solving skills utilizing traditional models. Able to balance competing demands and tends to see/create opportunity from problems. | Engages colleagues in looking at organization and industry trends, issues. Draws connections among them in order to make balanced decisions for his/her team. | Sees clearly how change in one part of the organization affects many others. Works with other departments to develop structures/processes in order to understand and address key issues. | Can conceive and think through systems seeing complex cause and effect relationships. Uses these to keep focus on macro-goals, service outcomes and the larger global context. Sees organization existing within larger industry/community, with attendant responsibilities, impact, and challenges. |
| 5. Development of effective differentiation strategies within organization. | Shows an intuitive sense about how his or her business unit can be/is unique in its products and services. | Engages team to identify strategies that will make the area unique, listens to customer needs, then positions business unit products/services accordingly in the marketplace. | Engages all levels of the business unit to examine their value to customers and finds new ways to build relationships that add value and distinctiveness from competitors. | Partners with customers, stakeholders, and the marketplace, to establish processes that support uniqueness strategies. Creates sustained, value-enhancing, competitive advantage. |

Source: *Leading Strategically © 2002: Competency Map.* Banff, AB: The Banff Centre 2002. www.banffcentre.ca/departments/leadership/competency.map. Reproduced with permission of The Banff Centre.

**Step 2:** *The learning contract.* The learning contract ensures individual focus and agreement between the participant, his or her supervisor, and the instructor on the critical elements for developmental success in the next six to nine months. Even the most capable adult can really only work on improving four or five attributes at once.

**Step 3:** *The learning process.* The competency profiling and learning contract helps focus the learning process, creating links and building strategies. The learning must be hands-on and provide participants with opportunities to try out new behaviour, receive feedback, and practise again several times.

**Step 4:** *Re-entry planning.* The learning contract helps the learner plan how he or she will start to apply the learning. Clear implementation plans with timelines and follow-up support will help ensure that the training actually results in changed behaviour and has an impact on the company.

**Step 5:** *Measurement of training effectiveness.* The competency profile and learning contract form the basis for measurement of successful changes in behaviour as well as levels of impact on the sponsoring organization. They can also be used to track continuous improvement by all parties in the learning partnership.

## 6.6 STEP 3: IMPLEMENTATION AND DELIVERY OF TRAINING

Once learning objectives have been written and training methods have been selected, trainers design the agenda for delivering the training. The agenda includes comprehensive details of content coverage, delivery methods, and timelines. Trainers also take into consideration adult learning principles—the guidelines and approaches that create a climate conducive to learning. This climate includes opportunities for trainees to practise new skills; setting up discussion forums to share personal knowledge, experiences, and insights; and the opportunity to receive recognition and constructive feedback to expand trainees' thinking and skill development. Trainers should know about and design training that satisfies trainees' learning-style

### In-class Notes

**Implementation and Delivery of Training**

- Design training agenda, including content coverage, how it will be delivered, and timelines
- Adult learning principles and learning style preferences set the stage for creating a climate conducive to learning
- Validation requires a pilot study to assess effectiveness of a program in achieving its objectives
- Revisions made to program based on results of validation study
- Implementation of program by training and development professionals
- Train-the-trainer sessions required if unfamiliar content or new presentation methods are involved

preferences. For example, people have three main learning styles: *auditory*, learning through talking and listening; *visual*, learning through pictures and print; and *kinesthetic*, learning by doing. Identifying learning styles and personalizing the training accordingly can enhance training effectiveness.[79]

Validation of the training or development program is an often-overlooked step in the training process. In order to ensure that a program will accomplish its objectives, it is necessary to conduct a pilot study or "run-through" with a representative group of trainees. The results of the pilot study are used to assess the effectiveness of the training.

Revisions to the program can be made to address any problems encountered by the pilot group of trainees in using the training and development material and experiences provided to them. Testing at the end of the pilot study can measure whether the program is producing the desired improvement in skill level. If the results fall below the level of the training or development objectives, then more work must be undertaken to strengthen the instructional design.

Once the training or development program has been validated, it is ready to be implemented by training and development professionals. In some cases, a train-the-trainer workshop may be required to familiarize trainers with unfamiliar content or with unique and innovative new methods for presenting the training content.

## 6.7 STEP 4: TRANSFER OF LEARNING

One of the most persistent and perplexing challenges faced by trainers is how to enhance the probability that learning from training classrooms is applied in workplace practice. Studies indicate that between 60 and 90 percent of learning acquired through training is not applied to the job.[80] A number of approaches can be used before, during, and after training to minimize barriers that impede transfer of learning and increase chances that learning will stick. Before training, trainees should be interviewed about their preferred learning styles, content they would like covered,

### In-class Notes

**Transfer of Learning**

- Enhance the probability that learning from the training classroom is applied in workplace practice
- Minimize the barriers that impede the transfer of learning from classroom to workplace
- Before training, seek trainees' input and create a learning contract to secure trainees' support for training
- During training, provide opportunities for trainees to practise new skills and explore potential obstacles to transfer of learning
- After training, encourage goal setting and relapse prevention

**succession planning** A process by which senior level openings are planned for and eventually filled.

The Bank of Montreal's Institute for Learning.

and training methods that suit their learning styles. When trainees' input is built into the training design, it increases the likelihood that they will support the training initiative. A learning contract should be generated between trainees and their supervisors so that there is an action plan in place to support new learning when trainees return to work. During training, opportunities should be provided for trainees to practice new skills and work through obstacles that might impede integration of new behaviours into practice. At the end of training, transfer interventions include goal setting and relapse prevention. Trainees should be encouraged to set measureable and observable goals and action strategies for moving new learning into everyday routines. **Relapse prevention** involves a follow-up session after training to check trainees' progress in achieving personal learning goals and to offer counsel if learning has derailed and trainees have returned to former behaviours. A buddy system is also advisable so that trainees can support each other as they transition to new ways of performing.

## 6.8 STEP 5: EVALUATION

After trainees complete their training (and at planned intervals during the training), the program should be evaluated to see how well its objectives have been met. For example, are trainees learning as *much* as they can? Is there a *better method* for training them? These are some of the questions that are answered by evaluating training efforts.

Overall, there is little doubt that training and development can be effective. For example, many companies that invested heavily in workplace training have substantially improved their results. Profitable companies spend the most on training. Those companies, rated among the 100 best companies to work for in Canada, spend the most per employee on training.[81]

There are two basic issues to address when evaluating a training program. The first is the design of the evaluation study and, in particular, whether controlled experimentation will be used. The second is the training effect to be measured. **Controlled experimentation** is the best method to use in evaluating a training program. A controlled experiment uses both a training group and a control group (which receives no training). Performance data should be obtained before and after the training effort in the training group and before and after a corresponding work period in the control group. In this way, it is possible to determine the extent to which any change in performance in the training

### *In-class Notes*

**Evaluation**

- Design evaluation study; determine whether to use controlled experimentation; determine training effect to be measured
- Four categories of training outcome: reaction, learning, behaviour, results

group resulted from the training itself rather than from some organization-wide change, such as a raise in pay, which would likely have affected employees in both groups equally. In terms of current practices, however, one survey found that less than half of the companies responding attempted to obtain before-and-after measures from trainees; the number of organizations using control groups was negligible.[82]

Four basic categories of training outcomes can be measured:[83]

1. *Reaction.* First, evaluate trainees' reactions to the program. Did they like the program? Did they think it was worthwhile? One expert suggests at least using an evaluation form like the one shown in Figure 6.3 to evaluate trainee reaction.[84]
2. *Learning.* Second, test the trainees to determine whether they learned the principles, skills, and facts they were supposed to learn.
3. *Behaviour.* Next, ask whether the trainees' behaviour on the job changed because of the training program. For example, are employees in a store's complaint department more courteous toward disgruntled customers than previously?
4. *Results.* Lastly, but probably most importantly, ask, "What final results were achieved in terms of the training objectives previously set? Did the number of customer complaints about employees drop? Did the reject rate improve? Was turnover reduced? Are production quotas now being met?" Improved results are, of course, especially important. The training program may succeed in terms of the reactions from trainees, increased learning, and even changes in behaviour, but if the results are not achieved, then in the final analysis, the training did not achieve its goals—especially its mandate to support the organization's strategic mission.

## *figure* 6.3 A Sample Training Evaluation Form

1. Considering everything, how would you rate this program? (Check one)
   Unsatisfactory ____ Satisfactory ____ Good ____ Outstanding ____
   Please explain briefly the reasons for the rating you have given:

2 Were your expectations (Check one) exceeded ____ matched ____ fallen below ____?

3. Are you going to recommend this training program to other members of your department?
   Yes ____ No ____. If you check "yes," please describe the job titles held by the people to whom you would recommend this program.

   ______________________________

4. Please rate the relative value (1 = very valuable; 2 = worthwhile; 3 = negligible)

| | | | |
|---|---|---|---|
| Videocassettes | ____ | Role-playing exercises | ____ |
| Workbooks | ____ | Lectures | ____ |
| Small group discussions | ____ | Readings: Articles | ____ |
| Cases | ____ | | |

5. Please rate the main lecturer's presentation (1 = not effective; 2 = somewhat effective; 3 = effective) in terms of:
   Ability to communicate ____
   Emphasis on key points ____
   Handout materials ____

continued

**relapse prevention** A follow-up session after training to check trainees' progress in achieving personal learning goals and to offer support if barriers stagnate the transfer of learning into practice.

**controlled experimentation** Formal methods for testing the effectiveness of a training program, preferably with before-and-after tests and a control group.

Succession Planning **www.emergingleader.com**

Business Training Media.com Inc. **www.business-marketing.com**

## *figure* 6.3 A Sample Training Evaluation Form—continued

6. Please rate the following cases, readings, and videocassettes by placing a check mark in the appropriate column:

| | Excellent | Good | Fair | Poor |
|---|---|---|---|---|
| Overcoming Resistance to Change | | | | |
| Reviewing Performance Goals | | | | |
| Setting Performance Goals | | | | |
| Handling Employee Complaints | | | | |
| Improving Employee Performance | | | | |
| Slade Co. | | | | |
| Superior Slate Quarry | | | | |
| McGregor's Theory X and Y | | | | |
| Henry Manufacturing | | | | |
| First Federal Savings | | | | |
| Claremont Industries | | | | |

7. Was the ratio of lectures to cases (Check one): High ____ OK ____ Low ____?
8. Were the videocassettes pertinent to your work? (Check one)
   To most of my work ____
   To some of my work ____
   To none of my work ____
9. To help the training director and the staff provide further improvements in future programs, please give us your frank opinion of each case discussion leader's contribution to your learning. (Place your check marks in the appropriate boxes.)

| | Excellent | Above Average | Average | Below Average | Poor |
|---|---|---|---|---|---|
| Davis | | | | | |
| Gleason | | | | | |
| Laird | | | | | |
| Martin | | | | | |
| Pontello | | | | | |
| Shall | | | | | |
| Sommers | | | | | |
| Wilson | | | | | |
| Zimmer | | | | | |

10. How would you evaluate your participation in the program? (Check)

| | | | |
|---|---|---|---|
| Overall workload: | Too heavy ____ | Just right ____ | Too light ____ |
| Case preparation: | Too much ____ | Just right ____ | Too light ____ |
| Homework assignments: | Too heavy ____ | Just right ____ | Too light ____ |

11. What suggestions do you have for improving the program?

    ______________________________________________

    ______________________________________________

12. Please add any additional comments, criticisms, or suggestions that you think might be helpful for the training group to know before scheduling future programs.

Source: K. N. Wexley and G. P. Latham, *Developing and Training Human Resources in Organizations*, 3rd ed. © 2002. Adapted by permission of Pearson Education Inc., Upper Saddle River, NJ.

As part of the evaluation process, a **return on investment (ROI)** should be conducted to ascertain if the benefits associated with developing and delivering the training outweigh the costs. Calculating the cost effectiveness of training helps to determine if the program should be delivered again in its current format or if revisions are required before it is delivered to a new audience. In some cases, trainers might need to find more efficient and cost-effective ways to deliver training within budget. Cost calculations enhance the credibility of the training and development function as one that is cost-sensitive and profit-oriented. The calculation of ROI is done using the following formula:

$$\text{Return on Investment} = \frac{\text{Net Program Benefits}}{\text{Cost of the Program}}$$

A **utility analysis** is also an important step in the training and development process. It is most beneficial to conduct at the beginning of the process and is used to forecast the net financial benefit from training and development. A utility analysis uses a complex statistical formula with which trainers calculate the dollar value of the net financial benefit of training by determining the extent of differences in performance among employees who are trained and those who are not. A break-even analysis can also be calculated to determine at what point training benefits equal costs.

One Canadian study that assessed organizational results from training found that organizations with greater investment in training had 14.1 percent higher profits, 13.7 percent higher productivity, and 5.7 percent higher revenues than organizations with lesser investment in training.[85] At TD Bank, the value of the bank's $50 million annual spending on training is measured very carefully, as illustrated in the Strategic HR box on page 204.

**RPC 6-17 >**

**Ensures participant and organizational feedback is documented and evaluated**

## 6.9 TRAINING FOR SPECIAL PURPOSES

Increasingly, training does more than just prepare employees to perform their jobs effectively. Training for special purposes, such as dealing with increased workforce diversity, is also required. The following is a sampling of such special-purpose training programs.

**RPC 6-18 >**

**Documents participant feedback to evaluate effectiveness of program delivery**

**RPC 6-19 >**

**Builds constructive and supportive relationships**

### Literacy Training Techniques

*frontLINE tips* Functional illiteracy is a serious problem for many employers. Nearly half of Canadians aged 16 and above have reading skills that are not up to international standards. Twenty-two percent have difficulty dealing with printed material, and another 26 percent can deal only with material that is simple and clearly laid out.[86] Yet as the Canadian economy shifts from goods to services, there is a corresponding need for workers who are more skilled, more literate, and better able to demonstrate at least basic arithmetic skills. Not only does enhanced literacy give employees a better chance for success in their careers, it improves the bottom-line performance of the employer—through time savings, lower costs, and improved quality of work.[87]

**RPC 6-20 >**

**Compiles, analyzes, and documents evaluation data based on feedback**

**return on investment (ROI)** A formula for calculating the cost effectiveness of training to determine if training benefits outweigh costs.

**utility analysis** A complex statistical formula used to forecast the net financial benefit from training and development.

National Adult Literacy Database **www.nald.ca**

Diversity at Work **www.diversityatwork.com**

Diversity in the Workplace **www.diversityintheworkplace.ca**

Ideas and Training **www.ideasandtraining.com**

**STRATEGIC HR**

## Measuring Training Effectiveness at TD Bank

Connie Karlsson is head of Learning Outcomes, a unit of six people inside the Learning and Development Department at TD Bank Financial Group. Their job is to measure the value of the bank's trainings pending. The group started out by picking an evaluation model that would work. Six Sigma was eliminated because banking is a sales and service environment, and a return on investment model was rejected as not simple enough. They wanted to institutionalize the measurement of training value.

The questionnaire the group developed for learners to fill out at the end of each training session was unique in that it went after indications of all four levels of measurement outlined in Kirkpatrick's training evaluation model—reaction, learning, behaviour, results. Karlsson sees the questionnaire as a reinforcement tool as it reminds trainees that they are being trained to improve their performance and to improve their ability to contribute to the achievement of business goals.

In working with business units within the bank to assess the results of training on business objectives, Karlsson says, "We've become business analysts. We've created partnerships. The people on my team are not perceived as training designers or facilitators. They're treated as business partners in helping the business align their business reporting with training. That was the real business win."

Source: Adapted from U. Vu, "Numbers-Cruncher Makes Impact on Training Culture at TD," *Canadian HR Reporter* (July 12, 2004), pp. 1–2. Reproduced by permission of *Canadian HR Reporter*, Carswell, One Corporate Plaza, 2075 Kennedy Road, Scarborough, ON, M1T 3V4.

Employers are responding to this issue in two main ways. First, companies are testing prospective employees' basic skills. Second, they are instituting basic skills and literacy programs. One approach is to use an interactive video disk (IVD). This technique combines the drama of video with the power of microcomputers.[88] An example is *Principles of Alphabet Literacy (PALs)*. This program uses animated video and a computer-stored voice to enable non-readers to associate sounds with letters and letters with words and to use the words to create sentences.[89] A second IVD program is called *SKILLPAC*. This program, subtitled *English for Industry*, was designed mostly for non–native-English speakers. It combines video, audio, and computer technologies to teach language skills in the context of the specific workplace situation in which those skills will be used.[90]

### Diversity Training

With an increasingly diverse workforce, many more firms are implementing diversity training programs. Diversity training enhances cross-cultural sensitivity with the aim of creating more harmonious working relationships among a firm's employees. It also enhances the abilities of salespeople to provide effective customer service when dealing with a diverse group of customers.[91]

Two broad approaches to diversity training are cross-cultural communication training and cultural sensitivity training. *Cross-cultural communication training* focuses on workplace cultural etiquette and interpersonal skills. *Cultural sensitivity training* focuses on sensitizing employees to the views of different cultural groups toward work so that employees from diverse backgrounds can work together more effectively. However, it is necessary to go beyond these approaches in order to gain the extra benefits of a diverse workforce. Diversity training should be seen as a business opportunity and be linked to long-term organizational development. According to one survey of HR directors, specific training programs aimed at offsetting problems associated with a diverse workforce include (from most used to least used) improving interpersonal skills, understanding/valuing cultural differences, improving technical skills, socializing employees into the corporate culture, reducing stress, indoctrinating into the North American work ethic, mentoring, improving English proficiency, improving basic math skills, and improving bilingual skills for English-speaking employees.[92] A unique example regarding diversity issues in Canadian banks is provided in the Workforce Diversity box on page 205.

Handidactis, a non-profit organization in Montreal, provides sensitivity training to help people deal with persons with disabilities, including those with

WORKFORCE DIVERSITY

## CIBC Trains Newcomers for Jobs in Canadian Banks

**BANK HIRES 15 OF 24 TRAINING PARTICIPANTS**

Having worked nine years in the banking industry in the Philippines and several more years in a family-run flower supply business in Manila, Gina Domingo immigrated to Canada with her husband and children last June.

A month after arriving in Toronto, she landed a job at a Roots warehouse as an order picker and then took a job at Starbucks as a barista. While she was working at Starbucks, she found out about a new program offered by CIBC and the YMCA of Greater Toronto to help newcomers to Canada prepare for jobs in the Canadian financial services sector.

"When I first came here to Canada, there were fears about giving up what we had back home, but the training program gave us the tools to be more effective and probably more marketable," said Domingo.

The six-week job readiness program, CIBC Connection to Employment, was free for newcomers with a background in the financial services sector. More than 665 candidates applied for the program. That number was narrowed down to 44 who met the English-language requirements.

"We saw it as both a business opportunity and a talent acquisition opportunity," said Sharon Wingfelder, vice-president of HR, resourcing, at CIBC. "We're always looking for creative channels to find great talent."

In the end, 24 candidates were chosen with a wide range of experiences, from entry-level customer service to senior-level positions, and from those who had just arrived in Canada to those who had been here for several years.

Over six weeks, participants learned how to put together a résumé, prepare for an interview and how to conduct themselves during the interview. They also learned about the culture of the financial services industry and bank-specific information relevant to Canada.

"Even though I had worked for a bank back home, the situation now is different, in terms of regulations in the bank," said Domingo.

But even more than the bank-specific training, it was the soft skills such as teamwork, conflict resolution and problem solving that Domingo found most helpful.

"That is most likely to help us out, being new in the country. You can apply it in any industry that you go to," she said.

Those are also the skills found most useful by Felix Quartey, who has worked as a supervisor in the financial services industry in Ghana and Australia, where he also taught finance and accounting.

"Those are the skill I believe I will carry with me throughout my career," said Quartey, who has been in Canada for five months. He said the opportunity to apply for jobs at CIBC after the program ended was a bonus.

So far CIBC has hired 15 of the participants for a wide range of positions, including commercial banking, retail banking, telephone banking and operations, and six more are in the pipeline, said Wingfelder. RBC also hired one of the participants.

Domingo has accepted a position as a customer service representative at a CIBC branch and Quartey has accepted a position as a CIBC loan operations officer.

With so many more people showing an interest in the program than could be accommodated, CIBC and the YMCA decided to offer a career fair and expo aimed at newcomers.

"There was a gap that was there and we really felt compelled to do something for these individuals," said Wingfelder.

More than 200 people attended the two-hour event, which included a one-hour session on interview and résumé writing skills, how to market yourself for different jobs and how to approach people. Afterward, attendees could check out different booths with relevant resources for newcomers, including language training.

CIBC also accumulated 20 leads for new hires from the event, said Wingfelder.

CIBC and the YMCA are discussing running another six-week program and looking at ways to expand, she said. These planned pleased Quartey who would like other newcomers to have the same opportunity to enter the Canadian job market as he did.

"There are a lot of newcomers in the country who are really looking for such opportunities—there just aren't that many opportunities available for newcomers. It's an excellent innovation on the part of CIBC and YMCA. I really would recommend this program to any newcomers who are wanting to access the Canadian workplace," said Quartey.

Source: S. Klie, "CIBC trains newcomers for jobs in Canadian banks," *Canadian HR Reporter*, January 26, 2009, p. 3. Reprinted with permission.

impaired vision or hearing and individuals who have a physical or mental disability. The first step is to ask the person with the disability if he or she needs anything special to do the job. This is often overlooked as people jump in to help someone with a disability, which, in effect, takes away that person's independence. Furthermore, the person may not need help. The training also involves discovering what it is like to have a disability through simulated visual and speech impediments.[93]

## Customer Service Training

More and more companies are finding it necessary to compete based on the quality of their service, and many are therefore implementing customer service training programs. The basic aim is to train all employees to treat the company's customers in a courteous and hospitable manner. Countless service companies today emphasize the saying, "The customer is always right."

The Canadian retail industry recently faced a crisis with respect to human resources. Understaffed and poorly trained workers were ill-equipped to provide quality customer service.[94] At the Liquor Control Board of Ontario, the crisis was met with a decision to train all 4500 employees through the "That's the Spirit" program, which enhanced customer-service skills and boosted knowledge about distilled spirits. The program stressed empowerment of front-line employees to help customers make better buying decisions. The results have been dramatic—sales of spirits, which had been declining since 1974, have begun to increase.[95]

**AN ETHICAL DILEMMA**

Should employees be required to participate in outdoor training if they do not want to because it is going to take time that they would otherwise be spending on personal and family responsibilities?

## Training for Teamwork and Empowerment

An increasing number of firms use work teams and empowerment to improve their effectiveness. However, many organizations find that teamwork does not just happen, and employees must be trained to be good team members. Some firms use outdoor training—such as Outward Bound programs—to build teamwork.[96] Outdoor training usually involves taking a group of employees out into rugged, mountainous terrain where, by overcoming physical obstacles, they learn team spirit, cooperation, and the need to trust and rely on each other. As one participant put it, "Every time I climbed over a rock, I needed someone's help."[97] The idea is to build trust in one's colleagues. Not all employees are eager to participate in such activities. Some feel that the outdoor activities are too contrived to be applicable back at work. However, they do illustrate the lengths to which employers will go to build teamwork.

Empowering employees (either individually or as teams) also almost always requires extensive training. It is rarely enough to just tell group members that they are "empowered" to do all the buying and

*In-class Notes*

**Training for Special Purposes**

- Literacy training addresses functional illiteracy in Canada's workforce
- Diversity training is necessary for effective use of diverse workforce
- Customer-service training is critical in the service-based economy
- Training for teamwork and empowerment intended to improve organizational effectiveness

selling and planning involved in producing the product for which they are responsible. Instead, extensive training is required to ensure they have the skills to do the job. Employees need to develop the problem-solving and analysis skills required to help the work team be empowered—in this case, to analyze and solve problems. Training in basic accounting is an example.

# Training and Development on the International Stage

Most organizations operate their businesses around the world through trade, flow of information technology, and finance. It is estimated that global trade in goods and services will triple to $27 trillion by 2030.[98] As organizations become truly global, the demand for exemplary leadership on the international stage will be more pronounced. Organizations will require more sophisticated leadership-development initiatives to groom staff for emerging leadership accountabilities. Leaders will be expected to exercise unparalleled strategic thinking, judgment, and decision-making intelligence to function in complex and uncertain times, challenge the status quo, cultivate extraordinary innovations, and develop high-performing teams to move forward aggressively with revitalized strategic priorities. Exemplary leadership that launches progressive strategic initiatives to propel organizations into uncharted and revolutionary terrain is the bedrock upon which organizational success and sustainability are built, and positions organizations for competitive advantage in the fluid, global economy.

In the past five years, Adobe, one of the world's leading software companies, has grown to more than 7000 employees worldwide. With expansion, there is a need for programs to develop exceptional leaders. Adobe recognizes that developing a global contingent of great leaders creates a competitive advantage as they reorganize to seize market opportunities and optimize performance. Adobe initiated "Adobe Leadership Experience" (ALE)—a tailor-made leadership development program that prepares leaders to engage global, cross-business teams and build collaborative networks with international partners. Participants in leadership training come from Canada, the United States, Europe, India, China, and Japan.

ALE consists of three integrated phases: (1) individual development, which includes 360-degree feedback and executive coaching to identify and hone strengths; (2) offsite classroom training at Berkeley's Haas School of Business at the University of California, where instruction in strategy, finance, marketing, and leading global teams is given (also included is a business simulation in which teams compete to demonstrate their leadership capacity in running a company and managing challenges); and, (3) an action-learning component in which participants work on an individual business challenge and a team business challenge with some of their ALE peers. The individual business challenge lasts three months and can relate to a new business opportunity, process improvement, change management initiative, or something specific that will help the leader stretch his or her abilities and contribute to Adobe. Each leader meets with an executive sponsor to track progress. The eight-week team-business challenge relates to a strategic project for the company, after which the participants present their recommendations and decide on next steps.

In 2008, 86 percent of Adobe's vice-presidential and general managerial positions were filled by internal candidates, up from 56 percent the previous year.[99]

# Chapter Review

## Answers to Test Yourself

1. What is the purpose of an orientation program from an employer's perspective?

   From an employer's perspective, a comprehensive orientation contributes to lower turnover, increased productivity, improved employee morale, and lower training costs. Developing strong orientation programs to lower turnover is especially critical at a time when Generation Y's definition of long-term commitment to an organization is one year and only one in five anticipates staying with the same company for six years or longer.

2. What are the three approaches to evaluating orientation programs?

   The three approaches to evaluating orientation programs are:

   *Employee Reaction:* Interview (either individually or in focus groups) or survey new employees for their opinions on the usefulness of the orientation program in helping them transition into the company and their new jobs.

   *Cost/Benefit Analysis:* Calculate the return on investment from orientation programs by comparing orientation costs (e.g., printing of handbooks, time spent orienting new employees by HR staff and immediate supervisors) and the benefits of orientation (e.g., reduction in errors, rate of productivity, efficiency levels, accident rates, reduction in turnover, and so on).

   *Employee Evaluation:* Assess degree to which orientation contributed to employee's on-the-job performance as part of the new employee's first performance evaluation.

3. What is the strategic relevance of training and development?

   Training and development equips employees with the skills, knowledge, and abilities needed to perform their jobs according to company standards so that the organization meets its goals. With a competent workforce that meets organizational goals, a company is able to maintain its competitive advantage in its industry.

4. What are the five steps in the training process?

   The training process consists of five steps: needs analysis, instructional design, implementation and delivery of training, transfer of learning, and evaluation.

5. Why has the need to deliver training through e-learning escalated in the past few years?

   The need to deliver training through e-learning has escalated with the arrival of Generation Y, who bring an impressive portfolio of requisite skills in technology to the workplace and expect that organizations are capitalizing on computer access and knowledge.

6. What is the organizational value of leadership development?

   In a complex and competitive global arena where success is measured by one's ability to respond to change quickly and effectively, exemplary leadership is the hallmark of competitive advantage. Studies affirm that an organization's leadership development initiatives have a direct impact on key financial metrics, including shareholder returns, growth in market share, and return in sales.

## Key Terms

action learning (p. 192)
behaviour modelling (p. 194)
case study method (p. 192)
controlled experimentation (p. 200)
deficiency of execution (p. 186)
deficiency of knowledge (p. 186)
development (p. 182)
developmental job rotation (p. 191)
e-learning (p. 189)
electronic performance support systems (EPSS) (p. 191)
employee orientation (p. 180)
in-house development centres (p. 194)
job instruction training (JIT) (p. 187)
leadership development (p. 194)
management game (p. 193)
on-the-job training (OJT) (p. 187)
organizational analysis (p. 185)
person analysis (p. 185)
programmed learning (p. 188)
reality shock (p. 180)

relapse prevention (p. 200)
return on investment (p. 203)
role-playing (p. 194)
socialization (p. 180)
succession planning (p. 196)
task analysis (p. 185)
training (p. 182)
utility analysis (p. 203)
vestibule or simulated training (p. 188)
virtual reality (p. 191)

## Required Professional Capabilities (RPCs)

RPC 6-1 > (p. 180)
RPC 6-2 > (p. 183)
RPC 6-3 > (p. 183)
RPC 6-4 > (p. 183)
RPC 6-5 > (p. 184)
RPC 6-6 > (p. 186)
RPC 6-7 > (p. 186)
RPC 6-8 > (p. 186)
RPC 6-9 > (p. 186)
RPC 6-10 > (p. 187)
RPC 6-11 > (p. 189)
RPC 6-12 > (p. 192)
RPC 6-13 > (p. 193)
RPC 6-14 > (p. 193)
RPC 6-15 > (p. 194)
RPC 6-16 > (p. 196)
RPC 6-17 > (p. 203)
RPC 6-18 > (p. 203)
RPC 6-19 > (p. 203)
RPC 6-20 > (p. 203)

# Cases and Exercises

**myHRlab**

For additional cases and exercises, go to www.pearsoned.ca/myhrlab.

## CASE INCIDENT

### Johnston Manufacturing

Ben Adams is the new training coordinator for Johnston Manufacturing, a large unionized facility that designs and produces health and safety equipment for the construction industry. Ben recently graduated with a Bachelor of Commerce specializing in Human Resources Management, with a strong background in training and leadership theory. One of the main reasons Ben was hired was to train first-line supervisors in current management practices. The company is experiencing an unusually high turnover rate among its skilled workers and the executive management team believes the additional training could help reduce turnover. One of Ben's first jobs was to design a series of management-development workshops for lower-level managers on how to motivate employees.

Ben worked hard preparing the first workshop. He put together a training manual, an impressive PowerPoint presentation, and had lots of examples to support his presentation. The president sent a memo to all managers requiring that they attend the training session. Ben was pleased to receive the president's support and he continued his efforts to prepare the best presentation possible.

On the first day of the workshop, all managers reported at the proper time. However, some were not happy to be there because they felt that their time could best be utilized working with their crews. They had pressing deadlines to meet. Each manager's unit was considered a profit centre, and they were evaluated weekly on the profit and loss statement of the unit. Ben assured everyone that they would find his presentation valuable, and proceeded with showing his first PowerPoint slide.

He began his presentation with a great description of Freud's personality theory. Ben then went on to describe Maslow's hierarchy of needs, Vroom's Expectancy Theory of Motivation, and Skinner's Behaviour Modification Theory.

At the end of the presentation, Ben was really pleased with his performance. He felt certain that the managers would have benefited from hearing about the theories.

However, his enthusiasm was completely destroyed when one of the managers approached him afterward and said, "Ben, on behalf of the managers, we really appreciated you telling us about all those interesting theories. You are a very good speaker. But can you please tell us how we can use this information to motivate our teams out there on the production line to produce more parts? None of that stuff is useful."

## Questions

1. Identify and discuss the root cause of the problem in this case scenario.
2. Discuss the approach Ben should take to correct this situation so that supervisors have the skills to deal with the turnover problem.
3. Discuss the specific training strategies Ben should put in place in order to reduce the probability of a similar response to his training in the future.

## Application Questions

1. You are designing an orientation program for new employees at Labatt Breweries of Canada that can be used in their facilities across the country.
   a. Identify the top three or four goals of the orientation.
   b. Discuss ways these goals can be achieved.
   c. Propose a plan for how you will evaluate whether the goals are met.
2. For the past three weeks, you have been facilitating a diversity-management training program for management and non-management staff at WestJet. Discuss the approaches you will use to evaluate the effectiveness of the training and present a strong business rationale for the evaluation methods you propose.
3. Conduct online research to gather data about training and development in Canada, such as what type of training is conducted in different organizations and how much training is provided in Canada as compared with other countries.
   a. What general conclusions can be drawn about the state of training and development in Canada in comparison to the global community?
   b. What are the business implications associated with your conclusions about the status of training and development in Canada?
4. Select one of your courses and convert its design and delivery into a computer-based course for students in the far north (include objectives, content, methods, and transfer of learning approaches). Now compare and contrast it to your classroom-based learning design and delivery.
   a. What are the advantages and disadvantages for students, instructors, and the academic institution?
   b. Which method do you prefer and why?
5. Two trainers are having a conversation about which training methods to use for a workshop on team development. One trainer wants to use a case study; the other wants to use a group activity. Regrettably, the tight timelines on the agenda only permit the use of one method. Discuss the key criteria that will be used to resolve this dilemma.
6. You are the facilitator of a one-week course on effective leadership skills for frontline supervisors. Discuss the most effective transfer of learning strategies you will use to increase the probability that learning is transferred from the training session to the workplace. Explain why each strategy is important.
7. Identify a potential training need in your part-time job or volunteer activity. Formulate a plan for how you will conduct an organizational, task, and person analysis. How would you go about presenting your plan to your supervisor to attain his or her buy-in and support for you to conduct the needs analysis?

## RUNNING CASE: LEARNINMOTION.COM

### The New Training Program

The case for Chapter 6, The New Training Program, describes problems that develop without a formal orientation and training program. Students must advise on how to create a suitable plan.

To read this case, go to www.pearsoned.ca/myhrlab and click on the *Management of Human Resources*, Third Canadian Edition, In-Class Edition, cover. Click on the case module in Chapter 6. The running case illustrates a variety of challenges confronted by HR professionals, small-business owners, and front-line supervisors. It places students in the role of HR management consultants to help the fledgling LearninMotion.com develop HR policies, strategies, and long-term goals. Each case is accompanied by assignments for the management consultants in the form of critical-thinking questions posed to the student.

## CONTROVERSIAL BUSINESS TOPIC EXERCISE

You have been hired as the trainer for a large telecommunications company that has service branches across Canada. You have identified a potential need for improving customer service in the call centres and would like to conduct a comprehensive needs analysis to determine the extent to which a training program would add value. Your supervisor can be described as "anti-needs analysis"—he perceives a needs analysis to be a waste of time and thinks that if you are an experienced trainer you should be able to quickly observe situations and determine if training is needed without going through a comprehensive process.

In teams of three (supervisor, trainer, and an observer), participate in a role play that represents the conversation you will have with your supervisor to convince him of the value inherent in needs analysis. At the end of the role play, your team is to provide feedback on the effectiveness of the trainer's argument and the supervisor's corresponding responses.

## IN THE BOARDROOM EXERCISE

The CEO of a large manufacturing facility has called his executive team to the boardroom to discuss the economic hardships currently facing the organization. For the past three quarters, there have been productivity decreases but they have not yet been substantial enough to lay off staff. Employees are anxious about their future and are waiting for management to exercise their leadership and carry them through the rough times. As part of his solution strategy, the CEO has proposed a complete elimination of the training budget for 2011–2012. As the director of training and development, you know this is not a viable business response to the organizational hardships. Discuss the approach you will use to argue that this elimination is not a sound business decision and to convince the CEO to reconsider reinstating the training and development budget. Present your recommendations in class to a team of five or six students and reach an agreement together on the best approach for dealing with this boardroom dilemma.

## TRAINING AND DEVELOPMENT ON THE INTERNATIONAL STAGE EXERCISE

*The exercise below relates to the Training and Development on the International Stage feature on p. 207.*

In "Training and Development on the International Stage" at the end of this chapter. you read about Adobe's leadership development program. Assume you are the training director for "Adobe's Leadership Experience," charged with designing the team-based business simulation in phase 2 of the program. Outline the details of the business simulation you would create to prepare participants for leadership roles in the global marketplace. Along with your design, include training objectives, transfer of learning approaches, and evaluation strategy.

## EXPERIENTIAL EXERCISE

For further study of text materials and development of practical skills, select the experiential exercise module for this chapter on www.pearsoned.ca/myhrlab. This module provides two to three individual or group-based assignments per chapter.

# QUIZ YOURSELF

## STUDY GUIDE QUESTIONS

Circle the correct answer. After completing this self-test, check your answers against the Answers to Study Guide Questions at the back of the book (p. 433).

1. Matthew joined his new place of work two days ago. On his first day, he was immediately put on an assignment. Matthew felt like a fish out of water. He was going through:
   a. panic attack
   b. reality shock
   c. anxiety shock
   d. orientation
   e. all of the above
2. Jennifer was recently appointed the training and development coordinator for Martin Industries. Management has emphasized leadership as a training requirement. However, when she talks to line managers, she hears that there are other areas of training requirements for staff. What could she do to address her dilemma?
   a. conduct one training session that covers all requirements
   b. conduct only leadership development training
   c. conduct a training needs analysis
   d. talk to staff about what they see as requirements
   e. conduct training sessions required by line managers
3. A training needs analysis is the first step in determining what training is required. There are three main approaches for conducting a needs analysis. They are:

a. task analysis, questionnaire surveys, return on investment
b. person analysis, surveys, task analysis
c. HR records, supervisor reports, utility analysis
d. task analysis, person analysis, organizational analysis
e. surveys, supervisor reports, focus groups

4. Sanjay is a new sales representative for a multinational pharmaceutical company. After a week of orientation, he is to team up with the regional sales manager to get to know the key customers and how to conduct product presentations. What kind of training technique is the company using to train Sanjay?
a. special assignment technique
b. on-the-job training technique
c. simulation technique
d. job instruction training
e. programmed learning

5. In simulated training, trainees learn their jobs on simulated equipment. This type of training is usually required if the actual training is too costly or too dangerous. One job requiring simulated training is:
a. vice-president
b. construction work
c. astronaut
d. forklift operator
e. all of the above

6. E-learning is a popular method used for training in Canada. There are three major types of e-learning used for employee training. They are:
a. simulated training, OTJ, CBT
b. multimedia, videoconferencing, online training
c. videoconferencing, CBT, EPSS
d. CBT, OTJ, videoconferencing
e. CBT, online training, EPSS

7. A company conducted a training program on leadership development for all senior executives. Before the participants began the program, they were evaluated on their leadership behaviours using a 360-degree feedback tool. After three months of training, the same survey was repeated to measure whether there were changes in their leadership behaviours. What stage of training evaluation is the company in with regards to the leadership training?
a. reaction
b. learning
c. behaviour
d. results
e. none of the above

8. Succession planning is a process that identifies senior-level openings and the key people who could fill those positions. It plays an important role in management development and is particularly challenging in today's small organizations. The Montana Company has a succession plan process in place and has just compiled a management skills inventory. What is the next step the company needs to take in the process?
a. make an organizational projection
b. identify development needs of successors
c. conduct an in-house development centre
d. draw a management replacement chart
e. conduct executive development activities

9. Management development plays a very important role in Canada, because 60 percent of Canadian organizations face a shortage of middle managers. It attempts to improve managerial performance by enhancing knowledge, skills, and attitudes. A number of different techniques are deployed for management development. On-the-job techniques that can be used are:
a. coaching, understudy
b. understudy, job rotation
c. job rotation, coaching
d. action learning, understudy
e. all of the above

10. One off-the-job management development technique does the following: presents the trainee with a written organizational problem; the trainee is then required to analyze the case on his or her own, diagnose the problem, and present findings and solutions in a discussion with other trainees. This method is called the:
a. role-play method
b. simulation method
c. case study method
d. seminar method
e. coaching method

11. A recent Conference Board of Canada survey found that only 5 percent of companies in Canada believe they have the leadership capability they need to face the challenges of the new millennium. The report concluded that Canadian companies need a fundamental overhaul of their leadership-development practices if they hope to keep up in today's business environment. Yet this is an uphill task, because leadership cannot necessarily be taught. What is a key competency required for leading strategically?
a. vision development
b. strategic planning
c. local/global trend creation
d. get buy-in from key stakeholders
e. all of the above

12. Identifying occupational orientation is an important factor in career choices. A leading career counsellor mentioned that a person's personality determines the occupational orientation. If a person is attracted to careers that involve cognitive activities rather than affective activities, what kind of a career is he or she most likely to choose?
a. social worker
b. entrepreneur
c. college professor
d. farmer
e. musician

7

chapter

# Performance Appraisal: The Key to Effective Performance Management

## Learning Objectives

1. Explain the strategic importance of managing performance.
2. Describe the three key steps in the performance appraisal process.
3. Define and explain performance expectations.
4. Discuss the process for appraising employees' performance.
5. Describe the qualities of effective feedback and the process for giving performance feedback.
6. Explain the legal and ethical issues associated with performance appraisals.

## Test Yourself

1. Why is it important to effectively manage performance and conduct appraisals?
2. What are the three major steps in conducting performance appraisals?
3. What are the six methods commonly used for performance appraisals, and who uses them?
4. What are the major problems inhibiting effective performance appraisals, and how can they be minimized?
5. What are some of the legal and ethical issues that need to be considered regarding performance appraisals?

## 7.1 THE STRATEGIC IMPORTANCE OF MANAGING PERFORMANCE

Performance management is of considerable strategic importance to today's organizations because the most effective way to differentiate a business in a highly competitive, service-oriented, global marketplace is through the quality of its employees.[1] The performance management process should link performance criteria to current strategic objectives and implementation plans.[2] Thus, it has been suggested that better performance management represents a largely untapped opportunity to improve company profitability.[3]

**Performance management** is a process encompassing all activities related to enhancing employee motivation, performance, productivity, and effectiveness. It includes goal setting, merit pay increases, acknowledging employee achievements and contributions, training and development, career management, and disciplinary action. The foundation of performance management is the performance appraisal process. Appraisals provide a systematic way to *look back* and *look forward.* In looking back, managers and employees review an employee's work performance, focusing on strengths and areas for improvement. In looking forward, managers and employees discuss goals each employee should set in order to change or enhance performance and develop action plans that chart the direction needed to reach those goals.

There are several reasons to appraise performance; these can be divided into two major categories: summative and formative.[4] Appraisals serve a **summative** purpose by providing information with which promotion and salary decisions can be made. They serve a **formative** or developmental purpose by providing an opportunity for managers and employees to review each employee's work-related behaviour, achievements, and contributions to the organization. This in turn enables the manager and employee to acknowledge the employee's strengths and develop an action plan whereby the employee sets goals to enhance strengths and to take corrective action to transform weaknesses into strengths. The appraisal should be central to a company's career-planning process because it provides a good opportunity to review each employee's career aspirations and work with them to map out a training plan that supports career development. Employees are more likely to stay with organizations that are interested in supporting their careers.[5]

Performance appraisals add value to mentoring programs by pairing employees who have a specific strength with employees who are seeking guidance in developing that skill.

### The Role of the Line Manager and HR Department in Performance Appraisal

The line manager who is the immediate supervisor of an employee usually does the actual appraising, so he or she must be familiar with basic appraisal techniques, understand and avoid problems that can cripple an appraisal, and conduct the appraisal fairly.

An HR department develops policies and procedures that support the performance appraisal process and serves in an advisory capacity to line managers. In one survey, for example, about 80 percent of the responding firms reported that their HR departments provide advice and assistance regarding the appraisal tool but leave final decisions on appraisal procedures to operating division heads. The rest of the firms reported that HR department staff members prepare detailed forms and procedures and ensure that all departments use them.[6] HR department staff members are also responsible for training managers to improve their appraisal skills. Finally, the HR department is responsible for monitoring the appraisal system's use and particularly for ensuring that the format and criteria being measured comply with human rights laws and do not become outdated. If an employee is not satisfied with his or her evaluation, the HR department facilitates the formal appeal process to review the appraisal results and bring a resolution to the situation.

Figure 7.1 outlines steps HR departments can take when developing a performance appraisal system for an organization.

## 7.2 THE PERFORMANCE APPRAISAL PROCESS

Conducting performance appraisal reviews is considered one of the most critical responsibilities of a line manager, as feedback has a strong impact on employee motivation and performance, which in turn affects the organization. Appraisals acknowledge and celebrate employee success in meeting and exceeding organizational expectations, pinpoint where performance improvement is needed, and focus on setting goals that stretch employees' skills and knowledge—which often benefits employees in the form of salary increases and career advancement and improves performance and productivity for the company.

## *figure* 7.1 Developing a Performance Appraisal System

1. **Preliminary investigation: Determine the type of program the organizational climate will support.**
   An appraisal needs to be consistent with company philosophy, method of operation, values, and objectives.
2. **Obtain support of top management to proceed with your proposed plan.**
   Top management needs to be willing to participate actively in the program, communicate support for the work being done by HR in rolling out this initiative, and demonstrate a willingness to be evaluated as well.
3. **Determine what specific existing needs the program would fulfill.**
   Conduct a focus group with stakeholder groups to determine
   - principles that should guide the development of the new performance appraisal system
   - summative and formative purposes of the evaluation
   - how results should be communicated and used in the organization
4. **Involve all key stakeholders in the design.**
   Work with all key stakeholders to determine
   - performance factors to be evaluated
   - method of evaluation/forms to be used
   - content communicated in appraisal interviews
   - guidelines for conductiing effective appraisal interviews
   - timelines for conducting evaluations
5. **Design a performance information system.**
   Based on feedback from stakeholders, design the evaluation system making use of available software to enhance efficiency of operations.
6. **Test the program.**
   Test drive the new program in one department to identify strengths and areas requiring modification.
7. **Develop policies, procedures, and guidelines in the form of an appraiser's manual.**
   Structured and standardized policies and practices enhance validity and reliability of the performance appraisal system. Publish manual widely, preferably online so chances in policies and procedures can be made and communicated in an efficient manner.
8. **Communicate the program.**
   Canvass top management's support in communicating the message alongside the HR department. Provide a comprehensive description of the entire system addressing key questions around who, why, when, how, etc.
9. **Train supervisor.**
   Provide comprehensive training program for all supervisors charged with performance appraisal responsibilities. Requires enhanced skill development in communication, problem solving, conflict resolution, planning, and coaching.
10. **Orient employees.**
    Recipients of performance evaluations should be fully versed in the policies and procedures so they know what to expect. All employees should be given job descriptions and copies of performance evaluation forms when hired so they know what is expected of them and how performance will be assessed.
11. **Proceed with appraisals.**
    HR to serve in an advisory capacity if supervisors and employees have questions.
12. **Use the results in making formative and summative decisions.**
13. **Monitor and revise the program.**
    Audit the quality of the system and how well it is achieving its intended purposes, provide feedback to management, and watch for ways to enhance the system.
14. **Train new supervisors.**
    As new supervisors are hired, they must be trained.

**performance management** The entire process affecting employee motivation, performance, productivity, and effectiveness.

**summative evaluation** Appraisals provide information for promotion and salary decisions.

**formative evaluation** Appraisals reveal opportunities for employees to develop goals and action plans for professional development.

Performance Management & Appraisal Help Centre **http://performance-appraisals.org**

Performance Appraisals **www.halogensoftware.com/products/halogen-eappraisal**

## In-class Notes

**The Strategic Importance of Managing Performance**

- Performance management process involves all activities related to enhancing employee motivation, performance, productivity, and effectiveness
- Quality of employees is an effective differentiation strategy for organizations
- Better performance management is a largely untapped opportunity to improve profitability
- Appraisals provide information for performance improvement, promotion and salary decisions, career planning, and mentoring

## Challenges with Performance Appraisals

Although there are many benefits of the performance appraisal process, it can be marred by a number of problems that threaten the positive impact they can have on employee and organizational development. When appraisals fail, they do so for reasons that parallel three steps—defining performance expectations, appraising performance, and providing feedback.[7] Some appraisals fail because employees are not told ahead of time exactly what is expected of them in terms of good performance, and managers are not trained to manage the performance appraisal process. Others fail because of problems with the method used to appraise performance or how managers complete the appraisal form. A lenient manager might rate all employees "high," for instance, although many are actually unsatisfactory. Still other problems arise during the feedback session, and these can include not communicating effectively or turning the session into an argument. Finally, failure to use appraisals in human resource decision making and career development negates the primary purpose of performance evaluations.

Many experts feel that traditional appraisals do not help in managing performance and may actually backfire. They argue that most performance appraisal systems neither motivate employees nor guide their development. Furthermore, "they cause conflict between supervisors and employees and lead to dysfunctional behaviours."[8] The traits measured are often personal in nature and "who likes the idea of being evaluated on his or her: honesty, integrity, teamwork, compassion, cooperation [objectivity] . . . ?"[9]

Similarly, proponents of quality management programs (including the late W. Edwards Deming) generally argue in favour of eliminating performance appraisals.[10] They believe that the organization is a system of interrelated parts and that an employee's performance is more a function of factors like training, communication, tools, and supervision than of his or her own motivation.[11] They also suggest that performance appraisals can have unanticipated consequences. Thus, employees might make themselves look better in terms of customer service by continually badgering customers to send in letters of support. Deming particularly argued against forced distribution appraisal systems because of their potential for undermining teamwork.[12]

Yet while these criticisms have merit, the solution is not the elimination of performance appraisals. The merits of well-designed and facilitated performance appraisal systems far outweigh the problems cited. The challenge and opportunity is to invest resources to develop a first-class system that makes it possible to manage performance given the realities of a new and increasingly complex business landscape that demands greater focus on quality and fiscal responsibility. This

*In-class Notes*

**The Performance Appraisal Process**

- Three steps:
  1. Defining performance expectations and standards
  2. Appraising employee performance by comparing actual performance to expectations
  3. Providing feedback to employees and planning future development
- Appraisal problems arise if these three steps are not carefully followed

chapter offers tools to develop performance appraisal systems that are valid, reliable, and legally defensible.

## Steps in Appraising Performance

A performance appraisal usually contains the following three steps:

1. *Defining performance expectations,* which means making sure that job duties and standards of performance are clear to all.
2. *Appraising performance,* which means comparing an employee's actual performance to the standards that have been set. This usually involves using one of the methods discussed later in the chapter.
3. *Providing feedback* sessions in which the employee's performance and progress are discussed and plans are made for any development that is required.

## 7.3 STEP 1: DEFINING PERFORMANCE EXPECTATIONS

The job description is the starting point for identifying the key components of a job. These key requirements are called **performance factors** and represent the core knowledge, skills, and abilities that will be used to evaluate employee performance. To operationalize these expectations, **performance standards** are developed for each major component of the job. Performance standards are the quantifiable and measureable criteria that communicate how well, how often, or how quickly tasks are to be completed. For example, sales associates may be expected to personally sell at least $600 000 worth of products per year, maintain a turnover rate of less than 10 percent in each of their departments, and sustain high levels of customer satisfaction by having no more than 10 customer complaints per year. The job description and performance standards should be communicated to employees when they are hired and should be reviewed with employees prior to the performance appraisal interview, so that workers are aware of the organization's expectations. A comprehensive explanation of the importance of performance standards should also be given to employees.

Performance factors should be aligned with the organization's values, objectives, and strategic direction so that employees understand how the work they are being evaluated on is relevant to the organization. The list of performance factors generated for each job should be scrutinized for criterion deficiency and

**performance factors** Key knowledge, skills, and abilities from an employee's job description that will be used to evaluate performance.

**performance standards** Quantifiable and measureable criteria that communicate how well, how often, and how quickly tasks are to be completed.

## In-class Notes

**Defining Performance Expectations (Step 1)**

- Job descriptions are the starting point for identifying the key ingredients of a job
- Quantifiable and measurable standards of performance are required
- Ensure employees clearly understand expectations
- Guard against criterion deficiency and criterion contamination
- Validate performance factors

criterion contamination. **Criterion deficiency** occurs when performance factors that are critical to job success are omitted and not assessed; for example, failure to acknowledge verbal communication skills for a flight attendant. **Criterion contamination** means that performance factors that are not relevant or are outside the employee's control are identified and assessed. For example, a general labourer in the mines of northern Ontario should not be assessed on the quality of his written communication skills, since report writing is unlikely to be a daily task. The best way to validate performance factors is to ask employees if the list of factors accurately represents the key ingredients of their job. Working with valid performance factors is integral to the next two steps in appraising performance and the legal defensibility of the evaluation.

## 7.4 STEP 2: APPRAISING PERFORMANCE

This section showcases several performance appraisal methods. Organizations occasionally mix the methods to create a hybrid when one is not an exact fit. Whether an appraisal method is used in its pure or hybrid form, organizations try to remain consistent in how all employees are evaluated. The exception to this rule is the use of different methods for evaluating management and non-management staff or office and factory staff, as there are likely to be significant differences in the performance factors.

Selecting a performance appraisal method is an important decision. Organizations need to consider the strengths and limitations of each and the purposes that the evaluation will serve. If a valid and reliable evaluation method is not selected, then it is less likely to have employee support, thus running the risk that decisions pertaining to promotions, transfers, salary increases, bonuses, training, and possibly terminations will be highly suspect and could prompt litigation. With a valid and reliable method, employees are more likely to trust decisions made as a result.

### Performance Appraisal Methods

**GRAPHIC RATING SCALE METHOD** The **graphic rating scale** is the simplest and most popular technique for appraising performance. Traditionally, it was based on assessing traits. Figure 7.2 shows a typical rating scale. It lists traits (such as quality and reliability) and a range of performance values (from unsatisfactory to outstanding) for each one. A supervisor rates each employee by circling or checking the score that best describes the employee's performance for each trait. The assigned values are then totalled.

Because appraising generic traits or factors (such as quality and quantity) may not be related to all jobs or be quantifiable, many firms specify the duties to be appraised instead. In this case, the job duties are taken from the job description and prioritized. The duties are listed by importance, and ratings are assigned.

The advantage of using rating scales is that they are relatively easy to develop and use. A major disadvantage *figure* 7.2 **One Page of a Two-Page Graphic Rating Scale with Space for Comments**

# Performance Appraisal

Employee Name ______________________ Title ______________________

Department ______________________ Employee Payroll Number ______________________

Reason for Review: ☐ Annual ☐ Promotion ☐ Unsatisfactory Performance

☐ Merit ☐ End Probation Period ☐ Other ______________

Date employee began present position ____/____/____

Date of last appraisal ____/____/____ Scheduled appraisal date ____/____/____

**Instructions**: Carefully evaluate employee's work performance in relation to current job requirements. Check rating box to indicate the employee's performance. Indicate N/A if not applicable. Assign points for each rating within the scale and indicate in the corresponding points box. Points will be totalled and averaged for an overall performance score.

**RATING IDENTIFICATION**

**O–Outstanding**–Performance is exceptional in all areas and is recognizable as being far superior to others.

**V–Very Good**–Results clearly exceed most position requirements. Performance is of high quality and is achieved on a consistent basis.

**G–Good**–Competent and dependable level of performance. Meets performance standards of the job.

**I–Improvement Needed**–Performance is deficient in certain areas. Improvement is necessary.

**U–Unsatisfactory**–Results are generally unacceptable and require immediate improvement. No merit increase should be granted to individuals with this rating.

**N–Not Rated**–Not applicable or too soon to rate.

| GENERAL FACTORS | RATING | SCALE | | SUPPORTIVE DETAILS OR COMMENTS |
|---|---|---|---|---|
| 1. **Quality**–The accuracy, thoroughness and acceptability of work performed. | O ☐<br>V ☐<br>G ☐<br>I ☐<br>U ☐ | 100–90<br>90–80<br>80–70<br>70–60<br>below 60 | Points ☐ | |
| 2. **Productivity**–The quantity and efficiency of work produced in a specified period of time. | O ☐<br>V ☐<br>G ☐<br>I ☐<br>U ☐ | 100–90<br>90–80<br>80–70<br>70–60<br>below 60 | Points ☐ | |
| 3. **Job Knowledge**–The practical/technical skills and information used on the job. | O ☐<br>V ☐<br>G ☐<br>I ☐<br>U ☐ | 100–90<br>90–80<br>80–70<br>70–60<br>below 60 | Points ☐ | |
| 4. **Reliability**–The extent to which an employee can be relied upon regarding task completion and follow-up. | O ☐<br>V ☐<br>G ☐<br>I ☐<br>U ☐ | 100–90<br>90–80<br>80–70<br>70–60<br>below 60 | Points ☐ | |
| 5. **Availability**–The extent to which an employee is punctual, observes prescribed work break/meal periods, and the overall attendance record. | O ☐<br>V ☐<br>G ☐<br>I ☐<br>U ☐ | 100–90<br>90–80<br>80–70<br>70–60<br>below 60 | Points ☐ | |
| 6. **Independence**–The extent of work performed with little or no supervision. | O ☐<br>V ☐<br>G ☐<br>I ☐<br>U ☐ | 100–90<br>90–80<br>80–70<br>70–60<br>below 60 | Points ☐ | |

is that appraising traits puts a focus on the person rather than the behaviour. They are also less legally defensible because of their subjective and ambiguous nature.

**FORCED DISTRIBUTION METHOD** The **forced distribution method** places predetermined percentages of ratees in performance categories. For example, it may be decided to distribute employees as follows:

- 15 percent high performers
- 20 percent high–average performers
- 30 percent average performers
- 20 percent low–average performers
- 15 percent low performers

Similar to bell-curve grading at school, this means that not everyone can get an "A," and one's performance is always rated relative to that of one's peers. One practical way to do this is to write each employee's name on a separate index card. Then, for each trait being appraised (quality of work, creativity, and so on), place the employee's card in one of the appropriate performance categories. This method has been criticized as demotivating for the considerable proportion of the workforce that is classified as less than average.[13] Yet forced distribution is used in some form by close to 30 percent of organizations. It is deemed an effective evaluation tool because it prevents the inflation of ratings and demands that managers have strong rationales for how they evaluate their staff. General Electric uses a forced distribution format referred to as their 20-70-10 program or "The Vitality Curve." Employees rated in the top 20 percent are given such extravagant rewards that they are unlikely to leave. Employees in the bottom 10 percent are either encouraged to make radical changes in their performance or prepare to leave.[14]

**CRITICAL INCIDENT METHOD** With the **critical incident method**, the supervisor keeps a log of desirable or undesirable examples or incidents of each employee's work-related behaviour. Then, every six months or so, the supervisor and employee meet and discuss the latter's performance using the specific incidents as examples.

This method can always be used to supplement another appraisal technique, and in that role, it has several advantages. It provides specific hard facts for explaining the appraisal. It also ensures that a manager thinks about the employee's appraisal throughout the year because the incidents must be accumulated; therefore, the rating does not just reflect the employee's most recent performance. Keeping a running list of critical incidents should also provide concrete examples of what an employee can do to eliminate any performance deficiencies.

The critical incident method can be adapted to the specific job expectations laid out for the employee at the beginning of the year. In the example presented in Table 7.1, one of the assistant plant manager's continuing duties is to supervise procurement and to minimize inventory costs. The critical incident shows that the

***table* 7.1 Examples of Critical Incidents for an Assistant Plant Manager**

| Continuing Duties | Targets | Critical Incidents |
|---|---|---|
| Schedule production for plant | Full utilization of employees and machinery in plant; orders delivered on time | Instituted new production scheduling system; decreased late orders by 10 percent last month; increased machine utilization in plant by 20 percent last month |
| Supervise procurement of raw materials and inventory control | Minimize inventory costs while keeping adequate supplies on hand | Let inventory storage costs rise by 15 percent last month; overordered parts "A" and "B" by 20 percent; underordered part "C" by 30 percent |
| Supervise machinery maintenance | No shutdowns due to faulty machinery | Instituted new preventative maintenance system for plant; prevented a machine breakdown by discovering faulty part |

assistant plant manager let inventory storage costs rise by 15 percent; this provides a specific example of what performance must be improved in the future.

The critical incident method is often used to supplement a ranking technique. It is useful for identifying specific examples of good or poor performance and planning how deficiencies can be corrected. It is not as useful by itself for comparing employees or, therefore, for making salary decisions.

**BEHAVIOURALLY ANCHORED RATING SCALES** A **behaviourally anchored rating scale (BARS)** combines the benefits of narratives, critical incidents, and quantified ratings by anchoring a quantified scale with specific behavioural examples of good and poor performance (as in Figure 7.3). Anchored statements on the scale are taken from the job description and used to communicate the key tasks and performance standards associated with the job. Its proponents

## *figure* 7.3 Behaviourally Anchored Rating Scale

**Sales Skills**

Skilfully persuading customers to purchase products; using product benefits and opportunities effectively; closing skills; adapting sales techniques appropriately to different customers; effectively overcoming objections to purchasing products.

5 — If a customer insists on a particular brand name, the salesperson perseveres. Although products with this particular brand name are not available, the salesperson does not give up; instead, the salesperson persuades the customer that his or her needs could be better met with another product.

4 — The salesperson treats objections to purchasing the product seriously; works hard to counter the objections with relevant positive arguments regarding the benefits of the product.

3 — When a customer is deciding on which product to purchase, the salesperson tries to sell the product with the highest profit magin.

2 — The salesperson insists on describing more features of the product even though the customer wants to purchase it right now.

When a customer states an objection to purchasing a product, the salesperson ends the conversation, assuming that the prospect must not be interested.

1

**criterion deficiency** Omission of performance factors that are integral to job success.

**criterion contamination** Inclusion of performance factors that are not relevant or are outside the employee's control.

**graphic rating scale** A scale that lists a number of traits and a range of performance for each trait. The employee is then rated by identifying the score that best describes his or her level of performance for each trait.

**forced distribution method** Predetermined percentages of ratees are placed in various performance categories.

**critical incident method** Keeping a record of uncommonly good or undesirable examples of an employee's work-related behaviour and reviewing it with the employee at predetermined times.

**behaviourally anchored rating scale (BARS)** An appraisal method that aims to combine the benefits of narratives, critical incident incidents, and quantified ratings by anchoring a quantified scale with specific behavioural examples of good and poor performance.

Sample Performance Appraisal Templates
**www.businessballs.com/performanceappraisals.htm**

claim that it provides better, more equitable appraisals than do the other tools that have been discussed.[15] Because it is so concrete, this method is more legally defensible than trait methods, for example. It also gives employees specific examples of the types of behaviours to do well in if they want to succeed in the organization. Studies have found that the BARS format contributes to enhanced clarity, commitment, and acceptance of goals, compared with graphic rating scales.[16] This method can also be time-consuming to develop, and it is difficult to keep the information current. A separate BARS form needs to be developed for each distinct job description in an organization in order to depict the unique set of critical incidents against which employees will be evaluated. The BARS format is considered a popular choice by many employers. Some employers pair the BARS format with the **Behaviour Observation Scale (BOS)**. Like BARS, it identifies critical incidents, but instead of evaluating how well an employee completed tasks, it assesses how frequently behaviours were demonstrated. For example, the BOS would evaluate how often a call centre representative effectively and efficiently resolved customer complaints.

**MANAGEMENT BY OBJECTIVES (MBO)** **Management by objectives (MBO)** is a structured, results-based evaluation system through which employees, in collaboration with their managers, set performance goals linked to the organization's strategic direction. Stripped to its essentials, MBO requires managers to set concrete and measurable goals and action plans with each employee and periodically discuss his or her progress toward these goals. The principle behind MBO is to ensure that employees understand what the organization is trying to achieve and how each employee is expected to contribute. MBO provides an opportunity to capitalize on the collective wisdom, skills, and abilities in the organization in the setting of goals and action plans to move the organization closer to its vision of the future. When employees have clarity on their roles and accountabilities and actively participate in shaping an organization's direction, it is likely to create an empowered and engaged workforce that is committed to making a difference in the organization.

The MBO process typically includes the following steps:

1. Develop strategic goals and plan for the entire organization.
2. Define key results areas.
3. Establish key performance indicators.
4. Major objectives are allocated among divisional and departmental units.
5. Unit managers and superiors jointly set specific objectives for their business units.
6. Managers and department members jointly set specific objectives and standards of performance.
7. Specific action plans defining how objectives are to be achieved are developed and agreed to by employees and their managers.
8. Action plans are implemented.
9. Progress is periodically reviewed and feedback is provided, usually on a quarterly basis.
10. Coaching and training are provided to employees who may require additional support and resources to meet goals.
11. Performance-based rewards are given based on successful achievement of objectives.
12. Continuing discussions occur between employees, supervisors, and managers to identify new objectives and standards of performance.

There are some disadvantages to using this method. The development of objectives can be an onerous task, because they need to be SMART: specific, measurable, attainable, results-oriented, and time-limited. A major criticism of writing objectives is they are often unclear and immeasurable. An objective such as, "Will do a better job of training" is useless. On the other hand, "Will have four employees promoted during the year" is a measurable objective.

Second, MBO is time-consuming. Taking the time to set objectives, measure progress, and provide feedback can take several hours per employee per year over and above the time already spent doing each person's appraisal.

Third, setting objectives with an employee sometimes turns into a tug of war, with the manager pushing for higher goals and the employee pushing for lower ones. It is thus important to know the job and the person's ability. To motivate performance, the objectives must be fair and attainable. The more a manager knows about the job and the employee's ability, the more confident he or she can be about the standards set.

However, using an outcome-based method provides unambiguous and clear objectives and standards by which performance can be appraised. It also can help eliminate subjectivity or bias on the part of the appraiser and, if designed properly, can be quite flexible and adaptable to changes the organization might experience. Figure 7.4 illustrates an example of MBO goals and supporting action plans.

## *figure* 7.4 Sample MBO Plan for a Product Marketing Manager

| Objectives | October, 2010 | November, 2010 | December, 2010 |
|---|---|---|---|
| **Strategic Business Objectives** | 1. **Product Launch** – Ensure a successful product launch (*from a marketing and MarCom perspective*), and confirm messaging integrity in market launch materials<br>2. **Market Planning** – Enhance overall quality of marketing department's decisions and planning<br>3. **Domain Expertise** – Reduce dependency on internal/external product/market experts | | |
| **Supporting Tactical Objectives** | 1. Complete positioning and value documents. Create product launch plan and provide input to MarCom<br>2. Create a competitive tracking and analysis process for gathering and analyzing market information<br>3. Establish comprehensive knowledge of the product (*including competition*) and market problems | | |
| **Action Items** | **October, 2010** | **November, 2010** | **December, 2010** |
| *Strategic Objective #1 Action Items – Product Launch* | 1. Validate customer use scenarios<br>2. Complete and sign-off value documents<br>3. Complete product positioning statements<br>4. Complete launch plan draft | 1. Present all messaging, value, identity; to MarCom and Marketing team members with an explanation on purpose/use<br>2. Choose marketing collateral items and media vehicles for launch | 1. Complete launch plan<br>2. Present possible co-marketing, and co-branding programs<br>3. Evangelize product to select prospects, partners, and analysts |
| *Strategic Objective #2 Action Items – Market Planning* | 1. Retain market research firm<br>2. Gather input from firm | 1. Draft data collection and analysis process | 1. Present draft of tracking and analysis process. Gain approval<br>2. Begin process implementation |
| *Strategic Objective #3 Action Items – Domain Expertise* | 1. Undergo product training with Product Manager<br>2. Exploratory visit to key customer | 1. Undergo product training with Product Manager<br>2. Attend industry conference<br>3. Exploratory visit to key customer | 1. Provide list of topics for articles and whitepapers<br>2. Write short article on product |
| *Miscellaneous* | None | Help MarCom find external advertising agency | None |

*figure* 7.5 **The Balanced Scorecard**

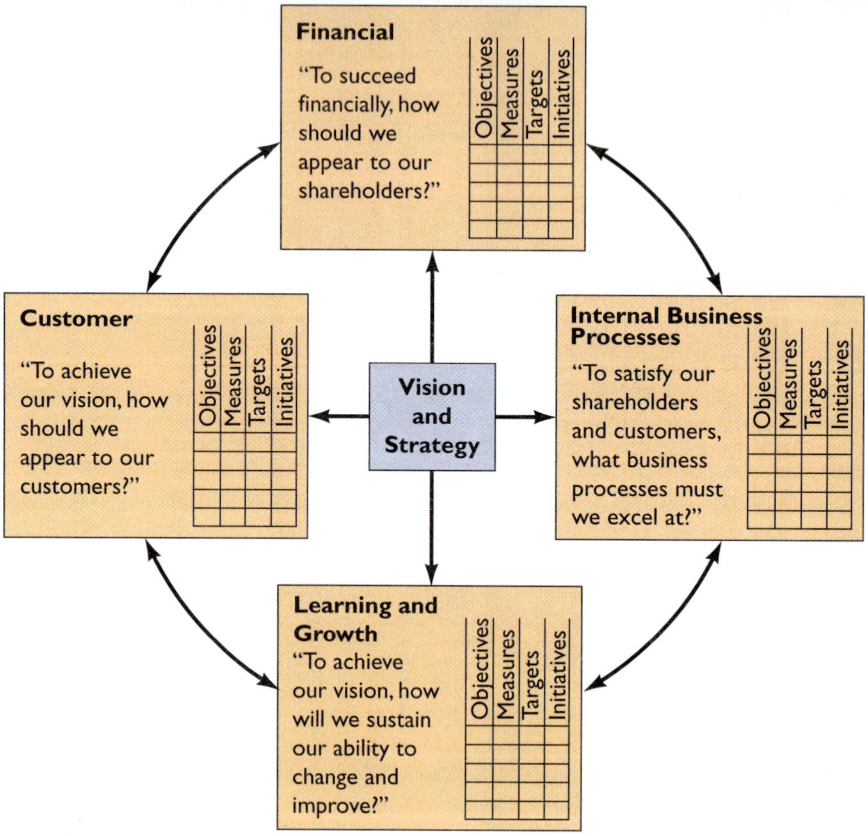


Source: R. Kaplan and D. Norton, "Strategic Learning and the Balanced Scorecard." *Strategy & Leadership* 24, no. 5, September/October 1996, pp. 18–24.


**BALANCED SCORECARD** The balanced scorecard is one of the most sophisticated tools for performance evaluation because it tracks and measures employee performance directly against an organization's strategy and metrics. The balanced scorecard was introduced by Robert Kaplan and David Norton and is used by over 50 percent of *Fortune* 500 companies.[17] It translates an organization's strategic priorities into a detailed set of performance measures and targets, and is more complex than the MBO approach in that it considers multiple sectors of the organization from which to develop employees' performance goals. Within the balanced scorecard framework, four key domains are measured: financial, internal business processes, learning and growth, and customer. In each domain, employees can commit to an objective, measures, targets, and initiatives. The strength of the balanced scorecard is threefold: (1) It can be used by individuals, teams, business units, or an entire organization, (2) it enables employees to focus on how they can make contributions in each of these four domains that are critical to organizational viability, and (3) it simplifies complicated organizational metrics so that they can be comprehended at individual and departmental levels.[18] Figure 7.5 gives

Technology has updated the appraisal process. New software programs enable employees to check their own performance against prescribed criteria.

## HR.NET

### Web-Based Performance Appraisal

emPerform is an online employee performance management system that enables organizations to improve performance through the active management and development of its people. With a unique collaborative yet controlled approach, employees and managers are able to track responsibilities, set and evaluate objectives and standards, and develop competencies and skills. emPerform permits organizations to take an integrated and ongoing approach to managing employee performance from the setup of performance criteria, to individual development plans, to final assessment and feedback. By creating a positive and continuous forum for performance-based communication, emPerform enables the entire organization to realize the benefits of effective employee performance management.

HR retains a large degree of control over a flexible and collaborative process and thorough grouped assignments of performance criteria and competencies. Employees and managers collaborate on development plans and achievement, and 360-degree evaluators provide broad insight from multiple sources. A unique colour-coded interface provides guidance to even novice Internet users, requiring little training. Users can choose from a large library of predefined web-based reports or create detailed reports, "on the fly," without any knowledge of the underlying database. emPerform empowers decision makers with the flexibility to access, analyze, and report on complete and detailed information spanning the entire organization.

Source: Used with the permission of the Corporate Renaissance Group. www.crgroup.com (February 26, 2005).

an example of the balanced scorecard and how it links strategy, resource allocation, and performance appraisal.

**TECHNOLOGY-BASED METHODS** Appraisal methods are appearing that are facilitated by software and Internet sites designed to help supervisors log and rate performance. The performance appraisal market is the fastest growing area of human resources software. In 2008, sales of performance management software skyrocketed to $490 million worldwide, a number that is expected to grow annually by 22 to 24 percent. Software firms sell a complete set of tools for managers, including appraisal forms in electronic format and software to track and manage employee performance goals, career plans, development plans, and progression in compensation.[19] Electronic Performance Monitoring (EPM) systems are also being used to provide managers access to employees' computers and telephones. EPMs allow mangers to monitor employees' work-related behaviour at any given time. One such system is described in the HR.Net box above.

It is also important to choose the right appraisal tool. Each tool has its own advantages and disadvantages, as shown in Table 7.2, and must be carefully weighed to ascertain which is best for an organization's needs.

## Who Should Do the Appraising?

The second aspect of this step involves who should appraise an employee's performance. Several options exist.

**APPRAISAL BY THE IMMEDIATE SUPERVISOR** Supervisors' ratings are still the heart of most appraisal systems. Getting a supervisor's appraisal is relatively easy and makes a great deal of sense. The supervisor should be—and usually is—in the best position to observe and evaluate the performance of employees reporting to him or her and is responsible for their performance.

**behaviour observation scale (BOS)** An appraisal method that identifies critical incidents and assesses how frequently behaviours were demonstrated.

**management by objectives (MBO)** Collaborative goal setting between manager and employee and then periodically reviewing progress made.

MBO **www.1000ventures.com/business_guide/mgmt_mbo_main.html**

Performance Appraisal Software **www.halogensoftware.com/products/halogen-eappraisal**

Performance Appraisal Software **www.successfactors.com**

*table* 7.2 **Important Advantages and Disadvantages of Appraisal Tools**

| | Advantages | Disadvantages |
|---|---|---|
| Graphic rating scale | Simple to use; provides a quantitative rating for each employee | Standards may be unclear; halo effect, central tendency, leniency, and bias can also be problems |
| Forced distribution method | Minimizes inflation of ratings | Can demotivate employees who receive scores less than the top 20% |
| Critical incident method | Helps specify what is "right" or "wrong" about the employee's performance; forces supervisor to evaluate employees on an ongoing basis | Difficult to rate or rank employees relative to one another |
| Behaviourally anchored rating scale | Provides behavioural "anchors." BARS is very accurate | Difficult to develop |
| Management by objectives | Tied to jointly agreed-upon performance objectives | Time-consuming |
| Balanced scorecard | Enhances employee commitment to strategic goals through their own actions | Time-consuming and resource intensive |

**USING PEER APPRAISALS** The appraisal of an employee by his or her peers can be effective in predicting future management success. There is a high correlation between peer and supervisor ratings.[20] Peers have more opportunity to observe ratees and to observe them at more revealing times than supervisors, which is likely to enhance the credibility of feedback received from one's peer group.[21] From a study of military officers, for example, we know that peer ratings were quite accurate in predicting which officers would be promoted and which would not.[22] In another study that involved more than 200 industrial managers, peer ratings were similarly useful in predicting who would be promoted.[23] One potential problem is *logrolling*, whereby all the peers simply get together to rate each other highly.

With more organizations using self-managing teams, peer or team appraisals are becoming more popular. Evaluations by cross-functional teams are also gaining popularity. For example, an employee who participates on a number of workplace committees, such as health and safety, change management, and diversity management, may request members from each committee to evaluate his or her performance. One study found that peer ratings had an immediate positive impact on perceptions of open communication, motivation, group cohesion, and satisfaction, and these were not dependent on the ratio of positive to negative feedback.[24] Thus, peer appraisals would appear to have great potential for work teams. At W.L. Gore & Associates, a manufacturer of fluoropolymer products with 8000 employees across 45 worldwide locations and annual revenues of U.S.$2 billion, peer review has been an integral part of their evaluation system for over 30 years. Several times a year, peer groups consisting of 10 colleagues provide feedback on each team member's contributions to the company's goals and strategize about how to improve performance.[25]

This food service supervisor is conducting a feedback session about an employee's performance during the day's major banquet to keep communications open and build employee commitment.

**RATING COMMITTEES** Many employers use rating committees to evaluate employees. These committees are usually composed of the employee's immediate supervisor and three or four other supervisors. Using multiple raters can be advantageous. While there may be a discrepancy in the ratings made by individual supervisors, the composite ratings tend to be more reliable, fair, and valid.[26] Several raters can help cancel out problems, such as personal bias, that might occur when using only one rater. Furthermore, when there are variations in raters' ratings, they usually stem from the fact that raters often observe different facets of an employee's performance; the appraisal ought to reflect these differences.[27] Even when a committee is not used, it is common to have the appraisal reviewed by the manager immediately above the one who makes the appraisal.

**SELF-ASSESSMENT** Self-assessment is a valuable evaluation technique when used for formative purposes because it allows employees to reflect on their professional growth and development. Self-assessment encourages employees to critique their past performance and reflect on where they want to set goals for improvement. Employees are encouraged to discuss their self-assessments at the appraisal interview. Regrettably, problems emerge when self-assessments are used for summative purposes. Employees usually rate themselves higher than they are rated by supervisors or peers, which can occur when self-assessments are tied to promotions, transfers, and salary increases.[28] In one study, for example, it was found that when asked to rate their own job performance, 40 percent of the employees in jobs of all types placed themselves in the top 10 percent ("one of the best"), while virtually all remaining employees rated themselves either in the top 25 percent ("well above average") or at least in the top 50 percent ("above average"). Usually, no more than 1 or 2 percent will place themselves in a below-average category and then, almost invariably, in the top below-average category. However, self-assessments have been found to correlate more highly with performance measures if employees know that this comparison will be made and if they are instructed to compare themselves with others.[29]

**MANAGEMENT APPRAISAL BY EMPLOYEES** Traditionally, supervisors feared that being appraised by their employees would undermine their management authority.[30] Over the past few years, a shift in organizational culture has created a climate that is more receptive to management appraisal by employees. At the forefront are more cross-functional committees that capitalize on joint collaborations between management and non-management staff, and management teams that realize the value of feedback to gauge how the organization is functioning. Thus, more organizations today are inviting employees to anonymously evaluate their supervisors' performance, a process many call *upward feedback*.[31] When conducted throughout the organization, the process helps upper management get an overview of how departmental managers are performing, The executive team learns about its managers' leadership styles and the implications of these approaches, identifies potential problems and takes corrective action with individual managers as required, and uncovers excellent work being done by some managers and finds ways to recognize their achievements. Such employee ratings are especially valuable when used for developmental rather than evaluative purposes.[32] Managers receiving feedback from employees who identify themselves view the upward appraisal process more positively than do managers who receive anonymous feedback; however, employees (not surprisingly) are more comfortable giving anonymous responses, and those who have to identify themselves tend to provide inflated ratings.[33] Research comparing employee and peer ratings of managers found them to be comparable.[34]

**360-DEGREE APPRAISAL** The **360-degree appraisal** or "multisource feedback" is one of the most popular methods of performance evaluation.[35] Here, as shown in Figure 7.6, performance feedback is anonymously collected "all around" an employee, from supervisors, managers, subordinates, peers, and internal or external customers.[36] The major purpose of 360-degree feedback is to reveal themes in employee performance, but to also capture the diversity of an employee's roles and contributions across an organization. This feedback was originally used only for training and development purposes,[37] but has rapidly spread to be incorporated in the management of performance and pay.[38] The 360-degree approach supports the activities of performance feedback, coaching, leadership development, succession

**360-degree appraisal** A performance appraisal technique that uses multiple raters including peers, employees reporting to the appraisee, supervisors, and customers.

### *figure* 7.6 360-Degree Performance Appraisals

Source: J. F. Milliman, R. A. Zawacki, C. Norman, L. Powell, and J. Kerksey, "Companies Evaluate Employees from All Perspectives," *Personnel Journal* 73(11), (November 1994), p. 100. Illustration by Tim Barker, copyright November 1994. Used with permission. All rights reserved.

planning, and rewards and recognition.[39] A sample of a 360-degree feedback form is shown in Figure 7.7.

There are a number of reasons for the rapid growth of 360-degree appraisal. Today's flatter organizations built on teamwork and participative management mean a more open communication climate conducive to such an approach, and it fits closely with the goals of organizations committed to continuous learning. A

## *figure* 7.7 360-Degree Feedback Survey

*RATEE: ____________________*

*PLEASE CIRCLE YOUR RATER TYPE:*

| Self | Supervisor | Peer / Colleague | Direct Report |
|---|---|---|---|

*USING THE FOLLOWING SCALE, CIRCLE THE APPROPRIATE RATING FOR EACH BEHAVIOUR/ACTION.*

| N/A | 1 | 2 | 3 | 4 | 5 | 6 | 7 | 8 | 9 | 10 |
|---|---|---|---|---|---|---|---|---|---|---|
| Don't Know | Poor – Development Critical | | Fair – Development Opportunity | | Acceptable | | Good | Very Good | Excellent | |

***LEADERSHIP***

1. **Champions the Values** — N/A 1 2 3 4 5 6 7 8 9 10
   Supports and champions the values and strategic objectives of the company.
2. **Communicates Vision** — N/A 1 2 3 4 5 6 7 8 9 10
   Sets and communicates a vision for their department that provides direction and inspires commitment.
3. **Plans Strategically** — N/A 1 2 3 4 5 6 7 8 9 10
   Thinks and plans strategically balancing short-term priorities with longer term objectives.
4. **Demonstrates Intelligent Risk Taking** — N/A 1 2 3 4 5 6 7 8 9 10
   Demonstrates intelligent and accountable risk taking through personal action, decision making and a willingness to challenge the status quo.
5. **Manages Corporate Resources** — N/A 1 2 3 4 5 6 7 8 9 10
   Manages corporate resources responsibly—"as if it were their own business," balancing the competing interests of customers, shareholders and employees in decision making.
6. **Takes Responsibility for Own Actions** — N/A 1 2 3 4 5 6 7 8 9 10
   Takes accountability and responsibility for their own actions and those of their direct reports, willingly admitting to mistakes as required.
7. **Makes Difficult Decisions** — N/A 1 2 3 4 5 6 7 8 9 10
   Steps up to and makes unpopular or difficult decisions.
8. **Recruits High Performers** — N/A 1 2 3 4 5 6 7 8 9 10
   Attracts and recruits people who have both the skills and values that lead to high performance.

multiple-rater system is also more meaningful in today's reality of complex jobs with matrix and team-reporting relationships. Further, the widespread lack of confidence in traditional performance appraisals conducted only by a supervisor and the fear associated with such appraisals on the part of both parties have reduced the credibility of that approach.[40] A 360-degree appraisal can be perceived as a jury of peers rather than the supervisor as a single judge, which enhances perceptions of fairness.[41]

The 360-degree appraisal is widely used in Canadian companies. For example, Toronto-based University Health Network (UHN) has adapted a 360-degree review with a twist. All key stakeholders provide feedback to the employee, and the employee in turn completes a self-assessment. Feedback is graphed, allowing comparison of stakeholders' ratings and comments against the self-assessment. While most workplaces protect the anonymity of staff who provide feedback, UHN encourages them to identify themselves so that employees can approach respondents for clarification. The 360-degree review is used exclusively for professional development and compensation is not tied to the results.[42] Rogers Communication also employs a 360-degree approach to evaluation. Rogers annually conducts these reviews for everyone in the company, including the entire leadership team of vice-presidents and directors. Rogers outsources the process to ensure complete anonymity.[43] Other Canadian companies using 360-degree appraisals include BC Gas Utility Ltd., Aetna Life Insurance, Scotiabank, Good Year Canada, and Hallmark.

**AN ETHICAL DILEMMA**
Is it fair for people other than your immediate supervisor to rate performance that will be used for summative purposes?

Internet-based 360-degree feedback systems are now available. One sample page of output from a feedback report is shown in Figure 7.8.

## Training for Appraisers

Training managers on their accountabilities during performance evaluations is essential to the success of the system. Court decisions in which employees challenged the validity of their evaluation ratings and research on

*figure* 7.8 **Summary of Internet-Based 360-Degree Feedback**

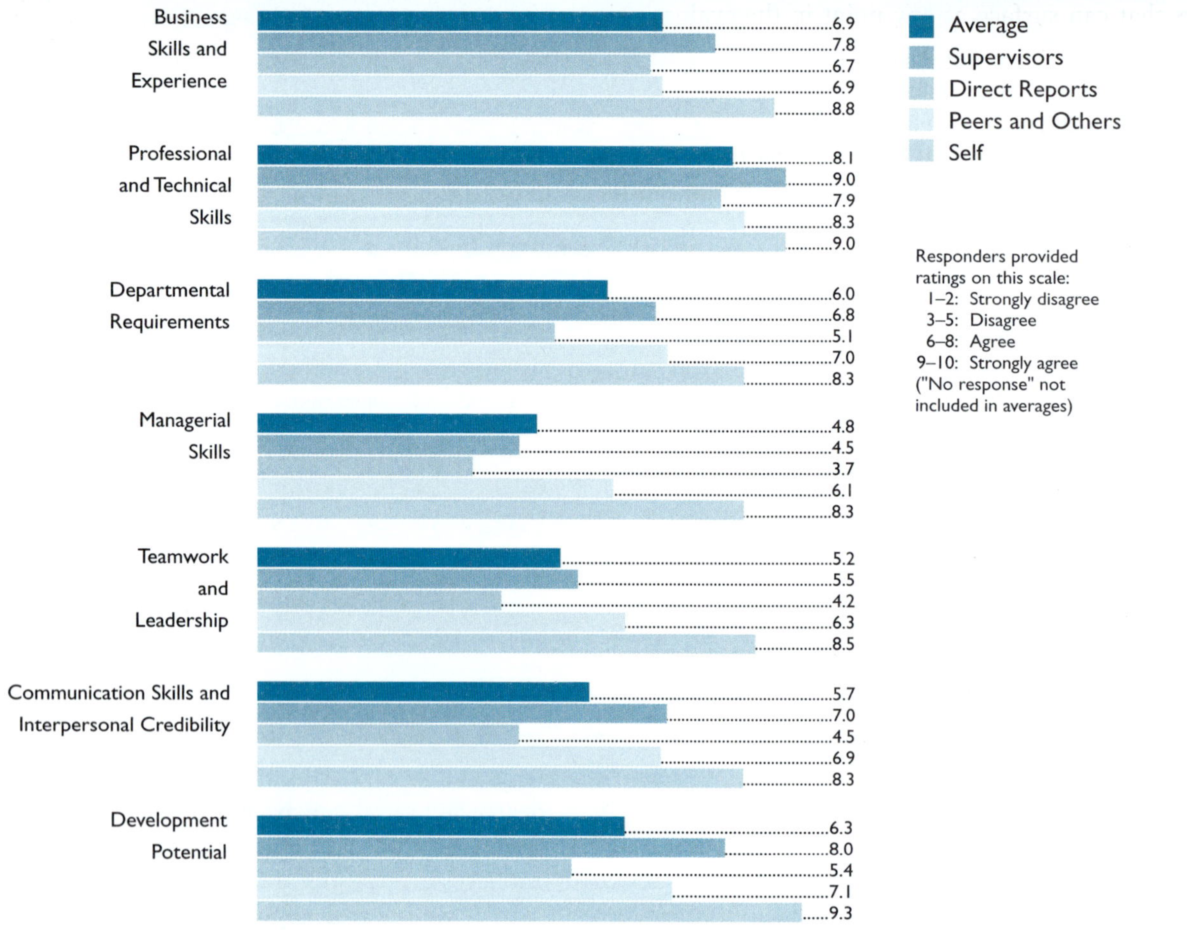


Source: "Panoramic Feedback," www.panoramicfeedback.com. January 2005. Reprinted with permission of Panometrics Inc.

performance evaluations both stress the significance of training managers. Being a good manager does not necessarily create a good evaluator, as the evaluation process demands a unique set of competencies. Training should also be extended to employees, so they know what to expected.[44]

The purpose of training is to enhance the likelihood that managers will use the same criteria in evaluating performance and conducting appraisal interviews. Unfortunately, studies have found that nearly 30 percent of companies do not provide managers with performance evaluation training.[45] The following topics are frequently covered in appraisal training: purpose of performance evaluations, the appraisal process and timing, preparation for the evaluation, completion of paperwork, conducting the appraisal interview, offering positive and constructive feedback, and coaching employees in performance improvement and goal setting.

One of the most important subjects covered in performance evaluation training is how to deal with rater errors that can surface at any point in the evaluation. Managers need to be aware of rater errors so that they can develop strategies to prevent them from adversely affecting the objective assessment of employee performance. The Royal Bank has an extensive training program for managers that uses role-plays to develop skills in eliminating rating errors. The role-plays are videotaped to allow managers to critique their performances and explore ways of preventing rater errors from creeping into real-life assessments of their employees.[46]

Rater errors include the halo effect, central tendency, leniency or strictness, appraisal bias, the recency effect, and the similar-to-me bias.

**HALO EFFECT** The **halo effect** means that the rating of an employee on one trait (such as "gets along with others") biases the way in which the person is rated on other traits (such as "quantity of work"). This problem often occurs with employees who are especially friendly (or unfriendly) toward a supervisor. For example, a very friendly employee will often be rated as satisfactory for all traits rather than just for the trait "gets along well with others." Being aware of this problem is a major step toward avoiding it. Supervisory training can also alleviate the problem.[47]

**CENTRAL TENDENCY** Many supervisors have a **central tendency** when filling in rating scales. For example, if the rating scale ranges from one to seven, they tend to avoid the highs (six and seven) and lows (one and two) and rate most of their employees between three and five. If a graphic rating scale is used, this central tendency could mean that all employees are simply rated "average." Such a restriction can distort the evaluations, making them less useful for promotion, salary, or counselling purposes. Ranking employees from best to worst can help offset this tendency.

**LENIENCY OR STRICTNESS** Some supervisors tend to rate all of their employees consistently high (or low), just as some instructors are notoriously high graders and others are not. This **strictness/leniency** problem is especially serious with graphic rating scales because supervisors are not necessarily required to avoid giving all of their employees high (or low) ratings. On the other hand, ranking employees as indicated above can help, because a manager is forced to distinguish between high and low performers.

**APPRAISAL BIAS** Individual differences among ratees in terms of a wide variety of characteristics, such as age, race, and gender, can affect their ratings, often quite apart from each ratee's actual performance.[48] This is known as **appraisal bias**. Not only does this bias result in inaccurate feedback, it is also illegal under human rights legislation. In one study, high-performing females were often rated significantly higher than were high-performing males. A related issue is described in the Workforce Diversity box on page 232.

**RECENCY EFFECT** The **recency effect** occurs when ratings are based on an employee's most recent performance, whether good or bad. The appraisal is biased to

**halo effect** In performance appraisal, the problem that occurs when a supervisor's rating of an employee on one trait biases the rating of that person on other traits.

**central tendency** A tendency to rate all employees in the middle of the scale.

**strictness/leniency** The problem that occurs when a supervisor has a tendency to rate all employees either high or low.

**appraisal bias** The tendency to allow individual differences, such as age, race, and gender, to affect the appraisal ratings that employees receive.

**recency effect** The rating error that occurs when ratings are based on an employee's most recent performance rather than performance throughout the appraisal period.

WORKFORCE DIVERSITY

## Gender and Performance Appraisal

Numerous studies have found that supervisors rate women lower than men for similar levels of performance, suggesting that for female employees, good performance alone may not lead to fair ratings. Two recent studies have provided further results regarding gender issues in performance appraisal.

One study investigated whether the gender composition of the supervisor–subordinate dyad affected ratings. Based on data from supervisor–subordinate dyads in four organizations, researchers found that both male and female supervisors exhibited a positive bias toward subordinates of the same gender and rated members of the same gender higher.[1]

Another study conducted among officers in the Israeli Defence Forces found that women's performance was rated lower than that of men when the women were token members of their units. However, the performance of women was rated higher than that of men when they constituted a higher proportion of officers in the unit.[2] Thus, the number of women in a work group may have some bearing on performance evaluation results. Both studies concluded that further investigation of gender differences in performance appraisal are needed to extend knowledge regarding this complex situation.

1. A. Varma and L. K. Stroh, "The Impact of Same-Sex LMX Dyads on Performance Evaluations," *Human Resource Management,* 40, Winter 2001, pp. 309–320.
2. A. Pazy and I. Oron, "Sex Proportion and Performance Evaluation Among High-Ranking Military Officers," *Journal of Organizational Behavior*, 22, September 2001, pp. 689–702.

## *In-class Notes*

**Appraising Performance (Step 2)**

- Methods
  - graphic rating scale
  - forced distribution
  - critical incident
  - behaviourally anchored rating scales
  - management by objectives
  - balanced scorecard
  - technology-based
- Raters can include immediate supervisor, peers, rating committees, self, subordinates, and 360-degree rating
- Rater errors, such as central tendency and the halo effect, can be minimized through helping raters understand the problem, rater training, and HR review of appraisals

the extent that this recent performance does not exemplify the employee's average performance over the appraisal period.

**SIMILAR-TO-ME BIAS** If a supervisor tends to give higher ratings to employees with whom he or she has something in common, the **similar-to-me bias** is occurring. This bias can be discriminatory if it is based on similarity in race, gender, or other prohibited grounds.

## 7.5 STEP 3: PROVIDING FEEDBACK

An appraisal typically culminates in an **appraisal interview**. This is an interview in which the manager and employee review the appraisal and make plans to remedy performance problems and reinforce strengths. This interview is a critical element in performance management, and how feedback is given to the employee can determine whether performance will improve or decline. All feedback should be directed to performance-related behaviours, should be nonjudgmental, and should not focus on the person. It would be counterproductive to ask a person why he is lazy instead of asking why pre-established standards of performance have not been met.

*frontLINE tips*

There should be no surprises for an employee during the interview. The conversation should exclusively focus on performance and development. It is not a time to discipline employees for past errors. Employees who breach company policies or procedures should be disciplined immediately after the incident and the issue should not be raised at the appraisal interview.

To communicate the importance of feedback beyond an annual performance evaluation event, Ernst & Young launched an online "Feedback Zone," where employees can request or post feedback at any time. Survey results indicate that the initiative is well received, especially by Generation Y employees, who place a high priority on frequent and candid performance feedback.[49]

### How to Prepare for the Appraisal Interview

Because the interview process is so critical, there are three things to do in preparation for the interview.[50] First, assemble the data. Study the person's job description and standards of performance, and compare records, notes, or logs of the employee's performance to the standards. If helpful, review the files of the employee's previous appraisals, although care should be taken not to let past performance affect your view of recent performance. Then prepare the employee. Give the employee at least a week's notice to review his or her work, read over the job description, analyze problems, complete a self-assessment, and gather questions and comments. Finally, choose the time and place. Find a mutually agreeable time for the interview and allow a period long enough for the entire interview. Interviews with non-supervisory staff (such as clerical workers and maintenance people) should take no more than an hour. Appraising management employees often takes two or three hours. Be sure the interview is done in a private place where there will be no interruptions by phone calls or visitors.

### How to Conduct the Interview

There are five things to keep in mind when conducting an appraisal interview:

1. *Be direct and specific.* Talk in terms of objective work-related behaviours. Use examples, such as absences, tardiness, quality records, inspection reports, scrap or waste, orders processed, productivity records, material used or consumed, timeliness of tasks or projects, control or reduction of costs, numbers of errors, costs compared with budgets, customers' comments, product returns, order processing time, inventory level and accuracy, accident reports, and so on.
2. *Focus on job-related behaviours.* Do not say, "You are too slow in producing those reports." Instead, try to compare the person's performance to a standard ("These reports should normally be done within 10 days"). Similarly, do not compare the

**similar-to-me bias** The tendency to give higher performance ratings to employees who are perceived to be similar to the rater in some way.

**appraisal interview** An interview in which the supervisor and employee review the appraisal and make plans to remedy deficiencies and reinforce strengths.

*figure* 7.9 **Example of an Action Plan**

**ACTION PLAN**

Date: May 18, 2005

For: John, Assistant Plant Manager

Problem: Parts inventory too high

Objective: Reduce plant parts inventory by 10% in June

| **Action Steps** | **When** | **Expected Results** |
|---|---|---|
| Determine average monthly parts inventory | 6/2 | Establish a base from which to measure progress |
| Review ordering quantities and parts usage | 6/15 | Identify overstocked items |
| Ship excess parts to regional warehouse and scrap obsolete parts | 6/20 | Clear stock space |
| Set new ordering quantities for all parts | 6/25 | Avoid future overstocking |
| Check records to measure where we are now | 7/1 | See how close we are to objective |

person's performance to that of other people ("He is quicker than you are"). If an employee is not performing to standard, try to find the root cause of the problem and offer support and training in how to move behaviour toward the expected performance standard.

3. *Encourage the person to talk.* Stop and listen to what the person is saying. Ask open-ended questions such as, "What do you think we can do to improve the situation?" Use such phrases as, "Go on" or, "Tell me more." Restate the person's last point as a question, such as, "Do you not think you can get the job done?" Studies have shown that the most effective appraisal interviews encourage employees to speak approximately 60 percent of the time.[51]
4. *Encourage collaboration.* Both managers and employees should actively participate in developing approaches for transforming weaknesses into strengths and charting performance goals. The more ownership employees have in mapping out the direction, the more likely they will commit to and reach performance targets.
5. *Post-Interview Follow-up.* Employees should leave the interview knowing specifically where they are doing well and where changes in behaviour are required. Get agreement before employees leave on how things will be improved and by when. After the interview, managers should follow up with employees to discuss progress and offer support.

If performance improvement is required, develop an action plan showing steps and expected results, as illustrated in Figure 7.9.

## How to Handle a Defensive Employee

Defences are a very important and familiar aspect of our lives. When a person is accused of poor performance, the first reaction will sometimes be denial. By denying the fault, the person avoids having to question his or her own competence. Others react to criticism with anger and aggression. This helps them let off steam and postpones confronting the immediate problem until they are able to cope with it. Still others react to criticism by retreating into a shell.

Understanding and dealing with defensiveness is an important appraisal skill. It is important to:

*** frontLINE tips**

1. *Recognize that defensive behaviour is normal.*
2. *Never attack a person's defences.* Do not try to "explain someone to themselves" by saying things like, "You know the real reason you are using that excuse is that you cannot bear to be blamed for anything." Instead try to concentrate on the act itself ("sales are down") rather than on the person ("you are not selling enough").
3. *Postpone action.* Sometimes, it is best to do nothing at all. People frequently react to sudden threats by instinctively hiding behind their "masks." Given sufficient time, however, a more rational reaction takes over.
4. *Recognize human limitations.* Do not expect to be able to solve every problem that comes up, especially the human ones. More importantly, remember that a supervisor should not try to be a psychologist. Offering employees understanding is one thing; trying to deal with deep psychological problems is another matter entirely.

## How to Constructively Criticize an Employee's Performance

When criticism is required, it should be done in a manner that lets the person maintain his or her dignity and sense of worth. Specifically, criticism should be provided constructively and in private. Provide examples of critical incidents and specific suggestions of what could be done and why. Avoid a once-a-year "critical broadside" by giving feedback on a daily basis so that at the formal review, there are no surprises. Never say the person is "always" wrong (since no one is ever "always" wrong or right). Finally, criticism should be objective and free of any personal biases.

## How to Ensure That the Appraisal Interview Leads to Improved Performance

It is important to clear up job-related problems by setting improvement goals and a schedule for achieving them. In one study, researchers found that whether employees expressed satisfaction with their appraisal interview depended mostly on three factors: not feeling threatened during the interview; having an opportunity to present their ideas and feelings and to influence the course of the interview; and having a helpful and constructive supervisor conduct the interview.[52]

### In-class Notes

**Providing Feedback (Step 3)**

- Appraisal interviews should be direct and specific and focus on job behaviours; the employee should be encouraged to talk; an action plan should be developed
- Defensive employee behaviour is normal; focus on behaviour, not on the person
- Provide constructive criticism
- Set performance-improvement goals
- Formal written warning may be required

However, the main objective is to get them to improve their subsequent performance. Here, researchers have found that clearing up job-related problems with the employee and setting measurable performance targets and a schedule for achieving them are the actions that consistently lead to improved performance.

## How to Handle a Formal Written Warning

There will be times when an employee's performance is so poor that a formal written warning is required. Such written warnings serve two purposes: (1) They may serve to shake the employee out of his or her bad habits, and (2) they can help the manager defend his or her rating of the employee both to his or her boss and (if needed) to a court or human rights commission.

LEGALcompliance

Written warnings should identify the standards under which the employee is judged, make it clear that the employee was aware of the standard, specify any violation of the standard, and indicate that the employee had an opportunity to correct his or her behaviour.

# 7.6 LEGAL AND ETHICAL ISSUES

The legal aspects of doing performance appraisal should always be considered. These and ethics should be the bedrock of a performance appraisal. In fact, most managers understand that an appraiser can "stick to the rules" and conduct a review of an employee's performance but still fail to provide an honest assessment. Accurate feedback is particularly important in defending against charges of bias based on grounds prohibited under human rights legislation such as age, sex, and so on. As one commentator puts it:

> The overall objective of high-ethics performance reviews should be to provide an honest assessment of performance and to mutually develop a plan to improve the individual's effectiveness. That requires that we tell people where they stand and that we be straight with them.[53]

LEGALcompliance

Guidelines for developing an effective (legal and ethical) appraisal process include:[54]

1. Conduct a job analysis to ascertain performance factors and performance standards required for job success.
2. Define each performance factor so there is consistency in how managers understand and assess each characteristic. Incorporate these performance factors into a rating instrument (the research literature recommends rating instruments that are tied to specific job behaviours, such as BARS).
3. Make sure that definitive standards of performance are communicated in writing to all raters and ratees. Provide opportunities for either party to ask questions about the performance factors and performance standards.
4. Use clearly defined and measurable individual dimensions of job performance (such as "punctuality") rather than undefined, global measures (such as "overall performance").
5. When using a graphic rating scale, avoid abstract trait names (for example, "loyalty," "honesty") unless they can be defined in terms of observable behaviours.
6. Employ subjective supervisory ratings or comments as only one component of the overall appraisal process.
7. Train supervisors to use the rating instrument properly. Give instructions on how to apply performance appraisal standards ("outstanding" and so on) when making judgments. Ensure that subjective standards are not subject to bias.[55]
8. Require appraisers to have regular contact with the employee being evaluated.
9. Whenever possible, have more than one appraiser conduct the appraisal, and conduct all appraisals independently. This process can help to cancel out individual errors and biases and enhance the reliability of the performance evaluation system. At a minimum, have someone else review the appraisal before it is shared with the employee.
10. Utilize formal appeal mechanisms and a review of ratings by upper-level managers.
11. Document evaluations and reasons for any termination decision.
12. Where appropriate, provide corrective guidance to assist poor performers in improving their performance.

**RELIABILITY AND VALIDITY** Appraisal systems must be based on performance criteria that are *valid* or accurate for the position being rated and *reliable* in that their application must produce consistent ratings for the same performance. Employee concerns about appraisal fairness are influenced by these characteristics of the performance appraisal system.

*table* 7.3 **A Graphic Rating Scale with Unclear Standards**

| | Excellent | Good | Fair | Poor |
|---|---|---|---|---|
| Quality of work | ______ | ______ | ______ | ______ |
| Quantity of work | ______ | ______ | ______ | ______ |
| Creativity | ______ | ______ | ______ | ______ |
| Integrity | ______ | ______ | ______ | ______ |

Note: For example, what exactly is meant by "good," "quantity of work," and so forth?

Criteria used in performance appraisal must be valid in order to produce useful results. Criteria must be (1) relevant to the job being appraised; (2) broad enough to cover all aspects of the job requirements; and (3) specific. For example, including a broad criterion such as "leadership" may not be relevant to non-management jobs and may be so vague that it can be interpreted in many different ways.

Effective appraisal criteria are precise enough to result in reliable, consistent measures of performance when applied across many employees by many different raters. This is difficult to achieve without quantifiable and measurable criteria.

The best performance appraisal systems are those in which the supervisor or manager makes an ongoing effort to coach and monitor employees instead of leaving evaluation to the last minute.

**UNCLEAR STANDARDS** The problem of **unclear performance standards** is illustrated in Table 7.3. Although the

## *In-class Notes*

**Legal and Ethical Issues**

- Use rating instruments based on specific job behaviours
- Provide an honest assessment of performance
- Require raters to have regular contact with employees
- Accurate feedback is critical to defend charges of bias based on prohibited grounds

______________________________

______________________________

______________________________

______________________________

______________________________

______________________________

**unclear performance standards** An appraisal scale that is too open to interpretation of traits and standards.

Canadian Human Rights Commission
**www.chrc-ccdp.ca**

graphic rating scale seems objective, it would probably result in unfair appraisals because the traits and degrees of merit are open to interpretation. For example, different supervisors would probably differently define "good" performance, "fair" performance, and so on. The same is true of such traits as "quality of work" or "creativity." There are several ways to rectify this problem. The best is to develop and include descriptive phrases that define each trait. For example, specifying the meanings of "outstanding," "very good," and "good" quality work results in appraisals that are more consistent and more easily explained.

# Performance Appraisals on the International Stage

A growing number of Canadians are crossing international borders to temporarily live and work in foreign countries. They are usually involved in one of four types of international assignments: (1) technical assignments that involve short-term projects in which they complete a specific task, such as implementing a new software program; (2) developmental assignments that involve training to enhance the knowledge capacity of foreign workers; (3) strategic assignments that focus on developing a balanced global perspective; and, (4) functional assignments that involve a two-way transfer of practices for the benefit of all participating companies.[56] A performance appraisal for international assignments is far more complex, with most companies selecting a management by objectives approach to evaluation. Since managers are not able to directly observe employees' daily performance or communicate with them frequently, performance appraisal ratings and feedback are predominantly focused on the degree to which employees achieve the goals and objectives of their assignment within the stated timelines. Managers and employees are required to engage in lengthy discussions about the goals, expectations, available resources, and timelines for task completion before employees leave on assignment so that employees have clarity around what is expected. There are differences in how these discussions are handled, however. In Germany and Sweden, employees actively contribute to the goal-setting process around international assignments, whereas in the U.S. job goals are assigned without opportunity for input.[57] In most cases, the appraisal is conducted by the employee's immediate supervisor at headquarters in consultation with the immediate host-country supervisor. Evaluation ratings and subsequent rewards for performance are based on reaching targeted goals within specified timelines.

# Chapter Review

## Answers to Test Yourself

1. Why is it important to effectively manage performance and conduct appraisals?

   Performance appraisals are an important component of an organization's performance management system. Performance appraisals provide (1) information on which to base salary or promotion decisions, (2) an opportunity to review and discuss work-related behaviour, and (3) an opportunity to facilitate career planning.

2. What are the three major steps in conducting performance appraisals?

   There are three steps in the performance appraisal process. The first is defining performance expectations to ensure that job duties and standards of performance are clear to all. The second step is appraising performance, which means comparing an employee's actual performance with the standards of performance that have been set. Various rating methods are available to conduct the appraisal. The third step is providing feedback based on the appraisal results. The employee's performance and progress are discussed, and plans are made for any development required.

3. What are the six methods commonly used for performance appraisals, and who uses them?

   Performance appraisal methods normally appraise traits, behaviour, or results and include the graphic rating scale, forced distribution method, BARS, MBO, balanced scorecard, and critical incident method. The line manager usually does the appraisal and provides feedback, with HR designing policies and procedures to support the performance appraisal system, serving in an advisory capacity to managers and employees, and monitoring the process. Appraisers can also include peers, rating committees, employees, customers, or a combination of these in the 360-degree process.

4. What are the major problems inhibiting effective performance appraisals, and how can they be minimized?

   Appraisal problems to be aware of are unclear standards and rater errors that include the halo effect, central tendency, leniency or strictness, appraisal bias, the recency effect, and similar-to-me bias. There are three key ways of minimizing these problems: raters being aware and familiar with rater errors; training supervisors to eliminate and avoid errors; and ensuring that the completed appraisals are reviewed by the supervisor's immediate boss and/or the HR department.

5. What are some of the legal and ethical issues that need to be considered regarding performance appraisals?

   Legal and ethical considerations are critical in performance appraisal. In order to provide appraisals, managers should ensure that performance standards are provided to all raters and ratees; train supervisors and managers to use the rating instrument properly; allow appraisers regular contact with the employee being evaluated; use multiple appraisers; include an appeal mechanism; and provide corrective guidance to assist poor performers.

## Key Terms

360-degree appraisal (p. 227)
appraisal bias (p. 231)
appraisal interview (p. 233)
behaviour observation scale (BOS) (p. 222)
behaviourally anchored rating scale (BARS) (p. 221)
central tendency (p. 231)
criterion contamination (p. 218)
criterion deficiency (p. 218)
critical incident method (p. 220)
forced distribution method (p. 220)
formative evaluation (p. 214)
graphic rating scale (p. 218)
halo effect (p. 231)
management by objectives (MBO) (p. 222)
performance factors (p. 217)
performance management (p. 214)
performance standards (p. 217)
recency effect (p. 231)
similar-to-me bias (p. 233)
strictness/leniency (p. 231)
summative evaluation (p. 214)
unclear performance standards (p. 237)

# Cases and Exercises

**myHRlab**
For additional cases and exercises, go to **www.pearsoned.ca/myhrlab.**

## CASE INCIDENT

### Another Eventful Appraisal Interview

Sam Maynard was nervous as he walked into John Adams's office for his annual performance evaluation. Sam dreaded the pilgrimage into his boss's office, as he never knew what to expect and always walked out of the interview with a desperate urge to quit. But Sam needed his job as a financial analyst and there were not many financial institutions like C.L. Carter & Company that offered great wages and benefits. He had been with the company for 15 years and always received very good performance evaluation results—until John Adams became his boss. Ever since Sam questioned a major policy change in how files are managed, John has been rather aloof and highly critical of everything Sam does.

"Come on in, Sam, and make yourself comfortable," began John. "I know we don't see each other often as I've been busy working with staff at the other branches across the city, but I think I can be candid with you about your performance. In the past six months, I've noticed a sharp decline in your performance and a really bad attitude. Your paperwork is substandard and I rarely see you in your office. You never attend the social events we host for staff after hours and you rarely make any important contributions in our staff meetings. I also noticed that one of your clients walked out of the office looking angry a few weeks ago and I was wondering what you did to upset her so much."

Sam was on the verge of speaking when John interrupted him. "I've heard from HR that you applied for the supervisory job we have posted. You realize with your questionable attitude and low performance that that's never going to happen. In my opinion, this job might be beyond your skill level. You need to make some serious changes in your personality and your behaviour, Sam. Take time over the weekend to make up your mind about what you are going to do, because I don't want to have this discussion with you again. Have I made myself clear?"

Sam smiled, "Yes, Mr. Adams. Perfectly clear. I definitely have a great deal to think about." Sam left the interview already planning in his mind what he will write in his resignation letter.

### Questions

1. Critique John's approach to appraising Sam's performance.
2. Besides Sam's decision to resign, what are other consequences of conducting appraisal interviews in this manner?
3. What corrective action would you recommend to the manager to improve his approach to conducting appraisal interviews?

### Application Questions

1. The executive team in your organization has sought your advice on how to create a valid and reliable performance evaluation system for the company. Discuss your recommendations in each of the following areas: (a) performance evaluation forms, (b) who should assess performance, and (c) topics to be included in performance appraisal training for managers.
2. You are the manager of a telemarketing firm with 80 percent of your sales staff working from homes three to four days a week. Map out the type of performance appraisal system that should be used to assess your employees' performance.
3. Select a job listed on the National Occupational Classification website (www5.hrsdc.gc.ca/NOC/English/NOC/2006/Welcome.aspx). Review the job description and create a performance appraisal form to be used to assess staff employed in this profession. Include your rationale for selecting this evaluation format.
4. In pairs, select one of the rater errors discussed in this chapter and through a role-play demonstrate how this error appears in an appraisal interview and the impact it has on employees. Present your role-play to the class to see if they can determine what rater error is demonstrated.
5. Bring a copy of a performance evaluation that you received in your current job or a former job. With reference to terminology associated with performance evaluation, critique the performance appraisal. What changes would you make to the evaluation form and why?

## RUNNING CASE: LEARNINMOTION.COM

### The Performance Appraisal

The case for Chapter 7, The Performance Appraisal, presents a disagreement among management concerning how to evaluate workers. What type of appraisal system is needed for LearninMotion.com?

To read this case, go to www.pearsoned.ca/myhrlab and click on the *Management of Human Resources*, Third Canadian Edition, In-Class Edition, cover. Click on the case module in Chapter 7. The running case illustrates a variety of challenges confronted by HR professionals, small-business owners, and front-line supervisors. It places students in the role of HR management consultants to help the fledgling LearninMotion.com develop HR policies, strategies, and long-term goals. Each case is accompanied by assignments for management consultants in the form of critical-thinking questions posed to the student.

## CONTROVERSIAL BUSINESS TOPIC EXERCISE

You are the operations supervisor overseeing a staff of 16 skilled labourers in a medium-sized manufacturing plant. Six months ago, you received a very favourable evaluation of your performance. You exceeded all performance targets, recommended cost containment strategies over $750 000, and received outstanding evaluations from your staff, who credited you as being one of the best supervisors in the business. At your appraisal interview, your director mapped out a plan for leadership training so that you can move into a more senior management role. Six months have passed and even though you have repeatedly asked your director about the status of the training, there have been no plans to start your leadership training. In fact, one of your colleagues in another department just returned from the leadership training program you were supposed to attend. There are rumours circulating that the vice-president does not want you to move up the corporate ladder as he sees you as a threat to his power. You start to believe there is some truth to this. How will you handle this situation?

## IN THE BOARDROOM EXERCISE

You are the director of HR for a large food distribution company with 1000 employees servicing clients in over 70 locations across Canada. You were asked by the CEO to review the current performance appraisal system and present your findings and recommendations to the board. In your 20-minute presentation, you present your critique of the graphic rating scale currently in use with emphasis on your concerns about the validity and reliability of the instrument. In its place, you recommend an MBO approach to evaluation. The CEO does not support your recommendation, stating, "The MBO is too time consuming. It will take much more time to set objectives, measure progress, and provide feedback over and above the time already spent doing appraisal. Setting objectives with our employees will turn into a tug of war, with managers pushing for higher goals and employees pushing for lower ones. This will take years to get properly implemented. I want something fast and efficient." Discuss the approach you would use to argue the value of switching from a graphic rating scale to an MBO appraisal system.

## PERFORMANCE APPRAISALS ON THE INTERNATIONAL STAGE EXERCISE

*The exercise below relates to the Performance Appraisals on the International Stage feature on p. 238.*

Imagine you work for an international emergency relief agency that provides aid to communities around the world. When a natural disaster such as an earthquake, tsunami, flood, or volcano hits a particular region anywhere in the world, your team immediately heads to that location to offer assistance. Create a sample of the performance appraisal form that would be used to assess the performance of emergency relief workers. Identify and explain the performance factors that would be used.

## EXPERIENTIAL EXERCISE

For further study of text materials and development of practical skills, select the experiential exercise module for this chapter on www.pearsoned.ca/myhrlab. This module provides two to three individual or group-based assignments per chapter.

# QUIZ YOURSELF

## STUDY GUIDE QUESTIONS

Circle the correct answer. After completing this self-test, check your answers against the Answers to Study Guide Questions at the back of the book (p. 433).

1. Performance management is of considerable importance to today's organizations because the quality of employees is an effective way to differentiate in a highly competitive, service oriented, global marketplace. Performance management is a:
   a. process that measures employee effectiveness in order to make decisions on salary reviews
   b. process that sets work standards and assesses employee performance against set standards
   c. process that includes all activities related to improving employee performance, productivity, and effectiveness
   d. process that identifies performance-related deficiencies and aims to address these by providing feedback
   e. none of the above
2. The performance appraisal process has three key steps. Which of the following combinations includes the three steps in the appropriate order?
   a. defining performance standards; identifying appraisal methods; conducting the interview
   b. appraising performance against set expectations; providing feedback; setting new goals

c. defining performance expectations; providing feedback; conducting the appraisal interview
d. job analysis; setting goals; identifying methods to appraise; appraising performance; feedback
e. defining performance expectations; appraising performance; providing feedback

3. The appraisal interview is generally conducted with the aid of predetermined and formal methods. What method is used for performance appraisals?
a. critical incident method
b. graphic rating scale
c. behaviourally anchored rating scale
d. forced distribution method
e. all of the above

4. Daniel & Associates uses a performance appraisal method that requires the line managers to set specific, measurable goals with each employee and periodically discuss their progress. This method is known as:
a. 360-degree appraisal
b. management by objectives
c. goal setting
d. supervisor evaluation
e. critical incident method

5. Dinesh had his appraisal interview two days ago. At the interview, he noticed that his supervisor brought specific examples of positive and negative behaviours and work-related examples to appraise Dinesh. The method used by the supervisor is called:
a. management by objectives
b. graphic rating scale
c. critical incident method
d. behaviour-based appraisal
e. forced distribution method

6. The following appraisal method is a combination of two appraisal methods that provides better, more equitable results than other methods and is also more legally defensible. The method is called:
a. critical incident technique
b. management of objectives
c. behaviourally anchored rating scale
d. graphic rating scale
e. technology-based method

7. If the performance appraisal process is not designed and conducted properly, it can lead to decreased performance. What is a key problem associated with an appraisal system?
a. reliable and valid performance criteria
b. using too many raters
c. unclear standards
d. performance improvement plans
e. all of the above

8. Typically, an employee's immediate supervisor conducts a performance appraisal. However, company X uses a method that captures information from multiple sources. This method is known as:
a. rating committee appraisal
b. 360-degree appraisal
c. peer appraisals
d. BARS appraisals
e. critical incident appraisal

9. For the past two years, Mona, despite achieving all her objectives and consistently going above and beyond her normal duties, has received ratings of 5 out of 10 from her supervisor. Other people in the department have a similar complaint. Mona's supervisor is exhibiting the following rater error:
a. halo effect
b. appraisal bias
c. recency bias
d. central tendency
e. strictness

10. Just before their annual performance reviews, employees in the marketing division remind each other to "do something that pleases the boss if you want to get a good performance rating." This is known as:
a. rater bias
b. strictness problem
c. recency bias
d. halo effect
e. appraisal bias

11. Rater errors can have a negative perception on the appraisal process. However, there are several ways to minimize the impact of rater-related problems. One effective way of addressing rater errors is:
a. conducting a 360-degree appraisal
b. HR conducting appraisals
c. training of supervisors to avoid errors
d. getting raters from outside the company
e. automating the appraisal process

12. The appraisal interview is a critical element in the appraisal process. It needs preparation and time. When conducting an appraisal interview, the supervisor should:
a. be direct and specific
b. focus on job-related examples
c. encourage the employee to talk
d. develop an action plan
e. all of the above

13. During his last three performance reviews, Joe received a below-average rating from his supervisor. Despite a performance improvement plan and extra training, Joe was unable to improve on his performance. The next step that Joe's supervisor should take is to:

a. terminate Joe
b. transfer Joe
c. ignore the problem
d. give Joe a formal written warning
e. send Joe to a training course

14. The legal aspects of performance appraisal should always be considered. Ethics should be the bedrock of a performance appraisal. The following are some guidelines that can be used for developing a legal, ethical appraisal process.
    a. conduct a job analysis to determine performance standards
    b. train supervisors to use rating instruments
    c. document evaluations
    d. provide defined performance standards in writing
    e. all of the above

15. Some critics argue that performance appraisals should be abolished because:
    a. they cause conflict between supervisors and employees
    b. traits measured are often personal in nature
    c. an employee's performance is more a function of such factors as training, communication, tools, and supervision than of his or her own motivation
    d. performance appraisal systems do not motivate employees
    e. all of the above.

# 8 chapter ESTABLISHING A STRATEGIC COMPENSATION SYSTEM

## Learning Objectives

1. Articulate the role of compensation as a strategic imperative.
2. Explain the basic considerations in determining pay rates.
3. Describe the steps in establishing pay rates and explain the purpose of each step.
4. Summarize the current trends in compensation.
5. Describe the pay system for managerial and professional jobs.
6. Identify and explain the types of incentive plans.
7. Explain the types of employee recognition programs.

## Test Yourself

1. What are the four basic factors determining pay rates?
2. What are the five basic steps in establishing pay rates?
3. What is job evaluation, and what are the common methods used to analyze jobs?
4. What are the pros and cons of salary plans and commission plans for salespeople?
5. What are the various types of organization-wide incentive plans?

## 8.1 STRATEGIC ASPECTS OF COMPENSATION

**Total compensation** refers to all forms of pay and benefits given to employees arising from their employment.[1] For a typical employer, payroll is the largest budget item, making up approximately 50 percent of operating costs. Compensation is widely used to improve performance, reward high performance, and contribute to the achievement of an organization's strategic goals. Compensation is used to communicate to employees the types of behaviours and standards of performance that an organization wants employees to repeat so that strategic goals can be achieved. Thus, compensation is an important issue for both employees and employers.[2] In this millennium, organizations are adopting new thinking, new practices, and more strategic direction in compensation as they experience reductions in organizational hierarchy and the evolution of more flexible jobs. Three strategic approaches are emerging:[3]

- paying an employee for his or her skills and competencies rather than on the basis of job description
- rewarding excellence through pay for performance
- individualizing pay systems by providing flexibility and choice to an increasingly diverse workforce.

Changes in the way pay for performance is calculated are explained in the Strategic HR box below.

Total compensation has two traditional components. There are direct financial payments in the form of wages, salaries, incentives, commissions, and

STRATEGIC HR

### Performance Pay Changing: Bonuses Tied to Individual Performance, Not Overall Company, Gaining Traction

Companies are changing the way performance-based pay is calculated for mid- and lower-level employees, according to an HR consultant.

Traditionally, bonuses have been determined based on a company's overall performance. While that is still a consideration, companies have begun taking a tiered approach to bonus calculation, which is increasingly defined based on division, says Robert Levasseur, a senior executive compensation consultant at Watson Wyatt in Toronto.

Incentive plans became prevalent after the recession in the early 1990s in an attempt to keep inflation down on compensation costs, says Levasseur. Since then, companies have been working to refine the calculation process.

Adding an increased level of accountability for employees, some companies are measuring bonuses through evaluations of individual goals and performance.

The work of an employee responsible for entering inventory data is an example of how the tiered approach works, he says. Because such a position would not have direct influence over stock performance or a company's profitability, some organizations are focusing on specific objectives within that individual's division. Managers evaluate the employee based on milestones or specific goals, such as improving the efficiency of filing systems, says Levasseur.

This evaluation process, combined with the overall performance of the company, are creating an individualized bonus structure more representative of employee contribution, he says.

**Fair treatment**

With a segmented system of bonus evaluation, companies face the challenge of balancing a desire to treat all employees fairly while, at the same time, recognizing key talent, says Lynn Stoudt, an Ottawa-based principal in the human capital group at consulting firm Mercer.

The evolving bonus calculation system is changing, she says, because organizations have realized the areas in which staff members are contributing the most must be recognized to achieve certain results.

"We're looking at performance-based pay but (also) the whole performance management program being part of a much larger talent system within an organization,"

**total compensation** All forms of pay and benefits given to employees arising from their employment.

says Stoudt. "It isn't just about pay, it's about development and leadership."

Organizations are also starting to examine the types of performance compensation given to employees, she says. To do that, company leaders need to understand the types of compensation employees value.

"For some—younger generations (aged) 25 to 35—a cash component is of real value. Others may be looking more in terms of stock and security," she says. "It's about understanding your workforce and what is meaningful to other employee groups."

**Performance pay for executives**

Increased public scrutiny of executive pay and bonuses has led company boards to re-evaluate the way compensation is calculated, says Jeffrey Gandz, a professor at the University of Western Ontario's Richard Ivey School of Business in London, Ont.

In March, it was revealed executives from struggling financial firm AIG collected millions in bonuses not long after the company received billions of dollars in bailout money from Washington. While most executives eventually gave the money back, the incident sparked a debate about the balance between compensation payouts for retention and reasonable rewards for corporate performance.

As boards observe the backlash caused by executive bonuses, they are becoming more sensitive to the overall performance of the organization when drafting compensation agreements, said Gandz.

The basic thinking is the right type of variable compensation will achieve alignment between the interests of shareholders and interests of executives, he says.

"One of the appalling problems of the last year is that you've had a huge amount of executive pay that was variable compensation, that was not aligned to the shareholder interests because it didn't take risk into account," said Gandz. "It took income into account but their income was in many, many cases obtained as a consequence of much increased risk on the balance sheet."

While outright payouts are being re-evaluated, boards have also virtually eliminated stock options for executives, he says. Now, there is a clear trend towards deferred stock units.

Providing stock options to executives created a misalignment in interests and created a situation where the company could do badly but the executive "could merely not gain," says Gandz.

"With real stock, if the shareholders lose, the executive loses, so there is a closer alignment when it is done with stock rather than stock options," he says.

In an effort to make executives more accountable, boards have begun to discuss deferred payments based on performance, says Gandz.

Last year, there were a couple of situations where compensation, to be paid the following year, was calculated based on positive business performance, he says. However, the severe deterioration between the time the bonus was calculated and the payout deadline led boards to re-evaluate the waiting period for compensation.

"Increasingly, there is a trend towards saying, 'Look, we will do executive compensation but it may be subject to what happens in the next couple of years of performance,'" says Gandz.

It's a deferred payment depending on the outcomes, he says. "If a CEO has magnificent performance until June 2009 and they are granted $2 million in compensation but the bottom falls out in the next year, that may not be a firm $2 million."

Source: A. Scappatura, "Performance pay changing: Bonuses tied to individual performance, not overall company, gaining traction," *Canadian Compensation & Benefits Reporter,* May 25, 2009, p. 22. Reproduced with permission.

bonuses, and indirect payments in the form of financial benefits such as employer-paid insurance and vacations. Increasing attention is being given to a third component—the work experience.

In turn, there are essentially two bases for direct financial payments to employees: increments of time and performance. Most employees are still paid primarily based on the time that they put in on the job. The second option is to pay for performance. Piecework is an example: It ties compensation directly to the amount of production (or number of "pieces") that a worker produces and is popular as an incentive pay plan.

Across Canada, there are variations in how employees are compensated for the work they do. For example, salary differences exist between the public and private sectors, with federal employees earning 17.3 percent higher wages than their private-sector counterparts in similar jobs. On average, there is a wage gap of 7.9 percent between comparable provincial government and private-sector jobs across Canada. When benefits are factored into the equation, the gap widens to 41.7 percent between employees in the private sector and federal public sector and to 24.9 percent at the provincial level.[4] Studies reveal that 81 percent of companies decreased their planned wage increases for employees in 2009 by one-half of a percentage point, and 14 percent froze 2009 pay across the board.[5] On average, 2009 salary increases across Canada hovered

*In-class Notes*

**Strategic Aspects of Total Compensation**

- Total compensation includes all forms of pay and benefits given to employees arising from their employment
- A strategic tool to improve performance, reward performance, and contribute to the achievement of strategic goals
- Two traditional components: direct financial payments (pay) and indirect payments (benefits)
- Work experience now being considered a third component of total compensation

around 3.46 percent, with Alberta leading at 3.83 percent and Quebec trailing at 3.24 percent.[6]

Psychologists know that people have many needs, of which only some can be satisfied directly with money. Other needs—for challenging work, affiliation, flexible hours, or career development, for instance—also motivate behaviour but can only be satisfied indirectly (if at all) by money.[7] As organizations face increasing pressure to win the war for talent, it is important to keep the relative importance of pay in perspective. Two Canadian reports issued in 2001 indicated that: (1) there is a persistent gap between what companies are offering employees and what the employees want; and (2) employees care more about having good relationships and other intrinsic rewards from work than about pay and benefits. Specifically, employees want a better working environment, more fairness and respect, more support and recognition, and more honesty and commitment on the part of employers.[8]

**RPC 8-1 >**

**Establishes payroll guidelines based on relevant legislation, tax laws, company policy, and contractual pay requirements**

## The Role of Human Resources in Compensation Management

In many organizations, a compensation specialist assumes a leadership role in managing the compensation system and works closely with managers to ensure an equitable system is in place. The compensation specialist is responsible for developing, communicating, and evaluating the compensation system. This includes evaluating jobs, conducting and analyzing pay surveys, establishing compensation policies, communicating and responding to questions about the pay structure and policies, and evaluating the effectiveness of the compensation system. Evaluation should be conducted annually to monitor trends and provide early intervention if problems emerge. HR metrics for evaluation of a compensation system include employee turnover, grievance rates, and employee satisfaction.

As well as understanding how the compensation system works, employees need to understand how they are doing in relation to performance standards and organizational goals. If employees are not clear about how to earn salary increases and incentives, or if they see goals as being unachievable, then the compensation system is not likely to influence their behaviour. Compensation specialists should be prepared to address the following question typically asked by employees:[9]

- Why did I receive this particular salary increase or bonus?
- How does what I earned reflect my personal performance and contributions?
- Do high performers earn more significant rewards than average or low performers? If so, how much more?

- How did considerations such as company or unit performance influence what I earned?
- What do I need to do to earn the same amount, or more, next year?
- What do I need to do to move into a higher salary range?
- Is my pay competitive with the market? How do you know?

It is also incumbent upon the compensation specialist to monitor internal organizational changes and to regularly canvass feedback from employees about whether the compensation system continues to meet their needs and where changes are needed. As well, external environmental scanning is required to be aware of new trends in compensation management and legislation affecting compensation in Canada.

## 8.2 BASIC CONSIDERATIONS IN DETERMINING PAY RATES

Four basic considerations influence the formulation of any pay plan: legal requirements, union issues, compensation policy, and equity.

### Legal Considerations in Compensation

**RPC 8-2 >**

**Performs a cost-benefit analysis of organizational and employee needs and preferences, including taxation considerations, legislative requirements, and funding requirements**

There are a number of laws affecting compensation in Canada. These laws vary between the provinces and territories, and there are similar laws at the federal level, which cover employees in interprovincial operations (including highway, rail, and air transportation, pipelines, telecommunications, banking, federal crown corporations, and others). Thus, HR managers must pay careful attention to legislation that affects their employees. Further, these laws are constantly changing and require continual monitoring to ensure compliance. Legislation affecting compensation administration includes:

**EMPLOYMENT/LABOUR STANDARDS ACTS** These laws set minimum standards regarding pay, which include minimum wage, maximum hours of work, overtime pay, paid vacation, paid statutory holidays, termination pay, record keeping of pay information, and more. Executive, administrative, and professional employees are generally exempt from overtime pay requirements.

**PAY EQUITY ACTS** Pay equity legislation has been enacted in the federal jurisdiction and in several provinces. These laws apply to public-sector employees only, except in Ontario and Quebec, where the laws cover employees in both the public and private sectors. Pay equity laws were enacted to redress the historical undervaluation of "women's work" by providing equal pay for work of equal (or comparable) value performed by men and women. Employers are required to identify male- and female-dominated jobs and then use a gender-neutral job evaluation system based on specific compensatable factors (such as skill, effort, responsibility, and working conditions) in order to evaluate them. Pay for female-dominated jobs that are equivalent in value to male-dominated jobs must be increased to the pay level of the comparable male-dominated jobs.

**RPC 8-3 >**

**Ensures accurate and timely delivery of pay**

**RPC 8-4 >**

**Ensures pay records are accurate and complete**

**RPC 8-5 >**

**Provides input into the development of employee feedback systems that support the organizational directions and culture**

**HUMAN RIGHTS ACTS** All jurisdictions have enacted human rights laws to protect Canadians from discrimination on a number of grounds (discussed in Chapter 2) in employment, including compensation.

**CANADA/QUEBEC PENSION PLAN** All employees and their employers must contribute to the Canada/Quebec Pension Plan throughout the employee's working lifetime. Details of these and other benefits are provided in Chapter 9.

**OTHER LEGISLATION AFFECTING COMPENSATION** Each of the provinces and territories, as well as the federal government, has its own workers' compensation laws. The objective of these laws is to provide income to victims of work-related accidents and illnesses. The *Employment Insurance Act* is aimed at protecting Canadian workers from total economic destitution in the event of employment termination that is beyond their control.

## Union Influences on Compensation Decisions

Unions and labour relations laws also influence how pay plans are designed. Historically, wage rates have been the main issue in collective bargaining. The Canada Labour Relations Board and similar bodies in each of the provinces and territories ensure that employees are treated in accordance with their legal rights. Thus, there is a need to involve union officials in developing a compensation package.

Several classic studies have shed light on union attitudes toward compensation plans and commonly held union fears.[10] Many union leaders fear that any system used to evaluate the worth of a job can become a tool for management malpractice. They tend to believe that no one can judge the relative value of jobs better than the workers themselves. The best way to gain the cooperation of union members in evaluating the worth of jobs is to get their active involvement in this process and in assigning fair rates of pay.

On the other hand, management has to ensure that its prerogatives—such as the right to use the appropriate job evaluation technique to assess the relative worth of jobs—are not surrendered.

Work stoppages may reflect employee dissatisfaction with pay plans and other forms of compensation, such as benefits.

## Compensation Policies

An employer's compensation policies provide important compensation guidelines regarding the wages and benefits it pays. One consideration is whether the organization wants to be a leader or a follower regarding pay. Some organizations may choose to lag in pay, meaning employees get less base pay than employees in similar positions elsewhere in the marketplace. Organizations that lag with base pay have impressive incentive programs that often result in employees getting an overall payout that exceeds what employees in similar positions elsewhere get paid. Lagging in pay communicates to employees that high performance is rewarded with high incentive payouts.

Other important policies include the basis for salary increases, promotion and demotion policies, overtime pay policy, and policies regarding probationary pay and leaves for military service, jury duty, and holidays. Compensation policies are usually written by the HR or compensation manager in conjunction with senior management.[11]

## Equity and Its Impact on Pay Rates

A crucial factor in determining pay rates is the need for equity, specifically *external equity* and *internal equity*. Externally, pay must compare favourably with rates in other organizations, or an employer will find it hard to attract and retain qualified employees. Pay rates must also be equitable internally; each employee should view his or her pay as equitable given other pay rates in the organization. Employees expect a) **procedural justice**, which means the policies and procedures for determining how pay is calculated are perceived as fair, and b) **distributive justice**, which means the rate of pay for a given job is perceived as fair. Distributive justice can be problematic when employees are not paid according to their performance output. For example, distributive injustice surfaces when a high-performing employee receives the same merit increase as an employee who is barely meeting performance standards. Pay inequity leads to disgruntled employees who are likely to file complaints, leave the company, organize a union to attain wage parity, or take an employer to court for wage inequities or wage discrimination.

**procedural justice** When the policies and procedures for determining how pay is calculated are perceived as fair.

**distributive justice** When the rate of pay for a given job is perceived as fair.

## In-class Notes

**Basic Considerations in Determining Pay Rates**

- Legal: employment/labour standards; pay equity; human rights; Canada/Quebec Pension Plan; Employment Insurance; workers' compensation
- Union influences: through collective bargaining
- Compensation policies: leader or follower regarding pay
- Equity: internal with pay for other employees and external with competitors

## 8.3 ESTABLISHING PAY RATES

In practice, the process of establishing pay rates while ensuring external and internal equity requires five steps:

1. Determine the worth of each job within the organization through job evaluation (to achieve internal equity).
2. Group similar jobs into pay grades.
3. Conduct a salary survey of what other employers are paying for comparable jobs (to achieve external equity).
4. Price each pay grade by using wage curves.
5. Fine-tune pay rates.

Each of these steps will now be explained.

**RPC 8-6 >**

**Monitors the competitiveness of the compensation program relative to comparable organizations**

### Step 1: Determine the Worth of Each Job

**JOB EVALUATION** **Job evaluation** is aimed at determining a job's relative worth. It is a formal and systematic comparison of jobs within a firm to determine the worth of one job relative to another, which eventually results in a job hierarchy. The basic procedure is to compare the content of jobs in relation to one another; for example, in terms of their skill, effort, responsibility, and working conditions. Once the compensation specialist knows (based on salary survey data and compensation policies) how to price key **benchmark jobs** and can use job evaluation to determine the worth of all the other jobs in the firm relative to these key jobs, he or she is well on the way to being able to pay all jobs in the organization equitably.

**COMPENSABLE FACTORS** There are two basic approaches for comparing jobs. The first is an intuitive approach. It might be decided that one job is "more important" or "of greater value or worth" than another without digging any deeper into why in terms of specific job-related factors.

As an alternative, focusing on certain basic factors that jobs have in common can help in comparing them. In compensation management, these basic factors are called **compensable factors**. They are the factors that determine the definition of job content, establish how the jobs compare with each other, and set the compensation paid for each job. Most employers use the four factors that are required by most of the pay equity acts in Canada: *skill, effort, responsibility,* and *working conditions.*

Identifying compensable factors plays a pivotal role in job evaluation. All jobs in each employee group, department, or business unit should be evaluated using the same compensable factors. An employer thus evaluates the same elemental components for each job within the work group and is then better able to compare jobs—for example, in terms of the degree of skill, effort, responsibility, and working conditions present in each.[12]

**PLANNING AND PREPARATION FOR JOB EVALUATION** Job evaluation is largely a judgmental process and one that demands close cooperation between supervisors, compensation specialists, and the employees and their union representatives. The main steps involved include identifying the need for the program, getting cooperation, and choosing a job evaluation committee; the committee then carries out the actual job evaluation.[13]

Identifying the need for job evaluation should not be difficult. In many cases, it is required by pay equity legislation. Employee dissatisfaction with the inequities of paying employees different rates for similar jobs and managerial uneasiness about an existing informal way of assigning pay rates to jobs may also make the need for job evaluation obvious.

Next, since employees may fear that a systematic evaluation of their jobs may actually reduce their wage rates, getting employee cooperation for the evaluation is a second important step. Employees can be told that as a result of the impending job evaluation program, wage rate decisions will no longer be made just by management whim; job evaluation will provide a mechanism for considering the complaints they have been expressing; and no present employee's rate will be adversely affected as a result of the job evaluation.[14]

The next step is choosing a job evaluation committee of about five members, usually including an HR specialist and a union representative (required by pay equity legislation in some cases). The committee should bring to bear the points of view, and, when the committee is composed at least partly of employees, this can help ensure greater acceptance of the job evaluation results by employees.

The evaluation committee performs three main functions. The members usually identify 10 or 15 key jobs to be evaluated first as anchors or benchmarks against which the relative importance or value of all other jobs can be compared. Next, the committee selects compensable factors. Finally, the committee turns to actually evaluating the worth of each job, usually using one of the following job evaluation methods:

*frontLINE tips*

the ranking method (common in smaller organizations), the job classification method (widely used in the public sector), and the point method (widely used in the private sector).

**RANKING METHOD OF JOB EVALUATION** The simplest job evaluation method ranks each job relative to all other jobs, usually based on some overall factor, such as "job difficulty." There are several steps in the job **ranking method**:

1. *Obtain job information.* Job analysis is the first step. Job descriptions for all jobs are prepared, and these are usually the basis on which the rankings are made.
2. *Group the jobs to be rated.* It is often not practical to make a single ranking of all jobs in an organization. The more usual procedure is to rank jobs by department or in "clusters" (such as factory or clerical workers).
3. *Select compensable factors.* In the ranking method, it is common to use just one factor (such as job difficulty) and to rank jobs on the basis of the whole job.
4. *Rank jobs.* Next, the jobs are ranked. The simplest way is to give each rater a set of index cards, each of which contains a brief description of a job. These cards are then ranked from lowest to highest. Some managers use an "alternation ranking method" for making the procedure more accurate. Here, the committee members arrange the cards by first choosing the highest and the lowest, then the next highest and next lowest, and so on until all of the cards have been ranked. A job ranking is illustrated in Table 8.1. Jobs in this small health facility are ranked from cleaner up to director of operations. The corresponding pay scales are shown on the right.
5. *Combine ratings.* It is usual for several raters to rank the jobs independently. Then the rating committee (or employer) can simply average the rankings.

**job evaluation** A systematic comparison to determine the relative worth of jobs within a firm.

**benchmark job** A job commonly found in other organizations and/or critical to a firm's operations that is used to anchor the employer's pay scale and act as a reference point around which other jobs are arranged in order of relative worth.

**compensable factors** Fundamental, compensable elements of a job, such as skill, effort, responsibility, and working conditions.

**ranking method** The simplest method of job evaluation, which involves ranking each job relative to all other jobs, usually based on overall difficulty.

Employment Insurance Act
**www1.servicecanada.gc.ca/en/ei/legislation/ei_act_tofprov_1.shtml**

Ontario Public Service Employees Union (OPSEU)
**www.opseu.org**

*table* 8.1 **Job Ranking by Olympia Health Care**

| Ranking Order | Annual Pay Scale |
|---|---|
| 1. Director of Operations | $60 000 |
| 2. Head nurse | $54 000 |
| 3. Accountant | $50 000 |
| 4. Nurse | $40 000 |
| 5. Cook | $26 000 |
| 6. Nurse's aide | $24 000 |
| 7. Cleaner | $20 000 |

After ranking, it becomes possible to slot additional jobs between those already ranked and to assign an appropriate wage rate.

**Pros and Cons** This is the simplest job evaluation method as well as the easiest to explain, and it usually takes less time to accomplish than other methods. However, there is a tendency to rely too heavily on "guesstimates." Ranking is often used by small organizations that are unable to afford the time or expense of developing a more elaborate system. Another potential drawback relates to legal compliance requirements. The "whole job" approach to ranking, just described, cannot be used by employers covered by pay equity legislation. Instead, separate rankings must be completed for each of the four compensable factors (skill, effort, responsibility, and working conditions) and then judgment is used to combine the results.

**CLASSIFICATION (OR GRADING) EVALUATION METHOD** The **classification (or grading) method** is a simple, widely used method in which jobs are categorized into groups. The groups are called **classes** if they contain similar jobs or **grades** if they contain jobs that are similar in difficulty but otherwise different. The federal government's AU (Auditor) job group is an example of a job class because it contains similar jobs, such as Auditor, Assessor, and Examiner. On the other hand, the PM (Program Management) job group is an example of a job grade because it contains dissimilar jobs, such as Program Consultant (an expert in one government program), Operations Officer (works on special projects), and Agent II (performs complex government benefit entitlement calculations for members of the public).

There are several ways to categorize jobs. One is to draw up class descriptions (similar to job descriptions) and place jobs into classes based on their correspondence to these descriptions. Another is to draw up a set of classifying rules for each class (for instance, the amount of independent judgment, skill, physical effort, and so on that the class of jobs requires). Then the jobs are categorized according to these rules. In either case, the usual procedure is to choose compensable factors and then develop class or grade descriptions that describe each class in terms of amount or level of compensable factor(s) in jobs. Based on these compensable factors, a **grade/group description** (like that shown in Figure 8.1) is written. Then the evaluation committee reviews all job descriptions and slots each job into its appropriate class or grade.

**Pros and Cons** The job classification method has several advantages. The main one is that most employers usually end up classifying jobs anyway, regardless of the job evaluation method they use. This avoids having to work with an unmanageable number of jobs; with the job classification method, all jobs are already grouped into several classes. The disadvantages are that it is difficult to write the class or grade descriptions, and considerable judgment is required in applying them. Yet many employers (including the Canadian government) use this method with success.

**POINT METHOD OF JOB EVALUATION** The **point method** (also known as the point factor method) is widely used. It requires identifying several compensable factors and defining several different degrees of each factor. A different number of points are then assigned for each degree of each factor. Next, the extent/degree to which each of these factors is present in the job is evaluated. Once the degree to which each factor is present in the job is determined, all that remains is to add up the corresponding number of points for each factor and arrive at an overall point value for the job.[15] The steps are as follows:

1. *Determine clusters of jobs to be evaluated.* Because jobs vary widely, the same point-rating plan is not usually used for all jobs in an organization. Therefore, the first step is usually to cluster jobs; for example, into plant jobs, administrative jobs, management jobs, and so on. Then the committee will generally develop a point plan for one group or cluster at a time.
2. *Collect job information.* Perform a job analysis and write job descriptions and job specifications.
3. *Select and define compensable factors.* Select compensable factors, such as skill, effort, responsibility, and working conditions. Often subfactors or specific components of the factor are also selected—physical effort and mental effort are commonly

## *figure* 8.1 Example of Group Definition in the Federal Government

### GROUP DEFINITION—AUDIT, COMMERCE AND PURCHASING (AV)

The Audit, Commerce and Purchasing Group comprises positions that are primarily involved in the application of a comprehensive knowledge of generally accepted accounting principles and auditing standards to the planning, delivery and management of external audit programs; the planning, delivery and management of economic development policies, programs, services and other activities; and the planning, development, delivery and management of policies, programs, systems or other activities dealing with purchasing and supply in the Public Service.

### Inclusions

Notwithstanding the generality of the foregoing, for greater certainty, it includes positions that have, as their primary purpose, responsibility for one or more of the following activities:

1. audit—the application of a comprehensive knowledge of generally accepted accounting principles and auditing standards to the auditing of the accounts and financial records of individuals, businesses, non-profit organizations, or provincial or municipal governments to determine their accuracy and reasonableness, to establish or verify costs, or to confirm the compliance of transactions with the provisions of statutes, regulations, agreements or contracts;
2. commerce—the planning, development, delivery and management of economic development policies, programs, services and other activities designed to promote the establishment, growth and improvement of industry, commerce and export trade; and the regulation of trade and commerce including:
   (a) the promotion of the more efficient use of resources in particular geographic areas through the conduct of studies and investigations and the implementation of programs and projects for this purpose;
   (b) the promotion of the development and use of modern industrial technologies;
   (c) the promotion of economic development directed towards groups, regions, industries or the Canadian economy as a whole;
   (d) the promotion of the export of Canadian goods and services, including the tourist industry;
   (e) the expansion of Canada's share of global trade by providing advice to Canadian companies, trade associations or other agencies of government, by safeguarding and promoting Canadian trading relationships, or by bringing the export aspects to bear in Canada's aid and financing programs;
   (f) the study and assessment of developments in international trade and trading arrangements, and their implications for the Canadian economy;
   (g) the administration and enforcement of competition legislation and legislation relating to restraints of trade; and
   (h) the examination of records and reports of registered insurance, trust and loan companies, money lenders and small loan companies, fraternal benefit societies and co-operative credit associations to ensure their solvency and compliance with legislation and regulations controlling their operations;
3. purchasing—the planning, development, delivery and management of purchasing and supply notices, programs, services and other activities to meet the needs of Public Service departments and agencies including one or more subsidiary activities, such as in the areas of asset management and disposal, contracting, procurement of goods and services, inventory management, cataloguing, warehousing or traffic management;
4. the provision of advice in the above fields; and
5. the leadership of any of the above activities.

continued

**classification (or grading) method** A method for categorizing jobs into groups.

**classes** Groups of jobs based on a set of rules for each class, such as amount of independent judgment, skill, physical effort, and so forth. Classes usually contain similar jobs—such as all secretaries.

**grades** Groups of jobs based on a set of rules for each grade, where jobs are similar in difficulty but otherwise different. Grades often contain dissimilar jobs, such as secretaries, mechanics, and firefighters.

**grade/group description** Written description of the level of compensable factors required by jobs in each grade. Used to combine similar jobs into grades or classes.

**point method** The job evaluation method in which a number of compensable factors are identified and then the degree to which each of these factors is present in the job is determined and an overall point value is calculated.

## *figure* 8.1 Example of Group Definition in the Federal Government—continued

### Exclusions

Positions excluded from the Audit, Commerce and Purchasing Group are those whose primary purpose is included in the definition of any other group or those in which one or more of the following activities is of primary importance:

1. the evaluation of actuarial liabilities and the determination of premiums and contributions in respect of insurance, annuity and pension plans;
2. the planning and conduct of internal financial audits;
3. the planning, development, delivery or management of the internal comprehensive audit of the operations of Public Service departments and agencies;
4. the application of a comprehensive knowledge of economics, sociology or statistics to the conduct of economic, socio-economic and sociological research, studies, forecasts and surveys;
5. the planning, development, delivery and promotion of Canada's diplomatic, commercial, human rights, cultural, promotional and international development policies and interests in other countries and in international organizations through the career rotational foreign service;
6. the design of trade exhibits or displays or activities dealing with the explanation, promotion and publication of federal government programs, policies and services;
7. the writing of specifications and technical descriptions that require the continuing application of technical knowledge; and
8. the receipt, storage, handling and issue of items held in stores.

Source: Example of Group Definition in the Federal Government, 2009, p. 1. www.canadagazette.gc.ca/archives/p1/1999/1999-03-27/html/notice-avis-eng.html. Government of Canada. Reproduced with the permission of the Minister of Public Works and Government Services Canada, 2009.

used subfactors of effort. Then carefully define each factor and subfactor. This is done in order to ensure that evaluation committee members will apply the factors with consistency. Examples of factor definitions are presented in Figure 8.2. The definitions are often drawn up or obtained by a human resources specialist.

4. *Define factor degrees.* Next, definitions of several degrees for each factor are prepared so that raters may judge the amount or degree of a factor existing in a job. Thus, the factor "mental effort" might have six degrees, ranging from "job is repetitive" through "requires initiative." (Definitions for each degree are shown in Figure 8.2.) The number of degrees usually does not exceed five or six, and the actual number depends mostly on judgment. Thus, if all employees work either in a quiet, air-conditioned office or in a noisy, hot factory, then two degrees would probably suffice for the factor "working conditions." It is not necessary to have the same number of degrees for each factor, and degrees should be limited to the number necessary to distinguish among jobs.
5. *Determine factor weights.* The next step is to decide the maximum number of points (weight) to assign to each factor. This is important because for each cluster of jobs, some factors are bound to be more important than others. Thus, for executives, the "responsibility" factor would carry far more weight than would "working conditions." The opposite might be true of factory jobs. For example,

| | |
|---|---|
| Skill | 25 percent |
| Effort | 30 percent |
| Responsibility | 35 percent |
| Working conditions | 10 percent |
| | 100 percent |

6. *Assign point values to factors and degrees.* Now points are assigned to each factor, as in Table 8.2. For example, suppose that it was decided to use a total number of 1000 points in the point plan. Then, since the factor "skill" had a weight of 25 percent, it would be assigned a total of $0.25 \times 1000 = 250$ points, so it was decided to assign 250 points to the skill factor. This automatically means that the highest degree for the skill factor

## *figure* 8.2 Example of One Factor in a Point Factor System

**Responsibility for the Safety of Others:**

This subfactor measures the degree of care required to prevent injury or harm to others

**Level Description of Characteristics and Measures**

1. Little degree of care required to prevent injury or harm to others
   e.g., closing of file drawers.
2. Some degree of care required to prevent injury or harm to others
   e.g., posting of "wet floor" signs; stacking supplies.
3. Considerable degree of care required to prevent injury or harm to others
   e.g., use of heavy equipment; yard duty.
4. High degree of care required to prevent injury or harm to others
   e.g., use of hazardous materials; administering medication; driving school bus.

Source: Adapted from the *CUPE Gender-Neutral Job Evaluation Plan.* Jointly developed by the Medicine Hat School District #76 and CUPE Local 829. Revised February 2000, p. 21. Used with permission.

would also carry 250 points. Points are then assigned to the other degrees for this factor, in equal amounts from the lowest to the highest degree. This step is repeated for each factor (as in Table 8.2).

7. *Write the job evaluation manual.* Developing a point plan like this usually culminates in a job evaluation manual. This simply consolidates the factor and degree definitions and point values into one convenient manual.
8. *Rate the jobs.* Once the manual is complete, the actual evaluations can begin. Raters (usually a committee) use the manual to evaluate jobs. Each job, based on its job description and job specification, is evaluated factor by factor to determine the number of points that should be assigned to it. First, committee members determine the degree (first degree, second degree, and so on) to which each factor is present in the job. Then they note the corresponding points (see Table 8.2) that were previously assigned to each of these degrees (in Step 6). Finally, they add up the points for all factors and arrive at a total point value for the job. Raters generally start with rating key jobs and obtain consensus on these, and then rate the rest of the jobs in the cluster.

**Pros and Cons** Point systems have their advantages, as their wide use suggests. They involve a quantitative technique that is easily explained to and used by employees. On the other hand, it can be difficult and time-consuming to develop a point plan and to effectively train the job evaluation user group. This is one reason that many organizations opt for a plan developed and marketed by a consulting firm. In fact, the availability of a number of ready-made plans probably accounts, in part, for the wide use of point plans in job evaluation.

The job evaluation step often takes the longest amount of time. Once it has been completed, the next step is to group similar jobs into pay grades.

## *table* 8.2 Evaluation Points Assigned to Factors and Degrees

| Factor | First-degree points | Second-degree points | Third-degree points | Fourth-degree points | Fifth-degree points |
|---|---|---|---|---|---|
| Skill | 50 | 100 | 150 | 200 | 250 |
| Effort | 60 | 120 | 180 | 240 | 300 |
| Responsibility | 70 | 140 | 210 | 280 | 350 |
| Working conditions | 20 | 40 | 60 | 80 | 100 |

**THE HAY SYSTEM OF JOB EVALUATION** The Hay System, created by the Hay Management Consulting Group, is a variation of the point method that is used to evaluate jobs held by professional, managerial, and executive employees. Three compensable factors are used to assign numerical values to each job. These three compensable factors and their subfactors are:

- *Know-how* (depth and breadth of specialized, technical or practical knowledge required on the job; managerial skills; and human relations)
- *Problem-solving ability* (the environment in which problem solving takes place, and challenges faced in exercising problem-solving ability)
- *Accountability* (freedom to act, job's impact on end result, and magnitude of the end result)

The Hay Guide Chart Method consists of a sophisticated set of charts used to evaluate each job. This procedure attempts to answer three questions about each position:

- What does the employee in this position need to know to perform the job to standard? (know-how)
- How much analytical thinking is needed to perform the job to standard? (problem solving)
- What does the position contribute toward the goals of the organization? (accountability)

The goal of the Hay System of job evaluation is to attempt to achieve internal equity in the salary ranges assigned to each position.

**Pros and Cons** The Hay System has the advantage of being a valid and reliable evaluation method because of its highly sophisticated mathematical calculations. On the other hand, it can be difficult to understand and often requires a trained compensation expert to administer and interpret the results.

## Step 2: Group Similar Jobs into Pay Grades

If a committee used the ranking, point, or factor comparison methods, it could assign pay rates to each individual job. For a larger employer, however, such a pay plan would be difficult to administer, since there might be different pay rates for hundreds or even thousands of jobs. Even in smaller organizations, there is a tendency to try to simplify wage and salary structures as much as possible. Therefore, the committee will probably want to group similar jobs (in terms of their ranking or number of points, for instance) into grades for pay purposes. Then instead of having to deal with hundreds of pay rates, it might only have to focus on, say, 10 or 12 groups of jobs.

A **pay grade** comprises jobs of approximately equal value or importance as determined by job evaluation. If the point method is used, the pay grade consists of jobs falling within a range of points. If the ranking plan is used, the grade consists of all jobs that fall within two or three ranks. If the classification system is used, then the jobs are already categorized into classes or grades. Under the factor comparison method, the grade consists of a specified range of pay rates. The next step is to obtain information on market pay rates by conducting a wage/salary survey.

## Step 3: Conduct a Wage/Salary Survey

Compensation or **wage/salary surveys** play a central role in the pricing of jobs, and virtually every employer uses such surveys.[16] First, survey data are used to price benchmark jobs that serve as reference points to anchor an employer's pay scale. Second, an increasing number of positions are priced directly in the marketplace (rather than relative to the firm's benchmark jobs) based on a formal or informal survey of what similar firms are paying for comparable jobs.[17] Surveys also collect data on benefits, such as insurance, sick leave, and vacation time, to provide a basis on which to make decisions regarding employee benefits.

To get the most value from surveys, compensation specialists need to know how to read survey reports. Salary data should be broken down as follows to provide compensation specialists with accurate information on which to base their compensation decisions:[18]

- by size of organizations
- by geographic regions
- by sectors and industries
- by roles (i.e. non-managerial and managerial; unionized and nonunionized)
- by data outlining differences in compensation design, communication, and administration for skilled labour and employee demographics

Benchmarking salaries became more challenging in 2007–2008 as organizations changed their compensation payouts to cope with the economic downturn. Prior to the recession, companies could get accurate data on what other companies were offering their staff in terms of wages, incentives, and benefits, and there appeared to be more consistency in how these payouts were decided and assigned. Companies began using more divergent approaches to save money, which resulted in a lack of consistency in compensation payouts. The greatest variations were in the allocation of bonuses and merit increases.[19]

There are many ways to conduct a salary survey, including formal and informal communication with other employers; reviewing newspaper and Internet job ads; and buying commercial or professional surveys from Statistics Canada, private consulting firms such as Watson Wyatt and Hewitt Associates, or professional organizations such as the Certified General Accountants Association.

Upward bias can be a problem regardless of the type of compensation survey used.[20] Because companies like to compare themselves against well-regarded, high-paying competitors, baseline salaries tend to be biased upward.[21] Problems can also arise when an organization's job descriptions only partially match the descriptions contained in the survey, the survey data were collected several months prior to the time of use, the participants in the survey may not represent the appropriate labour market for the jobs being matched, and so on.[22]

*figure* 8.3 **Plotting a Wage Curve**

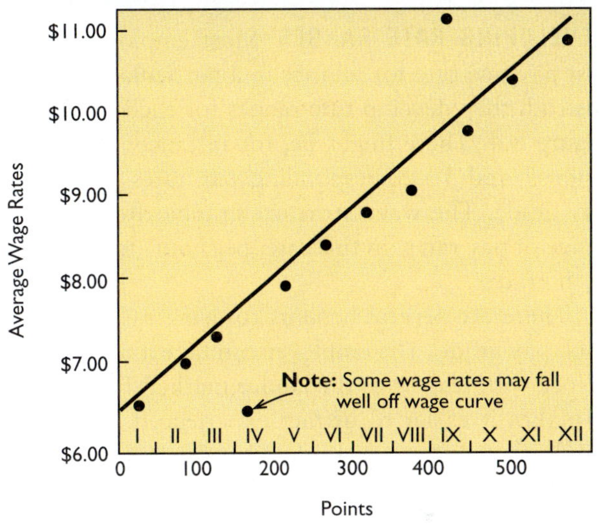


Note: The average pay rate for jobs in each grade (Grade I, Grade II, Grade III, etc.) are plotted, and the wage curve is fitted to the resulting points.

## Step 4: Price Each Pay Grade—Wage Curves

The next step is to assign pay rates to each of the pay grades (or to each job, if pay grades were not used).

*frontLINE tips*

Assigning pay rates to each pay grade (or each job) is usually accomplished with a **wage curve**. The wage curve graphically depicts the pay rates for jobs in each pay grade relative to the points or rankings assigned to each by the job evaluation committee. An example of a wage curve is presented in Figure 8.3. Note that pay rates are shown on the vertical axis, while pay grades (in terms of points) are shown along the horizontal axis. The purpose of the wage curve is to show the relationship between the value of the job as determined by one of the job evaluation methods and the current average pay rates for each job or grade.

The pay rates on the graph are traditionally those now paid by an organization. If there is reason to believe that the present pay rates are substantially out of step with the prevailing market pay rates for these jobs, then benchmark jobs within each pay grade are chosen and priced via a compensation survey. These new market-based pay rates are then used to plot a new wage curve.

There are several steps in pricing jobs with a wage curve using grades. First, find the average pay for each pay grade, since each of the pay grades consists of several jobs. Next, plot the pay rates for each pay grade, as was done in Figure 8.3. Then fit a line (called a *wage line*) through the points just plotted. This can be done either freehand or by using a statistical method known as regression analysis. Finally, price jobs. Wages along the wage line are the target wages or salary rates for the jobs in each pay grade. If the current rates being paid for any of the jobs or grades fall well above or well below the wage line, that rate may be "out of line"; raises or a pay freeze for that job may be in order. The next step is to fine-tune the pay rates.

**pay grade** A pay grade comprises jobs of approximately equal value.

**wage/salary surveys** Surveys aimed at determining prevailing wage rates. A good salary survey provides specific wage rates for comparable jobs; formal written questionnaire surveys are the most comprehensive.

**wage curve** A graphic description of the relationship between the value of a job and the average wage paid for that job.

## Step 5: Fine-Tune Pay Rates

Fine-tuning involves developing rate ranges and correcting out-of-line rates.

**DEVELOPING RATE RANGES** Most employers do not just pay one rate for all jobs in a particular pay grade. Instead, they develop **rate ranges** for each grade, as in Figure 8.4. There might be, for instance, 10 levels or "steps" and 10 corresponding pay rates within each pay grade. The wage structure graphically depicts the range of pay rates (in this case, per hour) to be paid for each grade.

There are several benefits to using rate ranges for each pay grade. The employer can take a more flexible stance with respect to the labour market. For example, it makes it easier to attract experienced, higher-paid employees into a pay grade where the starting salary for the lowest step may be too low to attract such experienced people. Rate ranges also allow employers to provide for performance differences among employees within the same grade or among those with differing seniority. As in Figure 8.4, most employers structure their rate ranges to overlap a bit so that an employee with greater experience or seniority may earn more than an entry-level person in the next-higher pay grade.

**BROADBANDING** The trend today is for employers to reduce their salary grades and ranges from 10 or more down to three to five, a process called **broadbanding**. Broadbanding means collapsing salary grades and ranges into a few wide levels or "bands," each of which then contains a relatively wide range of jobs and salary levels. Broadbanding a pay system involves deciding on a number of bands and assigning each a salary range,

*figure* 8.4 **Wage Structure**

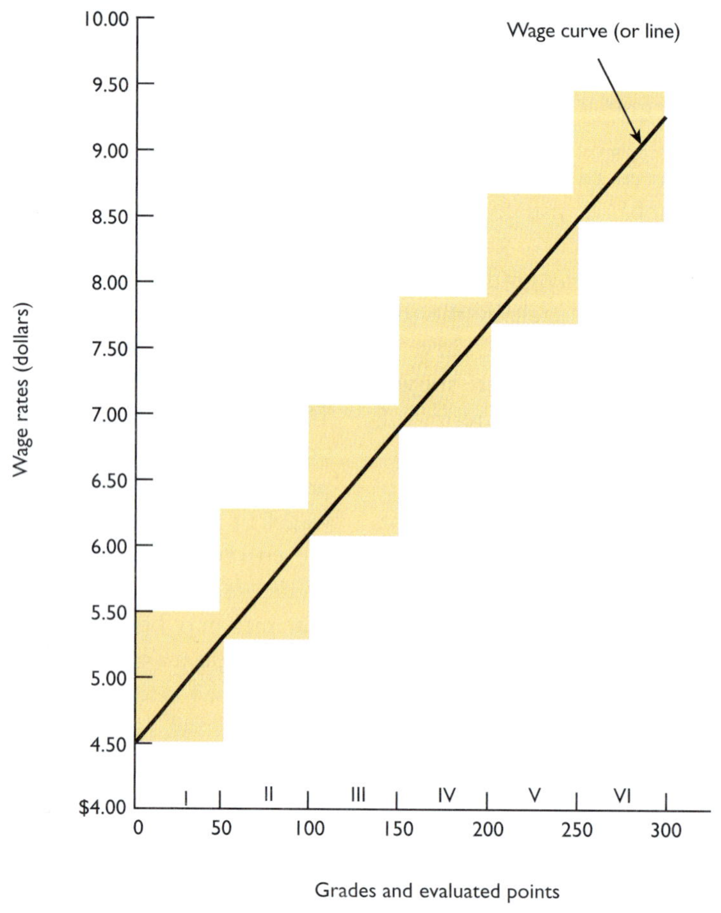

*figure* 8.5 **Broadbanding**

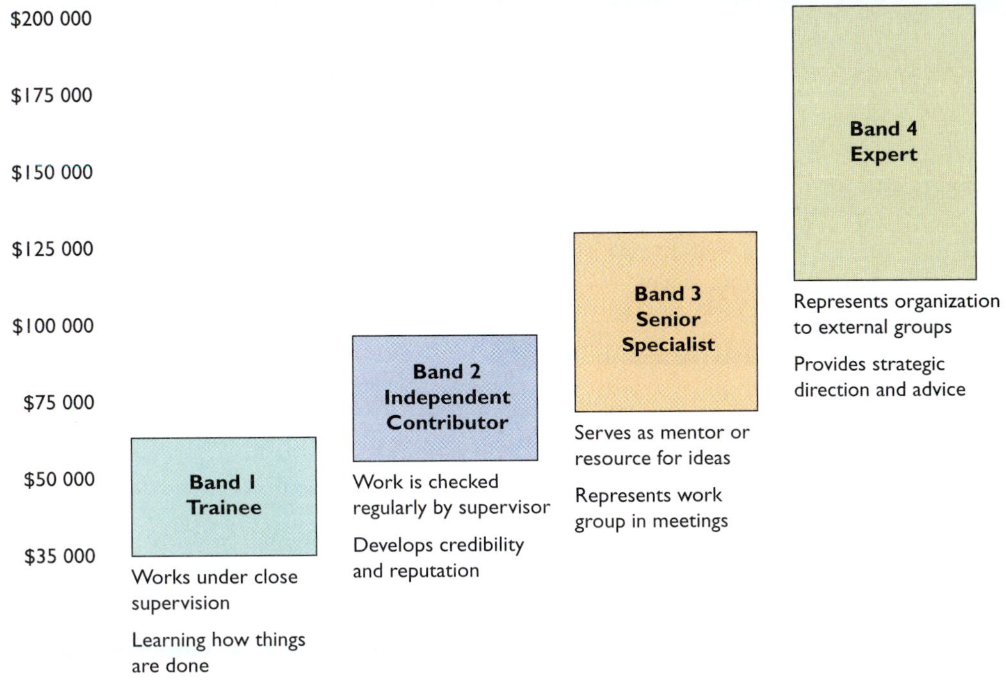


Source: H. Risher, "Planning a 'Next Generation' Salary System," *Compensation and Benefits Review*, November/December 2002, p. 16. © 2002. Reprinted with permission of Sage Publications, Inc. via Copyright Clearance Center.

as illustrated in Figure 8.5. The bands usually have wide salary ranges and also overlap substantially. As a result, there is much more flexibility to move employees from job to job within bands and less need to "promote" them to new grades just to get them higher salaries.

Broadbanding's basic advantage is that it injects greater flexibility into employee compensation.[23] It is especially appropriate when organizations flatten their hierarchies and organize around self-managing teams. The new broad salary bands can include both supervisors and those reporting to them and can also facilitate moving employees slightly up or down along the pay scale without accompanying promotional raises or demotional pay cuts. Broadbanding also facilitates the sorts of less specialized, boundaryless jobs and organizations being embraced by many organizations.

**CORRECTING OUT-OF-LINE RATES** The actual wage rate for a job may fall outside the rate range for its grade, as shown in Figure 8.3. This means that the average pay for that job is currently too high or too low relative to other jobs in the organization. If a point falls well below the line, a pay raise for the job may be required. If the plot falls well above the wage line, pay cuts or a pay freeze may be required.

## 8.4 CURRENT TRENDS IN COMPENSATION

Skill–competency-based pay, customized job evaluation, pay equity, and strategic pay are important trends in compensation. They give us a glimpse into the future of compensation management.

**rate ranges** A series of steps or levels within a pay grade, usually based upon years of service.

**broadbanding** Reducing the number of salary grades and ranges into a few wide levels or "bands," each of which then contains a relatively wide range of jobs and salary levels.

## *In-class Notes*

**Establishing Pay Rates**

- Evaluate jobs to ensure internal equity
- Group similar jobs into pay grades
- Conduct salary surveys to help ensure external equity
- Price each pay grade using wage curves
- Fine-tune pay rates using rate ranges

## Skill–Competency-Based Pay

**Competencies** are individual skills, knowledge, and behaviours that are critical to successful individual or corporate performance. With skill–competency-based pay, employees are paid for the range, depth, and types of skills and knowledge they are capable of using rather than for the job that they currently hold.[24] For many of today's leading organizations, key competencies reflect the importance of managing change, including technical knowledge, flexibility/adaptability, creativity/resourcefulness, and the ability to lead/manage.[25]

With job-based pay (JBP), employees receive the pay attached to their jobs regardless of whether they develop the competence needed to perform the job effectively. With skill-based pay (SBP), base pay is tied not to the job but to the employee's skills and competencies. With JBP, pay usually changes automatically when the employee switches jobs. With SBP, an employee must demonstrate proficiency at the skills/competencies required by the new job in order to get a pay raise. Pay in JBP systems is often tied to seniority, whereas pay in SBP systems is based on skills.

Construction workers today are often compensated for their work through the method of skill-based pay.

Experience has shown that skill-based pay is more efficient in the first years of its existence.[26] The greatest challenge is measurement of skills, abilities, and competencies. As time goes on, employees often become dissatisfied if skill measurements are not valid or if the people responsible for assessing competencies are considered incompetent or biased. Another major employee concern is that pay be linked sufficiently to performance as well as to skills/competencies. Some compensation consultants suggest that firms should not pay for competencies at the exclusion of rewards for high-performance results. For example, competencies could be linked to the determination of base salary combined with bonuses that are based on performance.[27]

## Customized Job Evaluation Plans

Despite the trend away from job-based pay, quantitative job evaluation systems (primarily the point plan) are still widely used in Canada, partly due to the requirements of pay equity legislation. In addition, individual differences in skill attainment can be taken into consideration even when point plans with salary ranges are used. Each individual's pay can vary within the range to reflect differences in skill levels.[28]

Furthermore, neither skill–competency-based pay or market-based pay entirely eliminates the need for evaluating the worth of one job relative to others. However, traditional job evaluation systems give little or no weight to teamwork, customer relations, or interpersonal communication, which have all become key behaviours for success. Responsibility has traditionally been defined in terms of the number of employees supervised but not for coaching and developing team members. Therefore, if an organization wants to reward technical knowledge and encourages teamwork, its job evaluation system needs to be updated and easily adaptable to the ever-increasing rate of change in organizations. As leading Canadian compensation consultant Nadine Winter says:[29]

> This means that traditional one-size-fits-all job evaluation systems are being rejected in favour of systems customized to reflect an organization's values, priorities and changing job roles.

In the final analysis, their relative ease of use and security are probably the major reasons for the continued widespread use of quantitative plans. Quantitative plans have also recently been facilitated by computerized packages, as explained in the HR.Net below.

**AN ETHICAL DILEMMA**

What should employers do when there is a shortage of a certain type of skills and they cannot attract any workers unless they pay a market rate above the maximum of their salary range for that job? How should other jobs in the same salary range be paid?

## Pay Equity

Historically, the average pay for Canadian women has been considerably lower than that for men. In 1967, women's average wages were 46.1 percent of men's

**HR.NET**

### Computerized Job Evaluation

Link HR Systems Inc., compensation specialists, has been applying information technology to more than 350 job evaluation processes over 15 years and has found that radical reductions in effort and cost can be achieved. Internet technology can change job evaluation from a bureaucratic committee-centred process to a simpler exercise where information is collected rapidly and inexpensively directly from employees and their managers over the Internet.[1]

HR-Dept.com is a virtual HR department that offers a variety of tools for HR management. One of these is the "Job Evaluation Assistant," which is intended to accomplish job evaluation while eliminating job evaluation committee meetings. The software provides a customizable job information questionnaire online; allows for prompted employee completion; and includes an embedded workflow for approval of the questionnaire. The job evaluation process is built in by allowing committee members to access the job questionnaires and the job evaluation plan and to enter their assessment of the job requirements. A rollup feature allows the compensation specialist to call up all of the results, deal with the exceptions, and manage the feedback reporting process all with a few clicks of the mouse. This software can reduce job evaluation time significantly without reducing the effectiveness of the process.[2]

Information technology also offers the possibility of improving the accuracy and integrity of the job evaluation process. A computerized job evaluation system can collect fact-based information as the basis for job evaluation, use analytical tools to ensure consistency across organizational units, and provide a complete audit trail of the decision process.[3]

1. T. Hull & R. Heneman, Submission to the Canadian Federal Pay Equity Task Force (June 2002), p. 3.
2. www.hr-dept.com/products/perforamnce/index.cfm (April 30, 2003).
3. Hull & Heneman, Submission to the Canadian Federal Pay Equity Task Force, p. 3.

Source: Excerpted from N. Winter, "Job Evaluation in a New Business Environment," *Canadian HR Reporter,* March 27, 2000, p. 17. Reproduced by permission of *Canadian HR Reporter,* Carswell, One Corporate Plaza, 2075 Kennedy Road, Scarborough, ON, M1T 3V4.

**competencies** Individual skills, knowledge, and behaviours that are critical to successful individual or corporate performance.

Certified General Accountants' Association of Canada
**www.cga-canada.org**

average wages. This "wage gap" of 53.9 percent meant that for every dollar earned by a man, a woman earned 46.1 cents. The gap slowly narrowed to about 29 percent in 2001. Studies in 2008 found that 23 percent of women perceive that they are paid less than equally qualified male counterparts; only 12 percent of men perceive the same about women. Women rationalize pay differences by saying that men are perceived to need more money to support their families (41 percent), men are more aggressive in compensation negotiations (35 percent), men receive more high-profile projects (33 percent), management shows favouritism to males (30 percent), and men network more with their bosses (25 percent).[30] It appears that systemic discrimination continues to affect women's wages.[31]

The purpose of pay equity legislation is to redress systemic gender discrimination in compensation for work performed by employees in female-dominated job classes. **Pay equity** requires that equal wages be paid for jobs of equal value to the employer as determined by gender-neutral (that is, free of any bias based on gender) job evaluation techniques. Pay equity reduced the wage gap in Ontario, to some extent.[32] However, although pay equity legislation has narrowed the gap, it has not eliminated it, and there is still no explanation other than systemic discrimination for much of the wage gap that persists.[33]

In 2008, the federal government introduced the *Public Sector Equitable Compensation Act*—controversial legislation that changed the pay equity rules. The Act states that issues of equal *pay* for men and women in the public service will be dealt with through collective bargaining between union and employer. Pay equity complaints are no longer addressed by the Canadian Human Rights Commission, but are resolved by the Public Service Labour Relations Board. Supporters believe this change leads to faster resolution of disputes, but critics claim the new legislation is ineffective in handling the right to equality in the workplace because it does not treat pay equity as a human right. The *Canadian Human Rights Act*, for instance, dictates that the value of work be assessed on skill, effort, responsibility, and working conditions. To those criteria, the new legislation adds a consideration of "qualifications and market forces."[34]

**PAY EQUITY AND JOB EVALUATION** Employers must ensure that there is no gender bias in the job evaluation plan itself. In particular, some traditional job evaluation point plans "tend to result in higher point totals for jobs traditionally held by males than for those traditionally held by females."[35]

As an example, the factor "responsibility" might heavily weight chain-of-command factors, such as number of employees supervised, and downplay the importance of functional authority or gaining the voluntary cooperation of other employees. The solution here is to rewrite the factor rules in job evaluation plans so as to give more weight to the sorts of activities that female-dominated positions frequently emphasize.[36]

In the long term, the best way to remove the portion of the wage gap resulting from systemic discrimination is to eliminate male- and female-dominated jobs by ensuring that women have equal access to, and are equally represented in, all jobs.

To avoid pay equity problems, it is important to ensure that job duties and responsibilities are clearly documented either by a job analysis questionnaire or a job description that is reviewed and updated annually. It is also important to review the pay system regularly. If more than three years have passed, serious inequities could exist. Maintenance of pay equity is a requirement of pay equity legislation. Organizations should ensure that pay equity laws are being monitored and adhered to in each province/territory in which a firm has employees. There are differences in the legislation among jurisdictions.

### Strategic Pay

LEGALcompliance

There is an increasing emphasis on paying employees for their competencies and results rather than just for job responsibilities. This is part of what is known as *strategic pay*. As two strategic pay consultants put it:[37]

> Today, compensation systems must support the mission and culture of the organization, and communicate to employees what is important, why they are important, and what their role is in ensuring the ongoing viability of the organization.

Figure 8.6 provides a strategic model for reward and organizational systems alignment. Organizations using strategically designed pay systems have been found to outperform those that do not based on financial measures such as earnings per share, return on assets, profit per employee, and cash flow.[38]

## 8.5 PAY FOR MANAGERIAL AND PROFESSIONAL JOBS

Developing a compensation plan to pay executive, managerial, and professional employees is similar in many respects to developing a plan for other employees.[39] Yet job evaluation provides only a partial answer to the *figure* 8.6 **Reward and Organizational Systems Alignment Model**

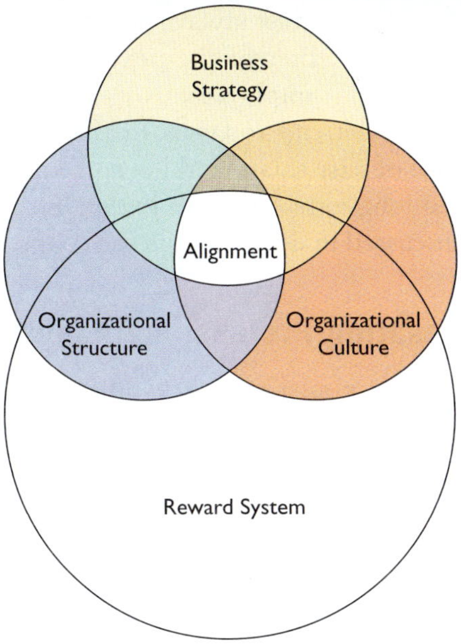


Source: R. L. Heneman and K. E. Dixon, "Reward and Organizational Systems Alignment: An Expert System," *Compensation and Benefits Review,* November/December 2001, p. 22. 

question of how to pay these employees. There is a tendency to pay managers and professionals based on their performance as well as on the value of their job. Job evaluation, while still important for determining base salary, usually plays a secondary role to nonsalary issues, such as bonuses, incentives, and benefits.

Studies have found that there is a disparity between what IT professionals want from the workplace and what organizations are offering. If the gap is not bridged, 43 percent of IT professionals are likely to resign from their companies in search of more money or a promotion within one to three years. IT professionals would stay longer than three years with their current employer if there was a stronger working relationship with their boss (70 percent), a positive work environment (60 percent), and compensation that recognizes their contributions (57 percent).[40]

## Compensating Managers

There are five elements in a manager's compensation package: salary, benefits, short-term incentives, long-term incentives, and perquisites (perks).[41] The amount of salary that managers are paid usually depends on the value of the work, which is determined through job evaluation and salary surveys and the resulting fine-tuning of salary levels.

*In-class Notes*

**Current Trends in Compensation**

- Skill–competency-based pay rather than job-based pay
- Customized job evaluation plans to reflect organizational values, priorities, and changing jobs
- Pay equity legislation requires equal pay for work of equal value
- Strategic pay for competencies and results rather than job duties

**pay equity** Providing equal pay to male-dominated job classes and female-dominated job classes of equal value to the employer.

Executive compensation tends to emphasize performance incentives more than do other employees' pay plans because organizational results are likely to reflect the contributions of executives more directly than those of other employees.[42] For example, the highest-paid Canadian executive in 2004 was Robert McEwen, CEO of Goldcorp Inc. He was paid a base salary of $346 712, other compensation of $26 732, and long-term incentives of $94 298 227, for a total 2004 compensation of $94 671 671. In general, bonuses today equal 25 percent or more of a typical executive's base salary in many countries.[43] Executive pay varies considerably by country. For example, one survey found that Canadian CEOs on average made 49 percent of what U.S. CEOs did, 137 percent of what Japanese CEOs were paid, and 99.7 percent of the average British CEO's earnings.[44]

**AN ETHICAL DILEMMA**

Is it fair that CEOs earn enormous amounts of money when most employees are getting small increases each year (sometimes even less than inflation)?

The Conference Board of Canada reports that the greatest decline in average salary increases in 2009 was at the senior executive level: Salary increases declined from 4.1 percent to 2.8 percent.[45]

Shareholder activism is combining with other changes to tighten up the restrictions on what organizations pay their top executives.[46] For example, the Ontario Securities Commission has rules regarding disclosure of executive compensation (salary, bonus, stock options, and other compensation) for companies listed on the Toronto Stock Exchange (TSX).[47] The chief executive officer's pay must always be disclosed as well as that of the next four highest paid employees.

The general trend today is to reduce the relative importance of base salary and boost the importance of short- and long-term executive incentives.[48] Incentives will be discussed in detail later in the chapter.

## Compensating Professional Employees

Compensating non-supervisory professional employees, such as engineers and scientists, presents unique problems. In theory, the job evaluation methods explained previously can be applied to evaluating professional jobs, using compensable factors such as problem solving, creativity, and technical knowledge and expertise.[49] In practice, traditional methods of job evaluation are rarely used for professional jobs, since it is so difficult to identify compensable factors that meaningfully capture the value of professional work.[50] As a result, most employers use a *market-pricing approach* in evaluating professional jobs to ensure that the employer remains competitive when bidding for professionals.[51]

*In-class Notes*

**Pay for Managerial and Professional Jobs**

- Pay based on performance as well as the value of the job
- Compensating managers: salary, benefits, short-term incentives, long-term incentives, perquisites
- Compensating professional employees: market pricing is common as it is difficult to identify compensable factors

## 8.6 INCENTIVE PLANS

Today's efforts to achieve an organization's strategy through motivated employees include financial incentives or monetary rewards paid to workers whose performance exceeds some predetermined standard. These incentives, also known as pay-for-performance and variable compensation plans, are now commonly called **variable pay**, meaning any plan that links pay with productivity, profitability, or some other measure of organizational performance. The fundamental premise of variable pay plans is that high performers who have a positive impact on a company's bottom line will share in the profits.[52] Thus, accurate performance appraisal or measurable outcomes are a precondition of effective pay-for-performance plans.

The number and types of variable compensation plans integrated into Canadian organizations has dramatically increased over the past 15 years. There has been a shift from 43 percent to 80 percent in the number of companies offering at least one variable compensation program. Organizations have moved in this direction in order to more strategically tie compensation to their business objectives. With this increased focus on variable compensation, attaining survey information about prevalence and types of variable pay plans broken down by industry, region. and role can be valuable for compensation planning purposes.[53]

The Conference Board of Canada reported that 95 percent of companies expected to have variable pay plan payouts in 2009, with 73 percent prepared to give all employees a payout. Variable plan pay outs were expected to be at or above target in 61 percent of organizations, at the same target in 53 percent of organizations, and below target in 2 percent of organizations.[54] Table 8.3 showcases annual variable pay plans for non-unionized employee groups.

Iogen, an Ottawa-based bio-tech company, role models an effective approach for how organizations should approach the development of total reward systems. Iogen's HR team facilitated focus groups with 10 or 12 different segments of employees, administered employee surveys, and conducted an environmental scan to ascertain the external competitiveness of its reward system. The company plans to make this an annual initiative in search of ways to enhance its total rewards system. Iogen uses a variety of metrics to gauge the program's success, including attrition, data collected when people leave the company, and participation data.[55]

Employers have put increasing emphasis on variable pay plans in order to maximize their return on "human capital," the only unlimited and self-renewing organizational resource.[56] Linking pay to performance has become a global trend, and the Global HRM box on page 267 provides details of the variable pay system in Singapore.[57]

There are several types of incentive plans.[58] *Individual incentive programs* give income over and above base salary to individual employees who meet a specific individual performance standard.[59] **Spot bonuses** are awarded, generally to individual employees, for accomplishments that are not readily measured by a standard, such as "to recognize the long hours that this employee put in last month" or "to recognize exemplary customer service this week."[60] For example, Cisco Systems provides up to a $2000 spot bonus for exceptional performance.[61] *Group incentive programs* are like individual incentive plans, but these programs pay over and above base salary to all team members when the group or team collectively meets a specified standard for performance, productivity, or other work-related behaviour.[62] *Profit-sharing plans* are generally organization-wide incentive programs that provide employees with a share of the organization's profits in a specified period.[63] *Gainsharing programs* are organization-wide pay plans designed to reward employees for improvements in organizational productivity. They generally include employee suggestion systems and focus on reducing labour costs through suggestions and participation.[64]

### Incentives for Operations Employees

**PIECEWORK PLANS** **Piecework** is the oldest incentive plan for operations employees and still the most commonly used. Earnings are tied directly to what a worker produces; the person is paid a *piece rate* for each unit that he or she produces. Thus, if Tom Smith gets $0.40 per piece for stamping out door jambs, then

**variable pay** Any plan that ties pay to productivity or profitability.

**spot bonuses** Spontaneous incentives awarded to individuals for accomplishments not readily measured by a standard.

**piecework** A system of pay based on the number of items processed by each individual worker in a unit of time, such as items per hour or items per day.

WorldatWork **www.worldatwork.org/canada/worldatwork-canada.jsp**

Canadian Payroll Association **www.payroll.ca**

American Society for Payroll Management **www.aspm.org**

*table* 8.3 **Annual Variable Plan Payouts, by Employee Group**

(expressed as percentage of base salary; non-unionized employees)

| 2008 Payouts* | (n=) | Average payout: Target payout | Actual payout | Receiving payouts*** | (n=) | Percentage of organizations: Exceeded target | Met target | Fell short of target |
|---|---|---|---|---|---|---|---|---|
| **Employee group** | | | | | | | | |
| Senior executives | 226 | 37.3 | 42.3 | 96.5 | 198 | 46 | 20 | 35 |
| Executives | 223 | 27.7 | 30.3 | 94.8 | 192 | 44 | 19 | 37 |
| Management | 265 | 16.0 | 16.8 | 91.8 | 230 | 42 | 18 | 40 |
| Professional—technical | 206 | 10.6 | 10.6 | 88.6 | 179 | 41 | 19 | 40 |
| Professional—non-technical | 199 | 10.2 | 11.0 | 91.3 | 174 | 43 | 20 | 37 |
| Technical and skilled trades | 98 | 7.3 | 7.9 | 92.7 | 84 | 45 | 21 | 33 |
| Clerical and support | 187 | 6.0 | 6.4 | 91.5 | 167 | 41 | 18 | 41 |
| Service and production | 88 | 6.2 | 7.5 | 91.2 | 77 | 40 | 25 | 35 |

| 2009 Projected Payouts** | (n=) | Target payout | Plan maximum |
|---|---|---|---|
| **Employee group** | | | |
| Senior executives | 203 | 38.2 | 67.0 |
| Executives | 191 | 27.7 | 48.0 |
| Management | 233 | 16.1 | 28.4 |
| Professional—technical | 186 | 10.8 | 19.2 |
| Professional—non-technical | 180 | 10.4 | 19.5 |
| Technical and skilled trades | 85 | 7.4 | 11.4 |
| Clerical and support | 167 | 6.2 | 11.8 |
| Service and production | 77 | 6.2 | 11.8 |

*2008 payouts refer to payouts based on 2007 results, paid in 2008. Sample size indicates the number of organizations providing a response for at least one of target or actual payout.
**2009 payouts refer to payouts based on 2008 results, to be paid in 2009. Sample size indicates the number of organizations providing a response for at least one target or plan maximum.
***Percentage of employees in category.
Source: The Conference Board of Canada, 2008, Annual Variable Pay Plan Payouts, by Employee Group.

he would make $40 for stamping out 100 a day and $80 for stamping out 200.

Piecework incentive plans have several advantages. They are simple to calculate and easily understood by employees. Piece-rate plans appear equitable in principle, and their incentive value can be powerful, since rewards are directly tied to performance.

Piecework also has some disadvantages. A main one is its somewhat unsavoury reputation among many employees based on some employers' habits of arbitrarily raising production standards whenever they found their workers earning "excessive" wages. In addition, piece rates are stated in monetary terms (such as $0.40 per piece). Thus, when a new job evaluation results in a new hourly wage rate, the piece rate must also be revised; this can be a big clerical chore. Another disadvantage is subtler. Since the piece rate is quoted on a per-piece basis, production standards become tied inseparably in workers' minds to the amount of money earned. When an attempt is made to revise production standards, it meets considerable worker resistance, even if the revision is fully justified.[65]

## GLOBAL HRM

# Variable Pay in Singapore

Singapore is a resource-scarce country and yet is often regarded as one of the most celebrated cases of economic development. Without doubt, it is the country's pool of human resources and the qualities of its workforce that have always been regarded by the government as the key factors in scaling the economic ladder. Income policy in Singapore shapes the country's competitiveness, and in order to understand the structure of the pay system and workers' wage expectations in Singapore, it is important to appreciate the role played by the National Wages Council (NWC), a tripartite body made up of representatives from unions, employers, and government. Although the wage and other recommendations given out by the NWC are not binding on individual employers and unions, they do provide a basis for constructive negotiation and reference. The aim of the NWC deliberations is to come up with a win-win situation so that the country's competitiveness and the welfare of its citizens will not be jeopardized. Because the underpinnings of these guidelines have been thoroughly discussed and agreed on, it is less likely that the outcome will be strongly in favour of one particular group of stakeholders.

Competitiveness at both the national and enterprise levels remains the foremost concern in the country's compensation structure. Over the years since the 1985–1986 recession, the pay system has been improved to enhance the responsiveness of its adjustment mechanisms. This was done through building up the variable component of the flexible wage system to 80 percent basic wage and 20 percent annual variable component. Almost 85 percent of the unionized companies and about 70 percent of the non-unionized ones in Singapore adopted the flexible wage system.

The 1997–1998 economic downturn gave the NWC a good opportunity to assess the variable component of the total pay package. It was found that the existing flexible wage structure was not flexible enough for companies to weather a sudden business downturn. The addition of a new component was strongly recommended by the NWC, resulting in a compensation structure of 70 percent basic wages, 20 percent annual variable component, and a 10 percent monthly variable component. These ongoing efforts to develop a flexible wage structure are intended to reduce the need for reductions in government unemployment/retirement programs and excessive corporate retrenchments in any future economic downturn.

Source: Adapted from D. Wan and C. H. Ong, "Compensation Systems in Singapore," *Compensation and Benefits Review*, July/August 2002, pp. 23–32. © 2002. Used with permission of Sage Publications, Inc. via Copyright Clearance Center.

**TEAM OR GROUP INCENTIVE PLANS** There are several ways to implement **team or group incentive plans.**[66] One is to set work standards for each member of a group and maintain a count of the output of each member. Members are then paid based on one of three formulas: (1) all members receive the pay earned by the highest producer; (2) all members receive the pay earned by the lowest producer; or (3) all members receive payment equal to the average pay earned by the group.

The second approach is to set a production standard based on the final output of the group as a whole; all members then receive the same pay based on the piece rate that exists for the group's job. The group incentive can be based on either the piece rate or the standard hour plan, but the latter is somewhat more prevalent.

A third option is to choose a measurable definition of group performance or productivity that the group can control. For instance, broad criteria, such as total labour-hours per final product, could be used; piecework's engineered standards are thus not necessarily required here.[67]

A growing trend in team or group incentives is the use of outdoor adventures, such as skiing, whitewater rafting, and kayaking, to reward employees, rather than cash. Studies have found that while cash incentives improve performance by 14.6 percent, those who worked toward a non-cash incentive of the same value enhanced performance by 38.6 percent. A cash incentive

**team or group incentive plans** Plans in which a production standard is set for a specific work group and its members are paid incentives if the group exceeds the production standard.

is quickly forgotten and is sometimes perceived as insufficient, whereas experiential rewards are team-bonding experiences that have long-term benefits on employee morale, engagement, and retention. Outdoor activities also reduce stress, provide opportunities for personal growth and development, and are more cost effective than cash payouts.[68]

**AN ETHICAL DILEMMA**

Is it ethical to provide potentially large bonuses to managers and executives on a purely discretionary basis?

## Incentives for Managers and Executives

Most employers award their managers and executives a bonus or incentive because of the role that managers play in determining divisional and corporate profitability.[69]

**SHORT-TERM INCENTIVES (ANNUAL BONUS)** More than 85 percent of firms in Canada with variable pay plans provide an **annual bonus**.[70] There are three basic issues to be considered when awarding short-term incentives: eligibility, fund-size determination, and individual awards. Eligibility is usually decided in one of three ways. The first criterion is *key position*. The second approach to determining eligibility is to set a *salary-level* cutoff point; all employees earning over that threshold amount are automatically eligible for consideration for short-term incentives. Finally, eligibility can be determined by *salary grade*. This is a refinement of the salary-level cutoff approach and assumes that all employees at a certain grade or above should be eligible for the short-term incentive program.[71]

Next, a decision must be made regarding fund size—the total amount of bonus money that will be available. Some companies use a non-deductible formula. Here, a straight percentage (usually of the company's net income) is used to create the short-term incentive fund. Others use a deductible formula on the assumption that the short-term incentive fund should begin to accumulate only after the firm has met a specified level of earnings.

The third issue is determining the individual awards to be paid. In some cases, the amount is determined on a discretionary basis (usually by the employee's boss), but typically a target bonus is set for each eligible position, and adjustments are then made for greater or less than targeted performance. A maximum amount, perhaps double the target bonus, may be set. Performance ratings are obtained for each manager, and preliminary bonus estimates are computed. Estimates for the total amount of money to be spent on short-term incentives are thereby made and compared with the bonus fund available. If necessary, the individual estimates are then adjusted.

**LONG-TERM INCENTIVES** Long-term incentives are intended to motivate and reward top management for the firm's long-term growth and prosperity and to inject a long-term perspective into executive decisions. If only short-term criteria are used, a manager could, for instance, increase profitability by reducing plant maintenance; this tactic might, of course, reduce profits over two or three years. Long-term incentives are also intended to encourage executives to stay with the company by giving them the opportunity to accumulate capital (such as company shares) based on the firm's long-term success. Long-term incentives or **capital accumulation programs** are most often reserved for senior executives but have more recently begun to be extended to employees at lower organizational levels.[72]

The **stock option** is by far the most popular long-term incentive in Canada. Over 80 percent of organizations using long-term incentives provide stock options.[73] A stock option is the right to purchase a specific number of shares of a company at a specific price during a period of time; the executive thus hopes to profit by exercising his or her option to buy the shares in the future but at today's price. The assumption is that the price of the shares will go up rather than going down or staying the same. (Stock options lost motivational power in 2001 when the post–September 11 economic downturn caused share prices to tumble.[74]) As shown in Figure 8.7, if shares provided at an option price of $20 each are exercised (bought) later for $20 when the market price is $60 per share and sold when the market price is $80 per share, a cash gain of $60 per share results if the shares are then sold on the stock market.

One of the interesting trends in stock options as long-term incentives is that, increasingly, they are not just for high-level managers and executives—or even just managers and executives—anymore. Pepsico, Starbucks, the Gap, and many other companies have broad-based stock option plans that include employees below the executive level.[75]

Compensation packages for chief executive officers in many large companies declined with the slow economy and faltering corporate performances of 2007–2009. For CEOs of the top 50 companies, compensation for 2007 was just under $14 million, a 15.8 percent reduction from 2006. Those at large companies received $9.4 million, unchanged from 2006, while CEOs of

*figure* 8.7 **Stock Options**

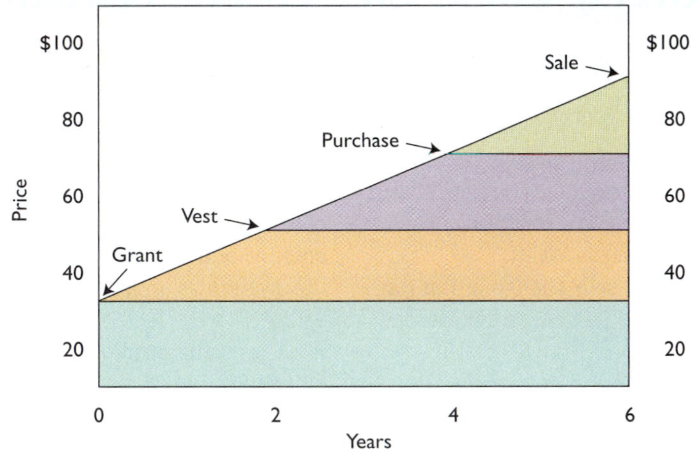


Source: B.R. Ellig, "Executive Pay: A Primer," *Compensation and Benefits Review,* January/February 2003, p. 48. © 2003. Reprinted with permission of Sage Publications, Inc. via Copyright Clearance Center.

mid-size companies earned $4.7 million, a decline of 4.6 percent. Long-term incentives, mostly in the form of equity, represent two-thirds of the total CEO pay package.[76]

The Strategic HR box on page 270 explains the changes in executive compensation resulting from heightened public and media scrutiny and pressure from shareholders to make changes.

## Incentives for Salespeople

Sales compensation plans have typically relied heavily on incentives (sales commissions), although this varies by industry. In the tobacco industry, for instance, salespeople are usually paid entirely via commissions, while in the transportation equipment industry salespeople tend to be paid a salary. However, the most prevalent approach is to use a combination of salary and commissions to compensate salespeople.[77]

**AN ETHICAL DILEMMA**

Is it fair to compensate sales employees on a 100-percent commission basis with no financial security?

**SALARY PLAN** In a salary plan, salespeople are paid a fixed salary. This works well when the main sales objective is prospecting (finding new clients) or when the salesperson is mostly involved in account servicing. The advantages of this approach are that salespeople know in advance what their income will be, and the employer also has fixed, predictable sales force expenses. Straight salary makes it simple to switch territories or quotas or to reassign salespeople, and it can develop a high degree of loyalty among sales staff. The main disadvantage is that salary plans do not depend on results.

**COMMISSION PLAN** Commission plans pay salespeople in direct proportion to their sales: They pay for results and only for results. The commission plan has several advantages. Salespeople have the greatest possible incentive, and there is a tendency to attract high-performing salespeople who see that effort will clearly lead to rewards. Sales costs are proportional to sales rather

**annual bonus** Plans that are designed to motivate short-term performance of managers and are tied to company profitability.

**capital accumulation programs** Long-term incentives most often reserved for senior executives.

**stock option** The right to purchase a stated number of shares of a company at today's price at some time in the future.

The Conference Board of Canada
**www.conferenceboard.ca**

STRATEGIC HR

# Bonus Controversy Could Change Compensation

**INCREASED SCRUTINY OF EXECUTIVE PAY COULD RESULT IN SMALLER BONUSES TIED STRICTLY TO PERFORMANCE**

Although executives can still expect some big bonuses in the future, company boards are moving towards a more conservative way of determining compensation, according to a senior executive compensation consultant at global consulting firm Watson Wyatt.

"There is probably going to be a change in the way executives are going to be paid," said Robert Levasseur, who is based in Toronto.

"There will be more concern in terms of looking at mitigating risk . . . because oftentimes the employees are (in) the position where they recorded vast amounts of compensation for decisions they've made, not knowing if the decisions are beneficial to the organization in the long term."

The way compensation is determined is beginning to change, in part because of the increased amount of public and media scrutiny, he said.

In March, it was revealed executives from struggling financial firm AIG collected $165 million US in bonuses not long after the company received billions of dollars in bailout money from Washington.

While some executives eventually gave the money back, the incident sparked a debate about the balance between compensation payouts for retention and reasonable rewards for corporate performance.

Although hearty financial compensation is still important for retaining and attracting quality executives, "it is a market after all," said Levasseur, and while executives are still playing the "retention card," there are fewer opportunities for them than there were nine months ago.

The downward shift in executive compensation means the system of bonuses is doing what it is supposed to do, said Jeffrey Gandz, a professor at the University of Western Ontario's Richard Ivey School of Business in London, Ont.

As boards observe the backlash caused by executive bonuses, they are becoming more sensitive to the overall performance of the organization when drafting compensation agreements, he said.

**Use market data**

When boards are determining compensation, it is important they avoid lumping all payments into the same category, said Gandz.

In order to decide what to pay a potential employee to retain her, company boards should look to market data to see what is competitive.

The next step involves deciding on the conditions they will attach to variable compensation—some for short- and long-term performance and some for financial goals.

"One of the things we are seeing is much greater care being taken to determine both the total amount and the various amounts of compensation so the system is more transparent and justifiable," he said.

The compensation package for retiring Manulife Financial CEO Dominic D'Alessandro is an example of the importance of performance-based compensation, said Gandz.

Although Manulife reported a $1.87-billion loss in the fourth quarter of last year, D'Alessandro received $12.35 million in total compensation for 2008. He will receive $12.6 million for 2009.

"If you take a look at it from March 29, it looks like a ridiculous decision—the shares were down yet (there) was a big bonus," said Gandz. However, D'Alessandro's compensation was agreed upon before "the bottom fell out," he said.

Now, the public will probably see fewer payments made because someone has done a good job and, instead, compensation will be tied to performance-based merits, said Gandz.

"There may well be bonus plans that have (provisions) in them saying 'dependent on such-and-such,'" he said.

**Retention without massive compensation**

The primary way to attract and retain executives without offering large compensation packages is to provide interesting and attractive jobs, said Gandz.

While that has always been important, it is even more so now because "the externalities facing companies are not that great. There is going to be a lot more focus on the nature of work and how to improve the conditions of work for people, other than in financial terms," he said.

"In the same token, there will be the need to be competitive," he said. "As perverse as it may seem, there will be pay increases when people are being laid off, essentially for the need to retain talent."

Source: A. Scappatura, "Bonus controversy could change compensation: Increased scrutiny of executive pay could result in smaller bonuses tied strictly to performance." *Canadian HR Reporter,* April 20, 2009. Reprinted with permission.

than fixed, and the company's selling investment is reduced. The commission basis is also easy to understand and compute.

The commission plan, too, has drawbacks. Salespeople focus on making a sale and on high-volume items; cultivating dedicated customers and working to push hard-to-sell items may be neglected. Wide variances in income between salespeople may occur; this can lead to a feeling that the plan is inequitable. More serious is the fact that salespeople are encouraged to neglect non-selling duties such as servicing small accounts. In addition, pay is often excessive in boom times and very low in recessions.

**COMBINATION PLAN** There has been a definite move away from the extremes of straight commission or fixed salary to combination plans for salespeople.[78] Combination plans provide some of the advantages of both straight salary and straight commission plans and also some of their disadvantages. Salespeople have a floor to their earnings. Furthermore, the company can direct its salespeople's activities by detailing what services the salary component is being paid for, while the commission component provides a built-in incentive for superior performance. However, the salary component is not tied to performance, and the employer is therefore trading away some incentive value. Combination plans also tend to become complicated, and misunderstandings can result.

The sales force also may get various special awards. Trips, home stereos, TVs, DVD players, and video cameras are commonly used as sales prizes. Access to the latest technology (such as notebook computers with customer and product databases, portable printers, digital cellphones, and so on) can also have a strong behavioural impact on field sales staff.[79]

## Incentives for Other Professionals

*frontLINE tips*

**MERIT PAY** Merit pay or a **merit raise** is any salary increase awarded to an employee based on his or her individual performance. It is different from a bonus in that it represents a continuing increment, whereas the bonus represents a one-time payment. Although the term *merit pay* can apply to the incentive raises given to any employees, it is more often used with respect to white-collar employees and particularly professional, office, and clerical employees.

Merit pay advocates argue that only pay or other rewards tied directly to performance can motivate improved performance. On the other hand, merit pay detractors present good reasons why merit pay can backfire. One is that the usefulness of the merit pay plan depends on the validity of the performance appraisal system, since if performance appraisals are viewed as unfair, so, too, will the merit pay that is based on them.[80] Second, supervisors often tend to minimize differences in employee performance when computing merit raises. A third problem is that almost every employee thinks that he or she is an above-average performer; being paid a below-average merit increase can thus be demoralizing.[81]

**OTHER INCENTIVES** Professional employees are those whose work involves the application of learned knowledge to the solution of the employer's problems. They include lawyers, doctors, economists, and engineers. Professionals almost always reach their positions through prolonged periods of formal study.[82]

Pay decisions regarding professional employees involve unique problems. One is that for most professionals, money has historically been somewhat less important as an incentive than it has been for other employees. This is not to say that professionals do not want financial incentives. However, professionals' bonuses tend to represent a relatively small portion of their total pay. The time cycle of the professionals' incentive plans also tends to be longer than a year, reflecting the long time spent in designing, developing, and marketing a new product.

There are also many non-salary items that professionals must get to do their best work. Not strictly incentives, these range from better equipment and facilities and a supportive management style to support for professional journal publications.

## Organization-Wide Incentive Plans

Many employers have incentive plans in which virtually all employees can participate. These include profit sharing, employee stock ownership, and gainsharing plans.

**merit pay (merit raise)** Any salary increase awarded to an employee based on his or her individual performance.

General Printers' president, David Fors, far left, credits an employee share ownership plan with the company's turnaround.

**PROFIT-SHARING PLANS** In a **profit-sharing plan,** most or all employees receive a share of the company's profits. Approximately 20 percent of Canadian organizations offer profit-sharing plans.[83] These plans are easy to administer and have a broad appeal to employees and other company stakeholders. The weakness of profit-sharing plans lies in the "line of sight." It is unlikely that most employees perceive that they personally have the ability to influence overall company profit. It has been found that these plans produce a one-time productivity improvement but no change thereafter. Another weakness of these plans is that they typically provide an annual payout, which is not as effective as more frequent payouts.[84]

There are several types of profit-sharing plans. In *cash plans*, the most popular, a percentage of profits (usually 15 percent to 20 percent) is distributed as profit shares at regular intervals. There are also *deferred profit-sharing plans*. Here, a predetermined portion of profits is placed in each employee's account under the supervision of a trustee. There is a tax advantage to such plans because income taxes are deferred, often until the employee retires and is taxed at a lower rate.

**EMPLOYEE SHARE PURCHASE/STOCK OWNERSHIP PLANS** **Employee share purchase/stock ownership plans (ESOPs)** are in place at approximately 50 percent of Canadian organizations with publicly traded shares.[85] A trust is established to purchase shares of the firm for employees, using cash from employee (and sometimes employer) contributions. The trust holds the shares in individual employee accounts and distributes them to employees, often upon retirement or other separation from service. Some plans distribute the shares to employees once a year.

ESOPs can encourage employees to develop a sense of ownership in and commitment to the firm, particularly when combined with good communication, employee involvement in decision making, and employee understanding of the business and the economic environment.[86] For example, General Printers in Oshawa achieved a dramatic turnaround following the introduction of an ESOP. The firm had been a chronic money loser but became profitable the year that the plan was introduced and has remained so in the years since that time. The value of the company has grown 80 percent since the ESOP was introduced, profits are up, spoiled orders are down 50 percent, and far less supervision of employees is required.[87]

## *In-class Notes*

**Incentive Plans**

- Variable pay linked to measure of performance
- Operations employees: piecework, team/group incentives
- Managers and executives: annual bonus, capital accumulation plans
- Salespeople: salary, commission, or a combination
- Other professionals: merit pay
- Organization-wide plans: profit sharing, employee stock ownership, gainsharing

**STRATEGIC HR**

## Maritime Life Assures Employee Rewards

Employees at Maritime Life Assurance in Halifax are given extra incentive to treat their customers right. The company reinforces top-notch service by offering a yearly bonus for all staff based on customer satisfaction. In fact, that's one of the reasons Maritime Life was listed as one of Canada's top 50 companies to work for two years in a row.

"Maritime Life has been measuring customer satisfaction for a long time. The intention is to ensure that customer service and satisfaction is high and it has been within the company's value system for years," said Steve Christie, Director of Compensation and Benefits at Maritime Life.

Maritime usually sets target satisfaction rates of about 90 percent and if that is achieved, staff will receive a bonus. Employees receive their payouts at the end of the year, and the bonus ranges from $500 to $1000 per worker. However, the overall payout is the same for everyone from senior manager to front-line worker, regardless of their position in the organization.

However, employees don't have to wait until the end of the year to get rewarded. They could receive a Lighthouse Award any time throughout the year, which recognizes individual contributions, and it doesn't have to be handed out by top management. Peers can award other peers, managers can recognize staff both in their departments and other departments, and vice-presidents can do the same. Staff can also give them to managers. The awards come complete with a certificate and voucher that can be used at the company's store, which sells Maritime Life paraphernalia. There is a maximum voucher of $75.

A cash bonus and vouchers aren't the only things on Maritime's recognition roster. Top management and HR make sure employees know there is room for advancement. Employees even have access to their own Career Investment Account to facilitate career growth. About 2 to 4 percent of every employee's salary is allocated to this account. They can use the account for learning in terms of attending conferences, seminars, or workshops. As part of the performance review process, when employees sit down with their managers, they're expected to look at what their development opportunities are and where they want to go in the company.

Source: Adapted from A. Tomlinson, "Maritime Life Assures Employee Rewards," *Canadian HR Reporter,* March 11, 2002, p. 7. Reproduced by permission of *Canadian HR Reporter,* Carswell, One Corporate Plaza, 2075 Kennedy Road, Scarborough, ON, M1T 3V4.

**GAINSHARING PLANS** A **gainsharing plan** is an incentive plan that engages many or all employees in a common effort to achieve a company's productivity objectives; any resulting incremental cost-saving gains are shared among employees and the company.[88]

The financial aspects of a gainsharing program can be quite straightforward.[89] Assume that a supplier wants to boost quality. Doing so would translate into fewer customer returns, less scrap and rework, and, therefore, higher profits. Historically, $1 million in output results in $20 000 (2 percent) in scrap, returns, and rework. The company tells its employees that if next month's production results in only 1 percent scrap, returns, and rework, the 1 percent saved would be a gain to be split 50/50 with the workforce, less a small amount for reserve for months in which scrap exceeds 2 percent. Awards are often posted monthly but allocated quarterly.[90]

Gainsharing works well in stable organizations with predictable goals and measures of performance but is less flexible and useful in dynamic industries that require rapid business adjustment. In general, most of the cost savings are generated in the early years.[91]

**profit-sharing plan** A plan whereby most or all employees share in a company's profits.

**employee share purchase/stock ownership plans** A trust is established to hold shares of company stock purchased for or issued to employees. The trust distributes the stock to employees on retirement, separation from service, or as otherwise prescribed by the plan.

**gainsharing plan** An incentive plan that engages employees in a common effort to achieve productivity objectives and share the gains.

ESOP Association Canada
**www.esop-canada.com**

Gainsharing Consultants
**www.bovino-consulting.com**

Reward Systems
**http://online-rewards.com/index.html**

Nelson Motivation, Inc.
**www.nelson-motivation.com**

Recognition Professionals International
**www.recognition.org**

Unfortunately, many companies find that variable pay plans do not produce desired business results. This is usually due to poor design and implementation of the plans.[92] The Strategic HR box on page 273 describes how one Canadian company, Maritime Life, has successfully implemented a variety of incentive plans.

## 8.7 EMPLOYEE RECOGNITION PROGRAMS

Although appreciated at the time of receipt, monetary rewards are quickly spent and offer no lasting symbol of recognition.[93] There is a growing awareness that demonstrating appreciation of employees' achievements is more important than ever.[94] Why? Because lack of recognition and praise is the number one reason that employees leave an organization.[95] The traditional role of recognition plans has been to reward employees for long service.

Employees consistently say that they receive little recognition. One study found that only 50 percent of managers give recognition for high performance and that up to 40 percent of workers feel they never get recognized for outstanding performance.[96] Another study found that 59 percent of human resources practitioners believe their recognition programs reinforce the strategy, values, and behaviours of the organization, but only 42 percent say the programs drive bottom-line results.[97] In today's fast-paced and constantly changing work world, managers are predominantly consumed with achieving bottom-line results, leaving little time and attention for the recognition of employees. However, when lack of recognition and praise results in the loss of valued employees, managers must recognize their employees' achievements.[98] Employees favour recognition from supervisors and managers by a margin of two-to-one over recognition from other sources.[99]

Stephanie Kwolek, a DuPont scientist, received the company's highest award, the Lavoisier Medal for Technical Achievement.

Recognition is also cost-effective. It takes 5 to 8 percent of pay to have an impact on behaviour when a cash reward is provided, but only 4 percent when a non-cash form of reward is used (such as recognition and modest gifts).[100] This is because employees find that the presentation process is as important as the gift itself.[101] Bob Nelson, author of *1001 Ways to Energize Employees*, says, "Cheap and meaningful is better than expensive and forgettable."[102]

As salary budgets are frozen, an increasing number of organizations are exploring creative and cost efficient ways to recognize and motivate staff, as outlined in the Strategic HR box on page 275.

Finally, recognition programs are key corporate communication tools that can achieve several goals—saying thank you, encouraging good workers, and encouraging good behaviour.[103] Northern Telecom, IBM, Labatt Breweries Ontario, Shell Canada, 3M Canada, and Warner Lambert are just some of the Canadian companies that are reaping the benefits of employee recognition programs.

### *In-class Notes*

**Employee Recognition Programs**

- Recognition and praise have more lasting value than financial rewards
- Recognition from supervisors is most effective
- Recognition is cost-effective
- Recognition is a key communication tool

STRATEGIC HR

## Recession-Proof Recognition

**SMALLER REWARDS, GIVEN OUT MORE OFTEN, CAN STOP EMPLOYEES FROM SLIPPING INTO "PSYCHOLOGICAL RECESSION"**

Dedicated and focused employees are the heart and soul of an organization. This is even more true in a recessionary economy, so it's imperative to recognize their contributions.

But as salary budgets are frozen and increases are scaled back, companies need to be creative to find cost-effective ways to recognize and motivate employees. A well-structured recognition program might just be the perfect recipe in a downturn.

When a company is looking to trim costs, a micro focus on expenses could suggest there is room to cut employee rewards and recognition initiatives. But when companies have had to slash the number of employees, either through layoffs or hiring freezes, it becomes important to gain high performance from those remaining.

These employees need to be assured of their value. Smaller awards given out more often can keep the attitudes and minds of employees from slipping into a psychological recession. Employees are also a great resource for ideas and any cost-saving suggestions should be rewarded during tough times.

Here are a few budget-pinching ways to recognize employees:

**Gift cards:** Employees want to know their employer cares about their personal lives. By rewarding them with gift cards, such as a $10 gas card or a $20 grocery store card, employees can share their success and rewards with their families while also saving on lifestyle expenses.

**Green initiatives:** To generate and engender loyalty, while saving the company money, encourage employees to explore options to make the company a more responsible, sustainable corporate citizen. Challenge employees to take on green initiatives such as car pooling, avoiding unnecessary printing, bringing in reusable cutlery and recycling paper.

Reward these initiatives with green rewards such as stainless steel water bottles, coffee mugs, lunch bags or totes made from recycled materials. Many of these items can be purchased and adorned with a company logo for less than $10. Ball caps made from recycled soda bottles and T-Shirts made from soybean protein, costing about $20, also add value by bringing together and motivating "green" teams.

**Group meals:** To help keep recognition top of mind, organize monthly or quarterly breakfasts or pizza lunches that give out individual rewards. This type of venue allows everyone to share their successes and talk openly with other departments, while affording the winners an opportunity to be recognized in front of their peers.

This reinforces the difference employees can make in the success of the company and links recognition to actions that reflect the company's goals and values. Open dialogue between departments also helps build team spirit and creates a culture of inclusion.

**Downgrades:** Take the opportunity to look at the rewards program and consider where it can be more economical without actually taking away rewards. Instead of awarding a 10-year employee with a set of wine glasses, choose a barbecue set. Instead of giving watches to notable employees, give out bracelets or cuff links.

If an employer chooses to reward specific behaviours to which it can assign a precise dollar value, a well-designed recognition program with nominal investment upfront will achieve desired results. As an example, if the behaviour recognized is worth $50 to your company, a $10 gift provides a 500-per-cent return on investment.

But clear, frequent communication is still the key driver of any successful rewards and recognition program. Objectives of the program should be outlined to include anticipated results and behaviours needed to achieve the goals. Put into place measurable results and clearly define the timelines and rewards attached to the goals achieved. Review the program as required but ensure all stakeholders know of any changes that have been made. And keep the communications upbeat as positive attitudes and reinforcement can be contagious.

Source: Reprinted courtesy of Karen Nixon.

# Total Compensation on the International Stage

The increasing number of employees working on overseas assignments has created a need for organizations to develop effective international compensation programs. Establishing international compensation programs requires knowledge of multinational employment and taxation law, customs, work environments, employment practices, currency, and the effect of inflation on compensation.[104] Fluency in compensation is needed, along with an understanding of the political, economic, and social landscapes of countries within which companies operate.[105] As well as extensive research on compensation practices in foreign countries, companies must also be aware of the needs and expectations of employees who reside overseas. They can then take local practices into consideration in addition to offering North American incentives. Even though managing international compensation is complex, the main objectives are similar to North American compensation—attract, motivate, and retain employees to achieve competitive advantage.[106]

There are two dominant approaches to developing an international compensation program: the going-rate approach and the balance-sheet approach. The going-rate approach uses local market rates in the host country as the basis for assigning wages. Data to make these decisions are gathered from local compensation surveys. The going-rate approach is simple to design and manage, easy for expatriates to understand, delivers wage parity with local employees, and helps expatriates identify with their host country. In cases where the wages in the host country are considerably lower than the wages given for comparable work in North America, base pay is supplemented by additional payouts or incentives. The balance-sheet approach is the most popular approach used by multinational firms. Expatriates are compensated according to the going rates in their home country with supplemental payment—a hardship premium—offered to make the overseas assignment desirable. One of the key advantages of the balance-sheet approach is that it provides equity between overseas assignments and expatriates of the same country.[107]

# Chapter Review

## Answers to Test Yourself

1. What are the four basic factors determining pay rates?

   The four basic factors that determine pay rates are legal requirements, union influences, compensation policies of the employer, and internal and external equity in pay.

2. What are the five basic steps in establishing pay rates?

   The five basic steps in establishing pay rates are determining the worth of the job within the organization through a job evaluation; grouping similar jobs into pay grades; conducting a salary survey of what other employers are paying for comparable jobs; pricing each pay grade by using wage curves; and fine-tuning pay rates.

3. What is job evaluation, and what are the common methods used to analyze jobs?

   Job evaluation is the formal and systematic comparison of jobs within a company to determine the worth of one job relative to another and eventually results in a job hierarchy. Commonly used job evaluation methods are the ranking method, the job classification method, and the point method.

4. What are the pros and cons of salary plans and commission plans for salespeople?

   Under a salary plan, salespeople receive a fixed salary. Employees have a fixed income, the organization has a predictable expense, and it is easier for the employer to change sales territories, to reassign salespeople, and to create loyalty. However, pay is not based on results. Under a commission plan, pay is directly proportionate to the amount of sales. This makes it easier to attract high performers, sales costs are proportionate to sales, and the plan is easy to understand and compute. However, commission plans can create large variances between high and low performers, resulting in inequity and leading salespeople to neglect hard-to-sell items, dedicated customers, and non-selling activities.

5. What are the various types of organization-wide incentive plans?

Common organization-wide incentive plans include profit sharing, where employees receive a share of the company's profits; employee stock ownership, where a trust is established to purchase shares of the company for employees using cash from employees and/or employer contributions; and gainsharing, where the company engages most employees in a common effort to achieve a company productivity objective and shares the resulting cost-saving gains.

## Key Terms

annual bonus (p. 268)
benchmark job (p. 250)
broadbanding (p. 258)
capital accumulation programs (p. 268)
classes (p. 252)
classification (or grading) method (p. 252)
compensable factors (p. 250)
competencies (p. 260)
distributive justice (p. 249)
employee share purchase/stock ownership plans (p. 272)
gainsharing plan (p. 273)
grade/group description (p. 252)
grades (p. 252)
job evaluation (p. 250)
merit pay (merit raise) (p. 271)
pay equity (p. 262)
pay grade (p. 277)
piecework (p. 265)
point method (p. 252)
procedural justice (p. 249)
profit-sharing plan (p. 272)
ranking method (p. 251)
rate ranges (p. 258)
spot bonuses (p. 265)
stock option (p. 268)
team or group incentive plans (p. 267)
total compensation (p. 245)
variable pay (p. 265)
wage curve (p. 257)
wage/salary surveys (p. 256)

## Required Professional Capabilities (RPCs)

**RPC 8-1 >** (p. 247)
**RPC 8-2 >** (p. 248)
**RPC 8-3 >** (p. 248)
**RPC 8-4 >** (p. 248)
**RPC 8-5 >** (p. 248)
**RPC 8-6 >** (p. 250)

# Cases and Exercises

**myHRlab**

For additional cases and exercises, go to **www.pearsoned.ca/myhrlab**.

## CASE INCIDENT

### Inserting the Team Concept into Compensation—or Not

One of the first things Sandy Caldwell wanted to do in his new position at Hathaway Manufacturing was improve productivity through teamwork at every level of the firm. As the new human resource manager for the suburban plant, Sandy set out to change the culture to accommodate the team-based approach he had become so enthusiastic about in his most recent position.

Sandy started by installing the concept of team management at the highest level, to oversee the operations of the entire plant. The new management team consisted of manufacturing, distribution, planning, technical, and human resource plant managers. Together they developed a new vision for the 500-employee facility, which they expressed in the simple phrase "Excellence Together." They drafted a new mission statement for the firm that focused on becoming customer driven and team based, and that called upon employees to raise their level of commitment and begin acting as "owners" of the firm.

The next step was to convey the team message to employees throughout the company. The communication process went surprisingly well, and Sandy was happy to see his idea of a "workforce of owners" begin to take shape. Teams trained together, developed production plans together, and embraced the technique of 360-degree feedback, in which an employee's performance evaluation is obtained from supervisors, subordinates, peers, and internal or external customers. Performance and morale improved, and productivity began to tick upward. The company even sponsored occasional celebrations to reward team achievements, and the team structure seemed firmly in place.

Sandy decided to change one more thing. Hathaway's long-standing policy had been to give all employees the same annual pay increase. But Sandy felt that in the new team environment, outstanding performance should be the criterion for pay raises. After consulting with CEO Regina Cioffi, Sandy sent a memo to all employees announcing the change to team-based pay for performance.

The reaction was immediate and 100% negative. None of the employees was happy with the change, and among their complaints, two stood out. First, because the 360-degree feedback system made everyone responsible in part for someone else's performance evaluation, no one was comfortable with the idea that pay raises might also somehow be linked to peer input. Second, there was a widespread perception that the way the change was decided upon, and the way it was announced, put the firm's commitment to team effort in doubt. Simply put, employees felt left out of the decision process.

Sandy and Regina arranged a meeting for early the next morning. Sitting in her office over their coffee, they began a painful debate. Should the new policy be rescinded as quickly as it was adopted, or should it be allowed to stand?

#### Questions

1. Does the pay-for-performance plan seem like a good idea? Why or why not?
2. What advice would you give Regina and Sandy as they consider their decision?
3. What mistakes did they make in adopting and communicating the new salary plan? How might Sandy have approached this major compensation change a little differently?
4. Assuming the new pay plan were eventually accepted, how would you address the fact that in the new performance evaluation system, employees' input affects their peers' pay levels?

*Note:* The incident in this case is based on an actual event at Frito-Lay's Kirkwood, New York, plant, as reported in C. James Novak, "Proceed with Caution When Paying Teams," *HR Magazine*, April 1997, p. 73.

#### Application Questions

1. What are some of the challenges related to pay equity that surface in a skill or competency–based pay system? Explain how these challenges should be managed.

2. Employees in your company are questioning the procedural and distributive justice in your compensation system. They claim that the system is not fair.
   a. Discuss the approaches you will take to establish procedural and distributive justice.
   b. How will you assess whether you are effective in establishing procedural and distributive justice?
   c. What courses of action will you take to minimize the probability that employees raise similar concerns in the future?
3. Compare and contrast the following job evaluation methods. Be specific with reference to terminology associated with each method.
   a. Similarities between the point method and the Hay System
   b. Differences between the point method and the job classification system
4. Your compensation committee has calculated graphically the minimum and maximum rates of pay for eight job classes. Four jobs fall below and above the pay boxes. Discuss the courses of action you will take to deal with this situation.
5. Identify and discuss key criteria an organization should take into consideration before broadbanding its pay structure.
6. Bring a copy of a job description to class—either your own or one that is available to you. In teams of three or four colleagues select one job description to analyze following these steps:
   a. Review the job description and identify the compensable factors that should be used to assess the job.
   b. For each compensable factor, define factor degrees and determine factor weights.
   c. Assign point values to factors and degrees.
   d. What are your significant learnings about the job evaluation process?

## RUNNING CASE: LEARNINMOTION.COM

### The New Pay Plan

The case for Chapter 8, The New Pay Plan, illustrates the need to evaluate LearninMotion.com's current wage structure as the company grows. The student is asked to comment on inequities in pay, the setting up of a formal salary structure, and the current pay scale.

To read this case, go to www.pearsoned.ca/myhrlab and click on the *Management of Human Resources*, Third Canadian Edition, In-Class Edition, cover. Click on the case module in Chapter 8.

## CONTROVERSIAL BUSINESS TOPIC EXERCISE

You recently graduated from college and were asked by your parents to join the family business as their human resources coordinator. Your parents diligently worked for the past 30 years to establish and manage a highly successful bakery that has 55 full-time employees in three locations across the city. Your first task is to familiarize yourself with the jobs and wages assigned to each position. As you begin your investigation, you notice that employees with the same job titles and job descriptions are getting significantly different rates of pay. In some cases the rates of pay far exceed the going rate for similar jobs in the region. When you address your concerns to your parents, they get quite angry, stating that several of the employees who are getting paid above the going rate are family members who are in dire need of money during these stressful economic times. They need all the support that the family can give them, and "family should always be treated better than anyone else." How will you handle this situation?

## IN THE BOARDROOM EXERCISE

The debate at the boardroom table is heating up. For the past two hours, the compensation team has been trying to decide which job evaluation method to use to assess the worth of jobs within the company. This is a medium-sized high technology company predominantly filled with IT experts in management and non-management positions and administrative staff that provide support to IT services. You have been called in as an external compensation consultant to help the team reach a decision. How will you exercise your leadership in helping the compensation team decide which job evaluation method to use? Discuss the key criteria the company should consider as they make this decision.

## TOTAL COMPENSATION ON THE INTERNATIONAL STAGE EXERCISE

*The exercise below relates to the Total Compensation on the International Stage feature on p. 276.*

Assume you are the compensation specialist of a large Canadian-based retail giant that is expanding its operations overseas. Select a country in which you would like to expand your business and conduct research to determine the international compensation program that should be put in place.

a. Present your findings in each of the following areas: employment and taxation law, customs, work environments, employment practices, currency, and the effect of inflation on compensation
b. Will you use a going-rate approach or a balance-sheet approach to allocating pay? Explain your answer.
c. Discuss the specific approaches you will use to determine the compensation needs and expectations of employees who are native to the country in which you are interested in establishing your business.
d. Discuss how you will assess the effectiveness of the international compensation system that you develop.

## EXPERIENTIAL EXERCISE

For further study of text materials and development of practical skills, select the experiential exercise module for this chapter on www.pearsoned.ca/myhrlab. This module provides two to three individual or group-based assignments per chapter.

# QUIZ YOURSELF

## STUDY GUIDE QUESTIONS

Circle the correct answer. After completing this self-test, check your answers against the Answers to Study Guide Questions at the back of the book (p. 433).

1. Total rewards refer to all forms of pay or other compensation (direct or indirect) going to employees arising from their employment. Direct pay is in the form of:
   a. work experience
   b. vacations
   c. paid insurance
   d. wages
   e. none of the above
2. Pay is a critical component in total rewards. However, there are number of factors that contribute to determining a pay rate, including which of the following?
   a. *Human Rights Act* and *Pay Equity Act*
   b. compensation policies of the employer
   c. Canada Labour Code
   d. internal and external pay equity
   e. all of the above
3. The Revlex Company did a salary survey, and the results showed that 10 of its key positions had lower wages than similar positions at key competitors. What is the problem faced by the company?
   a. compensation rates
   b. variable pay structure
   c. external inequity
   d. internal inequity
   e. none of the above
4. Determining pay rates is a five-step process. One of the steps in the process requires conducting a salary survey. What is the step that immediately follows this?
   a. job evaluation process
   b. grading of various jobs
   c. pricing pay grades
   d. designing pay grades
   e. fine-tuning pay rates
5. Job evaluation is a formal and systematic comparison of jobs within a firm to determine the worth of one job relative to another and eventually results in a job hierarchy. A company decided to conduct a job evaluation that required it to rank each job relative to all other jobs based on an assessment of overall job difficulty. What is the job evaluation method used by the company?
   a. point method
   b. grading method
   c. ranking method
   d. relative method
   e. factor comparison
6. One of the commonly used job evaluation methods employs the following steps: determine job clusters, collect job information, select and define compensable factors, define factor degrees, determine factor weights, assign points, write job evaluation manual, and rate the

jobs. Which method goes through this process to conduct job evaluation?
a. ranking method
b. grading method
c. classification method
d. point method
e. broadbanding

7. There are a number of methods used for the purpose of job evaluation. The most complex job evaluation method is:
a. point method
b. factor comparison method
c. classification method
d. ranking method
e. grading method

8. Pay equity requires that equal wages be paid for jobs of equal value to the employer as determined by gender-neutral job evaluation techniques. To date, pay equity has been found to reduce the wage gap in Ontario to some extent. To avoid pay equity problems, it is important to:
a. use a job analysis questionnaire
b. regularly update job descriptions
c. regularly review pay systems
d. monitor pay equity legislation
e. all of the above

9. Developing a compensation plan to pay executive, managerial, and professional employees is similar in many respects to developing a plan for other employees. The five elements in a manager's compensation package are:
a. salary, benefits, short-term and long-term incentives, perks
b. salary, benefits, variable pay, incentive plans, perks
c. salary, benefits, ESOP, long-term and short-term incentives, perks
d. salary, benefits, commissions, incentives, perks
e. salary, benefits, short-term and long-term incentives, pension plans

10. Biomedical Inc. is a leading research organization that employs more than 100 top research scientists. The company has plans to collapse its existing salary grades and ranges into just a few wide salary ranges that overlap substantially. This is called:
a. point method
b. salary survey
c. salary pricing method
d. broadbanding
e. none of the above

11. Jane is a production worker at an apparel manufacturer. She cuts 200 pieces of cloth a day that are then used to produce of a garment. She is paid $0.50 for each correctly cut piece. What kind of an incentive plan is Jane paid under?
a. daily incentive plan
b. piecework plan
c. production bonus
d. standard hour plan
e. team incentive plan

12. Most employers award their managers and executives a bonus or incentive because of the role that managers play in determining divisional and corporate profitability. A short-term incentive used to reward managers and executives is:
a. piecework plan
b. annual bonus
c. stock options
d. gainsharing
e. all of the above

13. Sales compensation plans typically rely heavily on incentives (sales commissions), although this varies by industry. Sales commissions, if implemented, can have positive as well as negative outcomes. What is a negative outcome that results from a sales commission plan?
a. easy for people to understand
b. attracting high performers
c. wide variances between people
d. computing is easy
e. sales costs are not fixed

14. Many employers have incentive plans in which virtually all employees can participate. The following are some organization-wide incentive plans that can be used:
a. profit-sharing, gainsharing, ESOPs
b. merit pay, RRSP, ESOPs
c. bonus plans, ESOPs, variable pay
d. gainsharing, piecework, RRSP
e. none of the above

15. There is a growing awareness that demonstrating appreciation of employees' achievements is more important than ever. The number one reason why employees leave an organization is:
a. lack of monetary rewards
b. lack of recognition
c. commission-based incentives
d. fixed pay methods
e. lack of work

# 9 chapter

# Employee Benefits and Services

## Learning Objectives

1. Articulate the strategic role of employee benefits.
2. Identify and explain legally required benefits.
3. Identify and explain voluntary company-sponsored benefits.
4. Discuss trends in employee services.
5. Critique flexible benefits programs.
6. Describe the benefits administration process.

## Test Yourself

1. What types of benefits are legally required in Canada?
2. What types of employee benefits do employers often voluntarily sponsor?
3. What are key legal and policy issues that need to be considered when developing pension plans?
4. What types of employee services are offered by organizations?
5. What are the advantages and disadvantages of flexible benefit programs?

## 9.1 THE STRATEGIC ROLE OF EMPLOYEE BENEFITS

**Employee benefits** and services can be defined as all of the indirect financial payments that an employee receives during his or her employment with an employer.[1] Employee benefits and services are an important part of most employees' compensation, but they have a different strategic purpose today from that in the last century. Employers traditionally used benefits to seek out and reward loyalty and tenure.[2] Employee services, formerly a minor aspect of compensation, are becoming more sought after by today's employees in the post–job-security era. Research indicates that benefits do matter to employees and that if benefits are aligned with business strategy, they can help attract and retain the right people to achieve business objectives.[3] For example, TD Bank Financial Group introduced health and family-friendly benefits that were well received by employees, as described in the Strategic HR box on page 284.

Benefits are generally available to all of an organization's employees and include such things as time off with pay, supplementary health and life insurances, and employee assistance plans. There may be some differences in the benefits offered to different pay groups in an organization. For example, hourly workers may not get the same amount of time off with pay, and their insurance benefits may be lower. On the other hand, executives may be offered a more lavish benefit package than salaried workers.

**RPC 9-1 >**

**Performs a cost-benefit analysis of organizational and employee needs and preferences relative to benefit plans, including taxation considerations and funding requirements**

Employee benefits are an important part of most employees' compensation, particularly given today's reality of modest salary increases.[4] For the aging workforce, health-care benefits are becoming increasingly important.[5] Employee benefits are in the midst of an evolution based on the aging population, the looming labour shortage in Canada, and advances in health care. Each of these factors is expected to increase the cost of benefits, which is already at an all-time high.[6]

Administering benefits today represents an increasingly specialized task because workers are more financially sophisticated and demanding and because benefit plans must comply with a wide variety of laws. Benefits as a percentage of payroll (for public and private sectors combined) are about 37 percent today (compared with about 15 percent in 1953). This translates to around $17 500 in total annual benefits per employee.[7] Industries with the highest benefit costs are the food, beverage, and tobacco industry (27.9 percent), and transportation and utilities (27.3 percent).[8]

Most employees do not realize the market value and high cost to the employer of their benefits, so prudent employers list the benefits' true costs on each employee's pay stub.

### *In-class Notes*

**The Strategic Role of Employee Benefits**

- Employee benefits are indirect financial payments received by an employee during his or her employment
- Traditionally rewarded loyalty; now to attract and retain
- Benefits average 37 percent of pay

## STRATEGIC HR

# TD Takes Family-Friendly Benefits to the Bank

Every year, TD Bank Financial Group asks employees to name two tangible things they would like to see improved within the company. Typically, the Toronto-based bank receives about 20 000 suggestions. Two consistent themes from that survey—more flexible work hours and improved benefits—have translated into successful policies that have earned TD Bank an exceptional rating in the area of health and family-friendly benefits.

"That's all part of our strategy to make sure we are viewed by our employees as a great place to work," says Peter McAdam, vice-president of consumer experience. "This ties back to our efforts to make sure we have the most engaged workforce out there."

Over the past few years, TD Bank has simplified its benefit plan while increasing its subsidy by $12 million annually. Every employee gets 100-percent coverage for basic life, health and medical insurance. They're also given credits to help with optional coverage for additional benefits. That subsidy is based on the number of dependants.

"Part of our philosophy is that they have an opportunity to create a personal benefits package that meets their needs throughout their entire life cycle while they work at TD," says Sherry Thodt, vice-president of retirement and benefit plans. "They pick and choose across a menu but when we deliver those benefit credits to them, we make it very clear and transparent how much we're providing to help them buy those additional benefits."

In addition, employees who work 15 hours a week receive health coverage, as do retirees with enough service. Employees can also register for pre-arranged emergency short-term daycare in cities where the service is available.

There's a strong business case for providing such extensive benefits, in terms of employee engagement, says McAdam. It's an argument the executive team not only understands but supports, especially since surveys show a measurable improvement in engagement over the past couple of years.

"They bought right in," he says. "We're fortunate that we have a senior executive who, besides understanding the business case, also feels very strongly that this is the right thing to do for our employees. We hope this is a bit of a virtuous circle. If the employees feel better, then it just looks after itself. So far, we've managed to afford all of this and still have great returns to shareholders."

HR doesn't necessarily go looking for new money every time it has a recommendation, says McAdam. Most often, these have to be budgeted into existing expense plans and HR has to either cut somewhere else or "just expect that the other revenues will keep rolling in." That may be more difficult in the days ahead, given the current economy, he admits.

Even in good times, increasing benefit subsidies and flexibility in the workplace is "never a slam dunk," says Thodt. Decisions have always been made after lengthy discussions with the entire senior management team, she says. Sometimes there is a "staging" of the delivery of the HR department's recommendations.

"The reality is that there's always lots of ways to spend money and there's never unlimited funds," she says. "We can't do everything all at once and it's not a matter of 'No, you can't do that.' It's about 'Let's do this one this year and then lay out that action B and action C for the years after.'"

Within the senior HR team, there has been a lot of debate about budgets as well as capacity, says Thodt. How much change can the bank and its people make at one time?

Fortunately, most of the team's initiatives have gone over well with senior executives, she says. This speaks to how well the bank listens to its employees.

"We're not going forward with things that are not aligned with them," she says.

One of the biggest changes to the benefits plan—that had the unequivocal support of senior leaders—was simplifying the language and design, says Thodt.

"Make the program and policies as simple as possible. The easier to understand the programs are, the more employees will value them," she says. "If a program is too complex, I don't think you reach the perceived value that really the program is worth to your employee group."

Flexibility is another area where TD Bank has performed well. The bank has opened up more opportunities for flexible hours, part-time work, shortened workweeks and telecommuting, says McAdam.

The challenge now is achieving consistency across the bank's vast network of locations, he says. It has more than 42 000 full- and part-time employees worldwide.

"It's not a tough sell to get the policy created and get senior management to buy in. They've been good at that," he says. "It's a challenge across an organization that has thousands of offices."

Source: Adapted from D. Harder. "TD takes family-friendly benefits to the bank," *Canadian HR Reporter,* February 23, 2009, p. 20. Reprinted with permission.

**RPC 9-2 >**

**Ensures compliance with legally required programs**

## 9.2 LEGALLY REQUIRED BENEFITS

Canada has one of the world's finest collections of social programs to protect its citizens when they are unable to earn an income. The following are the legally required, mandatory benefits an employer must provide.

### Employment Insurance (EI)

**Employment Insurance** is a federal program that provides weekly benefits to those who are unable to work through no fault of their own. It does not apply to workers who are self-employed, who represent 30 percent of the Canadian population. EI provides benefits for employees who are laid off, terminated without just cause, or quit their job for a justifiable reason such as harassment. EI benefits are not payable when an employee is terminated for just cause—for example, for theft of company property—or when an employee quits for no good reason. Workers may also be eligible for special EI benefits in cases of illness, injury, or quarantine when the employer has no sickness or disability benefits (or once such benefits have been exhausted), for maternity/parental leaves, and for compassionate-care leave when a relative is dying.[9] Canadians who are on EI can access retraining to help them get back into the workforce.

**RPC 9-3 >**

**Establishes sound operational practices to ensure confidentiality of employee information and compliance with regulatory requirements**

In order to receive benefits, an employee must first have worked a minimum number of hours during a minimum number of weeks, called a qualifying period (the number of hours and weeks varies from 420 to 700 hours per year depending on where you live). Then there is a waiting period from the last day of work until benefits begin. The waiting period varies but is often two weeks. If the employee was provided with severance pay or holiday pay at the time of losing the job, these payments must run out before the waiting period begins.

The EI benefit is generally 55 percent of average earnings during the last 20 weeks of the qualifying period. The benefit is payable for up to 45 weeks, depending on the regional unemployment rate and other factors. Illness benefits are payable for up to 15 weeks, and maternity/parental leave benefits are payable for up to 50 weeks.

However, studies have found that EI benefits in Canada are below the Organization for Economic Co-operation and Development (OECD) average. EI in Canada falls below other OECD countries in terms of access to benefits and the length of time benefits are available. It is anticipated that benefits for current EI recipients will be extinguished around February 2010, when the OECD estimates that unemployment will be substantially higher than current rates. The Canadian Centre for Policy Alternatives (CCPA) recommends eligibility requirements be relaxed and a second tier of unemployment benefits be established for people who are unemployed for long durations.[10]

Through EI, there is a work-share program to help employers avert layoffs. Under the work-share program, employees and the employer mutually agree to a reduced work week instead of layoffs and EI is paid to employees for the hours they no longer work. The work-share agreement lasts for 26 weeks, with the possibility of a 12-week extension that can be further extended by 14 weeks if deemed necessary. The mandate is to keep people working during difficult economic times. The program is estimated to cost $200 million over two years.[11]

The EI program is funded by contributions from eligible employees and their employers. Employee contributions are collected by payroll deduction, and employers pay 1.4 times the employee contribution. Employer contributions can be reduced if the employer provides a wage-loss replacement plan for employee sick leave.

**employee benefits** Indirect financial payments given to employees. They may include supplementary health and life insurance, vacation, pension, education plans, and discounts on company products.

**Employment Insurance** A federal program that provides income benefits if a person is unable to work through no fault of his or her own.

## Canada/Quebec Pension Plan (C/QPP)

The **C/QPP plans** were introduced in 1966 to provide working Canadians with a basic level of financial security upon retirement or disability. Over 30 years later, these benefits do, indeed, provide a significant part of most Canadians' retirement income. Almost all employed Canadians between the ages of 18 and 65 are covered, including self-employed individuals. Casual and migrant workers are excluded, as are people who are not earning any employment income, such as homemakers.

Employers and employees each make contributions of 4.95 percent of pay. Both contributions and benefits are based only on earnings up to the "Year's Maximum Pensionable Earnings" (intended to approximate the average industrial wage) as defined in the legislation. Benefits are adjusted based on inflation each year in line with the consumer price index and are not affected by job changes. However, the CPP is on shaky ground as it fell prey to the market crash in 2008, in which it lost more than $10 billion. The loss is expected to have a deep impact on Canadians and their retirement plans.[12]

Three types of benefits are provided: retirement pensions, disability benefits, and survivor benefits:

1. *Retirement pension* is calculated as 25 percent of the average earnings (adjusted for inflation up to the average inflation level during the last five years prior to retirement) over the years during which contributions were made. Plan members can choose to begin receiving benefits at any time between the ages of 60 and 70. Benefits are reduced upon early retirement before age 65 and are increased in the case of late retirement after age 65.
2. *Disability benefits* are only paid for severe disabilities that are expected to be permanent or to last for an extended period of time. The disability benefit is 75 percent of the pension benefit earned at the date of disability plus a flat-rate amount per child.
3. *Survivor benefits* are paid upon the death of a plan member. A lump sum payment is made to survivors and a monthly pension is also payable to the surviving spouse.

## Workers' Compensation

**Workers' compensation** laws are aimed at providing income and medical benefits to victims of work-related accidents or illnesses and/or their dependants, regardless of fault. Every province and territory and the federal jurisdiction has its own workers' compensation law. These laws impose compulsory collective liability for workplace accidents and work-related illnesses. This means that employees and employers cannot sue each other regarding the costs of workplace accidents or illnesses. Workers' compensation is, in effect, a "no fault" insurance plan designed to help injured or ill workers get well and return to work. For an injury or illness to be covered by workers' compensation, it must be proven that it arose while the employee was on the job. It does not matter that the employee may have been at fault; if he or she was on the job when the injury or illness occurred, he or she is entitled to workers' compensation. For example, suppose all employees are instructed to wear safety goggles when working at their machines and someone does not and is injured. Workers' compensation benefits will still be provided. The fact that the worker was at fault in no way waives his or her claim to benefits.

Employers collectively pay the full cost of the workers' compensation system, which can be an onerous financial burden for small businesses. The amount of the premiums (called assessments) varies by industry and by actual employer costs. Employer premiums are tax-deductible. Workers' Compensation Boards (e.g., the Workplace Safety and Insurance Board in Ontario) exist in each jurisdiction to determine and collect assessments from employers, determine rights to compensation, and pay workers the amount of benefit to which they are entitled under the legislation in their jurisdiction. Employers and employees have some representation on

Although safety gear is always recommended, failure to wear it does not invalidate an employee's claim for benefits under workers' compensation laws.

these boards, but usually both parties believe they should have more control.

Workers' compensation benefits are non-taxable and include payment of expenses for medical treatment and rehabilitation, and income benefits during the period of time in which the worker is unable to work (temporarily or permanently) due to his or her disability (partial or total). Survivor benefits are payable if a work-related death occurs. A recent study found that 45 percent of injured workers are not receiving any benefits from the Workers' Compensation Board and injured workers are four times more likely to live in poverty and utilize food banks. Many people with permanent disabilities fall by the wayside in the workers' compensation system and end up on social assistance. The study also uncovered that injured workers suffer from high rates of depression.[13]

**CONTROLLING WORKERS' COMPENSATION COSTS** In most provinces, workers' compensation costs continue to skyrocket. According to Ontario's Workplace Safety and Insurance Board (WSIB), total benefits paid escalated from $2.91 billion in 2005 to $2.98 billion in 2006. Total benefits include loss of earnings, health care, and labour market re-entry benefits.[14] Recently, a number of provinces amended their workers' compensation legislation to reduce benefit levels, limit benefit entitlements for stress-related illnesses and chronic pain, reduce inflation indexing of benefits, and put more emphasis on rehabilitation and returning to work.

All parties agree that a renewed focus on accident prevention is the best way to manage workers' compensation costs over the long term. Minimizing the number of workers' compensation claims is an important goal for all employers. While the Workers' Compensation Board pays the claims, the premiums for most employers depend on the number and amount of claims that are paid. Minimizing such claims is thus important.

In practice, there are two main approaches to reducing workers' compensation claims. First, organizations try to reduce accident- or illness-causing conditions in facilities by instituting effective safety and health programs and complying with government safety standards. Second, since workers' compensation costs increase the longer an employee is unable to return to work, employers have become involved in instituting rehabilitation programs for injured or ill employees. These include physical therapy programs and career counselling to guide such employees into new, less strenuous or less stressful jobs to reintegrate the recipients back into the workforce. Workers are required to cooperate with return-to-work initiatives, such as modified work.[15]

## Provincial Health-Care Plans

All provinces and territories sponsor **provincial health-care plans** that provide basic medical and hospital services with no direct fee to patients. The provinces of British Columbia and Alberta finance their health-care plans by requiring monthly premiums to be paid by each resident. Employers may subsidize these premiums. Ontario requires each taxpayer to pay an annual premium. Quebec, Manitoba, and Newfoundland levy a payroll tax to partially fund the cost of their health-care plans. Saskatchewan, Prince Edward Island, New Brunswick, Nova Scotia, the Northwest Territories, Nunavut, and the Yukon Territory use general tax revenues to pay for their plans.

The services paid for by these plans include medically required procedures provided by physicians, nurses, and other health-care professionals; standard ward hospital accommodation; drugs and medication administered in hospitals; laboratory and diagnostic procedures; and hospital facilities, such as operating rooms. Some of the services that are not covered by the provincial plans are prescription drugs, dental care, eyeglasses, private-duty nursing, cosmetic surgery, and semi-private or private hospital accommodation.

**C/QPP plans** Programs that provide three types of benefits: retirement income; survivor or death benefits payable to the employee's dependants regardless of age at time of death; and disability benefits payable to disabled employees and their dependants. Benefits are payable only to those individuals who make contributions to the plans and/or their family members.

**workers' compensation** Workers' compensation provides income and medical benefits to victims of work-related accidents or illnesses and/or their dependants regardless of fault.

**provincial health-care plans** Provincial health-care plans pay for basic medically required hospital and medical services with no direct fee to patients.

Canadian Pension and Benefits Institute
**www.cpbi-icra.ca**

Canada's Income Security Programs
**www.hrsdc.gc.ca/eng/oas-cpp/index.shtml**

Canada Pension Plan
**www.sdc.gc.ca/en/isp/cpp/cpptoc.shtml**

## Vacations and Holidays

Labour/employment standards legislation sets out a minimum amount of paid vacation that must be provided to employees, usually two weeks per year, but the requirements vary by jurisdiction. The actual number of paid employee vacation days also varies considerably from employer to employer. Even within the same organization, the number of vacation days usually depends on how long the employee has worked at the firm. For example, the Association of Management, Administrative and Professional Crown Employees of Ontario, a province-wide public sector bargaining agent, grants employees four weeks' vacation after one year of service and closes the office early before weekends in the summer. The Alberta-Pacific Forest Industries, a producer of kraft pulp used to manufacture paper products, gives employees 12 personal days off per year in addition to vacation time.[16]

The number of paid holidays similarly varies considerably from one jurisdiction to another from a minimum of five to a maximum of nine. The most common paid holidays include New Year's Day, Good Friday, Canada Day, Labour Day, Thanksgiving Day, and Christmas Day. Other common holidays include Victoria Day, Remembrance Day, and Boxing Day. Additional holidays may be observed in each province, such as Saint Jean-Baptiste Day in Quebec and Family Day in Alberta and Ontario.

## Leaves of Absence

All jurisdictions require unpaid leaves of absence to be provided to employees in certain circumstances. Maternity/pregnancy leave is provided in every jurisdiction and each has one or more of paternity, parental, and adoption leave available as well. The amount of maternity leave is 17 or 18 weeks in each jurisdiction (usually after one year of service), but parental and adoption leaves range from 8 to 52 weeks. At Simon Fraser University in British Columbia—ranked one of the top employers in Canada—new mothers, fathers, and adoptive parents are offered parental leave top-up payments that run to 100 percent for 37 weeks.[17] Carswell, a Thomson Reuters publisher for legal, academic, and financial communities, offers adoptive parents $5000 in assistance per child.[18] Employees who take these leaves of absence are guaranteed their old job or a similar job when they return to work.

## Compassionate Care Leave

In 2004, the federal government introduced the compassionate care benefit, through the EI program, so full-time employees would no longer feel that they would lose their jobs if they took time to care for a dying relative. The benefit protects an employee's job and pays 55 percent of the employee's earnings up to $414 a week for up to eight weeks. The Canadian Policy Research Networks argue that eight weeks is insufficient time for compassionate care and excludes many women who are unemployed, self-employed, or work part time. Some companies have exercised their own discretion for top-up payments in this area. For example, Carswell offers compassionate leave top-ups to 95 percent of salary for eight weeks.[19]

Bereavement leave upon the death of a family member is provided for employees in some but not all jurisdictions. The amount of time off varies by jurisdiction and depends on the closeness of the relationship between the employee and the deceased.

## Pay on Termination of Employment

Employment/labour standards legislation requires that employees whose employment is being terminated by the employer be provided with termination pay when they leave. In most cases, this is pay for time not worked. The amount to be paid varies between jurisdictions and with circumstances as follows:

**PAY IN LIEU OF NOTICE** An employee must be provided with advance written notice if the employer is going to terminate his or her employment (unless the employee is working on a short-term contract or is being fired for just cause). Many employers do not provide advance written notice. Instead, they ask the employee to cease working immediately and provide the employee with a lump sum equal to their pay for the notice period. This amount is called "pay in lieu of notice."

**SEVERANCE PAY** Some employers offer severance pay to employees who are terminated as a way to reduce the sting of being told to leave and to avoid lawsuits by having employees sign releases in exchange for the severance. A recent study found that 51 percent of companies offered one to two weeks of pay for every year of service with the company and 33 percent calculate payouts based on years of service, current salary level, and salary grade. In addition to cash payouts, most companies provide at least one benefit, such as health care

## In-class Notes

**Legally Required Benefits**

- Employment Insurance (EI) provides income for those unable to work
- Canada/Quebec Pension Plan (C/QPP) provides retirement benefits to formerly employed workers
- Workers' compensation provides income and health benefits to workers suffering work-related illness or injury regardless of fault
- Provincial health-care plans provide basic medical and hospital services with no direct fee
- Vacations and holidays—minimum amounts legislated
- Leaves of absence—unpaid parental/adoption, bereavement, sick leave
- Pay on termination of employment—pay in lieu of notice; severance pay; pay for mass layoffs

coverage, retirement benefits, outplacement services, references, waiving of loans, or disability insurance.[20]

**PAY FOR MASS LAYOFFS** The provinces of British Columbia, Manitoba, Ontario, New Brunswick, and Newfoundland require that additional pay be provided when a layoff of 50 or more employees occurs. In Nova Scotia and Saskatchewan, additional pay is required if 10 or more employees are being laid off.

## 9.3 VOLUNTARY COMPANY-SPONSORED BENEFITS

Many employers provide employee benefits that are not legally required. These include additional pay for time not worked over and above that legally required, insurance benefits, and retirement benefits. A sample of the type of employee provided benefits offered by some of Canada's top 100 employers appears in the Strategic HR box on page 290.

### Pay for Time Not Worked

**Pay for time not worked** is typically one of an employer's most expensive benefits because of the large amount of time off that many employees receive. It is a substantial part of almost every employer's payroll expense. Common examples of voluntarily provided paid time off include paid short-term disability/sick leave, additional vacations and holidays, and paid leaves of absence.

**Short-term disability plans** (also known as salary continuation plans) provide a continuation of all or part of an employee's earnings when the employee is absent from work due to non–work-related illness or injury. Usually, a medical certificate is required if the

**pay for time not worked** Benefits for time not worked, such as vacation and holiday pay and sick pay.

**short-term disability/sick leave plans** Plans that provide pay to an employee when he or she is unable to work because of a non–work-related illness or injury.

STRATEGIC HR

## Top Benefits Go Beyond Financials: Generous Top-Ups, Ample Vacation, Health-Care Options, Tuition Subsidies and Flexibility All Must-Haves for Canada's Top 100 Employers

Time off has been a big focus at AltaGas in the past year. The Calgary-based energy company changed its vacation policy for the third time in eight years and reduced its workday from eight hours to 7.5. It also gives employees eight "corporate" days off and workers enjoy provincial statutory holidays from outside their jurisdiction.

"We tried to listen to employees in terms of what's important and certainly time off stood out," says Kent Stout, vice-president of corporate resources at AltaGas. "Time off, quality of life, work-life balance are the issues we're taking to centre stage. And fun, we're trying to inject that as well."

AltaGas's range of generous benefits is typical of employers on Canada's Top 100 Employers list, published by Mediacorp Canada. To join the prestigious clan, organizations typically provide ample vacation, maternity leave top-ups, retirement savings options, bonuses, tuition subsidies and health benefits, along with fitness incentives and flexible work arrangements.

AltaGas evolves its benefits every year and tries to incorporate findings from annual employee surveys while balancing those desires with the resources of the company, says Stout.

"We have a highly competitive, challenging labour market in Calgary, particularly in the industry we operate in, so there's lots of competition out there, lots of big oil and gas producers that have very attractive compensation packages, including benefits, so somehow—we're not that large—we have to distinguish ourselves and attract and retain employees."

AltaGas offers three weeks' vacation to new employees but decided to steer away from flex days and instead offers five pre-designated corporate days aligned with long weekends, so employees can take a four-day break. Three other corporate days are given at Christmas, usually making for a 10-day break.

"Employees really like it because they don't have to feel guilty, worrying about others working, because the office shuts down, so they can relax more," says Stout.

Employees also enjoy quarterly events, contingent on financial success, that include scavenger hunts, cross-country skiing or dinners, with prizes such as WestJet gift certificates.

On the financial side, the 357-employee company provides signing bonuses, year-end bonuses up to $57 400, a share-purchase plan, a pension plan with employer contributions up to six percent, life and disability insurance and discounts on home computers.

AltaGas also pays 100 percent of health premiums and employees receive full family coverage. Family-friendly benefits include maternity leave top-up to 100 percent of salary for six weeks, emergency short-term daycare and compassionate top-up payment to 100 percent for one week.

"It's a very competitive marketplace but we seem to be attracting good quality employees," he says.

**Healthy options, generous leaves at Bayer**

Compensation is not the highest priority at Bayer. Instead, the Toronto-based pharmaceutical company focuses on the needs of its 963 employees by offering a range of benefits.

"We're not trying to be the top payer, trying to be competitive, because we believe when employees look at all the offerings we have, it's a very compelling package compared to the competitor," says Gord Johnston, vice-president of HR at Bayer.

Employee surveys prompted the launch of a Life at Work program to meet the physical and emotional needs of employees, with benefits such as healthy food options, fitness classes and a conservation area.

In addition to a health-care spending account, employees can contribute to a savings plan that is partly matched by the company. They can then transfer a portion of the match into the health-care spending account on a tax-free basis.

"We're finding people want that flexibility, they like the health-care spending account concept because they can transfer dollars in tax-free for larger purchases not covered by the plan, such as laser-eye surgery," he says, adding Bayer is considering the same option for the company bonus.

Employees can enjoy summer hours if they put in extra hours and Bayer now gives four weeks of vacation to managers instead of three, which other employees receive to start, along with four weeks at five years and five weeks at 10 years, depending on grade level.

The thresholds could change again, says Johnston.

"We could easily provide that to employees with no cost," he says. "It's not causing any recruitment issues, any internal issues, so it's the right balance for now."

When it comes to more traditional benefits, changes are made based on "basically what our competitors are doing, what the U.S. organization is doing and looking at our own demographics and what we think might be a value-added benefit," he says.

The company has a closed defined benefit pension plan and a defined contribution plan to which it contributes based on grade level. There is also a stock purchase plan matched by Bayer.

The employer provides up to $7000 in tuition subsidies for unrelated courses every year. And employee referrals have increased, from $1000 to $3000, with Bayer gaining about one-quarter of its hires this way, says Johnston.

The company pays 95 percent of health-care premiums and the plan is flexible. Employees receive full family coverage and there is retiree coverage with no age limit. Employees also receive discounted health-care products through an on-site store.

Bayer also provides a compassionate top-up payment of 100 percent of salary for eight weeks. Top-ups for maternity leave, paternity leave and adoptive leave are 100 percent for six weeks and are currently under review, says Johnston. (But if there is an increase, Bayer may introduce some kind of payback if an employee leaves shortly after returning from a leave, for retention value.)

While being a Top 100 employer has paid off in terms of attracting potential employees, he says, making the list isn't the only factor guiding the company's benefit decisions. "At the end of the day, it's got to make business sense to change those areas and the culture of the company."

**Ramped-up recognition at MUHC**

As part of Quebec's public health-care system, McGill University Health Centre's (MUHC) benefits are subject to collective agreements negotiated provincially. But two years ago the law changed, allowing employers to negotiate non-monetary clauses, so the Top 100 employer is focusing on areas such as vacation and access to promotions, says Vincent Altomonte, associate director of HR operations at the Montreal-based centre.

An academic health institution made up of five hospitals, MUHC recently raised vacation for managers from five weeks to six after five years, while other employees already have four weeks of vacation after their first year. The change was prompted by employee surveys, he says.

"Managers put in a lot of extra time, working weekends, evenings, so we were trying to find a way to compensate them and since we couldn't modify the pay scales, we had latitude to move the vacation package."

That approach applies to the development of most of the benefits at the 5467-employee centre, he says.

"We're trying to work on the non-monetary and put a lot of energy into recognition packages and accommodating flexible time, working within our boundaries to see how to accommodate employee needs, be they for family obligations or whatever."

The centre has introduced on-the-spot rewards and online nominations by coworkers and the milestones for service awards were reduced from 20, 25 and 30 years to five, 10 and 15 years.

Top-ups are 93 percent for 21 weeks for maternity leave, 100 percent for one week for paternity leave and 100 percent for 10 weeks for adoptive leave. There is also a generous compassionate leave that has been modified as many workers come from overseas.

"We rearranged leaves to try to meet the needs of our staff," says Altomonte.

MUHC also tries to accommodate the particular needs of nurses by offering a mix of traditional hours with compressed workweeks.

"This permits younger nurses and professionals coming in to buddy-up with employees who have tenure and more experience, versus other institutions where the shifts are fixed, where senior staff work days and junior people work evenings, nights and weekends. New staff really appreciate that," he says.

Just recently, the centre asked employees to come up with recommendations that could help the environment. One project involves the collection of batteries commonly used in pagers. There are also events, such as Christmas parties, a Halloween party for kids and departmental retreats. And the centre has improved its discount partnership with different corporations, such as the Montreal Ballet and the Brick.

The range of benefits has helped put MUHC on the Top 100 list but "the pressure's on to be on again and our aim definitely is to stay on it next year," says Altomonte.

Source: S. Dobson. "Top benefits go beyond financials: Generous top-ups, ample vacation, health-care options, tuition subsidies and flexibility all must-haves for Canada's Top 100 Employers." *Canadian HR Reporter,* September 8, 2008, pp. 15–16. Reprinted with permission.

absence extends beyond two or three days. These plans typically provide full pay for some period of time (often two or three weeks) and then gradually reduce the percentage of earnings paid as the period of absence lengthens. The benefits cease when the employee returns to work or when the employee qualifies for long-term disability. Short-term disability plans may be self-insured by the company or provided through an insurance company. Casual absences and short- and long-term disability cost employers $30 million in direct and indirect costs.[21]

**Sick leave plans** operate quite differently from short-term disability plans. Most sick leave policies grant full pay for a specified number of permissible sick days—usually up to about 12 per year (often accumulated at the rate of one day per month of service). Some jurisdictions require sick leave, as discussed above. Sick leave pay creates difficulty for many employers. The problem is that while many employees use their sick days only when they are legitimately sick, others simply utilize their sick leave as extensions to their vacations whether they are ill or not. Also, seriously ill or injured employees get no pay once their sick days are used up.

Employers have tried several tactics to eliminate or reduce this problem. Some now buy back unused sick leave at the end of the year by paying their employees a daily equivalent pay for each sick leave day not used. The drawback is that the policy can encourage legitimately ill employees to come to work despite their illness.[22]

**Presenteeism**, whereby employees report for work even though they are ill or exhausted, is a growing epidemic in the workplace. Approximately 80 percent of Canadians claim they have gone to work ill or exhausted to avoid getting behind in their work, meet pressing deadlines, and avoid burdening their colleagues. The central reason why employees go to work when not healthy is because missing work is frowned upon by their employer. Working when ill can result in errors, difficulty making decisions, irritability when working with others, an increased probability of accidents, and spreading illness.[23]

**ADDITIONAL PAID VACATIONS AND HOLIDAYS** Many employers provide additional paid holidays and paid vacation over and above the amount required by law. For example, long-service employees typically receive more vacation time than legally required.

**LEAVES OF ABSENCE** Some employers provide full or partial pay for all or part of legally required unpaid leaves. While not legally required to do so, some employers may choose to "top up" what employees receive from EI so that the total amount they receive more closely matches their regular salary. For example, in some cases, bereavement leave may be partially or fully paid by the employer.

Sabbatical leaves are becoming more common as a trend to retain employees, allow employees to pursue other life-fulfilling initiatives, and avoid employee burnout, particularly for employees struggling with work–life balance. Of the Canadian companies that offer sabbaticals, 50 percent are unpaid leaves and 13 percent are paid.[24] Sun Media Corp., McDonald's Restaurants of Canada Ltd., and HSBC championed the introduction of sabbaticals in Canadian organizations. Sabbaticals at HSBC consist of a six-month to one-year leave for employees with at least 10 years of service.[25] To ensure consistency and fair treatment, having clear policies and procedures for any leave of absence is essential. An application form, such as the one in Figure 9.1, should be part of any such procedure. In general, no employee should be given leave until it is clear what the leave is for. If the leave is for medical or family reasons, medical certification should be obtained from the attending physician or medical practitioner. A form like this also places the employee's expected return date on record, along with the fact that without an authorized extension, his or her employment may be terminated.

While many leaves are unpaid, it is incorrect to assume that the leave costs nothing to the employer. Even if the employer does not pay for the leave, one study concluded that the costs associated with recruiting new temporary-replacement workers, training replacement workers, and compensating for the lower level of productivity of these workers could represent a substantial expense over and above what employers would normally pay their full-time employees.[26]

## Insurance Benefits

The three standard insured benefits provided by most employers are group life insurance, supplementary health-care/medical insurance, and long-term disability insurance.

**GROUP LIFE INSURANCE** Virtually all employers provide **group life insurance plans** for their employees. As a group, employees can obtain lower rates than if they bought such insurance as individuals. In addition, group plans usually contain a provision for coverage of all employees, normally after a probationary period, regardless of health or physical condition.

*figure* 9.1 **Sample Application for Leave of Absence**

## APPLICATION FOR LEAVE OF ABSENCE WITHOUT PAY (OR PARTIAL PAY)

*The information on this form is collected under the authority of the Collective Agreements between the College and its bargaining units. The information provided will be used to process your leave. If you have any questions about the collection and use of this information, please contact HR.*

| | | | |
|---|---|---|---|
| | *SURNAME* | *FIRST NAME* | *INITIAL* |
| ***I.D. #*** | | | |

☐ **KEC** ☐ **CC** ☐ **IE CENTRE** ☐ **OTHER**__________________

***DEPARTMENT:***

☐ Support Staff (CUPE) ☐ Faculty (VCCFA)
☐ Administrators

**REASON FOR REQUEST:**

| **FOR ALL EMPLOYEE GROUPS** | **ADDITIONAL LEAVES FOR FACULTY ONLY** |
|---|---|
| ☐ **PERSONAL** @________% <br> ☐ **EDUCATION** @________% (NOTE: Faculty will be paid at 70% of salary and allowances) <br> ☐ **ILLNESS** *(Exhaustion of Sick Leave Credits)*__________ **First Date of Absence** <br> ☐ **MATERNITY** *(Please attach Doctor's note indicating Expected Date of Confinement)* <br> ☐ **PARENTAL** <br> ☐ **ADOPTION OF CHILD** *(Please attach proof of legal adoption)* <br> ☐ **OTHER**________________*(Please specify)* | ☐ **RENEWAL** <br> ☐ **RETIREMENT PREPARATION** @________% |

**PERIOD OF LEAVE REQUESTED *(Includes Weekends)*:**

| ***FROM (First Calendar Day of Leave):*** | ***TO (Last Calendar Day of Leave):*** |
|---|---|
| Day Month Year | Day Month Year |

**IF PERIOD OF LEAVE REQUESTED IS 15 (FIFTEEN) CALENDAR DAYS OR LESS, COMPLETE THIS SECTION:**

**Number of Duty Days on Leave:** ______________
**Total Number of Hours on Leave:** ______________
**Working under Compressed Work Week Schedule:** ☐ **Yes** ☐ **No**
**If Leave is One Duty Day or Less, Indicate Hours of Leave:** ______________
**For Faculty Members:**
This unpaid Leave of Absence will not count as *"duty days"* for the purpose of regularization of appointment nor for the purpose of time-status increase.

| | | | |
|---|---|---|---|
| ***EMPLOYEE'S SIGNATURE:*** | | ***DATE:*** | |
| ***APPROVAL-Supervisor/Department Head:*** | | ***DATE:*** | |
| ***APPROVAL-CUPE–Human Resources:*** <br> ***-VCCFA–Dean/Director:*** | | ***DATE:*** | |

***THIS SECTION FOR PAYROLL USE:***

***COMPLETED "ORIGINAL" FORM TO BE FORWARDED TO HUMAN RESOURCES FOR PROCESSING.***
***DEANS: Before submitting to HR, please take a copy for your file and a copy to give to the Dept. Head.***

J:\COMMON\FORMS\Human Resources Forms\College-wide\Leave-of-Absence-Without-Pay-Form.doc. June 8, 2005
CC: Personnel File

Source: Human Resources Department, Vancouver Community College. 

In most cases, the employer pays 100 percent of the base premium, which can provide life insurance equal to one, two, or even three years' salary. Additional life insurance coverage is sometimes made available to employees on an optional, employee-paid basis. *Accidental death and dismemberment* coverage provides a fixed lump-sum benefit in addition to life insurance benefits when death is accidental. It also provides a range of benefits in case of accidental loss of limbs or sight and is often paid for by the employer. *Critical illness insurance* provides a lump-sum benefit to an employee who is diagnosed with and/or survives a life-threatening illness. As discussed in the Workforce Diversity box below, this new benefit is one of several that will be of strategic importance in attracting and retaining older workers as the labour supply tightens over the next two decades.

## WORKFORCE DIVERSITY

### Employers Ill-Prepared to Woo Mature Workers: Organizations Should Be Targeting Workers over Age 50, Finds Conference Board Report

While many employers are anxious about a shrinking workforce, they're not doing enough to woo the one segment of workers who could really help them: those over the age of 50.

That's the conclusion from a report by the Conference Board of Canada, *Harnessing the Power: Recruiting, Engaging and Retaining Mature Workers,* that looked at 109 mid- to large-sized organizations across the country.

It found few of them, just 6 percent, focus on retaining mature workers, while 11 percent actively try to attract or recruit them.

"I'm not surprised at all," said Prem Benimadhu, vice-president of governance and HR management with the Conference Board. "There is always a time lag between awareness and execution."

Two things generally hold employers back—the "full-plate" syndrome and the likelihood a labour shortage will eventually be someone else's problem, said Benimadhu. Few executives have time to develop demographic-specific hiring strategies, which ultimately leads them to ignore the issue until it reaches a crisis.

Added to that is a "negative retirement mentality" on the part of both employers and the mature workers themselves, he said.

"Most of our human resources policies and practices were fashioned in the 1970s at a time when there was a labour surplus," he said. "We wanted people to take early retirement. That is something that has created a mindset among leaders in organizations and among mature workers themselves. We've had 10, 20 years of brainwashing to believe that after 50 they should start leaving the organization."

Almost one-half (47 percent) of employers surveyed consider the aging of the workforce to be an "important or critical issue" within the next 18 months, he said. That concern increases to 77 percent when looking ahead to the next three to five years. Yet only 7 percent of employers formally consider mature workers a distinct employee group.

"Organizations will need these people," he said. "There is a huge corporate memory gap that is going to emerge as a result of a massive number of older people leaving."

**What Calgary is doing**

It's a shortage already facing the City of Calgary. The city is Alberta's second largest employer, with 14 700 full-time and seasonal employees and the average age is 45. Most of them are expected to retire at 55, which would have led to a hiring crisis within the next decade.

Last year, in the face of these looming retirements, the city polled long-time employees about post-retirement plans. The results were surprising: 80 percent of near-retirees were interested in returning to work post-retirement, as long as the city met their need for flexibility and work diversity.

"We knew there was some interest, based on employee inquiries, but the level of positive response was more than expected," said Britt Wilson, acting manager of total rewards with the city.

As a result, the city instituted several policies. It can now hire former employees on a consultancy basis or following a 90-day break in service. Some non-unionized workers are also given the option to return to work immediately after retirement for a period of one year. This allows the retirees to collect a full salary plus pension benefits while the city buys time to focus on succession.

Calgary also established an internal employment agency that connects managers with retirees interested in working on short-term, non-union assignments in peak periods, or willing to cover vacations or take on special assignments.

Most employers that actively recruit and engage mature workers are successful, according to the Conference Board survey. Three-quarters of those that said they focus to a "great or very great" extent on this population have found the labour they're looking for. But those that use the same strategies to recruit a 20-year-old as a 50-year-old report much less success, with only about one-quarter of employers making older hires.

"We have to adapt our policies and practices for the new labour market—and that means greater flexibility," said Benimadhu.

**4 successful strategies**

Benimadhu said the four most successful strategies for engaging mature workers are:

- flexible work arrangements including part-time, shortened workweeks or working for blocks of time
- assigning special projects or offering challenging work
- providing mentorship opportunities
- tailoring the total rewards package.

HR policies also have to reflect the raison d'être that draws many mature workers back into the workforce, said Benimadhu.

"The fundamental thing that will retain these people is getting them to appreciate that there's meaning in the work they do," he said. "When these people are 55-plus, they're thinking of making a contribution. They have the money, they have the financial means. They don't want to work. 'Give me the opportunity to make a significant contribution to something bigger than the paycheque.'"

Few people know this better than Richard Evin, president of Evin Industries, a Montreal-based uniform manufacturer. His head shipper started there at the age of 63. He's still there at 80.

"You have a lot of older workers who have put in a lifetime's worth of work and enjoy the work and the good feeling that comes from it," he said.

The company's sales manager is also well past retirement. She's 75 and nowhere near ready to leave, said Evin. He has made certain accommodations to retain his older staff, such as shortened workweeks, but that's because of the value he gains from having them on staff.

"You have 40 years of experience of life under your belt," he said. "That 40 years is extremely valuable to what you can offer an organization."

**Make older workers feel welcome**

Aside from implementing demographic-specific strategies to engage mature workers, HR departments must also make them feel welcome, said Benimadhu. Some auto manufacturers in Europe are now equipping plants with robotics that swing the car bodies toward older employees so they can sit, instead of hunching over their work. Even small things, such as including older workers in corporate images, go a long way, he said.

At the City of Calgary, planning and preparing is especially important when re-engaging retirees, said Wilson. But employers should not underestimate the amount of administrative work involved, he said.

"Most human resource information systems are not designed to easily re-engage employees once they have retired," he said. "Other lessons include being aware of the implications of re-engaging retirees on your health, dental, life-insurance and LTD programs."

Source: D. Harder, "Employers ill-prepared to woo mature workers: Organizations should be targeting workers over age 50, finds Conference Board report." *Canadian HR Reporter,* November 3, 2009. Reprinted with permission.

## SUPPLEMENTARY HEALTH-CARE/MEDICAL INSURANCE

Most employers provide their employees with supplementary health-care/medical insurance (over and above that provided by provincial health-care plans). Along with life insurance and long-term disability, these benefits form the cornerstone of almost all benefit programs.[27] Supplementary health-care insurance is aimed at providing protection against medical costs arising from accidents or illness as a result of off-the-job causes.

**presenteeism** When employees report to work even though they are ill or exhausted.

**group life insurance** Insurance provided at lower rates for all employees, including new employees, regardless of health or physical condition.

Most supplementary health insurance plans provide insurance at group rates, which are usually lower than individual rates and are generally available to all employees after a probationary period regardless of health or physical condition. Supplementary health-care plans provide major medical coverage to meet medical expenses not covered by government health-care plans (including prescription drugs, private or semi-private hospital rooms, private-duty nursing, physiotherapy, medical supplies, ambulance services, and so on) that result from normal health problems or from long-term or serious illnesses. In many employer-sponsored drug plans, employees must pay a specified amount of **deductible** expense (typically $25 or $50) per year before plan benefits begin. Many employers also sponsor health-related insurance plans that cover such expenses as vision care, hearing aids, and dental services, often with deductibles. In many cases, the participants in such plans have their premiums paid for entirely by their employers.[28]

**Reducing Health Benefit Costs** A dramatic increase in health-care costs is the biggest issue facing benefits managers in Canada today. The Conference Board of Canada reported that the average annual health-care costs for employees are 7 percent of gross annual payroll, and 50 percent of employers report increases of 8.7 percent in these costs.[29]

Seventy-one percent of organizations have implemented strategies to manage the soaring costs of health care.[30] The simplest approach to reducing health-benefit costs is to increase the amount of health-care costs paid by employees. This can be accomplished by increasing employee premiums, increasing deductibles, reducing company **co-insurance** levels, instituting or lowering annual maximums on some services, or even eliminating coverage for spouses, private hospital rooms, and other benefits.[31] Another cost-reduction strategy is to publish a restricted list of the drugs that will be paid for under the plan, to encourage the use of generic rather than more expensive brand-name drugs. New drugs may not be covered if equally effective cheaper alternatives are available. This approach should be combined with employee education to effectively manage the demand for drugs.[32] A third approach is health promotion through various types of wellness programs. A fourth approach is to implement risk assessment programs.

**AN ETHICAL DILEMMA**

Should it be the employer's responsibility to cover health-care costs for early retirees until they become eligible for government heath-care benefits at age 65?

*frontLINE tips*

**Retiree Health Benefits** Another concern is the cost of health benefits provided to retirees. These benefits typically include life insurance, drugs, and private/semi-private hospital coverage. Some continue coverage to a surviving spouse.[33] Retiree benefits costs are already exceeding the costs for active employees in some organizations, partly due to encouragement of early retirement during the recession/restructuring of the 1990s.[34]

As members of the baby-boom generation retire with increasing life expectancies, retiree health benefit costs will increase rapidly. For example, Figure 9.2 shows the projected increases in hospital stays in Canada over the next 25 years. Almost 90 percent of the projected increase is attributable to seniors.[35] Employers can cut costs by increasing retiree contributions, increasing deductibles, tightening eligibility requirements, and reducing maximum payouts.[36] Although the temptation is to cut retiree health benefits, a growing number of companies on the "Top 100 Employers" list choose to protect the health-care benefits of their long-standing workers. Of employers that made the list, 35 percent offer health benefits to retirees, either up to age 75 or with no age limit at all, and the majority offer phased retirement plans.[37]

**LONG-TERM DISABILITY INSURANCE** Long-term disability insurance is aimed at providing income protection or compensation for loss of income due to long-term illness or injury that is not work-related. The disability payments usually begin when normal short-term disability/sick leave is used up and may continue to provide income to age 65 or beyond.[38] The disability benefits usually range from 50 percent to 75 percent of the employee's base pay.

The number of long-term disability claims in Canada is rising sharply.[39] An average disability claim can cost up to $78 000 per injury, including production delays, product and material damage due to inexperienced replacement staff, clerical and administrative time, and loss of expertise on top of the actual benefit payments.[40] Therefore, disability management programs with a goal of returning workers safely back to work are becoming a priority in many organizations.

*Disability management* is a proactive, employer-centred process that coordinates the activities of the employer, the insurance company, and health-care providers in an effort to minimize the impact of injury, *figure* 9.2 **Projected Hospital Stays in Canada**

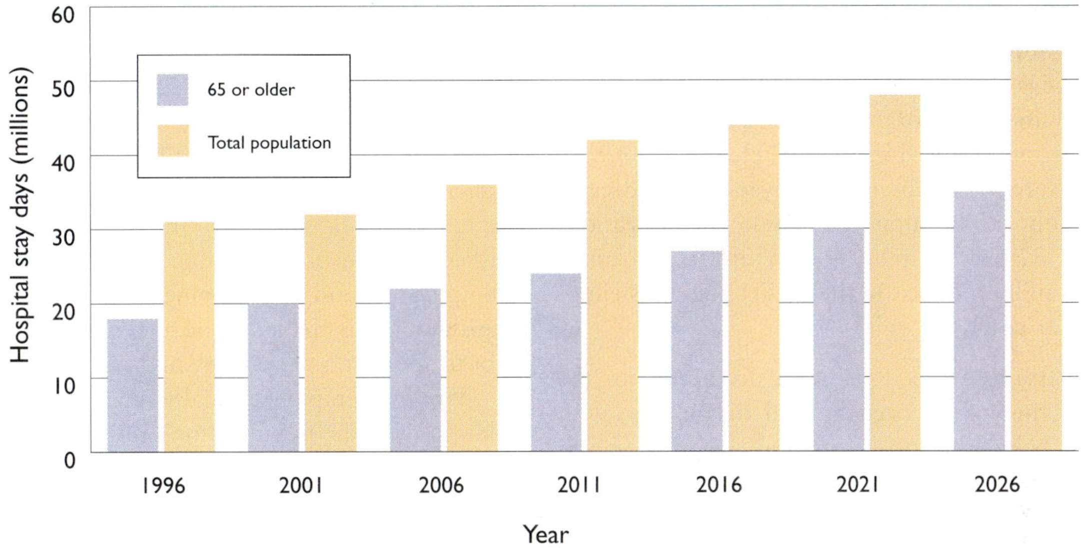


Source: M. Warren, "Retiree Benefits Coming of Age," *Benefits Canada* (May 2000), pp. 73–77. © Watson Wyatt. Reprinted with permission of *Benefits Canada.*

disability, or disease on a worker's capacity to successfully perform his or her job.[41] Maintaining contact with a worker who is ill or injured is imperative in disability management so that the worker can be involved in the return-to-work process from the beginning. Ongoing contact also allows the employer to monitor the employee's emotional well-being, which is always affected by illness and/or injury.[42]

**RPC 9-4 >**

**Integrates the basic benefits program with disability management**

The three most common approaches to returning a worker with a disability to work are reduced work hours, reduced work duties, and workstation modification.[43] Disability management programs in Canada have had dramatic results. BC Hydro's joint union–management program reduced long-term disability days off by almost 14 percent.[44] Canada Post saved $54.6 million per year with its return-to-work efforts due to a drop in employee absenteeism from 20 days to 10 days per employee per year.[45]

**Managing the Cost of Stress** The cost of stress-related absence has been growing at an alarming rate. A Statistics Canada study found that stress as a reason for work absence has increased by an alarming 316 percent since 1995.[46] In an employee survey conducted at Toronto's University Health Network, Canada's largest hospital, 63 percent of staff identified stress as their leading health risk.[47] In the week following the September 11 World Trade Center bombings in New York, 136 000 people missed part of the week for reasons other than sickness, vacation, or child care/maternity leave, according to Statistics Canada.[48] The impact of a crisis on attendance can be staggering.

**deductible** The annual amount of health/dental expenses that an employee must pay before insurance benefits will be paid.

**co-insurance** The percentage of expenses (in excess of the deductible) that is paid for by the insurance plan.

National Institute of Disability Management and Research **www.nidmar.ca**

Canadian Council on Rehabilitation and Work **www.ccrw.org**

Benefits Canada **www.benefitscanada.ca**

EmployEase **www.employease.com**

In the past, it was not unusual for employers to take a "hands off" approach to employees who were off because of stress, and employees were often left to cope on their own. With the dramatic increase in stress-related costs, employers and insurers are finding that they must implement comprehensive processes when an employee is absent due to a stress-related illness. For example, some large organizations established early intervention programs. Links with rehabilitation consultants ensured that absent employees received early rehabilitation and support. These organizations achieved a 32-percent reduction in disability claims, and the $5 million deficit in their LTD plan was eliminated in four years.[49]

**Mental Health Benefits** Psychiatric disabilities are the fastest growing of all occupational disabilities, with depression being the most common. Depression has been described as a "clear and present danger" to business, as it manifests itself in alcoholism, absenteeism, injury, physical illness, and lost productivity. Mental health claims account for 30 to 40 percent of disability claims in Canada.[50] Costs associated with mental health problems relate to short- or long-term disability and increased drug usage.[51] Estimates suggest that an employee with depression who goes untreated will cost the company twice the treatment cost per year.[52] Overall, depression, anxiety, and stress account for up to 25 percent of disability claims. At CIBC, anti-depressants are one of the most common drug claims. At Royal Bank of Canada, 31 percent of short-term absenteeism is related to mental illness and addiction.[53] Many companies are trying to reduce costs with prevention and early intervention programs, including psychiatric counselling and peer-support groups.[54]

**RETIREMENT BENEFITS** Employer-sponsored **pension plans** are intended to supplement an employee's government-sponsored retirement benefits, which, on average, make up 50 percent of the average Canadian's retirement income.[55] Unlike government-provided retirement benefits, employer-sponsored pension plans are prefunded. Money is set aside in a pension fund to accumulate with investment income until it is needed to pay benefits at retirement. Pension fund assets have grown rapidly over the past 35 years. Much of this money is invested in Canadian shares and bonds due to laws restricting the investment of these assets in foreign securities.

Most organizations (92 percent) report having a pension plan, with an average cost of 8 percent of their gross annual payroll. The public sector spends 9.4 percent of gross annual payroll on pension plans, compared to the private sector's 7.4 percent. Costs vary by industry, with the highest average pension costs in the transportation and utilities industry at 11.3 percent of gross annual payroll.[56]

The entire area of pension planning is complicated, partly because of the laws governing pensions. For example, companies want to ensure that their pension contributions are tax deductible and must, therefore, adhere to the *Income Tax Act*. Each province and the federal jurisdiction also have a law governing employer-sponsored pension plans.[57] Sometimes, the complicated and overlapping federal and provincial legislation can make employers question whether or not to sponsor a pension plan.[58]

While an employer usually must develop a pension plan to meet the organization's unique needs, there are several legal and policy issues to consider:[59]

LEGALcompliance

1. *Membership requirements*. For example, at what minimum number of years of service do employees become eligible to join the plan?
2. *Benefit formula* (defined benefits plans only). This usually ties the pension to the employee's final earnings or an average of his or her last three to five years' earnings.
3. *Retirement age*. The normal retirement age in Canada is 65, but mandatory retirement at age 65 is now illegal in many provinces. Employer plans usually permit early retirement with reduced benefits.
4. *Funding*. The question of how the plan is to be funded is another key issue. One aspect is whether the plan will be contributory or non-contributory. In the former, both employees and the employer make contributions to the pension fund. In a non-contributory fund, only the employer contributes.
5. *Vesting*. Employee vesting rights is another critical issue in pension planning. Vesting refers to the money that the employer has placed in the pension fund, which cannot be forfeited for any reason. The employees' contributions can never be forfeited. An employee is vested when he or she has met the requirements set out in the plan whereby upon termination of employment, he or she will receive future benefits based on the contributions made to the plan by the *employer* on behalf of the employee. In most provinces, pension legislation requires that employer contributions be vested

once the employee has completed two years of service.

6. *Portability*. Canadian employers today are being required by pension legislation to make their pensions more "portable" for employees upon termination of employment. This means that employees can take the money in their company pension account to a new employer's plan or roll it over into a locked-in RRSP.

**Portability** represents a shift in pension planning away from the original intent behind pension plans, which was to keep workers from changing jobs.

**AN ETHICAL DILEMMA**

Should an employer with a pension plan covering employees in several provinces give each group the minimum vesting and portability benefits for their province or take the most generous of these and provide it to all employees?

### Recent Trends in Retirement Benefits

Over the past several years, numerous court challenges based on human rights laws prohibiting discrimination on the basis of sexual orientation have led most jurisdictions in Canada to change their pension laws to permit same-sex couples to be entitled to spousal and survivor benefits in the same way as common-law couples and married couples would be entitled.[60] In most cases, the new definition of spouse applies to other benefits as well, such as health care.

The idea of **phased-in retirement**, whereby employees gradually ease into retirement using reduced workdays and/or shortened workweeks, has been in place in Europe for some time, and has become popular in North America.[61] Approximately three-quarters of Canadian employers view phased-in retirement programs as a critical organizational strategy over the next five years.[62] Phased-in retirement plans have been implemented in 52.5 percent of Canadian companies, with 33 percent interested in establishing one. Wal-Mart Canada is a leader in this area, having implemented "progressive retirement services" that invite employees to gradually retire by taking on part-time responsibilities, special projects, and training new recruits.[63] In 2007, Bill C-28 was passed, which allows employers with a federally registered pension plan to retain retired part-time workers on payroll while allowing the employee to collect a partial pension from their unreduced plan and simultaneously accrue benefits.[64] Even though phased-in retirement plans are gaining popularity, studies have found that 42 percent of employees are likely to delay their retirement by six years due to the unpredictable economic conditions wreaking havoc on their personal financial portfolios.[65]

Online retirement planning tools are the latest trend enabling employees to track and manage their retirement planning. For example, employees at Standard Life can access a site that provides a summary of their retirement planning activities, contributions, account balances, asset allocations, and projected retirement assets. Employees can customize their homepage, seek counsel, and calculate how much money they need to invest for their retirement. Standard Life launched this initiative when a recent study found that Canadians annually review their retirement statements but do not take proactive measures to secure a retirement plan that meets their long-term needs.[66]

**RPC 9-5 >**

**Develops specifications for the acquisition or redesign of pension plans and their administration**

## 9.4 EMPLOYEE SERVICES

While an employer's time off and insurance and retirement benefits account for the largest portion of its benefits costs, many employers also provide a range of services, including personal services (such as counselling), job-related services (such as child-care facilities),

**pension plans** Plans that provide income when employees reach a predetermined retirement age.

**portability** A provision such that employees who change jobs can transfer the lump-sum value of the pension they have earned into a locked-in RRSP or into their new employer's pension plan.

**phased-in retirement** An arrangement whereby employees gradually ease into retirement using reduced workdays and/or shortened workweeks.

Canadian Association for Retired Persons
www.carp.ca

Financial Planning for Retirement
www.wealthweb.ca/retireweb

Association of Canadian Pension Management
www.acpm.com

## In-class Notes

**Voluntary Company-Sponsored Benefits**

- Pay for time not worked—short-term disability/sick leave for non–work-related illness; paid leaves of absence
- Group life insurance—may also offer accidental death and dismemberment insurance and critical illness insurance
- Supplementary health-care/medical insurance—for costs not covered under provincial plans; costs increasing rapidly as workforce ages; retiree health benefits more common
- Long-term disability insurance (LTD)—for long-term, non–work-related disability; stress and mental health fastest-growing disabilities
- Employer-sponsored pension plans supplement government-sponsored retirement benefits

and executive perquisites (such as company cars and planes for executives).

**RPC 9-6 >**

**Reviews pension proposals submitted by third parties and evaluates the information received**

## Personal Services

Many companies provide personal services that most employees need at one time or another. These include credit unions, counselling, employee assistance plans, and social and recreational opportunities.

**RPC 9-7 >**

**Recommends the pension plan most suited to organizational objectives**

**CREDIT UNIONS** Credit unions are usually separate businesses established with the assistance of the employer. Employees usually become members of a credit union by purchasing a share of the credit union's stock for $5 or $10. Members can then deposit savings that accrue interest at a rate determined by the credit union's board of directors. Perhaps more importantly to most employees, loan eligibility and the rate of interest paid on the loan are usually more favourable than those found in banks and finance companies.

**RPC 9-8 >**

**Administers the reporting, funding, and fiduciary aspects of the plan**

**COUNSELLING SERVICES** Employers are also providing a wider range of counselling services to employees. These include *financial counselling* (for example, in terms of how to overcome existing indebtedness problems); *family counselling* (for marital problems and so on); *career counselling* (in terms of analyzing one's aptitudes and deciding on a career); *job placement counselling* (for helping terminated or disenchanted employees find new jobs); and *preretirement counselling* (aimed at preparing retiring employees for what many find is the trauma of retiring). Many employers

An on-site employee fitness centre.

also offer a full range of *legal counselling* through legal insurance plans available to employees.[67]

**EMPLOYEE ASSISTANCE PLANS (EAPS)** An **employee assistance plan (EAP)** is a formal employer program that provides employees with confidential counselling and/or treatment programs for such problems as mental health issues, marital/family problems, work–life balance issues, stress, legal problems, substance abuse, and other addictions, such as gambling.[68] They are particularly important for helping employees who suffer workplace trauma—ranging from harassment to physical assault.[69] The number of EAPs in Canada is growing because they are a proactive way for organizations to reduce absenteeism and disability costs. A very general estimate is that 10 percent of employees use EAP services. With supervisory training in how to identify employees who may need an EAP referral, usage can be expanded to more employees who require help.[70]

**OTHER PERSONAL SERVICES** Some employers also provide various social and recreational opportunities for their employees, including company-sponsored athletic events, dances, annual summer picnics, craft activities, and parties.[71] In practice, the benefits offered are limited only by creativity in thinking up new benefits. For example, pharmaceutical giant Pfizer Inc. provides employees with free drugs made by the company, including Viagra![72]

## Job-Related Services

Job-related services aimed directly at helping employees perform their jobs, such as educational subsidies and day-care centres, constitute a second group of services.

**SUBSIDIZED CHILD CARE** Today, large numbers of Canadian women with children under six years old are in the workforce. Subsidized day care is one increasingly popular benefit stemming directly from that trend.[73] Many employers simply investigate the day-care facilities in their communities and recommend certain ones to interested employees. However, more employers are setting up company-sponsored day-care facilities themselves, both to attract young mothers to the payroll and to reduce absenteeism. For example, Simon Fraser University has on-site and off-site child-care facilities with over 200 spots available for use by

Subsidizing day-care facilities for children of employees has many benefits for the employer, including lower employee absenteeism.

**employee assistance plan (EAP)** A company-sponsored program to help employees cope with personal problems that are interfering with or have the potential to interfere with their job performance as well as issues affecting their well-being and/or that of their families.

its employees.[74] An emerging benefit is day care for mildly ill children who are not accepted at regular day care. Day-care centres for the mildly ill are more expensive than regular day-care centres because they offer medical supervision, usually by a registered nurse, and infection-control measures.[75]

To date, the evidence regarding the actual effects of employer-sponsored child care on employee absenteeism, turnover, productivity, recruitment, and positive job satisfaction, particularly with respect to reducing obstacles to coming to work and improving workers' attitudes.[76]

**ELDER CARE** With the average age of the Canadian population rising, elder care is increasingly a concern for many employers and individuals. Elder care is designed to assist employees who must help elderly parents or relatives that are not fully able to care for themselves, up to and including palliative care of the dying.[77] Elder care is expected to become a more common workplace issue than child care as the baby boomer generation ages.[78] Statistics Canada reports that there are 2 million people 45 years of age and over providing care to seniors, with approximately 20 percent caring for seniors with a long-term health problem. One in 5 women and one in 10 men report they will likely retire sooner than planned because of elder care responsibilities.[79]

From an employer's point of view, elder-care benefits are important for much the same reason as are child-care benefits: The responsibility for caring for an aging relative can and will affect the employee's performance at work.[80] A number of employers are therefore instituting elder-care benefits, including flexible hours, support groups, counselling, free pagers, and adult day-care programs. Benefits also include access to a geriatric care manager who can refer employees to public and private programs and services.

**FAMILY-FRIENDLY BENEFITS** Recognition of the pressures of balancing work and family life has led many employers to bolster what they call their "family-friendly" benefits. Research has shown that one of the top drivers of workforce commitment in Canada is management's recognition of personal and family life.[81] Ninety percent of responding employees in one survey said work–life benefits were "important" or "very important" to them.[82] While there is no single list of what does or does not constitute "family-friendly" benefits, they generally include child care, elder care, providing light-duty work for pregnant women whose jobs require heavy lifting or long periods of standing, and flexible work hours that enable employees to better balance the demands of their family and work lives.[83] One recent Canadian survey found that 81 percent of firms polled provided leaves for family illness, and almost 75 percent provided leaves for other personal and family duties such as elder care.[84] Ford Motor Company now considers domestic violence a disability when a woman has to miss work to find shelter.[85]

**EDUCATIONAL SUBSIDIES** Educational subsidies, such as full or partial tuition refunds, have long been a popular benefit for employees seeking to continue or complete their education. Most companies pay for courses directly related to an employee's present job. Many also reimburse tuition for courses that are not job-related (such as a receptionist taking an accounting class) but pertain to the company business or are part of a degree or diploma program.[86]

## Executive Perquisites

Perquisites (perks, for short) are usually given to only a few top executives. Perks can range from the substantial to the almost insignificant, such as chauffeur-driven limousines, the use of company-owned property in the Caribbean, or the use of corporate jets for business travel.[87]

A multitude of popular perks falls between these extremes. These include management loans (which typically enable senior officers to use their stock options); salary guarantees (also known as *golden parachutes*) to protect executives if their firms are the targets of acquisitions or mergers; financial counselling (to handle top executives' investment programs); and relocation benefits, often including subsidized mortgages, purchase of an executive's current house, and payment for a move.[88] A potpourri of other executive perks includes cellphones, outplacement assistance, company cars, security systems, company planes and yachts, executive dining rooms, legal services, tax assistance, liberal expense accounts, club memberships, season tickets, credit cards, and subsidized children's education. An

**AN ETHICAL DILEMMA**

Is it fair that senior executives get financial perks, such as subsidized mortgages, in addition to their higher amounts of cash compensation when other lower-paid employees may be struggling to meet mortgage payments?

## In-class Notes

**Employee Services**

- Personal services—credit unions, counselling services, employee assistance plans (EAPs)
- Job-related services—subsidized child care, elder care, family-friendly benefits, educational subsidies
- Executive perquisites—loans, executive dining room, limousines, and others

increasingly popular new perk is concierge service intended to carry out errands for busy executives.[89] Employers have many ways of making their hard-working executives' lives as pleasant as possible!

## 9.5 FLEXIBLE BENEFITS PROGRAMS

Research conducted over 30 years ago found that an employee's age, marital status, and gender influenced his or her choice of benefits.[90] For example, preference for pensions increased significantly with employee age, and preference for family dental plans increased sharply as the number of dependants increased. Thus, benefits that one worker finds attractive may be unattractive to another. As a result, there is a trend toward **flexible benefits programs** that permit employees to develop individualized benefits packages for themselves by choosing the benefits options they prefer. Approximately 40 percent of organizations report that they have implemented a flexible benefits program for at least some of their employees as a cost-containment strategy.[91]

Flexible benefits plans allow an employee to put together his or her own benefit package, subject to two constraints. First, the employer must carefully limit total cost for each total benefits package. Second, each benefit plan must include certain non-optional items. These include, for example, Canada/Quebec Pension Plan, workers' compensation, and Employment Insurance.

Subject to these two constraints, employees can pick and choose from the available options. Thus, a young parent might opt for the company's life and dental insurance plans, while an older employee might opt for an improved pension plan. The list of possible options that the employer might offer can include many of the benefits discussed in this chapter: vacations, insurance benefits, pension plans, educational services, and so on. An example of how flexible benefits programs are structured can be found at UMA, a consulting engineering company with 15 locations across Canada. UMA developed a personal accountability approach to benefits administration, holding each employee responsible for benefit expenditures.

**flexible benefits programs** Individualized benefit plans to accommodate employee needs and preferences.

Benefits Design Inc. **www.benefitsdesign.com**

Benefits and Pensions Monitor
**www.bpmmagazine.com**

International Foundation of Employee Benefit Plans
**www.ifebp.org**

## *figure* 9.3 Advantages and Disadvantages of Flexible Benefits Programs

**ADVANTAGES**

1. Employees choose packages that best satisfy their unique needs.
2. Flexible benefits help firms meet the changing needs of a changing workforce.
3. Increased involvement of employees and families improves understanding of benefits.
4. Flexible plans make introduction of new benefits less costly. The new option is added merely as one among a wide variety of elements from which to choose.
5. Cost containment—the organization sets the dollar maximum. Employee chooses within that constraint.

**DISADVANTAGES**

1. Employees make bad choices and find themselves not covered for predictable emergencies.
2. Administrative burdens and expenses increase.
3. Adverse selection—employees pick only benefits they will use. The subsequent high benefit utilization increases its cost.

Source: Milkovich, Newman, and Cole. *Compensation*, First Canadian Edition (2005). (Whitby, ON: McGraw-Hill, 2005), p. 219. Reproduced with the permission of McGraw-Hill Ryerson.

Employees are given a personal spending account that allows them to decide how to allocate funds for the benefits they need. This initiative is part of a three-year plan to revitalize the entire benefit structure so that employees have ultimate flexibility in how money for benefits is allocated.[92]

Advantages and disadvantages of flexible benefit programs are summarized in Figure 9.3. The flexibility, of course, is the main advantage. Although most employees favour flexible benefits, some do not like to spend time choosing among available options, and some choose inappropriate benefits. Various organizations have developed user-friendly interactive software for personal computers that helps employees make choices under a flexible benefits program.[93]

A few organizations are moving beyond flexible benefits to "total flexible compensation," where employees at all levels design an individual compensation package (cash, benefits, vacation, incentives, and so on). Total flexible compensation provides employees with control over their compensation, and employers maximize the effectiveness of their compensation dollars.[94]

## 9.6 BENEFITS ADMINISTRATION

Administering benefits is an increasingly specialized task because workers are more financially sophisticated and demanding and because benefit plans must comply with a wide variety of laws. Providing and administering benefits is also an increasingly expensive task. Therefore, whether it is a flexible benefits plan or a more traditional one, benefits administration is a challenge. Even in a relatively small company with 40 to 50 employees, the administrative problems of keeping track of the benefits status of each employee can be a time-consuming task as employees are hired and separated and as they utilize or want to change their benefits. Many companies make use of benefits software to update information. For example, a program might track vacation eligibility and will trigger a memo to a supervisor when one of the employees in his or her department is overdue for some time off.

**RPC 9-9 >**

**Develops specifications for the acquisition and day-to-day management of employee benefit programs**

Another trend is outsourcing benefits administration, including record keeping, administration, and participant communication, to a third-party expert. Outsourcing benefits can offset the steep costs associated with managing an in-house benefits system, which include:[95]

- Staffing the benefits department with competent staff, which are in short supply in this field

*In-class Notes*

**Flexible Benefits Programs**

- Employees create individualized benefits packages by choosing benefit options they prefer based on family needs
- Employer limits total cost
- Government-sponsored benefits are mandatory

- The rising cost of keeping existing benefits software current when it becomes obsolete within a short period of time
- Administrative complexities of managing a benefits system, especially in light of mergers, acquisitions, restructuring, and downsizing

**RPC 9-10 >**

**Ensures the effectiveness of benefits programs by providing information, by ensuring accessibility of the program, and by minimizing the cost of the program**

## Communicating Benefits

Communicating benefits can be extremely beneficial to both the employer and employee. Often, employees do not know exactly what benefits they have, and, more importantly, they do not realize the cost of these benefits. Employers communicate the type and cost of benefits to employees in a variety of ways. For example, issuing a written benefit statement once a year to each employee can have a very positive effect on employees and can be very motivating. Often, employees take the benefits provided for granted. Once they realize that the company is spending hundreds, if not thousands, of dollars on their behalf, they can appreciate their total compensation package. In addition to providing benefit statements, organizations often use a variety of methods to inform employees about benefits packages. Benefit booklets, pamphlets, envelope stuffers, letters to the home, and face-to-face meetings are a few of the communication vehicles used. Electronic methods, such as email, web pages, and intranets, are also increasing in popularity. Specific approaches for effectively communicating benefits to employees appear in the Strategic HR box on page 306.

**RPC 9-11 >**

**Manages the transition to new plans, including communications, employee counselling, training, and discarding redundant practices**

**RPC 9-12 >**

**Provides necessary information and counselling to pension plan participants**

Benefits communication, particularly regarding pension plans and flexible benefits, is also increasingly important as a large number of people are approaching retirement.[96] Correct information must be provided in a timely, clear manner. Pension legislation across Canada specifies what information must be disclosed to plan members and their spouses. Court challenges concerning information on benefits plans are on the rise as people's awareness of their right to information grows.[97] Increasingly, organizations are utilizing new technology, such as an intranet, to ensure that up-to-date information on pensions, for example, is provided in a consistent manner.[98]

At Hewlett Packard (Canada) Ltd., an electronic pension booklet is available on the company's intranet and a pension-modelling tool can be accessed through the web. The modelling software allows employees to fill in their personal information to calculate various "what if" scenarios.[99]

**RPC 9-13 >**

**Manages the transition to new or revised plans by providing information to plan participants and providing appropriate training for administrative staff**

STRATEGIC HR

# The Benefits Are the Message: Total Rewards Program Useless If Not Understood by Employees

It is not just total rewards themselves that help engage and retain employees, it's the way employers communicate these rewards. The right communication shows employees how much an organization values them. That expression of value, in turn, supports retention.

Presenting a clear and concise summary of benefits can also be an effective tool for attracting new hires and reinforcing a company's value proposition relative to other opportunities in the job market.

Communicating benefits effectively should make use of all formats: Visual, oral and written. Program complexity, the number and size of work sites, IT capability and employee comfort with technology-based communication are all elements that can impact the approach.

Combining benefit communications with existing safety or corporate announcements can help employers lower the cost of face-to-face communication.

**Defining an end target**

Establishing goals and defining results is the best place to start. A written end target will make subsequent decisions easier to execute and provide the measuring stick for progress. It could state, for example, "We seek greater member appreciation and understanding of the benefits offered and link this understanding to measurable behaviour changes in service purchase."

The next step involves creating a road map. But take note—this transformation is not going to happen within six months. It will take at least 36 months to change existing practices and establish scheduled communications. It will also take time to make the necessary changes to communication approaches.

Next, consider other elements that could be included in the communication strategy. Is this the time to introduce that three-tier drug plan? Or is this the time to roll out that long dreamed about "choice benefits" plan?

Then, start plotting communication events. For each event consider the following: audience, purpose, delivery, where the communication will originate and who will execute this part of the plan. Some of the communication pieces may already exist.

The final step is choosing from an array of communication resources. Start simply to ensure the new habits generate momentum. Some easy-to-implement solutions include:

- streamlining a 50-page benefit booklet into a one-page summary
- a once-yearly bulletin communicating program performance and status
- the creation of a benefits board to provide relevant monthly articles on healthy living or dealing with stress
- an annual benefits meeting to revisit all aspects of the company's health and retirement benefits.

**Tailored approach**

Once the plan takes hold, the efforts can evolve into more sophisticated communications, such as customized member benefit statements that outline all programs per member (federal programs, provincial programs, company-sponsored programs) and costs associated with each. Implementing a series of customized information pieces to provide timely education relevant to the plan can provide the final nudge to transform member behaviour.

For example, use a drug pharmacy report to highlight shopping preferences. A one-page education piece highlighting dispensing fees, profit margins and the impact on the plan and what members pay out of pocket can assist in curbing this cost.

No communication or education strategy would be complete without targeting all affected parties. Providing high-level case studies for review by senior management is an excellent way to bring them along.

**Miscommunication**

*Most employees don't understand benefits: Survey*

Nine out of 10 employers think it's important employees understand and appreciate their benefits, but only about one-fifth (21 percent) of employees do, according to a September survey of 650 HR managers in the United States.

Methods used to communicate benefits to employees:

- Group meetings (80 percent).
- One-to-one meetings (58 percent, though 90 percent of employers say this would significantly improve employee understanding).
- Internet enrolment (44 percent).
- Self-enrolment (40 percent).

Source: R. Taylor, "The benefits are the message: Total rewards program useless if not understood by employees," *Canadian HR Reporter*, January 12, 2009, p. 15. Reprinted with permission of the author.

## In-class Notes

**Benefits Administration**

- Increasingly specialized task; many legal requirements
- Outsourcing to third-party experts becoming more common
- Benefits communication increasingly provided electronically

# Employee Benefits on the International Stage

Establishing a benefits plan that meets the needs and expectations of employees working in different companies is a challenging endeavour. A number of decisions need to be made in order to leverage local competitiveness and equity in what employees are receiving in different countries. Companies examine a number of factors: (1) national culture—understanding the relationship between cultural values and benefits helps determine which benefits are desired by employees; (2) industry—high tech and finance offer more generous benefits than manufacturing and transportation; (3) labour agreements, which define the benefits negotiated by employer and union; (4) corporate culture—understanding a company's global benefit strategy provides direction for implementing a benefits program in a new country; (5) availability of talent—competition to attract and retain talent, especially during a labour shortage, compels organizations to offer generous benefits packages; (6) stage of growth—younger companies tend to attract start-up staff with compensation; and (7) taxation—tax advantages play a major role in benefits design.

Cultures differ significantly in the benefits packages they value. For example, in Nordic countries people believe everyone should have equal rights, a value that is reflected in robust maternity, paternity, and parental leave policies and few, if any, executive plans or stock option plans. In Australia, companies offer sophisticated, flexible benefits plans to accommodate a society where individual decision making and actions are encouraged. In Singapore, people are comfortable with a high degree of uncertainty, which is reflected in their government-sponsored, defined contribution benefits plans.

National culture plays a role in some benefit practices, yet more empirical research needs to be conducted to discover which benefit practices and which measures of culture have significant relationships.[100]

# Chapter Review

## Answers to Test Yourself

1. What benefits are legally required in Canada?

   Employment Insurance provides weekly income benefits to those who are unable to work through no fault of their own. C/QPP plans provide three types of benefits—retirement income, survivor/death benefits, and disability benefits. Workers' compensation provides income and medical benefits to victims of work-related accidents or illnesses and/or their dependants regardless of fault. Provincial heath-care plans pay for basic hospital and medical services with no direct fee to patients. Paid vacations and holidays are required for all employees as well as leaves of absence for situations involving illness, maternity, and bereavement. Benefits must also be paid to employees whose employment is terminated by the employer without just cause.

2. What types of employee benefits do employers voluntarily sponsor?

   Employers often provide pay for time not worked, including leaves of absence (for maternity/parental/adoption leave, bereavement, compassionate care, sabbatical). Employers also often provide short-term disability or sick leave plans to provide a continuation of all or part of an employee's earnings when the employee is absent due to non–work-related illness or injury. Long-term disability plans provide income protection in the case of long-term illness or injury that is non–work-related. Other commonly provided benefits include life insurance and supplementary health-care/medical insurance to cover expenses that are not covered under provincial health-care plans and pension plans to provide retirement income.

3. What are key legal and policy issues that need to be considered when developing pension plans?

   Key legal and policy issues that need to be considered when developing pension plans include membership requirements regarding eligibility to join the plan; a benefits formula that ties either the contributions or the pension benefit amount to the employee's earnings; retirement age for normal, early, and late retirement; funding requirements for employees and the employer; vesting of employer money placed in the pension fund upon termination of employment; and portability of benefits to another employer's pension plan or to a locked-in RRSP upon termination of employment.

4. What types of employee services are offered by organizations?

   In addition to legally required benefits and employer-sponsored benefits, many employers also provide a range of services, including personal services, such as credit unions, counselling services, employee assistance programs, and social events; job-related services, such as subsidized child care, subsidized employee transportation, elder care, family-friendly benefits, food services, and educational subsidies; and executive perquisites, such as management loans, relocation benefits, club memberships, cellphones, and company cars.

5. What are the advantages and disadvantages of flexible benefits programs?

   Flexible benefits programs permit employees to choose individualized benefits packages for themselves. Advantages include employees choosing the options that best suit their needs, employer cost control, that the firm can meet the changing needs of a changing workforce, increased employee understanding of benefits, and that the introduction of new benefits is less costly. Disadvantages include the possibility that employees can make bad choices and find themselves not covered for certain emergencies, the administrative burden, and increased administrative expenses.

## Key Terms

C/QPP plans (p. 286)
co-insurance (p. 296)
deductible (p. 296)
employee assistance plan (EAP) (p. 301)
employee benefits (p. 283)
Employment Insurance (p. 285)
flexible benefits programs (p. 303)
group life insurance plans (p. 292)
pay for time not worked (p. 289)
pension plans (p. 298)

phased-in retirement (p. 299)
presenteeism (p. 292)
portability (p. 299)
provincial health-care plans (p. 287)
short-term disability/sick leave plans (p. 289)
sick leave plans (p. 292)
workers' compensation (p. 286)

## Required Professional Capabilities (RPCs)


RPC 9-1 > (p. 283)
RPC 9-2 > (p. 285)
RPC 9-3 > (p. 285)
RPC 9-4 > (p. 297)
RPC 9-5 > (p. 299)
RPC 9-6 > (p. 300)
RPC 9-7 > (p. 300)
RPC 9-8 > (p. 300)
RPC 9-9 > (p. 304)
RPC 9-10 > (p. 305)
RPC 9-11 > (p. 305)
RPC 9-12 > (p. 305)
RPC 9-13 > (p. 305)


# Cases and Exercises



## CASE INCIDENT

### Technology Plus's Benefit Dilemma

In order to stay competitive, many organizations today are choosing to restructure their benefit programs. Technology Plus is an example of such a company. Technology Plus employs 150 employees including upper management, skilled tradespersons, sales representatives, and customer service representatives. Five years ago, this company was enjoying huge profits and could afford their current benefits program; however, times have changed and now they need to find cost savings without laying off any of their staff.

Technology Plus to this point has offered all of their staff a premium benefits program, including much more than government-required benefits of employment insurance, Canada Pension Plan, worker's compensation, standard vacation of two weeks per year, and access to legislated leaves of absence. They offer group life insurance of three times salary, accidental death and dismemberment insurance of three times salary, extended health-care benefits (with vision care, dental care, hearing aids, and more), long-term disability of 75 percent of salary (employer-paid), and a defined benefit pension plan. They also provide a wellness program, an employee assistance plan, and many other services such as subsidized childcare and assistance with eldercare. However, now they need your help in deciding how to restructure their benefit plan to find significant cost savings but still provide meaningful benefit coverage for their employees.

### Questions

1. What voluntary employer-sponsored benefits should this company maintain and which ones should they not maintain in your opinion, and why?
2. Would a flexible benefit program save this organization money if administered properly?

### Application Questions

1. You have been asked to investigate whether your company should continue to finance an in-house benefits department or outsource all benefits. Discuss the internal and external factors that should be considered when making this decision.
2. Half of the members on the executive team in your company argue that benefits should be a top-down approach (i.e., management researches best practices in benefits and establishes benefits for the employees). The other half of the team support a bottom-up approach (i.e., employees offer their input and exercise their leadership in establishing a benefits program).
   a. Discuss the advantages and limitations of top-down and bottom-up approaches.
   b. What approach will you recommend to the executive team and why?

3. Discuss practices that should be integrated into benefits planning and communication in order to create a benefits program that attracts and retains employees.
4. The president of your company recently asserted that "Employee benefits and services are strictly administrative and do not play a strategic role within the organization."
   a. How will you respond to the president's comment?
   b. What steps need to be taken in a benefits department in order to communicate to everyone in the organization that employee benefits and services play a strategic role in the company?
5. With reference to your current or former part-time job, critique the voluntary company-sponsored benefits, identifying the strengths and limitations of the company's benefits package. Discuss the benefits that should be added to the mix, to help attract and retain employees.
6. The workers' compensation premiums your construction company is paying are skyrocketing beyond industry standards and you can no longer sustain the escalating payouts. Discuss the approach you will take to reduce your premium payments.
7. You are interested in implementing a phased-in retirement plan for employees who will be nearing retirement in the next three to four years. Propose a plan for what the phased-in retirement in your organization will look like.

## RUNNING CASE: LEARNINMOTION.COM

### The New Benefits Plan

The case for Chapter 9, The New Benefits Plan, follows LearninMotion.com as it continues to address new HR issues. It is clear that it does not have a consistent policy on sick leave, vacation, and other forms of time off. In addition, the group is considering establishing some type of retirement plan.

To read this case, go to www.pearsoned.ca/myhrlab and click on the *Management of Human Resources*, Third Canadian Edition, In-Class Edition, cover. Click on the case module in Chapter 9. The running case illustrates a variety of challenges confronted by HR professionals, small-business owners, and front-line supervisors. It places students in the role of HR management consultants to help the fledgling LearninMotion.com develop HR policies, strategies, and long-term goals. Each case is accompanied by assignments for the management consultants in the form of critical-thinking questions posed to the student.

## CONTROVERSIAL BUSINESS TOPIC EXERCISE

For the past year, you have served as the assistant vice president of human resources for a large clothing retailer, enjoying a number of executive perks—company car, 50 percent discount on all top-end clothing, fully furnished home office, mortgage rebates on your home, access to the company yacht and ski resort, company paid luxury vacations, and an unlimited expense account. In a recent conversation with two of the other assistant vice presidents in the organization, you discover they are not getting access to any of the executive perks that you have. The lack of equity is rather disturbing to you as you wonder what other areas of inequity exist in the company. As a senior representative of the human resources team, you should be concerned about internal equity, yet in reality you do not want to raise any flags that might cause the organization to take away the perks you have come to enjoy. Explain what you will do in this situation.

## IN THE BOARDROOM EXERCISE

The new CEO for a large manufacturing facility has been reviewing organizational reports to familiarize herself with the plant's operations. She discovered that employee benefits cost 48 percent of the company's payroll. At the boardroom meeting, she expresses her shock and dismay that the staff in the benefits department have been negligent in letting the costs soar beyond what the company can afford. The CEO wants the company to take immediate action to save money, which includes terminating the employment of all employees in the benefits department, eliminating all employee benefits, and giving employees a 15-percent pay increase so they can pay for benefits out of their own pockets. As manager of benefits, what is your response to the CEO's proposal?

## EMPLOYEE BENEFITS ON THE INTERNATIONAL STAGE EXERCISE

*The exercise below relates to the Employee Benefits on the International Stage feature on p. 307.*

You are the owner of your own company in Canada. Select a country of your choice in which you would like to expand your business.

a. Identify and describe the voluntary company-sponsored benefits you will offer to your Canadian employees to attract them to assignments in this overseas destination.

b. Map out the communication strategy you will use to explain the benefits package and convince employees to relocate.
c. Present your plan to the class. Ask half of your classmates to reject the benefits package you propose so that you can practise responding to employees' concerns.

## EXPERIENTIAL EXERCISE

For further study of text materials and development of practical skills, select the experiential exercise module for this chapter on www.pearsoned.ca/myhrlab. This module provides two to three individual or group-based assignments per chapter.

# QUIZ YOURSELF

STUDY GUIDE QUESTIONS

Circle the correct answer. After completing this self-test, check your answers against the Answers to Study Guide Questions at the back of the book (p. 433).

1. The indirect financial payments that an employee receives during his or her employment with an employer are called:
   a. employee compensation
   b. employee benefits
   c. employee remuneration
   d. employee assistance plans
   e. indirect monetary rewards
2. Employee benefits are an important part of compensation because:
   a. they reward loyalty and tenure
   b. they attract key talent
   c. most salary increases are very modest
   d. they can help to retain employees
   e. all of the above
3. Due to the aging population and increasing labour shortage in Canada, the cost of benefits, which is already at an all-time high, is estimated to increase further. It is estimated that benefits as a percentage of payroll amounts to approximately:
   a. 10 percent
   b. 15 percent
   c. 37 percent
   d. 47 percent
   e. 27 percent
4. Papol Inc. is a recently incorporated company. The CEO of the company plans to recruit four new employees. As an employer, what are the legally required benefits that the CEO has to provide for his new employees?
   a. workers' compensation, Canada/Quebec Pension Plan, Employment Insurance, long-term disability
   b. Employment Insurance, workers' compensation, Canada/Quebec Pension Plan
   c. employee assistance plans, workers' compensation, Canada/Quebec Pension Plan, Employment Insurance
   d. short-term disability benefits, paid vacations, Canada/Quebec Pension Plan
   e. employee assistance plans, extended health insurance, Employment Insurance
5. Which category/categories of people are excluded by the C/QPP?
   a. homemakers only
   b. casual workers only
   c. homemakers and casual workers
   d. homemakers, casual workers, and migrant workers
   e. all employees are covered by the C/QPP
6. Workers' compensation laws are aimed at providing income and medical benefits to victims of work-related accidents or illnesses regardless of fault. Leah is an employee of Stitches Ltd. As an employee, what are her entitlements under the workers' compensation laws?
   a. spousal benefits
   b. medical treatment for all disabilities
   c. health and safety costs
   d. benefits for non–work-related disabilities
   e. income benefits during the time of work-related disability
7. The management of Maxima Corporation declared that their health benefits costs have increased significantly during the past two years. They decided on the following strategy to help reduce the costs:
   a. introduce a short-term disability program
   b. introduce a dental plan
   c. increase employee premiums
   d. make health benefits non-contributory
   e. none of the above
8. The following benefits plans are used to attract and retain employees who are past retirement age:
   a. critical illness insurance
   b. elder care and home health-care benefits
   c. wellness programs
   d. long-term care insurance
   e. all of the above
9. Pay for time not worked is one of an employer's most expensive benefits. The following are common situations in which employees are paid for not working:
   a. short-term disability, sick leave, maternity leave
   b. adoption leave, vacation, sick leave
   c. holidays, vacations, sick leave
   d. holidays, paternity leave, short-term disability
   e. maternity leave, paternity leave, adoption leave

10. Long-term disability claims in Canada are rising sharply. It is estimated that an average disability claim costs up to $78 000. Long-term disabilities in workplace can:
    a. reduce productivity in the organization
    b. increase costs to the employer
    c. result in loss of expertise to the employer
    d. create production delays
    e. all of the above

11. Khalid is the HR manager of a leading pharmaceutical firm. He intends to introduce a pension plan for employees and is currently developing a proposal for board approval. Pension planning is complicated because of the laws that govern pensions. What are some of the legal and policy issues he needs to consider in his proposal?
    a. retirement age
    b. portability
    c. vesting
    d. funding
    e. all of the above

12. Mary is a recently divorced administrative assistant and is not her usual bubbly self. During the past two weeks, Mary's performance has been lagging. She has missed a few deadlines, and some of the instructions given by her superior have fallen on deaf ears. Her supervisor is considering using the following benefit to help her:
    a. workers' compensation
    b. employee assistance plan
    c. home health care
    d. elder care
    e. performance counselling

13. What is an emerging job-related service provided by employers?
    a. counselling
    b. child care
    c. day care for mildly ill children
    d. elder care for mildly ill elderly people
    e. EAPs

14. Kim is a new employee at Crevus.com. At her workplace, Kim was able to develop her own benefits package. What kind of a benefits program is Crevus.com offering its employees?
    a. flexible benefits program
    b. autonomous benefit program
    c. government benefits program
    d. employee assistance program
    e. long-term/short-term disability program

15. A trend in benefits administration is that companies are now turning toward outsourcing this activity. Why is benefits administration being outsourced?
    a. increasing expenses
    b. greater efficiency
    c. improved services
    d. greater consistency
    e. all of the above

# 10 chapter Occupational Health and Safety

## Learning Objectives

1. Explain the strategic importance of occupational health and safety.
2. Cite key facts about occupational health and safety legislation.
3. Outline approaches for handling and preventing workplace accidents.
4. Describe how to control workers' compensation costs.
5. Outline the value and ingredients of employee wellness programs.
6. Articulate and offer solutions to occupational health issues and challenges.

## Test Yourself

1. What are the major rights and responsibilities of employers and employees under occupational health and safety legislation?
2. What are the three basic causes of accidents?
3. How can accidents at work be prevented and what are the benefits of doing so?
4. What are employee wellness programs and why are they becoming increasingly popular?
5. What are the seven major employee health issues at work, and how should they be managed?

## 10.1 STRATEGIC IMPORTANCE OF OCCUPATIONAL HEALTH AND SAFETY

Health and safety initiatives are part of a strategic approach to human resources management. Service provided to clients and customers is a function of how employees are treated, and employee health, safety, and wellness management are important determinants of employee perceptions regarding fair treatment by an organization. Further, investment in disability management and proactive wellness programs create measurable bottom line returns.

In 2007, approximately 317 000 non-fatal injuries and 1055 deaths occurred in Canadian workplaces.[1] The average injury frequency rate in Canada based on 100 employees is 2.6, with the lowest rating in New Brunswick (1.3) and the highest in Manitoba (4.8).[2] These figures do not include minor injuries that do not involve time lost from work beyond the day of the accident. Further, these figures do not tell the full story, as it is estimated that 40 to 50 percent of work-related injuries in Canada go unreported.[3] The human suffering incurred by injured or ill workers and their families, and the economic costs incurred by employers, are not reflected in these numbers. Every year on April 28, a day of mourning is observed for Canadian workers killed or injured on the job.[4] Tables 10.1 and 10.2 depict the number of time-loss injuries and fatalities by jurisdiction from 1982 to 2008.

Workplace health concerns are widespread. One study found that two-thirds of employed Canadian adults believed they were being exposed to some sort of occupational health hazard, the most common being exposure to airborne dust and fibre and working with a computer screen or terminal. Thirty-two percent believed that these exposures had a negative effect on their health.[5]

The challenge and opportunity is to create and sustain a health and safety culture in the workplace that encourages everyone to exercise personal accountability for health and safety, to continually raise questions about policies and procedures around health and safety, and to offer recommendations that enhance safety and wellness. A new approach called the **shared responsibility model** communicates the importance of employer and employee cooperation to reduce accident rates. For example, the leadership team at GE Canada puts health and safety at the forefront of all discussions, especially when managers are walking the floor and talking to workers. As well, an extensive online training program is offered that enables managers to track employee use and progress and to report monthly performance metrics.[6]

**RPC 10-1 >**

**Implements and evaluates practices in the areas of health, safety, security, and workers' compensation**

### *In-class Notes*

**Strategic Importance of Occupational Health and Safety**

- Safety affects employee well-being, which in turn affects customer service
- Hundreds of thousands of costly workplace injuries occur across Canada each year
- Occupational health hazards are widespread

______________________

______________________

______________________

______________________

______________________

**shared responsibility model** A new approach to health and safety in the workplace that communicates the importance of employer and employee cooperation to reduce accident rates.

*table* 10.1 **Number of Accepted Time-Loss Injuries, by Jurisdiction, 1982–2008**

| Year | Total | NL | PE | NS | NB | QC | ON | MB | SK | AB | BC | NT/NU | YT |
|---|---|---|---|---|---|---|---|---|---|---|---|---|---|
| 1982 | 479 558 | 7766 | 1499 | 12 501 | 9696 | 159 288 | 141 917 | 18 558 | 15 239 | 44 941 | 66 882 | 1271 | ... |
| 1983 | 471 929 | 7808 | 1627 | 12 156 | 9530 | 160 796 | 145 412 | 17 759 | 15 507 | 37 346 | 62 949 | 1039 | ... |
| 1984 | 510 317 | 8223 | 1495 | 11 940 | 9704 | 176 001 | 167 748 | 21 358 | 15 700 | 37 665 | 59 319 | 1164 | ... |
| 1985 | 555 991 | 8743 | 1787 | 12 624 | 8986 | 194 377 | 186 648 | 22 440 | 16 666 | 41 376 | 61 146 | 1198 | ... |
| 1986 | 586 718 | 8624 | 1935 | 12 620 | 9909 | 213 366 | 195 937 | 23 495 | 15 916 | 42 249 | 61 711 | 956 | ... |
| 1987 | 602 531 | 9047 | 2068 | 11 732 | 10918 | 216 724 | 205 259 | 22 510 | 15 715 | 41 236 | 66 200 | 1122 | ... |
| 1988 | 617 997 | 10066 | 2435 | 11 219 | 12119 | 218 057 | 208 499 | 22 612 | 14 888 | 43 349 | 73 418 | 1335 | ... |
| 1989 | 620 979 | 10689 | 2450 | 13 897 | 13083 | 218 708 | 200 967 | 21 618 | 13 886 | 44 782 | 79 613 | 1286 | ... |
| 1990 | 593 952 | 10368 | 2551 | 12 870 | 12508 | 204 734 | 184 444 | 21 369 | 13 715 | 45 869 | 84 464 | 1060 | ... |
| 1991 | 520 706 | 9421 | 2250 | 12 730 | 11670 | 178 689 | 155 473 | 18 095 | 12 701 | 38 724 | 79 643 | 989 | 321 |
| 1992 | 456 326 | 7793 | 2108 | 12 181 | 10018 | 146 405 | 136 936 | 16 542 | 11 987 | 32 092 | 78 890 | 966 | 408 |
| 1993 | 424 848 | 6116 | 2009 | 13 332 | 5647 | 135 411 | 125 118 | 15 327 | 12 277 | 29 602 | 78 495 | 1058 | 456 |
| 1994 | 430 756 | 6646 | 2094 | 13 223 | 4784 | 135 482 | 125 638 | 17 740 | 13 337 | 30 801 | 79 428 | 1120 | 463 |
| 1995 | 410 464 | 6150 | 2443 | 10 463 | 4310 | 129 926 | 118 812 | 17 405 | 14 206 | 30 285 | 74 881 | 1049 | 534 |
| 1996 | 377 885 | 5272 | 2436 | 7940 | 3906 | 119 633 | 103 071 | 17 255 | 13 465 | 31 835 | 71 602 | 975 | 495 |
| 1997 | 379 851 | 5295 | 1794 | 8199 | 4212 | 117 407 | 101 806 | 17 738 | 14 345 | 35 234 | 72 428 | 873 | 520 |
| 1998 | 375 360 | 5879 | 2034 | 8159 | 4729 | 116 060 | 97190 | 18 658 | 13 872 | 36 104 | 71 502 | 780 | 393 |
| 1999 | 379 450 | 6640 | 2099 | 8547 | 5170 | 116 797 | 100 727 | 18 979 | 13 720 | 35 393 | 70 090 | 871 | 417 |
| 2000 | 392 502 | 6609 | 2066 | 9232 | 5354 | 119 135 | 104 154 | 19 721 | 14 945 | 39 393 | 70 661 | 835 | 397 |
| 2001 | 373 216 | 6173 | 1779 | 9082 | 5162 | 112 887 | 98359 | 18 544 | 15 065 | 38 755 | 66 076 | 889 | 445 |
| 2002 | 359 046 | 5517 | 1347 | 8724 | 4685 | 110 244 | 95568 | 17 919 | 15 623 | 38 426 | 59 530 | 968 | 495 |
| 2003 | 348 715 | 5247 | 1241 | 8849 | 4604 | 107 160 | 93234 | 17 586 | 15 135 | 37 335 | 56 946 | 936 | 442 |
| 2004 | 340 502 | 4834 | 1037 | 9173 | 4185 | 104 209 | 90397 | 17 260 | 13 880 | 35 969 | 58 289 | 817 | 452 |
| 2005 | 337 930 | 4821 | 876 | 8998 | 4439 | 99067 | 89734 | 17 785 | 14 170 | 36 305 | 60 340 | 950 | 445 |
| 2006 | 329 357 | 4577 | 812 | 8339 | 4261 | 93886 | 83179 | 18 134 | 14 148 | 37 577 | 63 042 | 908 | 494 |
| 2007 | 317 524 | 4365 | 870 | 8280 | 4480 | 87186 | 80863 | 17 318 | 13 856 | 35 083 | 63 718 | 927 | 578 |
| 2008 | 307 814 | 4239 | 877 | 8120 | 4686 | 83900 | 78256 | 17 091 | 13 731 | 32 248 | 63 159 | 948 | 559 |

2002 & 2003 PE Number restated

Source: National Work Injuries Statistics Program, Association of Workers' Compensation Boards of Canada.

*table* 10.2 **Number of Fatalities, by Province, 1993–2008**

| Year | Total | NL | PE | NS | NB | QC | ON | MB | SK | AB | BC | NT/NU | YT |
|---|---|---|---|---|---|---|---|---|---|---|---|---|---|
| 1993 | 758 | 11 | 2 | 40 | 14 | 134 | 292 | 25 | 33 | 77 | 124 | 5 | 1 |
| 1994 | 725 | 20 | 4 | 22 | 11 | 130 | 248 | 20 | 36 | 74 | 152 | 6 | 2 |
| 1995 | 748 | 26 | 2 | 20 | 17 | 148 | 245 | 22 | 26 | 93 | 134 | 12 | 3 |
| 1996 | 703 | 17 | 2 | 23 | 20 | 95 | 238 | 27 | 29 | 91 | 153 | 4 | 4 |
| 1997 | 833 | 19 | 3 | 20 | 17 | 202 | 225 | 21 | 38 | 120 | 164 | 4 | – |
| 1998 | 798 | 32 | 3 | 13 | 17 | 208 | 243 | 22 | 28 | 105 | 125 | 2 | – |
| 1999 | 787 | 27 | 3 | 17 | 20 | 164 | 283 | 23 | 34 | 66 | 147 | 2 | 1 |
| 2000 | 882 | 38 | – | 16 | 7 | 180 | 301 | 19 | 31 | 118 | 157 | 13 | 2 |
| 2001 | 919 | 26 | 5 | 8 | 15 | 180 | 328 | 25 | 35 | 118 | 168 | 11 | – |
| 2002 | 934 | 23 | 1 | 14 | 17 | 188 | 383 | 19 | 23 | 101 | 158 | 6 | 1 |
| 2003 | 963 | 23 | – | 18 | 7 | 175 | 378 | 24 | 35 | 127 | 170 | 5 | 1 |
| 2004 | 928 | 23 | 1 | 41 | 12 | 176 | 365 | 14 | 30 | 124 | 136 | 5 | 1 |
| 2005 | 1097 | 25 | 1 | 27 | 12 | 223 | 412 | 26 | 27 | 143 | 189 | 10 | 2 |
| 2006 | 976 | 18 | – | 12 | 15 | 206 | 373 | 27 | 30 | 124 | 160 | 8 | 3 |
| 2007 | 1055 | 23 | 2 | 14 | 9 | 206 | 439 | 28 | 29 | 154 | 140 | 9 | 2 |
| 2008 | 949 | 23 | 3 | 23 | 14 | 195 | 396 | 24 | 26 | 77 | 160 | 7 | 1 |

Alberta number corrected from 2004 publication

Source: National Work Injuries Statistics Program, Association of Workers' Compensation Boards of Canada.

The Strategic HR box on page 318 describes how organizations prepared for the outbreak of the H1N1 virus in 2009.

## 10.2 BASIC FACTS ABOUT OCCUPATIONAL HEALTH AND SAFETY LEGISLATION

All provinces, territories, and the federal jurisdiction have **occupational health and safety legislation** that is based on the principle of joint responsibility shared by workers and employers to maintain a hazard-free work environment and to enhance the health and safety of workers.[7]

### Purpose

These laws fall into three categories: general health and safety rules; rules for specific industries (for example, mining); and rules related to specific hazards (for example, asbestos). In some jurisdictions, these are combined into one overall law with regulations for specific industries and hazards, while in others they remain separate. The regulations are very complex and cover almost every conceivable hazard in great detail, as can be seen in Figure 10.1.

Provisions of occupational health and safety legislation differ significantly across Canada, but most provinces have some commonality, including responsibilities and rights of employers and employees and joint health and safety committees.

**occupational health and safety legislation** Laws intended to protect the health and safety of workers by minimizing work-related accidents and illnesses.

STRATEGIC HR

## Employers Prepare for Worst: Swine Flu Has Organizations Reviewing Pandemic Plans

It's early days for the onset of the H1N1 flu virus—also known as swine flu—in Canada but many employers have already started communicating with workers about the health risks and the possibility of a pandemic. Those organizations that still lack pandemic plans should start now, say industry experts.

The plans are important for more than just pandemics. They work for any kind of emergency, such as a terrorist attack, to help cope with the potential for high absenteeism and disrupted operations, said Diane Champagne, a Montreal-based principal for the health and benefits business at Mercer.

"Especially in the economic times we're in now, employers can't afford to have a high level of absenteeism when they may have already laid off people and may have just a sufficient number of people. It's really making sure your people can continue," she said. "Someone who doesn't have a plan now should be thinking about one."

Those creating plans should think about specific policies, such as employees staying at home, changes to travel plans and prevention measures, such as washing hands and keeping the workplace clean.

"That sort of thing employers could put in place quickly," said Champagne.

But there is no "boilerplate" approach, she said, because every organization is different and it depends on the industry, the size of the organization, the geographic reach and locations.

"Doing a preparedness plan does take some time because you have to think about all the policies you have to put in place, your backup systems, your critical paths and all that."

**Lessons from SARS outbreak**

Blakes law firm already has a formal process in place for such an event and the SARS outbreak in 2003 helped inform the protocol, said Mary Jackson, chief officer of legal personnel and professional development at Blakes in Toronto. Thus far, the law firm has monitored the news about the swine flu and sent out an email with suggestions on how employees can help prevent the virus' spread.

"It's finding a balance between taking the right precautions and being cautious and, on the other hand, not inflaming fear," said Jackson.

"You get so much news and information about it—that in itself raises the concern. It's important to show employees you care. Obviously we all look at things differently because of all the communication in the world. I think you have to respond."

The best time to plan is, of course, when there is no problem, but that goes against human nature, said S. Len Hong, president and CEO of the Canadian Centre for Occupational Health and Safety.

"This to me is a wake-up call. We actually had the luxury of a lull between SARS, Avian flu and now to get ready, but we'd better not get too many wake-up calls before we get into action. So now is the time to start doing things, start planning, start preparing employees, start preparing your business," he said. "Unfortunately, they do come and go so we should consider pandemics a normal business consideration and plan for them."

**How Scotiabank, L'Oréal are handling outbreak**

The health and welfare of employees is a top priority for Scotiabank, which is monitoring the situation and has sent out an executive letter to employees reinforcing proactive measures individuals can take, said Cory Garlough, Toronto-based vice-president of global employment strategies at Scotiabank. The company also has well-defined business continuity plans to ensure it can support customers should an unusual event occur, he said.

"These plans have been constantly evolving over the last several years and have been tested by the widespread power outage that occurred in 2003, SARS in 2003 and other events," he said. "We continue to refine and build on our strategies to ensure that we are as responsive as possible during a work interruption."

L'Oréal Canada is also monitoring the situation closely and keeping employees up to date through internal communications that relay information and recommendations put forth by health authorities such as the Public Health Agency of Canada.

"We also encourage employees to remain vigilant and invite them to visit the organizations' websites for additional information on any precautionary measures they can take to protect themselves," said Teresa Menna, manager of corporate citizenship and internal communications at L'Oréal in Montreal.

**Never too late to start**

Despite these examples, one-half of Canadian companies with 500 or more employees have no pandemic plan, according to a December 2008 survey by GlaxoSmithKline.

One-third do not intend to create one and only one percent of those companies with a plan have included the 15 key components recommended by authorities and experts, which include minimization of direct interaction among employees, identification of key employees and critical functions, extra stock of critical supplies and factoring day care closures and transportation disruptions into absenteeism projections.

There has been a lack of a sense of urgency, said Champagne, though the SARS crisis really was a wake-up call to a lot of organizations. Probably the most important part is the communication, ensuring employees have credible, up-to-date details on what to do and what not to do, said Champagne. Otherwise, they may start talking and spread false rumours, and things could get out of control.

"That's probably the most difficult part to manage, people's reactions and attitudes, everybody has different values," she said. "What you can't control are people's feelings and emotions when faced with a situation like that."

Source: S. Dobson, "Employers Prepare for Worst: Swine Flu has Organizations Reviewing Pandemic Plans," *Canadian HR Reporter*, May 18, 2009, p. 1. Reprinted with permission.

*figure* 10.1 **Ontario Occupational Health and Safety Act—Construction Regulations**

**O.REG.213/91**
**68. A sign used to direct traffic,**

(a) shall be diamond shaped, 450 millimetres wide and 450 millimetres long, with the diamond mounted at one corner on a pole 1.2 metres long;

(b) shall be made of material that has at least the rigidity of six millimetres thick plywood;

(c) shall be reflective fluorescent and coloured,

(i) red-orange on one side with the corner areas coloured black, so that the red-orange area forms a regular eight-sided figure, with the word "STOP" written in legible white letters 150 millimetres high in a central position on the sign, and

(ii) chartreuse on one side, with the word "SLOW" written in legible black letters 150 millimetres high in a central position on the sign; and

(d) shall be maintained in a clean condition.

## Responsibilities and Rights of Employers and Employees

In all jurisdictions, employers are responsible for taking every reasonable precaution to ensure the health and safety of their workers. This is called the "due diligence" requirement. Specific duties of the employer, as defined by legislation, include:

- filing government accident reports
- maintaining records
- posting safety notices and legislative information

**RPC 10-2 >**

**Ensures that security programs and policies minimize risks while considering the obligation of the employer and the rights of employees, the union, and third parties**

Employees have three basic rights under the joint responsibility model:

- the right to know about what hazards are present on the job, how these hazards affect the employee, and what health and safety training is available
- the right to participate in the occupational health and safety process
- the right to refuse unsafe work without fear of reprisals if they have "reasonable cause" to believe that the work is dangerous

This woman is not wearing a protective mask or goggles, which puts her at serious risk for an accident.

**RPC 10-3 >**

**Ensures due diligence and strict liability requirements are met; e.g., records are kept and formal procedures established**

"Reasonable cause" usually means that a complaint about a workplace hazard has not been satisfactorily resolved or a safety problem places employees in immediate danger. If performance of a task would adversely affect health and safety, an employee cannot be disciplined for refusing to do the job. An employee raises his or her concern to the supervisor, who collaborates with the health and safety representative and union member, if in a unionized environment, to investigate the situation and make a recommendation. If the employee is dissatisfied with the outcome, a government inspector is called to assess the situation and make a final ruling. If the inspector deems the work to be safe, the employee must return to work or face disciplinary action. These rights are limited in some emergency-response professions such as police, firefighters, and health-care practitioners, as refusal to work could put human lives in jeopardy. In these professions, there are other procedures to be followed.

**RPC 10-4 >**

**Responds to any refusals to perform work believed to be unsafe**

Employees also have responsibilities, which include taking reasonable care to protect their own health and safety and, in most cases, that of their coworkers. Specific requirements include wearing protective clothing and equipment and reporting any contravention of the law or regulations.

Health and safety professionals may be called upon to provide input on matters related to the drafting and/or application of legislation or regulations related to health, safety, security, and workers' compensation.

**RPC 10-5 >**

**Provides input on matters related to the drafting and/or application of legislation or regulations related to health, safety, security, and workers' compensation**

## Joint Health and Safety Committees

The function of joint health and safety committees is to provide a non-adversarial atmosphere where management and labour can work together to ensure a safe and healthy workplace. An effective committee has strong, consistent, and visible leadership and resource support, engages all employees to take an active role in health and safety, and attends senior management meetings and staff meetings to report on their work.[8] Most jurisdictions require a joint health and safety committee to be established in each workplace with 20 or more employees.

The committee is generally responsible for making regular inspections of the workplace to identify potential health and safety hazards, evaluating the hazards, and implementing solutions.[9] In order to effectively carry out these duties, committee members require training in health and safety, communications, problem solving, and teamwork.

A safety inspector visits the plant to check on reported violations of health and safety regulations.

## Enforcement of Occupational Health and Safety Laws

In all Canadian jurisdictions, occupational health and safety laws provide for government inspectors to periodically carry out safety inspections of workplaces. Health and safety inspectors have wide powers to conduct inspections, and employers are required to assist them.[10] Safety inspectors may enter a workplace at any time without a warrant or prior notification, and they may engage in any examination and inquiry that they believe necessary to ascertain whether the workplace is in compliance with the law. Safety inspectors may order a variety of actions on the part of employers and employees, including orders to stop work, stop using tools, install first aid equipment, and stop emission of contaminants.

Penalties consist of fines and/or jail terms. Governments across Canada are increasingly turning to prosecution as a means of enforcing health and safety standards. Bill C-45, known as the "corporate killing" amendment to the Criminal Code, imposes criminal liability on corporate executives and directors who fail to take reasonable measures in their company to protect employee and public safety. Under this legislation, the maximum fine on an organization for a summary conviction offence increased from \$25 000 to \$100 000. Penalties for negligence include up to 10 years in prison for injuries caused to an employee(s) or life imprisonment in the case of death. The first Canadian employer to be convicted for criminal charges in a workplace death faced a \$100 000 fine. At the hearing, the court heard how the company spent more than \$500 000 on safety improvements after the accident to reduce the probability of a repeat scenario.[11]

**RPC 10-6 >**

**Establishes a joint responsibility system as required by law (e.g., worker–management health and safety committees, investigations, audits, testing and training) to ensure employee safety**

## Control of Toxic Substances

Most occupational health and safety laws require basic precautions with respect to toxic substances, including chemicals, biohazards (such as HIV/AIDS), and physical agents (such as radiation, heat, and noise). An accurate inventory of these substances must be maintained, maximum exposure limits for airborne concentrations of these agents adhered to, the substances tested, and their use carefully controlled.

**WORKPLACE HAZARDOUS MATERIALS INFORMATION SYSTEM (WHMIS)** The **Workplace Hazardous Materials Information System (WHMIS)** is a Canada-wide legally mandated system designed to protect workers by providing crucial information about hazardous materials or substances in the workplace. WHMIS was the outcome of a cooperative effort between the federal, provincial, and territorial governments together with industry and organized labour. The WHMIS legislation has three components:[12]

1. Labelling of hazardous material containers to alert workers that there is a potentially hazardous product inside (see Figure 10.2 for examples of hazard symbols).
2. Material safety data sheets (MSDS) contain information on potential hazards (health, reactivity, fire, and environmental) and the procedures for safe handling of the product (see Figure 10.3 for a sample MSDS). The MSDS contain more explicit information than the label, including the use, storage, and emergency procedures related to the hazards of the product. Employees must know where the MSDS are filed at all times and the data sheets must be updated every three years or sooner if the product or product ingredients change.
3. WHMIS training is mandatory for all employees. Training includes how to identify WHMIS hazard symbols, read WHMIS supplier and workplace labels, and read and apply the information on an MSDS.

A movement is currently underway to align WHMIS with standardized hazard warnings and dangerous substance controls across the globe under the Globally Harmonized System of Classification and Labelling of Chemicals (GHS). This initiative is championed by the United Nations (UN), the International

**Workplace Hazardous Materials Information System (WHMIS)** A Canada-wide, legally mandated system designed to protect workers by providing information about hazardous materials in the workplace.

Canadian Centre for Occupational Health and Safety
**www.ccohs.ca**

Public Health Agency of Canada
**www.phac-aspc.gc.ca/index-eng.php**

*figure* 10.2 **WHMIS Symbols**

Source: WHMIS SYMBOLS, "Do you know these vital signs?" www.hc-sc.gc.ca/ewh-semt/alt_formats/hecs-sesc/pdf/occup-travail/whimis-simdut/poster_symbols-eng.pdf. Health Canada, 2005. Reproduced with the permission of the Minister of Public Works and Government Services Canada, 2009.

## *figure* 10.3 Material Safety Data Sheet

| | | | | |
|---|---|---|---|---|
| **SECTION 1—CHEMICAL PRODUCT AND COMPANY IDENTIFICATION** | | | | |
| Product identifier | | | [WHMIS Classification] | |
| Product Use | | | | |
| Manufacturer's Name | | Supplier's Name | | |
| Street Address | | Street Address | | |
| City | Province | City | Province | |
| Postal Code | Emergency Telephone | Postal Code | Emergency Telephone | |
| Date MSDS Prepared | MSDS Prepared by | | Phone Number | |
| **SECTION 2—COMPOSITION/INFORMATION ON INGREDIENTS** | | | | |
| Hazardous Ingredients *(specific)* | % | CAS Number | LD50 of Ingredients *(specific species and route)* | LC50 of Ingredients *(specify species)* |
| | | | | |
| | | | | |
| | | | | |
| | | | | |
| **SECTION 3—HAZARDS IDENTIFICATION** | | | | |
| Route of Entry | ☐ Skin Contact ☐ Skin Absorption ☐ Eye Contact ☐ Inhalation ☐ Ingestion | | | |
| [Emergency Overview] | | | | |
| | | | | |
| [WHMIS Symbols] | | | | |
| | | | | |
| [Potential Health Effects] | | | | |
| | | | | |
| | | | | |
| | | | | |
| **SECTION 4—FIRST AID MEASURES** | | | | |
| Skin Contact | | | | |
| Eye Contact | | | | |
| Inhalation | | | | |
| Ingestion | | | | |
| | | | | |

continued

## *figure* 10.3 Material Safety Data Sheet—continued

| Product Identifier | | |
|---|---|---|
| **SECTION 5—FIRE FIGHTING MEASURES** | | |
| Flammability ☐ Yes ☐ No | If yes, under which conditions? | |
| Means of Extinction | | |
| | | |
| | | |
| Flashpoint (°C) and Method | Upper Flammable Limit *(% of volume)* | Lower Flammable Limit *(% of volume)* |
| Autoignition Temperature (°C) | Explosion Data—Sensitivity to impact | |
| Hazardous Combustion Products | | |
| [NFPA] | | |
| **SECTION 6—ACCIDENTAL RELEASE MEASURES** | | |
| Leak and Spill Procedures | | |
| | | |
| | | |
| | | |
| **SECTION 7—HANDLING AND STORAGE** | | |
| Handling Procedures and Equipment | | |
| | | |
| | | |
| Storage Requirments | | |
| | | |
| | | |
| | | |
| **SECTION 8—EXPOSURE CONTROL/PERSONAL PROTECTION** | | |
| Exposure Limits ☐ ACGIH TLV ☐ OSHA PEL ☐ Other (specify) | | |
| Specific Engineering Controls *(such as ventilation, enclosed process)* | | |
| | | |
| | | |
| Personal Protective Equipment ☐ Gloves ☐ Respirator ☐ Eye ☐ Footwear ☐ Clothing ☐ Other | | |
| If checked, specify type | | |
| | | |
| | | |

| Product Identifier | | |
|---|---|---|
| **SECTION 9—PHYSICAL AND CHEMICAL PROPERTIES** | | |
| Physical State | Odour and Appearance | Odour Threshold (ppm) |
| Specific Gravity | Vapour Density (air = 1) | Vapour Pressure (mmHg) |
| Evaporation Rate | Boiling Point (°C) | Freezing Point (°C) |
| pH | Coefficient of Water/Oil Distribution | [Solubility in Water] |
| **SECTION 10—STABILITY AND REACTIVITY** | | |
| Chemical Stability | | |
| Incompatibility with Other Substances | | |
| | | |
| | | |
| Reactivity, and under what conditions? | | |
| | | |
| | | |
| Hazardous Decomposition Products | | |
| | | |
| | | |
| **SECTION 11—TOXICOLOGICAL INFORMATION** | | |
| Effects of Acute Exposure | | |
| | | |
| | | |
| | | |
| Effects of Chronic Exposure | | |
| | | |
| | | |
| | | |
| | | |
| Irritancy of Product | | |
| Skin Sensitization | Respiratory Sensitization | |
| Carcinogenicity–IARC | Carcinogenicity–ACGIH | |
| Reproductive Toxicity | Teratogenicity | |
| Embryotoxicity | Mutagenicity | |
| Name of Synergistic Products/Effects | | |

continued

## *figure* 10.3 Material Safety Data Sheet—continued

| **SECTION 12—ECOLOGICAL INFORMATION** |
|---|
| [Aquatic Toxicity] |
| |
| |
| |

| **SECTION 13—DISPOSAL CONSIDERATIONS** |
|---|
| Waste Disposal |
| |
| |
| |

| **SECTION 14—TRANSPORT INFORMATION** | |
|---|---|
| Special Shipping Information | |
| | PIN |
| TDG | [DOT] |
| | |
| [IMO] | [ICAO] |
| | |
| | |

| **SECTION 15—REGULATORY INFORMATION** | |
|---|---|
| [WHMIS Classification] | [OSHA] |
| | |
| [SERA] | [TSCA] |
| | |
| | |

***This product has been classified in accordance with the hazard criteria of the Controlled Products Regulations (CPR), and the MSDS contains all of the information required by CPR.***

| **SECTION 16—OTHER INFORMATION** |
|---|
| |
| |
| |
| |
| |

Source: Reprinted with permission of Saskatchewan Labour, www.labour.gov.sk.ca/safety/forms/MSDS-16.pdf (March 20, 2005).

Labour Organization, the Organization for Economic Co-operation and Development, and the European Union (EU). As international trade in chemical products grows, it is argued that a standardized system should be in place. A standardized system would be beneficial for underdeveloped countries that have few regulations of hazards; in remedying inconsistencies in national systems that have different classifications, labels, and safety data sheets for the same product sold in different countries; and in reducing costs and time associated with meeting classification and labelling requirements in each country.[13]

**RPC 10-7 >**

**Ensures that the organization complies with legislated and contractual requirements for information management (e.g., records of hours worked and records of exposure to hazardous substances)**

## Occupational Health and Safety and Other Legislation

Health and safety, human rights, labour relations, and employment standards laws are in force in every jurisdiction in Canada in an interlaced web of legislation. Situations arise in which it is difficult to know which law is applicable or which one takes precedence over another.[14] For example, are the human rights of one employee to wear a ceremonial knife related to a religion more important than the safety of other employees? How much discipline is acceptable to labour arbitrators for health and safety violations? Should fights in the workplace be considered a safety hazard? Is sexual harassment a safety hazard? How long does an employer have to tolerate poor performance from an alcoholic employee whose attempts at treatment fail? In Saskatchewan, human rights and occupational health and safety laws overlap because sexual harassment is considered to be a workplace hazard.[15]

## The Supervisor's Role in Safety

Most jurisdictions impose a personal duty on supervisors to ensure that workers comply with occupational health and safety regulations and place a specific obligation on supervisors to advise and instruct workers about safety.[16] In 2003, Great Lakes Power Ltd. was fined $250 000 for failing to train a 21-year old worker who was electrocuted and lost three of his limbs as a result.[17]

Safety-minded managers must aim to instil the desire to work safely in their workers. Minimizing hazards (by ensuring that spills are wiped up, machine guards are adequate, and so forth) is important, but no matter how safe the workplace is, there will be accidents unless workers want to and do act safely. Of course, supervisors try to watch each employee closely, but most managers know that this will not work. In the final analysis, the best (and perhaps only) alternative is to get workers to want to work safely. Then, when needed, supervisors should enforce safety rules.[18]

**TOP-MANAGEMENT COMMITMENT** Most safety experts agree that safety commitment begins with top management. If top managers are not committed to safety, that lack of commitment may extend down through the organization and be reflected in a company's safety record. On the other hand, if safety is seen as a priority starting at the top of the organization, it will usually be viewed as a priority by the rest of the company. One of the best examples of setting the highest possible priority for safety takes place at a DuPont plant in Germany. Each morning at the DuPont Polyester and Nylon Plant, the director and his assistants meet at 8:45 to review the previous 24 hours. The first matter they discuss is not production but safety. Only after they have examined reports of accidents and near misses and satisfied themselves that corrective action has been taken do they move on to look at output, quality, and cost matters.[19]

**RPC 10-8 >**

**Analyzes risk to the health and safety of employees and determines appropriate preventative measures, including training, provision of required safety equipment, and administrative practices**

In summary, without full commitment at all levels of management, any attempts to reduce unsafe acts by workers will likely meet with little success.

**RPC 10-9 >**

**Establishes effective programs for accident prevention, incident investigation, inspections, fire and emergency response, and required training**

## In-class Notes

**Basic Facts about Occupational Health and Safety Legislation**

- Employers are responsible for "due diligence" to maintain worker health and safety
- Employees have the right to refuse unsafe work
- Joint health and safety committees required to ensure a healthy workplace
- Workplace Hazardous Materials Information System (WHMIS) requires precautions regarding toxic substances
- Supervisors have personal duty for safety of their workers

# 10.3 WORKPLACE ACCIDENTS AND ACCIDENT PREVENTION

The causes of workplace accidents must be clearly understood in order to implement effective accident prevention programs.

## Causes of Workplace Accidents

There are three basic causes of workplace accidents: chance occurrences, unsafe conditions in the workplace, and unsafe acts on the part of employees.

An accident in a Toronto subway tunnel, in which three passengers were killed, provides a vivid example of all of these factors. Signal problems that had been reported by eight other drivers throughout the day had not been addressed as crews had been sent to the wrong tunnel. A rookie driver ran three red signal lights, a trip alarm failed, a call for help rang 15 times and then got a voice-mail direction to call another number, emergency crews were sent to look for an "odour," the radio system did not work in the tunnels, and the drivers had no evacuation training.[20]

**CHANCE OCCURRENCES** Chance occurrences (such as walking past a plate-glass window just as someone hits a ball through it) contribute to accidents but are more or less beyond management's control. We will therefore focus on *unsafe conditions* and *unsafe acts*.

**UNSAFE CONDITIONS** **Unsafe conditions** are one of the main causes of accidents. They include such factors as:

- improperly guarded or defective equipment
- hazardous procedures in, on, or around machinery or equipment
- unsafe storage (congestion, overloading)
- improper illumination (glare, insufficient light)
- improper ventilation (insufficient air change, impure air source)[21]

The basic remedy is to eliminate or minimize unsafe conditions. Government standards address the mechanical and physical conditions that cause accidents. A checklist of unsafe conditions can be used to conduct a job hazard analysis. Common indicators of job hazards include increased numbers of accidents, employee complaints, poor product quality, employee modifications to workstations, and higher levels of absenteeism and turnover.[22]

**RPC 10-10 >**

**Ensures internal environmental concerns, such as quality of air and water, are addressed**

**UNSAFE ACTS** Most safety experts and managers know it is impossible to eliminate accidents just by improving unsafe conditions. People cause accidents, and no one has found an effective way to eliminate **unsafe acts** by employees, such as:

**AN ETHICAL DILEMMA**

Is it ethical to provide safety training in English to immigrant workers who speak little English, in order to save money?

- operating or working at unsafe speeds (either too fast or too slow)
- making safety devices inoperative by removing, adjusting, or disconnecting them
- using unsafe equipment or using equipment unsafely
- using unsafe procedures in loading, placing, mixing, combining
- lifting or handling goods improperly
- distracting, teasing, abusing, startling, or quarrelling with coworkers or instigating horseplay

**THREE OTHER WORK-RELATED ACCIDENT FACTORS** In addition to unsafe conditions, three other work-related factors contribute to accidents: the *job itself*, the *work schedule*, and the *psychological climate* of the workplace.

Certain jobs are inherently more dangerous than others. According to one study, for example, the job of crane operator results in about three times more accident-related hospital visits than does the job of supervisor. Similarly, work is inherently safer in some departments than in others. An accounting department usually has fewer accidents than a shipping department, for example.

Work schedules and fatigue also affect accident rates. Accident rates usually do not increase too noticeably during the first five or six hours of the workday. Beyond that, however, the accident rate increases quickly as the number of hours worked increases. This is due partly to fatigue. It has also been found that accidents occur more often during night shifts.

Many experts believe that the psychological climate of the workplace affects the accident rate. For example, accidents occur more frequently in plants with a high seasonal layoff rate and those where there is hostility among employees, many garnished wages, and blighted living conditions. Temporary stress factors, such as high workplace temperature, poor illumination, and a congested workplace are also related to accident rates. It appears that workers who work under stress or who consider their jobs to be threatened or insecure have more accidents than those who do not. Figure 10.4 offers a sample of questions that should be asked to assess the root cause of an accident.

## Accident Prevention

No matter what the possible causes of accidents might be, in practice, accident prevention boils down to two basic activities: reducing unsafe conditions and reducing unsafe acts.

**REDUCING UNSAFE CONDITIONS** Reducing unsafe conditions is an employer's first line of defence. Safety engineers should design jobs to remove or reduce physical hazards. Supervisors and managers also play a role in reducing unsafe conditions. A brief checklist can be used to identify and remove potential hazards. However, only 4 percent of accidents stem from unsafe working conditions, so we will concentrate mainly on accident prevention methods that focus on changing behaviours.[23]

**REDUCING UNSAFE ACTS** Reducing unsafe acts is the second basic approach to accident prevention, and this can be done in a variety of ways, including:

1. Screening out accident-prone people or people who are not physically fit for the job requirements by using appropriate tests and by asking legally sanctioned questions according to human rights legislation. Any policy for required medical testing must fall within the limits of applicable legislation and contracts.
2. Training and educating employees in such areas as safe work practices and procedures and WHMIS. Safety associations, such as the Industrial Accident Prevention Association (IAPA), are available to partner in training efforts. Studies have shown that

**unsafe conditions** The mechanical and physical conditions that cause accidents.

**unsafe acts** Behavioural tendencies and undesirable attitudes that cause accidents. Unsafe acts can undermine even the best attempts to minimize unsafe conditions.

Health Canada **www.hc-sc.gc.ca**

WHMIS Training **www.whmis.net**

Occupational Exposure to Hazardous Agents **http://hazmap.nlm.nih.gov**

All Canadian Workers' Compensation Boards - **www.awcbc.org**

Canada Safety Council **www.safety-council.org**

Industrial Accident Prevention Association **www.iapa.on.ca**

## *figure* 10.4 Exercising Due Diligence When Investigating Workplace Accidents

The causes of any accident can be grouped into five categories—task, material, environment, personnel and management. Under each category there are several questions that need to be asked to assess the cause. The following are sample questions only and should not be considered a comprehensive checklist.

**Task**
Here the actual work procedure being used at the time of the accident is explored. Members of the accident investigation team will look for answers to questions such as:

- ❑ Was a safe work procedure used?
- ❑ Had conditions changed to make the normal procedure unsafe?
- ❑ Were the appropriate tools and materials available?
- ❑ Were they used?
- ❑ Were safety devices working properly?
- ❑ Was lockout used when necessary?

For most of these questions, an important follow-up question is "If not, why not?"

**Material**
To seek out possible causes resulting from the equipment and materials used, investigators might ask:

- ❑ Was there an equipment failure?
- ❑ What caused it to fail?
- ❑ Was the machinery poorly designed?
- ❑ Were hazardous substances involved?
- ❑ Were they clearly identified?
- ❑ Was a less hazardous alternative substance possible and available?
- ❑ Was the raw material substandard in some way?
- ❑ Should personal protective equipment (PPE) have been used?
- ❑ Was the PPE used?
- ❑ Were users of PPE properly trained?

**Environment**
The physical environment, and especially sudden changes to that environment, are factors that need to be identified. The situation at the time of the accident is what is important, not what the "usual" conditions were. For example, accident investigators may want to know:

- ❑ What were the weather conditions?
- ❑ Was poor housekeeping a problem?
- ❑ Was it too hot or too cold?
- ❑ Was noise a problem?
- ❑ Was there adequate light?
- ❑ Were toxic or hazardous gases, dusts, or fumes present?

**Personnel**
The physical and mental condition of those individuals directly involved in the event must be explored. The purpose for investigating the accident is not to establish blame against someone but the inquiry will not be complete unless personal characteristics are considered. Some factors will remain essentially constant while others may vary from day to day:

- ❑ Were workers experienced in the work being done?
- ❑ Had they been adequately trained?
- ❑ Can they physically do the work?
- ❑ What was the status of their health?
- ❑ Were they tired?
- ❑ Were they under stress (work or personal)?

**Management**
Management holds the legal responsibility for the safety of the workplace and therefore the role of supervisors and higher management and the role or presence of management systems must always be considered in an accident investigation. Failures of management systems are often found to be direct or indirect factors in accidents. Ask questions such as:

- ❑ Were safety rules communicated to and understood by all employees?
- ❑ Were written procedures and orientation available?
- ❑ Were they being enforced?
- ❑ Was there adequate supervision?
- ❑ Were workers trained to do the work?
- ❑ Had hazards been previously identified?
- ❑ Had procedures been developed to overcome them?
- ❑ Were unsafe conditions corrected?
- ❑ Was regular maintenance of equipment carried out?
- ❑ Were regular safety inspections carried out?

**Physical evidence**
Before attempting to gather information, examine the site for a quick overview, take steps to preserve evidence, and identify all witnesses. In some jurisdictions, an accident site must not be disturbed without prior approval from appropriate government officials such as the coroner, inspector, or police. Physical evidence is probably the most non-controversial information available. It is also subject to rapid change or obliteration; therefore, it should be the first to be recorded. Based on your knowledge of the work process, you may want to check items such as:

- ❑ positions of injured workers
- ❑ equipment being used
- ❑ materials or chemicals being used
- ❑ safety devices in use
- ❑ position of appropriate guards
- ❑ position of controls of machinery
- ❑ damage to equipment
- ❑ housekeeping of the area
- ❑ weather conditions
- ❑ lighting levels
- ❑ noise levels
- ❑ time of day.

**Interviewing witnesses**
Ask open-ended questions that cannot be answered "yes" or "no." The actual questions you ask the witness will naturally vary with each accident, but there are some general questions that should be asked each time:

- ❑ Where were you at the time of the accident?
- ❑ What were you doing at the time?
- ❑ What did you see, hear?
- ❑ What were the environmental conditions (weather, light, noise, etc.) at the time?
- ❑ What was (were) the injured worker(s) doing at the time?
- ❑ In your opinion, what caused the accident?
- ❑ How might similar accidents be prevented in the future?

Source: Adapted from Accident Investigation, www.ccohs.ca/oshanswers/hsprograms/investig.html, OSH Answers, Canadian Centre for Occupational Health and Safety (CCOHS), 2006. Reproduced with the permission of CCOHS, 2010.

only one in five employees in Canada receives safety training during their first year with a new employer.[24]

3. Building awareness and providing positive reinforcement for employees. Safety posters and other programs can be used to build awareness of the costs and benefits of good safety practices. Reinforcement in the form of charts or graphs showing the improved safety rate can also be used. Supervisors should praise employees individually or collectively at departmental meetings. Some companies may even offer such tangible rewards as coffee and doughnuts at the end of the shift after an accident-free week or month.
4. Providing top management commitment to employee health and safety. One of the most consistent findings in the literature is that successful health and safety programs require a strong management commitment.[25] This should be made evident to all workers by having top managers give safety a priority in company meetings, by giving the safety officer a high rank and status, and by having managers communicate the importance of health and safety to all workers.
5. Monitoring work overload and stress among employees. In one recent study, "role overload" (formally defined as the degree to which an employee's performance was seen as being affected by inadequate time, training, and resources) was significantly associated with unsafe behaviours.[26] Similarly, other researchers have suggested that as work overload increases, workers are more likely to adopt risky work methods. Thus, having employers and supervisors monitor employees (particularly those in relatively hazardous jobs) for signs of stress and overload may reduce unsafe acts.

**RPC 10-11 >**

**Contributes to and ensures that policies for required medical testing are in place and fall within the limits of statute and contract**

6. Educating younger workers. Younger workers under the age of 25 are at a much higher risk of injury than workers of any other age group. In 2006, more than 50 700 workers under the age of 24 lost time from workplace injuries and 51 died on the job.[27] This group suffers more injuries because of their inexperience and lack of training, a lack of confidence or understanding of their rights as workers, being asked to do more dangerous work, a sense of youthful invincibility, and unwillingness to ask questions. The most effective ways to prevent injuries to young workers are training and orientation (in particular, peer-to-peer training), health and safety training for supervisors, and more education for youth, parents, employers, and unions on workers' rights and responsibilities concerning workplace health and safety.[28]

**RPC 10-12 >**

**Provides information to employees and managers on available programs**

In Ontario, the Workplace Safety and Insurance Board (WSIB) created the Young Worker Awareness Program to give students the information they need to protect their health and safety on the job. It has two components, a general assembly presentation and a classroom instruction segment. Both the general assembly and classroom components stress student interaction. Using video and other materials, trained instructors will come to any Ontario high school to deliver this crucial message. Students receive a resource booklet and other information. There is no charge to the student or school for the program.[29]

Also in Ontario, the Ministry of Labour, the Ministry of Education, and the WSIB launched an effective workplace safety ad campaign aimed at 15- to 19-year-olds. It features animated ads that are shown in movie theatres, on public transit, and online. The Live Safe! Work Smart! program, which provides teachers with resources to help prepare high-school students for the job-specific safety training every employer must provide, is now being extended to elementary school students.[30]

**RPC 10-13 >**

**Ensures that mechanisms are in place for responding to crises in the workplace, including critical incident stress management**

Other actions management can take to reduce unsafe acts include establishing a safety policy, setting specific safety goals, having a safety manager, and conducting regular health and safety inspections. An innovative approach to safety in small businesses is outlined in the Entrepreneurs and HR box on page 332.

## ENTREPRENEURS AND HR

# An Innovative Occupational Health and Safety Initiative for Small Business

Small businesses have proportionately more injuries than big businesses, but small firm owners have often felt overburdened and underserved by health and safety agencies and workers' compensation boards. An innovative Canada-wide initiative is trying to improve this situation. The Safe Communities Foundation (SCF) was launched on April 23, 1996.

A health and safety incentive program was created through a partnership of the SCF and the Ontario Workplace Safety and Insurance Board (WSIB). Small- and medium-sized businesses in Ontario paying less than $90 000 in WSIB premiums can join the Safe Communities Incentive Plan (SCIP) and learn how to build and improve their health and safety systems. SCIP also offers a financial incentive for firms that complete the program.

SCIP is a two-part program where members can qualify for a WSIB rebate after attending training courses and workshops. Part 1 offers a five-percent rebate once the owner or senior manager of the firm attends the "5 Steps to Managing Health and Safety" training program and submits documents about their firm's strategy for implementing health and safety in the workplace. Once Part 1 is completed, a firm can qualify for another rebate of up to five percent based on completing Part 2, which entails forming a group with other firms and furthering their health and safety program development. The rebate is calculated based on the group reduction in injury costs. These rebates are in addition to any benefits an employer receives through their regular incentive program.

Employers benefit by being able to publicize their firms' status as safe places to work. By reducing injuries, firms will also enjoy such benefits as improved productivity, less downtime, and fewer missed deadlines.

So far, the program has been a great success. More than 6000 businesses in Ontario communities that participated in SCIP from 1997–2005 significantly reduced their claims costs and shared rebates that totalled more than $11 million from the WSIB.

Forty-six Safe Communities now cover about 22 percent of the Canadian population and 20 more communities are working toward the Safe Communities designation. The ultimate goal of the SCF is thousands of Safe Communities from sea to sea, creating a Canada-wide safety culture.

Source: Safe Communities Foundation. www.safecommunities.ca, February 2006. Used with permission.

## *In-class Notes*

**Workplace Accidents and Accident Prevention**

- Three basic causes of accidents:
    - chance occurrences
    - unsafe conditions
    - unsafe acts
- Other causes include the job itself, work schedule, psychological climate of the workplace
- Accident prevention through:
    - reducing unsafe working conditions through job hazard analysis
    - reducing unsafe acts by safety training, top management commitment to safety, monitoring work overload and stress, and educating young workers

## 10.4 CONTROLLING WORKERS' COMPENSATION COSTS

Workers' compensation premiums for employers are proportional to the amount of money paid to claimants. Thus, the more workers' compensation claims a company has, the more the company will pay in premiums. It is therefore important for health and safety professionals to coordinate workers' compensation benefits with other employee benefits, such as sick leave, long-term disability, and pension, so that any other applicable benefits are used to reduce the amount of a workers' compensation claim.

According to Ontario's Workplace Safety and Insurance Board, total benefits paid increased from $2.91 billion in 2005 to slightly over $3.0 billion in 2007. Total benefits include loss of earnings, health care, and labour market re-entry benefits. When an employer has one or more employees off work on a disability claim, they usually have most of the following costs: overtime, replacement worker, training, reduced productivity, increased absenteeism, reduced employee morale, and legal requirements.[31] Each year for the past 10 years, over 330 000 Ontario workers have made claims for injuries incurred while they were at work.[32] As WSIB officials like to state, however, while these numbers are high, they are able to process almost 97 percent of them within two months.[33]

**RPC 10-14 >**

**Coordinates workers' compensation benefits with other employee benefits, such as sick leave, long-term disability, and pension**

There are several steps in reducing workers' compensation claims:

**Step 1.** *Preventing the accident.* The appropriate time to begin controlling workers' compensation claims is before the accident happens, not after. This involves taking all of the steps previously summarized. For example, firms should remove unsafe conditions, screen out employees who might be accident-prone for the job in question (without violating human rights legislation), and establish a safety policy and loss-control goals.

**RPC 10-15 >**

**Establishes and implements strategies to minimize compensation costs**

**Step 2.** *Responding appropriately to the accident.* Occupational injury or illness can obviously be a traumatic event for the employee, and the employer's way of handling it can influence the injured worker's reaction. The employee is going to have specific needs and specific questions, such as where to go for medical help and whether he or she will be paid for any time off. Employers should provide first aid and make sure that the worker gets quick medical attention; make it clear that they are interested in the injured worker and his or her fears and questions; document the accident; file any required accident reports; and encourage a speedy return to work.[34]

**RPC 10-16 >**

**Analyzes rate grouping costs, early intervention and return-to-work programs, claims management programs, and claims appeals**

**Step 3.** *Facilitating the employee's return to work.* Controlling workers' compensation costs is vital to an organization, and one of the ways to do this is to facilitate the employee's return to work as soon as possible. Specific actions to encourage early return to work can be internal and/or external to the organization. Internally, an employer can set up rehabilitation committees, which include relevant stakeholders, such as the employee and his or her colleagues, HR professionals, union representatives, and managers, to identify modified work.

**Step 4.** *Conducting functional abilities evaluations (FAEs).* Functional abilities evaluations are an important step in facilitating return to work. A health-care professional conducts an FAE in order to:

- improve the chances that the injured worker will be safe on the job
- help the worker's performance by identifying problem areas of work that can be addressed by physical therapy or accommodated through job modification
- determine the level of disability so that the worker can either go back to his or her original job or be accommodated[35]

**RPC 10-17 >**

**Creates a strategy for effective liaison with the medical community**

**RPC 10-18 >**

**Ensures compliance with legislated reporting requirements**

*In-class Notes*

**Controlling Workers' Compensation Costs**

- Costs are proportional to amount of money paid to claimants
- Accident prevention
- Respond appropriately to accidents that do occur
- Facilitate employee return to work
- Conduct functional abilities evaluations

Externally, the employer can work with the employee's family to ensure that they are supportive, mobilize the resources of the EAP to help the employee, ensure that physical and occupational therapists are available, and make the family physician aware of workplace accommodation possibilities.[36] A study by consultants Sobeco, Ernst & Young found that 90 percent of companies have formal return-to-work programs but only 62 percent of those apply the program to all employees with disabilities.[37]

The City of Toronto uses software that can develop alternative career paths for employees who are physically or psychologically unable to perform a particular job by matching their restricted abilities with jobs whose physical and psychological demands they are able to meet. The City's savings from returning employees to productivity have been estimated to range from $800 000 to $1.2 million.[38]

**RPC 10-19 >**

**Ensures accommodation and graduated return-to-work programs are in place to meet the needs of disabled employees**

**RPC 10-20 >**

**Ensures that modifications to the work environment are consistent with the nature of worker disability (e.g., total versus partial and temporary versus permanent)**

## 10.5 EMPLOYEE WELLNESS PROGRAMS

There are three elements in a healthy workplace—the physical environment, the social environment, and health practices. **Employee wellness programs** take a proactive approach to all of these areas of employee well-being, unlike EAPs, which provide reactive management of employee health problems. Wellness should be viewed as a strategic health and safety initiative to achieve measurable outcomes related to increased levels of employee health, such as reduced health and safety costs, decreased absenteeism, lower workers' compensation costs, fewer long-term disability claims, reduced time off for short-term disability/sickness, increased morale, decreased health-care costs, and fewer employees in high-risk health categories (such as smokers).[39] With the cost of employee absenteeism soaring to $8.6 billion annually, health benefit costs increasing from 3.2 percent of payroll in 1990 to 7.3 percent of payroll in 2005, and the average days lost per worker due to illness increasing from 7.3 in 1997 to 9.2 in 2006, wellness is of paramount concern to Canadian employers. Studies have found that workplace wellness initiatives are an effective way to counter these costs, with data collected over the past 10 years showing that for every dollar invested in wellness, the returns have been cost savings between $2.30 and $10.00.[40]

Wellness initiatives often include stress management, nutrition and weight management, smoking-cessation programs, heart health (such as screening

Executives of the Federation des Caisses Desjardins du Québec lead a noon-hour walk in Montreal to launch a wellness campaign that challenges staff to exercise five times a week.

cholesterol and blood pressure levels), physical fitness programs, and workstation wellness through ergonomics.[41] At Husky Injection Molding, a $4.2 million investment in wellness helped save $9 million and has been very useful as a recruitment and retention tool.[42] North Atlantic Refining, a Newfoundland-based oil refinery, also takes pride in its wellness program, which was instrumental in helping it achieve a million employee hours without a lost-time injury in 2006, marking the second time in three years the organization reached this safety landmark. North Atlantic Refining was named as one of Canada's Top 100 Employers in 2008 for the third year in a row.[43]

Incentives are often used to encourage employees to engage in organization-sponsored wellness initiatives. For example, employees at IMB accumulate points for their workouts, which they trade in for extra money in their health-spending accounts. At Honeywell, employees who log a certain number of workout hours can save money on their fitness club fees through company subsidies. Organizations with good incentives, effective marketing, and strong promotion typically have a wellness participation rate of 30 to 60 percent. compared to a maximum 15 percent participation rate in companies with no incentives and poor marketing and promotion.[44]

**RPC 10-21 >**

**Develops or provides for wellness and employee assistance programs to support organizational effectiveness**

## *In-class Notes*

**Employee Wellness Programs**

- Strategic health and safety initiatives that take a proactive approach to employee well-being
- Wellness programs can include stress management, nutrition and weight management, smoking cessation, heart health, physical fitness, ergonomics
- Highly cost-effective

**employee wellness program** A program that takes a proactive approach to employee health and well-being.

## 10.6 OCCUPATIONAL HEALTH ISSUES AND CHALLENGES

A number of health-related issues and challenges can undermine employee performance at work.[45] These include alcoholism and substance abuse, stress, repetitive strain injuries, workplace toxins, workplace smoking, and workplace violence.

**RPC 10-22 >**

**Contributes to policy on the workplace environment (e.g., smoking, workplace violence, scent-free environment, communicable diseases, and addictions)**

### Alcoholism and Substance Abuse

Alcoholism is a serious and widespread disease with staggering costs. Substance abuse can cause a range of problems at work, including absenteeism, illness, reduced productivity, social withdrawal, psychological or stress-related effects, and engaging in illegal activities in the workplace, such as selling drugs and alcohol to other employees. The Canadian Centre on Substance Abuse estimates the annual lost productivity due to alcohol and drug abuse at close to $1.7 billion nationwide. Employers can expect between 3 and 7 percent of their workforce to be alcoholics, 10 to 30 percent of workers to drink to excess, and 2 to 7 percent to have a problem with illicit drug use, according to the Ontario Centre for Addiction and Mental Health.[46] Overall, about 30 percent of Canadian companies report having problems with drug and alcohol abuse in the workplace.[47]

#### WORKPLACE SUBSTANCE ABUSE AND THE LAW

Because of the seriousness of this problem, most employers take additional steps to deal with alcohol and substance abuse on the job. This is difficult in Canada because employers must balance conflicting legal obligations. On the one hand, Canadian human rights and privacy laws must be respected. Alcoholism and drug addiction are generally considered to be disabilities under human rights legislation. On the other hand, under occupational health and safety legislation, employers are responsible for maintaining due diligence.

**LEGALcompliance**

Alcohol and drug testing are only permitted under certain circumstances, as discussed in Chapter 5. Random drug testing is generally not permitted other than in "safety-sensitive" positions or upon reinstatement following a workplace incident where impairment affected performance and as part of a larger drug abuse investigation. "Safety sensitive" refers to the actual functions being carried out by the employee, rather than to his or her overall job.

A British Columbia arbitrator recently ruled on the legitimacy of drug and alcohol testing for safety-sensitive positions at Eurocan Pulp and Paper, which operates a mill and dock for its paper products in Kitimat. Safety is the company's priority and is enforced by a policy that prohibits reporting for work under the influence of drugs and alcohol, including hangovers. One of its ship loaders responsible for loading large cargo onto barges and cargo ships at the dock terminal reported to work smelling of alcohol and was asked to take an alcohol test. The employee filed a grievance claiming unjust cause for testing, but the arbitrator ruled that Eurocan had reasonable cause to ask for the test in a workplace where safety is paramount. The arbitrator also ruled that the employee was to meet with a substance abuse professional before returning to work.[48]

At present, it appears that employers can have a policy forbidding drugs and alcohol in the workplace; require random drug testing for employees in safety-sensitive jobs; and conduct mandatory drug testing after an accident or near-accident if the employer has reasonable or probable grounds to suspect that such abuse contributed to the accident.[49]

In general, a clear, well-communicated substance abuse policy that is reasonably and consistently enforced is the employer's best approach.

### Job Stress

Stress is the number-one health risk in the workplace and is called the "silent killer" because it is a taboo topic in most professional circles. North American culture espouses hyper-busyness as a measure of success in employees' personal and professional lives. References to personal struggle, the need for assistance, and anxieties associated with meeting expectations are buried because they suggest weakness and raise concerns about competency. These conversations are usually deemed off limits, and employees are expected to fend for themselves with solitary interventions. Hence, employees manage stress in silence.

In a nationwide poll, nearly half of all Canadian workers said that they experience "a great deal of stress at work."[50] Almost 40 percent of respondents to a 2008 survey declared that their workplace stress is so overwhelming that it made them physically ill. More troubling is that this statistic increased from 25 percent in 2002.[51] Studies have also found that 41 percent of employees are of the opinion that their employers are not doing "nearly enough" to help them manage stress in the workplace.

**AN ETHICAL DILEMMA**

Should a supervisor ignore an employee's claim that he/she is "stressed" until there is evidence that he/she is not meeting performance standards?

Organizations begin to suffer when too many employees feel that the relentless pace of work life is neither sustainable nor healthy.[52] Why is this happening? One reason is the burgeoning use of technology in the workplace—the sheer volume of email and voice mail is imposing terrific amounts of pressure and distraction on employees, taking a toll on their emotional equilibrium. Interestingly, Australians have condemned email as the number-one cause of workplace stress.[53] The effects of stress are not trivial—time lost as a result of stress-related absenteeism amounts to 19 million days per year, with a direct and indirect annual cost estimated at $4.5 to $6 billion.[54]

**BURNOUT** Many people fall victim to **burnout**—the total depletion of physical and mental resources—due to excessive striving to reach an unrealistic work-related goal. Burnout is often the result of too much job stress, especially when that stress is combined with a preoccupation with unattainable work-related goals. Burnout victims often do not lead well-balanced lives; virtually all of their energies are focused on achieving their work-related goals to the exclusion of other activities, leading to physical and sometimes mental collapse. This need not be limited to upwardly mobile executives. For instance, social-work counsellors caught up in their clients' problems are often burnout victims.

**REDUCING JOB STRESS** There are things that a person can do to alleviate stress, ranging from common-sense remedies such as getting more sleep, eating better, and taking vacation time to more exotic remedies such as biofeedback and meditation. Finding a more suitable job, getting counselling through an EAP or elsewhere, and planning and organizing each day's activities are other sensible responses.[55]

**WORKERS' COMPENSATION AND STRESS-RELATED DISABILITY CLAIMS**

Workers' compensation laws in several provinces prohibit compensation for chronic mental stress or impose severe limitations on what is covered. The rationale is that stress has multiple causes, including family situations and personal disposition. Research suggests, however, that a significant portion of chronic stress is often work-related. In particular, high-demand/low-control jobs (such as an administrative assistant with several demanding bosses) are known to be "psychotoxic."[56] Consequently, employees who are denied workers' compensation benefits for chronic stress that they believe to be work-related are suing their employers. The courts are recognizing these claims and holding employers responsible for actions of supervisors who create "poisoned work environments" through harassment and psychological abuse.[57] Courts are finding that a fundamental implied term of any employment relationship is that the employer will treat the employee fairly and with respect and dignity and that the due diligence requirement includes protection of employees from psychological as well as physical damage.[58]

## Mental Health Conditions

Mental illness will continue to be a leading cause of disability over the next 10 years, according to the World Health Organization. The Public Health Agency of Canada concurs, adding that an estimated 13 percent of the adult population in Canada has been diagnosed with a mental illness and that mental illnesses are misdiagnosed, on average, four times in someone's life. Approximately 48 percent of all workers at some point in their lives will experience depression, and people with chronic pain, chronic illness, or many health problems are 40 percent more likely to also have a mental health problem. What affects one part of the body is bound to affect other parts, including the brain and emotions.[59]

**burnout** The total depletion of physical and mental resources caused by excessive striving to reach an unrealistic work-related goal.

Canadian Injured Workers Alliance www.ciwa.ca

Bringing Health to Work www.ccohs.ca/healthyworkplaces

Institute for Work and Health www.iwh.on.ca

Newgate 180 www.newgate180.com

Bellwood Health Services www.bellwood.ca

Human Systems Incorporated www.humansys.com

Wellness Consultants www.wellnessproposals.com/wellness_consultant.htm

Mental health is a growing concern for employers, with nearly 80 percent indicating that mental health issues have increased in importance compared with three to five years ago. A recent study found that only 13 percent of senior executives have a strong awareness of the full impact of mental health on an organization and two-thirds underestimate the prevalence of mental illness in the workplace. It is estimated that 35 million workdays are lost every year in Canada due to mental illness.[60] Overall, the economic cost of depression is about $16 billion a year. Approximately 35 percent of depressed people suffer from depression as a result of work.[61]

There are several behaviours that signal that an employee potentially has a mental health issue. Changes are likely evident in the following areas: appearance, in which the employee becomes disinterested or overly preoccupied with hygiene; energy level, which usually wanes; lack of interest in socializing with others; quality of work falters; and either preoccupation with or disinterest in details.[62]

An example of organizational commitment to mental health is evident at Canada Post, which became the first major Canadian corporation to adopt mental health as its cause. Canada Post created an independent organization, the Canada Post Foundation for Mental Health, to raise awareness and champion the initiative. Led by an independent board, the Foundation supports front-line organizations serving patients, consumers, and caregivers while enhancing awareness of how mental illness affects the lives of all Canadians.[63]

## Repetitive Strain Injuries

Repetitive strain injuries (RSIs) cost the Canadian economy nearly $800 million each year.[64] The physical demands of new technologies have brought a new set of RSIs, most notably carpal tunnel syndrome (a tingling or numbness in the fingers caused by the narrowing of a tunnel of bones and ligaments in the wrist). RSIs have three causes: repetitive movements, awkward postures, and forceful exertion. The risk of developing RSIs increases with exposure to vibration and cold, and pre-existing conditions, such as arthritis, can exacerbate RSIs.[65] Warning signs of RSI include tightness or stiffness in the hands, elbow, wrists, shoulder, and neck; numbness and tingling in the fingertips; hands falling asleep; and frequent dropping of tools. The most common symptoms are neck and shoulder strain.[66]

**PREVENTING RSI** Fortunately, RSIs are extremely preventable. Poorly designed workstations and bad posture are among the primary conditions leading to RSI. **Ergonomics** is the art of fitting the workstation and work tools to the individual, which is necessary because there is no such thing as an average body. Typing with wrist guards (see Figure 10.5) minimizes the probability of employees suffering from carpal tunnel syndrome when spending prolonged periods of time on their computers. The most important preventive measure is to have employees take short breaks every half-hour or hour to do simple stretches at their workstations.[67] Software is now available that counts keystrokes over time and flashes a message to the employee to take a break and do the exercise shown on the screen.[68]

In the mid-1990s, Canadian Tire Acceptance Corporation Ltd. in Welland, Ontario, was facing increasing employee complaints of pain and stiffness but no related lost-time injuries. A root-cause analysis found that 60 percent of employees had RSI symptoms and 50 percent had sought medical attention for them. The company launched a comprehensive RSI-prevention program using internal and external community resources. The program included modification of workstations, wellness initiatives, stress management, education on risk factors, and proactive occupational therapy for RSI sufferers. Three years later, the company had no RSI-related disability claims. The success of the program was attributed to process champions, stakeholder participation, and management commitment to employees' well-being.[69]

**VIDEO DISPLAY TERMINALS** The fact that many workers must spend hours each day working with video display terminals (VDTs) is creating new health problems at work. Short-term eye problems, such as burning, itching, and tearing as well as eyestrain and eye soreness, are common complaints among VDT operators. Backaches and neck aches are also widespread. These often occur because employees try to compensate for display problems such as glare and immovable keyboards by manoeuvring into awkward body positions. Researchers have found that employees who used VDTs and had heavy workloads were prone to psychological distress, such as anxiety, irritability, and fatigue. There may also be a tendency for computer users to suffer from RSI, such as carpal tunnel syndrome, caused by repetitive use of the hands and arms at uncomfortable angles.[70]

General recommendations regarding the use of VDTs include:

1. Give employees rest breaks—15-minute breaks every hour for those with heavy workloads.

*figure* 10.5 **Typing with Wrist Guards**

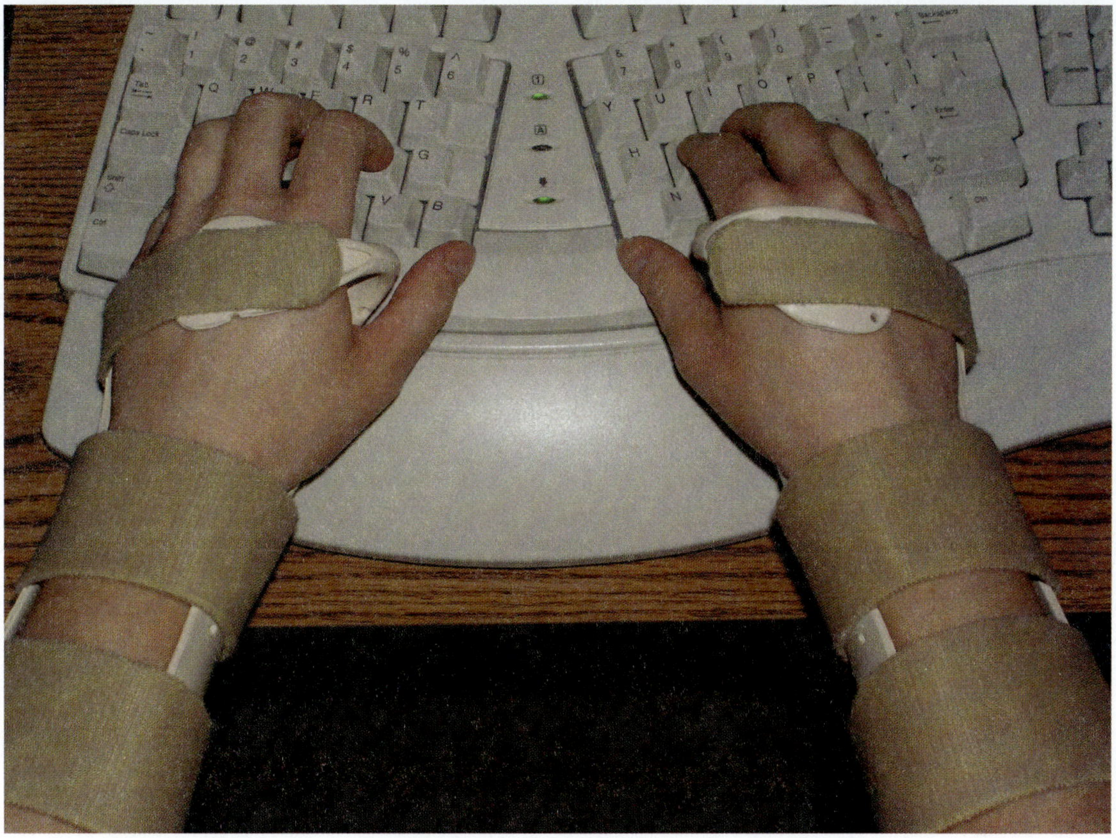

2. Design maximum flexibility into the workstation so that it can be adapted to the individual operator.
3. Reduce glare with such devices as shades over windows and terminal screens.
4. Give VDT workers a complete preplacement vision exam to ensure that vision is properly corrected for reduced visual strain.

## Workplace Toxins

The leading cause of work-related deaths around the world is cancer, as shown in Figure 10.6. Hundreds of

*** *front*LINE *tips*** Canadian workers die from occupational cancer each year, and according to the World Health Organization (WHO) at least 200 000 people die worldwide from occupational cancers on an annual basis.[71]

Exposure to carcinogens is not limited to a few industries. When it comes to radiation exposure, workers in health care, nuclear industries, industrial radiography, and even the veterinarian profession are exposed during their work day. Exposure to diesel is prevalent in mining, manufacturing, transportation, and among firefighters and paramedics. Exposure to benzene, a known

**ergonomics** The art of fitting the workstation and work tools to the individual.

*figure* 10.6 **Deaths Attributed to Work Worldwide**

According to the International Labour Organization, there were an estimated 2 million work-related deaths around the globe in the year 2000. Out of eight work-related diseases, cancer was cited as the number one cause of death.

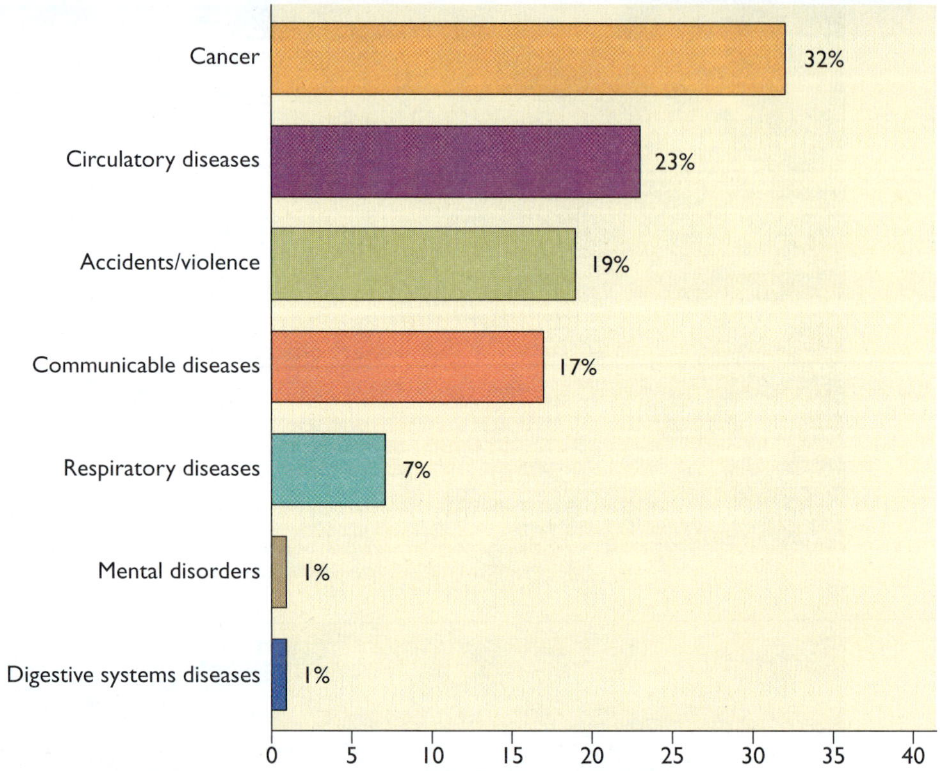


Source: *Introductory Report: Decent Work—Safe Work, Table 1* (www.ilo.org/public/english/protection/safework/wdcongrs/ilo_rep.pdf). Copyright © International Labour Organization, 2009.

carcinogen linked to leukemia, can occur in the transportation, petrochemical, rubber, and printing industries as well as with gas station attendants.[72]

Between January 2001 and December 2007, the WSIB approved 56 claims for occupational diseases from Algoma Steel Industries employees and retirees. Of those claims, 41 involved death. In total, 126 claims were received from Algoma, 64 of which were denied, including 11 deaths. Six cases are still pending. Of the 56 WSIB-approved cancer claims, there were 36 cases of lung cancer, nine cases of mesothelioma caused by exposure to asbestos, five gastrointestinal cancers, and three bladder cancers; the remaining were other cancers. After the initial round of claims was filed, another 442 employees who were sick or who had died from their illnesses were identified. The two most common types of diseases were chronic obstructive pulmonary disease (57 cases) and coronary artery disease (77 cases), but the majority of participants had cancer of one form or another.[73]

## Workplace Smoking

Smoking is a serious problem for employees and employers. Employers face higher costs deriving from higher supplementary health-care and disability insurance because smoking is associated with numerous health problems. The Conference Board of Canada found that the total costs to employers who hire smokers increased from $2565 per smoking employee in 1997 to $3396 in 2006. Employees who smoke cost companies between $2308 and $2613 more per year than non-smoking employees. The cost of smoker absenteeism increased from $230 to $323 and the cost of decreased productivity resulting from smoker breaks increased from $2175 to $3053.[74] In general, "smoking employees are less healthy than non-smokers, are absent more, make more and more expensive claims for health and disability benefits, and endanger coworkers who breathe smoky air." More than 47 000 Canadians die of smoking-related diseases every year.[75]

Governments across Canada have taken the lead in banning smoking in an increasing number of workplaces. British Columbia declared secondhand tobacco smoke to be an occupational hazard.[76]

## Workplace Violence

Violence against employees at work has become increasingly common in Canada. In fact, Canadians are more likely to be assaulted in their workplaces than are Americans.[77] Nearly one-fifth of physical assaults, robberies, and sexual assaults happen in the workplace, according to Statistics Canada's first study on violence at work. The study, *Criminal Victimization in the Workplace*, found that there were more than 356 000 violent incidents in Canadian workplaces in 2007, 66 percent of which were committed by someone known to the victim.[78]

Victims are often women in health-care professions.[79] A study of 45 000 nurses indicated that 68 percent had suffered physical violence, ranging from slaps to jaw-breaking punches. One author noted that when police officers are attacked, charges of assault or resisting arrest are laid, whereas when nurses are attacked, it is seen as part of their job.[80]

Workplace violence is about fear, about people losing control, and about implicit contracts between employer and employee being broken. Triggers for workplace violence include poor management relations, ambiguous work standards, inconsistent rule enforcement, ignoring cultural concerns, failure to address threats of violence, and insufficient worksite security.[81]

**Workplace bullying** is an escalating type of workplace violence. It is not easily recognized because it can take many different forms, ranging from social isolation to excessive criticism. Employees should be aware that bullying manifests in behaviours such as humiliation, discrediting a person, making rude remarks or gestures, making fun of personal or political choices, insults, name-calling, unsuitable language, over-monitoring of work, or withholding of job responsibilities. Organizations should ensure that supervisors know what symptoms to watch for and encourage employees to report a situation before it escalates. Confrontation of a bully rarely works because the bully is extremely defensive. It is best to talk to someone higher up in the organization and build a case of times, dates, and places where bullying occurred in order to provide substantial evidence to take disciplinary action.[82]

On April 4, 2007, Nova Scotia introduced Violence in the Workplace Regulations under the *Nova Scotia Occupational Health and Safety Act*, bringing the province in line with workplace-violence strategies in British Columbia, Alberta, Prince Edward Island, Manitoba, and Saskatchewan. The regulations only affect employers in certain sectors, such as retail sales, taxi and passenger transit services, and health services, but they apply a blueprint for best practices for employers in various industries across the country.[83]

Whether dealing with workplace bullying or any other type of workplace violence, employers want to avoid such violence on humanitarian grounds, but there are also legal reasons for doing so. Employers may be found liable for the violent acts of their employees.[84] For example, an employer may be sued directly by the victim of an employee's violent act on the basis that the employer negligently hired or negligently retained someone whom the employer should reasonably have known could cause the violent act.

There are several concrete steps that employers can take to reduce the incidence of workplace violence. These include instituting a workplace violence prevention policy that clearly communicates management's commitment to preventing violence. A company can also increase security measures, such as improving lighting, alarm, and surveillance systems. Improving screening processes to include such aspects as instituting sound pre-employment investigations, thorough reference checking, and implementing various training programs that identify causes and signs of violence and offer tips on how to prevent it and what to do when it occurs are also prudent steps to take.

**workplace bullying** An escalating type of workplace violence that can take a range of forms, from social isolation to excessive criticism.

Work Violence Solutions - www.workviolencesolutions.com

Registered Nurses Association of Ontario www.rnao.org/bestpractices

Canada Safety Council http://safety-council.org

Repetitive Strain Injury Treatment www.safecomputingtips.com/repetitive-strain-injury-treatment.html

Human Factors and Ergonomics Society www.hfes.org

## *In-class Notes*

**Occupational Health Issues and Challenges**

- Alcoholism and substance abuse are widespread and costly
- Job stress and burnout are very widespread and costly
- Repetitive strain injuries are common but can be prevented through ergonomics
- Workplace toxins are the leading cause of work-related death worldwide
- Workplace smoking is associated with numerous health problems
- Workplace violence is becoming increasingly common

# Occupational Health and Safety on the International Stage

Many employers send employees into regions with high business potential yet are plagued by economic and political turmoil and disease risks, extending concerns about employee safety beyond the typical work environment. Regional conflicts, terrorist attacks and difficult social and medical conditions are common problems for employees and their families in high-risk areas, and pose a real and immediate challenge for HR departments that prepare expatriates.

Assessing levels of risk, managing it, and deciding when a situation is simply too risky have never been more complicated or more necessary. Before staff are sent into high-risk regions, the organization should define what is considered safe in terms of working conditions. Employment contracts should clearly communicate the company's policy regarding the risks of the job, risks that come with working in foreign locations, and resources such as training in emergency response and management. A clear paper trail for this process is important and should include feedback from staff confirming that they have been properly briefed.[85]

HR departments should encourage employees to consider a number of factors before accepting long-term assignments in foreign countries, such as climate and physical conditions, housing availability and security, physical remoteness, accessibility to emergency services, risks to health, quality of the infrastructure including reliability and access to transportation and communication, the political landscape, and crime rate.

Employees who accept foreign assignments are to be fully trained in how to live and work among the locals. This includes security and emergency evacuation services, government and societal response to expatriates, and diplomatic relations between the host country and the employee's home country. To mitigate risks to employees, most employers house expatriates in compounds with other foreign nationals. By housing them in a secured location, risks to personal safety, access to other foreign nationals, and transportation can be reduced.

The return phase of the relocation has its own risks for expatriates and employers. Significant risks include the challenges of acclimatizing to one's home location and job after a prolonged absence and health risks such as returning home with a disease.[86]

# Chapter Review

## Answers to Test Yourself

1. What are the major rights and responsibilities of employers and employees under occupational health and safety legislation?

   The purpose of occupational health and safety laws is to protect the health and safety of workers by minimizing work-related accidents and illnesses. Employers are responsible for taking every reasonable precaution to ensure the health and safety of their workers, which is called "due diligence." Specific duties include filing government accident reports, maintaining records, and posting safety notices and legislative information.

   Employees have the right to know about workplace safety hazards, to participate in occupational heath and safety processes, and to refuse work if they have reasonable cause to believe that the work can be dangerous. Employee responsibilities include adhering to the health and safety rules of the organization, wearing protective clothing and equipment, and reporting any health and safety issues to the employer.

2. What are the three basic causes of accidents?

   There are three basic causes of accidents: chance occurrences, unsafe conditions, and unsafe acts on the part of employees. In addition, three other work-related factors—the job itself, the work schedule, and the psychological climate—also contribute to accidents.

3. How can accidents at work be prevented and what are the benefits of doing so?

   One approach to preventing accidents is to reduce unsafe conditions by identifying and removing potential hazards. Some approaches to improving safety by reducing unsafe acts include, for example, selection and placement strategies, education and training, positive reinforcement, monitoring work overload and stress, and establishing a safety policy.

   By preventing accidents, organizations can reduce workers' compensation costs, reduce absenteeism, and establish better morale by increasing employee perceptions of fair treatment by the organization.

4. What are employee wellness programs and why are they becoming increasingly popular?

   Wellness initiatives include physical fitness programs, smoking cessation programs, relaxation classes, and heart health monitoring. Employee wellness programs aim to improve employees' health and thus reduce costs for sickness and disability claims, workers' compensation, and absenteeism. Wellness programs can also increase employee morale.

5. What are the seven major employee health issues at work, and how should they be managed?

   Alcoholism and drug addiction are significant, continuing health issues among employees. Alcoholism is a particularly serious problem and one that can drastically reduce the effectiveness of an organization. Strategies to deal with employee substance abuse include in-house counselling, referrals to an outside agency, discipline, and discharge.

   Stress, depression, and burnout are also significant health problems. These problems can be reduced by employees taking vacations, eating and sleeping properly, making use of employee assistance plans, and having more control over their jobs.

   Mental health conditions include chronic and temporary depression. There is a growing body of research indicating that depression is linked to workplace experiences.

   Repetitive strain injuries are caused by the physical demands of new technologies and can be prevented through ergonomic fitting of the workstation and work tools to the individual worker.

   The leading cause of work-related deaths around the world is cancer from exposure to carcinogens. Workplace smoking is another serious health problem. Legislation is gradually being introduced to address these two issues.

   Workplace violence is a growing concern. It can be reduced by improving security arrangements, increasing employee screening, and providing workplace violence training.

## Key Terms

burnout (p. 337)
employee wellness programs (p. 334)
ergonomics (p. 338)
occupational health and safety legislation (p. 317)
shared responsibility model (p. 315)
unsafe acts (p. 329)
unsafe conditions (p. 328)
workplace bullying (p. 341)
Workplace Hazardous Materials Information System (WHMIS) (p. 321)

## Required Professional Capabilities (RPCs)

RPC 10-1 > (p. 315)
RPC 10-2 > (p. 319)
RPC 10-3 > (p. 320)
RPC 10-4 > (p. 320)
RPC 10-5 > (p. 320)
RPC 10-6 > (p. 321)
RPC 10-7 > (p. 327)
RPC 10-8 > (p. 327)
RPC 10-9 > (p. 327)
RPC 10-10 > (p. 328)
RPC 10-11 > (p. 331)
RPC 10-12 > (p. 331)
RPC 10-13 > (p. 331)
RPC 10-14 > (p. 333)
RPC 10-15 > (p. 333)
RPC 10-16 > (p. 333)
RPC 10-17 > (p. 333)
RPC 10-18 > (p. 333)
RPC 10-19 > (p. 334)
RPC 10-20 > (p. 334)
RPC 10-21 > (p. 335)
RPC 10-22 > (p. 336)

# Cases and Exercises

myHRlab
For additional cases and exercises, go to www.pearsoned.ca/myhrlab.

## CASE INCIDENT

### Swimming in the Deep End at Pools Are Us

Pools Are Us is a medium-sized wholesaler of industrial chemicals in Mississauga. The company has been in business for the past 20 years, handling swimming pool supplies and industrial solvents. It employs over 300 general labourers and 45 administrative staff. In the past year there has been a 200 percent growth in business, credited to increasingly hot and humid summer weather in Ontario, which has motivated many Ontarians to build pools in their backyards and many community centres to reopen pools that had been closed. With pools comes the need for service and general maintenance.

In order to meet workload demands, the company aggressively pushes everyone to work harder and faster. Most of the workers are offered overtime hours in the form of double and triple shifts to get the work done. Given the tight economic times, the workers are grateful to be given overtime and rarely, if ever, turn down the opportunity to make more money. Many of the workers are so attracted to the money that they work for three or four weeks without a day off. They have also started to experiment with short-cuts in the assembly process to cut down on the time it takes to get the job done. In their opinion, it does not matter how the work gets done; just deliver. The company recently introduced a bonus system to reward employees for working quickly.

As well as offering full-time employees overtime, the company needed to hire temporary staff to get through the peak period. Sixteen students from colleges and universities in the Toronto area were offered employment. Because of the high volume of work, the company scrambled to hire these students and get them working as soon as possible.

Since they would only be with the company for three months, it decided not to put the new recruits through formal training. There did not appear to be a good return on investment from training as it would take too long and be too expensive. In management's opinion, the jobs are really easy to learn and training can best be done on the job. Each new recruit was paired with a full-time worker responsible for training and mentoring.

On one typical hot and humid day in Ontario, everything changed at Pools Are Us. Kevin Seymour, a 22-year-old college student hired for the summer, had an accident. Kevin had only been on the job four days when a container of sulphuric acid was dropped, badly scalding his face, neck, and most of his upper body. You could hear the screams of pain echoing through the plant. Rob Clifford, the occupational health and safety manager, rushed to the scene and realized that Kevin was in desperate need of medical attention. Rob knew there was no time to wait for paramedics, so he lifted Kevin in his arms, ran out to the parking lot, put him in the passenger seat of his car, and drove him to the hospital. Kevin remained in hospital for seven months recovering from severe burns to his body. He required four plastic surgeries, extensive physiotherapy, and psychological counselling as part of this treatment. As a result, Kevin dropped out of school, unable to handle the rigour of an academic program while trying to recover.

A full investigation was launched into the accident at Pools Are Us.

### Questions

1. Outline the accident investigation steps that need to be followed.
2. What factors contributed to Kevin's accident?
3. Outline the recommendations that should emerge from the accident investigation to ensure that the company minimizes the probability of another accident of this magnitude.
4. What are the significant learnings from this case study for other companies?

### Application Questions

1. Select a location on your campus with which you are familiar. In teams of three or four, imagine you are the on-campus health and safety committee.
   a. Outline the criteria your committee will use to conduct a monthly health and safety audit of the facility.
   b. Based on the criteria identified, how will your committee evaluate this campus location and what recommendations will you propose?
2. Every year, the parks and recreation division in your community offers summer employment to 350 high school, college, and university students. Their jobs involve maintenance of pools and parks, including landscaping and clean-up. You reviewed the health and safety records for the past five years and discovered a high number of accidents involving summer employees. What courses of action will you take to minimize accidents in the upcoming season? Assume there are currently no supports in place for the students after they are interviewed and offered employment.
3. On Friday morning, a team of tradespeople were fixing the roof on the main building of your school. One of the roofers was hungover from a night of heavy drinking at the pub, and fell off the roof. He remained unconscious on the ground until the paramedics arrived and took him to the hospital. Discuss how you would conduct the accident investigation.
4. As the new health and safety officer for a medium-sized food processing plant, you have proposed a comprehensive health and safety plan to align the company with the Occupational Health and Safety Act in your province. Regrettably, employees do not support your initiative, claiming, "The OHSA is nothing more than government control, and we don't need to worry about all these policies and procedures unless we get caught." Discuss how you will respond to your employees' perception of health and safety. What will you do to change their mind on this matter?
5. With reference to the WHMIS symbols described in Figure 10.2, identify a product that employees might come in contact with in each of the eight categories. If you were responsible for designing and conducting WHMIS training in the workplace, what would you do to help employees remember the symbols and what they mean?

## RUNNING CASE: LEARNINMOTION.COM

### The New Health and Safety Program

The case for Chapter 10, *The New Health and Safety Program*, shows that even in a relatively safe environment, it is necessary to evaluate potential hazards in the workplace, including physical conditions as well as mental pressures.

To read this case, go to www.pearsoned.ca/myhrlab and click on the *Management of Human Resources*, Third Canadian Edition, In-Class Edition, cover. Click on the case module in Chapter 10. The running case illustrates a variety of challenges confronted by HR professionals, small-business owners, and front-line supervisors. It places students in the role of HR management consultants to help the fledgling LearninMotion.com develop HR policies, strategies, and long-term goals. Each case is accompanied by assignments for the management consultants in the form of critical-thinking questions posed to the student.

## CONTROVERSIAL BUSINESS TOPIC EXERCISE

The joint health and safety committee for a small community hospital met with the senior administrator to discuss its findings from the monthly health and safety audit. The committee reported that it had discovered a small leak coming from one of the radiation machines used in the treatment of cancer patients. The committee is not certain if the leak poses a threat to employee health, but does not want to take any chances, especially since staff in the radiation department spend 95 percent of their eight-hour shifts working in that room. The committee's recommendation is to close the facility for 72 hours in order to make the necessary repairs to the machine and to determine the extent of damage created by the leakage. The response from the senior administrator causes great concern. He tells the committee that it is exaggerating the situation and that he does not support the committee's recommendations. No one on staff in the radiation department has become ill over the past few weeks, which is, in his opinion, a strong indicator that the leak is not a health hazard. He argues that a hospital with a mandate to treat cancer patients cannot afford to close its operations for 72 hours, especially when the nearest cancer treatment facility is a four-hour drive away. The hospital is booked solid with patients over the next six months who are in dire need of treatment to save their lives.

Discuss how the joint health and safety committee should deal with this situation.

## IN THE BOARDROOM EXERCISE

You are the director of occupational health and safety for a car manufacturing plant in southern Ontario. Approval has been granted by the CEO for you to revitalize the health and safety program for the entire facility, including unionized workers in the plant and non-unionized staff in the office. Your intent is to develop and sustain a health and safety program that will be noted for its benchmark excellence in the manufacturing sector. Roll out your recommendations in each of the following areas:

a. Promoting safety awareness
b. Enforcing safety rules
c. Preventing accidents
d. Controlling workplace violence
e. Promoting work–life balance

## OCCUPATIONAL HEALTH AND SAFETY ON THE INTERNATIONAL STAGE EXERCISE

*The exercise below relates to the Occupational Health and Safety on the International Stage feature on p. 342.*

Select a company that operates its business in at least three different countries around the world. Imagine that this company offered you a "dream job" and asked you to travel to one of their overseas locations for a one-year assignment. Research the country, taking into consideration the health and safety factors both the employee and the employer should take into account when relocating. Based on what you discover from your research, will you accept the one-year assignment? Provide a rationale to support your decision.

## EXPERIENTIAL EXERCISE

For further study of text materials and development of practical skills, select the experiential exercise module for this chapter on www.pearsoned.ca/myhrlab. This module provides two to three individual or group-based assignments per chapter.

# QUIZ YOURSELF

**STUDY GUIDE QUESTIONS**

Circle the correct answer. After completing this self-test, check your answers against the Answers to Study Guide Questions at the back of the book (p. 433).

1. What is the key objective of occupational health and safety legislation?
   a. protecting the health and safety of workers by minimizing work-related stress
   b. requiring that hazardous materials in the workplace be labelled
   c. protecting the health and safety of workers by minimizing work-related accidents and illness
   d. protecting the health and safety of workers through wellness programs
   e. protecting workers who are prone to accidents and illnesses
2. Which of the following are requirements of "due diligence"?
   a. the employer's responsibility to post safety notices and legislative information
   b. the employee's right to refuse unsafe work if there is "reasonable cause"
   c. the employer's choice regarding when to maintain records and file government reports
   d. the employee's right to know about workplace safety hazards
   e. the employee's right to participate in the occupational health and safety process
3. A worker cannot be disciplined if he/she refuses to work due to "reasonable cause." "Reasonable cause" refers to:
   a. working with another employee with a communicable illness
   b. a psychological trauma that an employee has suffered during work that has not been resolved satisfactorily
   c. a complaint about a workplace hazard that has not been satisfactorily resolved or a safety problem that places employees in immediate danger
   d. working with another employee who has a work-related illness
   e. when an employee's back has been injured off the job
4. Recently, a supervisor of a worker killed in an unsecured trench where the walls collapsed was charged with a criminal offence. Under what law was the supervisor charged with this criminal offence?
   a. Occupational Health and Safety Act
   b. Workplace Safety Act
   c. Criminal Code amendment on corporate killing
   d. WHMIS
   e. none of the above
5. As the supervisor of a chemical plant, Tom is responsible for disseminating information to workers and ensuring appropriate labelling is carried on hazardous material containers as provided by:
   a. WHMIS
   b. SCF
   c. *Occupational Health and Safety Act*
   d. FAE
   e. EAP
6. Carlos is a forklift operator in a busy warehouse. At times, when there is a lot of loading to be done, Carlos tends to increase the speed of his forklift from the prescribed speed. What is Carlos doing by increasing the speed of his forklift?
   a. violating WHMIS
   b. violating occupational health and safety laws
   c. engaging in an unsafe act
   d. working under unsafe conditions
   e. not practising "due diligence"
7. Reducing unsafe conditions is an employer's first line of defence against workplace injury. What measures can an employer take to reduce unsafe conditions?
   a. introduce tougher rules and regulations
   b. train and educate employees
   c. put up safety posters within the organization
   d. partner with a safety association to create awareness
   e. none of the above
8. A functional abilities evaluation (FAE) is conducted by:
   a. a health-care professional
   b. the employee's supervisor
   c. the HR department
   d. workers' compensation staff
   e. a health and safety professional
9. Facilitating an employee's return to work plays an important role in controlling workers' compensation costs. In this context, what is the role of a "functional abilities evaluation"?
   a. assess future disability costs
   b. determine whether the disability will be permanent
   c. act as a deterrent to other employees
   d. assess an employee's performance capabilities
   e. none of the above

10. Burnout is caused by:
    a. physical exhaustion
    b. mental exhaustion
    c. total depletion of physical and mental resources
    d. excessive striving to meet an unrealistic goal
    e. poor physical health

11. A "poisoned work environment" is characterized by:
    a. toxic chemicals
    b. harassment and psychological abuse
    c. physical violence
    d. violations of WHMIS
    e. same-sex harassment

12. Chan is an ambitious, hardworking executive. His boss will retire next year, and Chan wants to be promoted into that position. As a result, he has established some objectives that are very ambitious but somewhat unrealistic. His colleagues notice that Chan has been working excessively and seems very stressed. What is Chan suffering from?
    a. chronic stress
    b. burnout
    c. work overload
    d. mental stress
    e. all of the above

13. Repetitive strain injuries (RSI) cost the Canadian economy $800 million each year. The primary conditions that lead to RSI are:
    a. poorly designed workstations and job stress
    b. bad posture and long hours of work
    c. tightness or stiffness in the hands
    d. bad posture and tightness or stiffness in the hands
    e. poorly designed workstations and bad posture

14. Ergonomics is used to minimize repetitive strain injuries by:
    a. designing work-related equipment to an average-sized employee
    b. fitting the individual to the workstation and work tools
    c. fitting the workstation and work tools to the individual
    d. preventing health and safety hazards at work
    e. preventing injuries from defective equipment and machinery

15. Violence against employees at work:
    a. is becoming increasingly common in Canada
    b. can be prevented if necessary precautions are taken
    c. has serious legal repercussions
    d. can be triggered by insufficient security
    e. all of the above

# 11 *chapter* THE FOUNDATION OF EFFECTIVE EMPLOYEE RELATIONS

## Learning Objectives

1. Articulate the strategic importance of effective employee relations.
2. Explain fair, ethical, and legal treatment.
3. Discuss the best approaches for managing dismissals.
4. Explain how to manage separations: layoffs and retirements.

## Test Yourself

1. What are the techniques used for building multidirectional communication systems in organizations?
2. What can an employer do to ensure a fair and just disciplinary process?
3. What constitutes wrongful dismissal and constructive dismissal?
4. What are important HR considerations in adjusting to downsizings, layoffs, acquisitions, and mergers?
5. What strategies can firms use to assist their employees in adjusting to retirement?

## 11.1 THE STRATEGIC IMPORTANCE OF EFFECTIVE EMPLOYEE RELATIONS

The objectives of HRM include establishing and maintaining a harmonious employer–employee relationship and retaining productive employees. Today more than ever, it is important to build a strategic competitive advantage, and it has long been recognized that organizations can do this though their human resources. From an economic and practical standpoint, it makes sense to keep the employees that companies have spent time and money recruiting, selecting, and training motivated and committed to the goals of the organization. In order to do this, organizations must also invest the time and money to establish programs that foster this commitment. They also need to ensure that employees are treated fairly, ethically, and within all legislative guidelines.

While it may not be possible to completely guarantee that all employees will be motivated and committed to an organization, there are steps that employers can take to move in that direction. This chapter will focus on programs and policies that constitute the foundations of effective employee relations.

**RPC 11-1 >**
Builds constructive and supportive relationships

### Communications Programs

It has been said that we live in an information economy. Certainly, managers cannot be effective without access to the information they need to help them make good decisions. Without information, today's knowledge workers cannot do their jobs. However, just as importantly, in order to remain motivated and committed, employees need information about the company, its goals, and their role in making the organization successful. Without sufficient information or sufficient opportunity to give their input, employees may suffer from stress and become dissatisfied. Most companies recognize this need and establish communications systems that facilitate downward, upward, and two-way communication.

**DOWNWARD COMMUNICATION** **Downward communication** is information about various aspects of an organization that is initiated by management and then proceeds down through the hierarchy. Various communications vehicles can be used to facilitate this, including:

- company magazines, newsletters, memorandums
- information booklets/pamphlets, flyers
- employee bulletins via physical or intranet bulletin boards
- video presentations, voice mail, email
- meetings or written reports on the company's economic performance, new products, major contracts or customers, annual results, and how these affect (or are affected by) employees

Some large organizations go to great lengths to ensure that the communications process is well planned and designed to be effective, and they may even hire an internal communications manager to do this. Some companies, such as Toyota, use a combination of these methods to keep employees informed. Toyota's management works hard to share what it knows with every team member. There are three-times-per-shift, five-minute team information meetings at job sites, where employees get the latest news about the plant. Monthly "roundtable" discussions are held between top management and selected non-supervisory staff. A bi-monthly news reporting current events in Toyota worldwide bulletin is distributed, and a bi-weekly newsletter provides local news. The firm's president is often in the plant fielding questions, providing performance information, and ensuring that all in the company are aware of Toyota's goals.

Studies have found that cutting middle-management positions as part of downsizing and restructuring damages communication and working relationships between management and employees, and, ultimately, productivity. Middle managers are noted for creating significant one-on-one relationships with employees that foster respect, trust, loyalty, and contribution. While upper management is focused on strategic direction, middle managers are charged with the responsibility of collaborating with employees to realize the organization's objectives and vision. Building strong communication channels between middle managers and employees leads to greater employee satisfaction, which translates into a more productive workforce.[1]

**RPC 11-2 >**
Provides input into the development of employee-feedback systems that support the organizational directions and culture

**UPWARD COMMUNICATION** No communications process would be complete without giving employees the opportunity to provide their opinions and ideas to management. **Upward communication** opportunities must be present in an organization, and can be more interactive than downward communication. Elements of upward communication might include the following:

- suggestion programs
- employee opinion surveys
- focus groups/small-group meetings
- rap sessions

**RPC 11-3 >**

**Develops and implements programs for employee involvement**

Probably the most effective communications systems are those that facilitate two-way communication, such as **management-by-walking-around (MBWA)**, which was introduced by Hewlett-Packard decades ago and has resurfaced as a means to engage and retain employees.[2] In MBWA, managers leave their offices to learn from others in the organization and to address questions by having casual, face-to-face conversations. When managers are visible in the workplace, employees are more likely to approach them with their problems and concerns, and offer insights about the organization. Employee concerns may run the gamut from malfunctioning vending machines and unlit parking lots to organizational restructuring and its impact on employees. Walking around the facility enables managers to address these concerns, answer questions about current and new organizational initiatives, and discover firsthand new ideas and opportunities for development. The organizational benefits associated with MBWA include increased profits, minimized losses, and improved retention. Companies that have successfully implemented MBWA include Hewlett-Packard, PepsiCo, Corning Glass, 3M, and WalMart.[3]

**RPC 11-4 >**

**Establishes and maintains the trust and support of one's manager and subordinates**

## Employee Opinion Surveys

Many firms also administer periodic anonymous **opinion surveys**. For maximum benefit, surveys should be conducted regularly, and the results must be provided to participants.[4] IBM Canada's organizational effectiveness survey regularly asks employees their opinions about the company, management, and work life. The survey's purpose is to assess the morale of employees. The standard practice is to have department heads conduct feedback sessions with their department members after the survey results are compiled in order to share the results and work on solutions.

Opinion surveys are conducted across Canada to gauge national sentiment about the workplace. A recent national survey revealed the following top-five reasons why employees leave their organizations: lack of trust in senior leaders, insufficient pay, unhealthy organizational culture, lack of honesty/integrity/ethics in the company, and insufficient training and development opportunities.[5] According to Leigh Branham, author of *The 7 Hidden Reasons Employees Leave,* opinion surveys give valuable information to probe deeper for the root causes of problems and to begin taking corrective action. The question to ask employees in exit interviews is not, "Why are you leaving?" but, "Why are you not staying?"[6]

**RPC 11-5 >**

**Gathers and analyzes employee feedback to assist decision making**

## Employee Engagement

Employee engagement gauges the level of connection employees feel with their employer, which is demonstrated by their ability and willingness to provide discretionary effort to help the company be successful.[7] Towers Perrin, an international firm that works with organizations to improve performance through effective people, risk, and financial management, refers to engagement as the process by which organizations

**upward communication** Communication that begins with employees and proceeds up through the organization as a way of informing/influencing management.

**management-by-walking-around (MBWA)** Managers leave their offices to learn from others in the organization and to address questions by having casual, face-to-face conversations.

**downward communication** Information about various aspects of an organization that is initiated by management and then proceeds down through the hierarchy.

**opinion surveys** Communication devices that use questionnaires to ask for employees' opinions about the company, management, and work life.

Performance Programs, Inc. - **www.performanceprograms.com**

Toyota Canada **www.toyota.ca**

activate the "head, hands, and heart." The "head" is the rational part of the equation—how employees connect with their company's goals and values. The "hands" refer to employees' willingness to contribute to the organization's success. The "heart" is the emotional connection between employee and employer, often described as commitment, pride, and loyalty.[8]

The 2008 Global Workforce Study involving 90 000 employees in 18 countries found that organizational factors such as leadership, learning and development, and image and reputation are the primary influencers of engagement. The study revealed that one in five Canadian employees (21 percent) are fully engaged on the job, 8 percent are fully disengaged, and 71 percent are in the "massive middle." The "massive middle" represent the greatest opportunity for employers because these employees can shift in either direction—become more engaged and contribute to the company or become more disengaged and possibly resign. Senior management received low scores in the study in areas such as accessibility (47 percent), embracing new ideas (45 percent), sincere interest in employees' well-being (38 percent), and communicating openly and honestly (36 percent). Although management maintains that employees are an organization's most valued asset, only 6 percent of employees believe this to be true.[9]

Companies that do not have an engaged workforce put themselves at competitive risk because engagement is highly correlated with business performance. Studies have found that companies with a highly engaged workforce experience a 19.2 percent growth in operating income while those with a disengaged workforce experience a 32.7 percent decrease. Engaged employees are more likely than disengaged employees to feel that they can affect key business drivers, such as work quality, customer satisfaction, and revenue, and are less likely to leave. Only 3 percent of engaged employees are actively looking for another job, compared to 33 percent of disengaged employees.[10]

Enhancing employee engagement has little to do with implementing employee programs. It starts with organizational leaders understanding what drivers are important to the workforce. Leaders need to ask employees what they care about and how they envision being involved in the organization. When this is fully realized, management and employees can co-create a workplace where both parties are accountable for how the organization achieves its vision and values and reaches its strategic mandate. At its core, engagement is about building and sustaining the interpersonal or relationship side of the work experience.[11] Employees care about what kind of leaders they have, the company's vision of the future, and how they can exercise their full capacity in making a difference in the organization. An employer that commits to understanding employees' needs and interests, and works with employees to realize the vision, is en route to improving employee engagement. The key to sustaining employee engagement is to continually assess levels of engagement, canvass employee feedback, and orchestrate changes to accommodate emerging workforce needs.

## *In-class Notes*

**The Strategic Importance of Effective Employee Relations**

- Motivated employees who are committed to the goals of the organization can provide a strategic advantage
- Communication programs, both downward and upward, are key to employee satisfaction
- Employee opinion surveys are also important communication tools

A number of ways to develop effective communication channels within an organization have been presented. In general, communications programs let management continuously monitor employees' feelings and concerns, and they make it clear that employees have several channels through which to communicate concerns and get responses. The net effect is that there is less likelihood of small problems growing into big ones. Another major benefit is that programs like these give employees an opportunity to be involved, and involvement usually contributes to increased commitment.

## 11.2 ETHICAL AND LEGAL TREATMENT

Another critical aspect of effective employee relations is the fair, ethical, and legal treatment of employees. Within the employer–employee relationship, it is important to remember that both have certain rights. **Management rights** can be defined as management's right to run the business and to make those decisions necessary to do so. **Employee rights** include the right to fair and ethical treatment and the right to due process. Employees also have certain **statutory rights**, which include protection from discrimination, the right to privacy, and the right to safe working conditions. They also have **contractual rights** that may arise from the employment contract, explicit or implied, or from the union contract if a union is in place.

Regardless of how fair an employer tries to be, there is always potential for employee grievances and discontent stemming from perceived unfairness. Discipline cases and seniority issues in promotions, transfers, and layoffs probably top the list. Others include grievances growing out of job evaluations and work assignments, overtime, vacations, incentive plans, and holidays. In order to ensure that these matters are resolved fairly and equitably and that employees have the right to due process, many companies have initiated **fair treatment programs** through which grievances can be aired. A grievance procedure helps to ensure that every employee's grievance is heard and treated fairly, and that unionized firms do not hold a monopoly on such fair treatment.

**RPC 11-6 >**

**Monitors application of HR policies**

Some programs, such as FedEx Canada's Guaranteed Fair Treatment Procedure (GFTP), go beyond most grievance procedures: (1) Special, easily available forms make filing a grievance easy; (2) employees are encouraged to use the system; and (3) the highest levels of top management are routinely involved in reviewing complaints. The net effect is twofold: complaints do not get a chance to accumulate, and all managers think twice before doing anything unfair, since their actions will likely be brought to their bosses' attention.

An **open-door program** gives every employee the right to appeal the actions of his or her supervisor by taking the concern to successively higher levels of management. IBM Canada has an open-door program

A public servant employee rallies along with other striking museum workers to protect employee rights.

**management rights** Management's right to run the business and make those decisions necessary to do so.

**employee rights** Rights belonging to the employee guaranteed by law, contract, or hiring conditions that relate to the employees' working conditions.

**statutory rights** Rights established by legislation.

**contractual rights** Rights arising out of an employment or union contract.

**fair treatment programs** Employer programs that are aimed at ensuring all employees are treated fairly, generally by providing formalized, well-documented, and highly publicized vehicles through which employees can appeal any eligible issues.

**open-door program** A fair treatment program that gives every employee the right to appeal the actions of his or her supervisor by taking the concern to successively higher levels of management.

Great Place to Work Institute Canada **www.greatplacetowork.ca**

Privacy Commissioner of Canada **www.privcom.gc.ca**

that gives employees the right to appeal a supervisor's actions. Programs like IBM's do not have as much structure and formality as FedEx's guaranteed fair treatment program, but they do help ensure that healthy communication occurs regarding disciplinary matters and that employees' voices are heard. Employees who report to supervisors with open-door programs maintain they can speak more candidly with their supervisors (73 percent) and credit their supervisors with genuinely listening to their concerns (84 percent). Seventy-six percent of employees say that closed doors ignite thoughts of being laid off.[12]

## Electronic Trespassing and Employee Privacy

The advent of the Internet and email has led to concerns about misuse of company time and property for personal and possibly illegal uses.[13] Individuals are concerned with privacy—their control over information about themselves and their freedom from unjustifiable interference in their personal lives. On the other hand, employers must maintain the ability to effectively manage their employees and prevent liability to the company because companies can be held legally liable for their actions.[14] In some cases, employee blogs can expose a company to claims of defamation, harassment, reputational damage, and unauthorized disclosure of confidential information. In an arbitration decision in Alberta, a government employee who used a weblog ("blog") to defame her coworkers, her department, and management was fired. Employers can discipline or fire an employee for blogging if the activity exposes confidential information, reveals company trade secrets, or defames colleagues, management, or the company.[15]

Today's employers are grappling with the problem of how to deal fairly with the issue of electronic trespassing and employee privacy. Around the world, about 27 million employees have their email and Internet use tracked.[16] Modern technological advances have put employees' privacy rights on a potential collision course with employer access and monitoring of information.[17] Research indicates that task performance declines when employees are being monitored, unless they have control over the monitoring.[18] Nevertheless, employers want to monitor the use of computer-related activities in the workplace to eliminate time wastage (on web surfing, playing computer games, and so on) and abuse of company resources.[19]

The issue boils down to the manner in which workers' privacy interests are balanced with the employer's "right to know." Potential justifications for access and/or monitoring include productivity measurement, harassment/defamation cases, activity involving obscenity and pornography, security issues, workplace investigations, and protection of confidentiality. For example, in 2002, the Catholic Children's Aid Society in Toronto fired six employees, suspended 26 others without pay, and sent letters of warning to six others for emailing hard-core pornography and offensive jokes.[20] Electronic monitoring is becoming easier and less expensive as new software is developed that can track websites visited by workers and time spent on each.

Canada's former privacy commissioner stated that "employees have a fundamental, inherent right to privacy in the workplace" and was opposed to broad monitoring of emails or computer use.[21] Privacy of employee information has recently been addressed in a new law stating that any information about an employee beyond name, title, business address, and telephone number is regarded as personal and private. This includes health-related information provided to insurers. Originally applicable to federally regulated employees, the law was extended to cover all employees across the country on January 1, 2004.[22]

In general, courts in Canada have permitted electronic surveillance as long as there is proper balancing of opposing interests. Because Internet and email usage occurs over telephone lines, previous case law determining that cellphone conversations are not "private" because the transmission is being done through a device that can be intercepted by someone other than the intended recipient has been deemed to apply. Thus, at the present time, employers are given substantial leeway in monitoring their employees' use of the Internet and email. Employers are in an even stronger position if there is a written policy in place. A typical policy includes the following elements:[23]

LEGALcompliance

- a caution alerting employees that email/Internet systems are for business use and that the employer retains the rights to all material sent over and stored in the system
- a warning that the computer system should not be used to communicate anything improper or illegal
- a warning that deletion of a message or file may not fully eliminate it from the system

- a clear statement that violation of the policy may result in disciplinary action
- a requirement that employees sign a consent form indicating their understanding of the company's policy

Employers are not the only ones engaged in electronic surveillance. A poll of 896 Canadian employees revealed that 47 percent search online for their colleagues' and managers' social networking pages, blogs they have commented on, and forums they are members of in hopes of unveiling additional information about those they work with. The motive for an online hunt for information is not only to uncover hidden secrets, but to give employees a better understanding of their colleagues' and managers interests, which may lead to stronger work relationships.[24] While companies may have clear policies governing Internet and computer use at work, it is much less common for a company to have a policy on personal computer use at home. The Strategic HR box on page 355 describes some of the challenges associated with employees' use of social networking websites after hours.

## STRATEGIC HR

### Dealing with the Social Media Monster: Off-Duty Conduct That Hurts Employers a Grey Area Causing Headaches for HR

Water-cooler gossip, lunch break chats and informal conversations with coworkers: That's how social networking in the workplace used to work. But the Internet changed everything.

Sites such as Facebook, YouTube and Twitter have completely rewritten the rules. While social media in the workplace is still in its infancy, the rate at which it is escalating is phenomenal. Facebook has about 80 million users, of which 8.8 million are Canadian. This widespread audience can have a significant impact—both useful and damaging—on employees and employers. Personal blogs have also become a common tool, usually created to keep in contact with family and friends and, in many cases, colleagues at work.

**Consequences of social media**

There are serious issues surrounding employees' use of social networking websites. While companies may have clear policies governing Internet and computer usage at work, it is much less common for a company to have a policy on personal computer use at home.

Depending on what's posted online, it could constitute workplace discrimination, bullying or harassment. Employees could also—accidentally or intentionally—divulge confidential information about a company, such as financial information or new product information, which could negatively impact the business.

**Understanding employer, employee rights**

HR professionals need to be aware of these new challenges and understand the rights of employees and employers regarding the use of electronic social networking. For example: What are the limits to employee freedoms? Can an employee be disciplined or dismissed for "improper" use of the Internet? And what constitutes grounds for discipline and dismissal?

It is HR's role to identify and understand the issues and challenges that can arise in the context of electronic social networking among employees.

**Disciplining off-duty conduct**

One grey area employers face is to what extent they can hold an employee responsible for online conduct that occurs after hours on a personal computer.

On the face of it, it would seem impossible to hold an employee responsible for such conduct. After all, what an employee does in his spare time out of the office is of no concern to the employer, right? Not always. Off-duty conduct can, and has, come into play when it comes to disciplining and terminating workers.

The basic rule of thumb is an employer has no authority over what employees do once they're off the clock—unless the employer can show its legitimate business interests are affected. Therefore, HR needs to understand the limits of freedom of expression when it comes to employee postings about the organization, management and coworkers.

Consider the following hypothetical scenario: Joe had a bad day at work. He was passed over for a promotion and, therefore, was annoyed. That evening, he posted a lengthy blog on his personal website. The blog discussed his feelings and how his boss mistreated him by failing to give him the promotion. It went on to suggest his colleague was given the promotion for political reasons. Joe's blog is accessible to anyone surfing the

Internet. The next day, Joe's boss tells him he is being let go for damaging the boss's reputation and the organization's reputation. Does Joe have a case against his employer? Should Joe have been dismissed for his Internet conduct outside of work hours?

This scenario raises a number of issues: What are the consequences, if any, for employees who post negative comments, gossip and offensive material online and who allow it to be accessible to employees, family, friends or the general public? How much freedom of expression are employees entitled to when it comes to discussing work-related issues? Is a negative personal blog about a boss slander? Do the disciplines imposed differ within unionized and non-unionized workplaces?

**Lessons from arbitration rulings**

There are myriad important questions that arise. Perhaps the best way to answer some of them is to look at decisions involving employees and employers in similar situations.

One case that is pertinent to the use of social media outside the workplace is *Chatham-Kent (Municipality) v. Clarke.* An employee who worked as a personal caregiver at the Home for the Aged, a retirement facility in Southwestern Ontario, set up a personal blog that was accessible to the public.

On her blog, the employee criticized management and her coworkers. The blog also contained inappropriate comments, confidential information and medical data about some of the residents. When the employer found out about the blog, the worker was fired.

The employee grieved the termination but the grievance was dismissed on the grounds of a breach of confidentiality, insubordination and conduct damaging to the employer's interest.

This decision shows workers have a responsibility to respect workplace confidentiality and not damage the employer's reputation.

A second case that deals with potentially harmful online conduct occurring outside the workplace is *EV Logistics v RWU.* In that case, the worker—a 22-year-old employee of EV Logistics—posted racist, violent and disturbing comments on his personal blog.

The entries celebrated Nazism, referred to extreme violence and targeted ethnic minorities. The entries on the blog clearly identified his employer and he was fired. The employer claimed the worker's conduct was particularly harmful because of the Internet's far reach.

In considering the gravity of the offence, the arbitrator took into consideration the age, inexperience, family history and health of the worker. In this case, the arbitrator reinstated the worker because his off-duty conduct was not specifically directed at the employer, nor were the attacks directed specifically at individual employees or customers.

While the ruling was favourable to the employee, the case nonetheless raises an important cautionary note for employees. Online behaviour that reflects poorly on an employee can also reflect poorly on a company. Though the blog did not raise concerns of breach of confidentiality or insubordination, and though the arbitrator ruled in favour of the worker, it was nevertheless potentially harmful to the employer.

There have been other cases where an employee was not as successful in defending her rights. One case that grabbed headlines involved a Delta Airlines flight attendant who was fired because of her personal blog. She posted pictures of herself in a Delta Airlines uniform and the pictures were considered inappropriate by her employer.

In another case, a woman was fired for complaining about her job on her personal blog called dooce.com. This firing created a new word—"dooced"—which means to be fired for blogging about work.

There are numerous cases of employees being fired for online misconduct—though HR departments on this side of the border would be wise to remember that high-profile firings upheld in the United States may not stand up to the scrutiny of Canadian courts.

**Tips for employers, employees**

Employers need to set out clear policies and guidelines when it comes to the use of social media, both inside and outside of work. The policy needs to be well-communicated and employees need to be clearly told of the ramifications of violating the policy. Employers should also be vigilant and consistent when enforcing these policies and guidelines.

Employees need to get the message that posting information about their employer can have serious consequences, including the employer's legal right to discipline. Among the concerns that should be communicated are: disclosure of confidential information; disparaging statements about the employer or employees; harassment; and anything that could damage the company's reputation.

Employees should recognize information posted online is a permanent record and could be read by the public. In general, a good rule of thumb may be: "Don't put anything in writing that you are not willing to say face to face." Finally, employees need to be aware their online conduct during work hours may be monitored.

Source: V. Lobo, "Dealing with the social media monster (Guest commentary): Off-duty conduct that hurts employers a grey area causing headaches for HR," *Canadian HR Reporter*, June 1, 2009, p. 27. Reprinted with the author's permission.

**RPC 11-7 >**

**Assesses requests for HR information in light of corporate policy, freedom of information legislation, evidentiary privileges, and contractual or other releases**

## Video Surveillance and Employee Privacy

Video surveillance in the workplace is an equally contentious issue. Employers have no absolute rights to video record employees either at work or away from the workplace. For employers who have a need for video surveillance, the challenge is to find a balance between the employer's right to manage and protect their businesses and employees' right to privacy.

In general, arbitrators have permitted video surveillance in the workplace as long as employers meet a strict set of criteria. These criteria were developed by the Federal Court after the case of *Eastmond v. Canadian Pacific Railway,* where employees in the mechanical facility area of the Toronto yard accused the railway giant of installing digital cameras that violated their privacy rights. The employees argued that the cameras were installed to monitor their performance. The arbitrator dismissed the application on grounds that the employer justified the cameras for security purposes and that the snapshot images captured on the video were insufficient for monitoring performance. Based on this ruling, employers can implement video surveillance in the workplace provided they meet the following conditions:[25]

- The company can show it cannot effectively address a persistent problem without the use of video surveillance.
- The video surveillance cameras must be conspicuous.
- The cameras will not be used to monitor employees for production or productivity purposes.
- The video is maintained for a stipulated period of time and then destroyed unless relevant for ongoing investigation purposes.
- The union and employees are advised, in advance, about the installation of the cameras and their purpose.

Stringent limitations are placed on the secret monitoring of employees in the workplace, especially at employee workstations. In *Unisource Canada Inc. v. Communications, Energy and Paperworkers' Union of Canada,* an arbitrator ruled that undisclosed surveillance is warranted only under the following conditions:[26]

- a substantial problem exists
- a strong possibility exists that surveillance will be effective
- no reasonable alternative to surreptitious surveillance is available

Off-site surveillance may be considered by employers when they suspect employees are misrepresenting themselves around employee disabilities and absences. If an employer suspects foul play, precautions must be taken in video surveillance to ensure that the company can legally use evidence gained from it. An arbitrator is likely to dismiss video evidence if the employee in question does not have a history of dishonesty, has no record of disciplinary action, and has no record of fraudulent claims. Arbitrators are more likely to rule in favour of off-site surveillance if the employer meets the following conditions:[27]

- There is a reasonable basis to initiate off-site surveillance.
- The extent and manner of the surveillance is confined to what is reasonable to accomplish a set purpose.
- The employee's seniority, discipline record, and cooperation are considered in supplying medical evidence during his/her absence when assessing whether reasonable grounds to conduct the surveillance exist and whether there are alternatives to obtaining the necessary information.
- Surveillance is to be conducted only on public property where an employee is open to public scrutiny and not in private places, such as an employee's home.
- The employer ensures that videos are accurate and not edited to mislead or distort facts.

**AN ETHICAL DILEMMA**

Is it ethical to apply disciplinary action in cases of ongoing absenteeism and tardiness due to family responsibilities? What other approach could be used?

## Fairness in Employee Discipline

The purpose of **discipline** is to encourage employees to adhere to rules and regulations. Courts have repeatedly articulated the rights of employees to fair treatment not only during the term of employment but also during the disciplinary and termination process.[28] A fair and just disciplinary process is based on three foundations: *rules and regulations*, a *system of progressive penalties*, and the right to due process through an *appeals process*.

A set of clear rules and regulations is the first foundation. These rules address such things as theft, destruction of company property, drinking on the job, and insubordination. Examples of rules include:

**RPC 11-8 >**

**Contributes to the development of information security measures**

1. Poor performance is not acceptable. Each employee is expected to perform his or her work properly and efficiently and to meet established standards of quality.
2. Liquor and drugs do not mix with work. The use of either during working hours and reporting for work under the influence of either are both strictly prohibited.
3. Vending anything in the plant without authorization is not allowed, nor is gambling permitted in any form.

The purpose of these rules is to inform employees ahead of time what is and what is not acceptable behaviour. Employees must be told, preferably in writing, what is not permitted. This is usually done during the employee's orientation. The rules and regulations are generally listed in the employee orientation handbook.

A system of progressive penalties is a second foundation of effective discipline. Penalties may range from verbal or written warnings, suspension from the job, or discharge. The severity of the penalty is usually a function of the type of offence and the number of times the offence has occurred. For example, most companies issue warnings for the first instance of unexcused lateness. However, for a fourth offence, discharge is the more usual disciplinary action.

Finally, as part of the disciplinary process, there should be an appeals process. This helps to ensure that discipline is meted out fairly and equitably and that employees have a right to due process. Programs like FedEx's GFTP and IBM's open-door program help ensure their employees' access to an effective appeals process. Several important discipline guidelines are summarized in Figure 11.1.

## *figure* 11.1 Discipline Guidelines

Make sure that the evidence supports the charge of employee wrongdoing. In one study, "the employer's evidence did not support the charge of employee wrongdoing" was the reason arbitrators gave most often for reinstating discharged employees or for reducing disciplinary suspensions.

Ensure that the employees' due process rights are protected. Arbitrators normally reverse discharges and suspensions that are imposed in a manner that violates basic notions of fairness of employee due process procedures. For example, follow established progressive discipline procedures, and do not deny the employee an opportunity to tell his or her side of the story.

Adequately warn the employee of the disciplinary consequences of his or her alleged misconduct.

Ensure that the rule that allegedly was violated is "reasonably related" to the efficient and safe operation of the particular work environment (since employees are usually allowed by arbitrators to question the reason behind any rule or order).

Management must fairly and adequately investigate the matter before administering discipline.

Ensure that the investigation produces substantial evidence of misconduct.

Apply rules, orders, or penalties even-handedly and without discrimination.

Ensure that the penalty is reasonably related to the misconduct and to the employee's past work history.

Maintain the employees' right to counsel. All union employees have the right to bring a union representative when they are called in for an interview that they reasonably believe might result in disciplinary action.

Do not rob the employee of his or her dignity. Discipline employees in private (unless they request counsel).

Remember that the burden of proof is on the employer. In Canadian society, a person is always considered innocent until proven guilty.

Get the facts. Do not base disciplinary decisions on hearsay evidence or on general impressions.

Do not act while angry. Very few people can be objective and sensible when they are angry.

There are six general components of fairness relating to a disciplinary discussion between a manager and an employee. Managers should do the following:[29]

1. Take a counselling approach to the problem.
2. Exhibit a positive, non-verbal, not angry or anxious demeanour.
3. Provide the employee with some control over the disciplinary process and outcome.
4. Provide a clear explanation of the problem behaviour.
5. Ensure that the discussion occurs in private.
6. Ensure that the discipline is not arbitrary; that is, that it is consistent with that used in other, similar situations.

**DISCIPLINE WITHOUT PUNISHMENT** Traditional discipline has two major potential flaws. First, although fairness guidelines like those previously mentioned can help, no one ever feels good about being punished. There may, therefore, be residual bad feelings among all involved. A second shortcoming is that forcing the rules on employees may gain their short-term compliance but not their active cooperation when supervisors are not on hand to enforce the rules.

Discipline without punishment (or non-punitive discipline) is aimed at avoiding these disciplinary problems. The supervisor moves into a coaching role, working with the employee to accept the rules, to take responsibility for his or her actions, and to exercise self-discipline in determining how to resolve the problematic behaviour.[30]

Here is an example: Assume there has been a breach of discipline (such as disregarding safety rules) or unsatisfactory work performance (such as carelessness in handling materials). In such cases, the following steps would constitute a typical non-punitive approach to discipline.[31]

**Step 1.** *Issue an oral reminder.* The goal is to get the employee to agree to solve the problem. Reminding the employee of the reason for the rule can do this, as can reminding the employee that he or she has a responsibility to meet performance standards. The supervisor should document this oral reminder.

**Step 2.** *Issue the employee a formal written reminder.* A copy is placed in the HR file should another incident arise within six weeks. In addition, hold a second private discussion with the employee to determine if there is a reasonable explanation as to why the employee is not performing job duties as required and to express confidence in the person's ability to act responsibly at work.

**Step 3.** *Give a paid one-day "decision-making leave."* If another incident occurs in the next six weeks or so after the written warning, tell the employee to take a one-day leave with pay. This time is to be used to consider whether the job is right for him or her and whether or not the person wants to abide by the company's rules. The fact that the person is paid for the day is a final expression of the company's hope that the employee can and will act responsibly with respect to following the rules. When the employee returns to work, he or she should be asked to provide a decision regarding whether the rules will be followed. Assuming there is a positive response, the supervisor should work out a brief action plan to help the person change his or her behaviour.

**Step 4.** *If no further incidents occur in the next year or so, the one-day paid suspension is purged from the person's file.* If the behaviour is repeated, dismissal is required.

The process must, of course, be changed in exceptional circumstances. Criminal behaviour or in-plant fighting might be grounds for immediate dismissal, for instance. All discussions and actions should be well documented.

Non-punitive discipline can be effective. Employees seem to welcome the less punitive aspects and tend not to abuse the system by misbehaving to get a day off with pay. Incidences of grievances, sick leave usage, and disciplinary incidents decrease in firms that use these procedures. Examples of company successes with non-punitive discipline include:[32]

- The Texas Department of Mental Health saw turnover drop from 48.5 to 31.3 to 18.5 percent in the two years following implementation. The system has now been in place for over two decades. In this time, employee turnover has consistently remained at a manageable 20 percent or less per year.
- A Vermont General Electric plant, one of many GE facilities that have adopted *discipline without punishment*, reported a drop in written warnings/reminders from 39 to 23 to 12 in a similar two-year period.
- GTE's Telephone Operations reduced all grievances by 63 percent and disciplinary grievances by 86 percent in the year after management implemented the approach.
- Tampa Electric Co. reduced sick-leave hours per employee from 66.7 in the year before implementation to 31.2 eight years later.

## In-class Notes

**Fair, Ethical, and Legal Treatment**

- Some organizations institute fair treatment programs for employee grievances
- Electronic surveillance technology creates challenging issues related to employees' right to privacy and employer's right to manage
- Fairness in employee discipline is based on clear rules and regulations, progressive penalties, and appeals process

# 11.3 MANAGING DISMISSALS

**Dismissal** is the most drastic disciplinary step that can be taken toward an employee and one that must be handled with deliberate care. Specifically, the dismissal should be fair in that *sufficient cause* exists for it. Further, the dismissal should occur only after *all reasonable steps* to rehabilitate or salvage the employee have failed. However, there are undoubtedly times when dismissal is required, and in these instances, it should be carried out forthrightly.[33]

## Grounds for Dismissal

There are four bases for dismissal: unsatisfactory performance, misconduct, lack of qualifications for the job, and changed requirements of (or elimination of) the job. *Unsatisfactory performance* may be defined as a persistent failure to perform assigned duties or to meet prescribed standards on the job.[34] Specific reasons include excessive absenteeism, tardiness, a persistent failure to meet normal job requirements, or an adverse attitude toward the company, supervisor, or fellow employees. *Misconduct* can be defined as deliberate and wilful violation of the employer's rules and may include stealing, rowdyism, disobedience, and insubordination. *Lack of qualifications* for the job is defined as an employee's inability to do the assigned work, although the person is diligent. Since the employee in this case may be trying to do the job, it is especially important that every effort be made to salvage him or her. An employee can also be dismissed for misrepresenting qualifications. *Changed requirements of the job* may be defined as an employee's incapability to do the assigned work after the nature of the job has been changed. Similarly, an employee may have to be dismissed when his or her job is eliminated. Here again, the employee may be industrious, and so every effort should be made to retrain or transfer this person, if possible.

**Insubordination**, a form of misconduct, is sometimes the grounds for dismissal, although it may be relatively difficult to prove. Stealing, chronic tardiness, and poor-quality work are fairly concrete grounds for dismissal, while insubordination can be harder to translate into words. To that end, it may be useful to remember that some acts are or should be considered insubordinate whenever and wherever they occur. These include:

1. Direct disregard of the boss's authority. At sea, this is called mutiny.
2. Flat-out disobedience of, or refusal to obey, the boss's orders—particularly in front of others.
3. Deliberate defiance of clearly stated company policies, rules, regulations, and procedures.
4. Criticism of the boss in public. Contradicting or arguing with him or her is also negative and inappropriate.
5. Blatant disregard of the boss's reasonable instructions.
6. Contemptuous display of disrespect; making insolent comments, for example; and, more

importantly, portraying these feelings in the attitude that is shown while on the job.

7. Disregard for the chain of command, shown by going around the immediate supervisor or manager with a complaint, suggestion, or political manoeuvre. Although the employee may be right, this may not be enough to save him or her from the charges of insubordination.
8. Participation in (or leadership of) an effort to undermine and remove the boss from power. If the effort does not work (and it seldom does), those involved will be "dead in the water."[35]

As in most human endeavours, there may be extenuating circumstances for apparent insubordination. The supervisor's boss should therefore review all such cases. For example, an Ontario millwright was fired when he pushed a company manager down the steps of a construction trailer, narrowly missing construction debris and a passing front-end loader. The manager had been reprimanding the millwright for taking a day off to go hunting, which had forced the company to hire a private electrical contractor. The millwright grieved his termination, and the arbitrator ruled that a four-month suspension would be more appropriate as the assault was not premeditated but the result of momentary anger in reaction to provocation by the supervisor.[36]

## The Employment Contract

In Canada, the employer–employee relationship is governed by an **employment contract**—a formal agreement (in writing or based on mutual understanding) made between the two parties. If the contract is for a specific length of time, the contract ends at the expiration date and the employee cannot be prematurely dismissed without just cause.

Employees are often hired under an implied contract, where the understanding is that employment is for an indefinite period of time and may be terminated by either party only when reasonable notice is given.[37] Employers cannot legally fire employees at will. Canadian employers can only terminate an employee's employment without reasonable notice when **just cause** exists. If just cause is not present, then a termination without notice is considered **wrongful dismissal.** For example, in *Alberta (Human Rights and Citizenship Commission) v. Elizabeth Metis Settlement*, two employees were terminated for refusing drug testing in accordance with the employer's policy that drug testing was key to maintaining a clean image. The Alberta Court of Appeal disagreed with the employer's reasoning, declared it wrongful dismissal, and refused to uphold the termination.[38]

Just cause is often an area of disagreement between employer and employee, but it is usually considered to include incompetence, dishonesty, insubordination, fighting, and persistent absence or lateness.[39] However, just cause cannot be assessed in isolation and may vary depending on the possible consequences of the misconduct, the status of the employee, and the circumstances of the case. The burden of proof rests with the employer. The employer must prove that the employee has irreparably damaged the working relationship to the point that it is unrealistic and unreasonable to expect the employer to work with the employee.[40] In Canada, courts often do not accept the assertion of just cause by the employer. One Canadian researcher found that. since 1980, the courts have agreed with employers in only 25 percent of cases alleging incompetence, 40 percent for misconduct, 54 percent for insubordination, and 66 percent for conflict of interest/competing with the employer.[41]

In any termination where just cause is not involved, the employer must provide, at a minimum, reasonable notice to the employee as defined by employment standards legislation. Depending on the length of service, this could be two or more weeks. The employee sometimes continues to work during the period of notice given but usually ceases work at the time that the notice of termination is given. In the latter case, the employee receives a lump sum of money equal to his or her pay for the period of notice.

Often, the amount considered reasonable is far beyond the minimum notice period required by employment/labour standards legislation. If an employer

**discipline** A procedure intended to correct an employee's behaviour when a rule or procedure has been violated.

**dismissal** Involuntary termination of an employee's employment.

**insubordination** Willful disregard or disobedience of the boss's authority or legitimate orders; criticizing the boss in public.

**employment contract** A contract defining the terms of the employment relationship for both the employer and the employee.

**just cause** A legally defensible reason or cause.

**wrongful dismissal** An employee dismissal that does not comply with the law or does not comply with a written or implied contractual arrangement.

gives the minimum notice and the employee considers this to be unacceptable, the employee can sue for wrongful dismissal. The court will review the circumstances of the dismissal and make a final decision on the amount of notice to be provided. The courts generally award a period of notice based on their assessment of how long it will take the employee to find alternative employment, taking into account the employee's age, salary, length of service, the level of the job, and other factors. Rarely have notice periods exceeded 24 months.[42]

**AN ETHICAL DILEMMA**

Is it ethical to "buy out" an undesirable employee with severance pay and a good letter of reference in order to avoid prolonged wrongful dismissal litigation, even when you know the letter is misleading to potential future employers?

A major change in the law of wrongful dismissal occurred in 1997 when the Supreme Court of Canada ruled that "bad faith conduct" on the part of the employer in dismissing an employee is a new factor to be considered in determining the period of reasonable notice.[43] At a minimum, employers are required to be candid, reasonable, honest, and forthright with their employees in the course of dismissal and should refrain from engaging in conduct that is unfair or in bad faith, such as being untruthful, misleading, or unduly insensitive. Since the Supreme Court decision, many employees suing for wrongful dismissal have claimed notice on the basis of "bad faith" conduct on the part of their employer, and there have been no limits on what kinds of conduct have been considered "bad faith." Employers were relieved in 2008 following the *Keays v. Honda Canada Inc.* ruling in which the Supreme Court of Canada overturned a precedent-setting award of punitive damages in a wrongful dismissal case. The ruling abolished extensions of a reasonable notice period for bad faith conduct during termination. Dismissed employees now have to prove actual, compensable damages to justify such an award. The decision also limited the availability of punitive damage awards to exceptional cases, where the employer's behaviour is so horrendous and offensive that they are deserving of punishment.[44]

In extreme cases, employers may also be ordered to pay punitive damages for harsh and vindictive treatment of an employee and/or damages for aggravated or mental distress if the employee suffered undue distress from not being given adequate notice of termination.[45] The employer has a legal responsibility to the employee to give a fair notice period and to treat the employee ethically. The employee, on the other hand, has the responsibility to make every effort to find alternative employment as soon as possible, although not at a position inferior to the one from which he or she was terminated.

In addition to the items shown in Figure 11.2, companies should also be careful not to:

1. discharge anyone who is about to become vested in employee benefits/pensions
2. discharge a female employee just before maternity leave
3. "constructively discharge" employees by placing them in a lower-paying job in hopes of a resignation
4. try to induce employees to waive existing rights in exchange for gaining other rights
5. deviate from internal complaint resolution guidelines and procedures[46]

In cases where employers want to protect themselves from employees seeking to compete after they leave the organization, a **restrictive covenant** should be included in the employment contract. A restrictive covenant is a clause that restricts employees' activities once they are no longer employed by the company. It includes limits on the employee's ability to solicit business of the former company's customers and clients, and limits the employee's right to work in a business that is in competition with the former employer. Courts have ruled that restrictive covenants will be enforced only if deemed reasonable, which is determined by answering the following questions:[47]

- Does the employer have a proprietary interest that is entitled to protection?
- Are the geographic limitations and time limits in the covenant reasonable?
- Is a clause reasonable in its restricted activities?

In addition, the restrictive covenant must be clear and precise in language. In the case of *Shafron v. KRG Insurance Brokers (Western) Inc.*, the restrictive covenant was not upheld because of its reference to activities in "metropolitan Vancouver." There is no defined understanding of what areas are housed under this umbrella term. The B.C. Court of Appeal applied the concept of notional severance—the striking or changing of ambiguous language—and replaced the term with a specific list of cities. The Supreme Court of Canada deemed it inappropriate to rewrite restrictive covenants, ruling that there are no second chances with employment contracts. Employers are reminded to pay close attention to the language in restrictive covenant

## *figure* 11.2 Avoiding Wrongful Dismissal Suits

In order to avoid wrongful dismissal suits, employers should consider doing the following:

- Review the employee manual to look for and delete statements that could prejudice the employer's defence in a wrongful dismissal case. For example, delete any reference to the fact that "employees can be terminated only for just cause" (unless the company really means that). Also consider not outlining progressive disciplinary procedures in the manual, since the employer may be obligated to stick with the rules and follow the steps exactly or be sued for failing to do so. Similarly, references to probationary periods or permanent employment may be unwise, since they imply a permanence that the company may not really mean to imply. Never limit the right to dismiss or list specific reasons for dismissal. Always add a sentence or paragraph that reserves for the employer the right to make changes to the handbook in the future.[1]
- Make sure that no one in a position of authority makes promises that the company does not intend to keep, such as "If you do your job here, you can't get fired."
- Have clear, written rules listing infractions that may require discipline and dismissal, and then make sure to adhere to the rules. Generally, employees must be given an opportunity to correct unacceptable behaviour, and supervisors should be careful not to discriminate in any way.
- Get both sides of the story if a rule is broken. Get the worker's side of the story in front of witnesses, and preferably get it signed. Then, make sure to check out the story, getting both sides of the issue. Document all testimonies.
- Be sure that employees are evaluated at least annually. If an employee is showing evidence of incompetence, give that person a warning, and provide a chance to improve. All evaluations should be put in writing and signed by the employee.[2]
- Keep careful records. Keep records of all actions, such as employee evaluations, warnings or notices, memos outlining how improvement should be accomplished, and so on. Keep all efforts at counselling or discipline confidential to avoid defamation charges.[3]
- Make sure the company's policy about probationary periods is clear. This way employees cannot infer that once they are past the probationary period their jobs are "safe."[4]
- Remember court protection for employees. Remember that there are a number of reasons used by the courts to protect employees from arbitrary dismissal, such as whistleblowing, complaining about equal pay or wage law violations, and filing a workers' compensation claim.[5]
- Review the person's HR file. Before taking any irreversible steps, review the person's HR file. For example, long-seniority employees may merit more opportunities to correct their actions than do newly hired workers.
- Consider "buying out" a wrongful dismissal claim with settlement pay. Do not stand in the way of a terminated employee's future employment, since a person with a new job is less likely to bring a lawsuit against the former employer than someone who remains unemployed.[6]

---

1. T. Brady, "Employee Handbooks: Contracts or Empty Promise?" *Management Review* (June 1993), pp. 33–35.
2. K. Jenero, "Employers Beware: You May Be Bound by the Terms of Your Old Employee Handbooks," *Employee Relations Law Journal* 20, no. 2 (Autumn 1994), pp. 299–312.
3. R. Paul & J. Townsend, "Wrongful Termination: Balancing Employer and Employee Rights—A Summary with Recommendations," *Employee Responsibilities and Rights Journal* 6, no. 1 (1993), pp. 69–82. Wrongful termination is particularly a problem when the employee is a "whistle-blower." See, for example, R. Costa-Clarke, "The Cost Implications of Terminating Whistle-Blowers," *Employment Relations Today* 21, No. 4 (Winter 1994), pp. 447–454.
4. Paul & Townsend, p. 81.
5. Paul & Townsend.
6. Paul & Townsend, p. 74.

**restrictive covenant** A clause added to an employment contract to restrict employees' activities once they are no longer employed by the company.

clauses so that they are specifically crafted to the employees in question.[48]

## Constructive Dismissal

**Constructive dismissal** occurs when the employer makes unilateral changes in the employment contract that are unacceptable to the employee, even though the employee has not been formally terminated.[49] The most common changes in employment status that are considered to constitute constructive dismissal are demotion, reduction in pay and benefits, forced resignation, forced early retirement, forced transfer, and changes in job duties and responsibilities. An employee who believes that he or she has been constructively dismissed can sue the employer for wrongful dismissal. If the judge agrees that constructive dismissal occurred, he or she will determine a period of notice to be provided to the employee. An executive at TD Bank, deemed to have been constructively dismissed when many of his duties were transferred to someone else, received $2 million as a result of wrongful dismissal litigation.[50]

## Dismissal Procedures

In the event of a dismissal, a number of steps should be followed:

*frontLINE tips*

1. Hold discussions with the employee before taking any final action. An employee must be made aware that he or she is not performing satisfactorily.
2. Give written confirmation of the final warning.
3. Prepare a checklist of all property that should be accounted for, including computer disks and manuals.
4. Change security codes and locks previously used by discharged individuals.
5. Always prepare for the possibility that the discharged individual may act irrationally or even violently either immediately or in the weeks to come.
6. Decide beforehand how other employees will be informed about this person's dismissal. An informal departmental meeting of those directly involved with this person is usually sufficient.
7. Prepare and secure approval for a news release if the dismissal involves large numbers of employees (say, 25 or more).

It is also wise to have a lawyer create an employee release form. Such releases are obtained from employees who have asserted claims against the company or who are the subject of employment actions, such as discharges and layoffs. They release the employer from claims by giving the employee something of value—"consideration" in legal terms.[51] Any such release should include (1) a general release of the employee's claims; (2) a covenant not to sue the employer; and (3) an indemnification and payback provision relating to breaches of the release.[52]

## The Termination Interview

Dismissing an employee is one of the most difficult tasks a manager will face at work.[53] The dismissed employee, even if warned many times in the past, will often still react with total disbelief, grief, or even violence. The employee's direct supervisor usually conducts the termination interview, with a second person present—usually an HR professional—to serve as a witness and to offer support. The HR professional provides advice to the manager regarding how to conduct the termination interview and how to communicate the dismissal to remaining employees. The HR professional is also the liaison to legal counsel, prepares the dismissal documentation and severance package, arranges for the collection of company property from the dismissed employee, and is available to answer questions after the employee has left.

When conducting the termination interview, managers are encouraged to remain objective, keep the discussion on topic, and control their own emotional reactions. They should refrain from making apologies, offering promises, and getting locked into a discussion with the employee about the rightness or wrongness of the decision. Questions to anticipate from dismissed employees include:

- Why me?
- Will you reconsider your decision if I commit to making changes?
- Who will do my job when I am gone?
- What will you tell my colleagues and my clients?
- Does my performance over the past few years not count for anything?
- Can I go around and say goodbye to everyone?
- How did you calculate my severance?
- What will you say to prospective employers if they call for a reference?
- What do I do now?

Guidelines for the **termination interview** itself are as follows:

**Step 1.** *Plan the interview carefully.* According to experts at Hay Associates, this means:

- schedule the meeting on a day early in the week
- never inform an employee over the phone
- allow 10 to 15 minutes as sufficient time for the interview
- avoid Fridays, pre-holidays, and vacation times, when possible
- use a neutral site, never your office
- have employee agreements, the human resources file, and release announcements (internal and external) prepared in advance
- be available at a time after the interview in case questions or problems arise
- have phone numbers ready for medical or security emergencies

**Step 2.** *Get to the point.* As soon as the employee arrives, give the person a moment to get comfortable, and then inform him or her of the decision.

**Step 3.** *Describe the situation.* Briefly, in three or four sentences, explain why the person is being let go and the effective date and time of the termination. Focus on work-related behaviours/situations. For instance, "Production in your area is down 4 percent, and we are continuing to have quality problems. We have talked about these problems several times in the past three months, and the solutions are not being followed through. We have to make a change."[54] Do not make a personal attack on the employee or engage in an extensive justification of the decision. An employee's stress level is very high during a termination interview, and therefore he or she is less likely to be actively listening. Keep messages simple and in writing, and ask the employee often if he or she understands what is being communicated.

**Step 4.** *Listen.* It is important to continue the interview until the person appears to be talking freely and reasonably calmly about the reasons for his or her termination and the severance package that he or she is to receive. Employees may react in many different ways. Some may try to bargain their way back into the company, and others may be very controlled or even stoic. Providing counselling/outplacement services can help employees deal with their various reactions and help them accept their fate.

**Step 5.** *Carefully review all elements of the severance package.* Describe severance payments, benefits, and how references will be handled. However, under no conditions should any promises or benefits beyond those already in the severance package be implied. The termination should be complete when the person leaves. Do not make a person sign a release at this time because it may contribute to undue stress and pressure. The courts may overturn a document signed under such conditions, and the employee may try to sue for additional monies due to the mental distress caused by such pressure.

**Step 6.** *Identify the next step.* Discuss office clear-out procedures and return of company property, and inform the dismissed employee of your plans regarding communication to colleagues and clients. The employee may be disoriented, so explain where he or she should go upon leaving the interview. Remind the person who to contact at the company regarding questions about the severance package or references. The outplacement counsellor often takes over at this point if outplacement counselling is being provided as a benefit in the severance package. If the dismissed employee is in a state of shock or confusion, be prepared to offer transportation home.

Termination interviews are among the most difficult tasks that managers face, but there are guidelines for making them less painful for both parties.

**constructive dismissal** The employer makes unilateral changes in the employment contract that are unacceptable to the employee, even though the employee has not been formally terminated.

**termination interview** The interview in which an employee is informed that he or she has been dismissed.

At the end of the interview, make a brief record of the proceedings in case the employee decides to charge the organization with unjust cause for dismissal.

## Outplacement Counselling

**Outplacement counselling** provides career counselling and job-search skills training for terminated employees.[55] Counselling helps employees focus on the future, reassess skills and options, and rejuvenate confidence. The counselling itself is done either by the employer's in-house specialist or by outside consultants.

Outplacement counselling is usually conducted by outplacement firms such as Drake Beam Moran Inc. and Right Management. Middle- and upper-level managers who are dismissed will typically have office space and secretarial services that they can use at local offices of such firms in addition to the counselling services. Some outplacement providers are experimenting with Internet-delivered services, as described in the HR.Net box below.

A recent study found that 94 percent of Canadian companies offer outplacement counselling for the following top five reasons:[56]

- considered the right thing to do (71 percent)
- makes good business sense (71 percent)
- sends positive signals to remaining employees (69 percent)
- ensures terminated employees receive training needed to transition quickly (67 percent)
- reduces threats of litigation (62 percent)

## Severance Packages

Severance packages consist of benefits offered to terminated employees that provide a cushion upon which to move forward in their careers. The benefits provided vary depending on what organizations deem appropriate and what their budgets can sustain. Benefits are categorized as assistance benefits and continued benefits. Assistance benefits consist of outplacement services,

### HR.NET

### Keeping Up with Outplacement

Traditional outplacement provided recently released employees with the work-like environment they were accustomed to and were unable to get while in a job search from home. Today, the services offered by such sites as Workopolis.com and Monster.ca have reduced the need for assistance with résumé writing and company research and have personally empowered the job seeker. Also, many employees have a comfortable setting and the necessary technology at home.

Therefore, some outplacement companies have offered Internet-delivered job search programs on a self-administered basis. However, these programs are missing the "human factor." When someone loses a job, they hurt and are in a great deal of emotional pain. A computer is about as sensitive as a vacuum cleaner or refrigerator. This problem has led some outplacement specialists to use a new hybrid approach, combining the efficiencies of technology with face-to-face personal coaching.

A professional outplacement counsellor can be in attendance at the termination to help the individual cope and will then meet again with the terminated employee to help design the outplacement program. Meetings can be held in coffee shops that provide a neutral setting close to the employee's home where they feel comfortable and can converse in a more candid and informal manner.

The employee has access to round-the-clock web-based and telephone support and is encouraged to at least start working on a résumé within 48 hours. It is during the first 48 hours that panic and anger set in and when the terminated employee is most likely to hire a lawyer and challenge the company's decision. By producing at least a starter résumé, the individual is challenged to move forward.

When a terminated individual regains employment quickly, litigation challenges drop significantly and the "survivor" employees who probably still remain in contact with the terminated employee are much happier, more stable, and productive.

Source: Adapted from B. Delaney, "Keeping up with Outplacement," *Canadian HR Reporter*, June 17, 2002, pp. 15, 19. Reproduced by permission of *Canadian HR Reporter*, Carswell, One Corporate Plaza, 2075 Kennedy Road, Scarborough, ON, M1T 3V4.

## In-class Notes

**Managing Dismissals**

- Grounds for dismissal include unsatisfactory performance, misconduct, lack of qualifications, and changed requirements for the job
- Employment contract often is not in writing, but the implied contract requires reasonable notice of termination (unless just cause for dismissal exists), otherwise a lawsuit alleging wrongful dismissal may result
- Careful preparation required for dismissals, particularly for dismissal interview
- Constructive dismissal when an employer's changes to the employment contract are unacceptable to the employee (such as demotion)
- Outplacement counselling is provided to dismissed employees to assist with job search and retraining
- Severance packages consist of benefits offered to terminated employees that provide a cushion upon which to move forward in their careers

retirement planning, financial planning, retraining, and secretarial services. Continued benefits include health-related and monetary benefits. A recent study found that Canadians terminated from professional and management positions receive greater severance packages than their counterparts anywhere in the world. Top Canadian executives receive, on average, 4.66 weeks of severance per year of service, compared to the global average of 3.52 weeks. Industry studies show that utilities employers provide the most benefits and the manufacturing and educational industries provide the least. Employees who are offered severance packages are asked to sign a release of all claims against the employer, which minimizes the number of legal claims against employers by terminated employees. In Canada, 43 percent of companies offer severance benefits regardless of an employees' seniority with the company, and 97 percent of companies require terminated employees to sign a waiver before they can access severance benefits.[57]

## 11.4 MANAGING SEPARATIONS: LAYOFFS AND RETIREMENTS

While it is important to treat employees who are being dismissed in an ethical and legal manner, there will be other situations in which employees are leaving the company through no fault of their own. Non-disciplinary separations are a fact of life in organizations and can be initiated by either employer or employee. For the employer, reduced sales or profits may require layoffs

**outplacement counselling** A systematic process by which a terminated person is trained and counselled in the techniques of self-appraisal and securing a new position.

Workers stand firm and protest the signing of free-trade agreements.

or downsizings, while employees may terminate their own employment in order to retire or to seek better jobs. Termination of one's employment, regardless of the situation, is a traumatic experience for most people. It is therefore equally important to treat these individuals fairly, ethically, and, of course, legally.

LEGALcompliance

**Group termination laws** require employers who are terminating a large group of employees to give them more notice than that required for termination of an individual employee. The laws are intended to assist employees in situations of plant closings and large downsizings. Most jurisdictions in Canada require employers who are terminating a group of employees (some specify 10 or more, others 25 or more, and some 50 or more) within a short period of time (some specify four weeks, others two months, and one specifies six months) to give advance notice to employees and sometimes to their union. The amount of notice varies by jurisdiction and with the number of employees being terminated, but such notice generally ranges from 4 to 16 weeks (except in Ontario, which specifies 1 week per year of service to a maximum of 26 weeks).

The laws do not prevent the employer from closing down, nor do they require saving jobs. They simply give employees time to seek other work or retraining by giving them advance notice of the termination. The law is not clear about how the notice to employees must be worded. However, a letter to the individual employees to be terminated might include a paragraph toward the end of the letter as follows:

> Please consider this letter to be your official notice, as required by law, that your current position with the company will end 60 days from today because of a (layoff or closing) that is now projected to take place on (date). After that day, your employment with the company will be terminated, and you will no longer be carried on our payroll records or be covered by any company benefit programs. Any questions concerning this notice will be answered in the HR office.[58]

Many companies offer a variety of services to employees affected by a downsizing or plant closure, including the formation of job-finding facilities complete with job posting boards, access to Internet job sites, and counselling regarding résumé writing, job hunting, and interview techniques.

## Managing Layoffs

A **layoff**—where workers are sent home temporarily—is a situation in which three conditions are present: (1) there is no work available for the employees; (2) management expects the no-work situation to be temporary and probably short-term; and (3) management intends to recall the employees when work is again available.[59] A layoff is therefore not a termination, which is a permanent severing of the employment relationship. However, some employers do use the term *layoff* as a euphemism for discharge or termination.

**ALTERNATIVES TO LAYOFFS** Many employers today recognize the enormous investment that they have in recruiting, screening, and training their employees. As a result, they are more hesitant to lay off employees at the first signs of business decline. Instead, they are using new approaches to either blunt the effects of the layoff or eliminate layoffs entirely.

There are several alternatives to layoff. With the *voluntary reduction in pay plan*, all employees agree to reductions in pay in order to keep everyone working. Other employers arrange to have all or most of their employees accumulate their vacation time and to concentrate vacations during slow periods. Some employees agree to take *voluntary time off*, which again has the effect of reducing the employer's payroll, avoiding the need for a layoff. Another way to avoid layoffs is the use of *contingent employees*. Temporary supplemental employees can be hired with the understanding that their work is of a temporary nature. Then, when layoffs come, the first group to be laid off is the cadre of contingent workers.[60] The use of contingent workers in Canada is growing and is expected to continue to increase.[61]

Another possible solution to downsizing is the work-sharing program offered by Service Canada, which allows employers who are facing cutbacks to avoid laying off workers by shortening the work week up to three days and reducing wages accordingly. Service Canada may then arrange for employees to draw employment insurance benefits to "top up" wages to help compensate for this loss. This program is subject to approval by Service Canada and requires the agreement of both the employer and employees.

## Downsizing and Mergers

**Downsizing** refers to the process of reducing, usually dramatically, the number of people employed by a firm. Although it is not clear why, most firms do not find that their operating earnings improve after major staff cuts are made. There are probably many ways to explain this anomaly, but declining employee morale as a result of downsizing is one plausible reason. Therefore, firms that are downsizing must also give attention to the remaining employees. Certainly, those "downsized-out" should be treated fairly, but it is around the "survivor" employees that the business will be built.

Mergers and acquisitions can also contribute to downsizing. When one company acquires another, it is often the employees of the latter company who find themselves looking for new jobs. In such a situation, the employees in the acquired firm will be hypersensitive to mistreatment of their colleagues. When dealing with the survivors immediately after the downsizing, one of two situations must be faced right away. First, if no further reductions are anticipated at that time, workers can be reassured accordingly. Second, if it is expected that more reductions will probably take place, be honest with employees who remain, explaining that while future downsizings will probably occur, employees will be informed of these reductions as soon as possible.

A critical responsibility of human resources managers in any downsizing is to ensure that the bad news is delivered in a humane manner.[62] Department managers need to be trained in how to deliver unwelcome news effectively (by participating in role-plays for practice). These managers also need to identify and recognize their own personal values that will anchor them during the difficult communication process. The responsibility for delivering tough news humanely, treating people with dignity and respect, and advising people of all the support services available to them must be emphasized. It helps if managers work with a partner who acts as a coach when preparing for a termination interview and debriefs them on the experience when it is over. Finally, every effort should be made to deliver downsizing news in a one-on-one manner and to anticipate emotional reactions from everyone involved, including the manager.

Employee contemplating different retirement options.

## Retirement

With Canada's rapidly aging population and the prevalence of companies offering early retirement in efforts to downsize, retirement issues are becoming increasingly important and complex. People are retiring anywhere from age 55 to 70, with many retirees choosing to return to work part-time or as consultants after taking a hiatus.[63] **Retirement** for most employees is bittersweet. For some, it is the culmination of their careers, a time when they can relax and enjoy the fruits of their labour without worrying about the problems of work.

**group termination laws** Laws that require an employer who is terminating a large group of employees to give them more notice than is required for termination of an individual employee.

**layoff** The temporary withdrawal of employment from workers for economic or business reasons.

**downsizing** Refers to the process of reducing, usually dramatically, the number of people employed by a firm.

**retirement** The point at which a person ceases full-time work, usually between the ages of 55 and 70, with an increasing number of people choosing to retire earlier because of attractive early retirement incentive plans.

For others, retirement is traumatic, as the once-busy employee tries to cope with suddenly being "non-productive." For many retirees, in fact, maintaining a sense of identity and self-worth without a full-time job is the single most important challenge they will face. It is one that employers are increasingly trying to help their retirees cope with as a logical last step in the career-management process.

**PRE-RETIREMENT COUNSELLING** Most employers provide some type of formal **pre-retirement counselling** aimed at easing the passage of their employees into retirement.[64] Court decisions have confirmed that employers do have some legal responsibility to help employees prepare for retirement.[65] Retirement education and planning firms provide services to assist upcoming retirees with such issues as lifestyle goals (including part-time or volunteer work and/or moving to another country), financial planning, relationship issues, and health issues. In the end, employees who are taking control of their retirement plans often have reduced absenteeism and health-care costs.[66]

### *In-class Notes*

**Managing Separations: Layoffs and Retirements**

- Group termination laws govern terms of plant closings and large downsizings
- Layoffs are short-term separations from employment with return to work expected
- Mergers and acquisitions often involve downsizings
- Retirement can be managed through pre-retirement counselling

# Terminating Employees on the International Stage

Employment laws vary significantly across the international workplace, making the task of dismissing employees from their positions in host countries a daunting task. It is incumbent upon employers to familiarize themselves with rules and laws around workforce reductions, layoffs, and terminations in foreign countries.

In general, the following guidelines should be taken into account when approaching a downsizing operation:

1. Knowing who can be dismissed. In Canada, an employer can dismiss an employee at any time for just cause, upon providing reasonable notice or pay in lieu of notice. In China, however, an employer is restricted from using workforce reduction to terminate employment of workers under a number of circumstances, including an employee who is pregnant, an employee who has worked for 15 years and is less than five years from legal retirement age, or an employee who suffers from an occupational disease or injury caused by the employment.
2. Getting the process right. In some countries, employees have procedural rights before a termination can become effective. Germany requires employers to

notify the local employment office in order for a mass dismissal to be valid. Terminations qualify as a mass dismissal if they are for more than five employees in a unit of 20 to 60; more than 25 in a unit of 60 to 500; and 30 or more in a unit with at least 500. These terminations must occur in a period of 30 days. The terminations cannot become effective earlier than one month after the information is filed with the employment office.

3. Signing the release. An employer must obtain separation agreements, waivers, or releases from terminated employees in exchange for providing them with notice or pay in lieu of notice. In Canada, for example, it is common practice for an employer to insist upon a full and final release from an employee who has received notice or pay in lieu of notice. In the United Kingdom, special rules apply to most statutory employment protection claims. Employees can only waive the majority of statutory claims by entering into a "compromise agreement" or a "COT3 agreement."
4. Knowing the local labour laws. Employers must have comprehensive knowledge of local labour laws so that they are not caught in an expensive predicament. For example, in Saudi Arabia, there is a large number of expatriate employees. If an employer in Saudi Arabia dismisses them, it is generally required to repatriate them at its own expense.[67]

# Chapter Review

## Answers to Test Yourself

1. What are the techniques used for building multidirectional communication systems in organizations?

   Companies can help ensure effective employee relations by implementing downward and upward communications processes, creating a two-way communication mechanism. Company magazines, newsletters, memos, information booklets/pamphlets, flyers, and employee bulletins (physical or intranet bulletin boards) are examples of downward communication methods. Suggestion programs, employee opinion surveys, and focus groups/small group meetings are upward communication methods. Companies should also assess employee engagement and work with employees to create a workplace where both management and employees are accountable for how the organization lives its vision and reaches its strategic mandate. Enhancing employee engagement has little to do with implementing employee programs, but starts with organizational leaders understanding what drivers are important to the workforce. Leaders need to ask employees what they care about and how they envision being involved in the organization. At its core, engagement is about building and sustaining the interpersonal or relationship side of the work experience.

2. What can an employer do to ensure a fair and just disciplinary process?

   A fair and just disciplinary process is based on three prerequisites: (1) establishing rules and regulations that inform employees ahead of time as to what is and what is not acceptable behaviour in the workplace; (2) a system or sequence of progressive penalties or disciplinary actions (warnings, suspensions) that are provided to the employee before a dismissal; and (3) an appeals process to ensure that discipline is administered fairly and equitably.

3. What constitutes wrongful dismissal and constructive dismissal?

   Wrongful dismissal occurs when an employee is dismissed without just cause, such as incompetence, dishonesty, insubordination, fighting, or persistent absence or lateness. The employer must provide the employee reasonable notice, which could vary from

**pre-retirement counselling** Counselling provided to employees some months (or even years) before retirement, which covers such matters as benefits advice, second careers, and so on.

Service Canada Work-Sharing Program **www.hrsdc.gc.ca/en/epb/sid/cia/grants/ws/desc_ws.shtml**

The Retirement Centre **www.iretire.org**

The Financial Institute of Canada **www.financialknowledgeinc.com**

two weeks to two years or more depending on the employee's length of service. Constructive dismissal occurs when the employer makes unilateral changes in the employment contract that are unacceptable to the employee, although the employee has not been formally terminated.

4. What are important HR considerations in adjusting to downsizings, layoffs, acquisitions, and mergers?

   During times of downsizing, mergers, and acquisitions, employers must ensure that employees who lose their jobs are treated fairly and in accordance with the law. The survivors must either be reassured that further downsizing is not planned or told honestly to expect more downsizing in the future. Department managers must be trained to communicate one on one with employees in a humane manner. Fair termination procedures must be followed. Emotional support services should be made available to all concerned. Alternatives to layoffs, such as voluntary reduction in pay, voluntary time off, or the use of contingent employees, should be considered first.

5. What strategies can firms use to assist employees in adjusting to retirement?

   The most important strategy to assist employees who are approaching retirement is pre-retirement counselling. Assistance for employees in dealing with such issues as lifestyle goals, financial planning, and health concerns can help make the transition to retirement less difficult.

## Key Terms

constructive dismissal (p. 364)
contractual rights (p. 353)
discipline (p. 357)
dismissal (p. 360)
downsizing (p. 369)
downward communication (p. 350)
employee rights (p. 353)
employment contract (p. 361)
fair treatment programs (p. 353)
group termination laws (p. 368)
insubordination (p. 360)
just cause (p. 361)
layoff (p. 368)
management-by-walking-around (p. 351)
management rights (p. 353)
open-door program (p. 353)
opinion surveys (p. 351)
outplacement counselling (p. 366)
pre-retirement counselling (p. 370)
restrictive covenant (p. 362)
retirement (p. 369)
statutory rights (p. 353)
termination interview (p. 364)
upward communication (p. 350)
wrongful dismissal (p. 361)

## Required Professional Capabilities (RPCs)

RPC 11-1 > (p. 350)
RPC 11-2 > (p. 350)
RPC 11-3 > (p. 351)
RPC 11-4 > (p. 351)
RPC 11-5 > (p. 351)
RPC 11-6 > (p. 353)
RPC 11-7 > (p. 357)
RPC 11-8 > (p. 358)

# CASES AND EXERCISES

PEARSON myHRlab

For additional cases and exercises, go to www.pearsoned.ca/myhrlab.

## CASE INCIDENT

### Do it yourself, Enviro-Man!

Ken Webster, a skilled labourer, has been working for Jansen's Manufacturing Ltd. for the past 23 years. Ken spends his days repairing machines when they break, monitoring schedules to ensure the plant has ample supplies for each shift, training new recruits on the machines, and helping out on the line when someone calls in sick. Ken has been in the same position for most of his career, and enjoys the work he does mainly because no one bothers him and he can exercise full autonomy in how he manages his day. He gets along with his colleagues and takes great pride in keeping all the machines humming on the shop floor. However, Ken is known for being outspoken, can be rebellious when things do not go his way, and often challenges management on changes made on the shop floor. He has no disciplinary record.

After lunch one day, Ken was hurrying back to his work station and inadvertently put a newspaper in the wrong recycling container. Bill Hamilton, the supervisor, happened to notice this and told Ken to retrieve the newspaper and put it in the proper recycling container. Ken turned to Bill and said, "I'm not paid to sort garbage." Bill replied, "We recycle around here. Get with the program! Put the newspaper in the right recycling container! What's wrong with you?!" Ken became angry and bellowed, "I have machines to fix, and I'm not going to stop and pick up garbage. Do it yourself, Enviro-man!" Ken continued to hurl unflattering names and remarks at Bill while everyone on the shop floor stopped to watch.

Bill has been trying for the past month to get everyone involved in the new recycling program as part of the company's commitment to environmental awareness and good citizenship. A number of staff meetings and environmental awareness campaigns were launched, with most employees supporting the new recycling initiative. However, Ken has been the most resistant to the change, voicing his concern that recycling in such a small plant will not make a difference.

After Ken ran out of oxygen being abusive, Bill called him into his office and suspended him for one week without pay for insubordination and use of abusive language when speaking with a supervisor. Ken was escorted by security out of the building, and Bill contacted the human resources department to inform them of the incident and the action taken.

### Questions

1. Analyze Bill's approach to disciplining Ken for not recycling according to new company protocol.
2. What, if anything, would you have done differently if you were in Bill's position? Explain why.
3. What, if anything, should Bill say to the employees who witnessed this incident?
4. What course of action should Bill take when Ken returns from his one-week suspension? Explain why.
5. If you were the HR manager in this organization, what advice would you give Bill to enhance his approach to discipline?

### Application Questions

1. For the past five years, employee turnover in your organization has been escalating.
   a. Discuss the communications programs you will implement to get a better understanding of the root cause of the problem and the changes needed to reduce turnover.
   b. What questions will you ask employees to get a better understanding of their concerns and needs?
2. There has been a rash of thefts in your factory during the third shift ("the midnight shift") over the past nine months. In an attempt to find the culprits, you decide to mount 12 cameras in the plant, yet only activate them during the third shift. Employees on the third shift are outraged by the decision and feel they are being discriminated against. How will you leverage employees' concerns with the need to protect your property?
3. You are the manager of a large retail outlet with eight locations across the city. Most of your time is spent at head office, leaving little, if any, time for you to oversee operations in each store. Staff in one location are complaining about a new employee. Apparently, she is rude to customers and staff, arrives late to work most mornings, and occasionally arrives under the influence

of drugs. Staff are pleading with you to fire her. What course of action will you take?

4. Reflect on a time when you were disciplined—either in a part-time or full-time job. Analyze the effectiveness of the person's approach to disciplining you and discuss the outcome of the disciplinary action taken.

## RUNNING CASE: LEARNINMOTION.COM

### Fair Treatment in Disciplinary Action

In the case for Chapter 11, *Fair Treatment in Disciplinary Action,* despite LearninMotion.com employees becoming more comfortable working in their surroundings and with each other, there is an increasing need for policies and rules concerning employee behaviour. Students are asked to determine what type of professional conduct policies are needed for the company.

To read this case, go to www.pearsoned.ca/myhrlab and click on the *Management of Human Resources,* Third Canadian Edition, In-Class Edition, cover. Click on the case module in Chapter 11.

## CONTROVERSIAL BUSINESS TOPIC EXERCISE

Your colleague, the manager of human resources at a large soft-drink manufacturer, has just alerted you to a very grave situation. The vice-president of marketing for your company—a competing soft-drink manufacturer—has been selling trade secrets to the competition. The vice-president for your company has been meeting with the CEO of the competition to share insider details about operations, product ingredients, company finances, strategic plans for the next five years, and confidential data about succession planning initiatives. Your colleague in HR overheard a number of conversations, but is not willing to take action as she does not want to jeopardize her career. You share similar concerns about raising the issue as you have recently been promoted to assistant manager of human resources. To make this situation even more difficult for you, the vice-president of marketing is your brother-in-law. What course of action will you take?

## IN THE BOARDROOM EXERCISE

The CEO sat quietly for several minutes after your presentation with a puzzled look on his face. You delivered a 30-minute presentation on non-punitive discipline in which you outlined how you envision implementing "discipline without punishment" practices. Eventually, the CEO takes a deep breath and says, "Non-punitive discipline is a waste of time and resources. I don't buy it and I know the union won't go for it either. Whoever heard of giving people a day off to think about how to correct their behaviour? People will only use the time to enjoy an extra day off at the company's expense. People aren't capable of being objective and self-directed when it comes to discipline. Management should take the leadership on discipline and treat this as a top-down decision-making process. If people get out of line around here, warn them and write them up, and if they don't change, fire them!" What is your response to the CEO? What will you say to convince the CEO to reconsider a non-punitive approach to discipline?

## TERMINATING EMPLOYEES ON THE INTERNATIONAL STAGE EXERCISE

*The exercise below relates to the Terminating Employees on the International Stage feature* *on p. 370.*

Select a country in which you would like to operate a branch of your Canadian business. Assume that one of your employees in this foreign country, who has worked for you for a year, does not meet the performance standards. You have given the employee verbal and written warnings, offered training and one-on-one coaching, and even established a job-shadowing arrangement so that the employee could learn from one of your star workers. However, the worker has not shown any marked change in behaviour. You have no other option but to terminate the employee.

a. Map out the dismissal procedures you will follow to prepare for the termination.

b. Outline how you will conduct the termination interview. Role-play the termination interview with a team of three classmates—one conducts the interview, one is the employee, and one is an observer to give feedback on how the interview was conducted.

## EXPERIENTIAL EXERCISE

For further study of text materials and development of practical skills, select the experiential exercise module for this chapter on www.pearsoned.ca/myhrlab. This module provides two to three individual or group-based assignments per chapter.

# QUIZ YOURSELF

STUDY GUIDE QUESTIONS

Circle the correct answer. After completing this self-test, check your answers against the Answers to Study Guide Questions at the back of the book (p. 433).

1. Managers need information to help them make decisions, and employees need information to keep them motivated and committed. Communications Inc. recognizes this need and would like to establish a mechanism that creates communication from bottom to top. The following is a method that can facilitate this process:
   a. newsletters
   b. suggestion programs
   c. bulletin boards
   d. memos
   e. all of the above

2. Karen is an HR generalist who wants to create a feedback mechanism to get information from staff on how they feel about the company, management, recognition and rewards systems, and work–life balance. If you were Karen, which of the following methods would you use to fulfill this purpose?
   a. suggestion programs
   b. Speak Up! programs
   c. opinion surveys
   d. bulletin boards
   e. mentoring

3. An important aspect of effective employee relations is the fair, ethical, and legal treatment of employees. Within an employee–employer relationship, both have certain rights. The right to ethical and fair treatment and the right to due process are known as:
   a. management rights
   b. employee rights
   c. statutory rights
   d. contractual rights
   e. none of the above

4. The use of the Internet and email has led to concerns about misuse of company time and property for personal and possibly illegal uses. Potential justifications for access and/or monitoring of personal use of Internet and email by the employer include:
   a. productivity measurement
   b. workplace investigations
   c. protecting confidentiality
   d. activity involving pornography
   e. all of the above

5. Virtuosa is an IT company that wants to establish a privacy policy to outline for staff what could be construed as unacceptable use of the Internet and email in the workplace. Which of the following is a key element that should be referred to in the privacy policy?
   a. a statement that company computers are not to be used for personal reasons
   b. a statement that disciplinary action will be taken for accessing the Internet
   c. a statement that if the policy is violated, disciplinary action will be taken
   d. a requirement that employees report any communication with external parties
   e. all of the above

6. The purpose of discipline is to encourage employees to adhere to rules and regulations. A fair and just disciplinary process is based on the following foundations:
   a. rules/regulations, system of progressive penalties, appeals process
   b. policies/procedures, dismissal process, appeals process
   c. just and fair treatment of employees within the legal framework
   d. establishment of disciplinary and grievance procedures
   e. rules/regulations, appeals process, and just and fair treatment

7. Dismissal is the most drastic disciplinary step that can be taken toward an employee. However, there are undoubtedly times when dismissal is required, and in these instances, it should be carried out forthrightly. Legitimate bases for dismissal include:
   a. elimination of job
   b. misconduct
   c. unsatisfactory performance
   d. lack of qualifications for job
   e. all of the above

8. Ameen had been given a number of verbal and written warnings, and measures were put into place to help him improve his customer service skills, but then he was terminated. Despite all efforts, his ability to deal effectively with customers did not increase. What was the reason Ameen was terminated?
   a. insubordination
   b. lack of qualifications

c. unsatisfactory performance
d. elimination of job
e. none of the above

9. Karen was recently terminated without any notice. The reason she was given was lack of performance. However, an investigation showed that during her five-year tenure with the company, she had received "excellent" performance review ratings on a consistent basis. Karen's dismissal is a:
a. performance dismissal
b. wrongful dismissal
c. constructive dismissal
d. unfair dismissal
e. none of the above

10. Ken is an administration manager with a construction company. Last week, he received a letter from the company informing him that he would be transferred to a new location as an administration coordinator. He can take action against the company on the grounds of:
a. wrongful dismissal
b. unfair treatment
c. constructive dismissal
d. workplace harassment
e. all of the above

11. The dismissed employee, even if warned many times in the past, will often still react with total disbelief or even violence. A termination interview should:
a. be held at a neutral site
b. not be held on Fridays
c. be prepared for in advance
d. not be done over the phone
e. all of the above

12. Outplacement counselling is usually done by external parties and provides the terminated employee with:
a. psychiatric counselling
b. job-search techniques
c. temporary work
d. legal counselling
e. job security

13. A layoff is a temporary situation in which there is no work available for employees. The following is an alternative to layoffs:
a. quality programs
b. casual employees
c. outsourcing
d. dismissals
e. work-sharing programs

14. Most companies resort to downsizing when the financial performance of the company suffers. However, there are other times when downsizing is required. One such occasion is:
a. mergers and acquisitions
b. labour market changes
c. strategic growth
d. international expansion
e. none of the above

15. Retirement for most employees is bittersweet. What measures can HR professionals provide to make the retirement process easier for those who retire?
a. retirement education
b. financial planning
c. management of health issues
d. pre-retirement counselling
e. all of the above

12 *chapter*

# Labour Relations, Collective Bargaining, and Contract Administration

## Learning Objectives

1. Summarize labour–management relations in Canada.
2. Explain Canada's labour laws, which regulate the working relationship between labour and management.
3. Explain the labour movement in Canada today.
4. Trace the steps in the labour relations process.
5. Explain the impact of unionization on HRM.

## Test Yourself

1. What are the key labour relations strategies that organizations can adopt in relation to unionization?
2. What are the common characteristics among Canadian labour relations laws?
3. What are the union organizing and recognition processes?
4. What is collective bargaining, and what are the critical steps involved?
5. What is the impact of unionization on HRM?

## 12.1 OVERVIEW OF LABOUR–MANAGEMENT RELATIONS

The term **labour–management relations** refers to the ongoing economic and social interactions between labour unions and management in organizations. A **labour union (or union)** is an officially recognized body representing a group of individuals who have joined together to present a united front and collective voice in working with management. The aim of unions is to secure and further the social and economic interests and well-being of their members. More specifically, the purposes of unionization are to achieve better pay and benefits, achieve greater control over the jobs being performed, obtain greater job security and improved working conditions, and influence the rules and procedures governing areas such as discipline, transfers, promotions, grievances, and layoffs.

A study conducted by the Canadian Auto Workers (CAW) union reports that unionized auto assembly-line employees in Canada are the most productive on the continent, outperforming labourers in Mexico and in the U.S. facilities of Japanese and European carmakers. Productivity in CAW-represented auto manufacturing plants is 8 percent higher than in unionized U.S. factories and 24 percent higher than in non-union U.S. plants of overseas-based automakers. It takes CAW workers 20.36 hours to assemble a vehicle, compared to 25.24 hours in U.S. plants and 32.54 hours in Mexican factories.[1]

The labour relations (LR) process changes the relationship between employees and an organization because it instills a collective agreement, which stipulates the nature of their working relationship and the procedures to be followed on a daily basis and when making decisions. In a unionized organization, a labour relations specialist in the HR department assumes a number of responsibilities, including grievance arbitration, informing management on labour legislation and interpretation of the collective agreement, and creating a positive working relationship between labour and management. The labour relations specialist is often a member of the management team that negotiates the collective agreement. First-line supervisors also play a critical role in shaping the labour–management relationship because of their day-to-day involvement in administering the collective agreement, promoting a positive work climate for employees, avoiding unfair labour practices, and resolving workers' complaints before they become official grievances.

Negotiating a collective agreement.

### Labour Relations Strategy

An organization's **labour relations (LR) strategy** is its overall plan for dealing with unions. An organization's LR strategy can result in a relationship ranging from hostility (open conflict) to co-operation.

**UNION ACCEPTANCE STRATEGY** Managers in organizations choosing a **union acceptance strategy** view the union as the legitimate representative of the organization's employees. They accept collective bargaining as an appropriate mechanism for establishing workplace rules and the terms and conditions of employment for the bargaining-unit members and work with the union toward a win-win outcome in the decision-making process. A union acceptance strategy is likely to result in labour–management cooperation and a harmonious working relationship.

**UNION AVOIDANCE STRATEGY** Managers select a **union avoidance strategy** when they believe that it is preferable to operate in a non-unionized environment. This may be based on the desire for greater flexibility in running the organization or fear that a union will have a disruptive influence or result in a loss of control over employees. There are two approaches that organizations can adopt to avoid unionization—one is proactive and the other employs hardball tactics.[2] A **union substitution (proactive HRM) approach** involves becoming so responsive to employees' needs that there is no incentive for them to unionize. For example, factories in Canada that are wholly owned by Toyota, Honda Motor Co., or Nissan Motor Co. have remained non-unionized by developing a reputation for fair treatment and concern for employee well-being, including first-rate working conditions, benefits and pay, opportunities for collective decision making, and extensive training and development. As long as the auto manufacturers remain profitable and lead the

## *In-class Notes*

**Overview of Labour–Management Relations**

- Labour–management relations is the ongoing economic and social interaction between labour unions and management in organizations
- A labour union is an officially recognized body representing a group of employees who have joined together collectively to deal with management
- Labour relations strategy is either union acceptance or union avoidance

industry in car sales, employees do not perceive a need for union representation.[3] Organizations adopt a **union suppression approach** when there is a desire to avoid a union at all costs. "Hardball tactics," which may or may not be legal, are employed to prevent a union from organizing the firm's employees or to get rid of an existing union. Hardball tactics can sometimes backfire. As will be explained shortly, a union may receive automatic certification if management is found guilty of unfair labour practices as set out in labour laws.

## 12.2 CANADA'S LABOUR LAWS

Canada's labour laws have two general purposes: to provide a common set of rules for fair negotiations and to ensure the protection of public interest by preventing the impact of labour disputes from inconveniencing the public. Protection of the public interest is an important political and social concern and explains why police officers, hospital employees, and firefighters are denied the right to strike in most jurisdictions.

Some of the key mandates of Canada's labour law applicable across federal, provincial, and territorial jurisdictions include:

- the right of employees to organize, join, and participate in a union of their choice
- "bargaining in good faith" by both union and management when negotiating a collective agreement
- the requirement that a collective agreement be in force for at least one year
- prohibition of strikes or lockouts during the life of a collective agreement
- mandatory conciliation process before a strike or lockout can be initiated

**labour–management relations** The ongoing economic and social interactions between labour unions and management in organizations.

**labour union (union)** An officially recognized association of employees practising a similar trade or employed in the same company or industry who have joined together to present a united front and collective voice in dealing with management.

**labour relations (LR) strategy** An organization's overall plan for dealing with unions, which sets the tone for its union–management relationship.

**union acceptance strategy** A labour relations strategy based on management's view that the union is the legitimate representative of the organization's employees.

**union avoidance strategy** A labour relations strategy based on management's preference to operate in a non-union environment. There are two possible approaches: union substitution and union suppression.

**union substitution (proactive HRM) approach** A union avoidance strategy that involves removing the incentives for unionization by ensuring that the needs of employees are met.

**union suppression approach** A union avoidance strategy that involves the use of hardball tactics, which may or may not be legal, to prevent a union from organizing the firm's employees or to get rid of an existing union.

Labour Management Services (Ontario)
**www.labour.gov.on.ca/english/index.html**

- the requirement that disputes over matters arising from interpretation of the collective agreement be settled by final and binding arbitration
- prohibition of certain specified "unfair practices" on the part of the union and management

There is a **Labour Relations Board (LRB)** in every Canadian jurisdiction except Quebec, where a Labour Court and 20 commissioners perform similar functions. The LRBs are tripartite—composed of representatives of union and management and a neutral chair or vice-chair, typically a government representative. They are empowered to interpret, administer, and enforce the Act and to investigate alleged violations. For example, the LRBs have the power to decide whether an individual is eligible for union membership, whether a union is the appropriate bargaining agent to represent employees, whether a collective agreement is in force, and whether the parties are bound by it. The LRBs also supervise certification of elections, investigate allegations of unfair labour practices, and mandate solutions.

When charges have been filed against an employer, the HR manager works with senior management and the organization's lawyer to prepare the case. After reviewing the case, the board's decisions are final and binding and cannot be appealed.

## Unfair Labour Practices by Management

To help protect employee rights, Canadian labour legislation prohibits specific **unfair labour practices** by management. Basically, managers are prohibited from interfering with and discriminating against employees who are exercising their rights under the LR legislation. Examples of prohibited unfair labour practices by employers include:[4]

LEGALcompliance

- interfering with the employees' right to select the union of their choice for collective bargaining purposes or discriminating against employees for union activity
- participating in the formation, selection, or support of unions representing the organization's employees
- unilaterally changing the terms of collective agreements or changing or threatening to change the wages and working conditions during certification proceedings or collective bargaining
- refusing to bargain in good faith—that is, failing to make a serious attempt to reach a collective agreement
- suspending, discharging, or imposing any penalty on an employee for refusing to perform the duties of another employee who is participating in a legal strike
- intimidating or threatening an employee regarding union activity

Penalties for bad faith bargaining can be severe. In 2001, the owners of Buhler Versatile Inc., a Winnipeg-based tractor plant, were ordered by the Manitoba Labour Board to pay $6 million to employees for bargain-

*In-class Notes*

**Canada's Labour Laws**

- Employees' right to organize, join, and participate in a union
- "Bargaining in good faith" by union and management
- Prohibition of unfair labour practices by both management and unions
- Labour Relations Boards investigate and resolve labour relations issues

ing in bad faith after Buhler offered progressively reduced wage rates without rationale during negotiations.[5]

## Unfair Labour Practices by Unions

Canadian labour laws also place limitations on the conduct of labour unions. Unfair labour practices by unions include:

- attempting to persuade an employee to become or continue to be a union member at the workplace during working hours unless employer consent has been obtained
- refusing to bargain in good faith
- discriminating against union members or employees in the bargaining unit on grounds prohibited by human rights legislation
- intimidating or coercing employees to become or remain members of the union
- failing to provide fair representation for all employees in the bargaining unit
- calling or authorizing an unlawful strike

**AN ETHICAL DILEMMA**

As an official card-carrying member of a union but not a strong union supporter, would you participate in union activities to support your colleagues who are pro-union?

## 12.3 THE LABOUR MOVEMENT IN CANADA TODAY

The primary goal of the labour unions active in Canada is to obtain economic benefits and improved treatment for their members. These activities are known as **business unionism.**[6] Unions strive to ensure job security for their members by providing a cushion against layoffs or terminations caused by fluctuations in economic conditions as well as protection against unjust treatment, such as arbitrary termination. The goal of attaining improved economic conditions for members is pursued by negotiating higher wages, benefits improvements, and cost of living adjustments (COLAs) to protect members' wages during inflationary times. Over the years, unions have successfully negotiated better working conditions for members and have been instrumental in convincing politicians of the need for stricter and more comprehensive health and safety legislation. More recently, unions have tried to narrow the wage gap between male and female workers, as discussed in the Workforce Diversity box on page 382.

Labour unions are also making progress in securing rights for casual workers. In a landmark decision in 2009, a New Brunswick court ruled that casual government employees in that province have the right to unionize. The court overturned legislation that prohibits unionization of casual workers, citing workers' right to freedom of association under the Charter of Rights and Freedoms. Under the new provision, casual workers can negotiate for benefits and vacation entitlement that were not part of their employment contract. The decision affected thousands of temporary and seasonal workers employed by the New Brunswick government.[7]

Many unions also choose to address broader political and social issues of concern to their members. Trying to influence economic and social policies of government at all levels is known as **social unionism.** The objectives of social unionism are often accomplished by lobbying and speaking out on proposed legislative reforms, such as the introduction of employment equity legislation or amendments to labour relations legislation.

In the current economic climate, plagued with job losses and plant closures, a union's negotiation skills are tested as it strives to protect the jobs of its members. For example, the CAW exercised its resourcefulness in negotiating a new collective agreement for workers at Lakeside Steel in Welland, Ontario—a steel pipe and tubing manufacturer facing massive layoffs as

**Labour Relations Board (LRB)** The legally recognized body in every Canadian jurisdiction (except Quebec) responsible for interpreting, administering, and enforcing the labour relations legislation. In Quebec, a Labour Court and 20 commissioners perform similar functions.

**unfair labour practices** Action by the employer or union that restrains persons from exercising their lawful rights under the labour relations statutes.

**business unionism** The activities of labour unions focusing on economic and welfare issues, which include pay and benefits, job security, and working conditions.

**social unionism** Activities of unions directed at furthering the interests of their members by influencing the social and economic policies of governments at all levels, such as speaking out on proposed legislative reforms.

WORKFORCE DIVERSITY

## An Excerpt from "Unions Taking Up the Mantle of Women's Issues"

With manufacturing jobs disappearing, gas prices soaring and the environment calling for attention, women's issues have not been front and centre in the media. However, the pay gap between the genders remains, the availability and cost of child care is still an issue, employment insurance is out of reach for many women who lack the requisite qualifying hours, and privatizing and contracting out in the public service sector have negatively affected many women's wages.

According to a March 2008 report by the Canadian Labour Congress (CLC), unions have been an important force in closing the economic inequality and pay gap between men and women. While women employed full time in Canada earned about 75 percent as much as their male counterparts in 2006, unionized women earned an average of 93 percent. The report, Women in the Workforce: Still a Long Way from Equity, notes union wages as a whole tend to be substantially higher than the average wage– anywhere from 7 percent to 14 percent depending on the sector, the worker's age and job classification.

**Pay equity still priority one**

However, unions are still working to improve women's financial fortunes. For example, the CLC is running a one-year campaign devoted to raising awareness of women's economic issues. One of the organizers, Gisèle Pageau, human rights director at the Communication, Energy and Paperworkers union (CEP), says the chief concern of the CLC's campaign is still pay equity.

She has been working to get women from all regions of Canada to participate in the year's activities and to lobby governments for change. Although she says the current federal government is not receptive to women's issues, that doesn't mean "we stop banging on the doors of government."

As well as lobbying governments and their agencies, CEP campaigns to "organize the unorganized," many of whom are women—often immigrants—in low-paying jobs. To bring the message to people who face language and cultural barriers, CEP trains women who are also immigrants and who better understand the situation of minimum-wage workers as they have often "walked in their shoes," says Pageau.

To help unionized women bring forward issues to fellow union members, CEP provides material on how to start a women's committee within a union local. Pageau says women's issues are often more nuanced than those for men in the union, chiefly because women are caregivers in their families.

"The guys are more inclined to say, 'Give me my pay and my pension' and that's it," says Pageau. But women are concerned about workplace violence, bullying, harassment, parental and other leaves, child care, and elder care, not to mention better salary levels, she says.

**Women's issues in collective agreements**

Unions also ensure language around women's issues is included in collective agreements, says Pageau. The contract at Laurentian University in Sudbury, where Pageau spent 25 years before joining CEP five years ago, contains one of the first references to paid leaves to handle emergencies involving children or other family members.

Another example is the agreement CEP recently negotiated with Dilico, an agency of about 230 employees, most of whom are women, serving the needs of Aboriginal children and their families in Thunder Bay, Ont. According to Pageau, CEP did not try to impose itself on the culture of the bargaining unit members, who work issues out by consensus. The collective bargaining process resulted in an agreement that Pageau described as "quite spectacular." For example, the grievance and arbitration process involves the use of healing circles and elders as arbitrators. The local developed an elders' handbook for handling such situations.

Julie White, director of women's programs for the Canadian Auto Workers (CAW) has also been involved in the CLC's equity campaign from the beginning and is organizing a CAW women's conference for mid-August. Participants will discuss how union women can respond in their communities and at the bargaining table to the federal government's decision to cut funding to women's programs and services, says White.

In 1985, when the CAW broke away from the United Auto Workers, only 11 percent of its members were female; now 34 percent are women. Over the years, and especially since a 1991 affirmative action document, women have been more involved in the union. They receive training, are encouraged to take advantage of staff opportunities and sit at the bargaining table. As a result, women's issues are heard by all union members both at the local level and three times a year when representatives of the rank and file meet with union leaders.

**CAW's Women's Advocate Program**

White points to the Women's Advocate Program, which began 15 years ago with 21 women in the automotive sector and now encompasses 113 women in various workplaces covered by CAW collective agreements.

Under this program, women are trained by the union as resource people to intervene on a woman's behalf in the event of workplace harassment or domestic violence. They make referrals to community resources and advocate for women not to be disciplined for taking time off to find emergency housing. Usually CAW collective agreement language states there is no loss of pay for the first three days under the sickness and accident plan if a woman goes into a shelter.

The advocate receives 40 hours of training initially and receives a three-day update each year, which is often paid for by the employer. Many employers embrace the idea enthusiastically, even to the extent of naming a management counterpart who understands the program and works with the union rep, while others are reluctant, fearing liability and need to be educated about their obligation under occupational health and safety legislation to provide a safe work environment, says White. Members of the Women's Advocate Program also advocate at the municipal and provincial level for women and for changes to occupational health and safety rules.

Source: Excerpted from L. Harris, "Unions Taking Up the Mantle of Women's Issues," *Canadian HR Reporter,* August 11, 2008, p. 17. Reprinted with permission.

a result of the downturn in the market. To reduce the extra costs associated with senior employees, such as higher wages and longer vacation entitlements, the union agreed to an increased retirement incentive from $12 000 to $20 000 to be offered to 70 employees eligible to retire. The retirement incentive encourages early retirement, which opens up jobs for junior staff, who are less expensive to hire and retain. To offset the loss of institutional knowledge resulting from so many senior staff leaving, the union agreed to an on-call workforce of retirees who are available as needed to fill in for vacations, sick leave, and training leave. This gives Lakeside more workforce flexibility and protects the employment of its workers.[8]

## Classification of Unions

Unions can be categorized according to the type of workers eligible for membership, geographic scope, and labour congress affiliation. **Craft unions** include only workers performing a certain type of skill or trade, such as carpenters or bricklayers. **Industrial unions** include skilled and unskilled workers in a particular company or industry, such as postal workers. Most unions in Canada are either international unions or national unions. Labour unions that charter branches in both Canada and the United States are known as **international unions**. The United Steelworkers of America is an international union. Labour unions that charter branches in Canada only are known as **national unions**. The Canadian AutoWorkers (CAW) and the Canadian Union of Public Employees (CUPE) are national unions. About 80 percent of unionized workers belong to unions that are affiliated with one of the three major labour congresses in Canada:

1. *CLC: Canadian Labour Congress*. The CLC is the largest democratic and popular organization in Canada, representing 70.7 percent of all unionized workers in Canada.[9] The Congress unites Canada's national and international unions, the provincial and territorial labour federations, and 136 district labour councils, and acts as a spokesperson for organized labour throughout Canada on economic, social and political issues from fair wages and safe working conditions to health care and equity rights.
2. *CSN: Confédération des syndicats nationaux* (in English, CNTU: Confederation of National Trade Unions). This federation is primarily composed of French-speaking unions and represents 6.6 percent

**craft unions** A union representing workers who practise the same craft or trade, such as carpentry or plumbing.

**industrial unions** A union representing both skilled and unskilled workers in a particular organization or industry.

**international unions** A union with branches and members in both Canada and the United States, the head office of which is in the United States.

**national unions** A union that charters branches in Canada only and has its head office in Canada.

of all unionized workers in Canada, mostly in civil service, hospitals, and education.[10] The CSN was instrumental in advocating for better working conditions for its members.

3. *AFL–CIO: American Federation of Labor–Congress of Industrial Organizations*. The AFL–CIO is the American counterpart of the CLC and includes a few Canadian unions such as the International Union of Painters and Allied Trades of the United States and Canada, the United Association of Journeymen and Apprentices of the Plumbing and Pipe Fitting Industry of the United States and Canada, and the American Federation of Musicians of the United States and Canada. The AFL-CIO represents 11 million workers across the United States and Canada.

## Union Membership in Canada

In the past decade, the number of Canadian unionized workers in the public service has remained the same, at 74.5 percent, but dropped in the private sector from 21.3 percent in 1997 to 18.7 percent in 2007. This equates to a total of 4.5 million workers currently represented by a union.[11] The unionization rate of men aged 25 to 34 fell by 20 percent, but the unionization rate of women aged 45 to 64 rose by 8 percent, from 32 to 40 percent. About 40 percent of the increase in the participation rate of women is credited to their employment in industries that are well represented by unions, such as public services.

Trends in union membership vary from industry to industry. In the past 20 years, forestry and mining experienced the sharpest decline in union membership, falling from 46 to 26 percent, followed by construction and manufacturing, which saw membership drop by 13 percent. Goods-producing and distributing industries, where union representation has historically been strong, also experienced decreases. Union membership has steadily dropped in all provinces, with Saskatchewan and Manitoba experiencing the smallest declines.[12]

With the percentage of unionized workers falling in Canada, union initiatives are underway to recruit new members, especially young people. Most recruitment initiatives occur in the service sector, where 84 percent of youth aged 17 to 24 are employed.[13] For example, the United Food and Commercial Workers Union (UFCW) sponsors the National Youth Internship Program (YIP) for youth activists, to help them learn bargaining skills and experience how unions operate by working with union representatives. As a result of UFCW's lobbying for youth representation in the union, some employers have included an availability clause in their collective agreements, entitling young people to return to their jobs after they have been away at school. The UFCW also runs a program in Ontario and Saskatchewan high schools called "Talking Union," in which union members speak with students about what unions do and what rights students have at work.[14] Union organizers across Canada are exploring the Internet as another vehicle for encouraging young people to join the labour movement. For example, the Canadian Labour Congress is examining the use of Facebook, YouTube, and blogs as part of their organizing campaign.

Unions recognize that equity-seeking groups identified under the *Employment Equity Act* have historically been marginalized and are not actively involved in union activities. Unions are exercising their leadership to rectify this situation. For example, in 2007, the Ontario Secondary School Teachers' Federation (OSSTF) established the Equity Survey Workgroup, which was charged with the task of conducting a three-year study on the level of union participation of members from equity-seeking groups and the institutional and structural barriers to their participation. The workgroup's recommendations for changes at the leadership level and throughout the union ranks in order to enhance union involvement of equity-seeking groups are slated for implementation in 2010. The goal is to ensure that OSSTF has a diversity of members shaping the union's collective future.[15]

The basic unit of the labour union movement in Canada is the **local**, formed in a particular plant or location. For HR managers and front-line supervisors, the union locals are generally the most important part of the union structure. An executive committee—headed by a president and vice-president, and sometimes a business agent—usually exercises power. Local unions are responsible for negotiating and administering the collective agreement, representing members who file grievances, educating members on the implications of organizational changes mandated by management, and speaking on behalf of members in response to organizational changes. As illustrated in Figure 12.1, there are generally a number of committees, each of which is assigned responsibility for specific activities.

Key players within the local are the elected officials known as **union stewards**, who are responsible for *figure* 12.1 **Structure of a Typical Union Local**

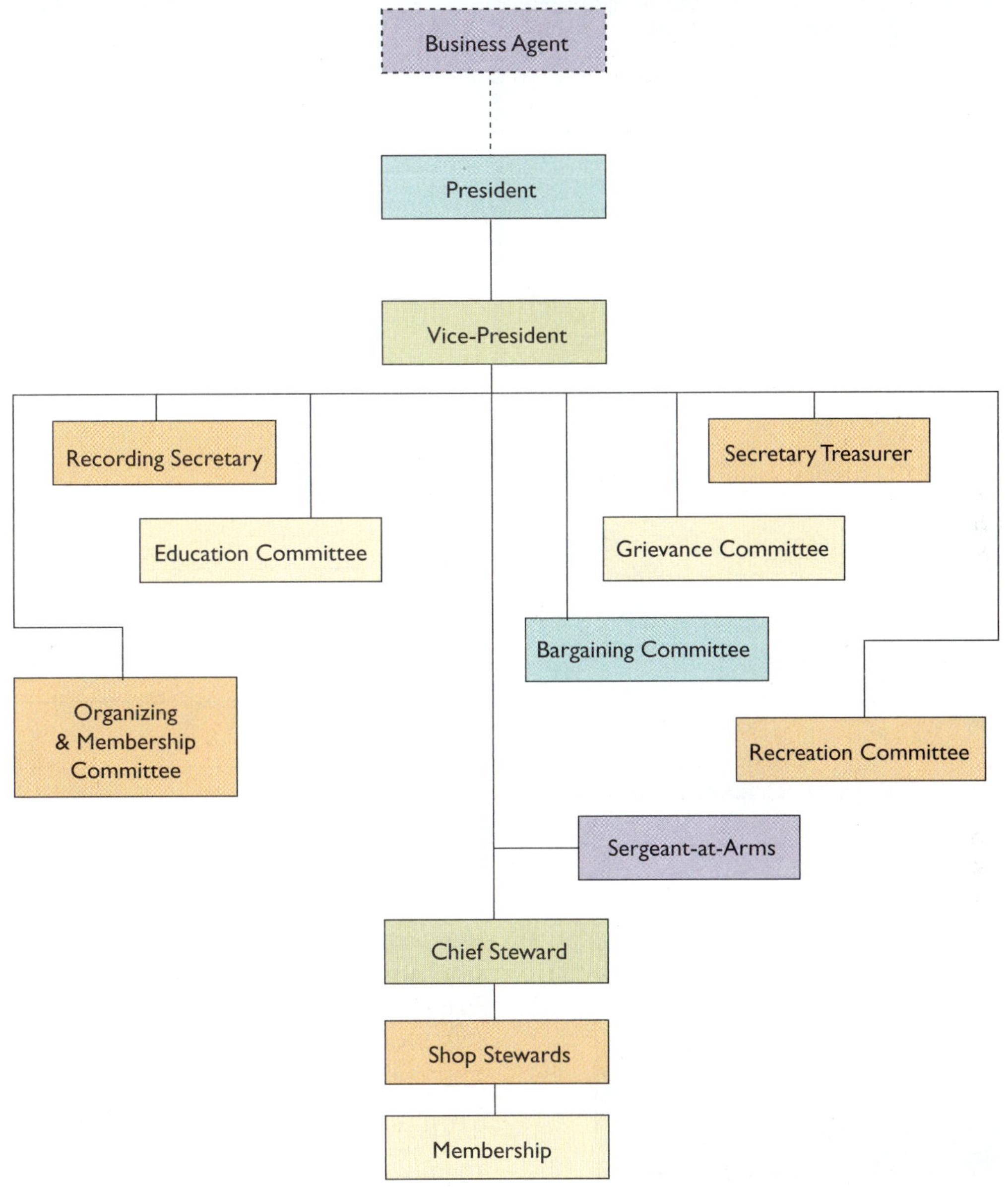


investigating and attempting to resolve complaints and grievances; interpreting the collective agreement for members; informing members about union policies and meetings; and recruiting new members. The senior steward for a particular area or division is known as the **chief steward**.

**local** The basic unit of the labour union movement in Canada formed in a particular plant or location.

**union stewards** A union member elected by workers in a particular department or area of a firm to act as their union representative.

**chief steward** The senior steward for a particular area or division.

## *In-class Notes*

**The Labour Movement in Canada Today**

- Goal is to obtain economic benefits and improved treatment for members as well as to influence government economic and social policies
- Unions categorized as craft versus industrial; international versus national
- Three major labour congresses in Canada:
  1. Canadian Labour Congress (2/3 of unionized workers)
  2. Confédération des syndicats nationaux (French)
  3. AFL-CIO (American, with a few Canadian unions)
- Declining union membership in Canada over the past two decades, except for increase in unionization rate of women
- Union initiatives are underway to enhance union involvement of youth and equity-seeking groups

This McDonald's, in Squamish, B.C., was the first to unionize among the chain's more than 15 000 North American outlets.

## 12.4 THE LABOUR RELATIONS PROCESS

The labour relations process is illustrated in Figure 12.2. The first three steps of the process relate to union organizing and recognition of the union by management. Step 4 involves preparing to negotiate a collective agreement; Step 5 covers the bargaining process, including face-to-face bargaining, contract approval, and strikes/lockouts. Step 6 summarizes the day-to-day administration of the collective agreement resulting from the negotiations.

### Step 1: Employees' Desire to Unionize

The first step in the labour relations process is the desire to unionize. A tremendous amount of time and money have been spent trying to analyze why workers unionize, and many theories have been proposed. It has become apparent that there is no simple answer, partly because each individual may become interested in unionizing for very unique reasons. Based on numerous research studies, however, there are a number of factors that can clearly be linked to the desire to unionize:[16]

- job dissatisfaction, especially with pay, benefits, working conditions, and leadership style

*frontLINE tips*

*figure* 12.2 **An Overview of the Labour Relations Process**

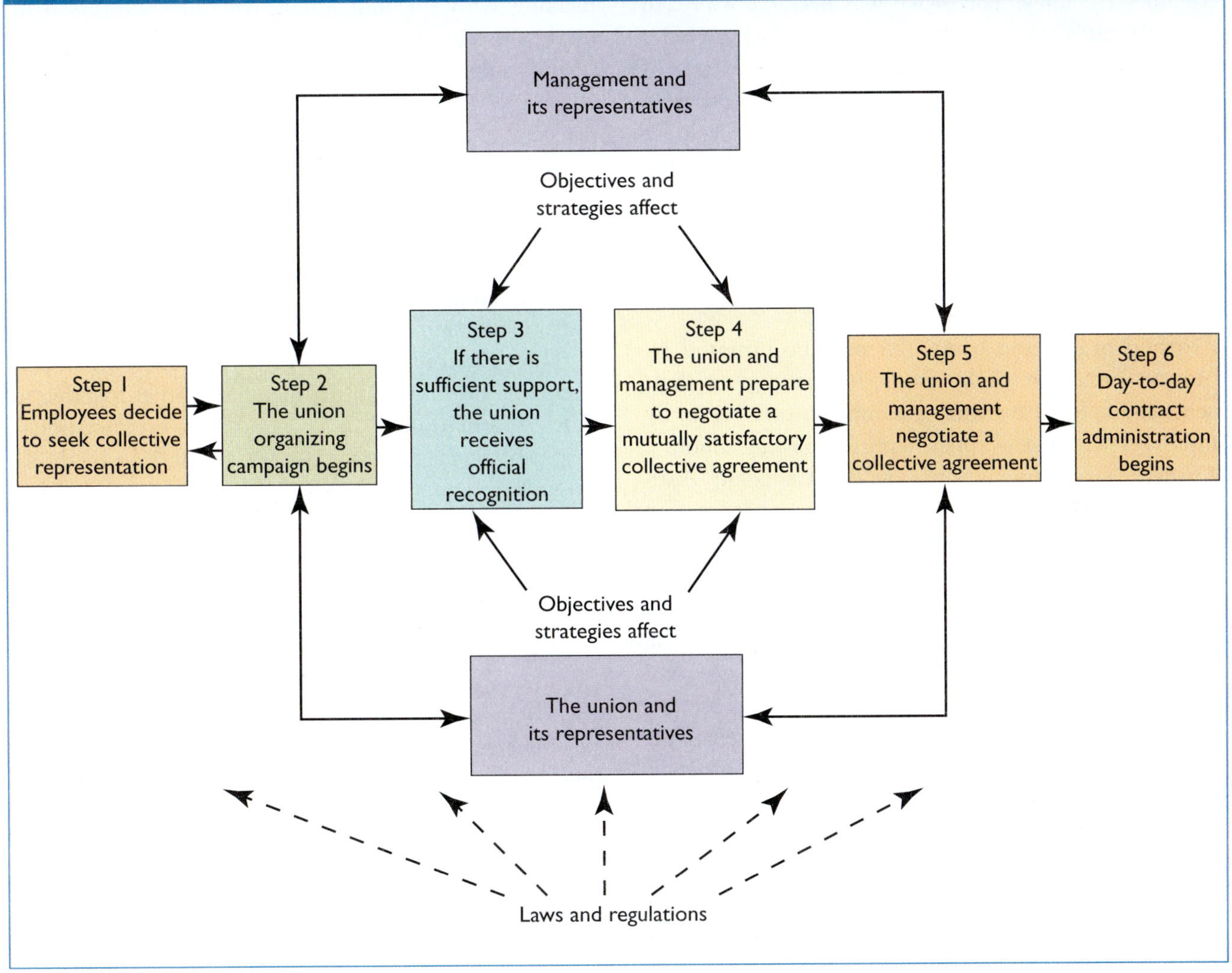


- lack of job stability and security
- unfair or biased administration of policies and practices
- perceived inequities in pay and how pay raises are determined
- lack of opportunity for advancement
- unfair decision making and lack of recognition by management
- abusive treatment by management
- lack of a desired amount of influence or participation in work-related decisions
- belief that unions can be effective in improving pay and working conditions

It should be pointed out, however, that research studies have made it quite clear that dissatisfaction alone will not lead to unionization. More important seems to be employees' belief that it is only through unity that they can get a fair share of the "pie" and protect themselves from the arbitrary whims of management. In other words, it is only when workers are dissatisfied and believe that they are without the ability to change the factors causing dissatisfaction, except through collective action, that they become interested in unionizing.[17]

At any time, a group of dissatisfied, non-unionized employees who feel a lack of power may come to believe that they would be better off as members of a labour union. This is when the union organizing process begins.

In 2009, the Ontario Superior Court ruled that the RCMP, Canada's largest police force, has the right to unionize. Since 1974, the RCMP had been under the

Staff Relations Representative Program (SRRP), which gave the staff of 22 000 the right to consult on workplace conditions and policies, but not to collectively bargain for change. The SRRP was declared a breach of the RCMP's freedom of association, which includes the right to collectively bargain under the Charter of Rights and Freedoms. This ruling comes into effect in 2010, giving the federal government time to develop a framework for bargaining. Employees eagerly await the change, as they are interested in collective bargaining around pension and wage rollbacks.[18]

## Step 2: Union Organizing Campaign

A formal organizing campaign may be initiated by a union organizer or by employees acting on their own behalf. Most organizing campaigns are begun by employees who get in touch with an existing union.[19] However, large unions such as the Canadian Auto Workers (CAW) and the Teamsters have on staff a number of **union organizers** who are responsible for identifying organizing opportunities and launching organizing campaigns. Recently, unions have established websites where employees can read about the benefits of joining the union, and they encourage email correspondence with employees to address concerns about unionization. However, the use of email is restricted to employees' home computers so that email traffic does not interfere with business operations. The United Food and Commercial Workers Union receives approximately 100 emails daily from non-unionized workers.[20] No matter how large or sophisticated a union's organizing department is, the outcome of an organizing campaign depends primarily on the employees. Even the most experienced organizers find it difficult to organize a truly well-managed, successful organization. In the words of Paul Forder, CAW's national director of organization, "We know thousands of people who need unions. The only time we are successful is when [employees] come to us."[21]

Promoting the benefits of unionization.

The union organizer generally schedules an initial meeting with the individuals who first expressed an interest in unionization and coworkers who subsequently expressed their support. The aim is to identify employees who would be willing to help the organizer direct the campaign. Then, an **in-house organizing committee** is formed, composed of a group of employees who are dedicated to the goal of unionization and who are willing to assist the union organizer. The role of such volunteers is to devote the time and effort necessary to contact employees, present the case for unionization, and sign members up.

Once the committee is formed, the union organizing campaign begins. First, the members gather together as much information as possible about the organization—its products, customers, finances, production methods, employees, managers, ownership, and attitude toward employees. The next step generally involves obtaining an accurate, up-to-date list of all employees who are eligible to join the proposed bargaining unit. Then, the committee members start contacting other employees. Usually, to get the campaign off to a good start, the employees who are believed to favour unionization are approached first. To avoid any suggestion of intimidation or coercion, personal contact is often made on a one-on-one basis. The goal of this contact is to encourage as many employees as possible to sign an **authorization card** that indicates their willingness to be represented by the union in question in collective bargaining with their employer. The number of signed cards is typically kept a closely guarded secret until a substantial number of eligible employees have been signed up. In doing so, management is less likely to know that a union organizing campaign is underway and subsequently persuade employees not to unionize.

Supervisors or small-business owners who suspect that a unionization attempt may be underway should watch for a number of the following signs:[22]

**frontLINE tips**

- disappearance of employee lists or directories
- more inquiries than usual about benefits, wages, promotions, and other HR policies and procedures
- questions about their opinions of unions
- an increase in the number or nature of employee complaints or grievances
- a change in the number, composition, and size of informal groups at lunch and coffee breaks

- employee discussions about past or future group meetings
- the sudden popularity of certain employees (especially if they are the informal leaders)
- the sudden cessation of employee conversation when a member of management approaches or an obvious change in employees' behaviour toward members of management that is expressed either formally or informally
- longer washroom breaks (a popular place for signing authorization cards)
- the appearance of strangers in the parking lot
- the distribution of cards, flyers, or pro-union buttons

External factors might also trigger employee interest in organizing a union, including:[23]

- recent changes in labour legislation that affect one's industry and might increase the attractiveness of unionization
- a spike in unionization activity in the community or industry
- a company's plans for mass hiring, which might motivate employees to organize a union before the company becomes too large and it becomes too expensive to organize

### EMPLOYER RESPONSE TO AN ORGANIZING CAMPAIGN

Once it is evident that an organizing campaign is underway, if the employer prefers that the group seeking unionization retain its non-union status, a careful campaign is usually mounted to counteract the union drive. The labour relations specialist plays a fundamental role in informing management about what they can and cannot say or do during the organizing campaign to ensure that they do not violate labour relations legislation and avoid actions that might inadvertently provide fuel for the union's campaign. When any member of management commits an unfair labour practice, it can lead to an expensive and time-consuming lawsuit and may result in automatic union certification.

LEGALcompliance

Answering questions is an important part of an effective counter-campaign. A good strategy is to set up an "information line" so that supervisors and employees can get quick answers to questions. Under the law, employers are granted the right to:

- express their views and opinions regarding unions in general and the organizing union in particular
- state their position regarding the desirability of remaining non-unionized
- prohibit distribution of union literature on their own property on company time
- increase wages, grant promotions, and take other HR actions as long as they would do so in the normal course of business
- assemble employees during working hours to state the company's position, as long as employees are advised of the purpose of the meeting in advance and attendance is optional

Employers must ensure that they do *not*:

- hold mandatory employee meetings regarding unionization
- question employees about union activities
- increase wages and benefits in a manner that could be perceived as a bribe for remaining non-unionized
- discipline employees for organizing a union or expressing pro-union sentiments
- interrogate employees about their voting intentions
- shut down an organization to avoid certification by a union
- terminate employees on the grounds of redundancy if this termination involves only union activists
- use coercion, intimidation, threats, promises, or "undue influence"
- refuse to answer legitimate employee questions about the impact of unionization

LEGALcompliance

The distinction between expressing one's views and exerting undue influence is not always clear. The highly

**union organizers** Full-time employees of the union whose role is to plan and execute union membership recruitment campaigns.

**in-house organizing committee** A group of employees dedicated to the goal of unionization who are willing to assist the union organizer.

**authorization card** A card signed by an employee that indicates his or her willingness to have the union act as his or her representative for purposes of collective bargaining.

Workplace Information Directorate, HRDC
**www.hrsdc.gc.ca/eng/labour/labour_relations/info_analysis/union_membership/index.shtml**

publicized Wal-Mart case provides an excellent example of the fine line that an employer must walk.[24]

The case arose out of a certification drive by the United Steelworkers of America at a Wal-Mart store in Windsor in April 1996. After obtaining 91 authorization cards from the 205 staff at the store, the union filed for certification. Based on the level of membership support indicated, the Board ordered that a certification vote be held. At the vote, the union was rejected by a margin of 151 to 43. The union subsequently alleged that the employer's conduct prior to the vote constituted unfair practices, which unlawfully influenced the outcome of the election. The allegation was sufficiently serious to justify disregarding the results of the vote and granting automatic certification to the union.

**AN ETHICAL DILEMMA**

You are a line manager in a telecommunications company who has discovered that the employees are involved in a secret union organizing campaign. As a strong union supporter, you think this move toward unionization is a good idea. Would you inform senior management that a campaign is underway? Why or why not?

After hearing the evidence, the LRB concluded that the union should succeed and certified the Steelworkers as the bargaining agent. Factors influencing the Board's decision included the fact that the company allowed an anti-union employee to make a speech at a company meeting, which, in the Board's opinion, contained the employee's belief that Wal-Mart would not stand for a union and that a union would harm job security. They also concluded that five managers who circulated throughout the store for a number of days exerted a subtle form of intimidation, since it appeared to be an effort to identify union supporters. Also, the LRB found that despite the company's open communication policy, management refused to answer the question as to whether the Wal-Mart store would close if it became unionized, which was perceived by the Board to be a subtle, but intentional, threat to employee job security.

Unionization challenges faced by Wal-Mart are not isolated to Ontario. For four years, United Food and Commercial Workers sought certification for workers at Wal-Mart in Weyburn, Saskatchewan, when over 50 percent signed authorization cards in 2004. To avert certification, the company took legal action, including two unsuccessful appeals to the Supreme Court of Canada. In December 2008, the Saskatchewan Labour Relations Board (SLRB) approved the certification of the Weyburn store, but in 2009 a Saskatchewan judge overturned the certification. The union certification was void because as of May 2008, seven months before the SLRB had approved the certification, a secret ballot vote was mandated to certify a union in Saskatchewan. The application was sent back to the Board, leaving the door open for union certification if the majority of store workers supported unionization through a secret ballot vote.[25] The SLRB is also considering applications for union representation at Wal-Marts in North Battleford and Moose Jaw.[26]

## Step 3: The Union Recognition Process

There are three basic ways a union can obtain recognition as the official and exclusive bargaining unit for a group of workers: (1) voluntary recognition, (2) the regular certification process, and (3) a pre-hearing vote.

**VOLUNTARY RECOGNITION** An employer in any Canadian jurisdiction (except Quebec) can voluntarily recognize a union as the bargaining agent for a group of its employees. The voluntary recognition process is an alternative to certification and does not require the involvement of a third party. Although fairly rare, it may occur if an employer has adopted a union acceptance strategy and believes that representation by that union is what the employees desire.

**REGULAR CERTIFICATION** The formal union certification procedure requires unions to present evidence of at least a minimum level of membership support for a bargaining unit that they have defined, in the form of signed authorization cards. The minimum level of membership support varies by jurisdiction, from 25 to 60 percent. Signed authorization cards, along with an application for certification, are sent to the appropriate LRB for review.

In most jurisdictions, LRBs can grant *automatic certification*, which means certification without a vote if the applicant union can demonstrate that it has a high enough level of support for the proposed bargaining unit (generally 50 or 55 percent).[27] Automatic certification may also be granted in some jurisdictions if the employer has engaged in unfair practices such that a vote would not or did not reflect the true wishes of the proposed bargaining unit members, as occurred in the Wal-Mart case. However, automatic certification is prohibited in Newfoundland and Labrador, Nova Scotia, Ontario, Alberta, and British Columbia. These provinces mandate a secret-ballot vote to gauge whether there is sufficient support for the union.

If the level of support is not sufficient for automatic certification, but is above a specified minimum level (between 25 and 45 percent, depending on jurisdiction), the Board will order a representation vote.[28] At an LRB-supervised **representation vote**, eligible employees have the opportunity to cast a secret ballot indicating whether they wish the union to be certified. In some jurisdictions, to gain certification, the voting results must indicate that *more than 50 percent* of the potential bargaining unit members are in support of the union. In other jurisdictions, the standard is the support of *more than 50 percent of those voting*.[29] If the union loses, another election cannot be held among the same employees for at least one year. Only about 20 percent of certifications are the result of a vote—roughly four out of five certifications are the result of authorization cards alone.[30]

In an unprecedented move, Magna International Inc., an Ontario-based automotive supplier, and the CAW mapped out a distinct recognition process in which Magna accepted the CAW as a partner and both parties signed a "Framework of Fairness" agreement that governs how they work together. Under the agreement, called the CAW-Magna National Collective Agreement, Magna—which repeatedly averted union organizing drives—invited in the union with conditional provisions. Instead of union stewards, "employee advocates" work with "fairness committees" in each plant to make local decisions. A "concern resolution process" replaces traditional grievance procedures, giving workers several pathways to pursue and resolve a concern. Strikes and lockouts are prohibited and replaced with final-offer arbitration. The "no strike clause" unleashed widespread criticism from other labour leaders, who see strikes as the best weapon when collective bargaining breaks down.[31]

**PRE-HEARING VOTES** In most jurisdictions, a **pre-hearing vote** may be conducted where there is evidence of irregularities early in an organizing campaign, such as an employer's use of unfair labour practices. The intent is to determine the level of support for the union as quickly as possible before the employer's intimidation tactics can taint the outcome. Then, if the Board concludes that the majority of bargaining unit members support the union on the basis of the ballots cast, the union is certified.

**TERMINATION OF BARGAINING RIGHTS** Just as it is possible for a labour union to become the legally certified or recognized bargaining agent for a group of employees, it is also possible for a union to lose such rights. Although there are many different grounds on which bargaining rights may be terminated, it should be stressed that such an event is quite uncommon.

Labour relations legislation provides procedures for workers to apply for the *decertification* of their unions. Generally, members may apply for decertification if the union has failed to negotiate a collective agreement within one year of certification or if they are dissatisfied with the performance of the union. The LRB then holds a secret-ballot vote. If more than 50 percent of the ballots cast (or bargaining unit members, depending on jurisdiction) are in opposition to the union, the union will be decertified.

If it is determined that the union obtained its certification through fraudulent acts, the union will be decertified immediately. Once the LRB has declared that the union no longer represents the bargaining unit employees, any collective agreement negotiated between the parties is void. A labour union also has the right to notify the LRB that it no longer wishes to continue to represent the employees in a particular bargaining unit. This is known as "termination on abandonment."

## Step 4: Preparing to Negotiate a Collective Agreement

Both union and management engage in extensive preparation for negotiations, which involves planning the bargaining strategy and process and assembling data to support bargaining proposals. Management's preparation includes the following activities:[32]

- reviewing the organization's strategic plan
- gathering data on economic trends and conducting wage and benefit surveys
- analyzing existing collective agreements and those of competitors

**representation vote** Employees in the bargaining unit indicate by secret ballot whether they wish to be represented by a labour union.

**pre-hearing vote** An alternative mechanism for certification used in situations where there is evidence of irregularities early in the organizing campaign, such as unfair labour practices on the part of management.

- obtaining supervisory input from those responsible for day-to-day contract administration
- conducting an analysis of grievances
- examining relevant arbitration awards and LRB rulings
- costing current and proposed contract provisions
- contingency planning for a possible strike or lockout

After research has been conducted, an initial bargaining plan and strategy are formulated and submitted to the senior management team for approval. The next steps are establishing a bargaining team based on an assessment of technical knowledge, experience, and personality required; establishing bargaining guidelines for the negotiating team; finalizing the bargaining strategy and proposals; and establishing a communication strategy with senior management.

**RPC 12-1 >**

**Advises clients on status of dependent and independent contractor and elements of employee status**

The union's preparation for negotiations involves a number of parallel steps, including:

- gathering data on general economic trends and collective bargaining trends
- obtaining data about the employer's finances
- analyzing existing collective agreements and those of competitors
- obtaining input from union members and stewards
- gathering demographic data about the bargaining unit members
- conducting an analysis of grievances
- costing of current and proposed contract
- contingency planning for a possible strike and/or lockout

The union then establishes a bargaining team and finalizes its bargaining strategy and proposals.

## Step 5: Collective Bargaining

A major function of a labour union is to bargain collectively over conditions of employment on behalf of those in the **bargaining unit** that it has received recognition to represent. **Collective bargaining** is the process by which a formal **collective agreement (union contract)** is established between labour and management. The negotiation of a collective agreement involves discussions, concessions, and mutual trade-offs between the union negotiating team and management representatives. Collective bargaining may also involve the use of third-party assistance and economic pressure by either the union (a strike) or management (a lockout), or third-party intervention.

**AN ETHICAL DILEMMA**

Is it ethical for a union negotiator to state in the opening bargaining session that the union is prepared to strike unless management grants a wage increase of 5 percent in year 1 and 4 percent in year 2, knowing that the membership will be satisfied with 3 percent and 2 percent, respectively?

LEGALcompliance

The collective agreement is the cornerstone of the Canadian labour relations system. To try to ensure that the process is as smooth as possible, both parties are legally required to bargain in good faith.

**Good faith bargaining** requires that union and management representatives communicate and negotiate, proposals be matched with counter-proposals, and both parties make every reasonable effort to arrive at an agreement.[33] The line between hard bargaining and bargaining in bad faith is not always clear. However, as interpreted by LRBs and the courts, activities that violate the requirement to bargain in good faith include **surface bargaining** (going through the motions of bargaining without any real intention of reaching a mutually acceptable agreement); failing to make concessions or withdrawing previously granted concessions; failing to make reasonable proposals and demands; delaying tactics, such as postponement of scheduled sessions; imposing unreasonable conditions; making unilateral changes in conditions; bypassing the official representatives of the other party; committing unfair labour practices during negotiations; and failing to provide accurate information requested by the other negotiating team.[34]

**The Collective Bargaining Process** Steps typically involved in the collective bargaining process include face-to-face negotiations and obtaining approval for the proposed contract. There are two possible additional steps when talks break down—third-party assistance and strike and/or lockout.

**Face-to-Face Negotiations.** Generally, the first meeting is a protocol meeting that sets the tone and parameters for collective bargaining. The meeting is devoted to an exchange of proposals and the establishment of rules and procedures that will be used during negotiations, such as length and duration of sessions, and the right to call a **caucus session** or

## *figure* 12.3 The Bargaining Zone and Characteristics of Distributive Bargaining

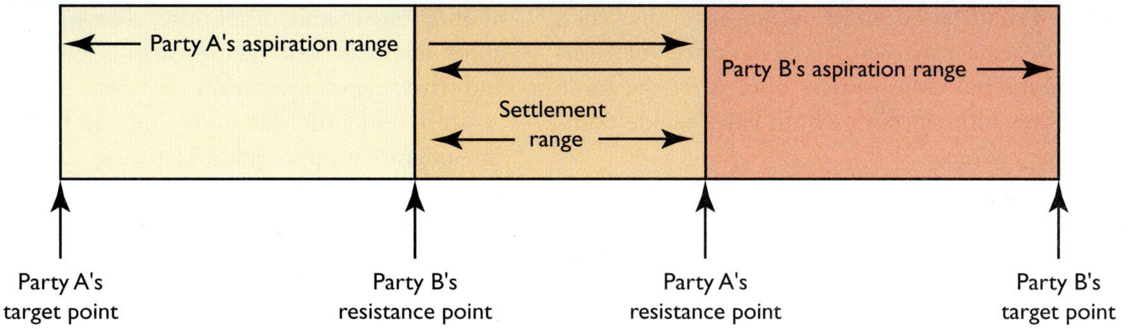


Source: S.P. Robbins and N. Langton, *Organizational Behaviour*, 3rd Edition. (Don Mills, ON: Pearson Education Canada, 2003), p. 307. Reprinted with permission by Pearson Education Canada Inc.

request adjournment. The initial meeting of the bargaining teams is extremely important in establishing the climate that will prevail during the negotiating sessions that follow. A cordial attitude can ensure that negotiations proceed smoothly.

At this stage, in a caucus session, the company and union negotiating teams generally make a private assessment of the other team's demands. Usually, each team finds some items with which they can agree quite readily and others on which compromise seems likely. Tentative conclusions are also made regarding which items, if any, are potential strike or lockout issues.

In subsequent bargaining sessions, each party argues for its demands and resists those of the other. At the same time, both are looking for compromise alternatives that will enable an agreement to be reached. Regardless of its degree of importance, every proposal submitted must be resolved in order to reach a settlement.

In order for each issue on the table to be resolved satisfactorily, the point at which agreement is reached must be within limits that the union and employer are willing to accept, often referred to as the **bargaining zone.** As illustrated in Figure 12.3, if the solution that is desired by one party exceeds the limits of the other party, then it is outside of the bargaining zone. Unless that party modifies its demands sufficiently to bring them within the bargaining zone or the other party extends its limits to accommodate such demands, a bargaining deadlock is the inevitable result.[35]

Very often, the parties separate the bargaining demands into two categories: monetary and non-monetary. Monetary issues include all items with direct cost implications, such as wages, overtime pay rates, shift premiums, changes in hours of work, vacation entitlement, and holidays. Non-monetary issues include such items as contract language, procedural matters, and

**bargaining unit** The group of employees in a firm, plant, or industry that has been recognized by an employer or certified by a Labour Relations Board (LRB) as appropriate for collective bargaining purposes.

**collective bargaining** The negotiations that take place between a labour union, collectively representing the employees of a firm or industry, and the employer or employer's association to arrive at a mutually acceptable collective agreement.

**collective agreement (union contract)** A signed, written agreement between an employer (or employer's organization) and the union representing a group of the organization's employees containing provisions outlining the terms and conditions of their employment.

**good faith bargaining** The legal requirement that the parties negotiating a collective agreement bargain honestly, fairly, and sincerely.

**surface bargaining** Going through the motions of collective bargaining with no intention of arriving at a mutually acceptable agreement.

**caucus session** A session in which only the members of one's own bargaining team are present to discuss the course of action they should take at the bargaining table.

**bargaining zone** The area defined by the bargaining limits (resistance points) of each side in which compromise is possible, as in the attainment of a settlement satisfactory to both parties.

Treasury Board of Canada Secretariat Collective Bargaining Update
**www.tbs-sct.gc.ca/media/lru-mnc/index-eng.asp**

International Labour Organization
**www.ilo.org**

administrative issues that do not involve direct cents-per-hour cost implications. It should be noted, however, that non-monetary items might have an indirect impact on an employer's costs. Typically, non-monetary issues are discussed first, based on the assumption that such items will be easier to resolve. Resolution of non-monetary items builds a positive climate at the table and establishes momentum as both sides tackle complex monetary issues.

**RPC 12-2 >**

**Collects and develops information required for good decision making throughout the bargaining process**

Negotiating is a relatively complex process consisting of four types of activity: distributive bargaining, integrative bargaining, the shaping of attitudes, and intra-organizational bargaining.

**Distributive bargaining** is an approach often typified as "win–lose" bargaining because the gains of one party are normally achieved at the expense of the other. These include such items as wage increases and benefits improvements.[36]

As indicated in Figure 12.3, distributive bargaining is characterized by three distinct components: the initial point, the target point, and the resistance point. The initial point for the union is usually higher than what the union expects to receive from management. The union target point is next and represents the negotiating team's assessment of what is realistically achievable from management. The union's bargaining zone limit is its resistance point (walk-away position), which represents its minimally acceptable level.

These points are essentially reversed for management. The management team's initial point is its lowest level, which is used at the beginning of negotiations. Next is its target point, the desired agreement level. Management's resistance point forms the other boundary of the bargaining zone. The actual settlement range generally lies in the bargaining zone between management's target and resistance points.[37]

**Integrative bargaining** is an approach that assumes a win–win solution can be found but also acknowledges that one or both sides can be losers if the bargaining is not handled effectively.[38] Integrative bargaining strategies require that both management and union negotiators adopt a genuine interest in the joint exploration of creative solutions to common problems. For example, in early 2002, employees at Algoma Steel in Sault Ste. Marie agreed to a 15-percent pay cut to save the company from bankruptcy, and the company agreed that salaries would return to their previous levels by the end of 2003.[39] Employers adopting a union acceptance strategy often try to use an effective mix of integrative and distributive bargaining. When the union–management relationship is based on integrity and trust, negotiating team members are more likely to be able to identify demands that can be handled using an integrative approach and to use such an approach whenever possible.

A relatively new integrative approach known as **mutual gains bargaining** (also called interest-based bargaining, consensus bargaining, and collaborative bargaining) is aimed at seeking win–win solutions to LR issues and problems. Mutual gains bargaining is grounded in the belief that the issues or concerns of union and management complement one another. For example, both parties agree with the organization's strategic direction and want the organization to prosper. This differs from traditional bargaining approaches, which declare that the parties' primary interests conflict with one another and the parties must find common ground through the bargaining process. As part of the mutual gains bargaining process, all key union and management negotiators are trained in the fundamentals of effective problem solving and conflict resolution. Mutual gains bargaining requires parties to respect the following principles:[40]

- focus on problems, not personalities
- base negotiation on the real interests of each party, not on predetermined positions
- examine a variety of options for mutual gains
- assess each option on the basis of objective criteria

The aim is to ensure that the principles of mutual gains bargaining are incorporated into the organization's value system so that promoting cooperation becomes a year-round corporate objective.[41] According to Kevin Mahoney, vice-president of HR at SaskPower (the electric utility serving Saskatchewan), a key benefit of the mutual gains process is that it encourages people to acknowledge their common ground and to focus their attention on solving real problems. This in turn provides a significant edge in a highly competitive marketplace.[42]

If union and management engage in ongoing problem solving and dialogue throughout the term of the collective agreement, instead of only at the bargaining table every three or four years, it will likely decrease the adversarial nature of labour relations and the likelihood of strikes and lockouts. Ongoing union–management conversation is common in Europe and accounts for the lower number of "person days not worked" (PDNW) due to work stoppages in many European countries as compared with Canada. Between 1997 and 2006, Canada earned the title of " highest PDNW rate" among the G-7 countries due to work stoppages such as strikes and lockouts.[43] Studies have found that 36 percent of employers and 42 percent of unions have used mutual gains bargaining techniques.[44]

The shaping of attitudes, such as trust or distrust and cooperation or hostility, has a major impact on bargaining outcomes. Bad relations outside the bargaining room can spill over into negotiations and vice versa. Attitudes that can assist in building a trusting relationship on which many successful negotiations are based include showing willingness to trust; checking to ensure that trusting signals being sent are being interpreted correctly by the other negotiating team; reinforcing the other party's willingness to trust; and sending signals regarding the adverse consequences of trust being offered and not reciprocated if all else fails.[45]

Intra-organizational bargaining also plays a major role in contract negotiations. The goal of this approach is to achieve a consensus within (rather than between) the union and management organizations. Within the union, the preferences and priorities of skilled workers, semi-skilled workers, and unskilled workers often differ, as do those of young, middle-aged, and older employees; and those of male and female members. On the employer's side, the sales and production managers may want a settlement regardless of cost while the accountant emphasizes the need for a modest settlement to protect the organization's financial position. For example, it might become evident to union negotiators during negotiations that management does not have the financial resources to accommodate a wage increase. The union negotiators must convince their membership that the message is accurate and that concessions should be accepted. Ken Lewenza, president of the CAW, found himself involved in intra-organizational bargaining with General Motors in 2009. The financially strapped automaker declared that union and management must work out the details of a cost-cutting contract that satisfies conditions outlined by the federal government in order to qualify for $6-billion in financial aid, or risk bankruptcy. Workers were skeptical and Lewenza assured them that the concessions were necessary for GM's financial recovery. Lewenza balanced the needs of the members, the union executive, and management to negotiate a cost-cutting plan that all parties would support.[46]

**The Contract Approval Process** The terms and conditions agreed to by the parties are usually reduced to a memorandum of settlement and submitted to the constituent groups for final approval. The formal collective agreement document is not usually finalized in writing until some time after the bargaining process has been completed.

Generally, final approval for the employer rests with the senior management team and/or the board of directors. In most cases, the union bargaining team submits the proposed collective agreement or memorandum of settlement to the bargaining unit members for ratification. If the majority of bargaining unit members vote in favour of the proposal, it goes into effect, replacing any prior agreement. If the proposed collective agreement is rejected, union and management negotiators must return to the bargaining table and seek a more acceptable compromise. In such instances, third-party assistance is often sought.

All Canadian jurisdictions provide for conciliation and mediation services. While the terms *conciliation* and *mediation* are often used interchangeably, they have quite distinct and different meanings. **Conciliation** is usually defined as the intervention of a neutral third party whose primary purpose is to bring the parties together and keep them talking to enable them to reach a mutually satisfactory collective agreement. The only means available to a conciliator to bring the parties to agreement is persuasion; he or she is not permitted to have any direct input into the negotiation process or to impose a settlement. In all jurisdictions except Saskatchewan, strikes and lockouts are prohibited

**distributive bargaining** A win–lose negotiating strategy such that one party gains at the expense of the other.

**integrative bargaining** A negotiating strategy in which there is acknowledgement that achieving a win–win outcome will depend on mutual trust and problem solving.

**mutual gains bargaining** A win–win approach based on training in the fundamentals of effective problem solving and conflict resolution in which trainees are taught to take the interests of all stakeholders into account so that the solutions developed are better and more permanent.

**conciliation** The use of a neutral third party to help an organization and the union continue negotiating.

until conciliation has been undertaken and failed and a specified time period has elapsed, usually two weeks after the submission of the conciliator's report to the minister.[47]

A conciliator is appointed by the applicable minister of labour at the request of management, union, or both parties, or at the discretion of the minister. Conciliation is typically requested after the parties have been negotiating for some length of time to reach a first agreement or renew an existing one and are starting to reach a deadlock or after talks have broken down.

**Mediation** can also be defined as the intervention of a neutral third party whose primary purpose is to help the parties fashion a mutually satisfactory agreement. Mediation is usually a voluntary process, with mediators called in at any time during the negotiations. The mediator's role is an active one. It often involves meeting with each side separately and then bringing them together in an attempt to assist in bridging the existing gaps. He or she is allowed to have direct input into the negotiation process but cannot impose a settlement.

When talks are reaching an impasse, unions will often hold a strike vote. Legally required in some jurisdictions, such a vote seeks authorization from bargaining unit members to strike if necessary. A favourable vote does not mean that a strike is inevitable. In fact, a highly favourable strike vote is often used as a bargaining ploy to gain concessions that will make a strike unnecessary. The results of a strike vote also help the union negotiating team members determine their relative bargaining strength. Unless strike action is supported by a substantial majority of bargaining unit members, union leaders are rarely prepared to risk a strike and must therefore be more willing to compromise, if necessary, to avoid a work stoppage.

A **strike** can be defined as a temporary refusal by bargaining unit members to continue working for the employer. Although strikes account for only a small percentage of total workdays lost each year, they are often costly for all involved. It should be noted that more than 95 percent of labour negotiations are settled without a work stoppage.[48] As illustrated in Figure 12.4, major work stoppages have declined. The economic downturn in 2008 led to relative labour peace in Canada as neither labour nor management could afford to strike. Companies were powerless as markets for their goods and services collapsed and profits decreased, making them susceptible in a work stoppage. Labour was also too weak to bargain for pay increases when employers were in survival mode.[49]

Although work stoppages have declined, they are longer in duration, however. For example, in 2008, the strike of York University's faculty lasted 84 days and the strike at the City of Ottawa ended after 51 days. A rise in union mergers has resulted in bigger unions with healthier strike funds. This means striking employees can last longer without a paycheque. Companies can also persevere longer during a strike with technology that enables them to run basic operations without unionized presence.[50]

Another factor that must be taken into consideration is the employer's ability to continue operating in the event of a strike through the use of supervisors and other non-striking employees and **replacement workers** where legally permitted. (Quebec has "anti-scab" legislation, forbidding the use of replacement workers during a strike, and B.C. has legislation that places some restrictions on the use of such workers).[51] The greater the organization's ability to continue operations, the less the union's chances of gaining its demands through strike action.

Yet there are cautions around the use of replacement workers. For example, in August 2000, Bridgestone/Firestone and Ford recalled 14.4 million tires that the National Highway Traffic and Safety Administration in the United States had linked to 271 deaths and over 800 injuries. Studies found a higher failure rate for tires produced at the Decatur, Illinois, plant during its two-year-long labour dispute than before or after the dispute. The production of defective tires was especially high during periods when large numbers of replacement workers had been hired. Poorly trained and under-supervised replacement workers and a strained work environment led to the production of defective goods.[52]

When a union goes on strike, bargaining unit members often **picket** the employer. Picketers stand at business entrances carrying signs advertising the issues in dispute and attempt to discourage people from entering or leaving the premises. Subjecting people who attempt to cross a picket line to verbal insults or physical restraint is illegal. For example, managers at Kanata's Corel Centre were successful in obtaining a court injunction to prevent up to 120 picketers from obstructing as many as 7500 vehicles seeking to enter the Centre's parking lots from Highway 417. This occurred on the eve of the Ottawa Senators' drive to the Stanley Cup playoffs during the spring of 1998 when the police presented evidence that they could not adequately protect innocent members of the public if violence erupted.[53]

## *figure* 12.4 Chronological Perspective on Work Stoppages in Canada

**Involving 500 or More Workers**
**1990–2009**
**Stoppages in existence during month, quarter, or year**

| Period | Number Beginning During Period | Total Number | Workers Involved | Person-Days Not Worked | % of Estimated Working Time[1] |
|---|---|---|---|---|---|
| **All industries** | | | | | |
| *Canada Total* | | | | | |
| 2009* | 5 | 7 | 13 343 | 390 250 | 0.01 |
| 2008 | 13 | 13 | 26 704 | 269 840 | 0.01 |
| 2007 | 26 | 27 | 49 172 | 1 243 190 | 0.03 |
| 2006 | 10 | 11 | 27 583 | 260 230 | 0.01 |
| 2005 | 39 | 41 | 179 482 | 3 645 060 | 0.10 |
| 2004 | 36 | 37 | 236 843 | 2 396 003 | 0.07 |
| 2003 | 23 | 26 | 56 730 | 1 076 560 | 0.03 |
| 2002 | 30 | 31 | 142 089 | 2 273 000 | 0.07 |
| 2001 | 41 | 44 | 189 240 | 1 296 960 | 0.04 |
| 2000 | 38 | 44 | 112 468 | 779 410 | 0.02 |
| 1999 | 54 | 56 | 127 372 | 1 415 010 | 0.04 |
| 1998 | 60 | 63 | 214 847 | 1 631 460 | 0.05 |
| 1997 | 30 | 32 | 237 246 | 2 855 740 | 0.09 |
| 1996 | 30 | 32 | 250 406 | 2 484 250 | 0.08 |
| 1995 | 35 | 39 | 125 531 | 993 430 | 0.03 |
| 1994 | 28 | 29 | 55 283 | 736 470 | 0.03 |
| 1993 | 23 | 25 | 73 757 | 498 680 | 0.02 |
| 1992 | 43 | 44 | 121 831 | 1 145 810 | 0.04 |
| 1991 | 34 | 36 | 218 377 | 1 452 400 | 0.05 |
| 1990 | 64 | 66 | 226 665 | 3 520 150 | 0.12 |

*2009 data reflects January–June

[1]Person-days not worked as a percentage of estimated working time is only available for All Industries and Canada Total.

Source: Chronological Perspective on Work Stoppages, http://srv131.services.gc.ca/dimt-wid/pcat-cpws/recherche-search.aspx?lang=eng, Human Resources and Social Development Canada, 2009. Reproduced with the permission of the Minister of Public Works and Government Services Canada, 2009.

Another economic weapon available to unions is a **boycott**, which is a refusal to patronize the employer. A boycott occurs when a union asks its members, other union members, the employer's customers/clients, and supporters in the general public not to patronize the business involved in the labour dispute. For example, in 2009, Petro-Canada refinery workers in Montreal organized a national boycott campaign against the oil company in response to the company's 13-month lock-out of its workers. The dispute was over the future of national pattern bargaining in Canada's oil, gas and petrochemical industries. The boycott was a landmark demonstration of Canadian labour solidarity, including international support from the International Federation

**mediation** The use of a neutral third party to help an organization and the union that represents its employees reach agreement.

**strike** The temporary refusal by bargaining unit members to continue working for the employer.

**replacement workers** Individuals hired to perform the work of striking employees and who are often referred to as "scabs."

**picket** Stationing groups of striking employees, usually carrying signs, at the entrances and exits of the struck operation to publicize the issues in dispute and discourage people from entering or leaving the premises.

**boycott** An organized refusal of bargaining unit members and supporters to buy the products or utilize the services of the organization whose employees are on strike in an effort to exert economic pressure on the employer.

of Chemical, Energy, Mine and General Workers' Union.[54]

Although not a widely used strategy in Canada, a **lockout** is legally permissible. This involves the employer prohibiting the bargaining unit employees from entering the company premises as a means of putting pressure on the union negotiating team to agree to the terms and conditions being offered by management. For example, the National Hockey League lockout lasted 301 days and wiped out the 2004–2005 hockey season, and ws followed by the eight-week lockout of 5500 CBC radio and television workers that summer.[55]

An unlawful strike or lockout is one that contravenes one or more provisions of the relevant labour relations legislation and lays the perpetrators open to charges and possible fines and/or periods of imprisonment if found guilty. A **wildcat strike** is a spontaneous walkout, not officially sanctioned by union leaders, which may be legal or illegal depending on its timing. For example, 8500 Toronto Transit Commission (TTC) employees in Toronto organized a sudden one-day wildcat strike in 2006, which shut down transit operations. Picket lines were formed by maintenance workers who were expected to take permanent night shifts and transit drivers concerned about safety when confronted with angry customers. About 800 000 commuters were affected by the walkout.[56]

**Arbitration** involves the use of an outside third party to investigate a dispute between an employer and union and impose a settlement. A sole arbitrator or three-person arbitration board may be involved. Arbitration decisions are final and binding and cannot be changed or revised, except in cases involving corruption, fraud, or breach of natural justice. Arbitration may be used to settle an **interest dispute** arising from the negotiation of a collective agreement. Arbitration is often used in the case of workers who are not permitted to strike, such as hospital and nursing home employees, police officers, and firefighters in most jurisdictions and public servants in some.[57] Arbitration is also used when special legislation is passed, ordering striking or locked-out parties back to work due to public hardship. Because the right to strike or lock out is, in effect, removed by such legislation, any terms of the collective agreement that are still in dispute are investigated by an arbitrator and a settlement is imposed based on his or her judgment of a fair course of action. This is known as **interest arbitration**.

Striking *Calgary Herald* journalists picketed and held a mock funeral for the "end of quality journalism" to raise public awareness and sympathy.

The wildcat strike at GM Canada in Oshawa in August 2000 was unlawful.

Molson's Barrie workers in front of the union's boycott bus preparing to distribute leaflets asking consumers not to purchase Molson's products.

## TYPICAL PROVISIONS OF THE COLLECTIVE AGREEMENT

The eventual outcome of collective bargaining, whether negotiated by the parties or imposed by an arbitrator, is a formal, written, collective agreement. The length and scope of this document varies depending on organization size, type of relationship between the parties, and duration of the bargaining relationship. Typical contract provisions include:

- union recognition clause
- union security/checkoff clause
- no strike or lockout provision
- management rights clause
- grievance procedure
- arbitration clause
- discharge and disciplinary procedures
- compensation rates and benefits
- hours of work and overtime pay provisions
- probationary period
- restrictions on contracting out
- health and safety provisions
- employee security/seniority provisions
- contract expiration date

Of the items listed above, five deserve closer scrutiny.

**Union Recognition Clause** A **union recognition clause** is a mandatory contract provision in most jurisdictions. It clarifies the scope of the bargaining unit by specifying the employee classifications included therein or listing those excluded. It is in this clause that the union is recognized as the exclusive bargaining agent for the employees in the bargaining unit (even those who choose not to be union members, where such choice is permitted) as specified in the LRB's certification order or the employer's voluntary recognition notice.

**Union Security/Checkoff Clause** All Canadian jurisdictions permit the inclusion of a **union security clause** in the collective agreement to protect the interests of the labour union. This clause deals with the issue of membership requirements and, often, the payment of union dues. There are various forms of union security clauses. The three most common of these forms are:[58]

1. The **Rand formula**, which is a popular union security arrangement that does not require union membership but does require that all members of the bargaining unit pay union dues.
2. A **union shop**, in which membership and dues payment are mandatory conditions of employment. Although individuals do not have to be union members at the time they are hired, they are required to join the union on the day on which they commence work or on completion of probation.
3. A **modified union shop**, in which the individuals who were bargaining unit members at the time of certification or when the collective agreement was signed are not obliged to join the union, although they must pay dues. However, all subsequently hired employees must do both.

**No Strike or Lockout Provision** There must be a clause in every contract in Canada forbidding strikes or lockouts while the collective agreement is in effect. The intent is to guarantee some degree of stability in the employment relationship during the life of the collective agreement, which must be at least a one-year period. It is interesting to note that Saskatchewan is the only jurisdiction that has established a maximum duration (three years), although a five-year limit is under consideration in Quebec.[59]

**Management Rights Clause** The **management rights clause** clarifies the areas in which management may exercise its prerogatives (exclusive rights) without agreement from the union and the issues that are not subject to collective bargaining. It typically refers to the

**lockout** Temporary refusal of a company to continue providing work for bargaining unit employees involved in a labour dispute, which may result in closure of the establishment for a period of time.

**wildcat strike** A spontaneous walkout not officially sanctioned by the union leadership, which may be legal or illegal depending on its timing.

**arbitration** The use of an outside third party to investigate a dispute between an employer and union and impose a settlement.

**interest dispute** A dispute arising between an organization and the union that represents its employees over the terms of a first collective agreement or revisions to an existing one.

**interest arbitration** The imposition of the final terms of a collective agreement.

**union recognition clause** A mandatory contract clause in most jurisdictions identifying the recognized trade union and clarifying its rights and responsibilities as the exclusive bargaining agent for the employees in the bargaining unit.

**union security clause** The contract provisions protecting the interests of the labour union dealing with the issue of membership requirements and, often, the payment of union dues.

**Rand formula** A popular security arrangement that does not require union membership but does require all bargaining unit members to pay union dues.

**union shop** A type of security arrangement in which union membership and dues payment are mandatory conditions of employment.

**modified union shop** A type of security arrangement in which the individuals who were bargaining unit members at the time of certification or when the collective agreement was signed are not obliged to join the union, although they must pay dues. However, all subsequently hired employees must do both.

**management rights clause** The clause that refers to the rights of management to operate the organization subject to the terms of the collective agreement. Any rights not limited by the clause are reserved to management.

STRATEGIC HR

## Union Hung Up on BlackBerrys

**PSAC WANTS CLEAR EXPECTATIONS ON OFF-HOURS USE OF DEVICE**

A manager expecting an employee to reply to an email on her BlackBerry at 11 p.m. had better start paying for the employee's availability, said the union representing federal public sector employees.

With seven bargaining units currently in contract negotiations, the Public Service Alliance of Canada (PSAC) said it wants to change two collective agreement provisions in an effort to curb widespread BlackBerry use within the bureaucracy.

"Emails are being sent at all hours, day and night. If people get them, if the BlackBerry is sitting on your dresser when it goes off, it's going to wake you up. And often, you feel you have to respond to it right away," said Maria Fitzpatrick, the incoming regional executive vice-president for PSAC's national capital region.

Ed Cashman, the outgoing regional executive vice-president for PSAC, said he couldn't quantify how prevalent BlackBerrys are, just that, like in the private sector, "everybody's got one, particularly among managers."

The problem is there has been no discussion across the federal Treasury Board about what the expectations are when employees get a BlackBerry, said Cashman. The union wants to update the clauses in the collective agreement that deal with call back and standby, he said.

When an employee is called back into the office, he is paid for four hours minimum to make up for the inconvenience of having to leave home, travel to the office and then home again. These days, an employee can do work without having to leave home and most times they're not compensated for the inconvenience, said Cashman.

Similarly, the standby clause was created at a time when, if the boss asked an employee to wait around for a development expected that weekend, she would have to stand by the phone. Today, the person could run errands or go to her son's game, but she might not be able to go to the golf course or the cottage if those places are out of cellphone range, said Fitzpatrick.

"It is our intention to make the cost prohibitive so that an employer would stop doing that. It's our experience that when employers have to pay something, they regulate their behaviour," said Cashman.

PSAC isn't the only party to have voiced concerns in Canada over excessive off-hours BlackBerry use. In November, an auditor's report conducted for Natural Resources Canada found employees in the department were using 900 BlackBerrys and 720 cellphones. According to the Canadian Press, which obtained the report, 20 percent of the devices were given out to employees who had no work-related reasons for having them.

"There are no policies, guidelines and procedures for voice telecommunications devices and service plans," the report stated. "Comprehensive corporate directives for the management and control of voice telecommunications do not exist."

In another federal department, a deputy minister issued a memo asking employees to implement a "blackout" on BlackBerrys between 7 p.m. and 7 a.m. and on weekends and holidays.

"Work-life quality is a priority for me and this organization because achieving it benefits us both as individuals and as a department," Citizenship and Immigration Canada deputy minister Richard Fadden reportedly wrote in the memo. "When we can 'balance' our work and personal responsibilities, we, as a team, stand to not only serve and perform more effectively, but also to attract and keep employees to help us build a stronger Canada."

In the United States, where lawsuits over overtime are more common, legal observers have been warning of oncoming litigation over off-hour BlackBerry use.

Under the Fair Labor Standards Act in the U.S., it isn't a defence to claim the employer didn't require the employee to do the extra work, wrote lawyers Jeffrey Schlossberg and Kimberly Malerba last year in a New York Law Journal article. If the employer knows the work is being performed, it must count the time as hours worked, stated the article.

Source: U. Vu, "Union hung up on BlackBerrys: PSAC wants clear expectations on off-hours use of device," *Canadian HR Reporter*, June 16, 2008, pp. 1–2. Reprinted with permission.

rights of management to operate the organization subject to the terms of the collective agreement.

**Arbitration Clause** All Canadian jurisdictions require that collective agreements contain an **arbitration clause** providing for the final and binding settlement, by arbitration, of all disputes arising during the term of a collective agreement. Such disputes may relate to the application, interpretation, or administration of that agreement as well as alleged contraventions by either party.

An increasing number of collective agreements also include provisions to limit BlackBerry use after work hours. The Strategic HR box above outlines the arguments in favour of reducing the expectation that employees respond to emails after office hours.

## Step 6: Contract Administration

After a collective agreement has been negotiated and signed, the contract administration process begins. Both union and management are required to abide by the contract provisions. It is also in day-to-day contract administration that the bulk of labour–management relations occurs. Regardless of the amount of time, effort, care, and attention put into the wording of the contract, it is almost inevitable that differences of opinion will arise regarding the application and interpretation of the agreement. Seniority and discipline issues are a major source of disagreement between union and management.

The collective agreement is a binding document that remains active for two to five years depending on the timeframe negotiated by union and management. However, the collapse of the auto manufacturing industry and the unprecedented economic crisis experienced by General Motors forced management and the CAW to open and make changes to their collective agreement before its expiration date for the sake of ensuring the company's survival. The Strategic HR box on page 402 outlines the concessions made to support General Motors's restructuring plan.

**SENIORITY** Unions typically prefer to have employee-related decisions determined by seniority, which refers to length of service in the bargaining unit. In many collective agreements, seniority is the governing factor in layoffs and recalls (the most-senior employees are the last to be laid off and the first to be recalled) and a determining factor in transfers and promotions. In some collective agreements, seniority is also the determining factor in decisions pertaining to work assignments, shift preferences, allocation of days off, and vacation time.

**RPC 12-3 >**

**Contributes to communication plan during work disruptions**

Managers often prefer to place greater weight on ability or merit, while unions want more emphasis placed on seniority. Thus, in some collective agreements, seniority is the sole basis for transfer, layoff, and promotion decisions; in others, seniority is the governing factor, provided that the senior applicant has sufficient ability to do the job; and in still others, seniority is the governing factor only in the case of two candidates with relatively equal skill and ability.

**AN ETHICAL DILEMMA**

Is it ethical to lay off senior workers who are within one year of retirement?

**DISCIPLINE** Almost all collective agreements give the employer the right to make reasonable rules and regulations governing employees' behaviour and to take disciplinary action if the rules are broken. In every collective agreement, bargaining unit members are given the right to file a grievance if they feel that any disciplinary action taken was too harsh or without just cause.

**RPC 12-4 >**

**Advises clients on matters related to interest arbitration**

Disciplinary action is a major source of grievances, and some unions challenge virtually all disciplinary action that is taken. Managers must therefore be extremely careful not only that the disciplinary issues are handled in accordance with the terms of the collective agreement but also that they are backed by evidence. It is important to provide evidence, first, that the employee actually engaged in some form of misconduct and, second, whether such misconduct warrants the particular discipline imposed.

**RPC 12-5 >**

**Provides consultation and risk assessment in issues involving arbitration**

**GRIEVANCES** A **grievance** is a written allegation of a contract violation generally involving a disagreement about its application or interpretation. When such alleged violations or disagreements arise, they are usually handled and settled through the **grievance procedure**, the last step of which is final and binding arbitration. The primary purpose of the grievance procedure is

**arbitration clause** The clause that requires final and binding arbitration of all disputes arising during the term of a collective agreement.

**grievance** A written allegation of a contract violation filed by an individual bargaining unit member, the union, or management.

**grievance procedure** The steps by which a dispute arising during the life of a collective agreement between an employer and bargaining unit member or between an employer and the union may be amicably settled.

STRATEGIC HR

## GM Freezes Wages, Pensions; Concessions a "Significant Sacrifice": CAW

The Canadian Auto Workers and General Motors Canada Ltd. reached a tentative agreement yesterday that will see wages and pensions frozen until 2012 and retirees pay part of their health care costs. Now it is up to Ottawa to determine whether enough concessions have been made to qualify the automaker for critical government aid.

"I am encouraged that GM and the CAW have reached a tentative agreement," Tony Clement, the Minister of Industry, said in a statement.

"These negotiations show that stakeholders realize how serious the auto-industry situation is and how important it is for everyone to come to the table and negotiate in good faith in order to fundamentally restructure the company. My officials and I continue to work closely with GM as we continue our due diligence. We will ensure that there is a viable, long-term sustainability plan involving all stakeholders in place before we commit any taxpayers' dollars."

The federal government said in December it was willing to offer up to US$6-billion in loans for GM Canada and US$2.25-billion to Chrysler Canada to help the carmakers stabilize their operations. GM is also asking for US$16-billion in aid from Washington. Ottawa has said everybody in the industry would have to give up something before any bailout could be considered.

CAW president Ken Lewenza said after a three-day bargaining session that ended yesterday morning at 5:30 that his members have done their part, adding that solving the auto sector's problem is not just about cutting wages. "The contract changes we have negotiated are a significant sacrifice, and they will cause hardship for our members and their families," Mr. Lewenza told reporters in Toronto. "The federal government demanded contract cuts as a condition of providing aid to the industry. Cuts in wages cannot save this company. If government does not provide emergency assistance, the company will surely fail."

In addition to wages being frozen until September, 2012, the union agreed to no cost-of-living adjustments to pensions for the remainder of the contract—a first for the CAW. By the end of the contract, GM could have as many as 50 000 retirees with only 8000 active workers. The autoworkers also agreed to a new monthly premium of $30 to be paid for health care costs for all active workers and pensioners under the age of 65. In another first, pensioners over 65 and survivors' spouses will have to pay $15 per month for their health care costs.

Other key cuts include: paid time off reduced by 40 hours per year; the elimination of an annual $1700 special bonus payment designed to help offset the cost of retiree health care benefits; and a 33 percent cut to union-sponsored programs such as child care.

The tentative agreement—GM's 10 000 members are to vote on it tomorrow and Wednesday—extends many of the main points that the two parties agreed to last year. That agreement was extended one year, until September, 2012.

The CAW would not put a dollar figure on the concessions it agreed to, but Mr. Lewenza said they "reduce active hourly labour costs by several dollars per hour, reinforcing Canada's investment advantage relative to U. S. facilities."

GM Canada officials were not available for comment, but the company said in a statement that the concessions would bring its labour costs to much more competitive levels and help ensure its long-term viability. "The agreement marks a positive further step in GM Canada's restructuring plan submitted to the Ontario and federal governments on February 20, 2009," the statement said.

Mr. Lewenza noted this is the second time in the past year the CAW has agreed to cuts, adding its 2008 contracts resulted in $300-million in savings across the industry. "This contract will cut labour costs much further," he said. The concessions agreed to yesterday could also affect talks with Ford Motor Co. of Canada and Chrysler Canada. "Pattern bargaining has been incredibly successful to us in good times and bad times. We'll make sure Chrysler and Ford get the information to analyze this agreement," Mr. Lewenza said. None of the concessions made yesterday will mean much if GM Canada's parent corporation does not survive. "The Canadian subsidiaries of the Big Three can't survive in isolation of the U. S. going down," Mr. Lewenza said. "If GM goes into [bankruptcy], there is not much we can do in Canada."

Source: G. Marr, "GM deal freezes wages, pensions; Concessions a 'significant sacrifice': CAW," *National Post,* March 9, 2009, p. A.1. Material reprinted with the express permission of "The National Post Company," a Canwest Partnership.

to ensure the application of the contract with a degree of justice for both parties. In addition, the grievance procedure resolves issues that were not anticipated by those at the bargaining table; provides the opportunity for the interpretation of contract language; serves as a communications device; fulfills an important political purpose by showcasing the important role that the union plays in assisting employees to protect their rights; and brings to the attention of the union leaders, management leaders, or both, those areas of the contract requiring clarification or modification in subsequent negotiations.

All collective agreements contain a grievance procedure, and most provide for arbitration as a final step. While the number of steps and people involved at each vary, Figure 12.5 illustrates a fairly typical grievance procedure. The usual first step of the grievance procedure occurs when an aggrieved employee or a union steward on his or her behalf files a written complaint with the employee's immediate supervisor. If the problem is not resolved to the satisfaction of the employee at the first step, he or she may then take the problem to the next higher managerial level designated in the contract and so on through all of the steps available. There are generally three internal steps prior to arbitration. Time limits are typically provided for resolution at each step. Ninety percent or more of all grievances are settled, abandoned, or withdrawn prior to arbitration.

**AN ETHICAL DILEMMA**

As the HR manager, how would you handle a situation in which a supervisor has knowingly violated the collective agreement when scheduling overtime?

**RPC 12-6 >**

Interprets the collective agreement

**RPC 12-7 >**

Advises clients of signatories' rights, including those with respect to grievance procedures

Grievance arbitration is an adjudicative process through which disputes arising out of the application and interpretation of a collective agreement are resolved. Such differences are known as **rights disputes**. Thus, if the parties are unable to resolve a grievance issue themselves, it must be referred to a sole arbitrator or three-person arbitration board for a final and binding decision. The process involved in resolving such issues is known as **rights arbitration**.

## *In-class Notes*

**The Labour Relations Process**

- Step 1: employees desire unionization due to dissatisfaction and lack of power
- Step 2: union organizing campaign and possible employer counter-campaign
- Step 3: union recognition process—certification procedures vary by jurisdiction
- Step 4: preparing to negotiate a collective agreement
- Step 5: negotiating a collective agreement, involving face-to-face collective bargaining; contract approval or strike/lockout
- Step 6: contract administration, including seniority, discipline, and grievances

*figure* 12.5 **A Typical Grievance Procedure**

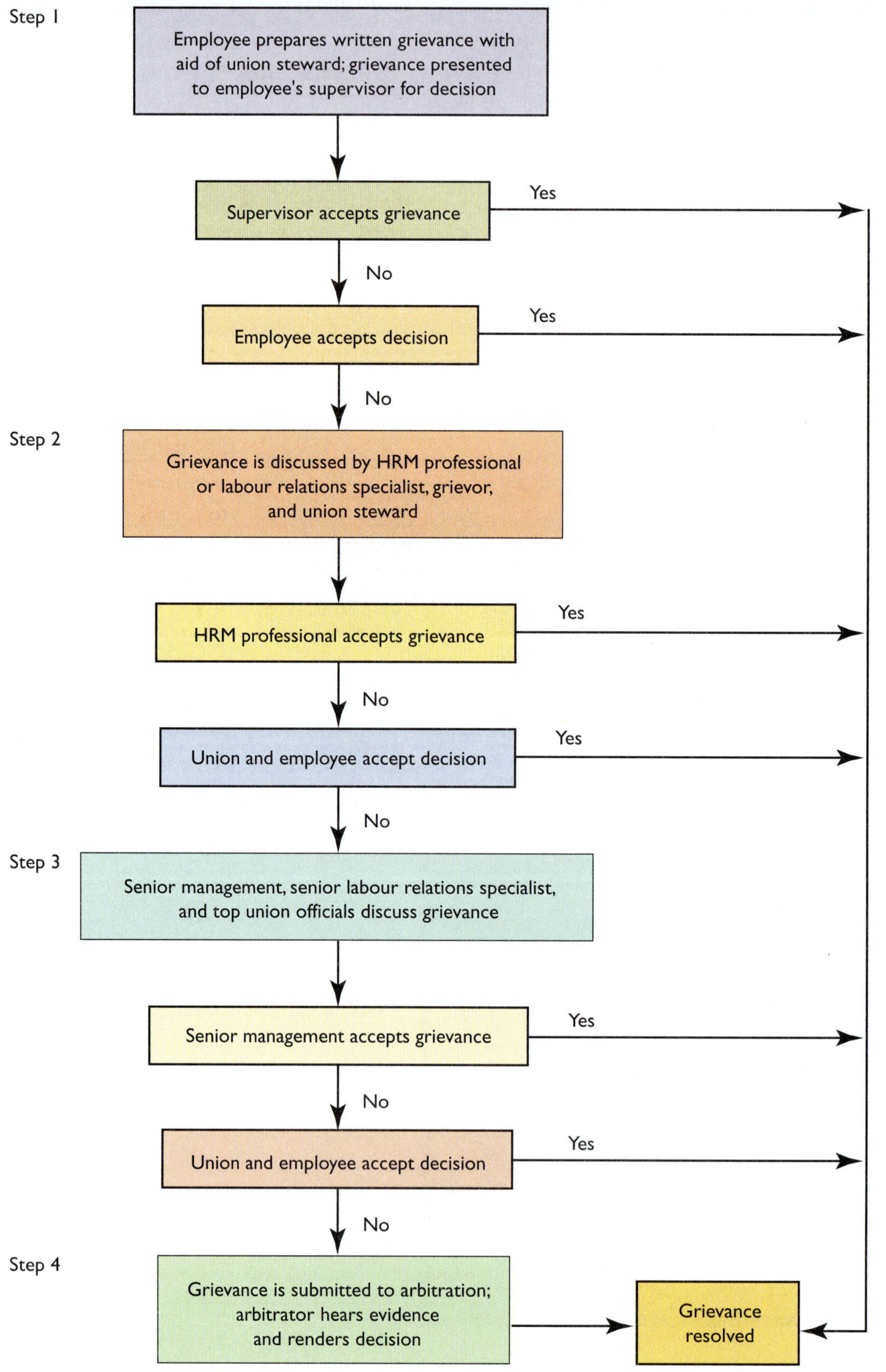

A written arbitration award is issued at the conclusion of most rights arbitration cases, indicating that the grievance has been upheld (which means that the grievor's arguments are deemed to be correct) or overturned (which means that the actions that launched the grievance have been deemed to be correct). In disciplinary cases, it is also possible for an arbitration award to substitute a penalty that is more or less severe than the one proposed by union or management.

## 12.5 THE IMPACT OF UNIONIZATION ON HRM

Once a collective agreement is signed, it must be administered by management and adhered to by both parties. This reality of unionization affects HRM in a number of ways, as described below.

**ORGANIZATIONAL STRUCTURE** Once an organization is unionized, the HR department is typically expanded by the addition of a labour relations specialist or group. In a large firm with a number of bargaining units, human resources and labour relations may form two divisions within a broader department often called industrial relations or labour relations.

**MANAGEMENT DECISION MAKING** Union leaders are typically involved in decisions pertaining to any issues that will affect bargaining unit members, such as subcontracting of work, productivity standards, and job content. This may lead supervisors to feel that they have lost some of their authority, which can cause resentment. They must ensure that all of their decisions and actions are in accordance with the terms of the collective agreement. The union may even challenge decisions that abide by the agreement.

**FORMULATION OF POLICIES AND PROCEDURES** In a unionized setting, management has less freedom to make unilateral changes. All HR policies regarding union members must be consistent with the terms of the collective agreement. Union representatives are often involved or at least consulted as such policies and procedures are being drafted.

**CENTRALIZATION OF RECORD KEEPING** Unionization generally results in greater centralization of employee record keeping. Supervisors are required to produce more written records than ever before, since documentation is critical at grievance and arbitration hearings.

### Building Effective Labour–Management Relations

In many organizations, union and management leaders recognize that an effective day-to-day working relationship is in their mutual interest. When managers wish to build a more harmonious and effective relationship, a number of strategies can help:

1. *Instituting an Open-Door Policy*. Many issues can be resolved informally if the president of the local knows that he or she can approach the labour relations manager "off the record" and that anything discussed in such sessions will be kept strictly confidential. Fewer grievances and a more trusting and harmonious relationship often result.
2. *Regular Meetings and Joint Study Committees*. Regularly scheduled union–management meetings can result in more effective communication and the resolution of problems/concerns before they become formal grievance issues. If any actions that might affect union members are discussed with the union executive first, the likelihood of grievances is greatly reduced. Forming joint labour/management committees to investigate and resolve complex issues can lead to innovative and creative solutions as well as to a better relationship.
3. *Demonstrating Genuine Concern for Employees*. When managers demonstrate genuine concern about employee well-being, mutual trust and respect are often established. This involves fair treatment and communication going well above and beyond the requirements of the collective agreement.
4. *Holding Joint Training Programs*. When a contract is first signed, it can be beneficial to hold a joint training program to ensure that supervisors and union stewards are familiar with the terms and conditions specified therein. Such training can

**rights disputes** Disagreements between an organization and the union that represents its employees regarding the interpretation or application of one or more clauses in the current collective agreement.

**rights arbitration** The process involved in the settlement of a rights dispute.

European Trade Union Confederation (ETUC)
**www.etuc.org**

reduce misunderstandings and the likelihood of disagreement regarding interpretation of contract language. Joint training programs can also be extremely helpful for dealing with employee health and safety issues.

5. *Using Third-Party Assistance*. It is often beneficial to bring in a consultant or a government representative to help identify common goals and objectives and ways in which trust and communication can be strengthened.

## In-class Notes

**The Impact of Unionization on HRM**

- Organizational structure adds labour relations department
- Management decision making may involve union participation
- Policies and procedures must be consistent with collective agreement
- Centralization of record keeping
- Building effective labour–management relations through an open door policy; prior consultation/joint study committees; genuine concern for employee well-being; joint training programs; third-party assistance

# Labour Relations on the International Stage

Labour relations systems and practices vary significantly around the world. Collective bargaining, which is a common practice for protecting union and management rights in Canada and the U.S., is viewed in many European unions as an incessant class struggle between labour and capital. In Sweden and Germany, collective bargaining refers to negotiations between an employer's organization and the industry's trade union, and in Japan negotiations are highly collaborative initiatives been enterprise unions and company management. In the United Kingdom, unions are affiliated with the Labour Party, and in Germany, unions are members of the company's board of directors.[60]

Labour relations on the international stage also differ in priorities. As discussed in this chapter, unions in Canada have predominantly economic priorities on pay, benefits, and job security. Canadian unions place less emphasis on priorities within the political arena. In sharp contrast, unions in France focus on political issues and do not devote as much time to economic concerns. Unions in France are closely affiliated with political parties, and strikes tend to focus on political change as a way of protecting and improving conditions for union members. Unions in Sweden leverage priorities in both the political and economic domains, with trade unions often represented on governmental commissions.[61]

Union membership as a percentage of the labour force is higher in most European countries than in Canada. Sweden tops the union participation list with 95 percent of their workers represented by unions, followed by Denmark with 88 percent. In the past two decades, there has been a decline in union membership in the United Kingdom, but unions still represent 51 percent of the workforce there, which equates to one and half times as many union workers as in Canada.[62]

# Chapter Review

## Answers to Test Yourself

1. What are the key labour relations strategies that organizations can adopt in relation to unionization?

   An organization's labour relations (LR) strategy is its overall plan for dealing with unions. Possible strategies include union acceptance and union avoidance. There are two avoidance strategies: union substitution and union suppression.

2. What are the common characteristics among Canadian labour relations laws?

   Common characteristics of LR legislation are procedures for the certification of a union collective agreement to be in force for a minimum of one year; procedures to be followed before a strike or lockout; prohibitions of strike or lockout during the life of a collective agreement; requirement that disputes over matters arising from interpretation of the collective agreement be settled by final and binding arbitration; prohibition of certain specified "unfair" practices; and establishment of a labour relations board or the equivalent.

3. What are the union organizing and recognition processes?

   The union organizing process typically includes employee–union contact; an initial organizational meeting; the formation of an in-house organizing committee; an organizing campaign; and the outcome—certification, recognition, or rejection. There are three basic ways a union can obtain recognition as a bargaining unit for a group of workers: (1) voluntary recognition, (2) the regular certification process, and (3) a prehearing vote.

4. What is collective bargaining, and what are the critical steps involved?

   Collective bargaining is a critical step in the labour relations process. It is the formal process used by management and labour to establish a collective agreement. The steps that are involved in the bargaining process include preparation for bargaining, face-to-face negotiations, and obtaining approval for the proposed contract.

5. What is the impact of unionization on HRM?

   Unionization has an impact on HRM in a number of ways. The HR department is expanded by the addition of an LR specialist or section. Union leaders are typically involved in decisions that will affect their members. Management has less freedom to make unilateral changes. Unions can cause greater centralization of employee record-keeping and standardization of decision making. Supervisors may feel that they have lost some of their authority while simultaneously experiencing an increase in responsibility.

## Key Terms

arbitration (p. 398)
arbitration clause (p. 400)
authorization card (p. 388)
bargaining unit (p. 392)
bargaining zone (p. 393)
boycott (p. 397)
business unionism (p. 381)
caucus session (p. 392)
chief steward (p. 385)
collective agreement (union contract) (p. 392)
collective bargaining (p. 392)
conciliation (p. 395)
craft unions (p. 383)
distributive bargaining (p. 394)
good faith bargaining (p. 392)
grievance (p. 401)
grievance procedure (p. 401)
industrial unions (p. 383)

in-house organizing committee (p. 388)
integrative bargaining (p. 394)
interest arbitration (p. 398)
interest dispute (p. 398)
international unions (p. 383)
labour–management relations (p. 378)
Labour Relations Board (LRB) (p. 380)
labour relations (LR) strategy (p. 378)
labour union (union) (p. 378)
local (p. 384)
lockout (p. 398)
management rights clause (p. 399)
mediation (p. 396)
modified union shop (p. 399)
mutual gains bargaining (p. 394)
national unions (p. 383)
picket (p. 396)
pre-hearing vote (p. 391)
Rand formula (p. 399)
replacement workers (p. 396)
representation vote (p. 391)
rights arbitration (p. 403)
rights disputes (p. 403)
social unionism (p. 381)
strike (p. 396)
surface bargaining (p. 392)
unfair labour practices (p. 380)
union acceptance strategy (p. 378)
union avoidance strategy (p. 378)
union organizers (p. 388)
union recognition clause (p. 399)
union security clause (p. 399)
union shop (p. 399)
union stewards (p. 384)
union substitution (proactive HRM) approach (p. 378)
union suppression approach (p. 379)
wildcat strike (p. 398)

## Required Professional Capabilities (RPCs)

RPC 12-1 > (p. 392)
RPC 12-2 > (p. 394)
RPC 12-3 > (p. 401)
RPC 12-4 > (p. 401)
RPC 12-5 > (p. 401)
RPC 12-6 > (p. 403)
RPC 12-7 > (p. 403)

# Cases and Exercises

> **myHRlab**
> For additional cases and exercises, go to www.pearsoned.ca/myhrlab.

## CASE INCIDENT

### Western College

Sean O'Sullivan is the HR manager at Western College, a medium-sized institution located in Bradley, Manitoba, which is approximately 240 km north of Winnipeg. Bradley has a population of 120 000, and many of the residents are employees of the federal or provincial governments or Via Rail Canada. Western College, like many other Canadian educational institutions, is under severe pressure to restrict and meet budgets in the wake of recent provincial government announcements of reduced spending on education. There have been some staff reductions already, and it is likely that there will be more that will affect virtually all areas of the college.

Sean is mulling over how he should handle a situation that Ruth Ann Zimmer, a supervisor in the maintenance and housekeeping department, has just brought to his attention. According to Ruth Ann, she is quite certain that an organizing campaign has begun among the employees reporting to her who maintain and clean the on-campus residences. She indicated that she actually witnessed a CUPE representative meeting with a number of the employees, urging them to sign union authorization cards. She also observed several of those who report to her "cornering" other employees to talk to them about joining the union and urging them to sign cards. Some of this activity occurred during working hours as the employees were carrying out their normal duties. She indicated that a number of employees have come to her asking her opinion about unions in general and CUPE in particular. They informed her that several other supervisors in the department had told their reporting employees not to sign any union authorization cards and not to talk about the union while they were on campus. Of particular concern to Sean is Ruth Ann's statement that one of her fellow supervisors told his reporting employees in a meeting that anyone who was caught talking about the union or signing an authorization card would be disciplined and perhaps terminated.

According to Ruth Ann, the employees are very dissatisfied with their wages and many of the conditions that they have endured because of students, supervisors, and other staff members. She said that several employees told her that they had signed union cards because they believed that the only way to get the college administrators to pay any attention to their concerns was to have a union represent them. Ruth Ann mentioned that she made a list of employees whom she felt had already signed authorization cards or were seriously considering doing so and said that she would be prepared to share this list with Sean if he wanted to deal with those individuals personally. Since her pager went off, she had to leave Sean's office rather abruptly. Just before departing, she stated that she and the other supervisors wanted to know what they should do in order to "stomp out" the threat of unionization in their department.

### Questions

1. Assuming that Ruth Ann is correct, why do you think some of the maintenance and housekeeping staff members might be interested in forming a union at this point in time? (What factors may have led to their contact with CUPE?)
2. How can Sean determine if Ruth Ann's information is correct?
3. What unfair labour practices have members of the union and/or management committed? Are there any legal ramifications?
4. How should Sean respond to Ruth Ann's offer to give him a list of those who have signed cards or are likely to do so?

### Application Questions

1. The CAW has become the official bargaining agent for your car manufacturing plant. What specific changes will occur in the management of human resources as the company transitions from a non-unionized to a unionized facility?
2. "Employees chose to unionize because of poor management practices. If companies had more effective leaders at the helm, employees would not be compelled to join unions." Do you agree or disagree with this position? Explain your response.
3. Employees at your food processing plant returned to work after a 62-day strike. What will you, as the labour relations specialist, do to create a positive work environment after a bitter and gruelling strike? What will you encourage the management team to do?
4. As the chief steward for a public service agency you realize that female union members are not participating in union meetings, running for elections, or volunteering for union committees. What courses of action will you take to enhance female participation rate in union activities?
5. After six weeks at the bargaining table, it is evident that management is bargaining in bad faith through a series of delaying tactics, such as repeatedly cancelling meetings at the last minute and not providing financial reports as requested. What should you do to address this issue with the management bargaining team?
6. Each student in the class is asked to find a copy of a collective agreement. In teams of four, compare and contrast the provisions negotiated in each collective agreement. Based on your analysis, what are your significant learnings about collective agreements?

## RUNNING CASE: LEARNINMOTION.COM

### Labour Relations

The case for Chapter 12, *Labour Relations,* asks students to give advice to management about the possible development of a union within the organization. To read this case, go to www.pearsoned.ca/myhrlab and click on the *Management of Human Resources,* Third Canadian Edition, In-Class Edition, cover. Click on the case module in Chapter 12.

## CONTROVERSIAL BUSINESS TOPIC EXERCISE

One of the most senior workers in your company filed a grievance claiming the violation of his seniority rights in the company's decision around layoffs. This is the fifth grievance in six months that this worker has filed. Management is infuriated with the amount of time and money devoted to grievance investigation and settlement generated by one worker who is intentionally aggravating management. As the labour relations specialist, you try to maintain civility between both parties, yet it is increasing difficult. You overhear a conversation between the CEO and the divisional plant supervisor, who are concocting a plan to get the worker fired for just cause. They are staging a major theft that will make it appear as if the employee is stealing from the company. How will you handle this situation?

## IN THE BOARDROOM EXERCISE

You are the labour relations specialist for a unionized pulp and paper facility in northern British Columbia. In the last two rounds of collective bargaining, you noticed a disturbing trend—union–management relations at the table have become increasingly adversarial, with both parties using hardball tactics to secure demands. At a recent management meeting, you raised your concerns and suggested that union and management adopt a mutual gains bargaining approach for the next round of negotiations. Laughter filled the room as you advocated for this change. "That is the most ludicrous idea I've heard all day," said the CEO. "How naive are you? Do you not realize we are in the pulp and paper industry that demands we bargain aggressively and fight to win? Mutual gains bargaining is fluff. Bargaining is not about collaboration. It's about putting pressure on the union and squeezing everything you can out of them."

Discuss the approach you will use to convince the CEO that a mutual gains approach to bargaining should be adopted. In teams of three, role-play the conversation that takes place between you, as the labour relations specialist, and the CEO. The third person on your team is the observer, who gives feedback on your argument and offers recommendations for handling the situation.

## LABOUR RELATIONS ON THE INTERNATIONAL STAGE EXERCISE

*The exercise below relates to the Labour Relations on the International Stage feature on p. 406.*

You are an entrepreneur expanding your business to the international market. Select a country in which you would like to do business and research the labour–management relations in that country. Examine (a) the system, practices, and priorities of unions and management in that country, and (b) the approach you will adapt to maintain strong relations with the union if your company becomes unionized.

## EXPERIENTIAL EXERCISE

For further study of text materials and development of practical skills, select the experiential exercise module for this chapter on www.pearsoned.ca/myhrlab. This module provides two to three individual or group-based assignments per chapter.

# QUIZ YOURSELF

## STUDY GUIDE QUESTIONS

Circle the correct answer. After completing this self-test, check your answers against the Answers to Study Guide Questions at the back of the book (p. 433).

1. A labour union is an officially recognized body representing a group of individuals who have joined together to present a united front and collective voice in dealing with management. The purpose of unionization is to:
   a. achieve better pay and benefits
   b. obtain greater job security
   c. obtain improved work conditions
   d. have better control over the jobs
   e. all of the above
2. Wal-Mart, a large multinational organization in the retail industry, believes that it is best to operate in a non-unionized environment. It believes that the good management practices it has adopted in the workplace are an incentive for employees to stay away from unions. The strategy adopted by Wal-Mart is a union:
   a. suppression approach
   b. substitution approach
   c. avoidance strategy
   d. relations strategy
   e. management approach

3. There are a number of common characteristics in the LR legislation across federal, provincial, and territorial jurisdictions. A common characteristic of labour relations legislation is/are:
   a. procedures for the certification of a union
   b. procedures to be followed for a strike or lockout
   c. prohibition of strikes or lockouts during the life of a collective agreement
   d. requirement that a collective agreement be in force for a minimum of one year
   e. all of the above

4. Canadian labour laws require the establishment of a labour relations board or the equivalent to administer and enforce the provisions of the legislation. The labour relations board is empowered to:
   a. interpret, administer, and enforce labour relations legislation
   b. assist unions in organizing workers
   c. help management decide on their labour relations strategy
   d. determine when to call a strike or lockout
   e. none of the above

5. Seasons Ltd. is an organization in the restaurant industry. They make sure that unions are not formed by seeing to it that those employees who try to initiate union formation are immediately identified and terminated from service. This is known as:
   a. unfair labour practice by the employees
   b. unfair labour practice by the management
   c. union substitution strategy
   d. dismissal for insubordination
   e. none of the above

6. What is the most recent business unionism initiative that unions have taken?
   a. better health and safety protection
   b. improved pay and benefits
   c. better working conditions
   d. narrowing the wage gap between men and women
   e. ensuring job security for members

7. The United Steelworkers of America is a union that is represented in Canada as well as in the United States. To which categorization of unions does the United Steelworkers of America belong?
   a. craft unions
   b. industrial unions
   c. national unions
   d. international unions
   e. management unions

8. An authorization card indicates an employee's willingness to:
   a. go on strike
   b. engage in a wildcat strike
   c. be represented by a union in collective bargaining with their employer
   d. deal with the employer on an individual basis
   e. pay union dues

9. Most employers want to identify reasons that may lead employees to form a union in an organization. As a labour relations advisor, which of the following are key factors that may result in employees wishing to form a union?
   a. lack of job security
   b. perceived inequities in pay
   c. unsatisfactory work conditions
   d. unfair policies/procedures
   e. all of the above

10. The Miller Company's employees supported the formation of a union with the intention that their union would be able to bargain for better pay, improved working conditions, and more health and safety measures. It has been almost a year and the union has not been able to live up to expectations, nor have they been able to negotiate a collective agreement. What can employees do in such a situation?
    a. go on strike
    b. decertify the union
    c. organize a protest
    d. take a vote
    e. none of the above

11. Mackenzie Corporation has a union, and its collective agreement is up for renewal this year. The management of the company has recently had their bargaining plan and strategy approved and identified their bargaining team. The union, too, has gone through a similar process. What is the next step that they have to take to enter into the bargaining process?
    a. prepare for negotiations
    b. have face-to-face negotiations
    c. contract approval
    d. draft the collective agreement
    e. ratification of the process

12. The Smith Corporation has just received a union proposal requesting a 20-percent wage increase across the board along with enhanced benefits packages. However, the company has been going through some tough financial times and is not willing to consider a wage increase. It also already has benefits packages in line with the industry. What is the bargaining approach that is exemplified here?
    a. collective bargaining
    b. mutual gains bargaining
    c. interest-based bargaining
    d. integrative bargaining
    e. distributive bargaining

13. The Smith Corporation management negotiating team refuses to consider any salary increase. It is also not agreeable to reviewing the benefits package. The union refuses to back down from its position. The following action is now available for the management to consider:
    a. strike
    b. lockout
    c. picket
    d. boycott
    e. all of the above

14. When alleged violations or disagreements arise with the contract, they are usually handled and settled through the grievance procedure. The primary purpose of grievance procedures is to:
    a. avoid strike situations
    b. manage terminations
    c. provide counselling
    d. ensure justice to both parties
    e. permit complaints about the union

15. Once a collective agreement has been signed, it must be administered by management and adhered to by both parties. This reality of unionization affects HRM in a number of ways. Two of these ways are:
    a. employee motivation and morale
    b. productivity and decision making
    c. decision making and organizational structure
    d. organizational structure and productivity
    e. all of the above

# Notes

## Chapter 1


1. R. Amit & M. Belcourt. 1999. "Human Resources Management Processes: A Value-Creating Source of Competitive Advantage." *European Management Journal.* April:174–181. See also G.R. Ferris, W.A. Hochwarter, M.R. Buckley, G. Harrell-Cook & D.D. Frink, 1999. "Human Resource Management: Some New Directions." *Journal of Management.* 25:385–415.
2. Quotation from Eric Cousineau, an HR professional in Toronto with 35 years experience, as referenced in S. Klie, "HR professionals full of pride: Survey." *Canadian HR Reporter,* August 10, 2009.
3. A. Lado & M. Wilson. 1994. "Human Resource Systems and Sustained Competitive Advantage: A Competency-Based Perspective." *Academy of Management Review.* 19(4):699–727. Quote from C. Truss & L. Gratton, 1994. "Strategic Human Resource Management: A Conceptual Approach." *The International Journal of Human Resource Management.* September:663.
4. See R. Saltonstall, "Who's Who in Personnel Administration," Harvard Business Review 33 (July–August 1955), pp. 75-83 reprinted in P. Pigors, C. Meyers & F.P. Malm, Management of Human Resources (New York: McGraw-Hill, 1969), pp. 61–73.
5. Truss & Gratton. "Strategic Human Resource Management," p. 663.
6. R. Saltonstall, "Who's Who?" p. 63.
7. D. Harder, "Limitless or limiting: What is the future of HR in the virtual world?" *Canadian HR Reporter,* July 14, 2008.
8. Based on the definition provided in the handout distributed by the Bell Canada trainer at Workshop One in the seminar series titled, "Be There: A Series of e-Business Workshops Presented by Bell Canada and the Peterborough Chamber of Commerce." (May 18, 2000), p. 2; Simke, "Emerging Trends in Outsourcing," *CMA Management* (February 2000), pp. 26–27.
9. T. Belford. "HR Focusing on How It Can Add Value." *Globe and Mail* (March 25, 2002):B11.
10. B. Kreissel, J. Lutz, & D. Giusto, "How strategic is your HR department?" *Canadian HR Reporter,* October 6, 2008.
11. M. Belcourt, "Making a Difference . . . and Measuring It with the 5 C's," *Human Resources Professional* (December 1996–January 1997), pp. 20–24.
12. T.H. Wagar, "Do HRM Practices and Policies Matter? The Survey Says . . ." *The HRM Research Quarterly* (Spring 1999), pp. 1–4.
13. Watson Wyatt, *Human Capital Index Study,* cited in D. Brown, "The 30 Ways HR Adds Value to the Bottom Line," *Canadian HR Reporter* (December 13, 1999), pp. 1, 20, 31.
14. "Good HR Equals Good Performance," *Workplace Today* (January 2002), p. 7.
15. D. Brown, "Profit Driven by Good HR, Study Finds," *Canadian HR Reporter* (November 19, 2001), p. 3.
16. S. Klie, "HR increasingly a business partner: Survey," *Canadian HR Reporter* (January 26, 2009), pp. 10–11.
17. S. Klie, "HR profession on path to higher status," *Canadian HR Reporter,* March 24, 2008.
18. "CEOs Talk," *Canadian HR Reporter* (March 11, 2002), pp. 17–19.
19. R. Stringer, *Leadership and Organizational Climate* (Upper Saddle River, NJ: Prentice-Hall, 2000).
20. "Highly Skilled Workers Still Hard to Find," *Canadian HR Reporter* (February 3, 1999), p. 6.
21. W.B. Werther, Jr., W.A. Ruch & L. McClure, *Productivity through People* (St. Paul: West Publishing, 1986), pp. 3–5.
22. S. Nador, "Designing Your Own Best Practices to Attract and Retain Talent," *HR Professional* (August–September 1999), pp. 42–43.
23. J. Zeidenberg, "HR and the Innovative Company," *Human Resources Professional* (June 1996), pp. 12–15.
24. J. Kettle, "Casual Work Gets Serious," *Globe and Mail* (November 20, 1997), p. B4.
25. S. Klie, "Part timers could go full time at grocery giant," *Canadian HR Reporter,* March 23, 2009.
26. S. Ostry & M.A. Zaidi, *Labour Economics in Canada,* 2nd ed. (Toronto: MacMillan of Canada, 1972).
27. G. Ferris, D. Frink, & M.C. Galang, "Diversity in the Workplace: The Human Resources Management Challenge," *Human Resource Planning,* 16(1):42.
28. Statistics Canada, 2007. "Profile of Canadian population by age and sex: Canada ages." Statistics Canada Catalogue, #96F0030XIE2005006, Ottawa, July 16. Analysis Series.
29. Conference Board of Canada, 2006. *Executive Action: Too Few People, Too Little Time. The Employer Challenge of An Aging Workforce.* July 2006, 1–5.
30. Statistics Canada, 2007. Profile of Canadian population by age and sex: Canada ages. Statistics Canada Catalogue, #96F0030XIE2005006. Ottawa, July 16. Analysis Series, 2006 Census.
31. J. Thompson, *If you can't measure it; you can't manage it,* The J. Walter Thompson Specialized Communications Consulting Group. Presentation: January 2003.
32. Drake Beam Morin, *DBM Survey finds companies have not prepared younger workers for senior leadership roles,* May 2003.
33. R. Carey, "Fight the brain drain," *Successful Meetings,* 2003, 52(2):31–35.
34. C. Barrett, "Performance and potential 2005–2006: Trends reshaping our future." Conference Board of Canada, 1–5.
35. B. Kaye & S. Jordan-Evans, *Love 'em or Lose 'em* (Barrett-Koehler Publishers, 2005).
36. Based on material cited in "News and Views: Flex Appeal," compiled by M. Griffin, *HR Professional* (February–March 1999), p. 10; and research reported by P.I. Nyhof in "Managing Generation X: The Millennial Challenge," *Canadian HR Reporter* (May 22, 2000), pp. 7–8.
37. J. Izzo, *Values Shift: The New Work Ethic and What it Means for Business* (Toronto: Prentice Hall Canada, 2002).
38. J. Wolburg & R. Pokrywczynski, "A psychographic analysis of generation Y college students," *Journal of Advertising Research.* 2001, 41(5):33–52.
39. C. Loughlin & J. Barling, "Young workers' values, attitudes, and behaviours," *Journal of Occupational and Organizational Psychology,* 2001, 74:543–558.

40. C. Martin & B. Tulgan, *Managing the Generation Mix,* (New York: HRD Press, 2002).
41. C. Martin, "From high maintenance to productivity: What managers need to know about Generation Y," *Industrial and Commercial Training,* 2005, 37(1):39–44.
42. M. Miller, "The New Entrant to the Work/Life Balancing Act: Eldercare," *HR Professional* (August–September 1999), pp. 40–41; D. Brown, "Senate Proposes Leave Benefits for Palliative Care," *Canadian HR Reporter* (July 17, 2000), p. 6.
43. D. Brown, "Employers Confused by Compassionate Care Benefits," *Canadian HR Reporter* (February 9, 2004), pp. 1, 9.
44. Statistics Canada, *The Canada Year Book 1999* (Ottawa: Minister of Industry, 1998), Catalogue No. 11-402-XPE, p. 158.
45. Statistics Canada, *The Canada Year Book 1999,* p. 160; International Adult Literacy Survey (IALS) definition cited in W. Clark, "Adult Literacy in Canada, the United States, and Germany," *Canadian Social Trends* (Winter 1996), Statistics Canada Catalogue No. 11-008-XPE, p. 28.
46. *Workforce 2000* (Toronto: Hudson Institute Canada and Towers Perrin, 1993).
47. Clark, "Adult Literacy in Canada," pp. 28–33; Statistics Canada, *The Canada Year Book 1999,* p. 160.
48. Clark, "Adult Literacy in Canada," pp. 28–33; Statistics Canada, *The Canada Year Book 1999,* p. 160.
49. S. Klie, "Diversity makes employers more attractive to candidates," *Canadian HR Reporter* (April 20, 2009), p. 20.
50. Statistics Canada, *The Canada Year Book 1999,* p. 228.
51. S. Crompton & M. Vickers, "One Hundred Years of the Labour Force," *Canadian Social Trends* (Summer 2000), Statistics Canada Catalogue No. 11-008, p. 8.
52. Study conducted by the Center for Work–Life Policy and the Harvard Business Review as published in *HR Magazine,* June/July 2009, 26(4):16.
53. "Women: Ivey Leadership Renewal Program," *HR Magazine,* June/July 2009, 26(4):16.
54. Canadian Human Rights Commission, Annual Report of 1998, p. 33.
55. Diversity: Mastering Aboriginal Inclusion, *HR Magazine,* June/July 2009, 26(4):13.
56. From a Royal Bank of Canada study cited in A.M. Tobin, "Increase Hiring of Disabled, Bank Urges," *Toronto Star* (April 4, 2000).
57. E. McGregor, "Emerging Careers," *Occupational Outlook Quarterly* 34 (Fall 1990), p. 22.
58. E. McGregor, "Emerging Careers," *Occupational Outlook Quarterly* 34 (Fall 1990), p. 22.
59. "HR's Quest for Status: Fantasy or Emerging Reality?" *Canadian HR Reporter* and Watson Wyatt (August 2001).
60. G. Betcherman, K. McMullen, N. Leckie, & C. Caron, *The Canadian Workplace in Transition* (Kingston: IRC Press, Queen's University, 1994).
61. C.W. Hill, *International Business* (Burr Ridge, IL: Irwin, 1994), p. 6.
62. B. O'Reilly, "Your New Global Workforce," *Fortune* (December 14, 1992), pp. 52–66.
63. S. Dobson, "Found in translation: Multilingual employees can be huge asset in global economy," *Canadian HR Reporter,* January 26, 2009.
64. R.E. Miles, *Theories of Management* (New York: McGraw-Hill, 1975).
65. F.W. Taylor, "The Principles of Scientific Management," J.M. Sharfritz & J.S. Ott (Eds.), *Classics of Organization Theory,* 2nd ed. (Chicago: The Dorsey Press, 1987), pp. 66–81.
66. D.G. Nickels, J.M. McHugh, S.M. McHugh, & P.D. Berman, *Understanding Canadian Business,* 2nd ed. (Toronto: Irwin, 1997), p. 220.
67. This discussion is based on E.E. Lawler III, "Human Resources Management," *Personnel* (January 1988), pp. 24–25.
68. R.J. Cattano & A.J. Templer, "Determining the Effectiveness of Human Resources Management," T.H. Stone (Ed.), *ASAC: Personnel and Human Resources Division Proceedings* (Halifax, NS: St. Mary's University, June 1988), p. 73.
69. L. Young, "National Public-Service Association Explores International Outreach Initiatives," *Canadian HR Reporter* (June 5, 2000), p. 2.
70. D. Brown, "Canada Gets National HR Designation," *Canadian HR Reporter* (July 15, 2002), pp. 1, 13.
71. HRPA website: Certification requirements, www.hrpa.org.
72. S. Klie, "Senior HR designation unveiled," *Canadian HR Reporter,* July 13, 2009, pp. 1–2.
73. KPMG's Ethics Survey 2000—Managing for Ethical Practice cited in Young, "Companies Not Doing Right," p. 17. Excerpted from Human Resources Professionals Association of Ontario, *Becoming a Certified Human Resources Professional (CHRP).* Copyright © 2005. Used with permission of the HRPAO.
74. Based on Walker Information Canada Inc. study cited in J. Martin, "Studies Suggest a Link Between Employees' Perception of a Firm's Ethics—and Loyalty," *Canadian HR Reporter* (September 20, 1999), p. G7; and McDougall, "Employees Want an Ethical Work Environment," p. 4.
75. W. Henn, "What the Strategist Asks from Human Resources," *Human Resource Planning,* 8(4) (1985), p. 195; quoted in Greer, *Strategy and Human Resources,* p. 105.
76. Government of Canada, 2008, APEX Conference on Public Service Renewal, Privy Council Office.
77. K. Lynch, *Fifteenth Annual Report of the Clerk to the Prime Minister on the Public Service of Canada,* Ottawa, Ontario, March 31, 2008.
78. B.E. Becker, M.A. Huselid, & D. Ulrich, *The HR Scorecard: Linking People, Strategy and Performance* (Boston, MA: Harvard Business School Press, 2001); see also D. Brown, "Measuring the Value of HR," *Canadian HR Reporter* (September 24, 2001), pp. 1, 5.
79. R. Schuler & S. Jackson, "Linking Competitive Strategies with Human Resource Management Practices," *Academy of Management Executive,* 1(3) (1987), pp. 207–219.
80. D. Brown, "HR Must Ensure Individual Goals Are Met," *Canadian HR Reporter* (February 25, 2002), p. 12.
81. A. Lado & M. Wilson, "Human Resource Systems and Sustained Competitive Advantage: A Competency-Based Perspective," *Academy of Management Review,* 19(4) (1994), pp. 699–727. Quote from C. Truss & L. Gratton, "Strategic Human Resource Management: A Conceptual Approach," *The International Journal of Human Resource Management* (September 1994), p. 663.
82. Truss & Gratton, "Strategic Human Resource Management," p. 663.
83. V. Scarpello, "New Paradigm Approaches in Strategic Human Resource Management," *Group and Organization Management,* 19(2) (June 1994), pp. 160–164; and S. Peck, "Exploring the Link between Organizational Strategy and the Employment Relationships: The Role of Human Resources Policies," *Journal of Management Studies* 31(5) (September 1994), pp. 715–736.
84. HR under pressure, *Canadian HR Reporter,* February 9, 2009 p. 4.
85. S. Klie, "HR divided on need for licensing; Survey," *Canadian HR Reporter,* January 12, 2009, p. 8.
86. Mercer's online report (2008). *Engaging Employees to Drive Global Business Success: Insights from Mercer's What's Working Research.*

## Chapter 2

1. J. Smith, "N.W.T. revamps employment standards law," *Canadian HR Reporter,* June 2, 2008.

2. Canadian Charter of Rights and Freedoms as part of the Constitution Act of 1982.
3. "Mandatory retirement of JPs at age 70 unlawful: Court Judge rewrites legislation to allow justices of the peace to work until age 75," *Canadian HR Reporter*, June 3, 2008.
4. Study conducted by Catalyst, a New York-based research and advisory organization, entitled "Career Advancement in Corporate Canada: A Focus on Visible Minorities—Workplace Fit and Stereotyping," reported in "Minorities not comfortable being themselves at work: Study," *Canadian HR Reporter*, June 26, 2008.
5. R. Minken, "Bona fide job requirement or just a convenience: Hiring male to clean men's washrooms was easy for employer but passing over female was discrimination," *Canadian HR Reporter*, February 19, 2009.
6. Ontario Human Rights Commission, Human Rights at Work (Toronto: Government of Ontario, 1999), pp. 63–64.
7. Annual Report of the Canadian Human Rights Commission (Ottawa: Government of Canada, 1991), p. 63.
8. Annual Report of the Canadian Human Rights Commission (Ottawa: Government of Canada, 1981), p. 29.
9. C. Milne, "Proving undue hardship not impossible (Legal view): Acting in haste hurts employers' chances of showing hardship," *Canadian HR Reporter*, January 26, 2009.
10. Canadian Human Rights Commission, Harassment Casebook (Ottawa: Minister of Supply and Services Canada, 1993), p. 2.
11. Employment Equity Annual Report 2008.
12. S. Rudner, "Psychological harassment hurts employees, productivity," *Canadian HR Reporter*, October 21, 2007.
13. A.P. Agarwal, *Sexual Harassment in the Workplace,* 2nd ed. (Toronto: Butterworths Canada, 1992), pp. 10–11.
14. M. MacKillop, "Dismissal If Necessary; Not Necessarily Dismissal," *Human Resources Professional* (April 1996), pp. 24–25.
15. Catalyst Census of Women Corporate Officers and Top Earners of Canada, 2009.
16. *Employment Equity Act* Annual Report 2008.
17. As part of its contribution to the dissemination of Census findings, *Canadian Social Trends* is highlighting some of the key social trends observed in the 2006 Census. In this issue, they present adaptations from the following Census analytical documents: *Aboriginal Peoples in Canada in 2006: Inuit, Métis and First Nations, 2006 Census* (Catalogue no. 97-558-XWE2006001); *Educational Portrait of Canada, 2006 Census: Findings* (Catalogue no. 97-560-XWE2006001); and *Canada's Changing Labour Force, 2006 Census* (Catalogue no. 97-559-XWE2006001), as well as Census data on income, housing affordability and home ownership.
18. S. Dobson, "Research report profiles Aboriginal partnerships: Communication, understanding, and consultation needed for success," *Canadian HR Reporter,* May 4, 2009.
19. Annual Report, *Employment Equity Act,* 2008.
20. Employment Equity Annual Report 2008.
21. Employment Equity Annual Report 2008.
22. Statistics Canada, "Recent Immigrants in the Work Force," as cited in "Talent Pool Overlooked by Employers," *Workplace News* (May 1999), p. 16.
23. Employment Equity Annual Report 2008.
24. R.S. Abella, *Equality in Employment: A Royal Commission Report* (Ottawa: Supply and Services Canada, 1984).
25. The discussion on the implementation of employment equity is based on *Equity Works Best* and other material provided by the Ontario Women's Directorate, and *Employment Equity: A Guide for Employers* (Ottawa: Employment and Immigration Canada, May 1991), Cat. No. LM-143, pp. 5–91, except as noted.
26. Cited in K. Toughill, "Firms Back Equity: To Some It's 'Good Business Sense' Despite Harris' Vow to Scrap It," *Toronto Star* (June 21, 1995), p. A2.
27. *Employment Equity: A Guide for Employers,* pp. 5–91.
28. Canadian Human Rights Commission, Annual Report 1999, www.chrc-cdp.ca/news-comm/2000/annual-report-news-releases (July 26, 2000).
29. Statistics Canada, "Women in Canada," as cited in D. Brown "Wage Gap Persists," *Canadian HR Reporter* (October 9, 2000), pp. 1, 11.
30. Statistics Canada, *The Persistent Gap: New Evidence on the Canadian Gender Wage Gap,* cited in D. Brown, "StatsCan Unable to Explain Gender Wage Gap," *Canadian HR Reporter* (January 31, 2000), p. 3.
31. M. Gunderson & R.E. Robb, "Equal Pay for Work of Equal Value: Canadian Experience," *Advances in Industrial and Labour Relations* 5 (1991), pp. 151–168. See also J.G. Kelly, *Pay Equity Management* (Toronto: CCH Canadian Ltd., 1988), pp. 45–54.
32. J. Coutts, "OCA to Hire Women for Next 10 Years," *Toronto Star* (January 9, 1990), p. A13.
33. Annual Report of the Canadian Human Rights Commission (Ottawa: Government of Canada, 1985).
34. S. Klie, "Lots of talk, not much action on diversity: Four in 10 organizations don't have a plan to foster diversity: Report," *Canadian HR Reporter,* January 15, 2007.
35. Study conducted by Catalyst, a New York-based research and advisory organization, entitled "Career Advancement in Corporate Canada: A Focus on Visible Minorities—Workplace Fit and Stereotyping," reported in "Minorities not comfortable being themselves at work: Study," *Canadian HR Reporter,* June 26, 2008.
36. L. Young, "Employers at diversity tipping point: Studies show employers only paying lip service to diversity, but demographics will force their hands," *Canadian HR Reporter,* January 14, 2008.
37. J. Samuel, cited in J. Schilder, "The Rainbow Connection," *Human Resources Professional* (April 1994), pp. 13–15.
38. Cited in Ministry of Citizenship, Culture and Recreation: *Equal Opportunity in Ontario,* p. 3.
39. A. Cuneo, "Diverse by Design," *Business Week* (October 23, 1992), p. 72.
40. J. Schilder, "The Rainbow Connection," pp. 13–15.
41. C.L. Taylor, "Building a Case for Business Diversity," *Canadian Business Review* 22(1) (1995), pp. 12–15.
42. S. Klie, "Workplaces not inclusive enough: Visible minorities less satisfied at work—Study," *Canadian HR Reporter,* July 16, 2007.
43. S. Dobson, "Changing the ranks: Police forces are stirring up the status quo by focusing on diversity in recruiting," *Canadian HR Reporter,* March 23, 2009, p. 15.
44. Employment Equity Annual Report 2008.
45. D. Davies, "Equity Equations," *Human Resources Professional* (May 1993), pp. 15–17.
46. L. Young, "Employers at diversity tipping point: Studies show employers only paying lip service to diversity, but demographics will force their hands," *Canadian HR Reporter,* January 14, 2008.
47. D. McCutcheon, "HR 101: Diversity plans," *HR Magazine,* February/March 2009, pp. 49–52.
48. S. Klie, "Diversity makes employers more attractive to candidates," *Canadian HR Reporter,* April 20, 2009, p. 20.
49. S. Klie, "Diversity makes employers more attractive to candidates," *Canadian HR Reporter,* April 20, 2009, p. 20.
50. Based on L. Young, "Mentoring Program Is One Diversity Step in a Series at Rogers," *Canadian HR Reporter* (March 27, 2000), p. 8.

51. B. Siu, "Making Sense of Diversity Assessment Approaches," *Canadian HR Reporter* (November 1, 1999), p. 10.
52. S. Klie, "Workplaces not inclusive enough: Visible minorities less satisfied at work—Study," *Canadian HR Reporter,* July 16, 2007.

## Chapter 3

1. S. Mohrman, " Designing Organizations for Growth: The Human Resource Contribution," *Human Resource Planning,* 2007, 30(4), pp. 34–46.
2. R. Giroux, "Downsizing in the Federal Public Service," Canadian Speeches, Issues of the Day, September 2003, 7(5), p. 48.
3. R. Ashkenas, D. Ulrich, T. Jick, & S. Kerr, "The Boundaryless Organization," Jossey-Bass, San Francisco, 1997.
4. D. Devine & L. Clayton, "Teams in Organizations," *Small Team Research,* 1999, 30(6), pp. 678–711.
5. P. Chisholm, "Redesigning Work," *Maclean's,* March 5, 2001, p. 36.
6. J. Hackman, *Leading Teams: Setting the Stage for Greater Performance* (Boston: Harvard Business School Press, 2002).
7. S. Mohrman, "Designing Organizations for Growth: The Human Resource Contribution," *Human Resource Planning,* 2007, 30(4), pp. 34–46.
8. D. Chalk, "Wild About Wikis and Big on Blogs," *PeopleTalk,* Spring 2007, p. 59.
9. R. Jones, R. Oyung, & L. Pace, "Working Virtually: Challenges of Virtual Teams," (Hershey: CyberTech, 2005).
10. C. Gibson & S. Cohen, *Virtual Teams that Work.* (San Francisco: Jossey-Bass, 2003).
11. M. Nicholls, "Going Global (Virtual Meetings)," *Meetings & Incentive Travel,* April 2001, 30(2), p. 20.
12. M. Hammer & J. Champy, *Reengineering the Corporation* (New York: Harper Business, 1993), p. 32.
13. M. Hammer & J. Champy, *Reengineering,* p. 51.
14. H. Coleman, "Learn Now, Lean Forever," *Electrical Wholesaling,* April 2009, 90(4), pp. 48–50.
15. For example, Charles Babbage listed six reasons for making jobs as specialized as possible. Such specialization results in: (1) less learning time; (2) less waste of material during the training period; (3) less time lost in switching from task to task; (4) increased proficiency with practice; (5) more efficient hiring; and (6) more uniform and interchangeable parts. C. Babbage, *On the Economy of Machinery and Manufacturers* (London: Charles Knight, 1832), pp. 169–176; reprinted in J. Litterer, *Organizations* (New York: John Wiley and Sons, 1969), pp. 73–75.
16. S. Mohrman, "Designing Organizations for Growth: The Human Resource Contribution," *Human Resource Planning,* 2007, 30(4), pp. 34–46.
17. F. Herzberg, "One More Time, How Do You Motivate Employees?" *Harvard Business Review* (January–February 1968), pp. 53–62.
18. J.R. Hackman & G. Oldham, "Motivation through the Design of Work: Test of a Theory," *Organizational Behavior and Human Performance,* 16(2) (1976), pp. 250–279.
19. J.R. Hackman & G. Oldham, "Motivation through the Design of Work," pp. 257–258.
20. D.A. Nadler, J.R. Hackman, & E.E. Lawler, *Managing Organizational Behavior* (Boston: Little, Brown, 1979).
21. J.R. Hackman & G. Oldham, "Motivation through the Design of Work," pp. 255–256.
22. P. MacInnis, "Ergonomics: A Good Fit for Ailing Workers," *Computing Canada,* September 10, 2004, 30(12), pp. 36–37.
23. D. Bailey & N. Kurland, N. "A Review of Telework Research: Findings, New Directions, and Lessons for the Study of Modern Work," *Journal of Organizational Dynamics,* Vol. 28, pp. 383–400.
24. T. Baker, "Practical Tips for Remote Employees." February 2009, 81(2), pp. 18–20.
25. Anonymous, "Quote, Unquote: Trouble with Telecommuting," *Industrial Engineer,* April 2009, 41(4), p. 14.
26. Anonymous, "2008 Was the Year that Redefined the Concept of "Telecommuting," *CPA Practice Management Forum,* March 2009, 5(3), pp. 18–19.
27. A. Felstead, N. Jewson, A. Phizacklea & S. Walters, "The Option to Work at Home: Another Privilege for the Favoured Few?" *New Technology, Work and Employment,* 17(3), pp. 204–223.
28. M. Collins, "The (not so simple) Case for Teleworking: A Study at Lloyd's of London," *New Technology, Work and Employment,* 2005, 20(2), pp. 115–32.
29. P. Browne, "Teleworking is Here to Stay: Bad Employees are Bad No Matter the Location," April 2, 2008, p. WK 4.
30. M. Morra, *HR Professional,* February/March 2009, p. 29.
31. C. Sullivan, "What's in a Name? Definitions and Conceptualisations of Teleworking and Homeworking," *New Technology, Work and Employment,* 2005, 18(3), pp. 158–65.
32. F. Clear & K. Dickson, "Teleworking Practice in Small and Medium-sized Firms: Management Style and Worker Autonomy," *New Technology, Work and Employment,* 2005, 20(3), pp. 218–233.
33. I. Cruickshank, "Telework Lessons from Telus," *Canadian HR Reporter,* October 6, 2008, 21(17), p. 15.
34. D. Bowen & E. Lawler, "The Empowerment of Service Workers: What, Why, How, When," *Sloan Management Review,* Spring 1992, 33(3), pp. 31–39.
35. I. Ugboro, "Organizational Commitment, Job Redesign, Employee Empowerment and Intent to Quit Among Survivors of Restructuring and Downsizing," *Journal of Behavioral and Applied Management,* May 2006, 7(3), pp. 232–245.
36. D. Irvine, "What is Employee Engagement: What It Is and Why You Need It," *Business Week* (online), May 11, 2009.
37. For a good discussion of job analysis, see J. Clifford, "Job Analysis: Why Do It, and How Should It Be Done?" *Public Personnel Management* (Summer 1994), pp. 321–340.
38. F.P. Morgeson & M.A. Campion, "Social and Cognitive Sources of Potential Inaccuracy in Job Analysis," *Journal of Applied Psychology* 85(5) (1997), pp. 627–655.
39. J.I. Sanchez & E.L. Levine, "Accuracy or Consequential Validity: Which Is the Better Standard for Job Analysis Data?" *Journal of Organizational Behavior* 21 (2000), pp. 809–818; F.P. Morgeson & M.A. Campion, "Accuracy in Job Analysis: Toward an Inference-Based Model," *Journal of Organizational Behavior* 21 (2000), pp. 819–827.
40. R.J. Harvey & M.A. Wilson, "Yes Virginia, There Is an Objective Reality in Job Analysis," *Journal of Organizational Behavior* 21 (2000), pp. 829–854.
41. D. Gayeski, T. Golden, S. Andrade & H. Mason, "Bringing Competency Analysis into the 21st Century," *Performance Improvement,* August 2007, 46(7), pp. 9–16.
42. N. Jagmin, "Assessing and Rewarding competencies: The Ten Year Tune Up at Frito Lay," *Presentation for the Centre for Organizational Effectiveness,* April 2003, Marina del Rey, California.
43. R. Henderson, *Compensation Management: Rewarding Performance* (Englewood Cliffs, NJ: Prentice-Hall, 1994), pp. 139–150. See also P.W. Wright & K. Wesley, "How to Choose the Kind of Job Analysis You Really Need," *Personnel* (May 1985), pp. 51–55; C.J. Cranny & M.E. Doherty,

"Importance Ratings in Job Analysis: Note on the Misinterpretation of Factor Analyses," *Journal of Applied Psychology* (May 1988), pp. 320–322.

44. Henderson, *Compensation Management,* pp. 148–152.
45. R. Pagliarini, "The World Cafe—Shaping Our Futures through Conversations that Matter," *Journal of Organizational Change Management,* 2006, 19(2), pp. 266–268.
46. The PAQ (and other quantitative techniques) can also be used for job evaluation.
47. Note that job evaluation is the process through which jobs are compared with one another and their values determined. Although usually viewed as a job analysis technique, the PAQ is, in practice, actually as much or more of a job evaluation technique. For a discussion of how to use the PAQ for classifying jobs, R.J. Harvey et al., "Dimensionality of the Job Element Inventory, A Simplified Worker-Oriented Job Analysis Questionnaire," *Journal of Applied Psychology* (November 1988), pp. 639–646; S. Butler & R. Harvey, "A Comparison of Holistic versus Decomposed Rating of Position Analysis Questionnaire Work Dimensions," *Personnel Psychology* (Winter 1988), pp. 761–772.
48. This discussion is based on H. Olson et al., "The Use of Functional Job Analysis in Establishing Performance Standards for Heavy Equipment Operators," *Personnel Psychology* 34 (1981), pp. 351–364.
49. Human Resources Development Canada, *National Occupation Classification Career Handbook,* p. 2.
50. Human Resources Development Canada, *National Occupation Classification Career Handbook,* p. 2.
51. J. Evered, "How to Write a Good Job Description," *Supervisory Management* (April 1981), pp. 14–19; R.J. Plachy, "Writing Job Descriptions That Get Results," *Personnel* (October 1987), pp. 56–58. See also M. Mariani, "Replace with a Database," *Occupational Outlook Quarterly* 43(1) (1999), pp. 2–9.
52. J. Evered, "How to Write," p. 16.
53. J. Evered, "How to Write," p. 16.
54. J. Evered, "How to Write," p. 17.
55. J. Evered, "How to Write," p. 18.
56. E. Dale, *Organizations* (New York: American Management Association, 1967).
57. Based on E.J. McCormick & Joseph Tiffin, *Industrial Psychology* (Englewood Cliffs, NJ: Prentice-Hall, 1974), pp. 56–61.
58. Human Resources Skills Development Canada, *National Occupation Classification Career Handbook,* pp. 8–23.
59. S. Leonard, "The Demise of Job Descriptions," *HR Magazine,* August 2000, 45(8), p. 184.
60. Anonyous, "Putting the Life Back into Employees," *China Staff,* October 2006, 12(9), pp 22–24.
61. A. Taylor, "Home-Working Requests Rarely Granted," *Financial Times,* May 26, 2008, p. 4.
62. C. Plaza, "International: Incentives to Work," *Employee Benefits,* December 2007, p. 29.

## Chapter 4

1. B. Parker & D. Caine, "Holonic Modelling: Human Resource Planning and the Two Faces of Janus," *International Journal of Manpower* 17(8), pp. 30–45.
2. M. Birchall-Spencer, interview: "Donna Wilson Shares her Gold Medal People Strategy for Vancouver's 2010 Olympic Winter Games," *HR Professional,* Dec/08–Jan/09, 26(1), pp. 53–56.
3. D. Bennett & M. Brush, "The Annual HR Strategic Planning Process: Design and Facilitation Lessons from Corning Incorporated Human Resources." *Organization Development Journal.* Chesterland: Fall 2007, Vol. 25, Iss. 3, p. 87.
4. L. Cassiani, "Looming Retirement Surge Takes on New Urgency," *Canadian HR Reporter* (May 21, 2001), pp. 1, 10.
5. E. Beauchesne, "Severe Labour Shortage Seen within 10 Years," *National Post* (September 8, 2003), pp. FP 1, FP 10; D. Brown, "HR and the Workforce 10 Years from Now," *Canadian HR Reporter* (October 20, 2003), pp. 1, 5; "Severe Labour Shortage Looming," *Toronto Star* (January 27, 2004), p. D3.
6. Conference Board of Canada. "Canadian Outlook Long-Term Forecast 2008: Economic Forecast," June 2008.
7. Conference Board of Canada. "Canadian Outlook Long-Term Forecast 2008: Economic Forecast," June 2008.
8. Government of Canada. "2008 APEX Conference on Public Service Renewal," Privy Council Office. www.pco.bcp.gc.ca.
9. H.G. Heneman, Jr. & G. Seitzer, "Manpower Planning and Forecasting in the Firm: An Exploratory Probe," in E. Burack and J. Walker, *Manpower Planning and Programming* (Boston: Allyn & Bacon, 1972), pp. 102–120; S. Zedeck & M. Blood, "Selection and Placement" from *Foundations of Behavioral Science Research in Organizations* (Monterey, CA: Brooks/Cole, 1974), in J.R. Hackman, E. Lawler III, & L. Porter, *Perspectives on Behavior in Organizations* (New York: McGraw-Hill, 1977), pp. 103–119.
10. R. Hawk, *The Recruitment Function* (New York: American Management Association, 1967). See also P. Pakchar, "Effective Manpower Planning," *Personnel Journal* 62(10) (1983), pp. 826–830.
11. R.B. Frantzreb, "Human Resource Planning: Forecasting Manpower Needs," *Personnel Journal* 60(11) (1981), pp. 850–857. See also J. Gridley, "Who Will Be Where When? Forecast the Easy Way," *Personnel Journal,* 65 (1986), pp. 50–58.
12. G. Milkovich, A.J. Annoni, & T.A. Mahoney, "The Use of Delphi Procedures in Manpower Forecasting," *Management Science* 19(4) (1972) pp. 381–388.
13. A.L. Delbecq, A.H. Van DelVen, & D.H. Gustafson, *Group Techniques for Program Planning: A Guide to Nominal and Delphi Processes* (Glenview, Illinois: Scott Foresman, 1975).
14. A. Alquest. "Managing in the Fog: Corporate Planning," *The Economist,* Feb. 28, 2009, 390 (8620), p. 67.
15. V. Mariga & D. Gambrill, "Future Planning," *Canadian Underwriter* (2007), 74(6), pp. 48–50.
16. N.C. Agarwal, "Human Resources Planning," p. 239.
17. For more information, visit the HRSDC Web site at www.hrdc-drhc.gc.ca.
18. C. Vander Doelen, "Canadian Workers to Get Buyouts: Sources Say Canadian Company Hopes 25% of Employees Take the Offer," *Times Colonist,* October 30, 2008, p. B4.
19. M. Evans, "Telus Offers Departure Packages to 11,000 Staff: Part of $300M in Cuts," *National Post,* June 8, 2002, p. 1.
20. D.A. Bratton, "Moving Away from Nine to Five," *Canadian Business Review* (Spring 1986), pp. 15–17.
21. O. Bertin, "Part-Time Work: Boom or Bust," *The Daily,* March 10, 2006, p. 8.
22. G. Surridge, "Printing Giant Cuts 1,500 Jobs: Clampdown on Advertising Spending Puts Squeeze on Transcontinental," *National Post,* February 19, 2009, p. 1.
23. Right Management Consultants Inc. Survey, reported in "HR Issues Sinking Mergers, Acquisitions," *Canadian HR Reporter* (May 31, 1999), p. 16.
24. T. Wagar, "The Death of Downsizing: Not Yet!" *HR Professional* (February–March 1999), pp. 41–43.
25. Based on J. Brockner, "The Effects of Work Layoffs on Survivors: Research, Theory, and Practice," in M. Staw & L.L. Cummings (Eds.),

*Research in Organizational Behavior* (Greenwich, CT: JAI, 1988), pp. 213–255 and D.M. Noer, *Healing the Wounds: Overcoming the Trauma of Layoffs and Revitalizing Downsized Organizations* (San Francisco: Jossey-Bass, 1993), pp. 87–185.
26. R.D. Gatewood & H.S. Field, *Human Resource Selection* (Chicago: The Dryden Press, 1990), p. 8.
27. Economic Council of Canada, 2006 national survey accessed through Deloitte website: www.deloitte.com.
28. J. Daum, "Internal Promotion—Psychological Asset or Debit? A Study of the Effects of Leader Origin," *Organizational Behavior and Human Performance* 13 (1975), pp. 404–413.
29. See, for example, A. Harris, "Hiring Middle Management: External Recruitment or Internal Promotion?" *Canadian HR Reporter* (April 10, 2000), pp. 8–10.
30. Career Mosaic Study, reported in "Internet Job Seekers Diversify," *Canadian HR Reporter* (December 13, 1999), p. 17; and "It Isn't Just for Techies Anymore," *HR Professional* (February–March 2000), p. 10.
31. Anonymous, "Online Recruitment: Shedding Light on Technology for the Future," *Recruiter,* December 10, 2008, p. 34.
32. H. Meredith & J. Lund, "New Recruiting Strategies: How Far Will You Go To Attract Top Talent?" *PeopleTalk,* Spring 2007, p. 37.
33. Cited in A. Altass, "E-Cruiting: A Gen-X Trend or Wave of the Future?" *HR Professional* 17(3) (June–July 2000), p. 29.
34. "Social Networking" Robert Half, *Law Office Management and Administration Report,* Dec. 2008, p. 11–15.
35. R. Half, "Social Networking for Recruitment," *Law Office Management and Administration Report,* December 2008.
36. A. Taylor, "Big Companies Hiring Staff via Own Websites," *Financial Times,* London, UK, June 28, 2007, p. 5.
37. Martell, "Résumé Volumes Push Firms to Web," p. 45.
38. Altass, "E-Cruiting: A Gen-X Trend or Wave of the Future?" p. 33.
39. Altass, "E-Cruiting: A Gen-X Trend or Wave of the Future?" p. 29.
40. L. Lines, "Canadian Employers Lagging Behind in Use of Corporate Websites for Recruitment," *Canadian HR Reporter,* November 19, 2001, p. 12.
41. Cited in Y. Lermusiaux, "Recruiting Effectively over the Internet," *Canadian HR Reporter* 12(7) (April 5, 1999), p. 2.
42. A. Da Luz, "Media Metrix, Comscore Networks," *Canadian HR Reporter,* December 2008, p. 7.
43. A. Pell, *Recruiting and Selecting Personnel* (New York: Regents, 1969, pp. 16–34). See also B. Hunger, "How to Choose a Recruitment Advertising Agency," *Personnel Journal* 64(12) (1985), pp. 60–62. For an excellent review of ads, see M. Magnus, *Personnel Journal* (August 1985 and August 1986), and R. Martin, "Recruitment Ad Ventures," *Personnel Journal* 66 (August 1987), pp. 46–63. For a discussion of how behaviour can influence the initial attraction to an advertisement, see T. Redman & B. Mathews, "Advertising for Effective Managerial Recruitment," *Journal of General Management* 18(2) (1992), pp. 29–42.
44. A. Tomlinson, "Finding Talented Grads Isn't Hard If You Play the Right Cards," *Canadian HR Reporter* (November 19, 2001), pp. 9, 11.
45. S. Jones, "You've Come a Long Way Baby: What the Staffing Industry Offers Today," *Canadian HR Reporter* (November 5, 2001), p. 15.
46. L. Young, "Headhunters Set Sights on Middle Management," *Canadian HR Reporter* (July 12, 1999), pp. 1, 5.
47. A. Pell, *Recruiting and Selecting Personnel,* pp. 16–34.
48. R. Ray, G. Silnicki, E. Pooley, & G. Scott, "Future Leaders," *Canadian Business,* October 22, 2007, 80(21), pp. 147–151.
49. C. Lachnit, "Employee Referral Saves Time, Saves Money, Delivers Quality," *Workforce Management,* 2001, 80(6), pp. 66–70.
50. C. Lachnit, "Employee Referral Saves Time, Saves Money, Delivers Quality," *Workforce Management,* 2001, 80(6), pp. 66–70.
51. R. Yerema, "The Top 100," *Maclean's,* October 13, 2008, 121(40), pp. 56–59.
52. L. Dickens, "Part-Time Employees: Workers Whose Time Has Come?" *Employee Relations* 14(2) (1992), pp. 3–12.
53. J. Pearce, "Toward an Organizational Behavior of Contract Laborers: Their Psychological Involvement and Effects on Employee Co-Workers," *Academy of Management Journal* 36 (1993), pp. 1082–1096; see also L. Corwin, "Now You See Them, Now You Don't: Using Contract Staff," *Canadian HR Reporter* (March 12, 2001), pp. 14, 16.
54. H. Hodgman, "The Next Office Temp Could Be You," *Human Resources Professional* 12(3) (May 1995), p. 17.
55. O. Parker & D. Gore, "The Changing Workforce: Are We Ready?" *Canadian HR Reporter* (August 13, 2001), p. 13; "Business, Government Unprepared for Worker Shortage," *Canadian HR Reporter* (November 5, 2001), p. 2.
56. P. Benimadhu, "Meet Needs of Older Workers, Firms Told," *The Province,* October 19, 2008, p. D4.
57. E. Miller, "Capitalizing on Older Workers," *Canadian HR Reporter* (June 16, 1997), p. 14.
58. E. Miller, "Capitalizing on Older Workers," p. 14.
59. E. Miller, "Capitalizing on Older Workers," p. 14, except Xerox example.
60. J. Izzo, "Values Shift: The New Work Ethic and What it Means for Business," 2002.
61. R. Zemke, "Here Come the Millenials," *Training,* 2001, 38(7), pp. 44–49.
62. C. Martin, "From High Maintenance to High Productivity: What Managers Need to Know About Generation Y," *Industrial and Commercial Training,* 2005, 37(1), pp. 39–44.
63. R. Wright, "From Exclusion to Inclusion," *Canadian HR Reporter* (February 11, 2002), pp. G7, G9.
64. www.ccab.com/monster.htm (March 22, 2005).
65. "Youth Equity at the Bank of Montreal," *Canadian HR Reporter* (October 20, 1997), p. 12.
66. S. LeBrun, "Booklets to Connect Disabled with Work," *Canadian HR Reporter* (October 20, 1997), p. 8.
67. A. Mirza, "Talent Management: Recruiting International Candidates," *HR Professional,* Dec 08/Jan 09, 26(1), p. 27.

## Chapter 5

1. R.D. Gatewood & H.S. Field, *Human Resources Selection* (Chicago: The Dryden Press, 1990), p. 3.
2. Hay Group and Business $ense Survey, cited in L. Young, "Organizations Searching for 'Fit' in Business Grads," *Canadian HR Reporter* (February 28, 2000), p. 3.
3. D. Bowers & B. Kleiner, "Behavioural Interviewing," *Management Research News* (2005), 28(11/12), pp. 107–114.
4. Angus Reid Survey for William M. Mercer Ltd., cited in E. Atkins, "Talent Rules," *Workplace News* (May 1999), pp. 1, 2.
5. Murray Axmith & Associates Survey (1999), cited in A. Macaulay, "Employers Getting Picky at Hiring Time," *Canadian HR Reporter* (August 14, 2000), pp. 1, 6.
6. D. Payne, "Staffing Can Cost You In More Ways Than One," *Medical Post* (2003), p. 15.
7. D. Hagel, "Why You Need to Hire the Best," *The Canadian Manager,* Spring 2007, 32(1), pp. 12–13.
8. D. Hagel, "Why You Need to Hire the Best," *The Canadian Manager,* Spring 2007, 32(1), pp. 12–13.

9. W.R.B. v. Plint, cited in J. Miller, "Employers Liable for Worker Crimes," (February 8, 1999), p. 5.
10. S.L. McShane, "Wrongful Dismissal Risks in Employee Selection," *Human Resources Professional* (February–March 1997), pp. 20–25.
11. S.A. Way & J.W. Thacker, "Selection Practices: Where Are Canadian Organizations?" *HR Professional* (October–November 1999), p. 33.
12. *Canadian HR Reporter,* April 20, 2009, p. 4.
13. D. Severyn, "Webcam Presentations as part of the Hiring Process," *Career Options Magazine,* Winter/Spring 2009, pp. 51–52.
14. D. Power, "Holt Renfrew Turns Around HR with Technology," *WWD New York,* April 4, 2007, 193(71), p. 12.
15. M. McDaniel et al., "The Validity of Employment Interviews: A Comprehensive Review and Meta-analysis," *Journal of Applied Psychology* 79(4) (1994), p. 599.
16. S. Simola, S. Taggar & G. Smith, "The Employment Selection Interview: Disparity Among Research-Based Recommendations, Current Practices, and What Matters to Human Rights Tribunals," *Canadian Journal of Administrative Sciences,* March 2007, 24(1), pp. 30–45.
17. D. Warmke & D. Weston, "Success Dispels Myths About Panel Interviewing," *Personnel Journal,* April 1992, 71(4), pp. 120–127.
18. S.A. Way & J.W. Thacker, "Selection Practices," p. 34.
19. A. Huffcutt et al., "A Meta-Analytic Investigation of Cognitive Ability in Employment Interview Evaluations: Moderating Characteristics and Implications for Incremental Validity," *Journal of Applied Psychology* 81(5) (1996), p. 459.
20. S.A. Way & J.W. Thacker, "Selection Practices," p. 34.
21. M. McDaniel et al., "The Validity of Employment Interviews," p. 602.
22. M. McDaniel et al., "The Validity of Employment Interviews," p. 601.
23. M. McDaniel et al., "The Validity of Employment Interviews," p. 601.
24. See P. Roth & J. McMillan, "The Behavior Description Interview," *The CPA Journal* (December 1993), pp. 76–79.
25. S. Simola, S. Taggar & G. Smith, "The Employment Selection Interview: Disparity Among Research-Based Recommendations, Current Practices, and What Matters to Human Rights Tribunals," *Canadian Journal of Administrative Sciences,* March 2007, 24(1), pp. 30–45.
26. A. Pell, *Recruiting and Selecting Personnel* (New York: Regents, 1969), p. 119.
27. M. Bolch, "Lights, Camera . . . Interview!" *HR Magazine,* March 2007, 52(3), pp. 99–102.
28. R. Dipboye, G. Fontenelle, & K. Garner, "Effect of Previewing the Application on Interview Process and Outcomes," *Journal of Applied Psychology* 69(1) (1984), pp. 118–128.
29. See R. Arvey & J. Campion, "The Employment Interview: A Summary and Review of Recent Research," *Personnel Psychology* 35 (1982), pp. 281–322.
30. See, for example, M. Heilmann & L. Saruwatari, "When Beauty Is Beastly: The Effects of Appearance and Sex on Evaluation of Job Applicants for Managerial and Nonmanagerial Jobs," *Organizational Behavior and Human Performance* 23 (1979), pp. 360–722. See also C. Marlowe, S. Schneider, & C. Nelson, "Gender and Attractiveness Biases in Hiring Decisions: Are More Experienced Managers Less Biased?" *Journal of Applied Psychology* 81(1) (1996), pp. 11–21.
31. C. Marlowe et al., "Gender and Attractiveness Biases," p. 11.
32. A. Pell, "Nine Interviewing Pitfalls," *Managers* (January 1994), p. 29.
33. T. Dougherty, D. Turban, & J. Callender, "Confirming First Impressions in the Employment Interview: A Field Study of Interviewer Behavior," *Journal of Applied Psychology* 79(5) (1994), p. 663.
34. See A. Pell, "Nine Interviewing Pitfalls," p. 29; P. Sarathi, "Making Selection Interviews Effective," *Management and Labor Studies* 18(1) (1993), pp. 5–7.
35. B. Losyk, "How to Hire the Right People," *Public Management,* June 2003, 85(5), p. 24.
36. See also P. Lowry, "The Structured Interview: An Alternative to the Assessment Center?" *Public Personnel Management* 23(2) (1994), pp. 201–215.
37. B. Paik, "Panel Interviews: Are Four Heads Better Than One," October 1996, 75(10), p. 111.
38. A. Pell, *Recruiting and Selecting Personnel,* pp. 103–115.
39. B. Paik, "Panel Interviews: Are Four Heads Better Than One," October 1996, 75(10), p. 111.
40. W.H. Wiesner & R.J. Oppenheimer, "Note-Taking in the Selection Interview: Its Effect upon Predictive Validity and Information Recall." Proceedings of the Annual Conference, Administrative Sciences Association of Canada (Personnel and Human Resources Division) 12(8) (1991), pp. 97–106.
41. S. Simola, S. Taggar & G. Smith, "The Employment Selection Interview: Disparity Among Research-Based Recommendations, Current Practices, and What Matters to Human Rights Tribunals," *Canadian Journal of Administrative Sciences,* March 2007, 24(1), pp. 30–45.
42. J.A. Breaugh, "Realistic Job Previews: A Critical Appraisal and Future Research Directions," *Academy of Management Review* 8(4) (1983), pp. 612–619.
43. J. Simmons, "Testing Techniques Provide Efficient, Standardized Procedures for Screening Candidates," *Journal of Human Resources,* Spring 2007.
44. J. Simmons, "Testing Techniques Provide Efficient, Standardized Procedures for Screening Candidates," *Journal of Human Resources,* Spring 2007.
45. R. Morin, "Hiring Shouldn't Be A Subjective Process," *Canadian HR Reporter,* March 26, 2007, 20(6), p. 31.
46. Way & Thacker, "Selection Practices," p. 34.
47. N. Williams, "Psychometric Tests Used for Staff Development," *Personnel Today,* March 3, 2009, p. 45.
48. R. Morin, "Hiring Shouldn't Be A Subjective Process," *Canadian HR Reporter,* March 26, 2007, 20(6), p. 31.
49. *Guidelines for Educational and Psychological Testing* (Old Chelsea, Quebec: Canadian Psychological Association, 1987).
50. Except as noted, this is based largely on L. Siegel & I. Lane, *Personnel and Organizational Psychology* (Homewood, IL: Irwin, 1982), pp. 170–185. See also Tyler, Tests and Measurements, pp. 38–79.
51. Except as noted, this is based largely on L. Siegel & I. Lane, *Personnel and Organizational Psychology* (Homewood, IL: Irwin, 1982), pp. 170–185. See also Tyler, Tests and Measurements, pp. 38–79.
52. R. Reilly, S. Zedeck, & M. Tenopyr, "Validity and Fairness of Physical Ability Tests for Predicting Performance in Craft Jobs," *Journal of Applied Psychology* 64(3) (1970), pp. 262–274. See also B. Daniel, "Strength and Endurance Testing," *Personnel Journal* (June 1987), pp. 112–122.
53. C. Colacci, "Testing Helps You Decrease Disability Costs," *Canadian HR Reporter* (June 14, 1999), p. G4.
54. This approach calls for construct validation, which, as was pointed out, is extremely difficult to demonstrate.
55. R. Tett, D. Jackson, & M. Rothstein, "Personality Measures as Predictors of Job Performance: A Meta-analytic Review," *Personnel Psychology* 44 (1991), p. 732. For a related study, see P. Raymark, M. Schmit, & R. Guion, "Identifying Potentially Useful Personality Constructs for Employee Selection," *Personnel Psychology* 50(3) (1997), pp. 723–736; and C. Fischer & G. Boyle, "Personality and Employee Selection: Credibility Regained," *Asia Pacific Journal of HRM* 35(2) (1997), pp. 26–40.
56. Tett, Jackson, & Rothstein, "Personality Measures," p. 732.

57. M.D. Dunnette & W.D. Borman, "Personnel Selection and Classification Systems," *Annual Review of Psychology* 30 (1979), pp. 477–525, quoted in Siegel & Lane, *Personnel and Organizational Psychology,* pp. 182–183.
58. S. Jackson, "Are You Hiring the Best Person for the Job," *Canadian HR Reporter,* September 2000, 13(16), pp. G 4–5.
59. H. Conn, "Zappos," *PeopleTalk,* Fall 2008, p. 11.
60. J. Weekley & C. Jones, "Video-Based Situational Testing," *Personnel Psychology* 50 (1997), p. 25.
61. J. Weekley & C. Jones, "Video-Based Situational Testing," pp. 26–30.
62. J. Weekley & C. Jones, "Video-Based Situational Testing," p. 46.
63. J. Jones & W. Terris, "Post-Polygraph Selection Techniques," *Recruitment Today* (May–June 1989), pp. 25–31.
64. For a discussion of such concerns, see, for example, K. Murphy, "Detecting Infrequent Deception," *Journal of Applied Psychology* 72(4) (1987), pp. 611–614.
65. M.B. Currrie and N. Eber, "Appealing Reasons," *OH&S Canada* (December 2002), pp. 18–21.
66. A. Tomlinson, "No Clear Cut Answers to Drug Test," *Canadian HR Reporter* (May 6, 2002), pp. 4, 11. See also Canadian Human Rights Commission Policy on Alcohol and Drug Testing. Canadian Human Rights Commission, June 2002.
67. C. Hoglund, "Mandatory Drug Testing," *Human Resources Professional* (January 1992), pp. 21–22.
68. Catano, "Alberta Suncor Says its Reviewing Drug Testing After Human Rights Ruling," *Canadian Press Newswire,* January 12, 2002.
69. M. Axmith, Survey 2000: Canadian Hiring, Retention and Dismissal Practices, p. 13.
70. K. Vermond, "Online Social Networking," *Profit,* May 2007, 26(2), p. 101.
71. L. Young, "Reference Checking Skills Sorely Lacking," *Canadian HR Reporter* (January 25, 1999), p. 1–2.
72. M. Stamler, "Employment Gaps, References Should Be Scrutinized," *Canadian HR Reporter* (April 8, 1996) p. 11, 15.
73. Stamler, "Employment Gaps," p. 15.
74. R.S. Echlin, "References Redux," *Human Resources Professional* 7(8) (September 1991), pp. 7–8.
75. B. Kleinmutz, "Why We Still Use Our Heads Instead of Formulas: Toward an Integrative Approach," *Psychological Bulletin* 107 (1990), pp. 296–310.
76. Gatewood & Field, *Human Resources Selection,* p. 89.
77. L. Tyler, Tests and Measurements (Englewood Cliffs, NJ: Prentice-Hall, 1971), p. 25. More technically, "validity refers to the degree of confidence one can have in inferences drawn from scores, considering the whole process by which the scores are obtained. Stated differently, validity refers to the confidence one has in the meaning attached to scores." See also R.M. Guion, "Changing Views for Personnel Selection Research," *Personnel Psychology* 40(2) (1987), p. 208.
78. L. Laroche, "Hiring Abroad," *CMA Management,* March 2002, 76(1), pp. 57–58.

## Chapter 6

1. See, for example, G. Chao et al., "Organizational Socialization: Its Content and Consequences," *Journal of Applied Psychology* 79(5) (1994), pp. 730–743.
2. M. Belcourt, "Working 101," *Canadian HR Reporter* (May 7, 2001), pp. 17–18.
3. C. Martin, "From High Maintenance to High Productivity: What Managers Need to Know About Generation Y." *Industrial and Commercial Training* 37(1) (2005), pp. 39–44.
4. R. Hastings, "Millennials Expect a Lot from Leaders," *HR Magazine* 53(1), p. 30.
5. R. Zemke, C. Raines & B. Filipczak, "Generations at Work: Managing the Clash of Veterans, Boomers, Xers, and Nexters in Your Workplace," (Washington, DC: American Management Association, 2000), pp. 45–54.
6. N. Tollinsky, "Technology Puts Employees in Orientation Program's Driver's Seat," *Canadian HR Reporter* (April 9, 2001), pp. 19–20.
7. R. Westwood, "Orientation: Taking it Online and the Trend to Blend," www.westwood-dynamics.com/all_about_orientation/article_taking_it_online.htm, downloaded December 16, 2008.
8. A. Macaulay, "The Long and Winding Road," *Canadian HR Reporter* (November 16, 1998), pp. G1–G10.
9. McKinsey Report, "Making Talent a Strategic Priority," *The McKinsey* Quarterly (Sept. 2008), pp. 3–5.
10. Statistics Canada (2007), "Profile of Canadian Population by Age and Sex: Canada Ages," Statistics Canada Catalogue, #96F0030XIE2005006. Ottawa, July 16. Analysis Series, 2006 Census.
11. G. McIntyre, "Rising to the Challenge," *Canadian Investment* Guide (12) pp. 5–8.
12. B. Kaye & S. Jordan-Evans, *Love 'Em or Lose 'Em* (New York: Barrett-Koehler Publishers, 2005), p. 28.
13. This is based on K. Wexley & G. Latham, *Developing and Training Human Resources in Organizations* (Glenview, IL: Scott, Foresman, 1981), pp. 22–27.
14. K. Sovereign, *Personnel Law* (Englewood Cliffs, NJ: Prentice-Hall, Inc., 1994), pp. 165–166.
15. These are based on Sovereign, *Personnel Law,* pp. 165–166.
16. S. Lebrun, "T & D Becoming More Strategic," *Canadian HR Reporter* (February 10, 1997), pp. 1, 2.
17. K. Wexley & G. Latham, *Developing and Training Human Resources in Organizations,* p. 107.
18. "German Training Model Imported," *BNA Bulletin to Management* (December 19, 1996), p. 408.
19. S. Harris-Lalonde, *Training and Development Outlook* (Ottawa: The Conference Board of Canada, 1999), p. 11.
20. M. Emery & M. Schubert, "A Trainer's Guide to Videoconferencing," *Training* (June 1993), p. 60.
21. G.N. Nash, J.P. Muczyk, & F.L. Vettori, "The Role and Practical Effectiveness of Programmed Instruction," *Personnel Psychology* 24 (1971), pp. 397–418.
22. K. Wexley & G. Latham, Developing and Training, p. 141. See also R. Wlozkowski, "Simulation," *Training and Development Journal* 39(6) (1985), pp. 38–43.
23. S. Lebrun, "T & D Becoming More Strategic," *Canadian HR Reporter* (February 10, 1997), pp. 1–2.
24. "Pros and Cons of E-learning," *Canadian HR Reporter* (July 16, 2001), pp. 11, 15.
25. D. Murray, E-learning for the Workplace (Ottawa ON: Conference Board of Canada, 2001). See also M. Rueda, "How to Make E-learning Work for Your Company," *Workspan* (December 2002), pp. 50–53; U. Vu, "Technology-Based Learning Comes of Age," *Canadian HR Reporter* (April 21, 2003), pp. 3, 17.
26. J. Mullich, "A Second Act for E-Learning," *Workforce Management* (Feb. 2004) (51), pp. 51–55.
27. A. Rosset & L. Schafer, "What to Do About E-Dropouts," *T+D* (June 2003), pp. 1–6.
28. D. Murray, *Keen for the Screen* (Ottawa: Conference Board of Canada, 2000).
29. S. Bolan, "Knowledge Is Out There," *Computing Canada* (February 23, 2001), p. 25.

30. C. Loughlin & J. Barling, "Young Workers' Work Values, Attitudes, and Behaviours," *Journal of Occupational and Organizational Psychology* (74), pp. 543–558.
31. See, for example, T. Falconer, "No More Pencils, No More Books!" *Canadian Banker* (March–April 1994), pp. 21–25.
32. W. Powell, "Like Life?" *Training and Development* (February 2002), pp. 32–38. See also A. Macaulay, "Reality-Based Computer Simulations Allow Staff to Grow through Failure," *Canadian HR Reporter* (October 23, 2000), pp. 11–12.
33. M. Shostak, "The Promise of New Media Learning," *Canadian HR Reporter* (April 7, 1997), pp. 15, 19.
34. S. Cohen, "A Guide to Multimedia in the Next Millennium," *Training and Development* (August 1997), pp. 33–44.
35. A. Czarnecki, "Interactive Learning Makes Big Dent in Time, Money Requirements for T&D," *Canadian HR Reporter* (November 18, 1996), pp. L30–L31.
36. L. Young, "Self-Directed Computer-Based Training That Works," *Canadian HR Reporter* (April 24, 2000), pp. 7–8.
37. M. Sani. "Mastering Healthcare Applications," *Health Management Technology* (May 2005), pp. 40–42.
38. These are summarized in R. Miller, "New Training Looms," *Hotel and Motel Management* (April 4, 1994), pp. 26, 30.
39. Shostak, "The Promise of New Media Learning."
40. M. Richmond, "Launching an Online Training Program," *Canadian HR Reporter* (August 9, 1999), pp. 16–17.
41. F. Manning, "The Misuse of Technology in Workplace Learning," *Canadian HR Reporter* (April 24, 2000), pp. 7, 10.
42. T. Purcell, "Training Anytime, Anywhere," *Canadian HR Reporter* (July 16, 2001), pp. 11, 15.
43. L. Cassini, "Student Participation Thrives in Online Learning Environments," *Canadian HR Reporter* (May 2, 2001), p. 2.
44. P. Weaver, "Preventing E-learning Failure," *Training and Development* (August 2002), pp. 45–50.
45. K. Oakes, "E-learning," *Training and Development* (March 2002), pp. 73–75. See also P. Harris, "E-learning: A Consolidation Update," *Training and Development* (April 2002), pp. 27–33.
46. C.R. Taylor, "The Second Wave," *Training and Development* (October 2002), pp. 24–31. See also P. Weaver, "Preventing E-learning Failure" and K. Oakes, "E-learning."
47. P. Weaver, "Preventing E-learning Failure."
48. E. Wareham, "The Educated Buyer," *Computing Canada* (February 18, 2000), p. 33. See also A. Tomlinson, "E-learning Won't Solve All Problems," *Canadian HR Reporter* (April 8, 2002), pp. 1, 6 and C.R. Taylor, "The Second Wave."
49. J. Webster & P. Hackley, "Teaching Effectiveness in Technology-Mediated Distance Learning," *Academy of Management Journal* 40(6) (1997), pp. 1282–1309.
50. C.D. Wetzel, P.H. Radtke & H.W. Stern, *Instructional Effectiveness of Video Media* (Hillsdale, NJ: Erlbaun, 1994).
51. J. Storck & L. Sproull, "Through a Glass Darkly: What do People Learn in Video Conferences?" *Human Communication Research* 22 (1995), pp. 197–219.
52. E. Welsh, "E-Learning: Emerging Uses, Empirical Results, and Future Directions," *International Journal of Training and Development* (7) (2003), pp. 245–251.
53. P. Weaver, "Preventing E-learning Failure."
54. W. Rothwell, H.C. Kazanas, & D. Haines, "Issues and Practices in Management Job Rotation Programs as Perceived by HRD Professionals," *Performance Improvement Quarterly* 5(1) (1992), pp. 49–69.
55. Yoder et al., *Handbook of Personnel Management and Labor Relations.* See also J. Phillips, "Training Supervisors Outside the Classroom," *Training and Development Journal* 40(2) (1986), pp. 46–49.
56. A. Tomlinson, "Going After the Best of the Best," *Canadian HR Reporter* (November 19, 2001), pp. 9–10.
57. K. Wexley & G. Latham, *Developing and Training Human Resources,* p. 207.
58. R. Noe, D. Greenberger, & S. Wang, "Mentoring: What We Know and Where We Might Go," *Research in Personnel and Human Resources Management* (2002) (21), pp. 129–173.
59. S. Kim, "Learning Goal Orientation, Formal Mentoring, and Leadership Competencies in HRD," *Journal of European Industrial Training* (1997) (31) (3), pp. 181–194.
60. N. Rosser, "Mentoring from the Top: CEO Perspectives," *Advances in Developing Human Resources* (2005) (7) (4), pp. 527–539.
61. V. Stead, "Mentoring: Model for Leadership Development," *International Journal of Training and Development* (2005) (9) (3), pp. 170–184.
62. This is based on N. Fox, "Action Learning Comes to Industry," *Harvard Business Review* (September–October, 1977), pp. 158–168.
63. Wexley & Latham, *Developing and Training Human Resources,* p. 193.
64. C.M. Solomon, "Simulation Training Builds Teams Through Experience," *Personnel Journal* (June 1993), pp. 100–105; K. Slack, "Training for the Real Thing," *Training and Development* (May 1993), pp. 79–89; B. Lierman, "How to Develop a Training Simulation," *Training and Development* (February 1994), pp. 50–52.
65. A. Macaulay, "Strategic Plan Off Base, Do Not Pass Go," *Canadian HR Reporter* (October 23, 2000), p. 12.
66. D. McKay-Stokes, "Sleeping in the Snow Together Does Wonders for Morale," *Financial Post* (April 25, 1995), p. 20.
67. For an interesting discussion of how to design a management game that is both educational and stimulating, see B.L. Taylor, "Around the World in 80 Questions," *Training and Development Journal* 40(3) (1986), pp. 67–70.
68. J. Hinrichs, "Personnel Testing," in M. Dunnette (Ed.), *Handbook of Industrial and Organizational Psychology* (Chicago: Rand McNally, 1976), p. 855.
69. D. Swink, "Role-Play Your Way to Learning," *Training and Development* (May 1993), pp. 91–97; A. Test, "Why I Do Not Like to Role Play," *The American Salesman* (August 1994), pp. 7–20.
70. This section based on A. Kraut, "Developing Managerial Skill via Modeling Techniques: Some Positive Research Findings—A Symposium," *Personnel Psychology* 29(3) (1976), pp. 325–361.
71. D. Conner, *Leading on the Edge of Chaos* (New York: John Wiley & Sons) (1999), p. 87.
72. Watson Wyatt, "Leadership: The Critical Key to Financial Success" *Drake Business Review* (2003) (1), pp. 21–25.
73. P. Bernthal & R. Wellins, *Leadership Forecast 2005/2006.* (Bridgeville, PA: Development Dimensions International, Inc.) (2006), p. 14.
74. Government of Canada, 2008 APEX Conference on Public Service Renewal. Privy Council Office. www.pco-bcp.gc.ca.
75. E. Michaels, H. Handfield-Jones, & B. Axelrod, *The War for Talent* (Boston, MA: Harvard Business School Press) (2001), p. 102.
76. For discussions of the steps in succession planning see, for example, K. Nowack, "The Secrets of Succession," *Training and Development* (November 1994), pp. 49–55, and D. Brookes, "In Management Succession, Who Moves Up?" *Human Resources* (January–February 1995), pp. 11–13.
77. D. Brown, "Succession in an Era of Turnover," *Canadian HR Reporter* (May 21, 2001), p. 7; "CEOs Talk," *Canadian HR Reporter* (June 4, 2001), pp. 17–19.

78. D. MacNamara, "Learning Contracts, Competency Profiles the New Wave in Executive Development," *Canadian HR Reporter* (November 16, 1998), pp. G8, G12.
79. D. LaMarche-Bisson, "There's More Than One Way to Learn," *Canadian HR Reporter* (November 18, 2003), p. 7.
80. J. Phillips & P. Phillips, "Eleven Reasons Why Training and Development Fails and What You Can Do About It," *Training* (2002) (39) (9), pp. 78–85.
81. M. Belcourt & P.C. Wright, *Managing Performance through Training and Development* (Toronto: Nelson Canada, 1996), p. 11.
82. R.E. Catalano & D.L. Kirkpatrick, "Evaluating Training Programs—The State of the Art," *Training and Development Journal* 22(5) (1968), pp. 2–9. See also A. Montebello & M. Haga, "To Justify Training, Test, Test Again," *Personnel Journal* 73(1) (1994), pp. 83–87.
83. G. Bickerstaffe, "Measuring the Gains from Training," *Personnel Management* (November 1993), pp. 48–51; J. Spoor, "You Can Quantify Training Dollars and Program Value," *HR Focus* (May 1993), p. 3; J. Trynor, "Is Training a Good Investment?" *Financial Analyst Journal* (September–October 1994), pp. 6–8; and S. Dolliver, "The Missing Link: Evaluating Training Programs," *Supervision* (November 1994), pp. 10–12.
84. N.L. Trainer, "Evaluating Training's Four Levels," *Canadian HR Reporter* (January 13, 1997), p. 10.
85. G. Betcherman, N. Leckie, & K. McMullen, *Developing Skills in the Canadian Workplace: The Results of the Ekos Workplace Training Survey, Study No. W/02* (Ottawa: Canadian Policy Research Networks Inc., 1997).
86. D. Heyman, "Illiteracy Called Risk to Nation's Progress," *Calgary Herald* (May 6, 1997), p. B3.
87. C. Knight, "Awards for Literacy Announced," *Canadian HR Reporter* (December 29, 1997), p. 10.
88. N.L. Bernardon, "Let's Erase Illiteracy from the Workplace," *Personnel* (January 1989), pp. 29–32.
89. N.L. Bernardon, "Let's Erase Illiteracy from the Workplace." The PALS course was developed by educator Dr. J.H. Martin.
90. N.L. Bernardon, "Let's Erase Illiteracy from the Workplace," p. 32. SKILLPAC was created by the Center for Applied Linguistics and Dr. A. Packer, senior research fellow at the Hudson Institute in Indianapolis, Indiana.
91. B. Siu, "Cross-Cultural Training and Customer Relations: What Every Manager Should Know," *Canadian HR Reporter* (November 15, 1999), pp. G3, G15.
92. W. Hopkins, K. Sterkel-Powell, & S. Hopkins, "Training Priorities for a Diverse Workforce," *Public Personnel Management* 23(3) (Fall 1994), p. 433.
93. C. Knight, "Training of, for and by the Disabled," *Canadian HR Reporter* (June 19, 1995), p. 11.
94. L. Young, "Retail Sector Seeks to Upgrade Education, Training to Solve Human Resource Woes," *Canadian HR Reporter* (February 8, 1999), p. 11.
95. P. Kulig, "LCBO Has Taste for Training," *Canadian HR Reporter* (August 10, 1998), pp. 1, 10.
96. This is based on J. Laabs, "Team Training Goes Outdoors," *Personnel Journal* (June 1991), pp. 56–63.
97. J. Laabs, "Team Training," p. 56. See also S. Caudron, "Teamwork Takes Work," *Personnel Journal* 73(2) (February 1994), pp. 41–49.
98. R. Sharma & J. Bhatnagar. "Talent Management—Competency Development: Key to Global Leadership" *Industrial and Commercial Training.* Guilsborough: 2009. Vol. 41, Iss. 3; p. 118.
99. D. Morris. "Leadership Experience," *T+D.* Alexandria: May 2009. Vol. 63, Iss. 5; p. 50, 5 pgs.

## Chapter 7

1. D. Brown, "HR Improving at Performance Management," *Canadian HR Reporter* (December 2, 2002), pp. 1, 14.
2. D. Brown, "Re-evaluating Evaluation," *Canadian HR Reporter* (April 8, 2002), p. 2.
3. J.T. Rich, "The Solutions for Employee Performance Management," *Workspan* (February 2002), pp. 32–37.
4. J. Cleveland et al., "Multiple Uses of Performance Appraisal: Prevalence and Correlates," *Journal of Applied Psychology* 74(1) (1989), pp. 130–135; I. Carlton & M. Sloman, "Performance Appraisal in Practice," *Human Resource Management Journal* 2(3) (Spring 1992), pp. 80–94.
5. S. Nador, "A Properly Crafted Performance-Management Program Aids Professional Development," *Canadian HR Reporter* (May 17, 1999), p. 10.
6. Keki Bhote, "Boss Performance Appraisal: A Metric Whose Time Has Gone," *Employment Relations* Today 21(1) (1994), pp. 1–9.
7. J.E. Oliver, "Performance Appraisals That Fit," *Personnel Journal* 64 (June 1985), p. 69.
8. Lawler, "Performance Management," p. 16.
9. M.M. Markowich, "Response: We Can Make Performance Appraisals Work," *Compensation and Benefits Review* (May–June 1995), p. 25.
10. See, for example, G. Boudreaux, "Response: What TQM Says About Performance Appraisal," *Compensation and Benefits Review* (May–June 1994), pp. 20–24.
11. G. Boudreaux, "What TQM Says About Performance Appraisal," p. 21.
12. See, for example, Lawler, "Performance Management: The Next Generation," p. 17.
13. C.L. Hughes, "The Bell-Shaped Curve That Inspires Guerilla Warfare," *Personnel Administrator* (May 1987), pp. 40–41.
14. M. Lowrey, "Forcing the Issue," *Human Resource Executive,* October 16, 2003, pp. 26–29.
15. J. Ivancevich, "A Longitudinal Study of Behavioral Expectation Scales: Attitudes and Performance," *Journal of Applied Psychology* (April 1980), pp. 139–146.
16. G. Greguras, J. Forg & S. Brutus, "Manager Attention to Multisource Feedback," *Journal of Management Development* 22, 2003, pp. 345–349.
17. D. Clements, "Bain & Company Survey," *PeopleTalk,* Fall 2008, pp. 13–14.
18. R. Kaplan & D. Norton, Strategic Learning and the Balanced Scorecard," *Strategy and Leadership,* Sept/Oct. 1996, 24(5), pp. 18–24.
19. D. Robb, "Appraising Appraisal Software," *HR Magazine,* October 2008, 53(10), pp. 65–68.
20. M.M. Harris & J. Schaubroeck, "A Meta-Analysis of Self-Supervisor, Self-Peer, and Peer-Supervisor Ratings," *Personnel Psychology* 41 (1988), pp. 43–62.
21. G.P. Latham & K.N. Wexley, *Increasing Productivity through Performance* Appraisal (2nd ed.) (Reading, MA: Addison-Wesley, 1994).
22. G. McEvoy & P. Buller, "User Acceptance of Peer Appraisals in an Industrial Setting," *Personnel Psychology* 40(4) (1987), pp. 785–798. See also J. Barclay & L. Harland, "Peer Performance Appraisals: The Impact of Rater Competence, Rater Location, and Rating Correctability on Fairness Perceptions," *Group and Organization Management* 20(1) (March 1995), pp. 39–60.
23. M. Mount, "Psychometric Properties of Subordinate Ratings of Managerial Performance," *Personnel Psychology* 37(4) (1984), pp. 687–702.
24. V.V. Druskat & S.B. Wolff, "Effects and Timing of Developmental Peer Appraisals in Self-Managing Work Groups," *Journal of Applied Psychology* 84 (1999), pp. 58–74.

25. P. Kamen, "360 Degree Review: A New Spin for Managers," *The Globe and Mail,* Sept. 23, 2002, p. B13.
26. R. Libby & R. Blashfield, "Performance of a Composite as a Function of the Number of Judges," *Organizational Behavior and Human Performance* 21 (April 1978), pp. 121–129; W. Borman, "Exploring Upper Limits of Reliability and Validity in Job Performance Ratings," *Journal of Applied Psychology* 63 (April 1978), pp. 135–44; M.M. Harris & J. Schaubroeck, "A Meta-analysis," pp. 43–62.
27. W.C. Borman, "The Rating of Individuals in Organizations: An Alternate Approach," *Organizational Behavior and Human Performance* 12 (1974), pp. 105–124.
28. S. Fox & Y. Dinur, "Validity of Self-assessment: A Field Evaluation," *Personnel Psychology* 41(3) (1988), pp. 581–592; and J.W. Lawrie "Your Performance: Appraise It Yourself!" *Personnel* 66(1) (January 1989), pp. 21–33.
29. P.A. Mabe III & S.G. West "Validity of Self-Evaluation of Ability: A Review and Meta-analysis," *Journal of Applied Psychology* 67(3) (1982), pp. 280–296.
30. G.P. Latham, D. Skarlicki, D. Irvine & J.P. Seigel, "The Increasing Importance of Performance Appraisals to Employee Effectiveness in Organizational Settings in North America." In C.L. Cooper & I.T. Robertson (Eds.), *International Review of Industrial and Organizational Psychology,* Volume 8 (1993), p. 103.
31. M. London & A. Wohlers, "Agreement between Subordinate and Self-Ratings in Upward Feedback," *Personnel Psychology* 44 (1991), pp. 375–90.
32. London & Wohlers, "Agreement between Subordinate and Self-Ratings," p. 376.
33. D. Antonioni, "The Effects of Feedback Accountability on Upward Appraisal Ratings," *Personnel Psychology* 47 (1994), pp. 349–355.
34. T.J. Maurer, N.S. Raju, & W.C. Collins, "Peer and Subordinate Performance Appraisal Measurement Equivalence," *Journal of Applied Psychology* 83 (1998), pp. 693–702.
35. R. Brillinger, "The Many Faces of 360-Degree Feedback," *Canadian HR Reporter* (December 16, 1996), pp. 20–21.
36. K. Nowack, "360-Degree Feedback: The Whole Story," *Training and Development* (January 1993), p. 69. For a description of some of the problems involved in implementing 360-degree feedback, see M. Budman, "The Rating Game," *Across the Board,* 31 (February 1994), pp. 35–38.
37. C. Romano, "Fear of Feedback," *Management Review* (December 1993), p. 39.
38. M.R. Edwards & A.J. Ewen, "How to Manage Performance and Pay with 360-Degree Feedback," *Compensation and Benefits Review* 28(3) (1996), pp. 41–46.
39. R. Brillinger, "The Many Faces," p. 21.
40. R. Brillinger, "The Many Faces," p. 20.
41. J.F. Milliman, R.A. Zawacki, C. Norman, L. Powell & J. Kirksey, "Companies Evaluate Employees from All Perspectives," *Personnel Journal* 73(11) (1994), pp. 99–103.
42. P. Kamen, "The Way That You Use It," *CMA Magazine,* April 2003, 77(2), pp. 10–12.
43. P. Kamen, "The Way That You Use It," *CMA Magazine,* April 2003, 77(2), pp. 10–12.
44. K. Hilgenfeldt, "Improved Performance Appraisal," *Law and Order,* 2004, 52(10), p. 90.
45. C. O'Neill & L. Holsinger, "Effective Performance Appraisal Systems," *WorldatWork,* Second Quarter, 2003, 61, p. 17.
46. M. Derayeh & S. Brutus, "Learning from Others' 360-degree Experiences," *Canadian HR Reporter,* February 10, 2003, p. 18.
47. Teel, "Performance Appraisal," pp. 297–298.
48. T.J. Maurer & M.A. Taylor, "Is Sex by Itself Enough? An Exploration of Gender Bias Issues in Performance Appraisal," *Organizational Behavior and Human Decision Processes* 60 (1994), pp. 231–251.
49. E. Chow, editorial, *PeopleTalk,* Spring 2009, pp. 10–11.
50. T. Lowe, "Eight Ways to Ruin a Performance Review," *Personnel Journal* 65 (January 1986).
51. S. Cook, "Appraisal Interveiws," *Training Journal,* November 2005, p. 50.
52. J. Pearce & L. Porter, "Employee Response to Formal Performance Appraisal Feedback," *Journal of Applied Psychology* 71 (May 1986), pp. 211–218.
53. L. Axline, "Ethical Considerations of Performance Appraisals," *Management Review* (March 1994), p. 62.
54. G. Barrett & M. Kernan, "Performance Appraisal and Terminations: A Review of Court Decisions Since Brito v. Zia with Implications for Personnel Practices," *Personnel Psychology* 40 (Autumn 1987), pp. 489–504.
55. G. Barrett & M. Kernan, "Performance Appraisal and Terminations," p. 501.
56. P. Caligiuir, "Performance Measurement in a Cross-Cultural Context," *Performance Management: Current Perspectives and Further Challenges,* pp. 227–244.
57. M. Tahvanainen, "Expatriate Performance Management," *Human Resources Management,* 39(2), pp. 267–276.


## Chapter 8


1. "Aligning Work and Rewards: A Round Table Discussion," *Compensation and Benefits Review* 26 (July–August 1994), pp. 47–63 and M. Morganstern, "Compensation and the New Employment Relationship," *Compensation and Benefits Review* 27 (March 1995), pp. 37–44.
2. H. Risher, "Exclusive CBR Survey: Pay Program Effectiveness," *Compensation and Benefits Review* 31 (November–December 1999), pp. 20–26.
3. E.E. Lawler III, "Pay Strategy: New Thinking for the New Millennium," *Compensation and Benefits Review* 32 (January–February 2000), pp. 7–12.
4. Canadian Federation of Independent Business, "Compensation: Huge wage, benefits gaps favour public sector," *HR Professional,* June/July 2009, Vol. 26(4), p. 15.
5. J. Janis, "Employers plan to reduce 2009 pay increases: Survey," *Canadian HR Reporter,* December 8, 2008.
6. Watson Wyatt's Annual Salary Survey, "Pay increases: Alberta leads in pay hikes," *HR Professional,* December 2008/ January 2009, Vol. 26 (1), p. 13.
7. S. Chadwick, "Using Rewards to Drive Commitment and Loyalty," *Canadian HR Reporter* (December 13, 1999), pp. 8–9.
8. G.S. Lower & G. Schellenberg, *What's a Good Job? The Importance of Employment Relationships* (Canadian Policy Network Study No. W05, March 2001); *Redefining Rewards* (Toronto: Winter Consulting Group, 2001).
9. C. Kapel & A. Mitchell, "Communication: The missing link in compensation," *Canadian HR Reporter,* April, 21, 2008.
10. H. Jones, "Union Views on Job Evaluations: 1971 vs. 1978," *Personnel Journal* 58 (February 1979), pp. 80–85.
11. R. Sahl, "Job Content Salary Surveys: Survey Design and Selection Features," *Compensation and Benefits Review* (May–June 1991), pp. 14–21.
12. Job analysis can be a useful source of information on compensable factors as well as on job descriptions and job specifications. For example, a quantitative job analysis technique like the position

analysis questionnaire generates quantitative information on the degree to which the following five basic factors are present in each job: having decision making/communication/social responsibilities, performing skilled activities, being physically active, operating vehicles or equipment, and processing information. As a result, a job analysis technique, such as the PAQ, is actually as appropriate as a job evaluation technique (or more, some say), in that jobs can be quantitatively compared with one another on those five dimensions and their relative worth thus ascertained.

13. E.J. Brennan, "Everything You Need to Know about Salary Ranges," *Personnel Journal* 63 (March 1984), pp. 10–17.
14. M.E. Lo Bosco, "Job Analysis, Job Evaluation, and Job Classification," *Personnel* 62 (May 1985), pp. 70–75. See also H. Risher, "Job Evaluation: Validity and Reliability," *Compensation and Benefits Review* 21 (January–February 1989), pp. 22–36; and D. Hahn & R. Dipboye, "Effects of Training and Information on the Accuracy and Reliability of Job Evaluations," *Journal of Applied Psychology* 73(2) (1988), pp. 146–153.
15. R. Plachy, "The Case for Effective Point-Factor Job Evaluation, Viewpoint I," *Compensation and Benefits Review* 19 (March–April 1987), pp. 45–48; R. Plachy, "The Point-Factor Job Evaluation System: A Step-by-Step Guide, Part II," *Compensation and Benefits Review* 19 (September–October 1987), pp. 9–24; and A. Candrilli & R. Armagast, "The Case for Effective Point-Factor Job Evaluation, Viewpoint II," *Compensation and Benefits Review* 19 (March–April 1987), pp. 49–54. See also R.J. Sahl, "How to Install a Point-Factor Job Evaluation System," *Personnel* 66 (March 1989), pp. 38–42.
16. S. Werner, R. Konopaske, & C. Touhey, "Ten Questions to Ask Yourself about Compensation Surveys," *Compensation and Benefits Review* 31 (May–June 1999), pp. 54–59.
17. P. Cappelli, *The New Deal at Work: Managing the Market-Driven Workforce* (Boston, MA: Harvard Business School Press, 1999).
18. J. Vathje & M. Campione, "What to do with all those numbers: Getting the most out of salary survey data," *Canadian HR Reporter,* August 11, 2008.
19. A. Scappatura, "Downturn wrinkles salary benchmarking: Diverging cost-cutting approaches make it hard to gauge competition," *Canadian HR Reporter,* June 15, 2009.
20. This is based on F.W. Cook, "Compensation Surveys Are Biased," *Compensation and Benefits Review* (September–October 1994), pp. 19–22.
21. F.W. Cook, "Compensation Surveys Are Biased," p. 19.
22. S. Werner, R. Konopaske, & C. Touhey, "Ten Questions to Ask Yourself about Compensation Surveys."
23. D. Hofrichter, "Broadbanding: A 'Second Generation' Approach." See also G. Bergel, "Choosing the Right Pay Delivery System to Fit Banding," *Compensation and Benefits Review* 26 (July–August 1994), pp. 34–38.
24. G. Ledford Jr., "Three Case Studies on Skill-Based Pay: An Overview," *Compensation and Benefits Review* (March–April 1991), pp. 11–23.
25. B. Orr, "Competencies Key in a Changing World," *Canadian HR Reporter* (November 30, 1998), pp. 10–11.
26. S. St.-Onge, "Competency-Based Pay Plans Revisited," *Human Resources Professional* (August–September 1998), pp. 29–34.
27. J. Kochanski & P. Leblanc, "Should Firms Pay for Competencies: Competencies Have to Help the Bottom Line," *Canadian HR Reporter* (February 22, 1999), p. 10.
28. This is based on L. Dufetel, "Job Evaluation: Still at the Frontier," *Compensation and Benefits Review* (July–August 1991), pp. 53–67.
29. N. Winter, "Job Evaluation in a New Business Environment," *Canadian HR Reporter* (March 27, 2000), p. 17.
30. J. Harper, "Mind the gap: Female workers feel males still better compensated," *Canadian HR Reporter,* September 26, 2008.
31. D. Brown, "StatsCan Unable to Explain Gender Wage Gap," *Canadian HR Reporter* (January 31, 2000), p. 3. See also M. Drolet, "The Male-Female Wage Gap," *Canadian Social Trends* (Spring 2002), pp. 29–35.
32. "Pay Equity Nets Gains for Women" *Ontario Pay Equity Commission Newsletter* (October 1995), p. 4.
33. D. Brown, "StatsCan Unable to Explain Gender Wage Gap."
34. A. Wherry, "Is this the quiet end to pay equity?" *Maclean's,* 00249262, March 2, 2009, Vol. 122(7).
35. M. Gray, "Pay Equity through Job Evaluation: A Case Study," *Compensation and Benefits Review* (July–August 1992), p. 46.
36. M. Gray, "Pay Equity through Job Evaluation," pp. 46–51.
37. V.L. Williams & J.E. Sunderland, "New Pay Programs Boost Retention," *Workforce* (May 1999), pp. 36–40.
38. J.R. Schuster & P.K. Zingheim, *The New Pay: Linking Employee and Organizational Performance* (San Francisco, CA: Jossey-Bass).
39. D. Yoder, *Personnel Management and Industrial Relations* (Englewood Cliffs, NJ: Prentice-Hall, 1970), pp. 643–645.
40. L. Young, "Disconnect between what IT wants, HR offers," *Canadian HR Reporter,* September 22, 2008.
41. B.J. Brooks, "Trends in International Executive Compensation," *Personnel* 64 (May 1987), pp. 67–71, and E. Lewis, "New Approaches to Executive Pay," *Directors and Boards* 18 (Spring 1994), pp. 57–58.
42. *Report on Business Magazine* (July 2000).
43. "Executive Pay," *The Wall Street Journal* (April 11, 1996), pp. r16, r17.
44. *Report on Business Magazine* (July 2000).
45. A. Cowan, "Compensation Planning Outlook 2009," Conference Board of Canada, Winter 2009.
46. This is based on W. White, "Managing the Board Review of Executive Pay," *Compensation and Benefits Review* (November–December 1992), pp. 35–41.
47. K. Howlett. "Pay Rules Signal Changes at OSC," *The Globe and Mail* (October 18, 1993), p. B1.
48. W. White & R. Fife, "New Challenges for Executive Compensation in the 1990s," *Compensation and Benefits Review* (January–February 1993), pp. 27–35.
49. For a discussion, see S. Schmdit, "The New Focus Career Development Programs in Business and Industry," *Journal of Employment Counseling* 31(1) (1994), pp. 22–28.
50. R. Sibson, *Compensation* (New York: AMACOM, 1981), p. 194.
51. J.R. Schuster & P.K. Zingheim, *The New Pay.*
52. D. Brown, "Top Performers Must Get Top Pay," *Canadian HR Reporter* (May 8, 2000), pp. 7, 10.
53. J. Vathje & M. Campione, "What to do with all those numbers: Getting the most out of salary survey data," *Canadian HR Reporter,* August 11, 2008.
54. A. Cowan, "Compensation Planning Outlook 2009," Conference Board of Canada, Winter 2009.
55. S. Dobson, "A small Ottawa company takes holistic approach to optimize attraction and retention," *Canadian HR Reporter,* November 3, 2008.
56. J. Hale & G. Bailey, "Seven Dimensions of Successful Reward Plans," *Compensation and Benefits Review* 30 (July–August 1998), pp. 71–77. See also I. Huss & C. Kapel, "Giving Employees What They Want and Linking It to Strategy," *Canadian HR Reporter* (May 8, 2000), pp. 7, 10.

57. Employability Skills 2000 (Ottawa: Conference Board of Canada, 2000).
58. Except as noted, this section is based on "Non-traditional Incentive Pay Programs," Personnel Policies Forum Survey, no. 148 (May 1991), The Bureau of National Affairs, Inc., Washington, D.C.
59. "Non-traditional Incentive Pay Programs," p. 3.
60. "Non-traditional Incentive Pay Programs," p. 9; A. Czarnecki, "'Spot Awards' Incentives Easily Administered, Flexible, Affordable," *Canadian HR Reporter* (March 13, 1995), p. 15.
61. R. Murrill, "Variations on Compensation," *Compensation and Benefits Update* 4 (February 2000), p. 5.
62. "Non-traditional Incentive Pay Programs," p. 13.
63. "Non-traditional Incentive Pay Programs," p. 19.
64. "Non-traditional Incentive Pay Programs," p. 24.
65. D. Belcher, *Compensation Administration* (Englewood Cliffs, NJ: Prentice-Hall, 1973), p. 314.
66. A. Saunier & E. Hawk, "Realizing the Potential of Teams through Team-Based Rewards," *Compensation and Benefits Review* (July–August 1994), pp. 24–33; and S. Caudron, "Tie Individual Pay to Team Success," *Personnel Journal* 73 (October 1994), pp. 40–46.
67. Another suggestion is as follows: equal payments to all members on the team; differential payments to team members based on their contributions to the team's performance; and differential payments determined by a ratio of each group member's base pay to the total base pay of the group. See K. Bartol & L. Hagmann, "Team-Based Pay Plans: A Key to Effective Teamwork," *Compensation and Benefits Review* (November–December 1992), pp. 24–29.
68. P. Brewer, "Experiential rewards: go for the money or memory?" *PeopleTalk,* Spring 2007, p. 51.
69. J. Nickel & S. O'Neal, "Small Group Incentives: Gainsharing in the Microcosm," *Compensation and Benefits Review* (March–April 1990), p. 24. See also J. Pickard, "How Incentives Can Drive Teamworking," *Personnel Management* (September 1993), pp. 26–32, and S. Caudron, "Tie Individual Pay to Team Success," *Personnel Journal* (October 1994), pp. 40–46.
70. D. Sidebottom, *Compensation Planning Outlook 2000,* Conference Board of Canada, p. 8.
71. B.R. Ellig, "Incentive Plans: Short-Term Design Issues," *Compensation Review* 16 (Third Quarter 1984), pp. 26–36.
72. R.M. Kanungo & M. Mendonca, *Compensation: Effective Reward Management* (Butterworths: 1997), p. 237.
73. D. Sidebottom, *Compensation Planning Outlook* 2000, p. 10.
74. A. Tomlinson, "Stock Options: Last Year's Darling, This Year's Headache," *Canadian HR Reporter* (October 8, 2001), p. 2; D. Brown, "Bringing Stock Options Back to the Surface," *Canadian HR Reporter* (May 7, 2001), p. 2.
75. S.J. Chadwick, "Extending Stock Option Plans to All Employees a Growing Trend," *Canadian HR Reporter* (October 5, 1998), pp. 10, 12. See also B. Cline, "Stock Option Plans . . . A New Trend?" *HR Professional* (June–July 1999), pp. 24–26; and I. Huss & M. Maclure, "Broad-Based Stock Option Plans Take Hold," *Canadian HR* Reporter (July 17, 2000), p. 18.
76. S. Dobson, "Executive compensation declining," *Canadian HR Reporter,* May 26, 2008.
77. J. Tallitsch & J. Moynahan, "Fine-Tuning Sales Compensation Programs," *Compensation and Benefits Review* 26 (March–April 1994), pp. 34–37.
78. C. Fellman & D. Johnston, "Pay Systems That Salespeople Will Buy," *Canadian HR Reporter* (April 20, 1998), pp. 16, 18.
79. E. Maggio, "Compensation Strategies Pulling You in Different Directions?" *Canadian HR Reporter* (October 4, 1999), pp. 11, 19.
80. N. Winstanley, "Are Merit Increases Really Effective?" *Personnel Administrator* 27 (April 1982), pp. 37–41. See also W. Seithel & J. Emans, "Calculating Merit Increases: A Structured Approach," *Personnel* 60 (June 1985), pp. 56–68.
81. D. Gilbert & G. Bassett, "Merit Pay Increases Are a Mistake," *Compensation and Benefits Review* 26 (March–April 1994), pp. 20–25.
82. This section based primarily on R. Sibson, *Compensation* (New York: AMACOM, 1981), pp. 189–207.
83. D. Sidebottom, *Compensation Planning Outlook 2000,* p. 8.
84. B. Duke, "Are Profit Sharing Plans Making the Grade?" *Canadian HR Reporter* (January 11, 1999), pp. 8–9.
85. D. Sidebottom, *Compensation Planning Outlook 2000,* p. 11.
86. P. Robertson, "Increasing Productivity through an Employee Share Purchase Plan," *Canadian HR Reporter* (September 20, 1999), pp. 7, 9.
87. S. Lebrun, "ESOP Saves the Day," *Canadian HR Reporter* (November 17, 1997), pp. 1–2. See also W. Smith, H. Lazarus & H.M. Kalkstein, "Employee Stock Ownership Plans: Motivation and Morale Issues," *Compensation and Benefits Review* (September–October 1990), pp. 37–46.
88. B.W. Thomas & M.H. Olson, "Gainsharing: The Design Guarantees Success," *Personnel Journal* (May 1988), pp. 73–79. See also "Aligning Compensation with Quality," *Bulletin to Management, BNA Policy and Practice Series* (April 1, 1993), p. 97.
89. This is paraphrased from W. Imberman, "Boosting Plant Performance with Gainsharing," *Business Horizons* (November–December 1992), p. 77.
90. For other examples, see T. Ross & L. Hatcher, "Gainsharing Drives Quality Improvement," *Personnel Journal* (November 1992), pp. 81–89. See also J. McAdams, "Employee Involvement and Performance Reward Plans: Design, Implementation, and Results," *Compensation and Benefits Review* 27 (March 1995), pp. 45–55.
91. P.K. Zingheim & J.R. Schuster, "Value Is the Goal," *Workforce* (February 2000), pp. 56–61.
92. P.K. Zingheim & J.R. Schuster, "Value Is the Goal," *Workforce* (February 2000), pp. 56–61.
93. D. Brown, "Variable Pay Programs Still the Way of the Future," *Canadian HR Reporter* (November 29, 1999), pp. 7, 13.
94. J. Mills, "A Matter of Pride: Rewarding Team Success," *Canadian HR Reporter* (March 8, 1999), p. 16.
95. A. Welsh, "The Give and Take of Recognition Programs," *Canadian HR Reporter* (September 22, 1997), pp. 16–17, 22.
96. J. Kouzes & B. Posner, *Encouraging the Heart: A Leader's Guide to Rewarding and Recognizing Others* (San Francisco, CA: Jossey Bass, 1999).
97. Globoforce, "Recognition needs improvement," *Canadian HR Reporter,* February 23, 2009, p. 5.
98. J. Mills, "A Matter of Pride: Rewarding Team Success."
99. L. Young, "How Can I Ever Thank You?" *Canadian HR Reporter* (January 31, 2000), pp. 7, 9.
100. E. Wright & K. Ryan, "Thanks a Million (More or Less)," *Canadian HR Reporter* (March 9, 1998), pp. 19, 21, 23. See also, "How to Sell Recognition to Top Management," *Canadian HR Reporter* (June 1, 1998), p. 21.
101. J. Mills, "A Matter of Pride: Rewarding Team Success."
102. B. Nelson, "Cheap and Meaningful Better Than Expensive and Forgettable," *Canadian HR Reporter* (August 13, 2001), p. 22.
103. A. Welsh, "The Give and Take of Recognition Programs"; E. Wright & K. Ryan, "Thanks a Million (More or Less)."

104. Kevin B. Lowe, John Milliman, Helen De Cieri, Peter J. Dowling, "International compensation practices: A ten-country comparative analysis," *Human Resource Management.* Hoboken. Spring 2002. Vol. 41(1), p. 45
105. P.J. Dowling, D.E. Welch, & R.S. Schuler. 1999. *International human resource management: Managing people in a multinational context* (3rd ed.) (Cincinnati, OH: South-West).
106. L.P. Crandall & M.I. Phelps. "Pay for a global work force," *Personnel Journal,* 1991, Vol. 70, pgs. 28–33.
107. R. Cui, "International compensation: The importance of acting globally," *WorldatWork Journal,* 2006, Vol. 15(4), pp. 18–23.

## Chapter 9

1. D. Brown, "Wellness Programs Bring Healthy Bottom Line," *Canadian HR Reporter* (December 17, 2001), pp. 1, 14.
2. L. Young, "Benefits Won't Bait Workers, Study Shows," *Canadian HR Reporter* (February 8, 1999), pp. 1, 8.
3. R.K. Platt, "A Strategic Approach to Benefits," *Workspan* (July 2002), pp. 23–24.
4. S. Beech & J. Tompkins, "Do Benefits Plans Attract and Retain Talent?" *Benefits Canada* (October 2002), pp. 49–53.
5. F. Holmes, "Talking About an Evolution," *Benefits Canada* (September 2001), pp. 30–32.
6. J. Thomas & M. Chilco, "Coming of Age," *Benefits Canada* (March 2001), pp. 36–38.
7. KPMG, *Employee Benefits Costs in Canada,* 1998.
8. A. Cowan, "Compensation Planning Outlook 2009," Conference Board of Canada, Winter 2009.
9. N. Spinks & C. Moore, "Compassionate Care Leave Takes Effect," *WorldatWork Canadian News* 12(2) (Second Quarter 2004), pp. 1, 21.
10. L. Osberg, "Canada's EI benefits well below OECD average," *Canadian HR Reporter,* July 3, 2009.
11. "Ottawa extends work-share agreements: Employers, workers can now access EI support to avoid layoffs for up to 52 weeks," *Canadian HR Reporter,* March 6, 2009.
12. S. Klie, "Workers delay retirement as economy tanks," *Canadian HR Reporter,* January 26, 2009, p. 7.
13. M. Endicott, "Injured workers 4 times more likely to be poor: Report," *Canadian HR Reporter,* June 8, 2009.
14. N. Rankin, "Mitigating the cost of disability: Why employers should treat all disability claims like workers' compensation claims," *Canadian HR Reporter,* May 2008.
15. H. Amolins, "Workers Must Cooperate in Return to Work," *Canadian HR Reporter* (November 3, 1997), p. 8; and C. Knight, "Ontario Businesses Ready for New WCB," *Canadian HR Reporter* (November 17, 1997), p. 9.
16. "Canada's Top 100 Employers for 2009," *Canadian HR Reporter,* October 20, 2008.
17. S. Dobson, "Benefits consultations make SFU top employer," *Canadian HR Reporter,* March 9, 2009, p. 12.
18. "Canada's Top 100 Employers for 2009," *Canadian HR Reporter,* October 20, 2008.
19. S. Klie, "Compassionate care benefit falls short of expectations," *Canadian HR Reporter,* January 30, 2006.
20. A. Maingault, E. Patton, & R. Dooley, "Layoff Criteria, Severance Pay, Student Interns," *HR Magazine,* July 2009, Vol. 54 (7), pp. 16–17.
21. S. Klie, "Mental health still the top cause of disability," *Canadian HR Reporter,* April 6, 2009.
22. M. Rothman, "Can Alternatives to Sick Pay Plans Reduce Absenteeism?" *Personnel Journal,* 60 (October 1981), pp. 788–791; Richard Bunning, "A Prescription for Sick Leave," *Personnel Journal* 67 (August 1988), pp. 44–49.
23. S. Klie, "Sick and tired in the workplace: Presenteeism can hurt productivity and cause serious illness," *Canadian HR Reporter,* June 2, 2008.
24. A. Cowan, "Compensation Planning Outlook 2009," Conference Board of Canada, Winter 2009.
25. S. Dobson, "An office in the mountains," *Canadian HR Reporter,* February 9, 2009, p. 13.
26. D. Gunch, "The Family Leave Act: A Financial Burden?" *Personnel Journal* (September 1993), p. 49.
27. "Employee Benefits in Small Firms," *BNA Bulletin to Management* (June 27, 1991), pp. 196–197.
28. R. Jain, "Employer-Sponsored Dental Insurance Eases the Pain," *Monthly Labor Review* (October 1988), p. 18; "Employee Benefits," *Commerce Clearing House Ideas and Trends in Personnel* (January 23, 1991).
29. A. Cowan, "Compensation Planning Outlook 2009," Conference Board of Canada, Winter 2009.
30. A. Cowan, "Compensation Planning Outlook 2009," Conference Board of Canada, Winter 2009.
31. C. Kapel, "Unitel Asks Employees to Share Costs," *Canadian HR Reporter* (June 17, 1996), p. 17.
32. J. Norton, "The New Drug Invasion," *Benefits Canada* (June 1999), pp. 29–32. See also S. Felix, "The New Drug Dilemma," *Benefits Canada* (March 1998), pp. 35–38.
33. K. Gay, "Post-Retirement Benefits Costing Firms a Fortune," *Financial Post* (June 2, 1995), p. 18.
34. S. Lebrun, "Turning a Blind Eye to Benefits," *Canadian HR Reporter* (February 24, 1997), p. 2.
35. M. Warren, "Retiree Benefits Come of Age," *Benefits Canada* (May 2000), pp. 73–77.
36. A. Khemani, "Post-Retirement Benefits Liability Grows," *Canadian HR Reporter* (November 4, 1996), p. 17. See also M. Warren, "Retiree Benefits Come of Age."
37. S. Klie, "Retiree perks growing among Top 100," *Canadian HR Reporter,* October 20, 2009.
38. A.N. Nash & S.J. Carroll, Jr., "Supplemental Compensation," in *Perspectives on Personnel: Human Resource Management,* H. Heneman III & D. Schwab (Eds.) (Homewood, IL: Irwin, 1978), p. 223.
39. K. Read, "Integration Key to Managing Lost Time," *Canadian HR Reporter* (May 18, 1998), pp. 10, 11.
40. M. Cusipag, "A Healthy Approach to Managing Disability Costs," *Human Resources Professional* (June–July 1997), p. 13.
41. A. Blake, "A New Approach to Disability Management," *Benefits Canada* (March 2000), pp. 58–64.
42. P. Kulig, "Returning the Whole Employee to Work," *Canadian HR Reporter* (March 9, 1998), p. 20.
43. N. Rankin, "A Guide to Disability Management," *Canadian HR Reporter* (March 22, 1999), pp. 14, 15.
44. S. Lebrun, "Employers Take Notice of Disability Costs," *Canadian HR Reporter* (December 29, 1997), pp. 1, 24.
45. D. Dyck, "Stating Your Case," *Benefits Canada* (February 1998), pp. 55–59.
46. A. Nicoll, "Employee Stress Claims Are Rising: What Can You Do About It?" *HR Professional* (February–March 2002).
47. M. Morra, "Return on Wellness," *HR Professional,* August/September 2009, Vol. 26(5), pp. 21–24.
48. A. Nicoll, "Employee Stress."
49. A. Nicoll, "Employee Stress."

50. M. Morra, "Return on Wellness," *HR Professional,* August/September 2009, Vol. 26(5), pp. 21–24.
51. This is based on S. Felix, "The Gloom Boom," *Benefits Canada* (January 1997), p. 32.
52. E. Vernarec, "The High Costs of Hidden Conditions," *Business and Health* 16 (1998), pp. 19–23. See also J. Kline Jr. & L. Sussman, "An Executive Guide to Workplace Depression," *Academy of Management Executive* 14 (August 2000), pp. 103–114.
53. M. Acharya, "Depressed Workers Cost Firms Billions, Business Panel Says."
54. M. Cusipag, "A Healthy Approach to Managing Disability Costs."
55. G.M. Hall, "Pensions: Death by Regulation?" *Canadian HR Reporter* (October 4, 1999), p. 6. See also S. Smolkin, "Changing Canadian Pension Standards," *Canadian HR Reporter* (November 29, 1999), pp. 24–26; S. Smolkin, "Proposals Add to Hodgepodge of Legislative Inconsistencies," *Canadian HR Reporter* (January 17, 2000), p. 8.
56. A. Cowan, "Compensation Planning Outlook 2009," Conference Board of Canada, Winter 2009.
57. T. Singeris & M. Mignault, "Tackling Pension Legislation Compliance," *Canadian HR Reporter* (January 31, 2000), p. 16. See also G.M. Hall, "Pensions: Death by Regulation?"
58. T. Singeris & M. Mignault, "Tackling Pension Legislation Compliance," *Canadian HR Reporter* (January 31, 2000), p. 16. See also G.M. Hall, "Pensions: Death by Regulation?"
59. T. Piskorski, "Minimizing Employee Benefits Litigation through Effective Claims Administration Procedures," *Employee Relations Law Journal* 20(3) (Winter 1994–1995), pp. 421–431.
60. A. Pun, "The Tide Turns on Same-Sex Spousal Benefits," *Canadian HR Reporter* (August 9, 1999), p. G4. See also "Same-Sex Legislation Rolls Out," *Canadian HR Reporter* (November 15, 1999), pp. 3, 6.
61. "Phased Retirement Gaining Converts," *Canadian HR Reporter* (June 1, 1998), p. 6. See also L. Ramsay, "Pliant Pension Rules Key to Phased-In Retirement," *Financial Post* (February 9, 1995), p. 19.
62. Hewitt Associates survey published in *Canadian HR Reporter,* January 2009.
63. Hewitt Associates survey published in *Canadian HR Reporter,* January 2009.
64. R. Castelli, "Phased Retirement Plans," *HR Magazine,* December 2008/January 2009, Vol. 26(1), p. 23.
65. S. Klie, "Workers delay retirement as economy tanks," *Canadian HR Reporter,* January 26, 2009, p. 7.
66. Standard Life, "Retirement: New online retirement planning tool," *HR Professional,* December 2008/January 2009, Vol. 26(1), p. 15. www.standardlife.ca.
67. See Henderson, *Compensation Management,* pp. 336–339. See also L. Burger, "Group Legal Service Plans: A Benefit Whose Time Has Come," *Compensation and Benefits Review* 18 (July–August 1986), pp. 28–34.
68. A. Davis, "Helping Hands," *Benefits Canada* (November 2000), pp. 117–121; and P. Davies, "Problem Gamblers in the Workplace," *Canadian HR Reporter* (November 4, 2002), p. 17.
69. F. Engel, "Lost Profits, Increased Costs: The Aftermath of Workplace Trauma," *Canadian HR Reporter* (September 7, 1998), pp. 21, 22.
70. A. Sharratt, "When a Tragedy Strikes," *Benefits Canada* (November 2002), pp. 101–105; D. Rosolen, "Situation Critical," *Benefits Canada* (November 2001), pp. 29–35; and J. Hobel, "EAPs Flounder Without Manager Support," *Canadian HR Reporter* (June 2, 2003), p. 7.
71. "Employee Benefit Costs," *BNA Bulletin to Management* (January 16, 1992), pp. 12–14.
72. "100 Best Companies to Work For," *Fortune* (January 2000).
73. C. Davenport, "Child Care Solutions for a Harried Work World," *Canadian HR Reporter* (April 21, 1997), p. 16. See also C. Eichman & B. Reisman, "How Small Employers Are Benefitting from Offering Child Care Assistance," *Employment Relations Today* (Spring 1992), pp. 51–62.
74. S. Dobson, "Beneftis consultations make SFU top employer," *Canadian HR Reporter,* March 9, 2009, p. 12.
75. D. Brown, "Bringing the Family to Work," *Canadian HR Reporter* (November 6, 2000), pp. 19–20.
76. L. Johnson, "Effectiveness of an Employee-Sponsored Child Care Center," *Applied H.R.M. Research* 2 (Summer 1991).
77. Commerce Clearing House, "As the Population Ages, There Is Growing Interest in Adding Elder Care to the Benefits Package," *Ideas and Trends* (August 21, 1987), pp. 129–131. See also "Elder Care to Eclipse Child Care, Report Says," *Canadian HR Reporter* (August 14, 1995), p. 11; and D. Brown, "Senate Proposes Leave Benefits for Palliative Care," *Canadian HR Reporter* (July 17, 2000), pp. 1, 6.
78. P. Kulig, "Eldercare Issues Loom for Canadian Organizations," *Canadian HR Reporter* (May 4, 1998), pp. 1, 2. See also A. Vincola, "Eldercare—What Firms Can Do to Help," *Canadian HR Reporter* (June 5, 2000), p. G3; D. Brown, "Senate Proposes Leave Benefits for Palliative Care."
79. A. Miller, "Retention: Elder Care Benefits," *HR Professional,* December 2008/January 2009, Vol. 26(1), p. 19.
80. K. Earhart, R.D. Middlemist, & W. Hopkins, "Elder Care: An Emerging Employee Assistance Issue," *Employee Assistance Quarterly* 8 (1993), pp. 1–10.
81. D. Dyck, "Make Your Workplace Family-Friendly," *Canadian HR Reporter* (December 13, 1999), pp. G5, G10.
82. "Work/Life Perks Often Avoided by Workers, Poll Finds," *BNA Bulletin to Management* (March 19, 1998), p. 81.
83. W. Burgoyne & P. Leblanc, "Pregnancy-Friendly Firms Create Loyalty, Improve Morale and Ease the Return to Work," *Canadian HR Reporter* (December 13, 1999), pp. 21–22.
84. N. Larin, "Progressive Companies Recognize Value of Family-Friendly Policies," *Canadian HR Reporter* (November 2, 1998), p. 4.
85. D. Brown, "Federal Government Jumps on Family-Friendly Bandwagon," *Canadian HR Reporter* (November 15, 1999), p. 2.
86. Hewitt Associates, *Survey of Educational Reimbursement Programs* (1984).
87. B. Ellig, *Executive Compensation—A Total Pay Perspective* (New York: McGraw-Hill, 1982), p. 141.
88. P. Clark, "Relocation Perks Are Tops With Executives," *Canadian HR Reporter* (June 1, 1998), p. G4.
89. J. Krauss, "Online Concierge," *Canadian HR Reporter* (August 14, 2000), p. 17.
90. W. White & J. Becker, "Increasing the Motivational Impact of Employee Benefits," *Personnel* (January–February 1980), pp. 32–37; and B. Olmsted & S. Smith, "Flex for Success!" *Personnel* 66(6) (June 1989), pp. 50–55.
91. A. Cowan, "Compensation Planning Outlook 2009," Conference Board of Canada, Winter 2009.
92. K. Jeffrey & D. Berrington, "UMA's benefits overhaul: Unique, flexible plan wins over sceptics," *PeopleTalk,* Spring 2007, pp. 35–36.
93. For information about this program, contact Towers, Perrin, Forster, and Crosby, 245 Park Avenue, New York, NY 10167. Hewitt Associates similarly has a program called FlexSystem (Hewitt Associates, New York, NY).

94. D. Woolf, "Total Flex Appeal," *Benefits Canada* (June 1998), pp. 40–42.
95. A. Minuskin, "Building the business case for outsourcing benefits administration," *HR Professional*, August/September 2009, Vol. 26(5), p. 18.
96. A. Czarnecki, "Employees Show Increasing Interest in Pension Communication Systems," *Canadian HR Reporter* (July 15, 1996), p. 18. See also J. Kopach, "Today's Flexible Benefits Programs Call for Greater Employee Education," *Canadian HR Reporter* (August 9, 1999), p. G3.
97. N. Chaplick, "Enter at Your Own Risk," *Benefits Canada* (May 2000), pp. 37–9. See also M. Reid, "Legal Aid," *Benefits Canada* (June 2000), pp. 46–48; S. Deller, "Five Hot Survival Tips for Communicating Benefits," *Canadian HR Reporter* (July 13, 1998), pp. 9, 19.
98. F.G. Kuzmits, "Communicating Benefits: A Double-Click Away," *Compensation and Benefits Review* (September–October 1998), pp. 60–64. See also D. McElroy, "Six Golden Rules of Intranet Benefit Communication," *Canadian HR Reporter* (October 18, 1999), pp. 6, 9; S. Felix, "Techno-Benefits," *Benefits Canada* (January 2000), pp. 27–34.
99. F.G. Kuzmits, "Communicating Benefits: A Double-Click Away," *Compensation and Benefits Review* (September–October 1998), pp. 60–64. See also D. McElroy, "Six Golden Rules of Intranet Benefit Communication," *Canadian HR Reporter* (October 18, 1999), pp. 6, 9; S. Felix, "Techno-Benefits," *Benefits Canada* (January 2000), pp. 27–34.
100. D. Mathieu & C. Barcelon, "Benefit programs for global workforce: Understanding culture of different countries can help companies craft effective benefit plans," *Canadian HR Reporter*, July 13, 2009.


## Chapter 10


1. www.awcbc.org/english/NWISP_STAT.htm (January 2006).
2. National Work Injuries Statistics Program, Association of Workers' Compensation Boards of Canada, www.awbc.org/english/NSWIP_Stats.htm.
3. A. Thompson, "From A Financial Perspective," *CMAJ*, January 30, 2007, 176(3), p. 10.
4. D. Brown, "Labour Says Some Accidents a Crime," *Canadian HR Reporter* (May 20, 2002), p. 3.
5. Statistics Canada, *Health Status of Canadians*, Chapter 6, 1994.
6. B. Rutten, "Building Competitive Advantage through Health and Safety," *Canadian HR Reporter*, April 20, 2009, p. 23.
7. This section is based on T.A. Opie & L. Bates, 1997, *Canadian Master Labour Guide* (CCH Canada Inc.), pp. 1015–1034.
8. Industrial Accident Prevention Association, "Making the Most of Health and Safety Committees," *Canadian HR Reporter*, April 20, 2009, p. 22.
9. M. Pilger, "Conducting a Hygiene Assessment," *Canadian HR Reporter*, April 10, 2000, pp. G3, G4.
10. J.E. Canto-Thaler, "Employers Should Be Ready for Inspectors' Visits," *Canadian HR Reporter*, April 10, 1995, p. 8.
11. "Crown recommends $100,000 fine in first Bill C-45 conviction." *Court to hand down sentence on March 17.*
12. J. Montgomery & K. Kelloway, *Management of Occupational Health and Safety*, 2nd ed. (Toronto: Nelson Canada, 2001).
13. A. Shaw, "Canada Ready to Go Global With Hazardous Materials Safety System, But Move On Hold Until U.S. Catches Up," *Canadian HR Reporter*, March 10, 2007.
14. P. Strahlendorf, "Tug of War," *OH&S Canada* (March 1997), pp. 36–54.
15. K. Prisciak, "Health, Safety & Harassment?" *OH&S Canada* (April–May 1997), pp. 20–21.
16. P. Strahlendorf, "What Supervisors Need to Know," *OH&S Canada* (January–February 1996), pp. 38–40.
17. M. Welsh & K. Sepkowski, "Corporation Fined After Young Man Lost 3 Limbs," *Toronto Star* (September 12, 2003), p. A4.
18. J.E. Canto-Thaler, "Employers Should Be Ready for Inspectors' Visits."
19. A.W. Hammer, *Occupational Safety Management and Engineering*, 3rd ed. (Upper Saddle River, NJ: Prentice Hall, 1985).
20. L. Jack, "Tunnel Vision," *OH&S Canada* (January–February 1997), pp. 31–37.
21. *A Safety Committee Man's Guide*, Aetna Life and Casualty Insurance Company, Catalog 872684.
22. J. Roughton, "Job Hazard Analysis," *OH&S Canada* (January–February 1996), pp. 41–44.
23. A. Fowler, "How to Make the Workplace Safer," *People Management* 1(2) (1995), pp. 38–39.
24. J. Cotter, "Young People Most Accident-Prone Employees on Canadian Job Sites," *Whitehorse Star*, June 16, 2008, p. 16.
25. J. Lutness, "Self-Managed Safety Program Gets Workers Involved," *Safety and Health* 135(4) (April 1987), pp. 42–45. See also F. Streff, M. Kalsher, & E.S. Geller, "Developing Efficient Workplace Safety Programs: Observations of Response Co-Variations," *Journal of Organizational Behavior Management* 13(2) (1993), pp. 3–14.
26. D. Hofman & A. Stetzer, "A Cross-Level Investigation of Factors Influencing Unsafe Behaviours and Accidents," *Personnel Psychology* 49 (1996), p. 329.
27. J. Cotter, "Young People Most Accident-Prone Employees on Canadian Job Sites," *Whitehorse Star*, June 16, 2008, p. 16.
28. http://youngworker.healthandsafetycentre.org/s/FAQ.asp (January 16, 2005).
29. www.youngworker.ca (July 24, 2005).
30. T. Hobel, "Promoting Career Options, Safety on Take Our Kids to Work Day," *Canadian HR Reporter*, November 11, 2007.
31. N. Rankin, "Mitigating the cost of disability," *Canadian HR Reporter*, May 5, 2008, 21(9), p. 30.
32. Workplace Safety and Insurance Board 2006.
33. R. Storey, "They Have All Been Faithful Workers: Injured Workers, Truth, and Workers' Compensation in Ontario, 1970–2008," *Journal of Canadian Studies*, Winter 2009, 43 (1), pp. 154–186.
34. *Workers' Compensation Manual for Managers and Supervisors*, pp. 36–39.
35. A. Bierbier, "Controlling Sky-High Absenteeism," *OH&S Canada* (January–February 1996), pp. 54–63.
36. C. Colacci, "Meet Your Return to Work Obligations With a Functional Abilities Evaluation," *Canadian HR Reporter* (April 10, 2000), p. G5.
37. S. Ritcey, "Psychological Job Matching," *OH&S Canada* (September–October 1996), pp. 50–56.
38. D. Dyck, "Wrapping Up the Wellness Package," *Benefits Canada* (January 1999), pp. 16–20.
39. S. Klie, "The Business of Health," *Canadian HR Reporter*, April 9, 2007, 20(7), p. 24.
40. A. Dranitsaris, "The (Not So) Hidden Costs of Illness: Building Better Business Through Wellness," *PeopleTalk*, Fall 2008, pp. 51–52.
41. L. Young, "Wellness: The Future of Traditional Health and Safety," *Canadian HR Reporter* (February 28, 2000), pp. 7, 11.
42. S. Felix, "Wellness Workout," *Benefits Canada* (January 1998), pp. 25–30.
43. L. Young, "Caring Culture Boosts North Atlantic Refining Company's Extensive EAP a Strong Asset," *Canadian HR Reporter*, October 18, 2007.
44. S. Klie, "Do incentives help change behaviour?" *Canadian HR Reporter*, April 21, 2008, 21(8), p. 21.

45. D. Brown, "Canada Trails U.S. in Wellness," *Canadian HR Reporter* (June 5, 2000), pp. 1, 6.
46. A. Chiu, "The Elements of Workplace Drug, Alcohol Policies."
47. K. Dorrell, "Making A Case," *Benefits Canada* (June 2000), p. 23.
48. J. Smith, "Employee's recent behaviour and smell of alcohol at safety-sensitive workplace made employer suspicious," *Canadian HR Reporter,* March 16, 2009.
49. J.E. Canto-Thaler, "Drug Testing Remains a Murky Legal Issue," *Canadian HR Reporter* (September 9, 1996), p. 8.
50. "Nearly Half of Workers Stressed Out," *Canadian HR Reporter* (June 5, 2000), p. 6A.
51. W. Bott, "An Important Engagement," *Benefits Canada,* June 2008, 32(6), p. 61.
52. P. Kulig, "Mental Health a Growing Business Concern," *Canadian HR Reporter* (October 19, 1998), pp. 1, 3.
53. "Email Overload Down Under," *Canadian HR Reporter* (August 14, 2000), p. 6.
54. L. Duxbury & C. Higgins. (2003) *Work Life conflict in the New Millennium.* Ottawa, Health Canada.
55. Bureau of National Affairs, "Work Place Stress: How to Curb Claims," *Bulletin to Management*, April 14, 1988, p. 120.
56. M. Gibb-Clark, "The Case for Compensating Stress Claims," *The Globe and Mail* (June 14, 1999), M1.
57. L. Young, "Stressed Workers Are Suing Employers," *Canadian HR Reporter,* May 3, 1999, pp. 1, 6.
58. D. Brown, "Liability Could Extend to Mental Damage," *Canadian HR Reporter,* October 9, 2000, pp. 1, 8.
59. K. Jurgens, "Labels don't help, but understanding does," *Canadian HR Reporter,* January 2007.
60. C. Sebastiano, "Employee Health and Unwellness," *Benefits Canada,* August 2008, 32(8), p. 11.
61. A. Shaw, "Toxic Workplaces as Bad as Unsafe Ones," *Canadian HR Reporter,* April 21, 2008.
62. K. Jurgens, "Labels don't help, but understanding does," *Canadian HR Reporter,* January 2007.
63. www.canadapost.ca.
64. I. Parvanova, "Repetitive Strain Injuries: Can You Afford Them?" *Workplace Today* (June 1999), pp. 36, 37, 43. See also "Ergonomics Not a Priority," www.workplace.ca/article3/wednesday.htm (September 20, 2000).
65. J. Tyson, "Pointing to the Problem," *OHS Canada* (April–May 1998), pp. 54–57.
66. J. Hampton, "RSIs: The Biggest Strain Is on the Bottom Line," *Canadian HR Reporter* (February 10, 1997), pp. 15, 19. See also G. Harrington, "Pushing Ergonomics Into Place," *Canadian HR Reporter* (April 24, 1995), pp. 11–12.
67. S.B. Hood, "Repetitive Strain Injury," *Human Resources Professional* (June–July 1997), pp. 29–34.
68. C. Knight, "Computer Tells Employees to Take a Break," *Canadian HR Reporter* (April 7, 1997), p. 9.
69. N.J. Gowan, "The Case for Integration," *OH&S Canada Buyer's Guide* (1997), pp. 68–77.
70. J.A. Savage, "Are Computer Terminals Zapping Workers' Health?" *Business and Society Review* (1994).
71. S. Klie, "Cancer Top Workplace Killer," *Canadian HR Reporter,* June 4, 2007.
72. S. Klie, "Cancer Top Workplace Killer," *Canadian HR Reporter,* June 4, 2007.
73. U. Vu, "Steel Union Gathers Workplace Cancer Data," *Canadian HR Reporter,* June 2, 2008.
74. A. Dranitsaris, "The (Not So) Hidden Costs of Illness: Building Better Business Through Wellness," *PeopleTalk,* Fall 2008, pp. 51–52.
75. N. Pankratz, "New season calls for new understanding of substance abuse," *Alaska Highway News,* March 4, 2008, p. A4.
76. R.G. Wyckham, "Regulating the Marketing of Tobacco Products in Controlling Smoking in Canada," *Canadian Journal of Administrative Sciences* 14(2) (June 1997), pp. 141–165. See also "Cigarettes: A B.C. Workplace Hazard," *Canadian HR Reporter* (November 7, 1997), p. 11.
77. G. Smith, "Violence at Work," *Benefits Canada* (June 1999), pp. 22–25.
78. S. Klie, "Workplace Violence Stats Tip of Iceberg," *Canadian HR Reporter,* March 12, 2007.
79. A. Tomlinson, "Manitoba Recognises Firefighting Cancer Risk," *Canadian HR Reporter* (June 17, 2002), pp. 2, 6. See also W.H. Glenn, "Finding the Right Balance," *OHS Canada* (June 2002), pp. 38–43; and W.H. Glenn, "What's Killing Canadian Workers?" *OHS Canada* (August 2002), p. 20.
80. D. Warner, "'We Do Not Hire Smokers': May Employers Discriminate Against Smokers?" *Employee Responsibilities and Rights Journal* 7(2) (1994), p. 129.
81. U. Vu, "New Rules to Prevent Violence," *Canadian HR Reporter* (October 6, 2003), pp. 1, 13.
82. S. Dobson, "Tackling the Bullies," *Canadian HR Reporter,* March 9, 2009.
83. R. Dunlop, "Nova Scotia Fights Workplace Violence," *Canadian HR Reporter,* December 17, 2007.
84. "Looking Out for Trouble," *OHS Canada* (March–April 1995), pp. 34–37.
85. M. Penrose, "Safety Extends to Employees Abroad," *Canadian HR Reporter,* May, 5, 2008.
86. T. Verbic, "Improving the odds on risky moves: What employers need to consider when sending staff to dangerous locations," *Canadian HR Reporter,* September 24, 2007.


## Chapter 11


1. S. Klie, "Middle managers boost productivity: One-on-one relationships with employees engender respect, trust, loyalty and contribution," *Canadian HR Reporter,* February 27, 2006.
2. A. Pace, "Leaving the Corner Office," *T+D,* August 2008, Vol. 62(8), p. 16.
3. A. Pace, "Leaving the Corner Office," *T+D,* August 2008, Vol. 62(8), p. 16.
4. P. Kulig, "The Importance of Being a Good Listener," *Canadian HR Reporter* (April 20, 1998), pp. 15, 19.
5. Survey conducted by David Aplin Recruiting, www.aplin.com as reported in the *HR Magazine,* August/September 2009, Vol. 26(5), p. 14.
6. L. Branham, *The 7 Hidden Reasons Employees Leave*, 2005, AMACOM Books.
7. An interview with Julie Gebauer, Towers Perrin Managing Director and lead on the 2008 Global Workforce Study, www.towersperrin.com/tp/showhtml.jsp?...global/...global.
8. An interview with Julie Gebauer, Towers Perrin Managing Director and lead on the 2008 Global Workforce Study, www.towersperrin.com/tp/showhtml.jsp?...global/...global.
9. Towers Perrin, 2008 Global Workforce Study, www.towersperrin.com/tp/showhtml.jsp?...global/...global.
10. S. Klie, "Senior leadership drives employee engagement: Study," *Canadian HR Reporter,* November 19, 2009.
11. An interview with Julie Gebauer, Towers Perrin Managing Director and lead on the 2008 Global Workforce Study, www.towersperrin.com/tp/showhtml.jsp?...global/...global.

12. M. Rhodes, "Kind bosses at heart of retention programs," *Canadian HR Reporter,* May 4, 2009.
13. B. Orr, "Privacy in the Workplace a Growing Challenge for Employers," *Canadian HR Reporter* (January 25, 1999), pp. 8, 10.
14. P. Israel, "Employee Misconduct . . . Employer Responsibility?" *Canadian HR Reporter* (May 20, 2002), p. 5. See also "Developing Internet Policies for Employees," *Canadian HR Reporter* (January 25, 1999), pp. 8, 10.
15. R. Ravary, "Employment law dominated HR news in 2008," *Canadian HR Reporter,* February 16, 2009.
16. "We Know Where You've Been," *Canadian HR Reporter* (August 13, 2001), p. 7.
17. J. Conforti, *Privacy in the Workplace: Access to Employee Records and Monitoring of Employees in the Internet Age.* Paper presented at the Human Resources Professional Association of Ontario Employment Law Conference (October 1999), Toronto.
18. E.A. Douthitt & J.R. Aiello, "The Role of Participation and Control in the Effects of Computer Monitoring on Fairness Perceptions, Task Satisfaction, and Performance," *Journal of Applied Psychology* 86 (2001), pp. 867–874.
19. P. Israel, "Spying on Employees . . . and It's Perfectly Legal," *Canadian HR Reporter* (April 21, 2003), p. 5. See also P. Bonifero, "Workplace Privacy and Surveillance Issues," *HR Professional* (February–March 1999), pp. 49–51.
20. "Inexcusable E-mail," *Canadian HR Reporter* (July 15, 2002), p. 2.
21. D. Brown, "10 Months to Get Ready," *Canadian HR Reporter* (February 24, 2003), pp. 1, 11.
22. R. Hiscock, "A Perspective on Canada's New Privacy Legislation," *Canadian HR Reporter* (June 18, 2001), pp. G8–G9. See also E. Kuzz, "More Rules for Employee Information Protection," *Canadian HR Reporter* (September 9, 2002), p. 16; and D. Brown, "10 Months to Get Ready."
23. N. Akerman, "Total Rewards on Guard," *Workspan* (December 2002), pp. 46–49; P.S. Eyres, "Impatience: High, Subject: Employee E-mail Policies," *Workspan* (December 2002), pp. 54–56; N. MacDonald, "You've Got E-mail Problems," *Canadian HR Reporter* (March 10, 2003), pp. G5, G10; and A. Tomlinson, "Heavy-Handed Net Policies Push Privacy Boundaries." See also J. Conforti, "Privacy in the Workplace: Access to Employee Records and Monitoring of Employees in the Internet Age."
24. Interview with Andy Barr of Yasni, "One-half of co-workers spy on each other: Survey," *Canadian HR Reporter,* August 13, 2009.
25. G. McFarlane & A. McPherson, "Big brother is watching: Do you know the legal limits on employee surveillance?" *PeopleTalk,* Spring 2007, pp. 55–56.
26. G. McFarlane & A. McPherson, "Big brother is watching: Do you know the legal limits on employee surveillance?" *PeopleTalk,* Spring 2007, pp. 55–56.
27. G. McFarlane & A. McPherson, "Big brother is watching: Do you know the legal limits on employee surveillance?" *PeopleTalk,* Spring 2007, pp. 55–56.
28. S. Ray & D. Holmes, "How to Discipline Without Exposure to Lawsuits," *Canadian HR Reporter* (September 6, 1999), p. 31. See also J. Miller, "Procedural Fairness toward Disciplined Workers an Issue before the Courts," *Canadian HR Reporter* (November 2, 1998), p. 5.
29. G.A. Ball, *Outcomes of Punishment Incidents: The Role of Subordinate Perceptions, Individual Differences, and Leader Behavior.* Unpublished doctoral dissertation. The Pennsylvania State University. See also N. Cole, "Yes, Employees Can React Positively to Discipline," *Canadian HR Reporter* (November 4, 1996), p. 11; and N.D. Cole & G.P. Latham, "Effects of Training in Procedural Justice on Perceptions of Disciplinary Fairness by Unionized Employees and Disciplinary Subject Matter Experts," *Journal of Applied Psychology* 82(5) (October 1997), pp. 699–705.
30. D. Campbell, R. Fleming, & R. Grote, "Discipline without punishment—at last." *Harvard Business Review,* July/August 1985, Vol. 63(4), pp. 162–169.
31. D. Grote, *Discipline Without Punishment.* (New York: American Management Association, 1995).
32. R. Grote, "Discipline without punishment," *Across the Board,* September/October 2001, Vol. 38(5).
33. J. Famularo, *Handbook of Modern Personnel Administration* (New York: McGraw-Hill, 1972), pp. 65.3–65.5.
34. Famularo, *Handbook of Modern Personnel Administration.*
35. Famularo, *Handbook of Modern Personnel Administration,* pp. 65.4–65.5.
36. K. Blair, "When Is a Firing Justified?" *Canadian HR Reporter* (April 21, 1997), p. 5. See also K. Blair, "Just How Just Does Just Cause Have to Be?" *Canadian HR Reporter* (November 3, 1997), p. 5.
37. E.E. Mole, *Wrongful Dismissal Practice Manual,* Chapter 7 (Toronto: Butterworths Canada Ltd., 1993).
38. J. Rubin & S. Sultan, "Drug and alcohol testing: Where are we now?" *Canadian HR Reporter,* March 9, 2009.
39. Mole, *Wrongful Dismissal,* Chapter 4.
40. S. Rudner, "Just cause termination still not clearcut," *Canadian HR Reporter,* March 23, 2009, p. 14.
41. T. Wagar, "Wrongful Dismissal: Perception vs. Reality," *Human Resources Professional* (June 1996), p. 10.
42. K. Blair, "Sports Editor Scores 28-Month Severance," *Canadian HR Reporter* (April 7, 1997), p. 5.
43. M.J. MacKillop, *The Perils of Dismissal: The Impact of the Wallace Decision on Reasonable Notice.* Paper presented at the Human Resources Professionals Association of Ontario Employment Law Conference (October 1999), Toronto. See also M.J. MacKillop, "Bad Faith Discharge Dismissed by S.C.C.," *HR Professional* (April–May 1998), pp. 11, 12; K. Blair, "The High Cost of Bad Faith Termination," *Canadian HR Reporter* (December 1, 1997), p. 5.
44. R. Ravary, "Employment law dominated HR news in 2008," *Canadian HR Reporter,* February 16, 2009.
45. K. Blair, "Pay in Lieu Just the Beginning," *Canadian HR Reporter* (July 14, 1997), p. 5. See also K. Blair, "Dismissal Damages, Thy Name Is Mitigation," *Canadian HR Reporter* (February 9, 1998), p. 5.
46. Based on a speech by Peter Panken and presented in *BNA Bulletin to Management* (June 20, 1985), pp. 11, 12.
47. M. Currie & C. Cunningham, "Competing Priorities: Restrictive Covenants," *HR Magazine,* August/September 2009, Vol. 26(5), p. 17.
48. M. Currie & C. Cunningham, "Competing Priorities: Restrictive Covenants," *HR Magazine,* August/September 2009, Vol. 26(5), p. 17.
49. Mole, *Wrongful Dismissal,* Chapter 3.
50. "Former TD Executive Awarded $2 Million," *Canadian HR Reporter* (February 14, 2000), p. 20.
51. This section was based on M. Rothman, "Employee Termination, I: A Four-Step Procedure," *Personnel* (February 1989), pp. 31–35; and S. Jesseph, "Employee Termination, II: Some Do's and Don'ts," *Personnel* (February 1989), pp. 36–38. For a good checklist, see Silbergeld, "Avoiding Wrongful Termination Claims: A Checklist for Employers," *Employment Relations Today* 20(4) (1993), pp. 447–454.
52. See J. Coil III & C. Rice, "Three Steps to Creating Effective Employee Releases," *Employment Relations Today* (Spring 1994), pp. 91–94. Wrongful termination is a problem for managerial employees as well.

See, for example, C. Longenecker & F. Post, "The Management Termination Trap," *Business Horizons* 37(3) (1994), pp. 71–79.

53. Based on Coil & Rice, "Three Steps to Creating Effective Employee Releases," p. 92.
54. S. Milne, "The Termination Interview," *Canadian Manager* (Spring 1994), pp. 15–16.
55. Morin & York, *Outplacement Techniques,* p. 117. See also S. Weide, "When You Terminate an Employee," *Employment Relations* Today (August 1994), pp. 287–293.
56. Global Research Report 2008, *Right Management,* www.right.com.
57. M. Morrow, "Severance trends for Canadian employees," *Canadian HR Reporter,* June/ July 2009, Vol. 26(4), p. 23.
58. J. Zarandona & M. Camuso, "A Study of Exit Interviews: Does the Last Word Count?" *Personnel* 62 (March 1985), pp. 47–48.
59. Commerce Clearing House, *Ideas and Trends in Personnel* (August 9, 1988), p. 133.
60. *Personnel Practices/Communications,* p. 1410.
61. P. Kulig, "Temporary Employment Changing the Character of Canada's Labour Force," *Canadian HR Reporter* (November 16, 1998), pp. 1, 15.
62. This is based on Mossop Cornelissen Report (August 1996).
63. S. Stephens, "When Two Worlds Collide," *HR Professional* (April–May 2000), pp. 27–35.
64. 1995 Canadian Dismissal Practices Survey, Murray Axmith & Associates, Toronto.
65. G. Golightly, "Preparing Employees for Retirement Transitions," *HR Professional* (December 1999–January 2000), pp. 27–33.
66. G. Golightly, "Preparing Employees for Retirement Transitions."
67. G. Avraam, A. Ishak, & T. Appleyard, "Terminating employees around the world: One size does not fit all when it comes to dismissing workers," *Canadian HR Reporter,* April 6, 2009.

## Chapter 12

1. N. Van Praet, "Canadian Auto Workers Most Productive," *Alberni Valley Times,* January 27, 2009, p. A17.
2. T. Kochan & H. Katz, *Collective Bargaining and Industrial Relations* (Homewood, IL: Irwin, 1988).
3. N. VanPraet, "Union Vote at Toyota Cancelled: Application Pulled," *National Post,* March 20, 2008, p. FP4.
4. Based on J. Pierce, *Canadian Industrial Relations* (Scarborough: Prentice-Hall Canada Inc., 2000), p. 276.
5. Bargaining in Bad Faith Costs Employer $6 Million," *Canadian HR Reporter* (August 13, 2001), p. 5.
6. P. Kumar, "Union Growth in Canada: Retrospect and Prospect" in W.C. Riddell (Ed.), *Canadian Labour Relations* (Toronto: University of Toronto Press, 1986), p. 103.
7. "Casual Government Workers in New Brunswick Win Right to Unionize: Court Rules Labour Relations Act Violates Charter Rights of Casual Workers," *Canadian HR Reporter,* June 29, 2009.
8. S. Klie, "Economic Crisis Changes Union Priorities: Focus of Collective Bargaining Shifts From Wage Increases to Job Security," *Canadian HR Reporter,* December 1, 2008.
9. Human Resources and Skills Development Canada, "Union Membership in Canada in 2008: Strategic Policy, Analysis, and Workplace Information," 2008.
10. Human Resources and Skills Development Canada, "Union Membership in Canada in 2008: Strategic Policy, Analysis, and Workplace Information," 2008.
11. L. Harris, "Technology Providing Organizing Options: Canadian Labour Congress Studies How to Increase Union Membership," *Canadian HR Reporter,* June 25, 2008.
12. Statistics Canada, "Rate of Union Coverage: Canada and Provinces 2008," data is adapted from Statistics Canada Labour Force Survey.
13. Statistics Canada 2006, "Diverging Trends in Unionization."
14. L. Harris, "Youthful Proposition From Unions," *Canadian HR Reporter,* October 20, 2008, Vol. 21(18), pp. 31–32.
15. C. Mancini, "Equity Survey Workgroup," *Update,* April 3, 2009, 36(7), p. 8.
16. A. Okafor, "White Collar Unionization: Why and What to Do," *Personnel* (August 1985), pp. 17–20; and M. E. Gordon & A. DiNisi, "A Re-examination of the Relationship between Union Membership and Job Satisfaction," *Industrial and Labor Relations Review* (January 1995), pp. 222–236.
17. C. Fullager & J. Barling, "A Longitudinal Test of a Model of the Antecedents and Consequences of Union Loyalty," *Journal of Applied Psychology* 74(2) (April 1989), pp. 213–227; A. Eaton, M. Gordon, & J. Keefe, "The Impact of Quality of Work Life Programs and Grievance Systems Effectiveness on Union Commitment," *Industrial and Labor Relations Review* (April 1992), pp. 592–604.
18. S. Klie, "Mounties Given Right to Unionize: Court says RCMP Has Right to Negotiate, Not Just Consult," *Canadian HR Reporter,* April 5, 2009.
19. L. Young, "Union Drives: Initiated Within, Prevented Within," *Canadian HR Reporter* (November 29, 1999), pp. 2, 14.
20. J. Darlington, "Casting the Net Wider: Twelve Tips for Taking the E-Union to the Next Level," 21 Conference, London, March 8, 2003.
21. Cited in Young, "Union Drives: Initiated Within, Prevented Within," p. 14.
22. Based in part on L. Field, "Early Signs," *Canadian HR Reporter* (November 29, 1999), p. 14.
23. H. Levitt, "Keep in Touch If You Want to Keep the Union at Bay," *Financial Post,* September 13, 1999, p. C11.
24. M.D. Failes, "Is Silence Really Golden?" *Human Resources Professional* (August–September 1997), pp. 33, 35.
25. J. Jones, "Wal-Mart Union Certification Overturned: Saskatchewan Court Rules Secret Ballot Vote Needed for Certification," *Canadian HR Reporter,* June 30, 2009.
26. L. Harris, "Another Wal-Mart is Unionized," *Canadian HR Reporter,* December 18, 2008.
27. M. Gunderson, A. Ponak, & D.G. Taras, *Union–Management Relations in Canada,* 4th ed. (Toronto: Pearson Education Canada, 2001), p. 186.
28. A.W.J. Craig & N.A. Solomon, *The System of Industrial Relations in Canada,* 5th ed. (Scarborough: Prentice-Hall Canada Inc., 1996), p. 217.
29. Craig & Solomon, *The System of Industrial Relations in Canada,* p. 218.
30. Craig & Solomon, *The System of Industrial Relations in Canada,* p. 216.
31. F. Stronach & B. Hargrove, "Unlikely Allies Team Up," *Canadian HR Reporter,* November 5, 2007.
32. Adapted from R.L. Miller, "Preparations for Negotiations," *Personnel Journal* (1978), pp. 36–39, 44.
33. M. Ballot, *Labour–Management Relations in a Changing Environment* (New York: John Wiley and Sons, 1992), pp. 169–425.
34. Based on R. Richardson, *Collective Bargaining by Objectives* (Englewood Cliffs, NJ: Prentice-Hall, 1977), p. 150.
35. R. Stagner & H. Rosen, *Psychology of Union–Management Relations* (Belmont, CA: Wadsworth, 1965), pp. 95–97.
36. The section on distributive bargaining is based on R.E. Walton & R.B. McKersie, *A Behavioral Theory of Labor Negotiations* (New York: McGraw-Hill, 1965), pp. 4–6.

37. H. Raiff, *The Art and Science of Negotiation* (Cambridge, MA: Belknap Harvard University Press, 1982), pp. 44–65.
38. The section on integrative bargaining is based on Walton and McKersie, *A Behavioral Theory,* pp. 4–6.
39. "Concessions Save Algoma." *Canadian HR Reporter* (January 28, 2002), p. 2.
40. R. Fisher, W. Ury & B. Patton, *Getting to Yes: Negotiating Agreement Without Giving In,* Penguin Books, 1991, 2nd ed.
41. Based on C. Kapel, "The Feeling's Mutual," *Human Resources Professional* (April 1995), pp. 9–13.
42. Kapel, "The Feeling's Mutual," p. 10.
43. S. Klie, "Rethink Labour Relations: Report. Move Away From Deadline Bargaining to Reduce Work Stoppages," *Canadian HR Reporter,* April 20, 2009.
44. J. Lendvay-Zwickl, "The Canadian Industrial Relations System: Current Challenges and Future Options," Ottawa: Conference Board of Canada, 2005.
45. R.E. Fells, "Developing Trust in Negotiation," *Employee Relations,* 14(1), 1993.
46. K. Merx & J. Green, "Governments 'Interfering' with GM Talks," *National Post,* May 20, 2009, p. FP.6.
47. Peirce, *Canadian Industrial Relations,* p. 431.
48. Cited in B. Tieleman, "Still Good Reason to Join a Union: Studies Show Union Workers Reap Better Wages and Benefits," *Financial Post* (July 5, 1999), C6.
49. S. Klie, "Labour Peace in 2009: Conference Board of Canada," *Canadian HR Reporter,* March 9, 2009, 22(5), pp. 1–2.
50. D. Akin, "Duration of Canadian Work Stoppages Growing," *The Vancouver Sun,* January 21, 2009, p. G5.
51. Gunderson et al., *Union–Management Relations in Canada,* p. 195.
52. A. Krueger, "Strikes, Scabs, and Tread Separations: Labour Strife and the Production of Defective Bridgestone/Firestone Tires," A study produced in collaboration with Princeton University, 2002.
53. M. Certosimo, "Hockey, Picketing and Injunctions," *Workplace News* (May 1999), p. 7.
54. D. Adams, "Petrocan Workers Win," *Our Times,* February/March 2009, 28(1), p. 5.
55. U. Vu, "Two Sides of the Same Coin," *Canadian HR Reporter,* February 27, 2007.
56. E. Drass, "May Took Toll on GTA's Streets: Deaths, TTC Strike," *National Post,* June 9, 2006, p. DT.20.
57. Based on Gunderson et al., *Union–Management Relations in Canada,* p. 429; and Peirce, *Canadian Industrial Relations,* p. 431.
58. This section is based on Gunderson et al., *Union–Management Relations in Canada,* pp. 282–283.
59. "Quebec Considers Limiting Contract Lengths," *Canadian HR Reporter,* September 25, 2000, p. 16.
60. A. Ferner, J. Quintanilla & C. Sanchez-Runde, *Multinationals and the Construction of Transnational Practices: Convergence and Diversity in the Global Economy* (London, UK: Palgrave Macmillan, P. Gunnigle, D. Collings & M. Morley, 2005).
61. M. Gilman & P. Marginson, "Negotiating European Works Councils: Contours of Constrained Choice," *Industrial Relations Journal,* 33(1), pp. 36–51.
62. C. Chang & C. Sorrentino, "Union Membership Statistics in 12 Countries," *Monthly Labor Review,* 2001, pp. 46–53.

# Answers to Study Guide Questions

## Chapter 1

1. a 2. e 3. c 4. a 5. b 6. c 7. b 8. c 9. e
10. b 11. c 12. b 13. e 14. b 15. d

## Chapter 2

1. a 2. c 3. a 4. b 5. c 6. e 7. b 8. e 9. b
10. e 11. a 12. e 13. c 14. b 15. e

## Chapter 3

1. b 2. c 3. a 4. c 5. b 6. e 7. a 8. d 9. a
10. e 11. b 12. c 13. a 14. e 15. c

## Chapter 4

1. b 2. d 3. b 4. c 5. e 6. c 7. d 8. e 9. a
10. b 11. a 12. c 13. c 14. a 15. c

## Chapter 5

1. a 2. a 3. d 4. b 5. c 6. b 7. e 8. e 9. c
10. e 11. d 12. b 13. c 14. b 15. d

## Chapter 6

1. b 2. c 3. d 4. b 5. c 6. e 7. c 8. d 9. e
10. c 11. e 12. c

## Chapter 7

1. c 2. e 3. e 4. b 5. c 6. c 7. c 8. b 9. e
10. c 11. c 12. e 13. d 14. e 15. e

## Chapter 8

1. d 2. e 3. c 4. c 5. c 6. d 7. b 8. e 9. a
10. d 11. b 12. b 13. c 14. a 15. b

## Chapter 9

1. b 2. e 3. c 4. b 5. d 6. e 7. c 8. e 9. c
10. e 11. e 12. b 13. c 14. a 15. e

## Chapter 10

1. c 2. a 3. c 4. c 5. a 6. c 7. e 8. a 9. d
10. d 11. b 12. b 13. e 14. c 15. e

## Chapter 11

1. b 2. c 3. b 4. e 5. c 6. a 7. e 8. c 9. b
10. c 11. e 12. b 13. e 14. a 15. e

## Chapter 12

1. e 2. b 3. e 4. a 5. b 6. d 7. d 8. c 9. e
10. b 11. b 12. e 13. b 14. d 15. c

# Name and Organization Index

## A



## B



## C

## V



## W



## Y



## Z

# Subject Index

*Note:* Key terms are boldface. Page numbers followed by *f* and *t* represent figures and tables, respectively.

## A



## B



## C

## D

## E

## I

## J



## K



## L

## M



## N



## O

## Q



## R



## S

# T

## U



## V



## W



## Y

# *Photo Credits*

## Chapter 1

**pp. 1, 28:** © hammondovi/iStockphoto; **p. 3:** Andy Levin/Photo Researchers, Inc.; **p. 18:** © dpa/Corbis; **p. 22:** Bettmann/Corbis.

## Chapter 2

**pp. 39, 47:** © INSADCO Photography/Alamy; **p. 45:** Eric Paul Zamora/Fresno Bee/MCT/Newscom; **p. 48:** © Steven Robertson/iStockphoto.

## Chapter 3

**pp. 69, 95:** Sean Prior/Shutterstock; **p. 77:** Monty Rakusen/Cultura/Getty.

## Chapter 4

**pp. 104, 108:** © Sean Locke/iStockphoto; **p. 117:** © Eliza Snow/iStockphoto; **p. 135:** Courtesy of Bank of Montreal.

## Chapter 5

**pp. 144, 158:** Adam Gregor/Shutterstock; **p. 150:** Zsolt Nyulaszi/Shutterstock; **p. 161:** Zsolt Nyulaszi/Shutterstock; **p. 164 (left):** Pixtal Images/Photolibrary; **p. 164 (right):** AVAVA/Shutterstock.

## Chapter 6

**pp. 179, 181:** © Steve Hix/Somos Images/Corbis; **p. 187:** Olaf Döring/imagebroker.net/photolibrary; **p. 189:** NASA/JSC/S98-03945; **p. 192:** The Slide Farm/Al Harvey; **p. 193:** Randy Lincks/All Canada Photos/Photolibrary; **p. 200:** Courtesy of Bank of Montreal.

## Chapter 7

**pp. 213, 237:** Blend Images/Photolibrary; **p. 224:** AVAVA/Shutterstock; **p. 226:** © Jon Feingersh/Blend Images/Corbis.

## Chapter 8

**pp. 244, 260:** Andrejs Pidjass/Shutterstock; **p. 249:** The Canadian Press (Pawel Dwulit Julie); **p. 272:** © Copyright by MPL Communications Inc. Photo reproduced by permission of *Canadian HR Reporter*; **p. 274:** E.I. DuPont De Nemours & Co., Inc.

## Chapter 9

**pp. 282, 301 (top):** Monkey Business Images/Shutterstock; **p. 286:** dragon_fang/Shutterstock; **p. 301 (bottom):** © Comstock/2010 Jupiterimages Unlimited, a division of Getty Images.

## Chapter 10

**pp. 314, 335:** In Vivio Media Lab/Desjardins Group; **p. 320 (top):** Paul Felix/Britain on View Non-Exclusive/Photolibrary; **p. 320 (bottom):** © Joe Carini/The Image Works; **p. 339:** © Lanica Klein/iStockphoto.

## Chapter 11

**pp. 349, 368:** The Canadian Press (Andrew Vaughan); **p. 353:** The Canadian Press (Pawel Dwulit Julie); **p. 365:** Paul Barton/Corbis/Bettmann; **p. 369:** Rubberball/Photolibrary.

## Chapter 12

**pp. 377, 378:** Francisco Cruz/SuperStock; **p. 386:** Ian Lindsey/*Vancouver Sun*; **p. 388:** Dick Hemingway; **p. 398 (bottom left):** *Canadian HR Reporter*; **p. 398 (top right):** Canadian Press (Adrian Wyld); **p. 398 (bottom right):** *Toronto Star*/Paul Irish/Canadian Press.

reduces reality shock, and clarifies job expectations. Assessment of orientation effectiveness includes: evaluating employee reactions and performance, and performing cost/benefit analyses.

**Five Steps in Training Process**
Steps include (1) needs analysis, (2) instructional design, (3) implementation and delivery of training, (4) transfer of learning, and (5) evaluation and follow-up.

**Traditional Training Techniques**
Techniques include on-the-job (coaching, job rotation), off-the-job (job instruction training, lectures, videoconferencing, programmed learning, simulations), and e-learning.

**Leadership Development**
Grooming employees to serve as organizational leaders. Development includes opportunities to participate in job rotation, coaching, mentoring, action learning, case studies, management games, role-playing, in house development centres, behaviour modelling, and seminars.

## Chapter 7

**Performance Appraisal**
Provides information on which to base salary or promotion decisions, an opportunity to review and discuss work-related behaviour and facilitate career planning.

**Three Steps in Conducting Performance Appraisals**
Steps include (1) define performance expectations to ensure job duties and standards of performance are clear, (2) compare employee's actual performance to standards of performance, and (3) provide feedback.

**Methods of Appraising Performance**
Methods include graphic rating scale, BARS, BOS, MBO, balanced scorecard, critical incident method.

**Problems with Performance Appraisals**
Problems include unclear performance standards and rater errors, including halo effect, central tendency, leniency or strictness, appraisal bias, recency effect, and similar-to-me bias. Ways of minimizing these problems: raters being aware of rater errors, training supervisors to eliminate and avoid errors, and ensuring completed appraisals are reviewed by supervisor's immediate boss and HR department.

**Legal and Ethical Issues**
Ensure performance standards are provided to raters and ratees; train supervisors on rating instruments; allow appraisers regular contact with employee being evaluated; use multiple appraisers; include appeal mechanism; provide corrective guidance to assist poor performers.

## Chapter 8

**Factors That Determine Pay Rates**
Include legal requirements, union influences, compensation policies of employer, and internal and external equity in pay.

**Steps in Establishing Pay Rates**
(1) Determine worth of job within organization, (2) group similar jobs into pay grades, (3) conduct salary surveys of what other employers are paying for comparable jobs, and (4) price each pay grade by using wage curves and fine tuning pay rates.

**Job Evaluation**
The formal and systematic comparison of jobs within a company to determine the worth of one job relative to another, resulting in a job hierarchy.

**Methods of Job Evaluation**
Methods include ranking, job classification, point, and Hay System.

**Types of Organization-Wide Incentive Plans**
- **Profit sharing**—employees receive a share of company profits
- **Employee stock ownership**—a trust is established to purchase shares of company stock for employees using employee and/or employer contributions
- **Gainsharing**—company engages employees in common effort to achieve company productivity objective and shares resulting cost-saving gains

**Current Trends in Compensation**
Trends include skill-competency-based pay, customized job evaluation, pay equity, strategic pay.

## Chapter 9

**Legally Required Benefits**
Employment Insurance, C/QPP plans, worker's compensation, provincial health-care plans, paid vacation and holidays, leaves of absence for situations involving illness, maternity, becoming a new parent, compassionate care leave, bereavement.

**Employer-Sponsored Benefits**
Maternity/parental/adoption leave, bereavement, compassionate care, sabbatical, short-term disability or sick leave plans, long-term disability plans, life insurance, supplementary health care/medical insurance, pension plans.

**Types of Employee Services**
- **Personal services**—credit unions, counselling services, employee assistance programs, social events
- **Job-related services**—subsidized child care, subsidized employee transportation, elder care, family-friendly benefits, food services, educational subsidies
- **Executive perquisites**—management loans, relocation benefits, club memberships, cell phones, company cars

## Chapter 10

**Occupational Health and Safety Laws**
Aim to protect health and safety of workers by minimizing work-related accidents and illnesses. Shared responsibility model communicates importance of employer and employee cooperation to reduce accident rates.

**Employer Responsibilities**
Include taking every reasonable precaution to ensure workers' health and safety (due diligence). Include filing government accident reports, maintaining records, and posting safety notices and legislative information.

**Employee Responsibilities**
Include adhering to health and safety rules of organization, wearing protective clothing and equipment, reporting health and safety issues to employer, refusing work where there is reasonable cause to believe the work is dangerous.

**Basic Causes of Accidents**
Include chance occurrences, unsafe conditions, unsafe acts on the part of employees.

**Accident Prevention at Work**
- **Reduce unsafe conditions**—identify and remove potential hazards
- **Reduce unsafe acts**—implement selection and placement strategies, education and training, and positive reinforcement; monitor work overload and stress; and establish safety policies

**Wellness Programs**
Aim to improve employees' health and thus reduce costs related to sickness and disability claims, workers' compensation, and absenteeism.

**Key Employee Health Issues**
Alcoholism, drug addiction, stress, depression, burnout, repetitive strain injuries, workplace smoking, mental illness, workplace violence.

## Chapter 11

**Fair and Just Disciplinary Process**
- Establishing rules and regulations that inform employees ahead of time as to what is and is not acceptable workplace behaviour
- Progressive penalties or disciplinary actions (warnings, suspensions) that are provided to employees before dismissal
- Appeals process to ensure discipline is administered fairly and equitably
- Appropriate use of restrictive covenants

**Wrongful Dismissal**
Employee is dismissed without just cause (such as for incompetence, dishonesty, insubordination, fighting, or persistent absence or lateness) and believes reasonable notice of dismissal was not provided.

**Constructive Dismissal**
Employer makes unilateral changes to employment contract that are unacceptable to employee although employee has not been formally terminated.

**Downsizings, Layoffs, Acquisitions, and Mergers**
- Genuinely communicate one-on-one to employees
- Treat those who lose their jobs with fairness and in accordance with the law
- Provide reassurance to survivors
- Provide emotional support
- Use fair termination process
- Use alternatives to layoffs

## Chapter 12

**Labour Relations Strategy**
An organization's plan for working with unions; strategies include union acceptance and union avoidance.

**Common Characteristics of Labour Relations Legislation:**
- Procedure for collective agreement to be in force for a minimum of one year
- Procedures to be followed before strike or lockout
- Prohibition of strikes or lockouts during life of collective agreement
- Requirement that disputes over matters arising from interpretation of collective agreement be settled by final and binding arbitration
- Prohibition of specified "unfair" practices
- Establishment of labour relations board or equivalent

**Union Organizing Process**
Involves (1) employee/union contact, (2) initial organizational meeting, (3) formation of in-house organizing committee, (4) organizing campaign, and (5) certification, recognition, or rejection.

**Collective Bargaining**
The formal process used by management and labour to establish a collective agreement. Bargaining includes preparation, face-to-face negotiations, and obtaining approval for proposed contract.

**Impact of Unionization on HRM**
- Expansion of HR department by addition of LR specialist or section
- Less freedom for management to make unilateral changes since union leaders are involved in decisions that will affect their members
- Greater centralization of employee record keeping and standardization of decision making

ISBN 978-0-13-814722-8
EAN
9 780138 147228
www.pearsoncanada.ca

# Management of Human Resources

Third Canadian Edition, In-Class Edition

## Study Card for Students

GARY DESSLER ■ CAROLIN REKAR MUNRO ■ NINA D. COLE

Chapter 1

**Human Resources Management (HRM)**
HRM is the management of people in organizations. Its goal is to attract the best qualified applicants, engage employees, maximize employees' contributions, and retain employees.

**HR's Impact on the Bottom Line**
HR professionals are internal organizational consultants offering advice to senior management on strategic directives and organizational change. HR departments are expected to justify their existence through metrics that illustrate the value-added contribution HR programs bring to an organization's bottom line.

**Environmental Factors Influencing HRM**

- **Internal factors** include organizational culture and management practices, such as a shift from traditional bureaucratic structures to flatter organizations.
- **External environmental factors** include labour market issues, demographic trends and increasing workforce diversity, technology, government, and globalization.

**Evolution of HRM**
Scientific management philosophy → human relations movement → personnel administration → human resources management.

The latest phase of HRM is ongoing and recognizes that highly trained and committed employees are an organization's best competitive advantage.

Chapter 2

**The Constitution Act of 1867**
Gives each province and territory power to legislate in relation to employment law for all workers, except those employed by federal government or in federally regulated industries.

**Human Rights Legislation**
Prohibits employers from exercising intentional or unintentional discrimination in their dealings with employees and the public, and in their policies pertaining to all employment terms and conditions.

**Equal Pay for Equal Work**
Specifies that employers cannot pay male and female employees differently if they perform the same work, and require the same degree of skill, effort, and responsibility under similar working conditions.

**Employment Equity**
Identifies and aims to eliminate systemic barriers to employment opportunities that adversely affect visible minorities, women, Aboriginal peoples, and persons with disabilities.

**Pay Equity**
Addresses pay imbalances in pay between male- and female-dominated job classes resulting from undervaluing work traditionally performed by women.

**Diversity Management**
Activities that aim to integrate all members of an organization's multicultural workforce and use their diversity to enhance organizational effectiveness. Requires top management commitment, recruitment, training, communication, celebrating diversity, mentoring and networking, audits, and management accountability.

Chapter 3

**Organizing Work**
Business landscapes are characterized by the global marketplace, international competition, shifts in demographic needs/expectations, and technological advancements. Organizations are reconfiguring their hierarchies and redesigning jobs in response to changes in the work world; changes include movements toward flatter/boundaryless structures, using virtual teams, and reengineering.

**Industrial Engineering**
Identifies, analyzes, and times elements of job cycles and uses the information to modify, eliminate, or rearrange work to reduce time required and improve efficiency.

**Behavioural Engineering**
Proposes job enlargement, job rotation, and job enrichment to overcome dehumanization and other problems associated with industrial engineering.

**Human Engineering**
Considers ergonomics and tries to adapt the entire job system to match human characteristics. Includes flexible work arrangements.

**Job Analysis**
Is concerned with collecting objective and verifiable data about job requirements. Information is used for developing job descriptions and job specifications.

**Competency Analysis**
Is the analysis of an organization's values, mission, and strategic direction in order to identify the KSAs employees are expected to demonstrate regardless of their positions. Reinforces capabilities that are valued by the organization.

**Job Description**
A written statement of what a jobholder does, how the job is done, and under what conditions the job is performed. It includes job identification, job summary, relationships, duties, performance standards, and working conditions.

**Techniques Used to Gather Job Analysis Data**

- **Conventional**—interviews, questionnaires, observation, diaries, and world cafe
- **Quantitative**—position analysis questionnaire (PQA) and functional job analysis (FJA)

**Employee Engagement in Job Redesign**
Involves all employees in sharing ideas about job redesign and enhances employees' commitment to change.

Chapter 4

**Steps in HR Planning**
Involves forecasting future human resources needs (demand), forecasting availability of internal and external candidates (supply), and planning and implementing HR programs to balance supply/demand.

**Forecasting HR Needs**

- **Quantitative approaches**—trend analysis, ratio analysis, scatter plots, regression analysis, and computerized forecasting
- **Qualitative approaches**—nominal group technique, Delphi technique and scenario planning

**Recruitment**
Involves searching for and attracting qualified candidates, from whom organization may select most qualified candidates for interviews.

**Job Posting**
Process of notifying current employees about vacant positions. Communicates title, duties, qualifications, hours of work, pay range, posting date, and closing date.

**Methods for External Recruitment**
Online recruiting, walk-ins/write-ins, employee referrals, educational institutions, HRSDC, private employment agencies, executive search firms, advertising, professional and trade associations, labour organizations, military personnel, open houses, and information sessions/job fairs.

**Evaluating Recruitment Effectiveness and Efficiency**
Uses measures of cost, time, quantity, and quality. A combination of cost and quantity measures is most often used to determine **costs per hire.** Organizations measure **costs per applicant** by dividing the cost of a recruiting method by the number of qualified applicants who respond to a recruitment drive.

**Strategies for Recruiting a More Diverse Workforce**
Includes overcoming stereotypes and biases, reevaluating HR policies and practices, developing flexible work options, redesigning jobs, and investing in training and career development.

Chapter 5

**Selection**
Involves interviewing individuals to find "best" candidate who possesses required KSAs and who fits the organizational culture.

**Five Steps in the Selection Process**
(1) pre-screening applicants, (2) selection interview, (3) selection testing, (4) background investigation and reference checking, and (5) hiring decision and job offer.

**Types of Selection Interviews**

- Structure—unstructured, structured, or mixed
- Type of questions—situational or behavioural
- Administration—serialized, panel, computerized, or by videoconference

**Factors that Undermine Effectiveness of Selection Interviews**
Include poor planning, making snap judgments, demonstrating negative or positive bias, not knowing job requirements, lowering standards under pressure to hire, not allowing for contrast effect, being unduly influenced by nonverbal behaviour, telegraphing desired responses to interviewee, and not providing realistic job previews.

**Selection Tests**
Online and paper-based tests include: intelligence tests, emotional intelligence tests, aptitude tests, tests of motor and physical abilities, personality tests, achievement tests, work-sampling, management assessment centres, honesty testing, and medical testing.

**Reference Checking**
Verifies information provided by the candidate and validates information obtained during other steps in the selection process.

Chapter 6

**Orientation/Socialization**
Provides information to new employee about company rules and practices,